Advance praise for the book

'Manu S. Pillai has once again given us an enthralling look into a neglected realm of Indian history. *False Allies* is at once lucid and accessible, all the while maintaining deep scholarly rigor . . . With the erudition that we've come to expect from his books, Pillai navigates the world of colonial Indian kingship and puts on display the complex and diverse personalities of the princes . . . and their interactions with their subjects and their colonizers, demonstrating that the period and its actors were far from monolithic. The result is a refreshing work that reframes the Indian princely states as both harbingers of tradition and agents of change, and demands we give them their due for their role in shaping modernity. *False Allies* is certainly a masterpiece of historical writing.'

Caleb Simmons, author of *Devotional Sovereignty: Kingship and Religion in India* (2020)

'Manu S. Pillai has done the double. He's written a book that general readers will relish and scholars will respect. Using the life and paintings of Ravi Varma, India's most famous artist of his time, Pillai re-examines some of India's princely states and their rulers – its maharajas. Through admirable research, he discovers skilful modernizers and deft political operators, struggling to keep the British at a distance and "modernize" in ways acceptable to themselves and their subjects. This cleverly crafted book will delight general readers and lead scholars to re-think ideas about the India of the 19th and early 20th centuries.'

Robin Jeffrey, editor of *People, Princes and Paramount Power: Society and Politics in the Indian Princely States* (1978)

'*False Allies* is a monumental achievement. Its sensitive portraits of India's princes rescue these long misunderstood figures from caricature and myth. By revealing how artfully India's princes addressed the challenges posed by colonialism and modernity, Manu S. Pillai makes them at once more human and more grand, and thereby grants them a more fitting place in our collective imagination. Learned, erudite, and wide-ranging, *False Allies* is a landmark contribution to our understanding of modern India.'

Rahul Sagar, author of *The Dewan: Raja Sir Tanjore Madhava Rao and the Making of Modern India* (forthcoming) and editor of *The Progressive Maharaja: Sir Madhava Rao's Hints on the Art and Science of Government* (2021)

'Manu Pillai proves once again why he is one of India's most popular writers of historical nonfiction. Taking the work of master artist Raja Ravi Varma as inspiration, Pillai here paints his own luminous portrait of some of the colonial subcontinent's most significant and flamboyant royals. With scholarly command, a meticulous eye for detail, and a sense of the dramatic, he mingles light and shadow to add rich texture to the region's much maligned maharajahs, revealing complex characters who sometimes managed through perspicacity and perseverance to challenge the might of the British Empire and usher in new, progressive ideas of a modern nation.'

Manu Bhagavan, author of *Sovereign Spheres: Princes, Education and Empire in Colonial India* (2003)

False Allies

False Allies

India's Maharajahs in the Age of Ravi Varma

Manu S. Pillai

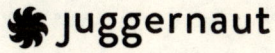

juggernaut

JUGGERNAUT BOOKS
C-I-128, First Floor, Sangam Vihar, Near Holi Chowk,
New Delhi 110080, India

First published by Juggernaut Books 2021

This book was made possible through a grant from the
Sandeep and Gitanjali Maini Foundation.

10 9 8 7 6 5 4 3

P-ISBN: 9789391165895
E-ISBN: 9789391165925

Typeset in Adobe Caslon Pro by R. Ajith Kumar, Noida

Printed and bound in India by Thomson Press India Ltd

For

T.M.P.
(1914–2006)

who couldn't read a word but made up for it with toughness and spirit

and

K.R.N.
(1931–2017)

who read widely and was the most decent person I knew

'Go ask the Maharajas how many wells they dug for the people in their States when they ruled them, how many roads they constructed, what they did to fight the slavery of the British. If you look at the account of their achievements before Independence, it is a big zero.'

Indira Gandhi, 1967

Contents

Introduction

The World of India's Princes

In 1887 a young man of ample proportions climbed on to a tricycle to pose for a famous painter. On his face was a look of doleful seriousness, and in the background were rolling hills and wiry trees. His gaze was directed at the viewer, and the hint of a double chin betrayed both solemnity and the advent of fatal obesity. On its own, the scenery around could belong to any part of the world really, but the subject himself was clearly meant to flaunt a picture of the modern Indian, in step with the times and its impulses. He wore English trousers and shiny shoes, with a dreary dark coat and pocket watch. Indeed, besides ear studs and an embroidered cap, there was no concession at all to the Western stereotype of Eastern opulence here – the brown Victorian was swathed in bureaucratic blandness, not silk and colour; if he was exotic, it was only as much as the English queen in whose name starchy civil servants – in matching uniform – governed his country. In fact, the whole purpose of the portrait, it would seem, was not so much to capture the sixteen-year-old's likeness or flatter his features as to parade his assumed personality. That the effort was received poorly is another matter: in Simla, the summer capital of the British Raj, a critic savaged the subject's 'matriculation examination kind of expression' and the anxious effort to project 'a modern and progressive air'. Instead, he sniffed, the artist – the celebrated Raja Ravi Varma – ought to have preserved convention. After

Prince Asvathi Tirunal of Travancore on his tricycle.

all, our distinguished tricycle rider was an Indian prince, and 'flowing white robes' with a jewel or three would have served him far better than this 'European travesty'.[1]

The tricycle, in fact, is the most revealing element in the portrait of Prince Asvathi Tirunal of Travancore (1871–1900).[2] By itself the machine was not uncommon in fashionable society. First marketed for ageing men and delicate ladies, its novelty had swiftly attracted the attentions of the rich and famous. Queen Victoria, for example, was dazzled when she saw a girl move about in a 'flashing mass of spinning spokes' some years before – immediately a Salvo Quad tricycle was acquired for the empress of India, causing the instrument itself to be rebranded as the *Royal* Salvo. The Ottoman viceroy in Egypt followed suit, outshining the queen by having his order plated in silver. Meanwhile, a Tricyclists' Association in London demanded special privileges in the city's parks: tricycle enthusiasts, they argued, were patently superior to the bores and mortals who rode bicycles.[3] Of course, in the larger scheme of things, it was the bicycle that prevailed, but for our prince posing atop a Royal Salvo, the objective was clear: he wished to be noted as a member of the cosmopolitan global elite despite his darker shade of skin. While in Europe, even as he sat for Ravi Varma, the tricycle was slowly admitting defeat before its two-wheeled cousin, in India the same object signalled a claim to equality with the British, if not in a racial or political sense, at least in the realm of interests and intellect. The art critic did not appreciate it, and others too might have preferred more glitter and flash in depictions of 'native' royalty. But to sitter and artist both, the idea was not to portray the man as yet another tropical exhibit as much as a serious gentleman of Eastern make but Western polish.

One can see why the prince wished to show himself to the world in this hybrid fashion, for all around were still clichés about India's maharajahs. Only six years before, for example, a Raj veteran had published a devastating picture of local rulers. It was a caricature really but asserted with force the theme of the hopeless oriental despot. 'Monstrous and bloated in bulk, hideous and disgusting in appearance, decked with earrings and necklaces like a dancing girl, and tricked out in silks and satins like a popinjay', the 'ghee-fed' Indian prince was little more than a 'hereditary scoundrel' to the censorious mind of this Englishman.[4] India itself, of course, was pretty, the writer conceded. 'Plenty appeared everywhere', 'gifts of Nature were scattered in rich profusion' and 'it was a place for the residence of Angels'. What was tragic, however, was that much of the land was in the hands of glorified dictators who, 'like a scorpion at the base of a beautiful lily', defaced it, violated it and frankly did not deserve it.[5] Indian princes were ignoble cretins who thought the world flat and parked on elephants and tortoises. They had little education and yet entertained outrageous pretensions to dignity. Power was to them a currency 'to gratify lusts', not 'a solemn trust' bestowed by providence.[6] Why, they were not even of decent blood, for 'from the Himalaya to Cape Komorin' sat on tinpot thrones the offspring of 'needy adventurers, lucky farmers, [and] successful freebooters'. Their states were physically the 'refuge of notorious criminals' and, morally, spaces 'where ideas stagnate'. It was unfortunate, the man suggested, that the British tolerated them at all.[7]

It was in this context that Ravi Varma depicted Asvathi Tirunal in that 1887 painting. It was not the first time the prince made an appearance in such a canvas, having as a boy posed with a brother. That frame presents Asvathi Tirunal with a book, its open page revealing the wonders of America, while his adolescent sibling rests his palm on a globe, tracing its location. Native princes supposedly knew little 'about countries and kingdoms beyond [their] narrow limits'.[8] And yet these royal sitters – here in Indian brocade – dispute such prejudice, laying claim to intelligence and knowledge.[9] Their principality too had made efforts to challenge the trope of native backwardness, earning respect for modernizing with a vengeance. Travancore's previous avatar as a case study in orthodox Hindu kingship was muted to accommodate a blended system in which engineering works were launched, schools were established, officials issued wordy reports in English about 'progress' and the ruler ceded many traditional prerogatives now past their expiry date. A year after Asvathi Tirunal posed on his tricycle, Travancore also became home to one of the first legislatures in the subcontinent. Admittedly, it was not a total transformation, and modernization was perennially at odds with the old ways: one ruler complained that the place remained 'the most priest-ridden Native State in the whole of India', expending fortunes on antiquated Brahminical ceremonies.[10] So even as Travancore earned praise for Western-style government, the *Times of India* named it 'the home of ultra-montane Brahminism', unusually 'intolerant' to social change.[11]

Our tricycle rider, however, was decidedly on the 'progressive' side of things. Where in upper India colonial authorities struggled to persuade rajahs to instruct their sons in British-approved methods of administration and thinking, this scion of Travancore keenly embraced English education. Where a forebear, when establishing a college, privately declared it the foundation stone for anti-royal anarchy,[12] Asvathi Tirunal after matriculating pursued a university degree with gusto. Even as his uncle prepared for a ritual that saw him weighed against a heap of gold, distributed promptly to 15,000 Brahmins,[13] the nephew obtained a Bachelor of Arts degree, acquiring the moniker 'B.A. Prince'. In 1892, when that charismatic advocate of reformed Hinduism, Vivekananda, visited Travancore, not only did Asvathi Tirunal 'interrogate' him about his travels and contacts with Indian progressives, he also whipped out a camera, flaunting a stylish new passion; impressed, the swami certified him as holding 'plenty of promise'.[14] Two years later, on a pan-Indian study tour, among the experiences he collected was that of viewing proceedings in a Bombay courtroom.[15] Even the viceroy Lord Curzon, notoriously hostile to Indian royalty, thought this specimen a 'man of culture, of travel, and of learning', who had earned his stripes by becoming the first graduate 'among all the Indian Princes'.[16] If there was that enduring notion of native rulers as 'grossly ignorant, grovelingly superstitious . . . without manners or power of conversation, without ideas or facility of speech', and 'selfish, cruel, fickle, and cowardly',[17] Asvathi Tirunal lived to challenge it.

Unfortunately, despite ticking boxes to match colonial standards, the man forgot to tick certain other essential areas. By 1899 he was 'far too stout, quite unwieldy, and [had] given up all exercise', with the result

that bad health intruded on his plans and brought death to his door
the following summer.[18] He never became maharajah, had no children
and his widow lapsed into obscurity, so that soon the prince faded from
memory, leaving his promise unfulfilled. His Ravi Varma portrait did
survive in his wife's house, however, commemorating the idealized
vision he held of himself: young, progressive, rebutting those who saw
Indian princes as human parasites. Critics wished the maharajahs to
admit 'their moral inferiority', that 'time and men have changed, that
it is their misfortune to be anachronisms, [and] that their antediluvian
ideas and wishes cannot be tolerated'.[19] Men like Asvathi Tirunal went
out of their way to take the sting out of such denunciations, joining
their culture with the drift of the modern age. But what the prince did
not realize – and what his peers would discover the hard way – was
that, for all their pontifications on progress in India, the British were
insincere masters. What they *really* sought was an arbitrary balance
between exoticism and modernity, between princely splendour and
administrative sobriety. As Sunil Khilnani notes, maharajahs were
'required to be at once conservative and liberal . . . to sport turbans
and read Bagehot'.[20] But they could never ascend to equality with their
imperial wardens – they would forever be *almost* modern, never fully so.
For if the second possibility were admitted, how would the Raj sustain
the myth that white men governed India for its own good?

The world Ravi Varma depicted in his canvases is one poorly understood
today. Indian princes and their states, when evoked now, are the stuff
of overstated romance or sneering disdain, if not a compound of both.
With palaces and processions, elephants and servitors, not to speak
of proverbial riches, Indian royalty recall that trite line by Rudyard
Kipling: 'Providence created the maharajahs to offer mankind a
spectacle.' Entertainment they were certainly capable of providing –
writing in 1931 a critic noted how an official princely conclave also
gave de facto competition to the New York Automobile Show. If one

maharajah flaunted a car with trendy security features, another showed
up with searchlights installed, of the kind that sat on warships. If some
royal vehicles were gold plated, others aimed for economy, if not variety
in taste, with silver.[21] Even personal eccentricities made the maharajahs
founts for transregional gossip. One thought himself an incarnation
of Vishnu, while another believed he was Louis XIV of France reborn
among Punjabis. The last nizam of Hyderabad owned truckloads of gems
but was also a miser who salvaged smokes from stubbed-out cigarettes.
Meanwhile, a ruler in the north-west had an appetite for sex, apocryphal
tales telling how, if the nizam was styled 'His Exalted Highness', this
fickle grandee was parodied as 'His *Exhausted* Highness'.[22] Why, in the
1880s, an Indian prince was even accused of harbouring a romantic
predisposition for elephants.[23] Unsurprisingly, then, the maharajahs
were typically cast as ludicrous idiots, who served no cause but their
own, and whose avarice and infirmity meant they played no role in
the making of modern India – precisely the kind of charge an Asvathi
Tirunal might resent.

But as with stereotypes generally, while there was a measure of truth to
this talk of excess, its circulation also served more insidious purposes. For
the British, it conveniently infantilized Indian rulers and cemented the
claim that natives were simply incapable of serious government. India's
traditional leaders were no good, except for frivolous sex and fancy dress,
thus justifying stern, manly imperial supervision. Similarly, for a younger
crop of nationalists, animated by democratic ideals, silken autocracy was
a relic of feudal yesterdays; India's destiny, recovered after a long struggle,
could not brook men who played no part in the battles that mattered. The
princes were British proxies, who cast their lot with the wrong side of
history, deserving little sympathy. Particularly in the closing stages of the
freedom struggle, they had tended towards repression – or as Jawaharlal
Nehru put it in the 1930s, 'Indian rulers and their ministers have spoken
and acted increasingly in the approved fascist manner.' His feud was not
personal: the fight, he clarified, was 'against autocracy and oppression
itself'. Yes, there were princes who 'may be good people', but in exercising
power they had generally proved 'inhuman'.[24] It did not help, as far as the

Indian National Congress was concerned, that the Hindu Mahasabha, championing a majoritarian vision of the nation, found welcome in the states. In the 1940s, thus, when Nehru spoke of republics and democracy, the Mahasabha was urging fidelity to the maharajahs as 'embodiments of Hindu pride'. Their ancestors had apparently saved India from Muslim domination, making them agreeable mascots for political Hinduism.[25] And what the Mahasabha endorsed, segments of the Congress leadership instinctively abhorred.[26]

As with most things pertaining to the past, however, the story of the princely states is also vastly more complex than simplistic readings suggest. And if the states are viewed on their own terms, they present a rather unexpected picture. To begin with, there was their sheer physical reach, for together the maharajahs controlled two-fifths of subcontinental territory, and about a quarter of its population.[27] Most

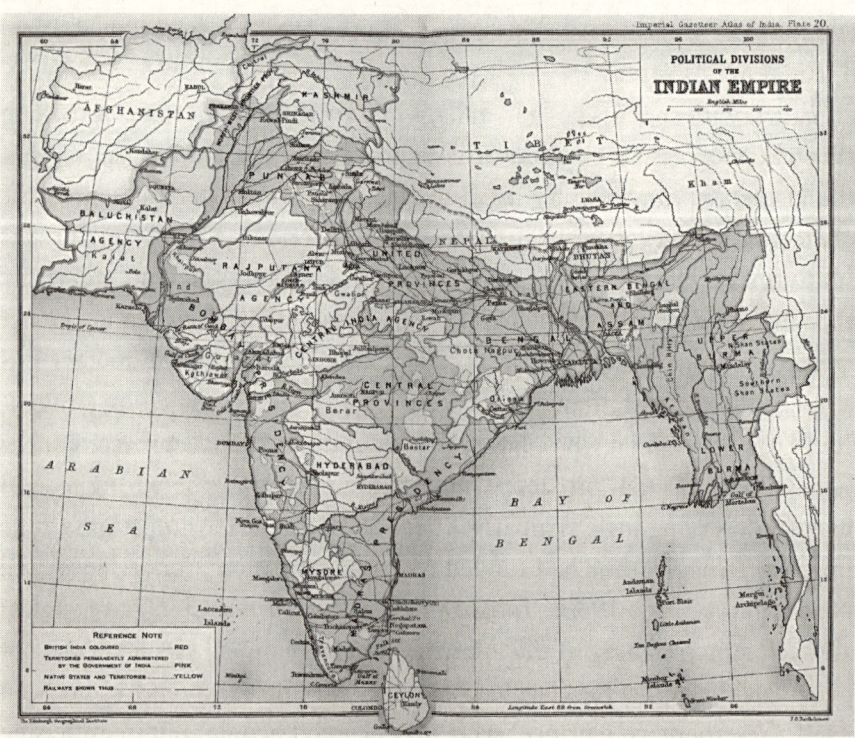

Map showing princely and British Indian territories.

discussions of 'Indian history', however, restrict themselves to *British*-ruled India, excluding this large slice of *Indian*-ruled India.[28] It is an approach that eclipses the experience of imperialism for millions who resided in the states, and *their* political evolution. Public mobilization here, for example, occurred not within nationalistic bounds of Indians versus the Raj, but along caste and religious lines – a detail which nuances general comprehension of that period.[29] In economic terms too, though the states included India's more industrially and educationally forward provinces like Mysore and Cochin, they attract scant notice: as Barbara Ramusack observes, 'In over a thousand pages of text, the second volume of *The Cambridge Economic History of India, c. 1757–c. 1970* has less than twenty references to the princely states.'[30] Even conceptually, the princely states are handicapped, described as being subject to 'indirect rule', that is, a system where token princes preserved a facade while the strings were pulled by white puppeteers.[31] The fact, however, is that the Raj's equation with the princes was one of constant negotiation and unending suspicion. The British were the stronger party, but the maharajahs had leverage too. And as their overlords made every attempt to dominate them, they also proved more than able to manipulate the system and resist colonial penetration – including sometimes by means of visual art and sitting on tricycles.

What the states deserve, then, is a more sophisticated approach and a more prominent place in general imagination. Even allowing the charge that they were nothing more than 'pillars of the empire', as is often alleged, the fact is that each pillar was of different design, and each had a unique story. Every major princely realm presents a historically dissimilar experience, and in any larger understanding of India, their incorporation is not just helpful but indispensable. The Maratha rulers of Gwalior, for instance, whose ancestors conquered territories dominated by others till the mid-eighteenth century, faced different challenges as compared to Rajput royalty, whose princely legitimacy went back a dozen generations; how political, economic and social dynamics evolved around these courts naturally varied. Some principalities were allies of the East India Company prior to being subordinated, while others began as inferiors in the first place, to the extent of being British creations – their cases too are unidentical. Thus, for every state they were able to pompously berate, as late as 1903 colonial officials were complaining of the nizam being 'too much on an equality' with the Raj, his state anything but a sham.[32] Similarly, where some kingdoms were divested of military muscle early in the day, counterparts elsewhere kept formidable armies till late in the nineteenth century. And as shall be seen, there is a surplus of evidence that these 'pillars' were often less than sturdy, needing constant surveillance to hold them in place. The maharajahs had their own calculations, and the Raj had to perpetually stay on its guard to ensure these did not threaten colonial goals and upset a delicate balance. To view Indian-ruled India as a circus of the absurd on the margins of British India, then, hardly furthers the cause of unravelling such complexities, and the country's many-layered colonial experience.

In terms of political structure too, the states offered variety. The larger the territory controlled by a 'native chief', greater were the factors at play, and more intricate its internal politics. Of 562 states, nearly 60 per cent were spread over a total of about 6,500 square miles of territory in western and central India, making them microscopic estates rather than kingdoms. On the other hand, 108 principalities with tens of millions of subjects covered well over 5,00,000 square miles, Kashmir alone holding 17 per cent of this figure.[33] Historical contingencies and accidents led to misleading classifications, betraying the ad-hoc manner in which British policy evolved, further muddying comprehension of the princes. Pudukkottai, for example, possessed 1,200 square miles of real estate and was classed with the states; Ramnad, once Pudukkottai's superior, held 2,000 square miles but sat with zamindars. Hyderabad, meanwhile, second to Kashmir in size, but inflated in prestige, had a complex 'multiethnic and multitiered political system' within its bounds.[34] Its Muslim nizams had arrived here as Mughal representatives in the eighteenth century, but local Hindu powers who paid them homage had been around for ages – just as the British managed a so-called system of 'indirect rule' with the maharajahs, many maharajahs in turn had similar internal arrangements with lower levels of indigenous authority.

In Hyderabad, some of these autonomous vassals traced their lines to the Kakatiya period, showing a fascinating historical continuity across many centuries. In Jaipur (Dhundar) it would take till the 1930s for its government to 'claim the minimal fiscal and legal powers characteristic of a modern state' from local chieftains, and even in 1938 a subordinate was able to attempt armed rebellion.[35] All this was alien, meanwhile, to bureaucratized Travancore – when conflict arose in this southern territory, it was not courtesy of recalcitrant feudatories but thanks to communists winning over the working classes.

In what may be awkward to register today, in terms of identity too, the states mattered, just as India's present-day federal units have distinct personalities. Baroda's Maratha rulers, for instance, ruled over a mass of Gujarati subjects. Though unwelcome invaders at first, the royal family came to terms with their people and created a stake for them in the court's survival. As a result, 'attempts to organize political protests on lines similar to those in British India were never a great success' in the state.[36] So much so that when the Raj was terminated, 'there was little enthusiasm in Baroda over [its] integration . . . into the new independent India'. Far from suffusing the land with nationalist delight, 'there was a feeling of depression and sorrow' here.[37] So too in Rampur, a sentiment of *Rampuriyat* (that is, a sense of belonging) was intense and its people felt an emotional bond of love and nostalgia for the state, manifested in cultural and literary forms.[38] Even with Pudukkottai, small though it was, the archive shows that the idea of physical integration with India elicited dismay. Officials under Sardar Patel – the 'Iron Man' who united princely units with British India – observed that the 'majority' of the rajah's subjects were not on board with merging the state with the ex-colonial districts around them.[39] The local legislature – and many states had legislative councils – went so far as to demand a plebiscite, insisting that Pudukkottai continue as Pudukkottai in independent India, because that identity and its physical bounds meant something.[40] The ruling family here, ironically, had not been terribly popular and could claim its fair share of scandal and ignominy; yet, evidently, their subjects identified with the principality. It is this emotional connection that makes descendants of former royal houses even today appealing candidates in democratic elections, giving namesake maharajahs conspicuous stature despite the loss of their ancestral powers.[41]

To simply dismiss the princely states as unworthy of historical interrogation, then – as a world of dancing girls and empty-headed despots – blurs intelligent perception. The cartoon idea that dominates nationalist retellings presents maharajahs as British clients, lost in sexual escapades while leeching off a weeping peasantry. It did not help that colonial narratives encouraged such disdain to sustain imperial interests: one nineteenth-century writer called the princes British 'tenants', erasing their character as well as histories.[42] They were presented by the Raj through a prism of expedience, as blingy tools for outsourced administrative labour. Lord Canning, the British Crown's first viceroy, for instance, labelled the states 'royal instruments' for the empire's security.[43] A successor, Lord Lytton, described the princes as not only a counter to 'Baboos' writing 'semi-seditious articles in the Native Press' and emerging as the first generation of Indian nationalists, but also as a means to 'strengthen very materially' British authority.[44] While they were not incorrect, there was more to the states than partisan packaging. For the maharajahs also transformed the Raj, and in negotiations with the princes, imperial authorities revealed their own vulnerabilities. One Victorian functionary asserted a little too loudly, thus, that the 'supremacy of the British Government is not derived … from any power inherited from the Moguls'. British paramountcy emerged, instead, 'partly by conquest; partly by Treaty; partly by usage'.[45] And yet flashy durbars orchestrated by successive viceroys were patently about reclaiming Mughal rituals to fortify British standing. After all the colonial enterprise in India had originated with merchants literally kissing Mughal feet.[46] Lining up maharajahs now in processions, bestowing titles and insisting on public fealty were exercises not just in projecting might, but also in seeking a legitimacy the Raj feared it did not possess.[47]

This was, in fact, admitted by Lytton, who observed to his London bosses that simply building roads and irrigation works, or putting up 'good government' was not adequate to win local support for the

Raj; Indian imagination was welded to the interests of its princes and hereditary leaders. 'They are a powerful aristocracy,' the viceroy recorded, and his conundrum was that 'whilst, on the one hand, we require their cordial and willing allegiance, we certainly cannot afford to give them any increased political power independent of our own'.[48] A racist slur Curzon unleashed on the Persians could have applied to India also, when he declared that 'the normal Asiatic would sooner be misgoverned by Asiatics than well governed by Europeans'.[49] History had already taught the authorities this much. While the Great Rebellion of 1857 had many sparks, ranging from agrarian discontent to religious provocation, a leading factor was also the toppling of esteemed royal houses. This too was the reason why leadership of the revolt was readily bestowed upon the princes who joined, just as its failure was linked to the refusal of a sizeable number to engage. Benjamin Disraeli correctly cautioned his colleagues in the House of Commons that the rebellion was no small mutiny. 'There must be no more annexation, no more conquest,' because India could not be governed 'by merely European agency'.[50] Nearly twenty years later, it was Disraeli who, as prime minister, helped Victoria fill Mughal shoes and proclaim herself India's empress, forging ritual bonds with the princes. The British possessed hard power in guns and were willing to use it too, but for stability in the subcontinent, they had to win over the maharajahs. That the latter knew this perfectly well rendered the imperial edifice itself susceptible to tremors.

Indeed, to merely view the maharajahs as stooges of the Raj would be an inadequate reading.[51] For while they were weak in physical strength, their cultural stature was not inconsiderable. As one scholar put it, people 'conceived of politics [itself] in terms of rajas and ranis, padishahs and begums',[52] which allowed Indian royalty to subtly remind the British of their foreignness. The princely alliance with the Raj was always a constantly readjusting transaction. In 1877, for example, the ruler of Indore spouted grovelling lines of loyalty. 'India has been till now a vast heap of stones,' the maharajah fawned, 'some of them big, some of them small.' It was thanks to the British that '[n]ow the house is built, and from roof to basement each stone of it is in the right place'.[53] On the face of it, this was as pro-Raj as princes could get. And yet, the same man was condemned by officials as 'a Chief whose disloyalty' was 'notorious' and who by 'intriguing in every possible manner' presented the Raj with 'persistent opposition'. The issue was simple: Indore was willing to flatter the British so long as they did not interfere in his domain; 'treaty rights', he explained, 'should always receive the most careful consideration', which was his way of telling the viceroy to mind his business.[54] Nothing vexed the Raj more than maharajahs deploying Western legalisms like this. So much so that as late as 1926, a viceroy had to assert that British supremacy 'exists quite independently' of treaties, and that 'no Ruler of an Indian State can justifiably claim to negotiate with the British Government on an equal footing'.[55] What is instructive here is not the statement itself, but the fact that only two decades before the final British withdrawal from India, supposedly servile princes needed such rebukes at all. Their language could border on oily, but friction was the founding principle of the maharajahs' dance with the Raj – including in such seemingly minor matters as ritual and vocabulary.

Much, in fact, has been made of the princely propensity for hollow pomp. As an administrator explained, 'loss of much of their real power makes [the maharajahs] more anxious to preserve forms that yet remain of royalty' through overblown pageantry. If the British suspended ritual intercourse, he felt, it would 'mortify them'.[56] In this view, ritualism was a sop for Indians divested of meaningful authority – a consolation prize, given that they had forfeited the trophy. In fact, however, the imperial power was just as keen to play this game. As early as the eighteenth century, their representatives in local courts clamoured for funds to keep up appearances; or as the Company's Hyderabad man conveyed, the nizam had so many people entitled to ceremonial distinctions about him, that 'for the sake of some appearance of equality', it was essential he match up.[57] Without ritual, the Company's agents were small fry and could be treated as such. The tables could be reversed too: helping a prince of Indore win the throne in 1843, Lord Ellenborough got him to present 101 coins to his envoy – with that quiet act, the ruler did the British homage, admitting inferiority.[58] By leading princes to their seats, determining how close the imperial agent's chair was kept and through other nitty-gritties, the Raj too conducted politics through ritual.[59] This, in fact, was also seen as a means to transfer 'recollections of the [Mughals'] imperial authority' to the British, yearning as they were to fit into an Indian cultural language, and to make 'princes and chiefs' cooperate 'cordially'.[60] Which then begs the question that if the maharajahs were slovenly heads of bogus states, why go to such prodigious lengths to court them in their own idiom?

On the Indian side, meanwhile, as British power swelled, ritual offered a platform for princes to taunt their suzerains even when official language was sugary. In 1861 the nizam was created a member of the Order of the Star of India. While intended as an honour, it also meant acknowledging the queen's supremacy, causing the man to avoid his investiture for as long as possible. When it could no longer be delayed, he refused to place the insignia around his neck, declaring it akin to a slave's collar. As for wearing a medal featuring Victoria's face, there was no chance at all. So at the ceremony, he 'simply grabbed it from [the British representative's] hand, deposited it on the *masnad* [throne], and sat on it'.[61] It was not resistance by street protest or armed force, but within princely settings and its powerful world of symbols, it was still a denial of legitimacy. Even trickery was not unprecedented. In 1877, another nizam went to Delhi, where his minister attempted to convey that Hyderabad was 'equal in sovereignty' to the Raj even if 'unequal in strength'. When the viceroy asked for the nizam's 'loyalty' and 'allegiance', the minister coolly rendered the chief words as 'friendship' and 'alliance'. 'My interpreter having noticed this, I corrected the intentional mistranslation,' the viceroy hissed, 'and caused the young Nizam to be informed that I meant …obedience and fidelity.'[62] Meanwhile, in 1871, Raj officials were aghast to find that Gwalior was still minting coins in the name of a Mughal emperor.[63] Resistance appears also in native ministers' regular use of the term 'royal family' for Indian princely lines, which the British saw as a violation – to them these were *ruling* families, for Victoria alone was 'royal'.[64] These negotiations on wording and ritual, moreover, were not bursts of pique; as one scholar put it, 'a slavishly subservient prince would have undercut his own legitimacy', making defiance, one way or another, and in whatever degree affordable, imperative to his political dignity.[65]

Subversion, in fact, was an inbuilt feature of the princely relationship with the British, though the extent to which it could be attempted depended on many factors, including the nature of their representative (generally called the Resident or Political Agent), the attitude of the higher authorities and the personality and pluck of each ruler. Indian princes often ventured, for example, to cloister British officers in their capitals, preventing free intercourse with their court and refusing audiences. In the mid-nineteenth century, the Hyderabad Resident, for instance, complained that he was 'purposely kept' in isolation from local 'men of rank and eminence'.[66] Decades later, in 1922, a successor gloomily repeated how he 'had not even been allowed a confidential conversation of five minutes' with the nizam.[67] Such unfriendliness was strategic, for why risk transmitting unnecessary intelligence to the British, who in their paranoia also ran an elaborate machine for hoovering gossip?[68] This did not mean maharajahs did not employ similar techniques: rulers in Lucknow, Jaipur and Hyderabad seduced Residents, giving bribes, employing their illegitimate offspring and even greasing the palms of Indian aides.[69] In Indore, a Resident was scandalized on being presented gold coins concealed in a fruit basket – when admonished, the sender apologetically asked whether he had expected a higher figure.[70] If a Resident remained nosey, other responses were invented. As Michael Fisher tells, excuses ranging from prayers to the 'operation of depilation' (that is, hair removal) were put forth to 'postpone unwanted discussions with British political agents, thus gaining these Rulers valuable time and sometimes negotiating advantage'.[71] In 1841 when told that approval was mandatory for ministerial appointees, one maharajah promptly declared his intention to rule sans minister.[72] Fudging accounts was another favourite technique: as late as 1906 the British were ruing 'scanty information' about Jaipur's finances, for example.[73] And when its head made donations to official charities, they recognized it as a clever tactic to 'ride the Government of India off from paying inconvenient attention' to his books of account.[74]

Such victories mattered, and if their armies were toothless, princes compensated through personal shrewdness. One Resident, for example, was astounded when he witnessed a ruler, who was sent disagreeable news, use boisterous ceremonial to spin this as the exact opposite. The nawab gave out robes of honour and ordered 'public rejoicings' till it appeared as though the 'fullest extent' of his wishes was permitted, not declined by the British.[75] Given how ritual was amenable to manipulation, this too, then, had to be policed by weary officials. They blocked, thus, the bestowal of ceremonial honours by the peshwa in Poona on Maratha chiefs after 1802, because they understood it gave the peshwa a risky aura of superiority. For the privilege of keeping shoes on in court, Residents waged battles for decades – in Hyderabad, the demand was resisted for two generations till the British finally succeeded in the reign of a three-year-old without an opinion.[76] So also they looked 'minutely on every point' in the exchange of gifts, because gifts held powerful meanings.[77] Lord Hastings avoided Delhi on a tour, for example, because convention required him to appear before the Mughal emperor and receive presents – a mark of servitude.[78] With the replacement of the emperor by an empress, however, the Raj insisted on Indians paying *her* ritual dues – Navaratri festivities in Ramnad in 1892, thus, featured Hindu rites, with the innovation that opposite the throne sat a portrait of the queen.[79] Interestingly, so much for the maharajahs being ciphers, it was really the empress who was in that position.[80] The princes, while troubled by interference, still taxed their people, presided over judicial matters and framed laws – powers denied to Victoria.[81] Their sovereignty was *divided*, in that foreign policy and similar subjects were surrendered, but the remainder stayed within their grasp, unlike the queen whose role was entirely titular.[82] So, when Curzon described princes as living in 'bejewelled and frivolous idleness', the critique applied less to its targets and more to his mighty empress.[83]

Over time, in fact, despite constant needling, the princes were able to extract even harder forms of power from their suzerains. Military matters are a case in point. As Britain's geopolitical contest with Russia ('The Great Game') gained pace in the closing decades of the nineteenth century, the maharajahs' armies – totalling 3,14,000 troops – suddenly looked appealing.[84] Till 1879 the policy was to limit their access to technology and weaponry, so as to reduce princely forces to a derelict gaggle rather than a meaningful threat to the Raj. And yet, in the end, ever-growing reliance was vested in them. Princely troops served in Afghanistan and Africa, and during the Boxer Rebellion in China, the maharajahs of Bikaner, Gwalior and Idar were personally present with their contingents.[85] In the First World War, 15 per cent of Punjabi enlistees in the British-Indian army came from the states.[86] Rajput principalities contributed as many as 48,611 combatants,[87] while Patiala alone provided 26,648 fighters.[88] The Bikaner maharajah was the only Indian signatory to the Treaty of Versailles alongside the United States president and other global powers. It may be tempting to view the princes as being 'used' here, but the fact is that the states also made gains. Not only did they wrest greater internal autonomy, they also boldly began to demand a share of power in *British* India – that is, in the running of the empire itself. The princes were also starting to lobby together, sending a shiver down colonial spines. As an official warned, 'The Native States, taken singly, cannot give us serious trouble, but by encouraging them to form themselves into a sort of trade union, we are calling into existence a formidable power which will most certainly be used to bring pressure to bear.'[89] That in 1917 the princes were still described as 'formidable' is revealing of the resources yet at their command.

The fact is that by the dawn of the twentieth century, sounds from the states were aggravating the Raj as much as nationalist clamour under the Congress. And the British had no option but to respond to this pressure – if Curzon acted like an overbearing nanny, his successor Minto changed course and conciliated. On the princely side there was logic to this growing ambition: as a ruler stated, 'We do not wish to become mere puppets and share the fate of some of the European aristocracies.'[90] Before the Imperial War Conference, the Bikaner maharajah also expressed hopes that Britain would not forget the 'just claims and aspirations of India' after the war – a lot like Mahatma Gandhi expected concessions in the post-war period as a reward for

Maharajah Ganga Singh of Bikaner (standing, in turban) featured in William Orpen's The Signing of Peace in the Hall of Mirrors *(1919).*

nationalist cooperation.[91] Indeed, Bikaner even asked for a categorical declaration that 'self-government within the British Empire is the object and goal of British rule'.[92] Providing unsolicited advice on 'liberal political reforms' in *British* India, he spoke of greater power for native legislators, and the creation of a princely council to consult with the government.[93] Ominously, he envisioned native royalty working in a 'complementary' fashion with the 'democratic element in British India'.[94] Naturally, the establishment was nervous – while they were cultivating princes as a *counter* to the Congress, here was free talk of cooperation. The man, then, was informed that 'just as the states resented any interference by the Government of India in their internal affairs, so the states must reciprocate by refraining from any interference in the affairs of British India'.[95] The last thing they wanted was 'intrigues between the Chiefs and the political leaders of British India', that is, pesky Congressmen.[96] While princes might be used *against* nationalists, a coalition of the two was dangerous; no room could be allowed for Indian prestige to unite with the nationalism of a pestilent Congress.[97]

Despite this discomfort about involving princes in British-Indian matters, however, there were moments when the Raj had to condone exactly that. In the mid-1910s, for example, when the government wished to construct irrigation works on the sacred river Ganga, they encountered opposition from Madan Mohan Malaviya, a Congressman and staunch Hindu. It took princely mediation to find a compromise, with the Raj carting to the negotiating table Maratha, Rajput, Sikh and Brahmin royalty to persuade the politician to give way.[98] Such cultural value could also be requisitioned in international matters. So, when the Ottoman empire entered the First World War, the British requested Hyderabad's nizam – the last great symbol of Mughal glory – to ask Indian Muslims to remain loyal to them, as opposed to the Ottoman king, who was also the caliph of Islam. This particular nizam, incidentally, was someone officials comprehensively disliked – by the 1940s some would openly pray for the day when 'His Exalted Highness may oblige us by joining his predecessors' in the afterlife.[99] For the time being, though, his support was urgently needed. To be clear, the nizam was not permitting himself to be exploited: he had his own interests, which when they were not met, saw him roll back assistance – a few years later, the same man was funding a conference on the *restoration* of the Caliphate, bringing disquiet to the viceroy.[100] In time he also got his heir married to the daughter of the last caliph, burnishing his credentials in the Islamic world. He was a notoriously bad ruler and sitting on a tinderbox of religious polarization. And yet the British dared not depose him – the nizam was too important, a viceroy qualifying the man as 'the spokesman and leader of Mahomedans in India'.[101]

In the end, then, the downfall of the princes was not due to the British but their own hesitation to move with the times. By the second decade of the twentieth century, the Raj was forced to respond to nationalist aspirations, but few maharajahs understood that they too would need to shift gears. If in the nineteenth century the idea of India as a nation was a novelty, into the twentieth, it fast became an emotional reality; to row against its currents was to write one's obituary. Even if only to protect their interests, the rulers failed at coordination. The viceroy in the 1920s had permitted the creation of a Chamber of Princes, but the body was handicapped: Rajput rajahs sneered at Maratha royalty, while senior rulers like the nizam were aghast at sitting on an equality with princelings of either kind. As Lord Irwin reported, the maharajahs were 'undoubtedly hampered' by a 'temperamental incapacity to agree among themselves'.[102] In some ways, they were still in an India that was a loose patchwork of entities rather than a nation, a point that also blinded princes to the appeal of democracy. So, in the inter-war period, when viceroys increasingly desisted from interference, Indian royalty utilized this room for manoeuvre not to reinvent themselves, but to resurrect paternalist rule.[103] When at last conceded more autonomy than ever, most maharajahs lapsed into anachronistic tendencies. The British knew why: 'The princes,' it was recorded in 1926, 'are afraid of the future . . . They are the last congenital autocrats in the world. Democracy has swept away others before their eyes . . . and they are terrified lest out of deference to clamour or fetish of the people's will we should let all the powers of the Government of India pass to a responsible Government' run by Congressmen.[104] Arguably, a savvy maharajah would have forged links with the Congress, but most shut doors and stifled dissent instead – an attitude that left a sour taste in nationalist mouths, and has since tarnished the princely legacy.

Looking back from the present, though, where the states are meticulously ignored in narratives of the period, it is in fact startling how even in the 1930s the maharajahs possessed opportunities to carve out a future in post-colonial India. They were invited to the Round Table Conferences, and while Congressmen like Nehru were cold, Gandhi himself was more circumspect, leaving the door ajar for engagement. In a sense, the mahatma, whose religiosity influenced his politics and who manifested a distinct conservatism, respected the cultural weight of the princes; he was, besides, born a princely subject, in a family with a history of royal service. He also admired many rulers personally: the Travancore maharani was an 'object of my envy' for her 'severe simplicity',[105] while Mysore's maharajah was a 'Rajarshi' – a royal sage – whose realm came close to Gandhi's utopian Ramrajya.[106] Other Congressmen too saw value in the rulers, and in this period imperial 'officials and Indian nationalists [both] pursued princely allies', revealing their importance.[107] Pressed into taking steps for Indian self-government, the British proposed a federal structure, with elected provincial governments as well as a national centre with a place for the states. In what would prove to be their undoing, however, the maharajahs failed to rise to the occasion – while some welcomed new equations, the majority were lost in myopia. They prevaricated on a settlement so that by the late 1930s, as Congress was forming ministries in British provinces and marching in from the street to govern, the princes were consumed by perilous trivialities. An official had succinctly captured the consequences of this attitude well in advance: 'British India is advancing along the lines of Evolution,' he declared, while 'the Indian States are on the road to Revolution.'[108]

And revolution it was. With the outbreak of the Second World War, the federation option was discarded. Congressmen resigned from government and were again on the streets and then in jail. While the states made remarkable contributions – financially and in military terms –

to the war on fascism, when it ended, they found they were no longer real partners at the negotiating table. Circumstances had altered, and there was little sympathy for princely grievances, which looked vulgar against such looming catastrophes as Partition. As an officer in the know reminisced, before the war the only way to realize a federation 'would have been to take the princes by the neck and compel them'.[109] At that time it was not an option because of the rulers' still-potent position. In the late 1940s, however, with the world itself transformed, the maharajahs were presented a fait accompli: they would hereafter be *tolerated*, not entertained, as equals. It also did not help that many experienced princes – including the Bikaner maharajah who spoke of cooperating with democratic forces – were dead. With the Raj set to terminate, and surprisingly swiftly, the fate of the maharajahs came to rest with the Congress. Where in the 1930s they had still had room to delay, now Sardar Patel towered over them with a dotted line on which to sign, wielding carrot and stick both. Most submitted quietly in a pall of gloom. With Hyderabad, however, the Indian government did not hesitate to launch a full-scale invasion, which included aerial bombing. Though played down through a more sedate term, the seriousness of the affair comes through in the suppression of an official report, which estimated that twenty-seven to forty thousand people were killed 'during and after' the so-called 'police action'.[110] When the British left, then, the face-off between the Congress and the maharajahs featured blood and violence – their states had become, in Patel's words, poisonous 'ulcers' to be excised for the viability of a hard-won nation.[111]

It was a strange gravestone for royal India, given its larger history. But the even greater irony is that the Congress and princes had originally been friends.

One of the prime witnesses to this ultimately doomed world of the maharajahs was Ravi Varma the artist. Though established in India's collective imagination for his mythological paintings, the man was also a public figure whose career straddled princely India as well as those urban pockets that were home to the early nationalists. His lucrative portrait-making enterprise saw him wield the brush in service of the most iconic princes of the age as well as that first generation of Congressmen. In a career spanning over four decades, he produced paintings of everyone from Edward VII to some of the most trenchant critics of the same monarch's imperium.[112] Indeed, through his art Ravi Varma captured a political universe itself, telling stories of the individuals who typified the age. He certainly knew that his work might one day serve purposes other than of artistic inquiry, writing: 'The historical importance of pictures is difficult to over-estimate. They throw as much light on the men and manners of a period as any amount of written record[s].'[113] By depicting princes and intellectuals, statesmen and politicians, and traversing the length and breadth of India to build his reputation, Ravi Varma created a visual archive through which may be plotted the story of a little-discussed political space. And his own experiences represent the contradictory forces at play: as much as he was admired by powerful Englishmen, in everyday encounters he was subject to quotidian racism. By the end of his life, as nationalism awakened his homeland, he not only participated in a Congress session, but also contributed to the process in his own distinct way.[114] And while he has been called the 'Painter of Colonial India', it is really a specific *chapter* we find represented in Ravi Varma's art, where nationalists and princes were still on the same page, and a future without the maharajahs was yet to be imagined.[115] It is this phase that is the subject of this book.

Writing in 1928, in fact, one of Curzon's former aides recalled how even in the early twentieth century it was entirely in order for politically conscious Indians in British territory to be in awe of their royal countrymen. 'I often watched', the man recalled, as maharajahs 'visited British India, and the profound respect and reverence' they commanded among 'the leading citizens of the various capitals'. Many of these progressives were anglicized lawyers, 'free and easy' in English society. Yet, 'in the presence of a real Raja' their 'manner and attitude changed', and they became surprisingly 'humble and deferential'. It was as if they

Raja Ravi Varma in 1904 after he was awarded the Kaiser-i-Hind medal.

'instinctively recognised their natural leaders and were glad and proud to see them'.[116] The official need not have been surprised, because he had already answered why the princes inspired veneration. Turning Curzon in his grave, his ex-secretary wrote: 'I regard the average Indian State as better suited to the happiness and temperament of the Indian than the huge unwieldy' British system. The native principality was more able to 'bring content and opportunities to the people' than the imperial bureaucracy, because it possessed a personal touch and had an ear to the ground.[117] Even if a bit too rosy, this was not an outlandish proposition: in 1910, a more senior figure had also blasphemed when he said, 'We have much to learn from Native States.' Yes, many presented 'a loose despotic system' but given their strong local roots, these governments did not 'press hard on the daily lives of the people'. On the other hand, the British machinery, though 'scientific', was rigid and not particularly better given the procedural harassment it inflicted.[118] Yet another colonial officer observed that where the princes were one up on the Raj was in their 'claim on the general regard of the people'. The idea of a maharajah, he believed, 'strikes [the Indian] imagination' in a way impossible for the file-bearing civil servant.[119]

Among those so struck, curiously enough, were founders of the Congress. To some extent their love was born of economics, for assorted maharajahs donated generously to the organization in its infancy. This included rulers such as of Baroda and Travancore as well as zamindars from Ramnad and Bobbili. Princely largesse, in fact, was showered so readily that it provoked alarm in imperial circles – in 1887 Mysore, whose family had only recently regained their kingdom after fifty years of colonial usurpation, was asked to cease making contributions.[120] Of course, all orders were not meekly obeyed: twelve years later the viceroy, interrogating the maharajah of Baroda, discovered that the latter was still giving to the Congress, while more than one ruler secretly financed the election of a Congressman to the House of Commons in London.[121] In fact, princely patronage was extended to regional nationalist clubs too. The Poona Sarvajanik Sabha in the Bombay presidency, for example, full of 'men with tainted views' and supposedly diabolical designs,[122] was funded not only by local rulers but also by southern maharajahs; the Deccan Education Society, which ran an institution attractive even to gun-wielding revolutionaries, obtained in excess of 2,00,000 rupees in princely gifts in its maiden twenty-five years of existence.[123] With the Congress, while support from Indian princes is presumed to have withered by the First World War – reflecting fears that nationalism might devour royalty too – there is evidently 'tantalizing evidence' of 'undocumented continuation of princely aid' behind the scenes.[124] After all, it is not impossible that at least some maharajahs confronting extinction attempted to negotiate with their executioner. Curzon, for instance, was convinced as late as 1925 that there were a 'number of Philippe Égalités' (after a Bourbon prince who supported the French Revolution) among the rajahs, with an 'ardent sympathy' for democracy.[125]

What is known for sure, however, is that in the period between the 1860s and the first decade of the twentieth century – the years chiefly covered in this book, and when Ravi Varma was active – Indian nationalists endorsed the legitimacy of the maharajahs.[126] Indeed, many rulers were seen as nationalists themselves, and several nationalists saw the states as rallying points in their fight against colonialism. As a historian of the Congress tells, at this juncture the party was 'less interested in whether chiefs lived up to the representative and liberal political principles' they espoused; irrespective of whether a ruler was good or bad, he was respected, the Congress's chief concern being whether 'the British honored the independence of the states'.[127] Territories under native control were spared the worst of imperialism, and both prestige and sentiment were tied to their survival. While many Congressmen did feel that absolutism would need to be jettisoned, it was *Indian* initiative they urged, not foreign interference. So, when the maharajah of Mysore died in 1894, the Congress officially mourned him. His 'constitutional reign', it was said, was proof that Indians could govern without the British intervention that masqueraded as guidance.[128] To these early nationalists, in fact, princes had a role even in a democratic future: M.G. Ranade, a Congress founder, visualized the Indian parliament as featuring an elected council resembling the Commons, with rulers constituting a corresponding House of Lords.[129] At this point, the right of the maharajahs to also speak for India was not questioned, and as we shall see through the states covered in this book, even conservative royal figures were treated with understanding and reverence.

There were other interactions too between nationalists and the states: in 1916 a Congress president praised rulers for rewarding Indian administrative talent with positions of authority – while brown men wasted away in minor posts in British India due to racial prejudice, in the states they found the platforms they deserved.[130] Indeed, this last point firmly punctured colonial biases. Belief that Indians were horrendously bad at governance dominated the highest echelons of the Raj. Curzon, for example, when asked to consider native representation in his council, declared: 'In the whole continent there is not one Indian fit for the post.'[131] When in 1892, as alluded to before, a Congressman won election to the British parliament, the governor of Bombay sent congratulations, but in private unleashed a jaundiced pen. 'I am very disgusted at Dadabhai Naoroji getting elected to the House,' said Lord Harris. 'Why England should elect natives I can't for the life of me see: they can't govern themselves. Why should they govern us?'[132] It was with relish, then, that nationalists highlighted the achievements of administrators in *princely* India, who established standards often superior to British rule – men like Seshiah Sastri, Dinkar Rao, Madhava Rao and Salar Jung, to name a few. Or as K.M. Panikkar argued, princes 'provided opportunities for Indians to demonstrate and develop their capacity for political and administrative affairs'. They helped develop 'a school for Indian statesmanship' and 'offered fields for men of capacity' whose complexion had placed a limit on what they could achieve in foreign-ruled parts of their own motherland.[133] Arguments on the native ability for self-rule could be won by pointing to royal India, thus, whose princes and ministers became heroes and much-needed icons in the fight against colonialism.

It was these very 'native statesmen' and maharajahs that Ravi Varma depicted with flair and glamour, and it is they who form the substance of this book – persons who, before nationalism moved to the phase of mass politics, manifested Indian aspirations, and gave many generations a sense of confidence. Ravi Varma was a favourite portraitist for these Victorian role models who demonstrated success and claimed Western modernity for native causes. Several of the statesmen – who would in time be associated with the Congress – began as British clerks but rose under maharajahs to pan-Indian prominence. They thought of politics and constitutions, of governance and development, and ultimately of beating the British at their own rigged game of 'progress'. Some became active spokespersons for nationalism – such as Naoroji, who before making history as a British parliamentarian was a princely minister – while others worked more discreetly. But they all rose to the challenge of imperialism, reflecting on questions about their own identity. The princes were part of this shared feeling: in stressing autonomy, in improving their systems and in supporting Indian aspirations, they stood up to their colonial bosses. Politics was a triangular contest between the Raj, princes and anglicized statesmen – precisely why the understandings they reached were specific to this context. They do not fit later trends when the masses entered the picture, and Congress and the maharajahs grew to view one another as antagonists. That is, the Congress of the 1890s differed from its 1940s' avatar, just as nineteenth-century princes were not like their twentieth-century heirs. While the final assessment of princely India draws from this last, troubled phase, the earlier is not without significance – and that is the story this book seeks to tell.

Of course, trying to offer a comprehensive record of princely politics is a daunting task. There are very many states to choose from, and quite a few remarkable figures. This is where Ravi Varma enters the picture. By following his professional peregrinations through five states, this book draws an account of their rulers and ministers, for all of whom the artist did portraits. Ravi Varma himself is not our subject, and though there are biographical snippets, in most chapters he makes only cameo appearances. It is his *world* that is of interest, and what the man offers is a thread to connect diverse kingdoms. We begin, thus, in Travancore, where he was born in the 1840s, and cover its transition from orthodox 'backwardness' to the vanguard of 'progress'. Ravi Varma's visit to Pudukkottai in the

1870s offers an opportunity to study how a feudal state, dominated by a certain caste, faced twin pressures to Brahminize as well as bureaucratize. In Baroda, where he went in the 1880s, we witness conflict between right and might under the Raj, as well as the career of a maharajah who proved one of colonial rule's sharpest princely critics. Mysore, where the artist did portraits for two generations of rulers, on the other hand, was home to a subtler brand of nationalism, with industrialization as its vehicle of resistance. Meanwhile, given how Ravi Varma was himself related to royalty, his family portraits open a window into intra-dynastic rivalries, gender, changing cultural mores and connected themes. The book concludes, finally, with Udaipur, whose ruler, defying all pressure to modernize, and eschewing even the English language, prevented British inroads into his realm; when he was toppled, it was not by the Raj but by peasant agitation – evidence, perhaps, that even without Congress-type politicians, the maharajahs would have faced trouble in the end.

All in all, princes and statesmen who appear in Ravi Varma's portraits are part of India's evolution in the colonial period. These protagonists were not mass leaders, but this should not blind us to their achievements. For in the end, resistance to British imperialism took multiple avatars – often in the most unusual places, in ways that were both deceptive and ingenious.

The 1971 commemorative stamp issued by the Government of India to honour Ravi Varma.

The following chapter provides a brief history of Travancore at the time of Ravi Varma's birth in 1848, and the state's experience of British colonialism, revelatory also of the general pressures and challenges nineteenth-century princes faced.

1

The Rajah in a Suit

Long before the tricycle-riding Prince Asvathi Tirunal memorialized himself in Ravi Varma's art, there had sat on the throne of Travancore a man called Uthram Tirunal (1814–60).[1] He was in every sense a fascinating character, negotiating a world of orthodoxy alongside the attractions of Western modernity. Born, it would seem, with a curious bent of mind, flattering reviews had piled up around him for decades before he became king. Aged six, at a reception for some British dignitaries, for instance, Uthram Tirunal unselfconsciously took possession of a military man's knee, demanding to know how 'all the gentlemen' in the East India Company's southern headquarters of Madras were doing.[2] As heir apparent, he met a reverend who left a rapturous recollection: his 'eagle eye' and 'dark, shining, intelligent countenance', John Abbs wrote, at once conveyed that 'you stood in the presence of royalty'. But 'when, after placing his hands on his forehead, he held it out and addressed you in English, you were instantly charmed by his benignant gracefulness'.[3] In the years while his brother was in power, Uthram Tirunal had all the time in the world to pursue interests outside of the typical routine imagined for conservative Hindu princes. He decided, for example, to channel his energies into the study of medicine, taking lessons from a British surgeon.[4] Not long afterwards, he opened a dispensary in the capital, Trivandrum, giving orders to procure hereon any 'new medicine discovered and advertised in the newspapers'.[5] The public implications of an amateur royal doctor were interesting; as a court chronicler put it,

> The Numboory Brahmans, who would not even touch English
> medicines, under the idea that most of the liquid substances contained
> spirits, began to take freely from His Highness' dispensary. His Highness
> would explain to them the good effects of European medicines and how
> speedily diseases could be cured by their means. Several of the Hindu
> gentry came from great distances, not only for the cure of ailments, but
> also for the purpose of having an opportunity of seeing His Highness
> while they were under treatment. Trevandrum is seldom without a
> religious ceremony of some kind being performed there, and the noted
> men among Numboory Brahmans who constantly resorted to the
> place, had spread throughout Malabar, among their community, reports
> regarding His Highness' medical knowledge and the virtues and efficacy
> of European medicines.[6]

Thus, we have Uthram Tirunal curing a pilgrim from Benares of
colic pain, while treating his brother – the maharajah – for crippling
diarrhoea. Now and then, 'minor surgical operations' were conducted,
with the prince's servants standing in (voluntarily, one hopes) as nurses
and assistants. All the palace establishment was vaccinated by his hands,
and soon there was a small laboratory at work, featuring devices ranging
from opera glasses and telescopes to an electric machine and ice maker.[7]
Indeed, after succeeding to power in 1846, Uthram Tirunal would order
even a skeleton made of ivory to continue his lessons in anatomy – as
a high-caste Hindu, handling human remains was not an option, so
craftsmen who hitherto designed pretty figurines were given the scientific
commission of making bones and joints.[8] His palace too was a museum
of curios, though the British thought it 'gaudy' and inclined towards
show more than taste. As one official saw it, Uthram Tirunal's residence
was full of 'mirrors, ottomans, statuary, clocks, couches, worked chairs,
and all the concomitant et-ceteras of glitter and parade'.[9] On another
occasion, the same visitor noticed a 'long room filled with tables covered
with all kinds of ornaments and knick-knacks', its walls 'crammed' with

pictures.[10] But it was never about taste to begin with, as much as an appetite to collect: anything that was remotely interesting was ordered, especially if it came from Europe.[11] This was not just because the prince was personally besotted with the West – Indian royalty of the day in general liked surrounding themselves with foreign goods as a signal of their international influence.[12] In that sense, a palace stuffed with trinkets and timepieces was precisely about show.

Socially too, Uthram Tirunal was fond of European company. As heir apparent in the 1830s, often, we read, he was 'the principal figure in a circle of [white] ladies and gentlemen, talking merrily' and completely at ease. In what was still unusual in his time, the prince appeared in English clothes on occasion, imported from British India's capital, Calcutta;[13] one visitor even reported seeing him in a 'really funny' 'half Hungarian outfit'.[14] Indeed, well before Ravi Varma depicted Asvathi Tirunal in Western dress, this great-uncle of that 'B.A. Prince' had posed in coat and trousers for a miniaturist. In his hand he held a book, while in the background on a desk appears a mantel clock, a lamp, a vase and other articles.[15] So too when a governor of Madras visited the state, Uthram Tirunal disarmed him by going aboard his steamer, throwing off both formality and his turban, and settling into a chat. He did, of course, have an agenda: a tour of the vessel and a demonstration of its engine operations.[16] In general, he loved the 'European style of living', and interacted with foreigners 'without the least show of superstition'. Why, despite caste taboos, he did not hesitate even in 'approaching tables where fish and animal food were served'.[17] At home, his vegetarian children were tutored in English, and having once made his daughter read to a guest, Uthram Tirunal added, as if to make sure its novelty were not missed, 'I believe it is very seldom Hindoo females are ever educated [in this style].'[18] In fact to some, all this anglicization even suggested that the prince might entertain a clandestine inclination to Christianity,[19] or at least break the religious ban on overseas travel to visit Victoria in her imperial capital.[20]

This, however, could not be. For Uthram Tirunal's fondness for Western culture did not mean a divorce from local tradition and its

*Uthram Tirunal in European dress,
painted by Alagiri Naidu.*

*Uthram Tirunal in Persianate
attire, painted by Alagiri Naidu.*

influence. As with several Hindu princes of the time, his attempt was very much to preserve what was valued at home with the best of the foreign world. The same officer to whom he showed off his English-speaking child, for example, observed how Uthram Tirunal was 'mad with vexation' when a rival prince's partisans stole a 'celebrated idol' from one of his temples: the maharajah was 'furious' and had 'abandoned all hopes of future happiness and glory because half-a-dozen crafty Brahmins have removed a piece of stone from one temple to another'.[21] The Englishman, of course, saw only stone and could afford sarcasm, but to his host this was an affront to his power as defender of that deity. In a more everyday sense, as much as the prince enjoyed strutting about in European clothes, his other great passion was to deck up in Kathakali costume and entertain himself. As royalty there was no question of performing on stage, so Uthram Tirunal spent hours admiring his skills in front of sundry mirrors instead.[22] A Kathakali troupe was attached to his palace, not only bringing innovation into this drama tradition but also producing star performers like Raman Unni (1807–65) and Easwara Pillai (1815–74).[23] Help was given in creative ways: in 1858 the latter with his master's support set up a press, and harnessing Western technology for local purposes, printed Kathakali plays for the first time.[24] Indeed, the anglicized Uthram Tirunal's reign was a veritable golden age for this old art form, described by an Englishman as that 'abominable Malabar play'.[25]

On the face of it, Uthram Tirunal seems an amiable dilettante, but the fact that he carried out his medical and sartorial experiments in an extremely orthodox state reveals the heterogeneous influences at work. It was a hundred years before that an ancestor forged Travancore, emerging from a political backwater on the southern tip of Kerala, to conquer and subjugate everything till Cochin. Deploying weapons supplied by the English, the military leadership of a European prisoner of war turned loyalist,[26] the strategic genius of a Tamil immigrant, and, where needed, mercenaries and bribery, he birthed a Malayali state that was a child of modern forces. But this king, Martanda Varma, was deeply conscious of his lack of legitimacy – a heap of noble houses were liquidated to launch his dominion; he then ejected various relations from their lands; and finally seized states belonging to other esteemed families. Not a little cunning and brutality was marshalled for these purposes. For instance, on attacking a Brahmin principality, his Hindu soldiers refused to spill sacred blood. So Martanda Varma shipped in Muslims and Christians to do what was needed.[27] Elsewhere, as his troops laid hands on a temple's property, its priests beat them back with brooms, inflicting injury not on their persons as much as their manhood.[28] In lore and song, his crimes include inviting a defiant cousin to see him, innocently taking his sword, and smiling 'with content' after cutting the man's throat ('like a chicken's gullet'), thrilled at the elimination of yet another rival.[29] Naturally, then, having obtained power by hook and crook, the king turned to religion to varnish his deeds in something better than gore; by this he would be reinvented, his actions imbued with an air of nobility.[30]

First Martanda Varma gave himself a caste upgrade through a ritual featuring a golden cow, in whose 'womb' he crouched to be 'reborn' into superior dignity.[31] He then 'surrendered' his conquests to his deity in the Padmanabhaswamy temple in Trivandrum: Travancore no longer belonged to its ruling family, but to god, making the king a divine servant. While broadcast as a spiritual act, this dedication of the kingdom to the almighty came with practical advantages. Criticism of the ruler was equivalent to 'blaspheming the deity' hereon,[32] and the position of the maharajah came to resemble that of 'the Pope in Rome'; Martanda Varma was recast from violent warrior into a faithful devotee, wiping away his bloody antecedents to reign in god's cleansing shadow.[33] The temple was reconstructed with fanfare, festivals were inaugurated, largesse distributed to win Brahmin validation and the royal family elevated from first among equals with their nobles to unquestioned primacy. As an observer later noted, even language, when referring to the ruler, acquired a 'highly artificial' character – the king's food was 'nectar', the maharajah was the 'golden king', every birth was the arrival of an 'incarnation' and so on.[34] The dynasty's everyday existence was sheathed in protocol, caste paranoias and interminable ritual – and as the advent of British authority gnawed away at hard power, these elements were re-

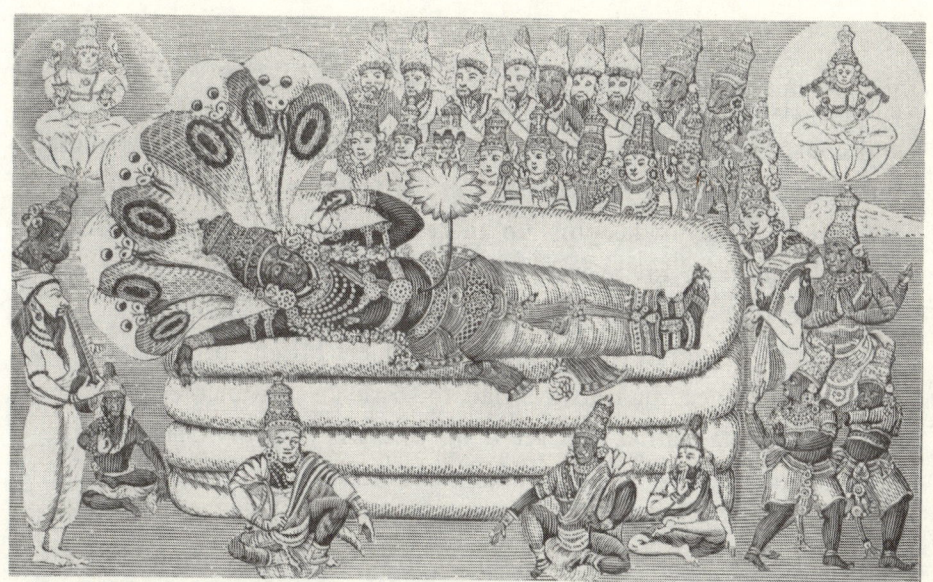

Sri Padmanabhaswamy as depicted in Samuel Mateer's The Land of Charity *(1871).*

The Sri Padmanabhaswamy temple in Thiruvananthapuram.

emphasized to transform the ruler into an even holier figure. Religion and conspicuous devotion, in other words, meant that no matter the turbulence of routine politics, the *sacred* legitimacy of the king was protected.[35] That, in keeping up these ceremonies, Uthram Tirunal's family would also invite imperial ridicule in the colonial period was another matter.

Though seemingly contradictory, in fact, Hindu orthodoxy and modern influences had always had to jostle in Travancore. In many ways Martanda Varma had set it up this way. On his deathbed the maharajah issued certain commandments to his heirs. Two stand out: that 'no deviation whatever' should be allowed in maintaining the deity as their theoretical sovereign; and that 'the friendship existing between' the British and the dynasty 'should be maintained at any risk'.[36] His successor lived by both orders, gaining by doing so – the godly aura consolidated power, while in 1790 the Christian Company saved the state from Tipu Sultan's aggressions. Unfortunately, the British had some calculations too. A treaty of 'perpetual friendship' signed soon after the war with Tipu required the maharajah to pay for troops who would spring to his defence if he were threatened.[37] In practice this meant that Travancore financed part of the Company's military, but it was accepted. Then in 1805, six years after the sultan's death, the British forced a scandalous agreement down the next ruler's throat. As the Company governor-general Lord Wellesley wrote, the earlier arrangement dealt with *foreign* enemies, not 'internal commotions'; its 'spirit', however, obliged the British to protect the royal family from turbulence within also. Troops were now stationed permanently in Travancore – thus ensuring that if a ruler reconsidered his 'friendship', English guns could surround the palace – and for this fishy privilege the state had to part with yet more money.[38] Though the wording presents the maharajah as a cheerful party to the contract, his complaints make clear an 'extremely vexatious' pressure. 'I was compelled', the ruler cried in vain, 'by the violence and oppression' of the local Company Resident.[39]

This, then, represented the other strong force in every colonial era court. In Travancore and elsewhere, the Resident was a strange beast,

neither an ambassador nor officially a supervisor; often, in the words
of a governor-general, he simply assumed the 'functions of a dictator'.[40]
All correspondence had to be channelled through this one-man outlet
for colonial power, even if they were complaints *about* the outlet itself.
Orders from the Company, meanwhile, depended on reports sent by the
same men who were not always objective – if they bungled up, they had
every incentive to blame the court, absolving their own indiscretions. Of
course, Residents did not all act uniformly – some were bored in their
postings, while others lived grandly, in a style close to royal.[41] Some were
conservative Christians, whereas others accepted with delight gifts of
titles and wives.[42] Much depended on personality: certain officers did not
interfere unless the state was in crisis; others poked their noses even in
tranquil waters.[43] Often, Residents staged haughtiness simply to sustain
the myth of the Company's omnipotence, leading some rulers to resist
in kind. In Gwalior, thus, Maharani Baizabai (1784–1864) made it a
point to treat her Resident as a nonentity. By keeping him poorly, she
emphasized *her* authority; or as was written, 'Her Highness is herself
anxious to have as little attention as possible paid to the Resident . . .
with the view of showing her own independence.'[44] After all, the British
were allowing a fifth column in the states – a ruler's internal enemies
simply had to win the white man's ear to make trouble.[45] Slighting the
Resident was a method to pre-empt this, though not all princes had the
requisite boldness or capacity.

Uthram Tirunal's brother, who ruled between 1829 and 1846, for
example, was paralysed by his predecessors' supineness before the
colonial bully. To a missionary observer Maharajah Swathi Tirunal
(1813–46) was 'of a mild disposition, secluding himself after the custom
of Eastern monarchs, living in state and barbaric luxury, in ill-health,
and devoting himself with bigoted attention to the rites, traditions, and
requirements of Hindooism'.[46] As a child, he was a 'very fine boy', but
less gregarious than his brother,[47] and even as ruler, people found him
'trembling with shyness'.[48] None of this augured well in facing British
pressure. In terms of intellectual capacities, however, he was Uthram
Tirunal's superior: besides supporting the arts, including professionals

who had lost patronage in states extinguished by the Company, he was himself a musical genius. While some doubt whether the prodigious number of compositions ascribed to him are all his,[49] he continues to be celebrated as a Sanskrit poet as well as one who composed Manipravala *padams*, with eighty-three works published as early as 1853.[50] His court supported not only Carnatic musicians, but also Hindustani experts from the north; there was even an Anglo-Indian playing Western music in his durbar.[51] Administratively too, in the first part of his reign, Swathi Tirunal showed promise, doing everything from promulgating a legal code to establishing an observatory and an English school. But then a Resident, William Cullen, arrived, with a scheming Indian assistant in tow – the ambitions of the latter, and the arrogance of the former (notorious also for his amorous adventures)[52] meant that for twenty years the 'Resident assumed almost sovereign authority' in Travancore.[53]

As the maharajah's standing dwindled and his government increasingly ran on the whim of the British agent, Swathi Tirunal considered abdication.[54] Though dissuaded, the remainder of his years were marked by political listlessness. 'His Highness now began,' a contemporary recalled, 'to devote his time more to religious devotions than to anything else, and spent his time mostly in prayer, ablutions, and in attending to the worship of the great pagoda at Trevandrum.' Large quantities of money were donated to the deity, and strenuous vows taken, entailing long fasts and solitude, so that even his brother no longer enjoyed free access; the chief minister, who was the Resident's toady, had to wait weeks for an audience. To this 'abyss of depression'[55] was added loss by the death of his father, a friend, a wife and children.[56] Only religious charity offered consolation: on a single occasion, Swathi Tirunal heaped up 1,00,000 rupees, a colossal sum, before his deity, spending an age emptying pouches into the temple's silver vessels. Money came to be 'considered by the Maha Rajah as dust, and the palace expenditure became most extravagant and lavish'. Unable to rule despite his talent, he focused now on the cultural and religious prerogatives of kingship – precisely the kind of turn that would later open maharajahs across India to the charge of mindless ostentation. His dislike of the British grew all along, meanwhile, and the Resident was contemptuously spoken of as a *vellah* (white), with no other European granted access to the royal presence if he could help it.[57] One wonders if in his songs addressed to Hindu deities, praising their destruction of demons and oppressors, Swathi Tirunal was also giving vent to his political feelings.[58] In any case, by the time he died, only in his early thirties, the maharajah was a broken man, though at least one official suspected that human intervention through poison may have hastened his end.[59]

Swathi Tirunal's helplessness and frustration was something several early colonial era princes would have known. On the one hand was the Company's power, while on the other was their own sovereignty, entirely legitimate in Indian eyes. A military response to creeping impotence would never have appealed to a man of Swathi Tirunal's retiring disposition, and adventurism in any case was risky, given how the British disposed of even more prominent rulers. In 1839, for example, they exiled the Satara rajah, a descendant of the founder of the Maratha empire. The Company's own officials deemed him a brilliant ruler – Mountstuart Elphinstone paid him the richest compliment, in colonial eyes at least, when he observed that this 'most civilised Maratha' ran his kingdom 'in a style that would credit a European'.[60] But as was only natural for a man of ability, the rajah got on the wrong side of the Resident, beginning to seem insufficiently docile – or as was reported, 'his disloyal conduct was due to exaggerated notions of his consequence'. He was accused of conspiracy, some alleging he 'thought of corresponding with Russia' when the person he contacted was the Portuguese viceroy in Goa.[61] In bypassing the Resident in external relations, however, he gave the British their excuse: 'Troops occupied his palace . . . The Rajah was torn from his couch, placed in a litter, carried for a distance of eight miles, and deposited in a cow-shed', after which he was removed to Benares. Meanwhile, over £300,000 in treasure was confiscated.[62] If this was the fate of the Maratha *chhatrapati*, Martanda Varma's more humble descendants could hardly entertain any comprehensive anti-colonial strategies – the only option was a middle path to preserve the king but also keep the Company content.[63] Travancore's rulers would have to reconcile to their peculiar position, and reframe how they wielded authority within its new, puzzling limits.

Succeeding his tragic sibling in 1846, then, Uthram Tirunal had his task cut out for him. Unlike Swathi Tirunal, his brother was better equipped to repair the bridges his predecessor had all but burned with their colonial overlords. The state itself seemed like a 'ship without a ballast or a compass in the midst of a storm', but now there was a man at the helm able to launch a charm offensive against the imperial power.[64] To begin with, the maharajah made a decision to 'be guided by the advice and counsel of the British Resident', bending the knee where his brother had quietly stewed till self-destruction.[65] The imperial agent's old assistant, whom Resident Cullen had tried for years to get installed as Dewan, or minister, and whom Swathi Tirunal called a 'vulgar minded man',[66] was finally granted this position. That he was useless in office was another matter, his chief quality being a capacity to exact obedience by flogging officials, and of course showing fidelity to his true master, the Resident.[67] Uthram Tirunal also found other ways of keeping the British happy. In 1849 when news arrived from London proposing the famous Great Exhibition in two years' time at the Crystal Palace, the maharajah prepared to send articles representative of his state's craft traditions. The chief present, however, was an ivory throne he originally meant to use himself, as the official Ivory Throne of the state; it was promptly shipped overseas instead. Whether the irony of his intended seat of power becoming a novelty for a foreign monarch struck him, encapsulating all at once his subordination, is not known.[68] But of the act's political intent, Uthram Tirunal was clear. As he wrote,

The transmission of articles from this country for the Exhibition has afforded me an opportunity of . . . forwarding also to London a chair of State, made of ivory, carved and ornamented . . . and which I request permission to offer for Your Majesty's acceptance as a curiosity, and at the same time as a slight token of my profound respect for Your Majesty's exalted person and for the numerous and great virtues for which Your Majesty is so eminently distinguished.

I beg Your Majesty will graciously condescend to receive this friendly, but humble tribute, from the Native Prince of a country situated at the very southern extremity of Your Majesty's vast Indian empire, who is, as every one of his predecessors has always been, a faithful ally and dependent of the British Government, which, on its part, has ever extended to us its protection and favor, a relation which I humbly trust will continue to the end of time.[69]

In a sense, it was the maharajah reaching out to the British *sovereign* as opposed to dealing with the Company, which held a certain significance – across princely India, in fact, the theory that they were in relations with the Crown and not the local administration would grow into a key tactical position. It was also propitious that the queen held a lifelong sympathy for India. A few years ago, thus, she had agreed with the then governor-general's words that if the country were governed for the 'interests of the People . . . and not the pecuniary advantages of [a] Nation of Strangers', there would be 'no limit' to its prosperity.[70] Later, after the Great Rebellion, when the Company was booted out and the Crown took over India, her proclamation guaranteeing freedom of religion and princely sovereignty did not actually satisfy her. Instead of vague words about 'obligations of Duty', she had desired for Indians to be 'placed on an equality with the [other] subjects of the British Crown' – it was elected politicians who rendered the wording less explicit.[71] Even so in a world of rajahs and ranis, the queen was a more reassuring figure than the disembodied Company, and she was localized in art as 'Victoria Maharani' and compared to goddesses like Lakshmi and Durga.[72] Poetry would be devoted to her in languages ranging from Sanskrit to Bengali, while she herself took Urdu lessons with a *munshi*. Of course, Indian intent was not innocent – the queen's proclamation offered a standard by which to evaluate the Raj, in a way the Company never could be held to account. As one figure wrote, the British 'may violate every one of its promises, but every promise will survive its own violation – and avenge it'.[73] In glorifying the queen, it was possible to make a point against her representatives actually on the ground, and even gain a higher moral position.

Rijksmuseum, Amsterdam

The ivory state chair sent by Uthram Tirunal to Queen Victoria.

Victoria Maharani with the Princess Royal: *The British queen as imagined by an unknown nineteenth-century Indian artist.*

Harvard Art Museums / Arthur M. Sackler Museum, Gift in gratitude to John Coolidge, Gift of Leslie Cheek, Jr. Anonymous Fund in memory of Henry Berg, Louise Haskell Daly, Alpheus Hyatt, Richard Norton Memorial Funds, and the generosity of Albert H. Gordon and Emily Rauh Pulitzer; formerly in the collection of Stuart Cary Welch, Jr.
Photo ©President and Fellows of Harvard College

So much so, in fact, that in 1851 when the queen replied to his letter, Uthram Tirunal conjured up a magnificent reception with 'all possible grandeur and pomp'. Even as tens of thousands of Brahmins gathered in his capital for a sexennial temple ceremony instituted by Martanda Varma,[74] the government was busy orchestrating this flattery of a Christian sovereign who lived oceans away in Buckingham Palace. The best state elephant was commandeered to carry, in a silver howdah, both the British agent and Victoria's letter, attended to by soldiers. When it was brought to the venue, 'The Maha Rajah advanced a few paces, and with a graceful air received the valued packet with a low bow, and raised the same thrice to his head to show His Highness' profound respect for the Queen.' He 'then opened the seal and perused the letter himself with a smile, while his eyes were filled with tears of joy'.[75] The durbar was smartly choreographed, and certainly made an impression on the British. Indeed, they would have had it no other way – imitating the Mughal tradition, where imperial presents were received with the same pomp as would be shown the emperor in person, here too the letter represented not paper but Victoria herself.[76] Sadly for Uthram Tirunal, demonstrations of loyalty, combined with his charisma, could only go so far in keeping at bay the nose of the Company. He had conceded much power to the Resident, but when trouble brewed again, accountability came conveniently to rest on his royal head. That is, if *blame* had to be apportioned, the buck stopped at the palace. And no matter how much the queen was impressed, she had little influence here, especially when news circulated even in London of Travancore's misgovernment.

The issue had old roots and shows how much policy in India depended on attitudes and public opinion in Britain. The first half of the nineteenth century saw Protestant evangelicalism enter India. And while Christian missions did much good – in education, uplifting the marginalized and exposing failures even of the Company – as far as Indian elites were concerned, they were a thorn in the side. In Travancore, for example, converts from low castes, empowered by their new identity, now aspired to equality with their ex-superiors. As a Dewan argued, by 'violating the existing social distinctions', the new Christians were bound to 'annoy the high castes', who demanded retribution. For generations, battles would be fought on dress, access to roads, temples, and even government buildings, and much of the reform Travancore grew famous for owed to this tension with missionaries, and the confidence they gave disempowered segments. Missionaries, however, also tended to magnify the evils they saw, to gain financial sympathy at home, for example. In 1848, thus, it was alleged that Travancore had a 'professed torturer', an expert in 'twenty-three modes' of abuse, on its payroll. In 1855 the state was described as 'a perfect pandemonium of torture and misgovernment'. But the core problem was a clash of moralities, causing even the maharajah 'great uneasiness'.[77] As a Hindu king his duty lay in preserving the way things were; or as he said: 'As my kingdom was in my predecessors' time, so let it remain, and so let it descend to my heir.'[78] His critics, however, wished to smash that caste-based order with a new conception of justice. Which side prevailed at any given moment depended also on higher-ups – Resident Cullen was sympathetic to the maharajah, while the infamous governor-general, Lord Dalhousie, showed personally an evangelical bent.[79]

But Travancore was in a soup for another reason: the state of its treasury. If the threat of social chaos gave the British a handle to interfere, a greater motivation for sternness was Uthram Tirunal's financial embarrassment. For if the government was in the red, it risked defaulting on tribute, which, more than anything else, the Company would not allow. Critics latched on, highlighting those elements of Hindu kingship that aggravated the crisis. The maharajah's prolonged coronation rites were one grievance: in 1850 when Uthram Tirunal was weighed in gold for the *tulabharam*, he spent over 2,00,000 rupees. 'The Rajah's weight was one and a half lakhs,' it was reported, 'the remaining half lakh spent in preparations and gifts.' The fact that most of this, 'taken from the cash-chest of a bankrupt state', was given to Brahmins – derided by the missionaries as an idolatrous priesthood – looked particularly egregious when 'salaries of nearly all the lower classes of public servants are now five or six months in arrear'.[80] Similarly, in 1851 expenditure on the maharajah's daughter's wedding attracted adverse comment.[81] So when, three years later, Uthram Tirunal decided to do the *hiranyagarbham* next (that golden cow ceremony), the British were incandescent. From the ruler's perspective, it was an essential rite of kingship; to his superiors, however, it was vain opulence. Of course, it was another matter that when it came to honouring Victoria, the Company never raised objections – austerity loomed only when Uthram Tirunal's own honour was at stake. But the authorities were in no mood to sympathize: when, as a future Dewan wrote, a remission of tribute was broached, the British 'threw out a broad hint that [they] would take charge of the State' if the maharajah failed to pay his dues.[82] If he persisted in his pursuit of kingly grandeur, that is, he would soon be king of nothing but air.

Interestingly, the maharajah seems to have been aware of the mixed feelings these expensive ceremonies and his patronage of temples, Brahmin feeding houses and other religious functions provoked. And he also knew that the old order did not fit well with transformations introduced by colonialism. Even so, it was impossible for him to avoid the rites, given how his ancestor had wedded the throne's standing with such rituals. In a possibly exaggerated account, we read how he revealed to a missionary his love for the Bible. 'I am sometimes,' the maharajah apparently remarked, 'inclined to renounce all my prospects of sovereignty, and become a Christian.' Unfortunately, he could not proceed, for, 'If I professed myself to be a Christian, there would be a revolution, and the Brahmins would not suffer me to live; and I fear that your Government instead of protecting me, would blame me as the cause of disorder.'[83] Whether Uthram Tirunal considered Christianity or whether he was simply trying to impress a member of a clamorous cultural opposition is not so much the point as his sense that he was duty-bound to a style of existence, and was 'legal protector' of his Hindu state and its practices.[84] The British perhaps would not understand that his prestige in local eyes depended on the performance of these rituals – to the colonial state, after all, ever since Travancore signed its treaties with them, its power was *their* political gift, not requiring indigenous legitimization. But to the ruler, imperial suzerainty did not negate his traditional situation; his political subordination to the Company did not

Uthram Tirunal receives a letter from Queen Victoria, attended to by his Dewan, nephews, sons and durbar.

erase his commitment to Padmanabhaswamy.[85] It was, in fact, a problem the British encountered in many states, failing always to comprehend the meaning such details held for Indian kingship. Instead, they dismissed what they did not know as blind superstition and hopeless extravagance.

In Uthram Tirunal's case, with a negative campaign under way thanks to the missionaries, and with the anaemic condition of his treasury, things began to look dire by the mid-1850s. The governor-general in Calcutta, none other than Dalhousie, had a habit of annexing principalities at the drop of a turban. Only recently, in 1854, he had taken Nagpur, a state ten times the size of Travancore, and immensely richer.[86] Not only was treasure seized, even household effects were confiscated and sold at auction, with scant regard for the ruling family's dignity.[87] Now, with Travancore too, 'annexation fever broke out afresh'.[88] The latest missionary petition even made it to parliament, though it mostly had only vague grievances: there was 'extortion' by the government of Christian converts; the police were an 'engine of iniquity'; prisoners were detained illegally while 'real criminals' committed 'outrages'; officials had 'bad' characters and were 'notoriously incompetent';

economic monopolies held by the government were 'evil'; accounts sent to Madras were 'cooked'; and more in this vein.[89] Though much of this was not the missionaries' business, the authorities bought into it, and in 1855 sent Uthram Tirunal a 'thunderbolt' of a letter.[90] Dalhousie had decided it was time for a 'formal and forcible expression' of British sentiments, instructing the maharajah via the governor of Madras to check the 'manifold abuses prevailing in his dominions' or prepare for intervention.[91] The order was couched as advice, but if disobeyed, would cause power to lapse from ruler to imperial master, irrespective of any deity's claims of divine sovereignty over this plum princely state.[92]

While agitated, Uthram Tirunal was not entirely submissive. In his reply not only did he make it clear that he would settle his obligations, he also highlighted that the Resident was always consulted, and that if there was misgovernment the British were party to it.[93] Given that Cullen had complete knowledge of things, how could the Company feign shock at so late a juncture?[94] He also sought the material aid of his gods; as his nephew wrote, 'The ancient vaults of the great Pagoda were ransacked, and five lakhs of rupees scraped out' to meet expenses.[95] While all this appears to have given the authorities pause, London urged an investigation. The gods, however, intervened again, and extraneous factors and slowness of communication saved the day. Before a decision was reached, the Dewan foisted on Uthram Tirunal by Cullen did everyone a favour by dying; his bosses – official and actual, brown and white – could quickly blame 'the evils which afflicted the Travancore State' on the dead man's 'maladministration'.[96] Calcutta and London were told that the state was now in more efficient hands. In fact, ever since the new minister took over in 1858, it was reported, 'petitions from Travancore have much abated . . . affording good grounds to hope that the administration is . . . being placed on an improved footing'.[97] Pan-Indian trends also gave relief: the Great Rebellion drew British energy away from Travancore to the question of their own survival. Sensing an opportunity for a diplomatic coup, Uthram Tirunal loudly professed loyalty, putting the imperial establishment in the position of having to reciprocate in grace. And in the end, while the maharajah's throne was saved, it was Company rule that terminated – the queen assumed authority over India, declaring in parallel that annexation as a policy had expired.

There was, however, a catch. As Maria Misra notes, while conquest ceased, the cultural pressure on the British at home to 'improve' India remained; the Raj began to espouse a model of 'conservative modernization' where native powers could remain autonomous so long as they participated in this mission.[98] In 1870, in fact, a viceroy would explicitly declare the terms for non-interference, as the British saw it, in an address to the princes of Rajputana:

> If we respect your rights and privileges, you should also respect the rights and regard the privileges of those who are placed beneath you. If we support you in your power, we expect in return good government. We demand that everywhere through the length and breadth of [the country] justice and order shall prevail; that every man's property shall be secure; that the traveller shall come and go in safety; that the cultivator shall enjoy the fruits of his labour, and the trader the produce of his commerce; that you shall make roads and undertake the construction of those works of irrigation which will improve the condition of the people and swell the revenues of your States; that you shall encourage education and provide for the relief of the sick . . . It is for such objects that the servants of the Queen rule in India; and Providence will ever sustain the rulers who govern for their people's good . . . The days of conquest are past; the age of improvement has begun.[99]

Of course, Uthram Tirunal did not need to be told such things – the maharajah who emerged from his close shave with annexation was a wiser man. Kingship, after the turmoil of conquest was out of the way, had hitherto been about preserving the status quo. It was imagined around sustaining temples, feeding Brahmins, performing grand rituals and preserving a caste-based political economy.[100] But whether the ruler liked it or not, the world had changed. Given his appetite for Western knowledge and objects, he could not have been blind to the direction in which the winds were blowing. Uthram Tirunal understood that Westernization in garb and social habits was inadequate. Beating British pressure would take a more agile approach, and only by meeting key parameters could future threats be avoided; only by removing the very grounds for complaint could intervention be pre-empted. And so it was that one of the brightest Indian products of the British system, imported some years earlier from Madras, was placed in full charge of the government. Fighting off talk of misgovernment, T. Madhava Rao was to help Travancore actively win encomiums, holding up its system as a model for princes across the land. By the time Uthram Tirunal died in 1860, still a charming man but a shrewder king, his state was on its way down this road, protecting itself by *owning* the change that otherwise might devour it. In his final years, thus, Padmanabhaswamy's servant gave that deity's kingdom a modern garb, and a fresh approach to survive the Raj.

It was into this transformed durbar that a young Ravi Varma made his entry.

A little after Uthram Tirunal came to Travancore's throne, a boy was born in a village called Kilimanoor, twenty miles from the royal capital. Many are the tales that speak of the child's predestined greatness: a favourite story has it that his mother, a poet called Umamba, was possessed by a *yakshi* who gave her the boon of gifted progeny. In keeping with tradition in her matrilineal family, Umamba had some years before taken a Brahmin husband. Years after she was 'given the cloth' (that is, married) by Neelakandan Bhattathiri, the couple still had no children – till in 1847 Umamba was possessed. An exorcist supposedly persuaded the spirit to spare the lady, offering the yakshi an alternative abode. The latter agreed, but as a gift to the mortal whose body briefly hosted her, she also issued a prophecy: Umamba would bear a son whose name would resound through the world.[101] In another version, Ravi Varma's mother is already pregnant when entranced – the

Jay Varma

The grove to the yakshi at Kilimanoor.

yakshi leaves her precisely because she finds that the baby in Umamba's womb is no ordinary child. Yet another retelling has the yakshi present a test: the couple could have either immense wealth, or a boy with talent. Wisely, the parents took the second option and impressed her.[102] And while Umamba would have more children in the years ahead, it was her eldest, born on 29 April 1848, who was ordained, it is said, for an uncommonly bright future, blessed by Kilimanoor's newest divine presence.

It is a feature of the Indian tradition to deify famous men and women through myth and legend. In Kilimanoor, the story around Ravi Varma is believed sincerely – the grove where the yakshi was installed survives, and to this day pregnant women perform rituals there. Either way, early on our protagonist is said to have shown signs that the prophecy would prove accurate. While he received an education in Sanskrit and Malayalam, Ravi Varma was restless about drawing. Whether it was a piece of charcoal with which he drew on the walls, or with a stick in the earth, an inclination towards art was constant. Posthumous myth-making and talk of yakshis aside, it probably helped that the boy was born into a family with multiple creative individuals, birthing a saying that 'in Kilimanoor, even the crows have talent'.[103]

In Swathi Tirunal's reign, for example, the family produced a Rajaraja Varma, styled *vidwan* (scholar) for his learning. He was the author of a revisionist Kathakali play, *Ravanavijayam*, in which the Ramayana's villain appears not as 'a wicked *asura*' but 'a human being endowed richly with human feelings'.[104] Artists, actors and scholars were frequent visitors to Kilimanoor, which had its own Kathakali troupe and poets, creating a distinct aesthetic environment – if Ravi Varma would later depict on canvas scenes from the epics, it was at home that he cultivated his knowledge of these stories. Umamba's cousin, also called Rajaraja Varma (1812–83) became a courtier to Uthram Tirunal, meanwhile – it was through this uncle that Ravi Varma was exposed to the possibilities of drawing, not so much as a distraction but as a lifelong pursuit and passion.

The Travancore durbar was a place already receptive to different kinds of art. The Kerala style of mural painting was, of course, popular: the palace in Padmanabhapuram houses spectacular work from Martanda Varma's day, as do walls in the temple in Trivandrum. But exposure to Western styles also increased with time, and possessing specimens was a mark of prestige. In the eighteenth century, for example, among gifts a maharajah received from a missionary were 'two European paintings', and in the early nineteenth, Uthram Tirunal's mother was delighted on obtaining from the Resident a selection of Western art.[105] It was only in Swathi Tirunal's reign, though, that Europeans received direct commissions. The Hungarian, Auguste Theodor Schoefft, who painted everyone from the Sikh emperor in Punjab to the Carnatic nawab, did seven portraits for this maharajah, receiving 12,000 rupees in payment. So too after the death of Serfoji II, the polyglot ruler of Tanjore (also, incidentally, the owner of an artificial skeleton for anatomical studies), painters from Tamil country accepted patronage in Trivandrum.[106] In 1841, the Russian Alexey Saltykov came to the state, making pictures and receiving presents from the maharajah of European-style paintings – an interesting reversal of roles, no doubt intended to impress.[107] And in Uthram Tirunal's reign, F.C. Lewis, Jr received a commission, doing a large painting of the maharajah's durbar as well as portraits of his sons and nephews.[108] In fact, even the controversial Resident Cullen made a contribution to art, supporting local talent in the form of one Muthukrishna who did for him a number of botanical paintings.[109]

It was in Uthram Tirunal's durbar that Ravi Varma's uncle Rajaraja met the painter Alagiri Naidu – the very man who depicted the maharajah in European dress. An expert in miniature as well as mural painting, Naidu was also trained in oil on canvas. Ravi Varma's uncle became a pupil, even if he did not pursue art with the professional enthusiasm his nephew would. For a dabbler, though, his output was impressive. In the family shrine in Kilimanoor, Rajaraja painted scenes from the epics, while within household buildings other evidence lives of his hand: a life-size horse, for instance, on an inner wall. He also acquired expertise with ivory – learning from families who practised the art of carving, he produced a figurine of the god Krishna as well as another of Indra on his elephant.[110] With portraits on ivory too he was a success; in the 1860s a visitor was 'astonished' by a picture of the maharajah, 'so accurate and so finished, that it looks like a coloured photograph of the highest class' – a painting likely produced by Rajaraja.[111] But while this uncle was the

The Sree Chitra Art Gallery, Thiruvananthapuram

Ravi Varma's uncle, Rajaraja Varma (1813–84).

most gifted in Ravi Varma's family, others about him too played around with the brush. In fact, as per tradition, it was *women* in the house who first demonstrated an aptitude for painting, with colours made from 'leaves, flowers, barks, seeds, the white of the egg and olive oil'.[112] So much so that given this long-standing exposure to art from Ravi Varma's grandmother's generation, one suspects his own instincts may have had a good deal to do with powers of observation, rather than supernatural forces; he merely grew into the most famous in a family full of artists, littérateurs and musicians.

Kilimanoor's connection with the royal house was rooted, though, not in paint and poetry but blood and war. The *Travancore State Manual*, published in the year of Ravi Varma's death, carries an account of the artist's ancestors. The Koil Tampurans (their family title) of Kilimanoor, we read, 'are the natives of Parappanad in Malabar', in north Kerala. Their forebears ruled as petty rajahs here, from a town called Beypore, subject to the suzerainty of the kings of Calicut (where Vasco da Gama had landed). In the late seventeenth century, however, they moved to what was shaping up into Travancore, and were at once allied to its rulers: for generations it was Kilimanoor that supplied husbands to the kingdom's matrilineal princesses (more on them later). 'The great Martanda Varma Maharajah, the founder of Travancore' was, we read, the 'issue of (this) alliance'. In fact, through the eighteenth century, down till 1829, every ruler was fathered by a Kilimanoor man – 'a circumstance', we are told, 'of which the members of the family always speak with just pride'.[113] An enduring tale about Ravi Varma casts him too as a prospective groom for a junior princess – the story goes that he was presented to the maharajah, who dismissed him on the grounds that he was too dark. But noting the boy's artistic capacities, he was permitted to remain in the durbar and train, with the ruler also throwing in a box of watercolours.[114] It is a charming tale and much repeated except for the little detail that by the time Ravi Varma got to Trivandrum in 1862, all the royal women were already wed.[115]

That said, supplying husbands to superior princely lines was not a novel experience for Ravi Varma's clan. Before his family transported itself from Beypore to southern Kerala, they were traditionally husbands to the princesses of Calicut. Unlike in Travancore where the names are known, though,[116] it is difficult to identify which of these northern kings were the offspring of Ravi Varma's forebears.[117] It was not their political authority, which was always modest, that made them attractive to matrilineal royal women as much as their ritual pre-eminence: in caste, the Beypore family ranked high, and was among the most esteemed local Kshatriya lineages. One legend suggests that their ancestors were Rajputs who abandoned their homeland to travel down India's west coast to the land of Malayalam.[118] And here, while they did not enjoy much political capital, their pedigree ensured they remained close to those men and women who *did* enjoy influence.[119] It may well be a lot of myth with a fragment of fact, but either way, this was the received tradition. And intermarriage with the ruling dynasty in Travancore meant that the family were close cousins of the maharajahs. However, as historian E.M.J. Venniyoor clarified, this did not mean 'that the men of Kilimanoor . . . were themselves rajas'. On the contrary, in keeping with 'the [matrilineal] arrangement obtaining in Kerala, they were just husbands living in the palace at the pleasure of the ruler, sometimes even of their wives'.[120] They had allowances and status, but no rank beyond that of 'consorts' – no Kilimanoor man was a king, even if he might father one through a princess (more on this in chapter five).

Even so, there was a certain tangential glamour to the family. Besides having helped birth a Martanda Varma, they had supplied a husband to that ruler's sister, giving the maharajah his heir by matrilineal succession. This brother-in-law was a brave man: in 1728 during a time of civil war, learning of an ambush as he escorted his royal wife and son, he sent them to safety and himself took a seat in their palanquin. So, when the enemy attacked, they were startled to see not Martanda Varma's sister but her husband rise before them. The 'Koil Thumpuran jumped out,' we read, 'and cut to pieces many of the assailants.'[121] He died in the process, but as a bona fide hero. The man's son, meanwhile, grew up as Martanda Varma's successor, and ruled Travancore for four decades. Where some knew him as Dharmarajah ('protector of the faith') for giving sanctuary to Brahmins and Hindu princes fleeing Tipu's invading army, this maharajah was also part of the Persianate Mughal world: subordination to the Carnatic nawab, himself feudatory to the Mughal emperor, brought Travancore into a fading but still respected imperial system in 1766.[122] So too when the pope wrote to him, the Carmelite father who acted as courier was amazed that the king spoke English 'exceedingly well'.[123] At a meeting, strikingly, the ruler was not in formal attire: all he had was a 'small piece of cloth fastened round the loins', with 'the only mark of distinction by which his royal dignity could be discovered' being a 'red velvet cap with gold fringes'.[124] The sight of an English-speaking Indian potentate in a loincloth must have been, by eighteenth-century standards, memorable.

The Kilimanoor family, naturally, entertained a degree of pride that this famous maharajah was fathered by their own revered ancestor. Besides, the stability that came with his reign meant that in their little fief too, the sword was steadily replaced by the pen, the musical instrument, and the brush. In the early nineteenth century, however, the family's monopoly over the supply of husbands to Travancore's princesses came to an end: among Malabar's royalty who chose exile here over defeat to Tipu were rivals who now entered the nuptial fray. Swathi Tirunal and Uthram Tirunal both, thus, were not sons of a Kilimanoor father but born of a rival clan. The family felt the loss but coped, winning acclaim by excelling in cultural pursuits instead of in the royal bedchamber. Ravi Varma especially brought fame of a pan-Indian scale to his village. In the first years of the twentieth century, in fact, he would inherit the headship of his clan, and formally enjoy its titles – he became one of the principal noblemen at the Travancore durbar. But if his social status helped his career, when men and messages came to Kilimanoor for him, it was to locate the *painter* who was part of a bigger world. In Baroda and Mysore, states mightier than Travancore, as well as metropolises like Bombay and Calcutta, it was Ravi Varma the professional who was feted. In a sense he became a bridge between two worlds: one with roots going back centuries, to an age of warriors and battles, of heroes and aristocrats, and a new one of emerging India, with its nationalists and viceroys.

And in his work too he married the two, creating something fresh and participating in something much greater than himself.

But that was into the future. Ravi Varma's arrival in 1862 in Trivandrum was a life-defining moment. Uthram Tirunal had died two years before, and his nephew, Ayilyam Tirunal (1832–80), was the maharajah.[125] Exposed hitherto to murals and miniatures thanks to his gifted uncle, it was under this ruler's patronage that Ravi Varma encountered oil paintings for the first time. 'In the palace,' Venniyoor tells, 'he wandered the halls and corridors, studied the artists paint, observed the paintings, saw colourful processions,' and 'pored over albums of European art' imported by Ayilyam Tirunal. He was struck, for instance, by what he could see of the works of the French painters Gustave Boulanger and William Adolphe Bouguereau, both of whom were senior contemporaries.[126] Edward Moor's *The Hindu Pantheon* (1810) was of particular interest for its depiction of the gods and goddesses Ravi Varma knew from the Puranas and Sanskrit texts.[127] This joining of a Western approach to Eastern subjects made an impression on him, far stronger than any temple fresco or Tanjore painting he had seen.[128] Soon it became clear to the boy that this was what he wanted to master: the European technique of painting with oils, and the depiction of Indian scenes in European style. In a time when Western modernity was being indigenized, he would take the Western *palette* and give it an Indian touch; Ravi Varma would do in art what the maharajah who supported him sought to achieve in politics, blending borrowed ideas with inherited tradition.

But none of this was easy, especially as formal instruction in this rare kind of art was not easy to find in the 1860s. The chief oil painter in the durbar, Ramaswamy Naidu,[129] does not seem to have had much time for the teenager from Kilimanoor. Generally, his refusal to instruct Ravi Varma is explained as stemming from a fear of being eclipsed: he knew how gifted the boy was, seeking to thwart his rise and avoid competition. But there may well have been factors other than professional territoriality. For example, class resentment – most court painters were at that time of Sudra background, and even Alagiri Naidu, 'the best painter of the day in

South India',[130] was viewed as a craftsman. In that context, the arrival of an aristocratic relative of the maharajah may have sparked a clannishness that Ravi Varma's cheerleaders read as envy. Indeed, in 1868 when the Danish artist Theodore Jensen came to Trivandrum, even his refusal to give lessons to the local painter was explained as emerging from fear of being outshone. But as art historian Partha Mitter explains, while it is possible Jensen wished to guard his technique and had a racist bone, his disregard for Ravi Varma came likely from the fact that he was an itinerant professional in town only briefly, unable therefore to entertain aspirants. Moreover, in comparing Jensen's portraits with Ravi Varma's work, Mitter observes that the Malayali *did* in fact pick up skills from the Dane, whom he was permitted to watch at work.[131] While the mythology around Ravi Varma tells one tale, with the artist as wronged hero and deliberately slighted by a white man, thus, viewed in context, its protest pales somewhat.

Of course, that Ravi Varma worked hard is not to be doubted. Naidu's refusal to teach him left him 'despondent' we learn, and 'with none to initiate him into the mysteries of perspective and chiaroscuro, of compositions and complementary colours', Ravi Varma 'marked his time'.[132] His official narrative has him face daunting barriers at every turn, till he overcomes them with 'the redoubled pace of a prodigy', beating both brown and white antagonists – as Geeta Kapur writes, 'What is at stake is not only native talent but national destiny.'[133] But the man was not, as has been observed, a 'self-created genius from the backwaters of Travancore who struggled in a basically artless surrounding'.[134] Moreover, his success was not based on just artistic talent but also a shrewd capacity for negotiating durbar politics, of which we don't hear enough. Naidu's unfriendliness did not put him off, for example: when a direct approach failed, Ravi Varma pursued an underhand method. The older man had an apprentice called Arumugham Pillai – somehow the latter, who assisted Naidu by day, was persuaded to give Ravi Varma lessons by night.[135] In the official account, what 'really sustained' the Kilimanoor boy 'during these years was his will to break through and excel, and an abiding faith in divine grace'.[136] But, arguably, what energized him was a combination of resolve and pragmatism. Pulling off a clandestine arrangement with the disciple of a hostile senior was not achieved through divine offices; more material incentives likely played a role.

Ravi Varma would, at more than one milestone in his life, have to find creative solutions of this nature, in fact. Unlike his uncle, who learnt to paint but never transgressed aristocratic bounds by becoming a professional, Ravi Varma challenged the orthodoxy. Great was the mockery he faced for his obsession with art and his desire for approval in the form of sales and commissions – painting, it was felt, was not a suitable vocation for the scion of a noble line, not least because it involved such pedestrian business as selling things for money. By allowing himself to become too seriously involved in art, it was argued, Ravi Varma was lowering himself from his natural station to the level of artisans. Some of these accusations do seem to have stung: it is said that the painter never personally handled money, refusing even to touch coins and bank-notes.[137] Irrespective of its truth, it hints at a man who, all said and done, tried to position himself as above the forces of the very market in which he was to become a celebrity; a man who set up a commercial press to sell prints of his works, and yet did not wish to be tainted by commerciality. He was accused of wandering across India, mingling with all kinds of castes, brush in hand, posing as a supplicant before diverse maharajahs. Indeed, even pan-Indian fame did not mitigate sneering attacks in family and caste circles. In that sense the real pressure Ravi Varma endured was not from fellow artists as much as his own lot. Where his elite status would open doors in other places, in Kerala itself it was at first used to brand him as a rebel and, in snooty circles, even an embarrassment.[138]

By 1870, at any rate, with many such questions playing on his mind, twenty-two-year-old Ravi Varma decided to leave Trivandrum briefly. He could count on the maharajah's support: if others saw painting as an inferior vocation, Ayilyam Tirunal viewed it as a gift ordained only to a few, in the process helping Ravi Varma navigate family tensions.[139] Still, the latter wished to find inner strength, and departed for Mookambika in what is now Karnataka state, for forty-one days of *bhajanam* (meditation) at its Sarasvati temple. When this was done, Ravi Varma fortified his decision: he would continue as an artist, no matter the condescension. All varieties of fantastic stories exist, in fact, about this pilgrimage – a sign of exactly how much appeal he won in popular narratives, which lapped up wondrous tales and a personality cult. In Kasargode, for example, he is supposed to have deployed occult knowledge to exorcise a spirit from the body of a Brahmin girl – locals, hearing of this, swarmed to him to be helped in various ways, till the artist fled one night.[140] In this tale, Ravi Varma is akin to a holy man. Another speaks of a lordly type who so liked the artist that he became determined to get his daughter married to him; again the man had to vanish in the dark hours to avoid unsolicited attraction.[141] Stories aside, what is of greater interest is that on the way back from Mookambika, Ravi Varma received his maiden commission outside the Travancore durbar – the very first private portrait he did shows a sub-judge of the Calicut court with wife and children.[142] It was, in other words, a mid-level British employee in British-ruled territory who gave the artist his first paid job, a man whose other claim to fame is that he would, in due course, become father-in-law to a future Congress president.[143]

It is not a particularly impressive work. While the painter got the drapery and ornaments on his five subjects nicely, their faces and features lack the finish he would in time become famous for as a society portraitist. Still, the receipt of a paid commission after weeks of prayer and introspection was a good omen: Ravi Varma was now reinforced in his choice of career. The story goes that soon after his return to court, he produced a portrait of the maharajah and his wife. Jensen had made one only two years before, but it was clear to everyone that Travancore's home-born artist had surpassed the European. A delighted Ayilyam Tirunal presented Ravi Varma with a *veerasringhala*, a bangle of honour once given to warriors and others of standing.[144] Ravi Varma also produced a state portrait of the ruler, transforming an otherwise unimpressive, egg-shaped man into a picture of kingliness. In any case, with this royal stamp of approval, the former's confidence grew. Three years later, after he was invited to participate by a visiting official, at an exhibition patronized by the governor of Madras, Ravi Varma won the gold medal.[145] In 1874, gold again landed in the Travancore artist's lap, all this especially delightful given his rivalry with Naidu who too submitted his work. British praise – including a meeting with the governor himself – cemented his sense of purpose, also making him an object of awe in Indian eyes; his career was starting to bloom. So much so that a popular story tells that in 1876, after he struck gold yet again, this time for his *Sakuntala Patralekhan*, Ravi Varma took a decision: he would no longer compete for medals. That way, lesser mortals might have a chance to win.[146]

For Ayilyam Tirunal, the adolescent he had supported had grown into a man of talent, one who brought his state a certain glow. But medals aside, the maharajah's true moment of pride had come a little before in a more prestigious setting. Late in 1875 Albert Edward, Victoria's son, landed in India for a tour of the subcontinent. Predictably, there were demonstrations of fealty, with rajahs tripping over each other in the process. The press was breathless with excitement: on the eve of his arrival, the *Native Public Opinion* noted how though they were of different complexions and costumes, 'We are all free-born British subjects.'[147] Indian rulers of 'five different soils', a Tamil reporter wrote, 'welcomed the Prince' who in return 'paid them respect by raising up his hand of crimson color'.[148] Edward was also loaded with presents through the trip, so valuable that, to his officers' chagrin, his own return gifts looked cheap.[149] The ruler of Mysore, for example, had given plates, trays and perfume holders of gold, while the Udaipur maharana presented a *sirpech* (head ornament) of diamonds, pearls and emeralds. Exquisite weapons were obtained from several princes; one rani even offered a 'boomerang of steel inlaid with silver and gold mountings'. From nutcrackers to stone sculptures, daggers to carved caskets, Edward collected over 2,000 objects in India.[150] Ayilyam Tirunal too gave gifts when they met in Madras, including an exquisite ivory bed and a painting of 'marvellous beauty and high finish'. According to a newspaper report, the future Edward VII admiring the second of these items had asked: 'Is it drawn by a veteran artist in England?' 'No,' replied the maharajah with a hint of smugness, 'it is the work of a young native genius at my Court.'[151]

That young genius was, of course, Ravi Varma.

This chapter covers the lives and work of two remarkable Travancore maharajahs, the first of whom was Ravi Varma's supporter, and the other, the exact opposite. Together, however, these maharajahs and their ministers preserved Travancore from British interference, setting it on the path of modernization.

2

The Brahmin Who Knew English

In many ways, as his exposure to Madras and an India outside Travancore grew in the 1870s, Ravi Varma understood what his aristocratic kinsmen, with their cushioned aloofness, were unable to comprehend: that the world was changing. The royal capital held all the evidence. There was, of course, the sanctified space of the fort and temple, which seemed almost to exist in a different age. And yet, beyond that quarter was emerging a new town of libraries, colleges and much else of patently modern make. As a missionary noted in 1869, there were 'fine roads in and around' the city, and 'engineering and architectural works', built by imported British technicians. Though under native rule, it was added with subtle condescension, Travancore looked as if it were run by 'a most enlightened European Government'.[1] Political life too was changing, and Ayilyam Tirunal was just the kind of prince to smooth the process. Laying the foundation stone for a state secretariat – which remains the Kerala government's headquarters 150 years later – the maharajah spoke of how British protection from 'external violence' meant it was now his 'pleasant' task to 'develop prosperity' and 'multiply the triumphs of peace'.[2] The Madras authorities were pleased: in 1868, less than a decade into his reign, they lauded Ayilyam Tirunal for finding a 'middle way' in the colonial refashioning of India: he made a point of 'avoiding all extremes', was 'conservative by temperament' but 'liberal by intelligence' and preserved 'the confidence of his own people' while meeting 'the discriminating expectation of a progressive age'.[3] And by so fitting the imperial vision of the ideal native, the man won for his kingdom – till recently subjected to threats – the coveted tag of a 'model state'.[4]

The process of Travancore's modernization, which had begun in Uthram Tirunal's final years, was originally about a ruler responding to colonial pressures. Under his heir, however, it grew into the state's mission to stand at the vanguard of 'progress'. But this could not happen without allies, and assisting Travancore – a seat of Brahminism by all accounts – navigate unfamiliar waters was, funnily enough, a new species of Brahmin: English speaking, English educated and inclined more to the office desk than the temple. The maharajah's right-hand man had such a visible Englishness about him, in fact, that he became an asset in wooing the British. Around 1850, shortly after he came to Trivandrum for the first time, a Residency official called him not only 'remarkably intelligent', capable of holding forth on everything from the American War of Independence to the Protestant Reformation, but also emphasized that he 'spoke English perfectly'. Why, he showed such 'ease and fluency', that he could pass off for someone brought up in England.[5] A decade later another amazed British agent repeated these sentiments: 'I have never yet met with a native of India who has obtained so thorough a mastery over our language, or so intimate a knowledge and appreciation of [our] modern views.'[6] In new India, in other words, where Sanskrit and Persian once served as portals to prestige, power now resided in the colonizer's language. The recipient of all this praise acknowledged this, writing how 'the honor and happiness' showered on him was thanks to 'the education which I owe entirely to the liberality of the British Government'.[7] But as far as the maharajah cared, to beat the British one had to first *know* the British – and that is what this civil servant brought to the table.

Raja Sir T. Madhava Rao (1828–91), came from a Marathi-speaking family, whose ancestors had abandoned the Deccan for openings in peninsular India under the Marathas.[8] And after the rise of the British, their community (Deshasthas) transferred its scribal loyalties to the Company.[9] Drifting with colonial officers, senior posts in princely states were arranged for them, where they became intermediaries between Hindu rulers (who appreciated their twice-born status) and the British (who valued their English). Long before Lord Macaulay envisioned a class 'Indian in blood and colour, but English in tastes, in opinions, in morals and in intellect', its prototype had already, in fact, surfaced with these Marathi Brahmins.[10] In 1811, thus, Resident John Munro brought an aide called Reddy Rao to Travancore, who was so attached to him that critics thought them 'one Soul in two bodies'.[11] Munro promoted his man – some years later, when the Dewan made the mistake of punishing a European, the Resident sacked him, and planted Rao in his place.[12] But such patronage was contingent on each British agent's tenure: when in 1819 a fresh Resident arrived, trotting along was *his* assistant, Venkata Rao – it did not take long for the new Rao to plot against the old Rao for the Dewanship.[13] Meanwhile, one of Munro's men had become English teacher to Swathi Tirunal; when this prince succeeded as king, it took only a year for the 'very clever' tutor to topple the second Rao.[14] Seven years passed till this third Rao fell out with his master – the second Rao returned triumphantly to claim his old position.[15] Finally, Resident Cullen imposed a Rao of his own on Uthram Tirunal. Though a reflection of British high-handedness towards maharajahs, this process can also be read another way: as an avenue for enterprising, mobile, high-caste Indians to cultivate English patrons; a back door through which brown bureaucrats began an ascent to power.[16]

Madhava Rao was the latest in this procession of Marathi Brahmins or, as locals would say, 'foreigners', who denied Travancore's home-born men the premier office in the land (indicating how national identities beyond the local had little appeal in this period).[17] Nephew to Venkata Rao of years before, as a boy he had been plucked from home and sent to study at the British government's high school in Madras, which later evolved into Presidency College.[18] Joined to his intelligence and appetite for exertion was that extraordinary flair for English, which put Rao in an enviable position insofar as employment went. For a brief time, he was a mathematics teacher in his alma mater, after which he joined the office of Madras's accountant general. But then in 1849, a life-altering

Sir T. Madhava Rao as depicted in The Indian Charivari *(1875).*

knock landed on his door: Uthram Tirunal was seeking a tutor for his nephews, and wondered if Rao would take up the post. At 200 rupees a month, the job was not vastly better than what Madras offered, so the man turned for advice to John Bruce Norton, a pro-Indian legal luminary who lambasted his own countrymen for ruling more 'to extract revenue' and less for the good of the people.[19] Norton, who for all his criticism of the colonial system also believed that natives needed to be trained to govern first, advised Rao that it was his 'bounden duty' to accept; 'because if he excited in the breast of those young Princes a thirst for knowledge and a love of virtue' (as defined by the West, of course), 'he might become the benefactor of millions of his fellow countrymen'. Rao, who reportedly was at first fretting about court intrigues and princely unpredictability, took the advice.[20]

As Rao began a professional journey of uncommon success, Norton would repeatedly present him as a trailblazer. He was, the Englishman said in 1855, 'an example and a pride to all Hindus', because he had gained important offices 'not by any intrigue . . . by back-stair or Court influence; but by a noble perseverance in the path of duty'.[21] Two years later, Norton described Rao as a 'splendid example of what education may do for the Native'.[22] Leaving the racist undertones aside, what he was referring to was his protégé's swift rise in Travancore. Joining in 1849, Rao taught Uthram Tirunal's nephews for four years; he was then made deputy *peishkar*, that is, placed in a post two steps below that of the Dewan. Thereafter, in 1855 he was appointed deputy Dewan on a generous salary of 600 rupees a month.[23] As with Ravi Varma – and as claimed by Norton – Rao's official narrative frames his rise entirely as a consequence of merit; as the inevitable triumph of (British-approved) talent. In reality, however, here also personal networks and family antecedents played a role – it was his own brother, Vasudeva Rao, for instance, who first recommended him to Uthram Tirunal as a potential royal tutor, no doubt aware that this could become the first rung on a rewarding ladder.[24] Indian as well as friendly British networks were exploited, in other words, in the making of this future statesman.

Soon Rao gained a sway over the princes and the maharajah, whom he served as English secretary during his crisis years.[25] As deputy Dewan, for example, he proposed straight to the ruler and Resident, over the head of his superior, that he be given territorial divisions to govern. The deputies till then, we are told, 'scarcely did any work of real importance' and were at the receiving end of the Dewan's jealousy, if they were not themselves plotting against him.[26] The idea was accepted, showing Rao's ability to topple hierarchies that got in his way, much like Ravi Varma got past unfriendly court painters.[27] Then we read, in the words of one of his royal wards, that no sooner had Rao's wishes been granted than he proved himself in a heroic style – a knight in shining armour beating back dark forces. If the British claimed to 'civilise' India and bring 'order', here that exaggerated language was appropriated for an Indian; darkness itself was not denied, but credit for doing something about it was placed in native hands:

> Though the districts delivered to Madava Row contained the most turbulent race of men ... though they were parched and famine-stricken ... though they were thickly interspersed by fierce dacoits, though they formed the high road for the contraband trade of tobacco, yet, in a short year ... they improved in their physical and social features, irrigation works being carried on a large scale, corruption and violence being suppressed, and crimes of all natures being crushed; scarcely a just grievance reached him, which did not speedily receive that relief which was in his power to give. All the notorious robbers and criminals who had hitherto eluded detection were apprehended ... In fact, Madava Row's division furnished a worthy model to the others. The unanimous opinion of the honest and unbiased missionaries has testified to the excellence of Madava Row's administration.[28]

In other words, missionaries – not actually the most unbiased observers – liked him; the British liked him, because of his English; the young princes he mentored were fond of him; and, of course, he was efficient, all of which combined to locate Rao in a towering position. With the anglophone Uthram Tirunal, for instance, his relationship was not entirely formal. As Rao wrote to a friend in 1855, 'His Highness once when jesting told me that my salary of Rs. 600 is regulated at the rate of one hundred for each child [for he had six]. I said in reply that if that was the principle of promotion, I could soon entitle myself to further additions [that is, produce more babies], till His Highness be compelled' to pay more.[29] It wasn't too many government servants who could engage in playful banter with a semi-divine sovereign. So, it is no surprise that in late 1857 when Cullen's Dewan, increasingly eclipsed and blamed for every grievance against the state, died, Rao was propelled into his place over the head of a senior. Where his classmates from Madras were still at salaries of under 300 rupees, instantly this thirty-year-old began to receive a purse of 2,000.[30] Indeed, the British themselves would note that Rao's salary as Dewan was 'double that of the best appointment held by any Native under the Madras Government'.[31] He had pleased Uthram Tirunal, and cultivated bonds with his nephews who would in future become maharajahs: this influence and British backing helped him as much as what Norton loftily described as a selfless regard for duty.[32] If he had remained in Madras, on the other hand, he would still be plodding through a clerical line – it was transfer to a *princely state* that gave him an opportunity to scale real heights; this is what brought him renown.[33]

Rao's work as Dewan, particularly the bureaucratic structures he developed, would survive till Travancore's dissolution. The judicial system was modified, portions of the Indian Penal Code came into force in the state and the minister's attention was drawn to everything from revenue to the postal services. Clever as he was, Rao also knew that success meant little if it were not advertised. So, year after year, reports were published, packed with statistics on how many miles of roads were added, what number of schools were opened, and more in this vein. With such determination did the man bombard colonial authorities with data, that in another state where he would later serve, an officer sarcastically prayed for 'somewhat less enlightened and talented persons' at the helm. For that way the reports would be 'a few hundred pages shorter' and they would be spared Rao's 'lectures'.[34] It was a compliment really that the Raj had, insofar as administration went, little to complain about.

Madhava Rao (right) with his royal wards, Ayilyam Tirunal (centre) and Visakham Tirunal (left), as depicted in Samuel Mateer's The Land of Charity *(1871).*

In the early years, in fact, his updates on the progress of 'progress' in Travancore were welcomed: noting the Dewan's record for 1864–65, for instance, higher-ups commented that not only were the state's finances 'creditable', matters were also proceeding on 'enlightened principles'.[35] Fears of falling behind on tribute receded as revenues rose in Rao's first decade from 43 lakh to 51 lakh rupees.[36] The maharajah too was for modernization: pious speeches were made about his desire to do 'all that lies in my power' in 'making Travancore an honourable example of Native good government'.[37] In a world where enlightenment was viewed as a British monopoly, and backwardness irradicably Indian, this was not without a larger meaning.

Rao too, of course, was aware that he was helming a grander mission than merely managing departments.[38] He knew that the power he enjoyed was a scarce commodity among natives, and that he was making history. So, having been given a platform, he brought initiative and spirit to it. In a note to the assistant Resident, for example, Rao waxed eloquent about attracting foreign investment to the state, to 'rouse the energies of the native capitalist'. Concluding the missive, he apologized for its length: 'one's self control is heavily taxed when he has to resist the temptation of such a subject as the improvement of this fine country.'[39]

In 1866, when he was knighted, the governor of Madras reminded him that his legacy would not be limited to one state: 'The mission in which you are engaged,' said Lord Napier, 'has more than a local and transitory significance. Remember that the spectacle of a good Indian Minister serving a good Indian Sovereign is one which may have a very lasting influence on the policy of England, and on the future of Native Governments.'[40] It was precisely the philosophy Rao believed in – that Indians only needed to prove that they could govern well, and the empire would shower rewards and respect. Or as he wrote to a junior who later became Dewan himself,

> I have only to add my hope that by continuing to render faithful, diligent and willing service, you will advance in the [government] service. Remember that much more than your individual interests are at stake; in short the national character is under trial. If educated young men can show that they can equal Europeans not only in the capacity to do good service, but in the strictest integrity in every sense of the word, it will be a great thing accomplished for our community. I am glad that in your conduct hitherto you have shown yourself quite alive to the importance of this point.[41]

This did not mean, however, that Rao was incapable of pointing out failings on the part of the Raj. In 1854, when he was still at a relatively junior place, and could have been shown the door for his candour, he permitted Norton to publish his views on flaws in British-inspired revenue models. In eliminating middlemen and landlords to extract taxes directly from the cultivator, the authorities believed they had lifted peasants to the peak of contentment. But as Rao wrote, 'experience shows that such is not the case'. The British tehsildar (collector's deputy) was a 'far greater and bolder oppressor' than the traditional man he had displaced; these officers were hand in glove with others in the collector's office, so that together they demanded from farmers not only the government's dues, but also illegal commissions. In other words, if the Raj thought it had successfully replaced the feudal with the bureaucratic, in reality Indians were feudalizing the bureaucracy; if the British believed they had ended caste-based power structures, their Indian employees brought caste into the civil service.[42] These men were capable of inflicting even torture on peasants to claim their dues. 'Incredible as this may seem to an Englishman,' Rao finished, 'it is nevertheless true.'[43] Thus, where defects were visible in the colonial apparatus, the man was capable of pointing it out – he believed in Western ideals of governance and accountability, making it his duty to point out lapses even if they were by the British.[44]

Interestingly, the young officer who raged against corruption and a culture of rent-seeking in the 1850s, only three years into Ayilyam Tirunal's reign in the next decade was himself accused of impropriety. In 1863 a Madras newspaper carried a report that the Dewan had received suspiciously large sums of money from the maharajah in recent times. Who leaked this is not clear,[45] but it caused enough of a furore for the governor to demand clarification. As it turned out, Rao had wanted a raise in salary of 500 rupees, making a total (and enormous) receipt of 2,500.[46] Ayilyam Tirunal – his ex-student, who in these years deferred a great deal to his tutor-turned-minister – was unkeen. But because the Dewan was 'anxious to have some addition', the maharajah offered to pay the sum as a stipend to Rao's sons instead. That way, Rao would get what he desired, without raising expectations in future Dewans by setting an undesirable precedent.[47] In person, however, the maharajah admitted to the Resident that 'the request for an increase in pay had been greatly pressed, advantage being taken of his [that is, Ayilyam Tirunal's] anxiety to avoid all unpleasantness and annoyance which it was in the Minister's power to create'. In fact, he had acceded 'contrary to his own real wishes'.[48] Further inquiries showed that besides this, the Dewan also received substantial gifts from the ruler. So much so that the authorities in Madras were horrified when the full report reached them, noting that all this tended 'greatly to modify the high opinion' they had hitherto held of Rao, now the centre of gossip in the press.[49]

Soon Rao was notified 'that his conduct in thus aggrandizing himself was not what the [British] Government had been led to expect from his previous character'. While things were forgiven, they hoped to see a 'greater disinterestedness, and a better sense of what was due to his position' in future.[50] In internal correspondence, however, the governor was blunter (if also a tad blind to irony). By acting as he had done, it was said, Rao resembled 'a vulture preying on a carcass', not 'a responsible Minister' – words Indians would one day use with greater force against the British. He was to be reminded that he 'holds his office during the pleasure of the Government', and that he had better behave.[51] With news also circulating that Rao was importing relations and granting them official positions, another inquiry followed. One relative was a royal tutor, it was found, while another was in charge of the state charities and temples. A cousin, who was also Rao's son-in-law, had become deputy Dewan. Though these men were in service from long before, they had, it was argued, 'swiftly risen in his tenure'.[52] In a sense this suggests that while anglicized to a degree, caste feeling and the pull of older Indian tendencies coexisted in Rao. And just as the British had their patronage systems, this powerful native was also building something similar for himself. Besides, very likely Rao had made enemies in the state, who with or without the ruler's connivance, found a weak point with which to discredit him. As for Travancore, the continued descent of 'foreign' Raos into the state even under an enlightened minister would become a serious political problem a few decades later.

The episode also reveals larger complexities. On the one hand were the British who wished for grateful, English-speaking natives to help manage the empire; on the other were those natives themselves who showed ambition and a nascent nationalism, but were equally susceptible to caste prejudice and nepotism. And, of course, there were maharajahs like Ayilyam Tirunal, seeking to preserve their kingship from both the Raj as well as overglamorous ministers. Power had to be balanced, then, between three players – Ayilyam Tirunal, acquiesced in Rao's desire for more money, only to use the Resident to dish out a reprimand. The British, no doubt also keen to prevent natives from becoming *too* big, found an occasion to inhibit Rao. And the latter also, as we shall see, played ball with the Raj at the maharajah's expense. But in the end since neither the British nor the king could be dislodged, he, as a paid employee, would lose. Ayilyam Tirunal was no pushover. Norton, having met him in the 1860s with his brother, Visakham Tirunal, wrote of the 'pleasure and astonishment' they caused in Madras with their 'European turn of thought, and the enlightenment and liberality of their opinions'.[53] While Rao's help in saving the last maharajah's reputation was valued, this clever new maharajah would resent how the Dewan seemed to eclipse the ruler. Or as the Resident reported, over time Rao went 'astray' with 'an overweening sense' of his own importance; he had forgotten 'the bounds of proper subordination'.[54] So the maharajah naturally retaliated. The Resident was already a clamp on his authority – letting the Dewan become another was dangerous.

Ayilyam Tirunal was a complicated man – physically unprepossessing, industrious, sensitive, cunning, a stammering polyglot, and a Sanskrit scholar.[55] As a prince, he had seen his uncle's struggle to reconcile Brahminical ideals of kingship with British pressure and a vacant treasury. He also served Uthram Tirunal as an apprentice; without him, we read, his uncle 'seldom moved beyond the palace' or 'transacted any important business'. For example, the prince, aided by his 'calm reasoning power', formulated Uthram Tirunal's response to that 1855 threat of annexation, along with Rao.[56] Indeed, Rao's rise owed much to him: when the old Dewan died, state officials and the Resident were happy to recognize an older Malayali deputy as his successor. Uthram Tirunal, in consultation with his nephew, however, decided to offer the position to our Madras man instead. This, Ayilyam Tirunal argued, was 'the best' plan in terms of repairing relations with the British – particularly because the rival candidate spoke no English[57] – and so Rao was appointed.[58] While the rejected officer resigned in bitterness, the decision helped Travancore: in the words of a durbar historian, Rao's pen played an instant role in 'disabusing the minds of several great officers' of negative ideas they had formed about the state.[59] He was able to turn the page and chart out a new beginning, marshalling also his network of friends in Madras and in the British bureaucracy to reinvent the state's image.

With his succession in 1860, Ayilyam Tirunal directly joined forces with the Dewan to claim respect for Travancore, using the Raj's own political and economic language of 'improvement'. Where five years earlier public works received 38,000 rupees, a little over a decade into his reign, the new maharajah was disbursing twelve lakh for building roads and bridges.[60] While an English school had long existed in Trivandrum, now access to vernacular education was systematically widened. It was not as though the maharajah did not face his uncle's conundrum in managing the way things were with the demands of an intimidating modernity – in 1865, 1868 and 1871 he found himself answering British interrogation on outlays of money for which the chief beneficiaries were

Ayilyam Tirunal in the late 1870s.

well-fed Brahmins.[61] If these had to be sustained, he understood, the state would have to simultaneously 'progress'; that is, if the maharajah wanted to perform his great Hindu rites and ceremonies, funds would also have to be made available for schools and hospitals. Unlike Rao, who was building a professional reputation, the maharajah had also to preserve tradition and older institutions.

Significantly, Ayilyam Tirunal was also clear that the royal family must be seen at the helm of all this 'progress'; allowing the Dewan to claim all credit was unwise. In Cochin next door, for example, the rajah was weakened by his minister and Resident. In 1862, when he ordered certain religious ceremonies, the Dewan responded that they should be 'performed at His Highness's private expense' because such rituals had brought the state in the past to 'the brink of bankruptcy'; the combination of an unsympathetic minister and Resident turned the Cochin rajah into a supplicant in his own kingdom.[62] This Ayilyam Tirunal would not allow in his own context, so he transformed even his appearance: where in 1862 dignitaries saw him in formal clothes of the old Persianate style, by the next decade he acquired a businesslike European look, for instance. Or as a visitor wrote, 'It is a great pity that he should lay aside his handsome native robes and jewelled turban for a shabby-looking alpaca coat and white trousers, such as cost about 3 [shillings and] 6 [pence] at some marine store shop.'[63] But for the maharajah, niggardly appearance was strategic. A dull outfit was preferred to flashy fabric, to deny naysayers the opportunity to reduce him to an exotic installation. Nobody could suggest that he stay in the back seat and look pretty, while 'real men' rolled up their sleeves and did the actual governing. Under Ayilyam Tirunal, that trope of Hindu effeminacy would not be allowed anywhere near his dynasty – he wished to be an *active* king, not a rubber stamp leaning completely on his minister or the Resident.

These efforts by Ayilyam Tirunal yielded dividends – in 1867, just over a decade after the threat of annexation, Travancore's gun salute was raised from seventeen to nineteen in the imperial honours system. Its ruler was permitted to style himself 'maharajah' instead of 'rajah' – a privilege hitherto denied.[64] The maharajah would in time receive the Kaiser-i-Hind medal too – one day to be awarded to Ravi Varma – and a knighthood. Socially, meanwhile, he managed to conciliate orthodox expectations. As the same visitor who saw the ruler in Western clothes added, 'Although a very enlightened man as to the interests of his country, and the advantages of European intercourse, he [remains] in close subjection to the customs of his religion and the authority of the Brahmans.'[65] The aura around the royal family and their ceremonious lives did not make it easy to move freely in European society, for example. So, while white visitors were received in a 'thoroughly English' apartment, meetings took place at 7 a.m.– this way the maharajah could have his morning bath *afterwards*, and stay 'pure' the rest of the day.[66] In matters of policy too, as historian Robin Jeffrey observes, physical modernization did not coincide with adequate *social* reform. Both maharajah and Dewan wanted to 'improve' things in a material sense, without risking too much in complicated areas of caste and custom. In 1870, for instance, after the Resident objected to low castes being barred from roads, these were in 'a calculated gesture' thrown open; in fact, however, this 'liberality continued for many years to exist mainly on paper'.[67] Similarly, the state abolished the use of degrading language by *avarnas* (outcastes) when addressing their superiors[68] – this too translated poorly on the ground. In at least some areas, then, 'progress' could be a sham.

What the paper orders did do, however, was address British standards of enlightened rule. In Raj circles, the maharajah became a model prince: sufficiently amenable to 'advice', well educated in English, and with a minister popular in colonial society. The progressive posture of the state was widely publicized, winning narrative battles for Travancore against imperial condescension. In fact, in what is remarkable, even when Ayilyam Tirunal fell out with Rao, the two attempted a secret accord to avoid undue British involvement. Trouble had begun between them in the mid-1860s, with the Dewan's growing power annoying the ruler. Outwardly, of course, deference was shown. A visiting Englishwoman wrote how at a banquet Rao did not join, waiting in an adjacent room instead – in keeping with protocol, he could not sit in the royal presence.[69] But formal considerations aside, the maharajah felt he was being treated as a puppet. Indeed, some of Rao's actions at this time do not reflect well even insofar as the state's interests went. In 1865, for example, he committed Travancore to an Interportal Trading Convention with the colonial government. It was a miscalculation of Himalayan proportions, some decades later estimated to be depriving the state of about four million rupees in revenue.[70] That this lopsided, pro-British agreement was signed not long after Rao was pulled up for extracting money from the ruler raises questions on whether he was attempting to reingratiate himself with the Raj. Ayilyam Tirunal, of course, signed off on the deal, but that it took place amidst a growing coldness with the Dewan is not without significance.

By the end of the decade, thereafter, relations took a turn for the worse. In 1868–69 Rao alleged that military honours – such as troops lining up at his arrival, presenting arms and so on – had been summarily terminated. As we saw in the Introduction, these outward forms and rituals were also a conduit for politics, and the fact that the maharajah wanted to ensure 'a marked distinction' in honours 'between royalty and any of His Highness's subjects' betrays tension.[71] That is, just as Rao became ever more famous and talked about, we witness the maharajah signalling displeasure. While this matter was closed quietly, by 1871 a fresh controversy reared its head: 'differences' arose between master and Dewan in the course of an investigation into a corruption case. Rao had 'secretly' summoned 'servants of the palace', interrogating them without the ruler's knowledge. Naturally the episode, which may well have been the minister flexing muscles, left Ayilyam Tirunal infuriated.[72] Those seeking to 'aggravate the unfriendly feelings which the maharajah already entertained towards' Rao took advantage: where in the last year Ayilyam Tirunal had *broached* the idea of getting rid of the Dewan, now he grew determined, even talking of abdication if the British insisted otherwise.[73] In a private discussion,

The Maharajah . . . dwelt at some length upon the causes for his dissatisfaction with the Dewan. He said that for several years the Dewan's treatment of him had not been what he considered it ought to be, and that this had been especially the case during the time the late [Henry] Newill held the office of Resident [that is, 1864–69, the time when the problematic trade agreement was also signed]; that at that time matters were constantly settled between the Dewan and the Resident without his being consulted until all the details had been arranged, and that he constantly had reason to feel that he was regarded as a mere cipher.[74]

On another occasion, the maharajah 'spoke with unmistakeable and almost painful emotion', saying of recent experiences with Rao: 'I have never felt such grief in all my life.'[75] The British were sympathetic, admitting, 'if we are to speak plainly', that the servant had really become the master in Travancore, and that this was only bound, sooner or later, to spark resentment.[76] But given Rao's competence, the Madras government was loath to lose him. So, reconciliation was attempted, a senior official visiting the state for negotiations. In January 1871, thus, the Dewan was prevailed upon to write a letter to Ayilyam Tirunal, professing loyalty and regret. He 'never in the remotest degree intended offence', and hoped the maharajah would 'forgive my errors, which I shall be doubly careful to avoid in the future'. In fact, he wished to continue as Dewan 'to enjoy the great privilege of being the humble instrument of giving effect to Your Highness' benevolent views' and to bring 'happiness of Your Highness' subjects'.[77] The maharajah took the apology, and it looked like the gulf was bridged – all was well again in India's model state.

But no sooner had the British representative departed than Rao and the ruler came to their own arrangement. Ayilyam Tirunal's opinion of the Dewan had not changed, and the latter too realized that it was better to end on a decent note instead of waiting for a breakdown. To keep colonial interference at a minimum, the two fixed secret terms: Rao would stay a year, while the maharajah would provide him a pension of 700 rupees in addition to a sinecure of 300 per month thereafter. Besides, a job in the state was also ensured for the retiring Dewan's son.[78] When news leaked out, as it was bound to, that old emissary who had patched things up – now acting governor – felt resoundingly betrayed. 'The want of candour manifested by the secrecy of the transaction disappointed us greatly,' he wrote, amazed that a princely ally and his seemingly pro-British Dewan would wish to cut them out of such dealings. But there was no point pressing the matter: both maharajah and minister were determined, and would part ways regardless of views in Madras.[79] The British did not seek a second reconciliation, but, to score at least a symbolic point, refused to recognize the agreement. It was a damp squib, of course, for in the end Rao was still given 1,000 rupees in pension. Correspondence followed thereafter on whether or not the Dewan should stay in the capital or remove himself, so as to break his networks and permit his successor a clean slate.[80] In the end, though, Rao received an offer to become minister elsewhere, leaving Travancore for good.

Rao's departure from the helm was the end of an era. But it also left the maharajah, who had 'chafed under the constraint' of his authority,[81] paranoid of ever again employing a man who might demean royalty – an insoluble problem, given that the very desire to modernize entailed a curtailment of autocratic princely powers. This was especially stark when, as happened with Travancore, the Dewan was such a dramatic success – future ministers would expect the same level of autonomy. As one florid account put it in Rao's case, 'He brought sunshine into a land covered with darkness. He secured the blessings of good government to a people harassed by anarchy. He obtained freedom of person and property to those who were constantly assailed by hereditary robbers. He reared costly edifices in a city covered with mud huts. He constructed various works of public utility, such as roads, bridges, canals and tunnels . . . Peace and plenty reigned supreme.'[82] That this tribute emerged from the pen of G. Parameswaran Pillai (1864–1903) makes it more interesting – this was a journalist who would excoriate the trend of 'foreign' Dewans in the state; in 1889 he would declare 'Travancore for Travancoreans' and two years later orchestrate public agitation.[83] With Rao, however, he was speaking not just as a princely subject but as an *Indian*; that he had praise for a 'foreigner' suggests that he saw him as a *national* icon. For the Dewan, this kind of praise augmented his prospects on the pan-Indian stage; but for the maharajah, who had only one kingdom, larger-than-life ministers were tricky allies who could easily also become threats to royal power.

In the final assessment, though Rao deserves the lion's share of credit for Travancore's growth, he would have achieved little were it not for a ruler who shared most of his political goals. Unfortunately, Ayilyam Tirunal's reputation has not survived as well as that of his Dewan, who still gazes in statue form at the secretariat he occupied. With time, a notoriety came to rest on the maharajah: he was, it is alleged, 'a moral wreck and a sexual pervert', with a 'flood of local stories' about his 'perversions'. Tales circulated of 'indiscriminate advances' towards women,[84] and in the words of his brother, he 'never subjected himself to strict moral discipline'.[85] He also became highly suspicious. Rao's successor, for instance, was a 'man of excellent abilities, great experience, and very high character'.[86] His selection, though, was tricky: Ayilyam Tirunal wanted a year-long probation before finalizing the appointment. Having been perceived as weak before, he believed that 'the introduction of a stranger as Dewan' so readily after the last one's departure 'would, in the eyes of his people and of the public generally, make it appear that a Dewan had been forced upon him' by the Raj. As the irritated Resident wrote, the ruler attached 'undue importance to this point, with the idea, apparently, that his regulating [the appointment] himself is a sort of crucial test of his independence'.[87] It did matter to Ayilyam Tirunal, for he could afford neither another Rao, nor a British satellite. So, after a pile of names was rejected,[88] the royal hand fell on a Tamil Brahmin called Seshiah Sastri. He was to last five years before falling out with the maharajah, who then appointed the more submissive Nanoo Pillai. Not long after this, in 1880, Ayilyam Tirunal died, leaving a sparkling legacy, if not a pristine personal report card.

What is most telling, however, is that even in the end, the maharajah clung with determination to the Hindu character of his kingship. His much-touted Western education and the progressive reputation he had painstakingly constructed did not lead to a rejection of even some bizarre traditions. This was exemplified in his final hours in a curious ritual all monarchs followed in Travancore. As the maharajah lay dying, a man was found who, for a generous fee, agreed 'to bear the responsibility for the Rajah's sins'. At the appointed hour, the candidate entered the royal bedchamber, and 'after the performance of certain ceremonies by the Brahmans, was tenderly embraced by the sick man'. By this the maharajah unloaded his sins on to the soul of this unnamed alien. And so it was that Ayilyam Tirunal could depart this world unblemished and guaranteed, to a reasonable extent, a shot at salvation. His scapegoat, on the other hand, with a pocket full of cash but carrying the burden of another man's misdeeds, was 'conducted out of Travancore into the Tinnevelly district with orders never to return'.[89] What is amusing here is not just the ritual itself but also its geography: for while the maharajah purified himself in Travancore, it was into British territory that he expelled his sins.

As with royal successions around the world, the death of a king was often followed not only by his heir's enthronement but also by a purge in the palace. In Trivandrum, forty-three-year-old Visakham Tirunal (1837–85) had waited years in the wings. To call his relations with Ayilyam Tirunal frosty would be an understatement: the brothers were not even on speaking terms, and 'whom the ruler approved, the heir apparent did not' and vice versa.[90] Visakham Tirunal was fond of Rao, for example, and did not conceal this when the Dewan fell out with the maharajah; on the contrary, when Rao retired, the prince published a thirty-nine-page tribute praising the man to the heavens and then some.[91] So too while the maharajah was glad to see the back of his next minister, Visakham Tirunal personally called on him, writing how he had 'won the esteem and appreciation of all whose esteem and appreciation are worth winning' – a broadside against his brother.[92] Indeed, he did not hesitate to air catty views even to junior officials: to a sidelined bureaucrat Visakham Tirunal said, 'I cannot think much of a Government which is indifferent to a young man of your stamp and promise.'[93] Some of this was just evidence of his opinionated style, but a great deal also drew from the fact that as heir to the throne, Ayilyam Tirunal's brother was placed in a frustrating position – he was neither a minor figure, nor in possession of power, stuck in a political limbo till his brother's death. The longer a ruler sat on the throne, the shorter became the reign of his sibling successor.[94]

Outwardly, of course, respect was usually demonstrated. As we read, in Travancore, 'A junior member, even the immediate heir to the throne, behaves himself in the presence of his senior as an ordinary member of society in his bearing, address, and deportment. The junior member, in addressing the sovereign, says "your holy self" and in speaking of himself "your vassal". None would dare to say "you" or "I".'[95] Behind this punctilious facade, however, lay uneasy truths and discontent – and with good reason. Years before, when Ayilyam Tirunal was heir apparent, his uncle, Uthram Tirunal, had allowed him the role of an adviser, which ensured a smooth relationship – the maharajah's successor was in the thick of things. But where Ayilyam Tirunal and his own sibling were concerned, a healthy arrangement was never found. Separated only by a few years in age, tutored by the same man, it did not take long for the brothers to mark each other as rivals. It could also be that their uncle favoured Ayilyam Tirunal, for Visakham Tirunal was not always obedient.[96] He had a mind of his own that did not brook commands from a much older Uthram Tirunal – it is not surprising, then, that his brother's orders fared worse. This animosity in the palace had political implications too: one ministerial candidate had to wait a decade for appointment for the reason that, though Ayilyam Tirunal recognized his ability, he was also aware that his brother endorsed him – this was enough for the maharajah to deny his hopes.[97] Not to be one-upped, Visakham Tirunal, after becoming ruler, lashed out at his brother's favourites: the sitting Dewan was replaced by the bypassed man, this reshuffle at court affecting others associated with Ayilyam Tirunal – including his pet painter, Ravi Varma.

In the years our artist spent under the late maharajah's patronage, he had grown in skill and in his commitment to art. Why, recognition in Madras also transformed him into something of a celebrity, as senior

A young Visakham Tirunal,
painted presumably
by his favourite artist,
Ramaswami Naidu (Ravi
Varma's rival).

Detail from Ravi Varma's painting of Visakham Tirunal and his Dewan,
V. Ramiengar, receiving the governor of Madras in 1880.

figures collected his works and gave him portrait commissions. Ayilyam Tirunal had revelled in the attention the young talent generated, allowing him – as we shall see in the next chapter – to accept work even in another state. Visakham Tirunal, however, partly due to his blanket dislike of his brother's courtiers, but also because he preferred Ravi Varma's rival, Ramaswamy Naidu, showed no such magnanimity. An incident in October 1880, when the governor of Madras came calling, makes this clear. Incidentally, the latter knew Ravi Varma: he once commented how this native artist, with very few sittings, produced a portrait superior to that of a European who had demanded eighteen.[98] Now, upon arrival, the visitor wished to renew their friendship. The story goes that when Visakham Tirunal summoned Ravi Varma, not only did the governor go to the door, but he also invited the artist to sit with them. The painter declined for it was *lèse majesté* to presume equality with the maharajah. This, however, led to more awkwardness, for the governor elected to converse standing. Visakham Tirunal, who could hardly remain in his seat with his British guest on his feet, also ended up rising, seething at all this fuss for a painter.[99] While the governor departed – and Ravi Varma produced a painting depicting his visit – the chill at court did not. The writing on the wall was clear: after eighteen years, Ravi Varma left Trivandrum, a casualty of the vendetta between two royal brothers.[100]

Pettiness aside, however, Visakham Tirunal was intellectually his brother's equal but more fully inspired by his tutor.[101] In fact, it was a matter of pride to him that he was made a Fellow of the Madras University *before* Rao himself.[102] Having lost his mother (Uthram Tirunal's sister) when only months old, he was raised by a great-aunt, who too died when he was in his teens. The prince was, furthermore, 'of a delicate constitution', and pronounced consumptive.[103] Two notches down in the succession, Visakham Tirunal knew it would be some time before – if ever – he ascended the throne. So, he drove his energies into other pursuits. As a youth, for example, he sent an essay on 'The Education of Native Princes' to the *Madras Athenaeum*, only for its editor to reject it. This 'naturally galled the Prince', who applied himself with resolve to a second piece; this time, his 'Political Sketch of Travancore' was published.[104]

An amateur botanist, his circle of correspondents included Darwin's friend Joseph Hooker in London and John Bennett in Australia.[105] Visakham Tirunal also made sounds that appealed to the British. In 1872, he railed against the 'drain on the public treasury' in Travancore through the money 'frequently squandered on the Brahmans'.[106] It was probably a convenient method to attack his brother's government, for the fact is that as maharajah, Visakham Tirunal had no qualms expending his own share on these rites. Or as he sheepishly justified, 'These ceremonies may be viewed as anachronisms . . . but as long as one continues to be in the midst of a whole body of these . . . there is no good in half-performing and half-condemning them.'[107]

His newspaper dissertations, at any rate, impressed its audience. As early as 1861, the governor of Madras called Visakham Tirunal 'the most intelligent Native I have seen',[108] while another occupant of that office complimented him on his language skills, observing: 'I doubt if there is a Prince in Europe who could write so well in a foreign language as your Highness does in English.'[109] When Victoria's heir, Edward, came to the country in 1875, Visakham Tirunal did not fail to try and impress him; he had no opportunity to do so in person, so he achieved this via the press. As a journal put it with a touch of sarcasm, the latter had 'strangely seized the occasion of the Prince of Wales's visit to India to advocate publicly his views as to the execution of criminals'. Describing Visakham Tirunal as 'one of the best educated and most enlightened of Hindus', the paper lauded his exhortation that 'criminals should be executed under the influence of chloroform'. The idea was, it finished magnanimously, 'an example of how deeply European abhorrence of the infliction of unnecessary pain has impressed the enlightened Asiatic mind'.[110] Of course, what Visakham Tirunal was doing was advertising his modernity to a future British sovereign. But it was not all flattery that came from the man's pen. In future he would urge the Raj to redouble investments in Indian higher education. This was at a time when the governor of Madras, M.E. Grant Duff, was allegedly contemplating a withdrawal of state support to universities. As Visakham Tirunal wrote,

That the higher education . . . has simply reared a race of pedants or discontented men is a gross calumny. That the native portion of the Government Service and of the Bar has immensely improved during these past forty years is a fact which the most cavilling critic will not deny. If this result, full of public importance, is not to be traced to the higher education given by Government, to what else is it due? The result is a happy one equally to the governing and governed classes . . . At this moment four Native States are being administered by four men who belong to the earlier harvests of the late High School of Madras, and who would do credit to any nation in the world. Under such men . . . Baroda, Mysore, Travancore and Pudukotta enjoy a good government . . . Every educated native in or out of Government service is a radiant point of enlightenment, possessing manly self-respect and grateful loyalty . . . The argument that the Government apprehends political danger from the spread of higher education is one which may be worthy of Russia, but not of the just, free and enlightened British nation.[111]

In other words, here was a prince, like Congress politicians emerging in the same period, gently reminding the British of their own declared standards: a comparison with Russia was intended to stress this point. And it was not the first time. In the 1860s Visakham Tirunal used to publish essays under the nom de plume 'Brutus' in the *Indian Statesman*, proffering advice to Travancore Residents – a risky line for royalty when technically it was the Resident who was in the advice-giving trade.[112] In 1872 we find him first flattering the British empire as a 'glorious landmark' in history, before highlighting an 'important truth' for its benefit. As he argued, the ruling race ought not to forget that while railways and roads were welcome, *education* was key. Yes, it would make natives 'think and reason', and 'the most inviting field to which a mind sharpened and invigorated by education would turn' was politics. But to fear that this would launch an 'army of Bengalis, Purbiahs, Sikhs, Parsis, and Madrassis, under a Babu Wellington and a Chetti Blucher' to destroy the Raj was 'alarmist'. Instead, the appropriate attitude was to look to a day 'when the British . . . shall present to the world the noblest spectacle it has yet beheld, by making over to the people of India, when they have fitted themselves for its rule, this magnificent Empire, enlightened and ennobled under British guardianship'. Listing men like Ramaprasad Roy (son of Rammohun Roy), Sambunath Pandit (the first brown judge of the Calcutta High Court), Rajendralal Mitra (the antiquarian) and others, Visakham Tirunal felt it was inevitable that Indians would one day rule themselves – he just hoped the British would not construe this as a calamity but see it instead as an achievement.[113] Only by doing so would the empire have a happy ending, having served a moral purpose.

In his decades as heir apparent, Visakham Tirunal also had time for productive employment, by which he hoped to set Indians an example. With Rao, he invested in a coffee plantation,[114] besides also experimenting with tobacco and cotton.[115] From travels, 'he would return loaded with large collections of plants and seeds, ferns and orchids, stones and minerals, butterflies and moths, stuffed birds and sundry reptiles', besides 'innumerable drawings of indigenous medicinal herbs, flowers and berries'.[116] The grounds of his palace became a farm, and in 1876 he was featured in a British newspaper for 'pointing . . . to the poorest classes of Hindoos how they could with hardly any cost and labour procure a very nutritious vegetable' in tapioca.[117] It would catch on, becoming today's staple and quintessential *kappa*.[118] Meanwhile, his study of tobacco brought him to the conclusion that 'good cigars and cheroots' capable of rivalling Manilla and Cuba could be manufactured in Travancore – promptly, the press noted, he imported American machines and Spanish workmen to set up a factory.[119] Indeed, just as Ravi Varma won medals at colonial art shows, the prince won laurels at its industrial parallels: in Madras, his coffee was deemed best at an exhibition, and when he sent Travancore fibre to Vienna, it won a medal.[120] In time he would be elected to the Linnean Society of London, whose members were distinguished for botanical researches and studies in natural history.[121] All along Visakham Tirunal also produced a pile of writing, advocating religious neutrality in education one moment, writing an essay on Sanskrit literature the next – in 1884, even when busy with state matters, he found time to comment on the fourteenth-century *Sukasandesam*, because existing scholarly material was 'either too prolix or too meagre'.[122]

These were not the doings of a jobless prince as much as a man bursting with ideas but denied, thanks to primogeniture, the power to do much about them. Equally, however, in his own way, he was also smashing clichés about natives. It was his resultant popularity in intellectual and political circles that rankled Ayilyam Tirunal. In fact, while still heir apparent, his younger brother was offered a seat on the viceroy's council; though he declined, this was evidence of an appeal that threatened the maharajah.[123] When in 1880 Visakham Tirunal finally succeeded to power, in his installation speech he quoted Lord Ripon, the pro-India viceroy who famously pledged himself not only to the queen but also to the Indian people, and in turn pledged himself to Travancore – he would be a new kind of king.[124] Only weeks later, addressing students, the maharajah painted a future, somewhat idealistically, where 'every field-labourer and every day-labourer can find a couple of spare hours every day to sit under a shady tree and read his manual of Travancore history and Travancore geography, his little arithmetic, his twelve-page catechism of moral duties, and his Robinson Crusoe or Hitopadesam'.[125] He wished to make well-rounded citizens of his subjects. Since his reign lasted only five years, the man did not get a chance to realize all his schemes, but the British were aware of his ambition. As the Resident wrote, 'few Princes have ever succeeded to a throne with more opportunities of earning a great name', and if this one devoted himself, its benefits will 'not be confined to Travancore but will be reflected far and wide over Hindustan'.[126] His brother had already set an example, but there was every chance the new maharajah might pull off the task of surpassing it.

As it happened, however, though the maharajah was driven, he suffered also from mulishness and overenthusiasm. Rao, who visited Travancore soon after his installation, hearing frenzied chants of 'reform' quipped: 'I suppose you know that all changes are not necessarily reforms.'[127] The maharajah's keenness for speed over durability may have stemmed from frustration at being denied a chance to contribute for years, as much as from fear of death. As he wrote, 'I am already in the 44th year of my life. None of my predecessors even touched their 50th year . . . I am myself of a weak and sickly constitution. Humanly speaking, my reign cannot be a long one, and my sole ambition is to leave behind me a name which posterity may bless and gratefully remember.'[128] So many reforms were introduced, only for the state to acknowledge within twenty years that some of these were 'not beneficial'. But because 'His Highness had made up his mind' in favour of 'drastic changes', he would neither 'tarry nor allow himself to be thwarted'.[129] Still, Visakham Tirunal was not without his triumphs – in his influential 1897 book *Representative Indians*, Parameswaran Pillai, the journalist mentioned before, included the maharajah, making him the only royal alongside bureaucrats and statesmen to impress young India.[130] Regardless of his failures, the fact that he worked hard, burning the midnight oil, and possibly extinguishing his life under strain, earned the maharajah respect. Capable of irrational fury (as with Ravi Varma) and of nurturing grudges for years (as with his brother), the ruler was by all accounts a flawed man; and yet, he also had a vision, his early demise in 1885 genuinely lamented across the land.[131]

On his death, this younger of Uthram Tirunal's nephews was succeeded in turn by *his* sister's son – a ruler Ravi Varma would paint and later lobby to set up an art gallery in Trivandrum. Sadly, the new man was mediocre, chiefly interested in religious affairs and led by a succession of sycophants through his nearly forty-year reign. Why, things got so bad that a junior prince allegedly tried to bribe the Resident for redress, besides seeking legal aid to rein in the ruler and his favourites – it took Madhava Rao's intercession to buy peace in the palace.[132] But it did not obscure the fact that the new maharajah was weak. Unlike his uncles, who worked proactively to bridge their kingship with modernity, this ruler put things on autopilot. His reasons were clear: as he said, since the kingdom was doing well, 'I have therefore only to work on the lines [already] chalked out for me.'[133] Indeed, because of the 'great ease and buoyancy' in the government's accounts, the maharajah early on performed those grand Hindu rituals of state that caused tension with the British.[134] In 1892 he achieved the tulabharam, which cost more than

Maharajah Mulam Tirunal of Travancore (r. 1885–1924), nephew to Ayilyam Tirunal and Visakham Tirunal. This photograph was the basis of Ravi Varma's state portrait of the maharajah (see plates section).

the yearly police budget, and a little less than education; charities and temples also cost the government over a million rupees.[135] But while a strong bank balance kept the British at bay, fresh pressures were emerging: thanks to Rao's policies that threw open access to education and bold new ideas, young men embraced politics, threatening royal power from *within*. The principal allegations made in Madras now were no longer about misgovernment but corruption and bias in the royal government. The result was that in 1904, for the first time in generations, the Raj specifically denied the maharajah a minister of his choice – instead, to unseat the coterie controlling him, a Dewan was practically imposed on the state.

The great irony, of course, is that this was precisely what the previous maharajahs had worked to prevent. Both Ayilyam Tirunal and Visakham Tirunal asserted royal power but were hands-on rulers; they modernized actively while preserving their ceremonial turf, making the correct noises in public to help shape the idea of the enlightened Indian prince. Constantly, they and their ministers adapted the narrative to frame their future and the identity of the state. Their nephew, however, let his guard down, and failed to present anything that resembled a vision of modern kingship. And for this he paid the price – Travancore in the early twentieth century was given a minister who was more loyal to Madras than to its ruler.[136]

In the late 1870s Ravi Varma, seen here with his brother (standing) and a friend, for the first time accepted a royal commission outside Travancore. The following pages tell the story of Pudukkottai state and of its royal family, which struggled to manage progress with tradition, and battled its own minister for control and power.

3

Of Robber Kings and Civil Servants

In 1894 when Ravi Varma, by then a famous man, joined Travancore's prince Asvathi Tirunal on an all-India tour,[1] among the places they visited was Kumbakonam in Tamil territory. This was the town where Madhava Rao had spent his childhood years, and by this time it had earned a reputation also as the 'Eton of Southern India' for its modern educational facilities.[2] But more significantly for the visitors, the place was retirement home to Rao's successor as Dewan: Sir A. Seshiah Sastri (1828–1903).[3] The prince, the artist and the latter's brother were received at the station by a deputation of local notables, following which they went to Sastri's 'palatial residence'. As Rajaraja Varma – Ravi Varma's sibling and assistant, himself a gifted painter – observed, the ex-Dewan's home was full of reminders of his time in Travancore in the 1870s. 'The paintings, the huge elephant's tusks, the ivory knick-knacks, nay, the very beams and door-posts of massive teak in the house, were reminiscences of our host's connection' with the state. 'He himself,' added Rajaraja, 'never speaks of the country, its scenery, or its people, except in terms of the highest praise and admiration.'[4] Ravi Varma too was fond of Sastri. Not only had he done his portrait,[5] the latter owned half a dozen of his other works. In a letter Sastri once wrote to the artist, we read, for example:

Lady with a Flower is too large for my drawing room. But I would like to have Harishchandra and Taramati. It is true; I do not like to keep

The Wellcome Collection, London

Chromolithograph prints of Ravi Varma's Krishna with Gopis *and* Sita's Swayambara, *which Seshiah Sastri admired.*

paintings depicting tragic scenes in my house. I am not interested in Bombay Singer, which is only a social scene. By constantly looking at your paintings, I have started admiring the pretty faces of your women. So I would like to have paintings of Krishna with Gopis; Coronation of Rama and Sita's Swayambara . . . I would like to have a copy of Nair Lady Inside the Mosquito Net, which you had presented to the Prince of Wales.[6]

Sastri was a talented man, and another icon from that generation of Indians who slowly proved their administrative mettle to claim power and prestige within the British establishment. Born in 1828 in rural Tanjore as the fifth son of a Brahmin priest, such a future would not have been his obvious path if it weren't for an uncle who sent him to Madras for an English education.[7] While here he would meet Rao, becoming a lifelong friend, it was not easy getting by: fees took a toll, and it was only by means of a scholarship that Sastri was able to continue his studies. He was prone to sweeping up prizes, ranging from one for best essay on

'What is Civilisation' to a cartload for his handwriting.[8] Their master, E.B. Powell, with his 'instincts of a born teacher' and 'single-minded devotion' to his students, was a fount of motivation.[9] When Sastri graduated in 1848, for example, the man sent out a glowing recommendation: he had 'a very high idea of Sashiah's integrity and would not hesitate to place the utmost confidence in him. I trust,' he added, 'his success in life may be commensurate with his talents, industry, and good conduct.'[10] Powell was not disappointed – before he died, many of his pupils had become men of standing. And Sastri too never forgot his debt to this 'Guru', fifty years on still paying him tributes.[11] It was not empty praise: at one time, the headmaster himself settled the boy's fees when his family was out of means.[12]

His teacher's recommendation, and his writing and language skills – as with Rao – were to help Sastri's rise in the colonial bureaucracy. Unlike his friend, however, this Tamilian did not come with a family history of government service or the associated networks; he was the first of his house to go down this new path.[13] English, then as today, was a passport to economic mobility, and even before he left school, Sastri had begun to look for an income. At eighteen, he became tutor to the boys of a prominent native figure – the head sheristadar of Tanjore (a kind of chief secretary working under the white collector) – which, though not as grand as Rao's impending assignment in Travancore, gave him a welcome twenty-five rupees a month. In any case, the arrangement was a stopgap; what Sastri *really* wanted was the security of a government job. By the eve of his graduation, he was lining up at a British dignitary's gate, hoping to be noticed so he could seek a position or at least a reference. At twenty, he got what he desired: he became a clerk to Madras's Board of Revenue.[14] Starting on twelve and a half rupees, doubled after a few months,[15] Sastri had a foot now on the official ladder. At its end lay a ministerial term in Travancore, and regency of another princely state. The boy from Amaravati was on the way to greatness.

Indeed, the influence Sastri and his classmates acquired, and the inspiration they became to their countrymen, was such that their personal stories were embellished into heroic narratives. With Sastri, eminence was prophesied the moment he took breath. His mother wanted a girl, we learn, and on hearing sighs of disappointment at his birth, the midwife supposedly declared, 'This son of yours will be the luckiest in the family.'[16] Mama eventually did warm to him, while he, when departing for Madras, announced: 'I now go a poor boy, but I shall return in another style – with pack-bullocks laden with jingling coins.'[17] So too his uncle's dying advice was, 'Be honest, my boy, and God will bless you,' which is supposed to explain his incorruptibility.[18] In all such tales there is also an inevitability as far as greatness is concerned. Of course, the real platform from which Sastri rose was his school. Besides Rao, a second classmate, V. Ramiengar (1826–87), would also become Dewan of Travancore, showing how much being in the right place at the right time in a *single* British institution, not destiny or midwives' prognostications, made all the difference.[19] That each of them ran with the opportunity and founded a native hall of fame is, of course, to their credit.

In fact, these Indians also watched out for one another, sharing their successes and anxieties. Before Sastri finished school, in 1846, for example, Rao wrote to him demanding a letter on 'what your prospects are, what course you have chalked out . . . whether you intend venturing into the outstations for employment or look to establishing yourself in some independent position in life, to become a man of profession, to turn an architect, an engineer, a lawyer or a judge'. Sastri must have expressed uncertainty, for in his next dispatch Rao reassured him that he would surely find his place 'in the wide world without assistance'.[20] After he joined government service, we find Ramiengar, who also was in a clerical position (and of whom too Ravi Varma would do a portrait),[21] share a similar bond. In 1849, for instance, when Sastri was away, Ramiengar wrote how 'Everything is remarkably quiet . . . I am even more barren now than we used to be on some of those occasions in which we used to sit face to face in the [office] dunning each other for news.'[22] At another time Ramiengar helped his friend with a transfer so the latter could stop working with a troublesome boss.[23] Though they would all become idolized 'native statesmen', at this juncture they were novices. All they wished for was that their steady salaries would lift up their families, and the most ambitious office they could divine was that of a district sheristadar.[24]

Over time, however, Powell's boys also grew willing to take risks and seize opportunities. If Rao embraced the unpredictability of a disorderly Travancore durbar, Sastri took up an assignment outside Madras for a roving commission in the Northern Circars – a coastal unit of the province – where the administration was in a shambles. Here the Tamilian worked hard, even finding a way to make extra bucks giving tuition. As Rao wrote, 'You seem to have marched away at a very rapid rate . . . I cannot help admiring your spirit. You have availed yourself of a capital opportunity of advancing your interests and gratifying your curiosity simultaneously.'[25] Their teacher continued to guide them; in the same year, Powell responded to doubts Sastri was having, telling him 'not to form a hasty judgment'. 'Sacrifice the Present to secure the Future,' was the man's advice.[26] And so, Sastri stuck to his job. It paid off: by 1851, he was at fifty rupees per month, having also become right-hand man to his boss. And when, in the course of their wanderings, they reached Masulipatam, the twenty-three-year-old received a recommendation for a tehsildarship. An impressed British officer is said to have declared, 'Young man, when an hour back you entered this room you were an ordinary clerk. You now go as a Tahsildar – the responsible wielder of the destinies of a taluq [a division within a district]. I hope you will justify my choice.'[27]

From today's perspective these offices sound paltry, but at a time when few Indians held posts of responsibility, each promotion occasioned celebration. Sastri justified the decision to put him in charge with sheer zeal – for only by surpassing British expectations could his fellows and he claim places they knew they deserved.[28] It was not, of course, an easy job. Local power structures rooted in caste and history had to be negotiated alongside the agendas of the colonial state. As Ramiengar expressed to Sastri, 'I am now anxious to hear how you get on, for you must find yourself in a dreadfully strange position. It is commonly believed that an honest, upright, kind-hearted man can never make a good Tahsildar . . . The greatest rogues pass off for the cleverest and

honestest of men and really sensible and straightforward people for
the veriest dunces. Pray tell me how you get on.'[29] Today a minor post,
in the mid-nineteenth century tehsildars commanded lordly airs. As a
future Congress president recalled of his father, they could live 'in great
state. I remember he [daddy] had belted peons carrying swords before
him when he went anywhere.'[30] Men in this position could be tempted
by extravagance to pursue illicit wealth, and generally feudalize their
authority. But Sastri, while keeping up show, was not content with small
victories: he worked hard, delivered results and got noticed in *British*
circles, which is what ultimately mattered.

Slowly, through perseverance and diligent plodding, Sastri's
career advanced, albeit without the leaps we witnessed with Rao. In
Masulipatam, for example, he handled law and order, took a town
census, attended to tax matters, intervened in religious feuds, snuffed
out corruption, and even founded a debating club. Years later he would
tell of his 'almost quixotic' desire to 'set everything to right'.[31] Such
energy and efficiency meant that his name was mentioned in the
right quarters, which brought new offices and better pay. In 1854, for
example, two British functionaries got into a spat with one asking for
Sastri's services, and his existing boss unwilling to part with him. The
former won by wooing the man with a better title and 175 rupees in
pay. Shortly after this, in 1855, Sastri became head sheristadar: the
collector's 'minister' and the district's 'virtual ruler'.[32] Rao wrote to him
delighted: 'I was rejoiced to hear that so early you are in the highest post
accessible to natives in the Revenue line. There is not the least doubt
that you deserve . . . far higher. Perhaps and probably, *you* will be the
means of opening to our countrymen the higher walks of the service.
You are probably destined to enter them first, bidding your brethren to
follow you!'[33] By their late twenties, then, Powell's students had moved
from seeking security to pursuing ambition. While it was tough to beat
Rao, Sastri hammered away. Five years later, after 'improving' his earlier
office, he was appointed special assistant to what was called the Inam
Commission, with a staff of 250 under him.[34] It was the kind of power
Indians in British territory could only dream of.

To be clear, it was not as if these men faced no obstacles. In 1855, when a new commissioner arrived, he was offended that someone as junior as Sastri was head sheristadar. He admitted his 'education and application to duty' but was unwilling to give up the principle of seniority.[35] So too Sastri had a run-in with a white bureaucrat in Masulipatam who seemed keen to insult him: when he went to see him for the first time, he was kept waiting for an age – the man, it was said later, was 'absorbed in some pressing work' and had not taken notice of his brown colleague.[36] Interestingly, this officer was none other than Henry Newill, who as Resident in Travancore in the next decade would be accused by Ayilyam Tirunal of colluding with Rao to belittle him. Then, when in 1859 Sastri became one of the first Indian deputy collectors, he was denied a raise – it took a protest for this to be corrected.[37] Such hurdles and racial challenges aside, Sastri's ascent continued through a calm tenacity and the fact that his Indian friends were rising simultaneously to influence; together they set a trend and gave each other confidence. By 1866 Sastri was back in his home district, Tanjore, where his superior certified him as a 'first rate officer' of 'unblemished character'.[38] Four years later, at 1,000 rupees a month, he became sheristadar of the Board of Revenue in Madras: his highest ever position in British service, in the very office where he had begun his career as an impoverished clerk.

That was when, in 1872, Sastri was asked if he wanted Travancore's Dewanship, which his old schoolmate was vacating. He agreed, and at once his salary was doubled to 2,000, bringing also immense prestige.[39] The man who began life twenty-four years ago at a dozen rupees, was now earning over 150 times that amount. The Madras authorities too had 'every reason to be satisfied': the 'distinguished' Sastri had 'risen, with the approval of one and all, to one of the highest posts held by a Native of India'. He 'worthily possesses,' the governor wrote, 'the confidence of all with whom he has been associated in official life.' 'We anticipate,' thus, 'the best results from his appointment.'[40] But if their delight drew from a Madras man being placed in charge of a princely state, on the Indian side there was also a sense of national pride. In fact, just as states needed trained ministers to help navigate colonial pressures, English-educated

Indians also needed princely patrons to shine and, more importantly, prove equality with their white peers. As Sir William Robinson, who would briefly act as governor of Madras, wrote understandingly to Sastri, 'I had heard that you had accepted the office of Dewan . . . with great pleasure. For though we miss you . . . I consider the [ministerial] post you have, as quite the highest open to natives in this Presidency. For there you are truly a native ruling your own countrymen. Under British Rule this can never be, though much do I long . . . to see natives with a more potential voice in the governing of the country.'[41]

Given Ayilyam Tirunal's bad relations with Rao, he was, however, hesitant to confirm too soon someone of such strikingly close background. He 'wished for a minister who could both govern well and yield graciously', which was to say that the royal command should be supreme.[42] And so Sastri was on probation for a year, in which time he soothed his employer's nerves; as the Resident reported, the maharajah soon spoke 'very favourably' of his new Dewan.[43] Ayilyam Tirunal himself affirmed to Sastri how he was 'convinced of [his] excellent ability, tact and above all your sincerely faithful attachment and true loyalty to me'.[44] This – the princely expectation of *personal* loyalty versus the inclination of Western-educated statesmen to build bureaucratic *institutional* machineries – was, in practice, however, easier said than done. Sastri's term, therefore, had ups and downs. Initially, he took care not to upset the ruler – he played the diplomat, and when the maharajah tried to plant favourites in state positions, for example, let it pass. So too it helped that the Resident at the time was a friend from Masulipatam, which allowed for a healthy relationship. Overall, thus, Sastri enjoyed a fairly free hand, till in time he couldn't help but express himself more frankly. Once, for instance, he cautioned Ayilyam Tirunal about unconstitutionality in a judicial intervention; 'I thought,' the maharajah replied dryly, 'I had done with all reference to "constitutional" with Sir Madhava Rao.'[45] Another time, Ayilyam Tirunal is supposed to have exclaimed, only half in jest, 'Oh, these Powell's boys! I wonder how Powell had the art to mould them all alike!'[46]

But in what would please the maharajah, Sastri proved a valiant

Sir A. Seshiah Sastri in later life. His portrait by Ravi Varma could not be traced.

protector of the principality's traditional practices. In this the Tamil Brahmin seems to have been different from his Marathi prior, who apparently had 'no liking' for orthodox elements at court, seeing them as 'ignorant bigots'.[47] Progress for Sastri did not mean relinquishing the state's Brahminical character. He spent vast sums, despite revenue contraction, on the Padmanabhaswamy temple.[48] So too he deployed statistics to disprove that the state was spending disproportionately on temples. Citing how it was under Resident Munro sixty years ago that hundreds of endowed shrines were annexed by the government, he pointed out that income from the temple lands so gained was many times *more* than the cost of maintaining those sites of worship.[49] 'His mind was essentially conservative,' his biographer explained, 'though, whenever he felt the need, he strenuously advocated progress and reform. He approached the study of all national institutions in a sympathetic spirit and he was loath to end them even where he could not mend them.'[50] In 1876, he even made time for a pilgrimage, writing to the maharajah of the many dips he was taking in sacred waters in Ramesvaram and at Tirupati. Years later, contemplating British attempts to end child marriage and the debate around the age of consummation, again Sastri sided with conservatives.[51] This, then, was no deracinated Indian; he was very much a product of colonial modernity but also wedded to Brahminical ideals of old.

In dealings with the Raj too, Sastri grew in confidence. His appointment in 1872 was welcome in Madras because he was seen as a loyal civil servant; as a royal Dewan, however, he proved capable of asserting himself in Travancore's interests, against those of the British. A major feud, for instance, was about state judges' jurisdiction over whites; the powers above unilaterally denied it. The only concession they were willing to consider was that princely governments could appoint *British* judges who might in turn try white defendants. This too was framed as an overlord's gift to a vassal: as London declared, the 'conferring of a limited jurisdiction on certain magistrates' in states like Travancore was 'a fitting acknowledgment of the efforts made by [its] rulers ... to improve the administration of justice'. It was the patronizing opposite of a just compromise; or as Sastri wrote, 'only the shadow of a favour without the substance'.[52] He made a strong argument that until Travancore, by *treaty*, ceded rights in these matters to the imperial power, the latter had no business giving notes on how the maharajah might try Europeans, or what the state judges' complexion should be.[53] It was all in vain, of course, for at the end of the day, the white man's writ weighed more than the brown man's reasoned argument. Perhaps in retaliation, then, Sastri acquired a reputation for being hard on Europeans in Travancore – his admirers justified this 'want of cordiality' as merely misconstrued ministerial 'firmness', but it is possible that racism in this case was repaid in a matching coin.[54]

In fact, liberation from British service into a powerful position under Indian rule gave Sastri's pen a distinct sharpness. This comes across in his contribution to debates on colonial policy. When Lord Ripon, seen as more sympathetic to Indian aspirations, was appointed viceroy in 1880, he introduced legislation for local self-government, with proactive native participation. Even as British society went up in arms, Sastri's views provide an overarching sense of his political ideas, despite thirty-odd years in colonial service. It was a textbook case of moderation and did not question the Raj's legitimacy, but yet dismissed hysterical sounds from British partisans. What to Sastri was the real threat was an Indian 'class of penniless patriots or demagogues who have nothing at stake in the system'—the answer to which was the *creation* of a stake, as Ripon was attempting to do, by happily welcoming brown men in greater numbers into the administration. As he added,

The spread of education is slowly revolutionizing national ideas and raising national aspirations, and, unless the Government takes note and keeps pace, discontent, if not disaffection, must spring in the minds of the leading classes and ere long danger to the State must ensue. It is therefore a graceful and statesmanlike move on the part of Government to invite the people to take a share in the discussion and management of matters . . . The people on their part must thankfully accept the invitation and show themselves worthy of confidence and capable of discussing public matters in a public spirit . . . The educated natives, whether engaged in Government service or in other walks of life must, for a long time to come, continue to be interpreters between their own countrymen and the rulers. To say [as the British party argued] that they [English-speaking Indians] are selfish and unsympathetic and not likely to take interest in, or sacrifice time and convenience for, the common good of the country, is a libel on their character and a libel on education itself.[55]

So too when Ripon introduced what was called the Ilbert Bill in 1883, by which Indian judicial officers were finally to be allowed to sentence

European defendants, there was a furore. Rao, for example, while calling the fuss regrettable, suggested a rollback in the interests of 'practical statesmanship'. 'I would not', he wrote, 'incur the risk of such widespread irritation' and would 'rather wait until the prevailing misconceptions and exaggerated views pass away'.[56] Sastri, however, showed no such reserve, eager to correct the 'abnormal' nature of judicial practice. Writing one of his fiercest notes, he observed how 'I have carefully studied the petition of protest [from the British side] and have searched in vain for a solid argument'. Instead, the only thing he could see was 'that worst of prejudices – namely, race prejudice'.[57] 'Why should it hurt the feelings of an Englishman,' he asked, 'to be tried by a scion of the Zamorin or the Maharajah of Benares? It would be a very strange commentary on the advance of civilisation', on which the colonial power gave so many sermons, 'if it be declared that the best of natives – the very cream of the intellectual aristocracy of India', despite university degrees and exposure to the West, were still not equals.[58] Indeed, the Brahmin bureaucrat even held up America's example:

> Is not the United States of America, perhaps the greatest and the most powerful empire on Earth, an example where all nationalities are absorbed and moulded into one great nation for purposes of Government and all men, be he Scotch, Irish, Swiss, French, German, or Spanish, or Negro or Chinaman, live in peace under equal laws administered without reference to race or colour?[59]

Again, he was disappointed, in that while the bill was passed, outrage forced in modifications that kept Indian judges, in the end, unequal to their British counterparts. If an Indian sat in judgement over a European, a jury fifty per cent white would be arranged. It is no surprise, then, that after the Congress was founded in 1885, Sastri went from general ambivalence to a willingness to give the movement a chance. To a friend who resented this new crop of younger men agitating for rights, Sastri would write:

Are you not a little too hard on the Congress? Of course we old people cannot go so fast: but still even the Congresswallahs are sobering down and the noise they make is such a big chorus that it has some influence upon the nation of rulers [that is, the British public at home], if not on the rulers direct [that is, uppity bureaucrats in India]. The periodical meeting of so many people from distant provinces for a common purpose is itself a preliminary step in political education ... I should think the enlargement of the Legislative Councils and the right of interpellation is not a bad fruit of the Congress movement. Of course there will be some blundering at first but it will not prevent eventual success.[60]

Sastri, in other words, was able to contemplate an eventuality where Indians would be placed in charge of their own destiny. And though he was willing to be patient, when a man of his stature, who had earned his stripes, played by lopsided rules, and *still* made a mark, spoke up for natives, it not only drew attention but also generated public confidence.

Wikimedia Commons

The popular viceroy, Lord Ripon.

But this was in the future. In Travancore of the 1870s, meanwhile, the maharajah was again restless. A bone of contention was Sastri's desire to increase official salaries. Ayilyam Tirunal, parsimonious in the extreme, given his uncle's financial misadventures, could not comprehend this determination to pay bureaucrats well. In the end, a first round of salary reforms, proposed in 1872, was accepted by the ruler a full two years later.[61] Other innovations were easier to digest, such as a scheme for the Dewan's office to absorb young graduates as apprentices.[62] So too Sastri found pleasant ways to harmonize tradition with the modern: *asans* or village teachers, were given roles in government schools.[63] But money matters were different. The 1870s saw a decline in revenue, against which Sastri had to manage high expenses, made worse by famine.[64] Between the maharajah's tendency to watch the treasury and Sastri's efforts to spend liberally, tension between ruler and minister escalated. In fact, on three occasions, the Dewan – who 'concealed an iron hand within a silken glove'[65] – threatened to resign, and Ayilyam Tirunal backed off.[66] Though they had much in common, Sastri's idea of his official powers and the maharajah's desire for control ended up creating conflict. The idea of the minister really governing, while the ruler took a constitutional back seat was untenable; indeed, fearing again that his sovereign prerogatives were being sacrificed, Ayilyam Tirunal saw in his new Dewan the spectre of his predecessor.

As a disgruntled maharajah told Sastri once: 'Whatever may be the excellence of your motives, this is a spirit of Madhava Rao and when I see such a spirit my feelings will be in the same manner irritated.'[67] Not one to go down without a fight, the Dewan also complained of lack of faith: 'Certain passages in your Highness' note of yesterday have wounded me deeply and render it imperative that I should defend myself not only against the charge of reckless extravagance, whimsical and capricious action . . . but also in respect of my financial management which is now so utterly distrusted by your Highness.'[68] He made it clear he would leave Travancore at the end of his term, without seeking a renewal – and thus, maharajah and Dewan parted in August 1877. Of course, a pension was provided,[69] and Sastri wrote warmly to thank Ayilyam Tirunal. 'The bread thus given will not be eaten in ungratefulness or sulky discontent,' he declared, for '[t]he brightest chapter of my life is my service under your Highness. The little name and fame I have acquired is in reality but the light reflected on the servant by an illustrious master, to serve whom, even for a brief period, has been my pride and privilege.'[70] In a sense, despite dissensions and quarrels, there was sympathy for the state itself, and awareness that they were all on the same side of the larger debate – one where natives had to stick together.

Sastri had left a decent record overall, if not one of such spectacular success as his friend, Rao, and would long be remembered fondly, including by officials he mentored. Content, it was time now, the statesman felt, for retirement – he had won official distinction, and though childless, had raised his siblings' families, giving them education.[71] The rest of his years he planned to spend quietly. Indeed, hearing talk of his being offered a commissionership over temples and religious endowments in Madras, he alerted the authorities to his disinterest. '[A]fter being Dewan of Travancore (notwithstanding it was no bed of roses!),' Sastri explained, 'I don't wish to be anything else or anything less ... I am quite content with the career I have run under God's blessing and with the little competence He has measured out to me for my support in the evening of life.'[72] Of course, this was wishful thinking by a man of about fifty. For another princely state beckoned, which would claim the next *sixteen* years of the Dewan's existence. And here, more than in Travancore, Sastri would have a free hand to realize his special conception of kingship, uniting his vision as a Brahmin with wisdom about constitutionality. It was to a land ruled by Kallars – translated often as 'thieves' – that the man now travelled, becoming an unlikely Dewan to a seemingly hopeless prince.

In 1878, a young Ravi Varma unexpectedly ran into Sastri at the Trichinopoly railway station. The artist was waiting for a train connection on his way home from Madras, after an exhibition. Now, this reunion proved fortuitous, opening doors to a new durbar, and a professional world beyond Kerala and Madras for the first time. For Sastri, who was an admirer of the painter, offered him a commission on the spot: if the Travancore maharajah permitted it, he would be delighted to welcome Ravi Varma to the Tondaiman dynasty's kingdom of Pudukkottai, where he was now *sirkele* (minister).

For the ex-Dewan, Pudukkottai was a real step down (with half the pay too) from governing a principality like Travancore. But he had been pressed to step in and practically 'save' the state from British intervention. No less a figure than Rao made its gravity and patriotic intent clear, when he wrote: 'You should by no means refuse to that state the benefit of your knowledge and experience. As natives we cannot but be the well-wishers of native states. Therefore let us do our utmost to set Pudukottah on a sound footing.' Rao was 'anxious' to lift up the Tondaimans from their 'unenviable position', and who better than Sastri to get this done? For, '[h]ere is a suffering patient, and here is a first-rate Doctor . . . What can be more desirable than that they should be brought together!'[73] In a second missive, Rao stressed his point again: Pudukkottai was, he elaborated, like a poor insect 'struggling for life on the surface of water'; at least out of humanitarian concern, it was essential someone helped it out. As Indians, this was urgent business because '[m]any native states have gone'. While Travancore and Cochin were 'pretty safe', he was 'sincerely and earnestly anxious' about the Tondaiman Raj being swallowed up by Madras. 'In these circumstances I must again press you to vouchsafe to Pudukota what it so much requires – the services of a first-rate man.'[74]

And so in August 1878, a year after he bid farewell to Travancore, Sastri assumed charge of a principality one-sixth its size, with a government groaning under administrative chaos and lack of direction.[75] Soon enough, Ravi Varma arrived to enshrine in portraits the dramatis personae the new minister would deal with here. There was Ramachandra Tondaiman, the ageing rajah; there was the shrewd junior rani, Janaki Subbamma; and, finally, their daughter and her child, Martanda Bhairava, adopted as heir to the throne.[76] The first of these was friendly to Sastri and desperate for his services; in fact, when initially the latter showed a disinclination, the rajah implored him to reconsider. As he wrote, Sastri would truly 'oblige me and my state by coming here and assuming the office as my Sirkele'. For his part, the rajah would give 'every possible assistance' if Sastri could help 'promote my dignity and honour and restore me to the good will of the British Government'.[77] The rani, on the other hand, was suspicious and, like Ayilyam Tirunal, on her guard so royal privileges were not surrendered to a hired stranger in this fetish for modernization. As for the prince – he was to grow up into the dramatic *opposite* of what Sastri planned for him, though luckily for the old man, he would be long dead by the time the boy set British and Indian society afire with scandal.

At under 1,200 square miles of territory and a quarter million rupees in revenue, Pudukkottai ought to have been a cakewalk for Sastri. But it had an interesting history. To begin with, the ruling caste here were Kallars. As a publication, *Notes on Criminal Classes of the Madras Presidency* (1892), would put it (with all the ethnographic judgement that characterized such colonial texts), this was a 'dark race of small stature', who were the 'principal criminals' of southern Tamil country. Their very name, translating as 'robbers', indicated 'their peculiar mode of earning a livelihood' and 'lawless habits'. 'Their profession,' the document added, 'is that of stealing with or without violence as opportunities offer,' and till the British arrived, they were 'in constant warfare with their neighbours'.[78] Some of this was true in that Kallars were originally predatory tribes, with a reputation as highwaymen. In the official manual of Pudukkottai, for instance, we read how, historically, 'They issued from their woods every night, sometimes five or six hundred in number, and went to plunder the territories' around them.[79] Retreating just as swiftly into the hills by dawn, there was little local powers could do to deliver retribution.[80] Naturally, besides the Raj, many elite Indian groups also looked down on the Kallars with disdain.

That said, however, much of this was also a convenient imperial reading to discredit a group that was defiant of colonial power. Kallars, to begin with, had a clear role in agrarian society. When medieval kings cleared forests and brought in cultivators, these tribes were co-opted as security

Map of south India, with Pudukkottai visible towards the west coast.

men, watchers of highways and travellers' escorts. The very people whom
the British called a 'fraternity of thieves'[81] even had a role protecting
temples, though with their kinship bonds and clan-based system, they
could become a power unto themselves.[82] In Pudukkottai, *they* were
the dominant force, serving as soldiers, headmen, temple trustees and
even throwing forth a nobility with pretensions to Kshatriya rank. And

instead of rejection, Brahminical society made room for integration: in Sanskrit chronicles, Kallars are the offspring of Indra, king of gods.[83] Concurrent to this construction of narrative and genealogy was their growing political strength, as earlier powers – the *rayas* of Vijayanagara and their successor states – recognized Kallars as legitimate, even if not fully controllable, members of the diverse societies they governed. Thus, just as cultivators paid the state its dues, they also paid the Kallars protection fees, the government having little say in the transaction. They became a law enforcement agency of sorts, but outside the official grasp, giving them a predatory appearance.[84]

This is not to say that the Kallars' reputation was a colonial creation. If, for example, villages did not pay them their dues, they simply took it by force.[85] Equally, however, if people under their protection suffered losses due to the *Kallars'* lapses, they were compensated.[86] The coming of the Company, however, changed things. Unlike previous rulers, the British forced their way in and smashed such autonomy: starting in 1755, campaigns were launched, one of which saw 3,000 Kallars massacred, and when they still would not surrender, another 2,000 added.[87] The conflict was over control – the Kallars would not submit to the Company, which not only deprived them of their dues, but also branded them as genetically prone to thieving. And as local states bowed to the British, this group, spread across large areas, became a problem. With agricultural classes coming to terms with the Company as their new taxing authority, the Kallars now fell *outside* the system, and indeed began to resemble robbers. In the end, the Raj branded them a criminal tribe, though as late as the 1920s, given the limits to government penetration in rural areas, the Kallars often remained preservers of order and security in several places.[88] Even so, the colonial narrative acquired a resonance: in a late-nineteenth-century novel, a character states: 'Stealing is our business. You Brahmins chant the Vedas, and we Kallars steal.'[89]

Royal Kallars, however, had their own story. Pudukkottai's Tondaimans, originally migrants from Telugu territory, rose to prominence in the seventeenth century serving Sriranga III, the Vijayanagara emperor. The founder of the line supposedly impressed

A Kallar man as depicted in Charles Gold's Oriental Drawings *(1806).*

him by subduing an elephant, and Sriranga, in turn, granted him
privileges and marks of regality. This validation constituted the
dynasty's first toehold on the rise to kingship.[90] When Vijayanagara
split into successor states in the seventeenth century, the Tondaimans
were linked to the *nayakas* of Madurai.[91] In the following generation, a
daughter married the Ramnad rajah, becoming one of his forty-seven
wives. Her brother, who assembled a more modest harem of six wives,
seven mistresses and thirty-two children, meanwhile served that rajah
in a military capacity. For this he received an estate and a new roster

of honours.[92] This was the nucleus of Pudukkottai state, and slowly the Tondaimans absorbed more parcels of land around them. By the mid-eighteenth century, they were vassals of the Carnatic nawab, drawn also, thus, into the Mughal universe.[93] And in the process, they became little kings in their own right: royalty among 'robbers'.

As rulers, the Tondaimans naturally also needed legitimacy. As we saw with Martanda Varma in Travancore, promoting Brahminical ideas was a means to this end.[94] In fact, the new rajahs surpassed earlier kings of the area in endowing Hindu shrines, including many outside the state. They invited Brahmin settlers with land grants, established charities and feeding houses, and distributed largesse to construct a courtly standard.[95] As Navaratri had been Vijayanagara's state festival, in Pudukkottai too celebrations were put up, marking, as Nicholas Dirks tells, its rulers' 'full transition from local chiefs to important regional kings'.[96] All along engagement with the Persianate world held – the Tondaimans were thrilled when the Carnatic nawab bestowed on them the title 'Bahadur', and they would later press the British also to grant them marks of distinction. The designation 'maharajah' would have been ideal, but all they got was the privilege of using white umbrellas – a sign of royal status – and gold staffs.[97] In other words, Kallar kings cemented authority not only by adopting Hindu rituals, but also through elements designed by powers of Muslim and Christian provenance. These Kallars were not outside the system; in Pudukkottai, they *became* the system.

Significantly, in wars against third parties that the nawab and Company fought, the rajah sided with them – Kallars were used as auxiliaries for 'cutting off small [enemy] parties, surprising convoys or stealing or disabling horses or cattle, at which they were most expert'.[98] Throwing their hat in with the British would go a long way in preserving their position. As a Tondaiman acolyte varnished it later, 'When the English came into the South of India, this house being satisfied as to the just and equitable rule with which they governed India, allied itself with that power.'[99] In 1799, importantly, as a major Tamil chieftain rose in revolt against the British, it was thanks to the Tondaimans that he was apprehended.[100] The rajah wrote: 'I am ready with my life to serve the Company' so much so that 'their service is the essence of my existence'.[101] In another message he told of how there was nothing 'so good as the Service of the Company; it is fit for me by zeal and diligence to obtain their favor'.[102] This may seem like slavish flattery but as kings of recent vintage, the rajahs were courting a superior power not only to preserve what they had earned, but also to survive on a shifting political chessboard.

This fidelity paid. For when the British brought peninsular India under their sway, Pudukkottai was spared. While Ramnad's rajahs, who first bestowed land on the Tondaimans, were reduced to mere zamindars,[103] Pudukkotai became an autonomous state. In fact, in what was a special privilege, neither did it pay tribute to the British, nor was there a treaty between the two parties, revealing the many forms of the Company's ties with Indian princes.[104] Of course, the British intervened in the state's affairs, and there was no doubt as to which power was the master; not even in theory was this an alliance of equals. In 1807, significantly, when the reigning rajah died, he left two boys as heirs. Supervision fell to William Blackburne, Resident in nearby Tanjore, whose interventions would have enduring effects. Both the ruler and his brother were fond of their guardian, virtually adopting him as their 'father'.[105] He, in return, gave them well-intentioned lectures (and English lessons), hoping to shape them into princes matching Western standards.[106] His affection was genuine: when the older boy died in 1825, the man wrote feelingly how 'It would be fruitless to describe the effect which the loss of our children, so beloved, so respected, so highly praised, has upon us'. He used 'children' knowingly, 'for such we always considered and loved you'.[107]

But personal sentiments aside, the Resident was peeved by Pudukkottai's administration: it had no bureaucracy, no records for the realm, no central judiciary, and, nothing, in other words, that gave its British overlords a full sense of the country.[108] Power was dispersed with Kallar chiefs, in contradiction to the administrative model the British espoused. It evaded him, that an emphasis on centralization was essential to *colonizers* – to Indian rulers, decentralized traditional networks allowed for factions to be integrated and balance to be maintained between myriad interest groups, and for kings to *share* power. The state did not just belong to one family; it was built by a *network* of Kallars, linked through ritual and marriage, down multiple levels, holding together the polity. The king, in other words, sat at the head of a pyramid – to hollow this out was to trample on his subordinates' prerogatives. While the white man's conception of administration was clinical, for a rajah it was personal, with honour, prestige and tradition all entwined. From Blackburne's day, however, such arrangements began to look like impediments; 'progress' meant discarding these forms and transforming the state. Pudukkottai would have to become a centralized, bureaucratic state, with all power rooted in the capital. Here the royal family would retain a traditional facade, while exercising authority through British-approved ministers.

Colonial attitudes also threatened existing economic structures. As late as the mid-nineteenth century, 45,000 acres of land in the most fertile parts of this drought-prone state was held tax-free by Brahmins. One hundred and thirty-six villages were set apart for temples.[109] Only 30 per cent of the principality's taxable extent was under royal control; the remainder was *inam* or freehold. More than half of this was with royal cousins, nobles, military retainers, village heads and hereditary servants.[110] Reflective of Pudukkottai's evolution, now, under British dominance, the chiefs were replaced by a salaried bureaucracy. Ignoring local complexities, Blackburne carted in a crop of Marathi Brahmins.[111] It was a definitive shift and as late as 1875, a Resident would note that if there was a subject of 'universal complaint' in the land, it was the 'paramount influence of Maratta Brahmins, bound together by the closest ties of relationship and interest', and who dominated the administrative services.[112] Why, even state accounts came to be maintained not in Tamil (the local language), Telugu (Vijayanagara's old courtly language), or even Persian (preferred for pan-Indian diplomacy), but in Marathi.[113]

Naturally, these changes fuelled resentment, even if at first its symptoms were muted. Indeed, in the reigns of both the Resident's 'children', there was little visible trouble.[114] Unfortunately, the next king, Ramachandra (1829–86) – later Sastri's master – would prove unable to navigate British expectations on modernization alongside the natural resistance such changes provoked among those invested in older forms. In fact, the price of creeping innovations made in previous reigns began to catch up in this period. As Dirks observes, the most senior class of the nobility did not feel the pinch badly – with court positions, wealth and status, they could weather these times. But the middle rung was disenfranchised. Those who assembled militias, for instance, served no purpose now, with peace in the state, and the British having brought stability outside. This class realized that it was becoming 'obsolete', and that reforms in administrative priorities would affect their privileges the most.[115] Resistance was inevitable: in 1854 there was open defiance of the rajah. Taxes went uncollected, armed bands sparked unrest, and commerce broke down. The whole affair was squashed by the display of British boots, but it also supplied the colonial state an opening to interfere.[116] The Tondaiman kingdom was no longer at peace within, and so intervention took the form less of 'advice' and more of orders and commands.

To make things worse, the rajah was the wrong man in the wrong seat at the wrong time. Only ten years old when installed, Ramachandra's reign began with a council in charge, after which he assumed full powers in 1844. Not long after, he was married – first to the daughter of the Kallakkottai zamindar, and some years later to Janaki, from the Neduvasal zamindar's house. The first lady belonged to the rajah's sub-caste, and their union was to reinforce bonds with the Kallar aristocracy. But the junior rani was 'not connected by any kinship relations' with the country's leading families; she was an outsider.[117] This would have serious consequences given her influence. Soon, not only was the senior rani ignored, even her daughters by Ramachandra were ill-treated.[118] To make things worse, the rajah's largesse – earlier distributed among his nobility, and thus expended to preserve political loyalties – was directed now towards the junior rani and her relations from *outside* the state. Prior rulers deployed pomp and gave gifts as a means of fortifying relationships; munificence represented the ruler's regard for his lords, with the honour he showed them, in turn, reinforcing their positions with *their* power bases. This kept the system well oiled. Now, however, not only was the rajah cut off, but he was spending chiefly for private entertainment. Shielded from internal as well as external crises by the British, the rajah had no incentive to invest in the bonds on which power once rested.

What Ramachandra also did not realize, furthermore, was that for the privilege of cushioning him from threats, the colonial state would extract a price. Ironically, *they* were able to see the damage the ruler was doing. As the Resident observed, the chief nobles deserved 'to be treated by the Rajah with respect'. He was urged at least to give them an 'occasional reception', which would serve him better than pleasing his second wife's kin.[119] The leader of the 1854 rebellion too, for example, categorically noted the 'extravagance of the Rajah, and his maintaining in his service a number of young men who pandered to his vices': men who were not courtiers, but foreign interlopers.[120] The British confirmed the charge: besides the fact that 'low and disreputable parasites' sealed Ramachandra off from his durbar, these people obtained 'money, cloths, and jewels' of great value.[121] After the rebellion, therefore, the rajah was deprived of power – the Resident and the sirkele would now handle matters, with a fixed privy purse for the palace. The rajah was reduced to begging his own minister for money, and five years later, managed to pile up debt to the tune of over 5,00,000 rupees. In a punitive move, the British withdrew the style of 'His Excellency' from him.[122] The rajah now had neither the loyalty of the old regime, nor the respect of his overlords – he was lost between two worlds.

Ramachandra never did manage to rein in his financial profligacy, though he did make a 'most favourable impression' on visitors, given the 'fluency, correctness and elegance' of his English. But that he made a bad ruler was never in doubt.[123] In 1870, amidst deepening trouble, for example, we find the rajah applying for funds to buy a pet cheetah,[124] while a few years later he wanted cash for a bird. 'They have got a self-acting singing bird for sale,' he informed the Resident. 'It is very curious indeed. I am very anxious to have it in my possession. You know my pecuniary difficulties. I shall really feel indebted if you would kindly direct the Sirkele to buy the bird box for me.'[125] Combined with the unpopularity of the junior rani, and the supplicant position in which Ramachandra found himself, it is no wonder that even official state publications acknowledged his reign as disturbed. As we read, 'Some years after the Raja was entrusted with the sole charge of the affairs of the State, he was misled by evil advisers in spite of the remonstrances of the successive [British] Political Agents, who advised him . . . that he should regain the good name of his family by forbidding all his bad counsellors from entering his presence.' But unheedful, Ramachandra 'plunged himself deeper and deeper into debt till at last the state of affairs became critical'.[126]

In fact, by 1861 the rajah's stock was so poor that he was severely embarrassed by a creditor, who issued the following stinging public announcement:

Take notice . . . Rajah of Poodoocottah. That, on and after the 10th of December, in the year one thousand eight hundred and sixty one, unless the sum of rupees [28,200] in full is previously sent by you to

Ramachandra Tondaiman with his courtiers in 1858.

my house, as intimated in my last notice . . . your second wife, son, and daughter, begotten of her, will be put up conjointly, and nominally sold to the highest bidder, in my Receiving Hall, in satisfaction of the claim in question . . . But should you, Maharajah Rama Chundra Tondimon Bahadoor, of Poodoocottah, fail either to send down the above-said amount, or your second wife, son, and daughter by her . . . Know you for certain that my old shoes or slippers will be issued and sent to you, to compel and demand of you to fulfil the terms of this condition; for you must bear in mind that you are not supposed to trample upon the rights and liberties of others with impunity, when you yourself wish and expect your own rights, liberties, and privileges . . . to be respected.[127]

The notice summarizes the crisis in Pudukkottai succinctly: the rajah's addiction to purposeless and self-involved luxury; the hatred directed at the junior rani and her 'outsider' relations who replaced the traditional aristocracy in the ruler's affections; and the overall breakdown of the old order, besieged by colonial forces. It was into this mess that Sastri landed in 1878, to save the teetering state. Resurrecting the old system was not a workable option in the Victorian age; and yet the better parts of tradition also had, the Brahmin Dewan believed, to be preserved. Unlike in Travancore, which was already 'settled' by the time he got there, Sastri's attitude in the Kallar Raj was, therefore, different: that, as Rao put it, of a doctor treating a sick patient. It was to have mixed results, and Sastri's own lurking casteism would intrude into his work. But even so, as Rao had hinted, at least it was an *Indian* doctor treating an invalid of the same colour – of the available options, a native statesman was preferable any day to the British Resident.

Ravi Varma's 1879 portraits of the Tondaimans do not betray this complicated background. Indeed, the rajah we see through the artist's eyes is the very personification of confidence. Ramachandra is dressed in rich clothes ('dark blue embroidered in gold with small squares in

*Ravi Varma's state portrait of
Ramachandra Tondaiman.*

*Rani Janaki Subamma
of Pudukkottai.*

each of which appears a man on horseback'), destined, in a macabre way, though, to one day burn on his funeral pyre.[128] His left hand rests on a book, the spine of which is turned towards the viewer, revealing its English title. In furniture and other details, the painting is European, but in the background, through an arch, one obtains a view of a temple in the capital – a glimpse of tradition in a depiction otherwise modern. In fact, Ravi Varma appears to have been inspired by an old portrait done by F.C. Lewis, Jr – who painted Uthram Tirunal in Travancore in the 1850s, and whose work our painter, thus, knew – given how he presents a near-exact stance and background. Either way, the ruler we see in this frame is a fantasy figure, not the besieged, emasculated Ramachandra of reality. It was a depiction of the rajah as he *wished* to be seen (or as Sastri wished him to be seen), rather than the man he had proved to be. In so flattering him, Ravi Varma brushed over the infamy and humiliation the ruler faced. In that sense, the junior rani's portrait was more honest: Janaki, laden with costly jewels, and in a blazing red sari, is all aplomb. In her demeanour there is authority, which she certainly made every effort to wield.

The rani, in fact, was to become Sastri's chief enemy in Pudukkottai during his long stay. There would be two phases to this. For the first eight years he held the title of sirkele and served the rajah. And then, after Ramachandra died, he became Dewan-Regent, holding the fort till the minor heir came of age; it was chiefly here that the rani and he crossed swords. In fact, before Sastri came to the state, the British had already branded Janaki as a 'thoroughly dangerous' woman.[129] Her love of luxury exacerbated royal debts, just as her toadies were responsible for alienating the rajah from his court.[130] There was truth to these charges, but not a little sexism also in blaming the lady for *all* the man's failings. Thus, for instance, just before Sastri appeared we have the Resident declare, 'No doubt [the ruler] is inexcusably weak and extravagant; but what can be expected of a Rajah whose only associates are narrow-minded, jealous wives, and intriguing parasites?'[131] The 'parasites' – a word used a lot by white sahibs – were the rani's servants, while reference to the wives acknowledged tensions between Janaki and her rival.[132] That the rani, screened away in the palace, achieved everything she set her mind to made her doubly ominous to white gentlemen outside. For instance, the desire to have her daughter's son installed as heir (after her own died) flew in the face of the rajah's nephews' rights. The British consistently opposed this, till in 1877 the boy was secretly adopted.[133] Ramachandra having presented a fait accompli, Janaki's grandson was grudgingly accepted.[134]

Sastri, however, did not have patience for durbar politics. To begin with, the new sirkele had a certain contempt for Kallars, approaching them like a puritanical schoolmarm. Shortly into his term, we find him dismissing the community's leading families as prone to 'sensual pleasures, improvidence, extravagance, and consequently indebtedness'. In his headmasterly opinion, nothing 'but constant supervision and check in all pecuniary matters can keep persons of this class within the limits of propriety'.[135] The wording is revealing – what Residents said of Indian princes, here a Western-educated statesman repeated of native courtiers, mimicking the British Raj with a Brahmin Raj. And here too, moral lectures had material goals – Sastri made these remarks while seizing an estate held by a junior branch of the royal family. Hitherto its heads were chiefs; now they were unwillingly reduced to political pensioners. It was another move to centralize power and bureaucratize the state; as a civil servant, it is not surprising that Sastri thought this style of government ideal. The sirkele in fact did not even permit the family to appoint its own manager – a move that could be written off as stemming from his authoritarian style had it not featured a whiff of casteism. For the manager, he insisted, had to be Brahmin, not Kallar.[136] Viewed alongside Sastri's views on issues like child marriage, we see in him not just a desire to govern, but also to Sanskritize the state's 'robber caste' rulers.

From the sirkele's perspective, this was how things were to be set right: English-educated men of high standing (and, apparently, high caste), capable of matching European standards as well as his Brahminical ideals would man the administration. The Kallar aristocracy were backward relics and were allowed no place in the modern remoulding of the kingdom they helped make in the first place. Indeed, like the British,

Sastri too was appalled that so little of cultivated land in the state paid taxes to the capital; it was unacceptable that at over 3,11,000 acres, freeholds were in excess of the 2,28,000 acres that brought in revenue to the centre. By the end of the 1880s, thus, he would resume many Kallar estates, riding roughshod over the old order. A commission studied tax-free lands to 'verify' whether they deserved that status. Since these had been granted for various services, the new standard was to check whether these were 'useful' in the modern age. Lands given for military purposes, for example, were not, because men at arms were no longer required.[137] Rejecting claims that these were permanent grants, Sastri added 1,50,000 extra acres to the exchequer's share.[138] By doing so, he achieved his goal of raising revenues as well as of impressing the British. In fact, as early as 1883 Sastri proclaimed how '[f]or the first time in the history of Pudukota there was literally no room in the Treasury for the money that had accumulated in it'.[139] But – for better or worse – this came at the cost of inflicting a blow on the old way of life.

To be fair, a number of Sastri's reforms were favourably received by the people. Converting tenants on government lands into proprietors, freeing them from the demands of middlemen, meant that agriculture received a boost.[140] Land revenue rose from 2,75,000 rupees to 6,00,000 rupees,[141] and in his final years Sastri was working on a permanent tax settlement, hoping to 'bequeath it as a real Magna Carta' to the peasants.[142] New buildings, roads, bridges, irrigation facilities, a hospital, college and other structures were erected – in fact, we are told that the government, hitherto housed haphazardly, was given a headquarters that struck visitors with 'wonder and admiration'.[143] As Sastri himself wrote, 'People who have known the town well ten years ago can hardly recognize it now.'[144] At one level, the Dewan-Regent was trying to exhibit tangible 'progress' in Pudukkottai. But equally, all this might have had something to do with a desire to leave behind a physical monument to his work.[145] And the best way to do this was to pave roads, raise striking structures, and have an army of clerks working at desks. 'There is scarcely a morning I don't drive out to see the progress and suggest improvements,' Sastri once explained. 'With a treasury containing six lacs at my back I now feel that

I can indulge myself to the fullest extent in the luxury of doing public good – But I am forgetting myself and drifting into "Vanity Fair".'[146] It was a Freudian slip because a good deal of this does appear to have been about the Dewan validating his own saviour complex.

Indeed, Sastri believed it was his destiny to rescue Pudukkottai. In his mind, interim pain was bitter but necessary medicine. Blind to his own biases, he even saw himself as the victim. As early as 1879, certain reforms had invited a threat of assassination. When the disenfranchised aristocracy forwarded complaints to Madras, the man chuckled. 'I wish them success with all my heart!'[147] But he did have doubts, confessing a few years later, 'My position here is getting more and more unpleasant ... and I long to be out of it ... If I care I might stay as long as I please; but the question is – Is it worth while?'[148] On the rare occasions when Ramachandra showed displeasure, he patiently (though again in that schoolmasterly tone which so infuriated Ayilyam Tirunal) explained himself. 'In the course of my duty and according to the dictates of my conscience, I have sometimes to do things which are very unpleasant'. But they were all for good, and once 'the first effects of disappointment and anger' passed, he hoped the ruler would see 'my motives and acts in their proper light'.[149] Divorced from local history, contemptuous of the ruling caste, and yet, as an Indian, keen to see Pudukkottai satisfy progressive parameters, it was natural that Sastri justified himself through lofty references to duty and conscience.[150] When he became regent, he claimed: 'It is after all the hand of Providence that invisibly, though none the less certainly, guides us and controls our own destinies and the destinies of Native States and of all kingdoms on earth.' Here, Sastri became God's instrument slogging away in Kallar territory to 'save' them from the British and themselves.[151]

With such heroic ideas of his own place, it is no wonder that Janaki could not stand the man.[152] In fact, when appointed regent, Sastri reported how 'There is nothing but prickly pear all around the direction of the palace'.[153] This is no surprise, for now the Dewan had a free pass to interfere even in the royal household, as guardian to Martanda Bhairava (1875–1928). He appointed, for example, his nephew to the rajah's retinue, a man Janaki described as Sastri's 'replica', placed there to relay 'all of the tittle-tattle of the palace'.[154] Devadasis who attended to royal women were, meanwhile, barred. Yes, when the governor of Madras visited, 'it rained wreaths and nautch girls';[155] but Sastri shared a Victorian disdain for such women. Janaki was furious, for the devadasis were a window to the outside world and intelligence. Where the Dewan spoke with pride of stopping the 'ingress of all dancing girls', to the royal ladies it seemed an assault on them.[156] Why, Sastri even nailed up a door to prevent 'wicked and debaucherous' people from having access.[157] He attacked the rani by referring to the 'disgrace and ruin' she brought upon her husband; not to be outdone, she and her daughter retaliated by alleging that the Dewan wished to murder them, even organizing 'a sacrifice of one hundred cobras' to rally spirits.[158] Sastri was unaffected, for the 'British Government', he wrote, was 'a Constitutional Government not easily moved by sensational telegrams'.[159] Or simply put, he was in step with reigning attitudes; they, on the other hand, were exhibits of backwardness, and illicit influence.

The chief tussle, however, between Dewan and rani was about custody of the rajah. Nearly eighty years before, Blackburne had observed that a regency was 'the appropriate and probably the only time for making substantial reforms' in Pudukkottai.[160] Sastri shared the belief, making use of the ruler's minority for not only administrative innovations, but also a transformation of the *kind* of king the state would have. Already in Ramachandra's day he had Brahminized the throne: this was the logic behind giving the king a new title. Imitating the Travancore custom, where rulers were 'Padmanabha Dasas' ('Servants of Padmanabhaswamy', their deity), Sastri recast Ramachandra as 'Sri Brihadamba Dasa' ('Servant of Brihadamba', Pudukkottai's own god).[161] With Martanda Bhairava, now, Sastri was determined not only to keep him away from Janaki, but also to 'mould the character of the young Rajah'.[162] Long before, Rao had opined privately that if Ramachandra was a bad ruler, it was because of 'defective education and a bad company in early years';[163] the same mistake could not be repeated. An English tutor kept the boy away in Trichinopoly for much of his time, 'as that

station furnished facilities for games and field sports', and put him in
'European society'.[164] Tours across India were arranged to expose him
to good governance, while exposing him rather less to his own state
and its people. In his *Instructions for the Guidance of the Guardian of
the Maharaja*, Sastri not only defined ideal royal companions, but also
argued the importance of 'guarding . . . His Highness's morals'.[165] As
his assumption of power approached, Martanda Bhairava's tutor gave
an optimistic certificate: the rajah's character and behaviour were such
that there was every hope of 'an honourable and useful career'.[166]

And thus, in 1894, with the new ruler installed, Sastri departed from
Pudukkottai, having made it, as Joanne Punzo Waghorne puts it, 'a
country of laws and not men'.[167] At the durbar on the occasion, rich
tributes were paid him. As the governor of Madras said to the rajah,

> The inheritance upon which you are this day entering was twenty years
> ago financially and in every other respect in a most dilapidated condition.
> The aspect of affairs is now very different; you will have made over to
> you a State not only unencumbered with debt, but possessing a balance
> of more than three lakhs, while there is every prospect of its yielding
> an increasing revenue if it is administered with due care. On every side
> material improvements are visible. Every branch of the administration
> has been more or less reformed, the revenue has improved, the roads
> are excellent, and the capital is adorned with modern public buildings.
> All these are due to the untiring energy and devotion to his duties of
> Dewan-Regent, Mr Sashiah Sastri . . . The result of his labours has been
> so successful that what was at the time of his accession to office almost a
> wreck is at the present moment a prosperous possession . . .[168]

It was not hollow praise – in due course the ex-Dewan would be
rewarded with a knighthood. And Sastri too wished the state well. He
hoped that 'the high education and excellent training which . . . the
Rajah has received under the directions of the Madras Government will
bear good fruit' so that 'His Highness will far excel his predecessors in
the excellent manner in which he holds his sway over his people'.[169] The

old man now retired to his mansion in Kumbakonam – a house, he told his schoolmaster, Powell, was so 'comfortable' that locals thought it a palace.[170] Sastri spent his final decade there, in active correspondence with his British as well as Indian connections, and in reflection about all that he and his fellows had achieved. His old friend Rao was dead by now, but the feelings he expressed a few years before probably resonated with Sastri. 'When we used to meet in our early years,' Rao had written, 'and eat tiffin together, little did we dream that we were destined to become such eminent men!! God be praised for the good fortune which has attended us.'[171] It was true – Powell's boys had gone out and conquered important corners of their world. They won laurels and proved that they were as good as white officials. But if Rao praised the almighty for their rise, Sastri politely gave credit to one more force. As he declared at

From an important private collection

The young Martanda Bhairava Tondaiman, as painted by Ravi Varma in the mid-1880s.

Martanda Bhairava's installation, if things had 'prospered beyond all my expectation', allowing him to close his career with esteem, it was thanks to the 'blessings of God and the Madras Government'.[172]

Sastri's challenge was one many statesmen of the time faced: the pull of patriotism against the hold of conservatism; the desire to birth in India a modern system, against the painful business of hacking away what was (seemingly) rotten. Nor was it easy to negotiate British pressure against Indian aspirations, or grapple with the challenges of royal courts. These men did their best to chart out a new road map and accommodate what they thought needed salvaging, constructing an empowering future. They were not always successful. By 1903, for example, a critic would write that while Sastri could claim a 'happy combination of moderation, prudence, patriotism and practical common sense', this once-penniless man, no sooner had he risen through the ranks, assumed aristocratic airs and *became* the establishment. He showed support for the Congress as an idea, but manifested an 'aversion' to align with it. 'It is,' the critic added, 'of little use to say that a man sympathized with a movement when he did nothing for it himself, when he withheld from it all the support he could easily give.' The least he could have done was to place 'the prestige of his position, and the benefit of his large experience' directly at the service of the nationalist cause. Instead, the scathing conclusion went, 'He fought no battle for the public. He made no sacrifice for his countrymen.' It was somewhat unkind to this ageing generation whose battles were of a different type, but then, again, the world was changing by the early twentieth century, and a new time needed new idols.[173]

Ironically, even his work in Pudukkottai, where he closed his career with so much honour, did not fare well. For all the wonderful statistics on roads and buildings, the *ruler* Sastri placed on the throne proved a disappointment. The Dewan's effort with the Raj to make him modern, while also distancing him from his family, had the following consequence: between Martanda Bhairava's installation in 1894 and the close of 1897, he could be persuaded to spend only a grand total of two months in his own kingdom.[174] Soon it was said that 'the Raja is more a coloured European gentleman, with entirely European tastes, than a Native Prince'; he had become an 'absentee chief', 'addicted to amusements'.[175] Power was delegated to a council in 1898, and a decade later he installed his brother as Dewan. Rival claimants to the throne sent petitions to the British, while the people grew agitated with the ruler's neglect. By 1908, when the rajah had been away for two years, it was clear he had 'a regrettable tendency to prefer his private interests to those of his people'.[176] At least his grandfather, for all his flaws, lived among his subjects; this successor, exemplifying the civilizing power of the Raj, could not be bothered. Finally, in 1926, at the Pudukkottai People's Conference it was declared: 'The Kingdom is Desolate. Tears of blood shed by the poor are running. There is famine everywhere. People are emigrating from the country for their livelihood. All round there is scarcity. There are no handicrafts. How long are the people to suffer in this way?'[177]

In fact, Martanda Bhairava's deracination was such that he couldn't, apparently, even find a local wife – he was entirely de-Kallarized. After a long bachelorhood he shocked both Indian and British society by marrying an Australian he met in a hotel. The prospect of a white rani opened a can of worms, as did the notion of a mixed-race Tondaiman. But the rajah was determined. Speaking on his return to Pudukkottai, he cleverly pointed to his 'training and travels', which had 'formed certain ideas' about the kind of spouse he wished to have. After 'much looking out', he regretted that 'it was impossible' to find a brown lady of his 'standard'. So, instead, he presented Molly Fink of Melbourne. Under their 'joint guidance' Pudukkottai would, he promised, grow 'even more prosperous and happy'.[178] As it happened, they stayed less than a year.[179] The British, meanwhile, were horrified, with the monarch in London crying, 'Miss Molly Fink! What a name!'[180] In India too the authorities asked: did not 'the State . . . require the presence of His Highness? Is it safe to allow the bond between him and his people on which the happiness and safety of the State has depended to be entirely broken?

. . . [And] once even an elementary consciousness of their "rights" has awakened . . . is it not a factor in the situation which no wise ruler can afford to ignore?'[181] In the end, the rajah surrendered ruling functions and moved abroad. When he died, he was succeeded by a cousin: a descendant of that very Tondaiman relative who was deprived of his lands in Sastri's day.

Sastri himself, of course, was no more by this time, but if he had had a grave, he would have taken a turn in it. If there was any consolation, it was that in the end Pudukkottai *did* get in its next prince, Rajagopala Tondaiman (1922–97), a ruler who had the qualities that mattered. Of his character, his tutor (who, incidentally, would also serve Ravi Varma's great-grandson, the last maharajah of Travancore, in a similar capacity) had no doubts: he was 'upright, moderate' and 'kindly', 'amenable to progressive ideas, unassuming, unselfish' with neither 'extravagant tastes' nor a propensity for 'injudicious spending'.[182] So too post-independence India's government would speak of him as a 'man of character' who was 'frugal' and popular.[183] Why, Rajagopala had no property, no fortune, no estates – nothing other than his rulership of Kallars.[184] There was only one complication in this promising story: that he was a child when he came to the throne, so that from 1928 until 1944 the state was under a minority and British control. These years were spent in an effort to ensure the boy would become all that his predecessor had failed to be. And just when it looked like the British finally got things right, the world changed: three years into his reign, Rajagopala signed the instrument of accession, joining the destiny of his state to that of the Congress-led Indian Union. By the time there was a Kallar prince suited for the modern age in Pudukkottai – a rajah of Sastri's dreams – it was simply too late.

Portrait by Mangala Bayi, Ravi Varma's sister.

In 1881, after patronage at the Travancore durbar was withdrawn, Ravi Varma received a major commission in Baroda state. This chapter tells the story of one of the most fascinating maharajahs of this Maratha principality in Gujarat, as well as the tale of his predecessor who fell afoul of the Raj.

4

A Patron of Sedition

On the morning of 9 November 1874, an Englishman called Robert Phayre suddenly felt an attack of nausea in princely Baroda. The middle-aged Colonel Phayre was British Resident at the Maratha court here and had been somewhat under the weather for several days prior. That morning, though, was different. He had, as usual, returned from his walk and taken a few sips of the pummelo sherbet his servants always kept ready. Sitting down to write a letter, however, a 'sudden squeamishness' possessed him. Deciding it was the juice, he threw out the rest, only to notice something odd. 'As I was replacing the tumbler on the wash-hand stand,' Phayre recalled, 'I saw a dark sediment collected at the bottom.' Holding it closer to the eye, 'the thought occurred at once to my mind that it was poison'.[1] He sent off the substance for analysis, and telegrammed his superiors: 'Bold attempt to poison me this day has been providentially frustrated.'[2] Interestingly, despite the gravity of the claim, when the local maharajah came to see him hours later, the Resident kept mum; it was days before the incident was broached, news having reached the palace through other channels. In his official commiseration, the ruler expressed horror at this plot by 'some bad man' to liquidate the Resident. 'If it becomes necessary for you to obtain my assistance in proving the criminal's guilt,' the maharajah offered, 'the same will be given.'[3]

MULHARRAO, GUICOWAR OF BARODA
Arrested by the Indian Government for Attempting to Poison Colonel Phayre

COLONEL R. PHAYRE, C.B.
Late British Political Resident at Baroda

Wikimedia Commons

Malhar Rao Gaekwad and Robert Phayre as depicted in The Graphic *(1875).*

Unfortunately for Malhar Rao Gaekwad of Baroda (1831–82), in Phayre's mind the 'criminal' was none other than the maharajah himself. Ever since his arrival in the principality, the colonel had found himself unable to get along with its ruler. Neither was, to be fair, a particularly placatory type. Described as an 'overbearing, irascible British official . . . dreaded and detested by all Indians', Phayre had left his last posting in a muddle.[4] The maharajah, meanwhile, was textbook dubious. A little over a decade ago, when his brother sat on the throne, he was locked up for conspiring to murder him.[5] His sibling's death, however, restored Malhar Rao to liberty, and succeeding to power, he showed 'a most sweeping and vindictive character'. The minister who had investigated the murder conspiracy, for example, was left to rot in prison, where he died mysteriously.[6] So too Malhar Rao developed a habit of seizing women he liked and forcing them into palace service: as *The Hitechhu* reported, girls were 'taken like pigeons' and subjected to 'filthy violations'.[7] Then there was the matter of his newest wife, 'Luxmeebaee', who was first the ruler's mistress, marrying him while already pregnant; when the maharajah expressed a desire to proclaim his son by her as heir, Phayre demurred.[8] Furious, Malhar Rao apparently issued orders that anybody who did not refer to his wife as the 'Chotee Rani' (junior queen) was liable for a fine of fifteen rupees.[9]

Baroda was a case study in what the British deemed misgovernment. Its Maratha rulers were originally conquerors in Mughal Gujarat, subject to the Peshwas of Poona. By the nineteenth century, however, they obtained independence from the Peshwas with aid from the East India Company. Territories were carved up between the British and the Gaekwads in a way that the kingdom came to comprise several disconnected tracts.[10] Then, in 1857, during the Great Rebellion, Khande Rao (elder brother to Malhar Rao) stayed loyal to the Company, for which the dynasty was granted second highest rank among India's princes.[11] This was why, despite a deepening crisis, colonial authorities did not intervene excessively in the state's affairs. In Khande Rao's time, for example, '[n]ew cesses and levies were recklessly imposed to pay for court extravagancies and collected by the harshest measures', we read. 'No complaints were listened to' till 'discontent became general among all classes'.[12] The Maratha elite were disconnected from their Gujarati subjects, and Malhar Rao did little to improve things when he succeeded his brother. On the contrary, he seemed capable of surpassing him in immoderation. Where the old maharajah commissioned a carpet of gems and pearls,[13] his heir cast cannons of gold to fan his competitive vanity. Residents ventured the occasional menacing 'advice' but wrote much of this off as typical oriental conduct – that is, till Phayre decided to tutor Malhar Rao in good governance as well as princely morality.

The new Resident did not have a propitious start in Baroda. Indeed, on the very day he arrived in March 1873, eight men were flogged on the streets of the capital, resulting in several deaths. The colonel demanded an explanation from the ruler, who in turn viewed having to provide one as demeaning.[14] He justified his actions on the ground that the men had tried to poison him, but to the British the issue was whether they had gone through any kind of judicial process before being sentenced.[15]

There could be no place for arbitrary decisions in a modern society, and this maharajah in particular, who was 'taken from a prison' and parked on the throne, had to 'be guided'.[16] As time passed, then, Phayre catalogued more evidence of despotism on the part of the 'deranged' court, and at his urging, his bosses constituted a commission of inquiry.[17] Its raison d'être was simple: that disturbances in Baroda could also 'injuriously . . . affect British interests'.[18] And soon the commission confirmed that bankers were indeed oppressed, the nobility was coerced into delivering 'presents' to the maharajah, and women were enslaved regularly by palace henchmen.

But, as the commissioners saw it, these were symptoms of a larger problem: the fact that the government was run by sycophants, in a violently feudal style. The men in charge, they claimed, had no conception of what to do with power other than to mine it for self-aggrandizement. There was little sense of moral and public accountability, and the maharajah could not alone modify this state of affairs. And so, the commission recommended:

> . . . we deem it to be essential that the [future] Minister of the Baroda State shall be selected with reference to his administrative experience, and personal and other special qualifications for the post, and while enjoined to secure the Chief's good-will and confidence and to work in respectful subordination . . . have such support from the Resident, as . . . to enable him to carry out, efficiently and satisfactorily, the important functions of his office . . . [Moreover,] while we should deprecate any *needless* introduction of other than Baroda subjects into the service of the State, the employment of a few carefully selected men, who have already received adequate training in the British public service, will . . . be absolutely necessary to enable the minister to carry out the changes so urgently called for.[19]

In other words, progressive individuals from *outside* were to be placed in charge, albeit under the maharajah's direction. According to the commissioners, things were bad but could yet be rectified, if this were done. It was a gentler reprimand for Malhar Rao than the fireworks Phayre wanted and set off a quarrel within the British establishment. Baroda was supervised by the governor of Bombay, whose men had hoped for untrammelled intervention; the viceroy in Calcutta, however, did not wish to rock the boat too much.[20] With the current report, therefore, two members of the governor's council submitted notes of dissent. Henry Tucker, for example, believed that Phayre had 'in no way exaggerated the evils' of Baroda – it was the investigators who had erred with their 'mild condemnation'. Indeed, to Tucker this was not about Baroda alone but the Raj's moral function, for a 'refusal to recognise and terminate' misgovernment would 'bring great discredit' to the British nation. Judged by this yardstick, the commission's willingness to allow Malhar Rao a second chance was scandalous. A critical paragraph, in fact, reveals not only Tucker's views but also evolving ideas on how princely states ought to consider their long-term prospects – ideas that were also playing on the minds of India's nationalists:[21]

> . . . I consider that a gradual change from arbitrary to constitutional government is absolutely necessary for the preservation of the integrity of these States and for the prevention of their ultimate annihilation . . . It seems to be unreasonable to hope for any improvement in a Native State where everything is made to depend on the will of the ruler; and the natural check upon such a system, viz., the rising of the people against tyranny and oppression, is rendered inoperative by the overwhelming force of the British nation, which serves to protect a wicked or incompetent Ruler from any serious revolt . . . It is impossible for the Native States to stand still among the changes of thought and growth of civilization which is slowly but surely developing around them; and if nothing be done to provide the means of improvement within themselves, they must steadily deteriorate . . . till their extinction is called for by the general voice of the country.[22]

Leaving aside the irony of the British lecturing others on the moral weight of power, this was a compelling general observation. On the one hand it acknowledged that, unlike in the past when subjects might throw off a ruler's yoke, today's native princes were cushioned by the British and protected from internal turmoil. This birthed stagnation, for the maharajahs no longer needed to mollify local society, whether in terms of caste networks, commercial guilds, the nobility, or otherwise. So long as they paid tribute to the Raj, they could be left in security, and this in turn caused them to neglect their people.[23] It is indeed a fact that in earlier days, far from being a meek and oppressed peasantry, the cultivating Indian masses had considerable leverage.[24] Or as a rajah elsewhere once put it, if the peasants were ill-treated, they would 'fly to another part of the country' rather than 'sell their plough and cattle to pay their rents'.[25] A maharajah, in other words, did not exist in isolation, with the world revolving around his whims; on the contrary, his power depended on a series of negotiations with his people, and *their* satisfaction.

This pattern extended to the ruler's courtly subordinates as well. So, chiefs and noblemen had rights, which if trampled upon could lead to conspiracy. So too if bankers were dragooned into writing off royal debts, they could move their business elsewhere, or even plot with the ruler's enemies.[26] This was precisely why, given Malhar Rao's conduct, his own sirdars, merchants, and even a man claiming to be his latest wife's cuckolded husband were able to undermine him via appeals to the Resident. If the ruler did not moderate his conduct, that is, his people would seek foreign aid. But with Phayre in charge, it was not as though the British were dispassionate parties either. As a royal descendant wrote, 'The Residency's clerks and secretaries . . . began to wield far more power than the Maharaja's ministers, and, to be sure, made an excellent living out of it.'[27] Indeed, the Resident may well have become the centre of power in the state, but for the fact that Calcutta was against harsh punitive actions.[28] As the viceroy saw it, no matter how monstrously incompetent Malhar Rao was, *legally* the maharajah had the right to introduce reforms himself.[29] However lofty their intentions, the British could not arrogate a vassal's authority without giving him a chance. So, in July 1874 the maharajah was placed on probation: he had under eighteen months to address grievances about his government.[30]

The various territorial segments of Baroda, surrounded by British India.

As it happened, Malhar Rao too had gauged that reform was a form of defence. So much so that months before the viceroy's communique arrived, the maharajah had already selected a new Dewan – a figure Phayre described as his 'principal adviser' from as far back as 1872.[31] The Resident did not approve, because the appointment was made without consulting him; eight months later, in fact, the colonel was still urging his superiors to refuse to recognize the Dewan, not only because he was 'incapable', but also because his 'line of conduct' left much to be desired. He was constantly 'insulting the Resident and endeavouring to rid himself and his master' of his 'advice'; in fact, allowing this minister would be 'absolutely subversive of . . . [British] interests, as well as our own honour'.[32] But it did not have the intended effect. 'You have been made acquainted in the clearest language,' Bombay wrote in response, 'not to fetter the Gaekwar' for now. Instead of upbraiding the ruler, they called out Phayre's own 'decided hostility' and 'personal opposition'.[33] As far as they were concerned, the matter was closed. But Phayre was not chastened. After all, the new Dewan was none other than Dadabhai Naoroji, one day to be celebrated as the Grand Old Man of India, and declared by Gandhi himself as the father of the nation and a veritable mahatma.[34]

The suave, erudite and anglicized Naoroji (1825–1917) was an unusual choice for Dewan in a state where, so far, the cabinet had featured the maharajah's brothers-in-law and a host of royal toadies. Baroda seemed to be in a state of decay, unlike cosmopolitan Bombay where Naoroji was reared. And yet the man embraced the opportunity, sailing all the way from London, where he was living. As his biographer Dinyar Patel explains, to Naoroji, who lamented the drain of wealth from India to Britain, a key strategy in response was to advocate for Indians, rather than Europeans, to take charge of public administration. Any serious hope of self-government in the subcontinent would depend, he felt moreover, on experiments in the *princely* states, where native rule could distinguish itself. 'What a splendid prospect is in store for the future', he exclaimed, if only the British allowed princes to govern without interference.[35] After all, the states did not have to pay exorbitant salaries to white officials who then repatriated this money to foreign shores; their economies were controlled by local bankers and merchants, not directly by foreigners; and despite losing sums by paying tribute, they had resources to beat the British.[36] It would, of course, entail the maharajahs surrendering some traditional powers, but it was a small price to pay for the nation. This, more than attractions of durbar service, was Naoroji's motivation; or as he wrote after accepting his post in Baroda, 'We have not come to serve the man; we have come to serve the cause.'[37]

The Sree Chitra Art Gallery, Thiruvananthapuram

Ravi Varma's portrait of Dadabhai Naoroji.

Naoroji, who by family tradition may well have lived as a Zoroastrian priest, was another early product of English education in India. While Rao and Sastri graduated from what became Presidency College in Madras, this Parsi emerged from Bombay's Elphinstone College. Like them, he too was witness to the failure of the 1857 rebellion, choosing constitutional means to fight the British instead. Travelling to Britain for business interests, he also became a spokesman for his homeland. His East India Association served as a platform to inform white audiences of the poverty and enervation the British sowed in their colony. In his first speech on 'England's Duties to India', he bluntly declared: 'Security of life and property we have better in these times' of British rule, 'but the destruction of a million and a half lives in one famine is a strange illustration of the worth of the life and property thus secured'.[38] Mastering official statistics, he showed British audiences the dire circumstances in which Indians lived, puncturing the exotic idea of India – a land of palaces and elephants – with the reality of its malnourished masses. All along, large sums of money were donated to the Association by Indian

princes, to sustain a native platform under the nose of the very queen
to whom they pledged loyalty.[39] In time, Naoroji would also serve as a
parliamentarian, to directly push reform.[40] But that was in the 1880s – in
1873, no sooner did an invitation arrive to run a native state than Naoroji
sailed east, hoping to make a practical demonstration that Indian-ruled
India could prosper.

Understandably, Phayre was not thrilled with the new minister's
nationalist propensities. As he reported, 'a perceptible difference in tone
was at once apparent in all official communications from the Durbar'
ever since the Parsi landed.[41] Soon, Naoroji declared open war, helping
the maharajah complain about the Resident to his higher-ups. The
colonel, it was stated, not only inflicted 'petty slights, discourtesies, and
harsh expressions' on the ruler, but was 'continuously unkind'. Why, he
even subjected Malhar Rao to a 'public insult' by avoiding his wedding
with the controversial Lakshmibai.[42] Her antecedents did not matter;
by refusing to participate in an important ritual, he had sent a damaging
message. Phayre, furious at this boldness, railed against Naoroji. In
the Resident's mind, the Dewan exploited his 'excellent knowledge of
English customs and habits' to push the maharajah's unworthy cause.
He used a language and terminology designed to impress British
readers and win sympathy for a wicked ruler. Indeed, more than a
deferential minister, his work in Baroda unmasked him as a 'mischievous
political agitator'.[43]

Here the Resident was not incorrect, in that the Parsi statesman
viewed his duties in light of his larger nationalist project rather than
simply as a job. Even the people he invited to join him betrayed these
sympathies. Though he did not accept, M.G. Ranade was one person
Naoroji tried to import.[44] Another officer who was successfully wooed
was Kazi Shahabuddin, who had worked both in a princely state and
Bombay, besides also possessing international experience.[45] Phayre's
prejudice against these men becomes clear in that he took only months
to write off Shahabuddin as hopeless, when the man in a few years
would himself become Dewan. All along, Naoroji was also attempting
to persuade the maharajah towards an elevated outlook. 'The chief

foundation of the State,' the Dewan explained, 'must be laid upon justice and fairness.'[46] Malhar Rao was half-hearted, and yet Naoroji was able to cut the sale of official appointments, the use of torture, that custom of coercing women into royal service, all while attempting to formulate a legal code and reform taxes.[47] Many had no faith that the Baroda experiment would triumph – its maharajah was not the kind of 'enlightened' prince who would wholeheartedly back a progressive Dewan. But Naoroji persevered anyway, clearly invigorated (or perhaps blinded) by patriotic fervour.[48]

Unfortunately, with this particular statesman, the naysayers were proved right. It did not take long for the minister to learn that he was handicapped in multiple ways. On the one hand was the bitter obstructionism of the Resident, who took an age to acknowledge even Naoroji's existence. Then, on the other, was the fact that while some officials from the earlier system were dismissed, many were not; indeed, the last minister was retained in a palace post, resulting in a kitchen cabinet at odds with the Dewan. Unlike Ayilyam Tirunal in Travancore who embraced reform, Malhar Rao wished only for its appearance. When, for instance, Naoroji suggested he sign an 'agreement of 25 articles' delineating a division of powers with the Dewan, not only did the durbar thwart this, even the Resident protested, asserting that the proposal was 'an offence against [British] sovereignty'.[49] As *The Hitechhu*, which otherwise had praise for Naoroji, rued, 'Mr Dadabhai has become perfectly useless.'[50] Ironically, it was Phayre's superiors who showed sympathy for the beleaguered minister. While the Resident was anxious to certify him a failure, Bombay felt that he had not had a fair chance. 'Mr Dadabhai Nowrojee himself may be fairly open to the objection of being inexperienced in matters of administration,' they wrote, 'but a very high opinion is entertained in many quarters of his character and abilities.'[51] It did little to amend Phayre's attitude, and soon relations between ruler, Resident and Dewan were comprehensively fractured.

It was in this disturbed context, then, that Phayre discovered diamond dust and arsenic in his sherbet that November morning in 1874. And from his perspective, there was reason to suspect the ruler. On the one hand was the maharajah's continued umbrage at the delay in recognizing his son as heir to the throne. British inquiries revealed that baby's mother was once 'employed as a cooly [sic] in Surat' before she was taken to the palace; but though she was of inferior caste and pregnant at the time of her wedding, given that Malhar Rao had acknowledged the child as his, there was no way to withhold recognition.[52] Then there was political animosity. A week before the poisoning, on the same day that the maharajah fired off a volley of complaints against the Resident to the viceroy, the latter too submitted a 174-point 'progress report' that showed Baroda as doomed. It was intended to damage the Dewan as well as the still-on-probation ruler.[53] Frustrated, Naoroji realized he had had enough, deciding to resign.[54] British officials in Calcutta were, naturally, in a bind. Having themselves reprimanded Phayre, they could hardly evade the maharajah's charge that the Resident 'prejudged' everything and had produced a biased report.[55] Equally, though, Malhar Rao was not the kind of ruler who inspired sympathy. The only course available, in the viceroy's mind, then, was to sack Phayre and send in a mature man – a decision that in turn inflamed the governor in Bombay, who registered a grievance about viceregal overreach into matters that were *his* jurisdictional concern.

Phayre, true to form, did not take these developments in the right spirit. At first, he tried to dig his heels in, and when he left, made an almighty fuss.[56] His successor in Baroda, meanwhile – Lewis Pelly, who, interestingly, would win a Commons seat in the same election where Naoroji first stood as candidate – decided to investigate the poisoning. This was chiefly because though '[n]o evidence of any value was procured', Phayre kept insisting the matter be looked into. His perseverance paid off: Pelly found that the ruler had 'secret communications' with Residency servants, two of whom confessed to the poisoning.[57] After seeking legal opinion in Bombay and Calcutta, then, the viceroy decided there was a prima facie case against Malhar Rao. From here on, things moved fast. By January 1875, troops were landed, the maharajah was placed under house arrest, and the government – just as Naoroji departed – was assumed by the Raj. Though Malhar Rao, by the viceroy's own acknowledgement, had not had a chance to put up a defence, examine witnesses or explain his version, the British opted to pre-emptively seize power till he was cleared. 'This action,' the viceroy explained, 'was not based on considerations of law. It was an act of State, carried out by the Paramount Power.'[58] Elements in the press too had paved the way for this. As an editor put it, 'The only way to clear the Vessel of Baroda is, to throw over-board its cargo of Rogues.'[59]

But trying a maharajah was no easy business: he could not be dragged before a British court, nor was a public inquiry fitted to his dignity. Still, in the end, an inquiry was less embarrassing. Notwithstanding Malhar Rao's reputation, this too, in native circles, caused protests – insulting one of the country's princes was seen as an assault on Indians as a people. Did this dangerous precedent mean, additionally, that other thrones too were not secure?[60] Among the general public agitation grew; it was, we read, 'not limited to processions to the temples and prayers' but also 'modernized by the educated natives into the form of public meetings and memorials to' the viceroy.[61] In Poona, thus, the Sarvajanik Sabha called for a fundraising campaign for the ruler's defence.[62] Under pressure, therefore, the British were forced into a 'gesture of equality': of six commissioners chosen for the inquiry, three were Indians: the Maratha king of Gwalior, the Jaipur maharajah and Sir Dinkar Rao, north India's leading statesman.[63] In the meantime, Malhar Rao too, hoping to fight fire with fire, imported the British barrister William Ballantine to argue his case. The choice was strategic, for, as Judith Rowbotham tells, while this genius was a spectacular misogynist, the one thing he was not, by contemporary standards, was a racist.[64] Ballantine, who till then had had no idea even of Baroda's existence, decided to do what he did best – try and win.[65] For he too was aware that this was more than just a court battle. The contest, it seemed, was between native prestige and British supremacy.[66]

On 23 February 1875 proceedings opened in Baroda. To begin with, the language chosen was English, which put not only the maharajah but also Dinkar Rao at a disadvantage, as neither spoke it with ease.[67] Bombay's advocate-general presented the case against Malhar Rao: his

Sir Dinkar Rao and the Gwalior and Jaipur maharajahs.

bribery of Residency employees, the poisoning of November as merely the last in a series of attempts and the confession of even the royal secretary.[68] But Ballantine proved a formidable cross-examiner. The servant who had served the pummelo juice, for instance, despite claiming to have been bribed, had not *actually* received any money. When grilled, the man mumbled that since he had failed at the task of murdering Phayre, his conscience did not allow him to accept remuneration.[69] More stinging was the barrister's attack on the ex-Resident. Days after doctors generically confirmed that the sediment in his tumbler was poison, Phayre cited 'secret and confidential' information specifying it as '1. Common arsenic; 2. Finely powdered diamond dust; 3. Copper'.[70] This was linked to an alleged purchase of diamonds by Malhar Rao, thus connecting the substance to the prince. But Ballantine was curious: from whom had Phayre received such precise intelligence?[71] Here the ex-Resident stumbled. Vaguely stating that he had very many sources, he claimed he could not recall 'which particular person' conveyed these details.[72] Smelling blood, Ballantine wondered how on such a grave matter Phayre had forgotten the origin of critical information.

When after sustained cross-examination a name was at last revealed, it happened to be that of one Bhau Punekar, 'notoriously the bitterest enemy of the Gaekwar . . . who had been for years fostering charges against him'.[73] Who, demanded Malhar Rao's lawyer then, was to say that it was not Punekar himself who had framed the ruler? After all, given their mutual hatred of the maharajah, Punekar enjoyed 'complete access' to the Resident and, conveniently, happened to also be present that fateful morning.[74] Could he have added the poison to Phayre's drink? Moreover, the man from whom the diamonds were allegedly purchased by the maharajah also declared that he was coerced into stating so. Why, even the ruler's secretary who had confessed did so after having been kept under arrest, and then given a deal.[75] One by one, flaws began to appear in the prosecution's evidence, with the press adding to the shame. The *Daily Telegraph* wrote, for instance, how 'the meanest pickpocket would not be convicted on the evidence upon which it was sought to deprive a Sovereign of his throne'.[76] Even the *Times of India*, as pro-British a paper as could be, thought the evidence 'worthless'.[77] The British commissioners, however, ignored these inconvenient revelations.[78] After all, it was common sense that natives were 'instinctively untruthful' and 'incompetent witnesses', so small quibbles were not allowed to get in the way.[79] The whole trial was fast becoming a farce that said more about the hold of racial stereotypes than cool and calm modern justice.

On 17 March 1875 public proceedings closed. Soon after, the viceroy informed London that while the white commissioners found the maharajah guilty, their brown colleagues felt the opposite – poisoning was indeed attempted, but Malhar Rao had not convincingly been linked to it. It was here, finally, that British duplicity discarded its lofty veneer. For, while the natives were theoretically equal members on the commission, their English peers alone guided the government. The maharajah's 'previous character' left no doubt, as far as the Raj was concerned, that he was guilty. To restore him to the throne would be a 'miscarriage of justice', besides also being 'a fatal political error' that could 'seriously weaken the authority of the British Government'.[80] In fact, it was baldly admitted that 'we did not consider that the circumstance of an equal division of opinion rendered it obligatory upon the Government of India to give the accused party the benefit of the doubt'.[81] London, however, still had a fraction of ethical concern left. They agreed that the maharajah had to be deposed because he was a confirmed disaster, but his removal was to be 'upon general grounds' and *not* his alleged culpability in the crime.[82] And so it was that in the viceroy's order of 19 April, Malhar Rao and his son by that 'cooly' wife – to kill two birds with one stone – were stripped of claims to the throne, due to the father's 'gross misgovernment', his 'incapacity to carry into effect the necessary reforms' and – in what was a convenient trump card – for the 'interests of the people of Baroda'.[83]

The whole case was writ with irony. For all his flaws, Malhar Rao was legally entitled to quite a different kind of treatment, but with the British set against him, no amount of legalese could save him. Queen Victoria had promised in 1858 that her agents in India would never again absorb any native states; here, the letter of that proclamation was maintained, but not its spirit. Most tellingly, the decision went against even the viceroy's publicly announced assurance. In 1874, after all, he

Malhar Rao's famous golden guns.

Los Angeles County Museum of Art

had granted Malhar Rao till December 1875 to bring reform to Baroda; now, eight months *before* the term's expiry, the maharajah was deposed – and not for conspiracy to murder, but for failing to reform! Nothing, however, could be done. It was three days after the orders arrived that Malhar Rao was informed of his fate. 'His Highness,' we read, 'wept and entreated, but finally submitted.'[84] On a special train, he was bundled away in the dead of the night to Madras, where he was to spend the rest of his days. Phayre, of course, did not suffer any consequences: a few years later, having reverted to military service, he distinguished himself in the Third Anglo-Afghan War, winning a knighthood. The armed forces, rather than political diplomacy, proved a better profession for him. As for Naoroji, whom Phayre thought a 'traitor' instigating princes against the British, he established an agency in London, precisely with the intent of lobbying for assorted maharajahs aggrieved by the Raj.[85]

The tragic figure in all this, of course, was Malhar Rao. He had many defects of character and was guilty of numerous lapses. But to the last he denied grinding diamonds with arsenic to rid himself of the Resident. His life in banishment was gloomy, not aided by the fact that in 1880, his son died. The boy did, funnily enough, briefly occupy the throne of Baroda, thanks to the people, who felt some loyalty towards the ex-maharajah after all. On 28 April 1875, less than a week after Malhar Rao was shipped away, tradesmen in the capital shut their shops, 'saying there could be no trade while there was no Gaekwar'. A mob gathered, and assaulting the police, marched to the palace. And then, the 'populace took Luxmeebaee's child, placed it on the *gadee* [throne], and proclaimed it Gaekwar'.[86] It was a short-lived reign, though, for as soon as reinforcements arrived, the crowd dissolved; days later, Malhar Rao's son and wives were themselves put on a train to Madras. Here the ex-ruler became extra-religious, so that in a few years, even when ill, he was refusing to 'take food in any shape until he [had] said his prayers and bathed an hour or two'. Permanently suspicious of his captors, he accepted neither British doctors readily, nor their medicines, relying instead on ayurvedic powders 'compounded in his presence.' And then, on 26 July 1882 the world received news that Malhar Rao Gaekwad, ex-maharajah of Baroda, was dead.[87] One wouldn't be surprised if some thought he had been poisoned.

Exactly ten days after Malhar Rao was sent into exile, a most striking lady entered Baroda city. Conducted the next morning into the palace, she was waited on by the nobles, anxious to pay homage. Maharani Jamnabai enjoyed the attention, though she did not appear in the durbar herself, planting her daughter, Tarabai, on the throne instead; it was to this little proxy that the old men of the state pledged fealty.[88] It was a personal triumph for the widow of Khande Rao (Malhar Rao's brother), who had been away in Poona. A woman of ambition, during her time there, she went so far as to sell jewellery to fund complaints against her brother-in-law, bribing even Residency staff to fan Phayre's animosity.[89] All along, Jamnabai also kept communications open with the British, so that in the proclamation that announced Malhar Rao's deposition, tribute was paid to Khande Rao's loyalty in 1857. And, as a mark of thanks, it was announced that his lady would now be 'allowed to adopt some [male] member of the Gaekwar House' as the next ruler.[90] Of course, colonial officials would 'select' a 'suitable person', but Jamnabai would have a key role in shaping the future. For her part, meanwhile, she was happy to play ball with the British, who viewed her as an asset. A writer would later note how this 'august widow' was 'extremely popular'. 'Brahmins worship her name more fervently than they worship Brahma', while in political affairs, she showed herself as both 'firm of hand and strong of will'.[91] And so it was that the Raj with a Gaekwad widow began remaking the durbar.

Born Tanhibai in 1853, the maharani came from a village close to Rahimatpur near Satara. Though her father was only a village headman, he belonged to the high-status Mane clan. This meant that, despite her family's middle-class means, Tanhibai's bloodline made her a suitable Gaekwad consort.[92] In a hagiography published shortly after the maharani's death in 1898, she is, not unpredictably, cast as predestined for glory. As a child, she studies her father, a 'little king in the village', as he handles finances, cares for the poor, and more in this vein. During games, she instinctively plays the princess. She also possesses equestrian talents and loves elephants – royal animals par excellence. Romantic retellings aside, it was good luck and shrewd timing that transported the girl from agrarian settings to the palace. Tanhibai's mother was the daughter of a Baroda nobleman.[93] In 1866 the lady arrived with her daughter on a casual visit, just when the ruling maharajah, Khande Rao – childless and twice widowed – was looking for a wife. Chances are that Tanhibai was brought precisely because the royal net had been cast. Soon the objective was achieved: the maharajah, in his forties, made the thirteen-year-old from Rahimatpur his queen. In keeping with custom, she was reincarnated as Maharani Jamnabai, and, in the four years they lived together, her biographer asserts, not only did she assist her husband in official matters, she also cooked meals for him, like a pious Hindu wife. Why, she even won the approval of a mighty pet dog, cementing her place in the ruler's heart via this canine favourite.[94]

The formidable Maharani Jamnabai by Chelvaranga Naidu. The biologist Marianne North described her as 'very slight and graceful, with eyes like a deer'.

Incidentally, that dog, Motya, was to prove critical in securing Jamnabai's life. For when in 1870 her husband died and Malhar Rao was released from prison, her position was imperilled. The brother-in-law, in fact, had every reason to dislike the widow. She had, suspiciously in his eyes, declared herself pregnant soon after Khande Rao's death; until she gave birth, Malhar Rao had no security, for if her offspring were a boy, *he* would be the heir. Both sides, naturally, became suspicious of one another. By the maharani's side was Motya, standing guard day and night, while her attendants and she warded off everything from black magic to that familiar thing: poison.[95] Malhar Rao, for his part, was convinced that his sister-in-law's pregnancy was bogus. Indeed, he first insisted that she was not with child, and when proved to the contrary, maintained that the father was someone other than Khande Rao.[96] In the end, in March 1871, Jamnabai, who had been sleeping with a dagger by her side, did something unprecedented – she obtained permission to deliver her baby in the Residency. And when in July she went into labour, waiting outside was Malhar Rao, to personally ensure that the woman did not replace a female with a male surrogate. One can imagine his delight, then, when the newborn Tarabai was shown; now confirmed as ruler, he 'set out on a triumphal procession through the town, showering gold mohurs'.[97] His day in the sun had finally come, short though it would prove.

Still only eighteen, Jamnabai did not give up – moving to Poona, supposedly with just the clothes on her back and the jewels she wore,[98] she watched as Malhar Rao made blunder after blunder, adding fat to the fire by sponsoring his enemies. And when, three and a half years later, the maharajah was deposed, she was ready to combine forces with the British so long as it featured her reinstation. She certainly had personality. When Prince Edward visited Baroda in 1875 – as part of an imperial sop to smooth over public anger after Malhar Rao's deposition – his staff was mesmerized by the maharani. She had already met them in Bombay, and did not keep purdah. Noting her 'pleasant face, bright eyes, and agreeable smile', not to speak of 'particularly small and well-shaped' hands and feet, they were struck that her movements were constrained by, of all things, a bejewelled toe ring. During their meeting, she also made it a point to introduce Tarabai and announce that her daughter 'would have been a Gaekwar had she been a boy'. When, late at night, Edward took leave, Jamnabai even walked to the palace steps to bid him goodbye.[99] The only detail in Baroda which startled the visitor was one of Khande Rao's eccentric bequests: having seen a highland regiment, that maharajah decided to dress one of his own battalions in Scottish uniform, complete with kilts. As a chronicler of Edward's trip observed, this suited 'the brown faces wonderfully well' and would have been 'quite correct' had Khande Rao not also drawn pink tights over all the dark soldierly legs.[100]

Importantly, for a place that had recently seen a mini rebellion after Malhar Rao's removal, Baroda now looked perfectly calm.[101] In reality, however, it had taken swift action to settle the public. London had hoped, when deposing Malhar Rao, that a successor could be named simultaneously to pre-empt panic. But this was not possible, because multiple heirs had sprung up. One person rejected instantly was Malhar Rao's grandson through a daughter – having denied his own son, the British could not entertain another lineal descendant.[102] Three other men then appeared. The dynasty's founder, the family tree showed, had several brothers. The three candidates were descendants of one of these, aged thirty-two, twenty-six and twenty-two respectively. The eldest, Sadashiv Rao, had an especial advantage, in that his father had already been adopted by an earlier prince's widow – this technically made him a member of the ruling house, tying him closer than others to succession.[103] Even before Malhar Rao's trial, in fact, he had submitted a letter on why his nomination was strongest, shrewdly deploying 'progressive' jargon to try and win the Raj over.[104] That may have been the end of the issue had not another group of claimants showed up, this time not even from Baroda but from British territory.

While Sadashiv Rao was descended from a brother of the dynasty's founder, the founder had a younger *son*. This late-eighteenth-century prince's line had fallen upon hard times, ending up in a village called Kavalane in Nasik. Though alienated from the royal family, they carried the founder's blood, and thus claimed an 'undoubted right' to the throne.[105] Furious with the development, Sadashiv Rao insisted that this clan, while of princely descent, was illegitimate. As happened many times in more than one state, then, here too the Raj set out to investigate. Records in Kavalane were studied, and a fortnight after Malhar Rao was deposed, the Resident confirmed that the branch was *not* illegitimate and did indeed enjoy a right to the gaddi.[106] Final orders on whether Sadashiv Rao or one of three Kavalane boys, aged between ten and twelve, should be picked was left, though, to the viceroy. Unsurprisingly he opted for the latter, for this held strategic advantages.[107] As was admitted, 'a youth ... who could be carefully trained' was preferable to an adult. In other words, a young ruler would be more amenable to 'advice' than a grown man with a formed mind. And to neutralize Sadashiv Rao, it was asserted that the 'right of the new Gaekwar' depended 'solely upon his selection by the British Government'.[108] This too, then, was 'no mere question of law or ... right'. It was, conveniently again, 'an act of State', tailored to a colonial design.[109]

Having opted for the Kavalane adolescents, however, the actual decision on which one of them specifically should succeed was left to Jamnabai. The maharani's finger landed on twelve-year-old Gopal Rao, described as 'the eldest and perhaps the most promising of the three'.[110] All kinds of stories exist as to why he was favoured. One tells that when the candidates first arrived at the palace, they were questioned on why they had come; while the others mumbled, Gopal Rao declared, 'To be a Maharaja!' A second tale states that during a dinner, the other boys, village bumpkins, looked bewildered by the etiquette; Gopal Rao, however, cleverly imitated the maharani's actions.[111] The intent behind these tales, of course, is to communicate an innate kingliness in the chosen heir. Either way, weeks after the maharani's return to Baroda, the principality had a new ruler. And just as the girl from Rahimatpur went from Tanhibai to Jamnabai, Gopal Rao of Kavalane now became Sayaji Rao III (1863–1939) of Baroda. From living as an illiterate farmhand, he was now a prince.[112] Interestingly, the new maharajah was proclaimed not as successor to Malhar Rao, but to Khande Rao – after the installation, he was escorted to Jamnabai, and placed in her arms by Resident Pelly,

The young Sayaji Rao as depicted in The Indian Charivari *(1875).*

its symbolism clear to all.[113] Meanwhile, arrangements were made for the other claimants – debts were paid, allowances granted, and they were 'treated with every consideration'. Sadashiv Rao alone continued to be peeved. In the end, by 'persistently and perversely' refusing to give up his claim, he invited Malhar Rao's fate: he was sent into exile.[114]

Sayaji Rao's ascent was the stuff of dreams. Or as a commentator put it, 'He became a prince by a freak of fortune that could not be paralleled in the most extravagant prayers of oriental romance.'[115] To begin with, there was no looking back – having come to Baroda, the teenager did not visit his village again for fifty years.[116] Physically too, he was transformed. Small for his age, of swarthy complexion, he looked, as one of Prince Edward's party wrote, like any other local boy.[117] But this was more than made up for by how he was 'weighted, head, neck, chest, arms, fingers, ankles with ... vast diamonds, emeralds, rubies, and pearls'.[118] While Edward and his friends were in awe, Sayaji Rao himself would, in time, eschew shimmering clothes and jewellery. Years later, he would be described as bearing the 'look of the clever, well-educated man, and the indefinable expression of one who is accustomed to be obeyed'; it was demeanour rather than dress that marked his identity.[119] Indeed, while the British preferred to have India's princes sparkle in 'Asiatic finery', this maharajah would consciously position himself as a new-age ruler, avoiding clichés of this variety. And it was not a private question of dress, for at a critical moment his sartorial choices would be added to an inventory of charges against him, amounting, in imperial eyes, to sedition.[120] The British had wanted a 'malleable' boy who 'might be shaped according to the right ideas'; to their regret, though, the new maharajah was to prove his own man, and too strong-minded for a subordinate native prince.[121]

In the viceroy's 1875 proclamation deposing Malhar Rao, there were several elements designed to calm public nerves by clarifying the principality's future. The chief promise, of course, was that a new maharajah would be installed, but other guarantees were also given. So, for instance, though the British were tempted to exploit the opening and demand self-serving amendments in their treaty with the state, in the end they did not risk the uproar this would generate[122] – instead, the proclamation pledged outright that 'no alteration will be made' to existing terms, and that 'the new Gaekwar will enjoy all the privileges and advantages' of his predecessors. Queen Victoria's supremacy was asserted, of course, and other immediate aspects were similarly covered. But towards the end of the document appears the following line, which reveals what the imperial authorities planned in terms of administrative prospects. A statesman of distinction was deputed, the proclamation announced, to 'proceed to Baroda, and conduct the administration of the State as Prime Minister, under instructions . . . from the Governor-General's Agent', Pelly. And this new minister, charged with the onerous task of modernizing, correcting and lifting up the Maratha principality, was none other than Madhava Rao.[123] On the very day, in fact, that Khande Rao's widow received the durbar's obeisance, Rao quietly entered the state, taking over as Dewan soon thereafter.

When his long term in Trivandrum came to an end in 1872, Madhava Rao, to great surprise, declined membership in the viceroy's legislative council. In fact, negotiations with Ayilyam Tirunal pertaining to his retirement suggest that he had no plan to leave Travancore at all. But then the man was prevailed upon to accept a fresh posting, becoming, the next year, Dewan of Indore, ruled by the Holkars. During Malhar Rao's trial, moreover, the Holkar maharajah and Rao were both privately consulted. The former, for example, was certain that Malhar Rao was hopeless, and in favour of deposition – the important thing was to 'save the state', not its prince. As a champion of the princely order the maharajah could see how bad eggs like Malhar Rao made the whole basket reek.[124] Madhava Rao, for his part, meanwhile, had tendered advice as early as 1873–74, when the first commission looked into allegations of misgovernment. Henry Tucker, whom we encountered earlier, sought Rao's opinion, specifically concerning his idea that the maharajah be forced to agree to formal checks on his power. This – the notion of a written constitution by which to conduct the government – was a novel concept in India, but, as Tucker wrote, when it was broached to 'an eminent Native administrator', the latter 'informed me that he had long ago come to the conclusion' of its necessity himself.[125] This statesman even sent in a copy of what has been described as the 'first constitution drafted in modern India'. Though unnamed in Tucker's minute, as his biographer Rahul Sagar shows, the document's author was Rao in Indore.[126]

Indeed, more and more eminent Indians – from Naoroji, with his statistical analyses, to Dinkar Rao, who had offered a detailed opinion on how to govern India as early as 1862 – were engaging not just with practical administration, but also its theoretical nuances.[127] However, it is in Rao's draft constitution that we find, for the first time as Sagar observes, a guidebook for Indian-ruled India. It was positioned as a device to reform poorly run states without opting for the drastic measure of annexation; that is, if a ruler were not up to the mark, 'fundamental principles' could be prescribed in a 'plan of Government' from above.[128] Its goals were simple: to put an end to 'arbitrary will' (so patent in Malhar Rao) with well-framed laws; to create a formal mechanism for making those laws; to ensure such laws were obeyed; to protect public funds from royal misappropriation; to 'preserve the rights and liberties of the people'; and to do justice without bias, all while staying loyal to the Raj.[129] Furthermore, as Rao noted, these

... principles will, I am sure, bear good fruit even in the Native States to whom they are not directly prescribed. Other Princes will easily perceive that to the extent they spontaneously conform to those principles, they will render unpleasant interference from the Paramount Power unnecessary. This will be an immense gain ... An earnest and warm well-wisher as I am of the Native States, my strong belief is that their future existence and prosperity will depend upon their conforming themselves to [such] principles ... I am convinced that if unqualified personal and arbitrary rule continue in Native States, they must inevitably collapse one after another, the event being only a question of time.[130]

That said, Rao's proposals were conservative. This alone could persuade princes to entertain them, as any hint of radicalism would spark suspicion. For example, while Rao hoped for lawmaking to become the preserve of a specialized body, he also clarified that all legislation would require princely ratification. The ruler, on his part, meanwhile, would have to promise not to negate laws unilaterally once passed. So too he believed, the public should be invited to give (non-binding) views on proposed legal changes. And borrowing from the British system – which Seshiah Sastri enacted in Pudukkottai also – the Dewan was to become the ruler's sole mouthpiece in all matters; a maharajah ought neither to bypass him, nor allow his stature to be diminished.[131] Interestingly, even as Rao drafted his constitution, Naoroji too was thinking along similar lines. That twenty-five-point agreement he wished Malhar Rao to sign expressed almost the exact sentiments as Rao.[132] Both the south Indian statesman and the Parsi thinker, then, were on the same page as far as hopes for princely India were concerned. One came from within the administrative system, and the other from without, but their goal as Indians was not dissimilar.

While Rao's draft – an early milestone in India's constitutional history – went nowhere at the time, having been assigned Baroda, the man could now test his ideas. Additionally, Rao enjoyed an edge over his predecessor: where Naoroji had to constantly fight two battles, one against a combative British agent and the other with durbar elements, the new Dewan arrived with the fullest confidence of the colonial state. Not only did Rao possess decades of accumulated administrative acumen, the experience with Ayilyam Tirunal had also armed him with enough tact to handle royal sensitivities.[133] Despite something of a saviour complex like Sastri,[134] on the ground it was obvious to the Resident too that the minister 'desires to prove the degree of excellence to which [a native] administration can rise'.[135] But he also demanded a free hand – Rao was, we read, 'very sensitive' and dreaded 'interference from any quarter that may be exercised in a form or manner to weaken his influence . . . or to imperil the success of [his] measures'.[136] Perhaps having observed Naoroji's struggles, Rao was determined to ensure he would not go down as a failure for similar reasons. What is also obvious, however, is that while both men brought similar ideas and energies to Baroda, only he with imperial validation was able to prevail.[137]

For the next six years, Rao went about modernizing, bureaucratizing and reinventing the state. Or as a writer put it, in this 'most uncleanable of Augean stables', with 'brooms and mops and spades' he 'swept away' the flawed system of before.[138] It was not an unqualified success, however, for as in Pudukkottai, all development came at the cost of the earlier order. Malhar Rao's daughter, for example, claimed in 1876 that estates her father gave her were resumed on untenable grounds,[139] while three years later forty-five sirdars alleged not only that the Dewan was trampling on long-standing usages, but that he was also making a sinister effort to subject them to the same laws as commoners.[140] Rao, who had little patience for feudal classes, was unperturbed. While noting that some of the aristocracy did merit special consideration, having contributed historically to Baroda, others were of 'recent growth' with no 'service or pedigree to boast of, and who became what they are from mere favor or caprice'. So, it was his conscious intention to apply 'great discrimination' as to who deserved honours, and whose claims were best ignored.[141] In his own mind, he was bringing 'every branch of administration' into 'harmony with the spirit of the age', for the 'first time in the annals of the State' articulating the 'fundamental principle' that the 'object of Government is to promote the happiness of all classes alike', not the 'happiness of the Sovereign and of his friends'.[142] Whether or not the traditional court liked it, it could no longer be avoided.

Some of Rao's innovations, seemingly small, were quite significant in the context. For instance, within weeks of his arrival, he moved the Dewan's offices to buildings outside the palace, so as to stress a division between court and government.[143] Antiquated punishments were ended, revenue collection was reformed, and – to the chagrin of local bankers – the state's moneys were no longer channelled through their establishments, but via a central treasury.[144] As Sastri did in Pudukkottai, Rao too in Baroda was divesting the old order of

Madhava Rao in later life, as featured in
G. Parameswaran Pillai's Representative Indians
(1897). See plates section for his posthumous portrait
by Ravi Varma.

everything but ceremonial significance, consolidating authority in his
secretariat. Equally, he also acknowledged Gujarati grievances. Of 119
senior officials, a disproportionate seventy-six were Marathas, allowing
only twenty-nine 'sons of the soil' a share of the pie; Rao ordered 'good
rules' for further selection, hoping to conciliate local aspirations instead
of courting the Maratha elite.[145] Unlike Sastri, though, who was a little
too authoritarian, Rao was in theory prepared to devolve power. As he
explained, 'regular and rigid laws' would not serve the people. What they
wanted was not a 'system of technicalities' but 'substantial justice'. So,
while enunciating 'sound principles', the Dewan left subordinates on the
ground 'free and flexible' in how these were implemented.[146] Conceptually,
this was wise, though whether it was successful remains open to debate.

Every new system, besides, always produces winners and losers, and
it was not as though Rao escaped criticism. Behramji M. Malabari,

the activist, conceded, for example, that the minister had 'changed the face of Baroda'.[147] In a satirical passage, he lampoons the aristocracy for bewailing the pre-Rao era: 'where are thy great institutions, such as the Sathmari in which human beings were trampled under the elephant's foot . . . where alleged offenders were buried alive, thrown down steep hills, pinned to the wall, rolled in barrels nailed inside? Where are thy Holi festivals, during which a hundred hired houris frolicked in naked charms . . . and invited . . . the whizzing liquid of the royal pichkari . . . Where is thy bracing fever, thy benignant cholera, O land of my birth? Gone, gone are all thy glories . . . And instead I see the jail and the court-house, parks and palaces, roads and tanks, schools and colleges; and that monster of a Municipal Commissioner!'[148] That said, however, to Malabari too, Rao was rather 'servile' an 'imitator' of the British method which 'worship[ed] routine and centralization'. For all the Dewan's talk about devolution of power, the fact was that paper-pushing bureaucrats now sent peasants running from pillar to post. In the old feudal system, a villager could seek justice from his local liege, and for better or worse, it was at once given; now he had to 'carry his grievance from village to town, and thence to the district and finally to the capital' in a frustrating system of appeals ill-fitted to an illiterate society.[149] In seeking to make a point to the British, native rule had become in its own damaging way quite English.

Others viewed Rao as an imperial Trojan horse,[150] and newspapers like the *Kesari* and *Maratha* lambasted his alleged meekness in resisting colonial inroads. Indeed, even members of the royal family would tell that he allowed the British 'to establish precedents that were never envisaged in the treaties'.[151] He was, it was said, 'a strong administrator but a weak negotiator'.[152] A disused but sentimentally cherished right to manufacture arms was given up, while opium and salt production was modified to fit British needs, for example.[153] 'From what Sir T. Madhava Rao has to say of himself,' another critic thundered, 'it would seem that . . . civilization began [only] with [his] arrival.'[154] British officials too noted that while the man had done 'immense good', it was believed 'that his administration looks its best in a report'.[155] But Rao viewed things differently. In his words: 'Perfect tranquility prevails. Life and property are secure. Justice is fairly administered. The finances are in a highly flourishing condition. Public works have been liberally provided. Medical agencies are well at work.'[156] M.G. Ranade too rose to his defence in time: if the Dewan yielded to the Raj, it was always after a fight; if Baroda lost privileges, it was because the British asserted their power, not because Rao lacked a spine.[157] But what mattered most was the impression he made on the ruler. Sayaji Rao would remember the Dewan as 'a striking figure with a statesmanlike face', calling him 'a thorough courtier and a typical man of the world of his time'.[158] But reading between the lines, there is no praise here, for apparently the maharajah too never quite liked the man.[159]

One can sympathize with Sayaji Rao. There were three men in his life at the time: the Dewan, the new Resident, P.S. Melvill, and his tutor, F.A.H. Elliot. In 1876, it was reported that the maharajah had between six and seven hours of lessons each day, excluding games. A year after his adoption, the former illiterate was able to read and write Marathi 'tolerably well' and was 'beginning to speak English' too.[160] Of the three mentors, though, it was only the last who was able to bond with him, and, judging by a book he did on Baroda, Elliot also took an interest in the state.[161] Then, by the boy's seventeenth birthday, discussions were afoot not only about finding him a wife, but also on whether he was 'fit' to take the throne on attaining majority the next year. On the question of marriage, there was no reservation: scouts were sent out to identify brides, the Dewan himself interviewing their parents. Eventually a niece of the Tanjore rani was chosen, and the wedding took place in early 1881. On the matter of bestowing power, however, both Dewan and Resident were hesitant. Between teaching the alphabet and readying him for government, Elliot had only had six years' time with the maharajah; to Rao and Melvill, thus, the ruler was not prepared, and twenty-one, not eighteen, seemed a better age to entrust him with the weight of state. He needed, they felt, special training, over and above Elliot's instruction – a line that also betrays the rivalry that existed between the Dewan and teacher.

Surprisingly, the idea did not receive sympathy from above. When choosing Sayaji Rao as heir, the viceroy, Lord Northbrook, felt there was 'a distinct advantage . . . in a minority, for the sink of iniquity surrounding the old Court can be thoroughly purged' and the British – without soiling their own hands – would 'direct the administration'.[162] By this standard, a prolonged regency was in the imperial interest. Now, however, Lord Ripon, with his pro-India leanings, shifted gears. So, in late 1880 when the Resident and Dewan recommended a delay in the investiture, their boss was not in a mood to listen. Melvill, for example, wished to 'indoctrinate' the maharajah with details: he was to be taught about customs, stamps, mapping, police, the 'history of extradition', jails, printing, the functioning of the medical department and so on.[163] Rao proposed similar ideas, only with a grand moral gloss. 'If any ruler stands in need of such special education,' he wrote, 'it is the Native Prince.' For unlike 'rulers of civilized countries' who had restraints on their power, in India much rested on the ruler's 'personal intelligence'. This made it important to impart lessons in 'duties and responsibilities' and not rely on 'mere general education'. So, we read how the ruler was to be taught that he was 'made for the people, and not that the people are made for him'; that 'arbitrary and capricious will' could not be the source of law; that merit should be the 'chief guide' in selecting officers; that 'His Highness should be in his life and daily conduct a bright moral example'; and so on, bordering on cliché.[164]

Calcutta was horrified with this combined wisdom. As an official observed, it looked like the maharajah was to be 'kept away from all the realities of administration, and to be crammed with prolix platitudes and dreary truisms'. Why, if Melvill and Rao had their way, far from fostering ability, they would 'thoroughly disgust the young Chief with his duties, and thus throw all power into the hands of the Minister'.[165] Another figure described the plan as 'alarming', 'bad and unpractical', and crafted to birth boredom.[166] 'It seems to me,' he added, 'that you might as well expect to teach a man swimming on dry land as expect to turn out a ready-made ruler in the way proposed.' Some suspected that the Resident and Dewan were perhaps troubled by their impending loss of power. 'Sir Madhava Rao', wrote the political secretary, 'will prophesy innumerable evils if his own almost despotic rule is brought to an end', so his words were better taken with a pinch of salt.[167] Yet another adviser highlighted conceptual infirmities in the received arguments. 'The principle that no hereditary ruler is to succeed until he is fit to rule a State,' the man scribbled, 'would bar every King or Prince throughout the world, and utterly subvert the whole system of hereditary monarchy.'[168] No, the maharajah could not be kept waiting three more years; it was Sayaji Rao's *right* to reign, so long as nothing suggested he would prove an abject disaster. The Dewan's 'tedious exposition of the general duties of a model prince', while coming from 'good intentions', was thus politely rubbished.[169]

Instead, by February 1881, soon after the arrival of the maharajah's bride, it was made clear that the viceroy wished to 'place him as soon as possible in the actual exercise of responsible authority'. This was ideally with the Resident's and Dewan's guidance, and by the creation of an advisory council.[170] Rao, while acquiescing, did not let his other scheme completely lapse, though. Through 1881, the maharajah was bombarded with lectures, the whole lot compiled into a 357-page volume, unironically called *Minor Hints*.[171] It covered everything from what kind of correspondence deserved the ruler's attention to matters of state policy. In a section on sifting honest well-wishers from self-seekers, two columns were prepared, with such infantilizing lines as 'an intriguer is base metal . . . coated with gold' while the well-wisher 'is a solid mass of gold'. A lesson was given on anger management, while in another Rao was shown as an example of a man 'guided by principles'. Sayaji Rao, in the Dewan's mind, was always to walk the path of conciliation. So, if the Resident tendered 'advice' that was not to his liking, he should not 'attribute the advice to a desire on the part of the Resident to weaken' him but 'to his desire to save the Maharaja needless trouble'.[172] So too if a minister rounded up a servitor for misdeeds, it should not be viewed as coming from 'bad motives' but from more noble intentions (one wonders if Rao spoke from his own bitter experience interrogating Ayilyam Tirunal's favourites).[173] But on the whole, it was almost as though the Dewan was readying Sayaji Rao to bear the attitude of a cautious bureaucrat rather than a prince.

One long lecture delivered in April 1881, in fact, reveals a great deal about how the Dewan felt the maharajah should view his relationship with the British. Citing the fact that the paramount power had become the 'judge' as to good government in India, Rao argued that princes 'must constantly take care that the British Government is fairly satisfied that [they] are governing well – that, at least, we are not misgoverning'. Indeed, a smart maharajah 'should study what the British Government would consider good and bad government' and stay on the better side of that lane.[174] This was not only for strategic reasons, but also because, in Rao's eyes, there was genuine good the Raj had brought India. As he explained,

> With all the unavoidable disadvantages of being a foreign government, [British rule] is really far more powerful and far more durable than any that had preceded it. Why? Mainly because its first principle is to promote the happiness of the people as a whole. Here and there the British Government may have made errors, – may have failed in this respect – may have exposed itself to adverse criticism. Yet, on the whole, I feel, and every thoughtful man must feel, that India cannot have any better or even an equally or nearly equally good Government. Such a feeling is one of the strongest securities for the durability of the British Government in India.[175]

This, then, was Rao at his loyalist best. He was convinced that the British, guided by admirable political traditions, would bestow incremental benefits upon Indians. Indeed, as he suggested later, modern Indianness owed a debt to British rule: 'What a glorious change the railway has made in old and long neglected India!' wrote the statesman in 1885. 'The young generation cannot fully realize it. In passing from the banks of the Tambrapurny to those of the Ganges, what varied scenes, what successive nationalities and languages flit across the view!

Tamil, Telegu, Canarese, Marathi, Guzerati, Hindustani, Bengali – populations which had been isolated for unmeasured ages, now easily mingle in civilized confusion.' Why, 'it has repeatedly struck me that if India is to become a homogenous nation . . . it must be by means of the Railways . . . and . . . the English language'.[176] While the British had, of course, constructed the railways for their own advantage, to Rao's generation it served also as an instrument to knit together the land, helping in everything from famine relief to cementing identity.[177] Or as Ravi Varma's brother too would tell, 'the Railways and the telegraph' not only 'annihilated time and distance, the general feeling of security of persons and property, which prevails from Cape Cameron [sic] to the Himalayas under the benign rule of the British Government, [also] increased ten fold the number of visitors to the sacred banks of the Ganges'.[178] From their point of view, colonial rule was, thus, a prime *catalyst* for nationalism.

Equally, however, the Dewan was also attempting to ensure the maharajah never found himself colliding with the imperial state. Rao's words, which were expressed during Ripon's popular viceregal term, should of course be read in context, but there is little doubt that he saw the future of the princes as predicated on acknowledging the Raj's superiority, and on respecting boundaries. And he was not alone in this. The early Congress too proceeded along similar lines. Naoroji in his 1886 address, for example, called it India's 'good fortune' that it was governed by the British; it was 'under the civilizing rule of the Queen' that Indians were 'freely allowed to speak our minds without the least fear' for the first time. Without the 'blessings of British rule' the Congress could not have gathered at all, and far from being a 'nursery for sedition', it was 'another stone in the foundation' of the British government.[179] So too Rao, in his own words to that political gathering in the next year, would reiterate that their very existence was 'the soundest triumph of British administration, and a crown of glory to the great British nation'. It is likely, given how fragile nationalist ideas were, that such language was tactical to avoid provoking the worst elements in the Raj. For as Rao counselled Congressmen and the British alike:

. . . permit me to advice you to be moderate and forbearing. It is in the nature of vaulting ambition to overleap itself. It is the character of renovated youth to be carried away by excessive zeal. Steer clear of such shoals and quicksands. Discuss without prejudice, judge without bias, and submit your proposals with the diffidence that must necessarily mark suggestions that are tentative in their character. Much irritation and retaliation will be avoided if the mutual dependence of the rulers and the ruled is steadily kept in view . . . By the rulers it must be taken for granted that when subjects petition and expostulate, it is not in a spirit of disputation or cavilling, much less of disaffection or disloyalty, but only to enlighten those holding sway over them, and in a peaceful and constitutional manner . . . [180]

Rao was to die in 1891, three years after this speech, when nationalism was still emerging, and statements like these were not yet jarring to patriotic ears.[181] But his ward, Sayaji Rao, belonged to a new generation that chose a less diplomatic approach. While famous instances exist from his later career, a demonstration of this, in fact, came early on, even as the Dewan was inflicting his lectures on conciliation. The viceroy had decided to grant the maharajah his powers in December 1881. While in June the Resident described Sayaji Rao as 'extremely amiable', 'most anxious to learn' and a 'happy selection' for the throne,[182] only weeks later the boy was asking questions that would lead to a revision of this assessment. When informed that his actions were to be moderated by a council, the maharajah asked if this was a 'provisional or permanent' arrangement. When told he could eventually make changes, the eighteen-year-old demanded a specific time frame; or as a viceregal officer wrote, he wished to be 'distinctly assured' that the council was of 'a provisional character'. This was entirely, Sayaji Rao explained, to avoid talk that 'he had allowed material encroachments' that would 'lower his status as an independent Chief'.[183] Rao, incidentally, was 'favourable to the maintenance of some kind of constitutional machinery, whereby the influence of responsible advisers will be brought to bear on the ruler' (that is, prevent absolute power), but Sayaji Rao refused to give in. So, in the end, a two-year limit was negotiated, and the young ruler got his way.[184]

This early assertion of independence did not, understandably, please Calcutta. It was suspected that the prince was in touch with the Holkar maharajah, who was eternally protesting British overreach in princely dominions. Indeed, no sooner had he challenged his advisers than Sayaji Rao was characterized as an 'obscure Mahratta boy, raised by the favour' of the Raj, and who, instead of gratitude, showed 'a sudden disposition to stand on his prerogative and object to all interference'.[185] In other words, after training and educating him to fit their dreams, the instant Sayaji Rao showed a hint of personality, the establishment was disaffected. They had presumed that the boy would be more deferential than evidence now suggested. In fact, once the two-year deadline was accepted, and Rao prepared its guidelines, Sayaji Rao took his own time to study them and suggest modifications. As Melvill reported, 'His Highness by no means took a secondary part in the consideration of these rules. He has taken an immense deal of trouble to understand Sir Madava Row's original draft, and exhibited intense anxiety to have matters put in a way as favorable as possible to his own wishes.'[186] The village boy had not only grown up, but also grown *into* his status as a prince.

On 28 December 1881, Sayaji Rao was invested with his powers. At the ceremony, the maharajah was given yet another lecture by his guest, the governor of Bombay, while the Resident paid tribute to Rao. 'Until I came here,' stated Melvill, 'I was utterly ignorant of the extent to which the character of a highly educated native gentleman could be carried. I assert with the fullest confidence and with satisfaction . . . that Sir Madava Row is a man who acts from as high principles as any English gentleman . . . [H]e has proceeded and acted regardless of the opinions of others, and solely guided by his own opinion of what is right, after taking counsel from those whom he should take counsel.'[187] It was meant as a compliment but is also telling of prevailing attitudes, which Sayaji Rao was to challenge: that even the best of native statesmen were only *almost* English; that brown opinion had to be moderated by white counsel. Rao, meanwhile, thanked the Resident for his help, and in the next year retired from Baroda with a substantial purse for his services. He spent the final decade of his life in Madras, attending public meetings and contributing newspaper articles. Then, in 1891, having suffered a stroke the previous winter, news was transmitted across the empire that the old man was no more. As *The Bombay Gazette* reported:

A telegram from Madras announces that Sir T. Madhava Rao died at his residence at Mylapore at eleven o'clock on Saturday morning. He had long outlived his period of practical usefulness, and the contributions which in his later years he made to the discussions of questions of public interest scarcely led the younger generation to endorse the high opinion in which their fathers had held this erstwhile eminently capable man. They know him as the 'Native Thinker' who now and again wrote scrappy little notes upon the events of the day . . . But herein he did himself scant justice, and once more an obituary notice must be made use of to demonstrate that good and great men are in danger of being misjudged by those who have known them only by their later life . . . No argument in demonstration of the fitness of natives of India for high office in their own country was ever put forward without finding point and illustration in the career of this most excellent of men . . . What Stein was to Prussia . . . Sir Madhava Rao was to Baroda.[188]

Despite the grudging opening, this was perhaps an accurate remembrance of the man's life; an acknowledgement that while he was once an icon to Indians, he had not been able to note shifts in sentiment. Still, considering the pre-1857 India where Rao began his career, and what he had achieved, his was not a legacy that could be brushed aside. He had built roads, established courts, proved that Indians could rule, and demonstrated through years of hard work in three states that the British ought to trust native talent. 'England is not the power that seeks security from darkness,' he once remarked, intending it not as flattery but as a reminder to the Raj not to forget higher values. 'England desires to be a great illuminating agent, and bids Princes and people alike be enlightened and happy.'[189] One wonders, had Rao survived another decade, whether he would have altered his views, and recognized that this Western luminosity and enlightenment was only a facade; that the British love of India was much more transactional than viceregal speeches admitted. We will, of course, never know. And perhaps it is only apposite, then, that the last grand portrait done of this eminent statesman, a posthumous work by Ravi Varma, depicts him in splendid robes, with all his imperial honours and badges. And it is to this day housed in Calcutta, in a building named, befittingly, after Queen Victoria.

In 1881, as Ravi Varma fell out with Visakham Tirunal, he decided to seek patronage outside Travancore. It was a decision with momentous consequences for Indian art itself. As historian Rupika Chawla tells: 'Had Ravi Varma not taken the road least travelled but rather continued to play out his life in Travancore he would not have become the Ravi Varma that we know.'[190] And to give him a leg up, the artist turned to Madhava Rao. 'I think,' he began, 'you had kindly promised to write to me when it would be safe for me to make my appearance at Baroda. I am most impatiently waiting.'[191] In particular, he added, he was anxious to widen his horizon. 'I have established some reputation in southern India ... But my ambition has ... enlarged ... and I have a mind now to undertake a tour to northern India provided I could place myself under your august patronage.'[192] It was a clever move, for Rao had earned a name for supporting Indian artists, just as Residents in princely courts promoted European painters. Thus, for instance, if Valentine Prinsep received a commission in Baroda through Melvill's good offices, Indian talent was welcomed thanks to the Dewan.[193] Not long after Prinsep, we find the south Indian painter M.C. Tiruvengada Naidu in the state, beginning a professional relationship that would last years. Now, with Ravi Varma making his application, the Dewan invited him for Sayaji Rao's investiture, granting the Malayali artist the privilege of doing, on Gujarati soil, a Maratha maharajah's state portrait.

Finished in 1882, the painting, at a glance, resembles other royal depictions: Sayaji Rao wears a magnificent diamond necklace, with a sirpech and pearl tassel on his turban. Pinned to his chest is a medal commemorating Prince Edward's visit, while his sword marks the Delhi Durbar of 1877, with a miniature of a viceroy on its scabbard. In his demeanour, however, there is no standard regality; instead, Ravi Varma shows Sayaji Rao with a brooding seriousness.[194] In many ways he was unlike any other prince the artist painted, reigning nearly sixty years, and showing a most forthright attitude towards the Raj. Where Visakham Tirunal and his brother in Travancore, even in their criticism of imperial policy, erred on the side of polite caution, the Baroda maharajah – representing an impatient, restless generation – was to evolve a pointedly blunt approach. While Madhava Rao's south Indian princely wards, even if they did not always see eye to eye with him, worked within his framework of meeting British standards, his youngest student would question the framework itself, demanding it be remoulded. This did not occur in a vacuum: Sayaji Rao's conflict with the Raj coincided with the rise of unabashed nationalist feeling in India; just as the last years of the nineteenth century marked the rise of aggressive voices within Congress, the same period underlined this maharajah's policy of assertion.

Of course, the build-up was slow, in that during the first phase of his reign the ruler's focus was largely inward: he attended to administrative advancements, improved government machinery, broadened his mind, while also stamping his authority as ruler. For instance, early on the maharajah had to prevent his adoptive mother, Jamnabai, from positioning herself as a rival force. Rao had tried to keep the maharani happy, for had 'it not been for her steady sympathy and support', he knew his job would have been 'much more difficult'.[195] With the maharajah, however, things were complicated. In 1883, Jamnabai even petitioned the British asking that they 'direct' him to grant her twelve lakh rupees in allowances, have the state bear all her expenses, guarantee her a right to 'advice' the ruler and so on.[196] When asked to reconsider, Jamnabai doubled down. 'I am certain,' she wrote, 'that the Maharaja has not up to this time acted up to *your* advice, nor is there any possibility of his

Ravi Varma's state portrait of Sayaji Rao.

doing so in future.' So, unless instructions were issued 'to put a stop to his self-sufficiency', neither she nor the Raj would be satisfied.[197] It was patent that Jamnabai was attempting not only to check the ruler's autonomy, but she also expected the British to join forces – an ominous development for Sayaji Rao, no doubt also given how the dowager had played a role in fatally damaging his predecessor's reputation.

Moreover, Jamnabai believed *she* was the head of the family. When, for example, the Resident reminded her that the people were her son's subjects, not hers, she described this as a 'more theoretical than practical' distinction.[198] Calcutta knew too that she had 'character and power enough' to become not only 'disagreeable', but also 'dangerous'.[199] However, they were not prepared to exploit Jamnabai to clip the ruler's wings. To begin with, Sayaji Rao treated her generously. It also turned out that the prime hiccup between mother and son was that the ruler disliked her adviser. This 'dangerous person' had at one time even organized a 'number of Brahmins and astrologers, and practised magic arts' against Sayaji Rao, causing Bombay to warn of poison plots.[200] Besides, the maharajah, while providing *material* luxuries, felt 'relieved from [any] moral obligations' to Jamnabai on account of 'the tenor of Her Highness's private life'.[201] In fact, as early as 1876 allegations had circulated about the maharani's 'criminal intercourse' with certain men,[202] and Prinsep, the painter too heard 'all kinds of rumours'.[203] So in the end, in a mix of Victorian disapproval of her lifestyle, and the fact that Sayaji Rao had not diminished her in a monetary sense, he was allowed to prevail. It was, however, a battle he had not expected to fight, and showed the ever-present risk of internal dissensions providing the Raj a window for interference.

The maharajah also suffered domestic tragedy in this first phase. In 1884, his wife died (and of this princess, Ravi Varma did a posthumous portrait). He would marry again, but the loss was felt keenly. In time, pain was also inflicted by the death of his sister, Tarabai. Despite his strain with Jamnabai, the maharajah had what the Resident called 'a pleasant and quite natural' attachment to her daughter.[204] Madhava Rao too had fond memories of this 'most interesting girl, beaming with beauty and intelligence'. While sex denied her the throne, Tarabai received a good education, with her mother inviting the Resident and Dewan 'at intervals to examine the young Princess'.[205] Ravi Varma did two portraits of this promising lady, in the first of which she radiates confidence and style, posing with an arm on her waist, as though interrogating the viewer. Sadly, Tarabai died young in 1897. When news reached her mother, she was crushed – Sayaji Rao went out to console Jamnabai, and perhaps they were reconciled.[206] But soon the maharani went into decline. As the *Times of India* reported the next year, 'when she found that her end was approaching, she went on pilgrimage . . . and then returned to Baroda to die amongst her own people'.[207]

Alongside these events, the maharajah had to also *learn* government; he later regretted that his education had not been practical enough,[208] as suddenly all things, small and big, landed on his plate, leaving him 'very much alone'.[209] Things were so centralized that even the purchase of a door handle required his approval.[210] Besides, he lacked familiarity with his state, so tours were set up, taking him for the first time into his own territories beyond the capital. But this did not mean intellectual exercise came to a standstill, for early on Sayaji Rao built contacts with thinking men, many of whom held ideas at variance with Madhava Rao's tutorials. 'He had a special affinity,' his great-grandson would write, 'for the intellectuals of Poona whom the British . . . tended to regard as seditionists.'[211] One of them, the anti-caste leader Jotirao Phule was hopeful enough about Sayaji Rao to give him a pre-publication preview of his *Shetkaryaca Asud* (Cultivator's Whipcord, 1883), which lambasts everything from Brahminism to the Raj's ignorance of Indian realities.[212] Phule also urged the maharajah to cease customary patronage of Brahmins, and to use that money for the poor.[213] While even Madhava Rao – noting how 7,000 Hindus and 3,000 Muslims were fed daily in the capital – had called for reform,[214] he had treaded cautiously. The maharajah, however, cut things down. Instead, resources were diverted to an orphanage, boarding houses for backward caste children and scholarships.[215] It was this shift in priorities that soon enabled the Baroda government to support a bright Dalit student's studies, for example – a boy named B.R. Ambedkar.[216]

In fact, Sayaji Rao was also to rail against caste in general. Certainly, as a Maratha prince, he was not immune to its hold – he went, for example, to some length to marry a granddaughter into the Kolhapur family (who as Shivaji's descendants claimed high rank) and was furious when his daughter broke off her engagement with Gwalior, the other big Maratha in the land. But equally, he was aware that caste was an impediment for a modern future. 'Our country's prosperity is greatly hindered' by the institution, he declared in 1893, for '[m]en are good and bad according to [their] virtues and capacities', not parentage. Education could even things, so in this his government would make 'no distinction between man and man'.[217] This was not posturing, for in private too, Sayaji Rao expressed such sentiments. Writing to Ranade once, he explained how '[s]ocial reforms are of greater importance than even gaining political rights' – a point Ambedkar, who crafted post-colonial India's constitution, would push.[218] In another address the maharajah reiterated: 'The system which divided us into innumerable castes . . . is a whole tissue of injustice, splitting men equal by nature into divisions high and low, based . . . on the accident of birth.' Besides, it was also a hurdle in the construction of a national identity, causing 'ill-feeling' and 'nepotism, heart burning, and consequent mutual distrust'.[219] In other words, the maharajah was not merely talking material progress but also touching delicate *social* questions – areas princes like Ayilyam Tirunal had avoided.

Indeed, Sayaji Rao's vision of a reformed Hindu society found reflection even in Ravi Varma's art. While Madhava Rao helped the artist get a foot in the door, the latter made the most of it, impressing the maharajah. So much so that the painter was invited to do a second set of portraits, followed, between 1888 and 1891, by a series depicting epic scenes. Ravi Varma had long been tapping into Sanskrit literature for inspiration, partly also because it impressed the British. From the eighteenth century, when the first translation of Kalidas's *Abhijnana Sakuntalam* appeared in English, many in the West had had a love affair with Sanskrit. It commanded admiration as much from Europeans as native elites, allowing a certain intellectual equality between colonizer

Chromolithograph prints of Ravi Varma's new-age mythological depictions of (clockwise) Lakshmi, Sarasvati, Savitri and Yashoda–Krishna.

and colonized. Of all people, in fact, a Madras governor in 1871 announced how the epics offered 'the most inexhaustible . . . stores for pictorial representation'. All natives had to do was 'engage the service of the national pencil', and as mythology had 'fastened on the national memory and animated the national voice' it could also generate a national imagery.[220] In other words, in a country of seemingly irreconcilable diversity, the epics were a common passion, amenable to encapsulating pan-Indian aspirations. And here Ravi Varma was 'unrivalled in his strategy for re-creating a romantic past' for modern India.[221] He was to idealize a heritage capable of moving audiences in Kerala as much as in Calcutta; in Gwalior as well as Gujarat, giving visual confirmation of a *shared* cultural inheritance. And urging him on was Sayaji Rao.

With Baroda, when Ravi Varma first came here in 1881, he brought with him a depiction from the Ramayana which was acquired for the palace. But when seven years later Sayaji Rao asked for fourteen Puranic paintings, things moved into another league. The maharajah's seriousness comes across in how Ravi Varma was paid a princely 50,000 rupees for the project. And the artist, on his part, took the commission seriously, for unlike earlier patrons, this was a man with a vision. Ayilyam Tirunal, for instance, had backed Ravi Varma, but belonged to a generation yet to imagine India as a whole; in his time, the subcontinent was a patchwork of identities and territories. Baroda's ruler, however, did not want art to appeal merely to his Maharashtrian roots or Gujarati landscape, but to transcend provincialism. Ravi Varma, in fact, went on a pan-Indian tour to live up to the challenge. While it exposed him to everything from miniature traditions to sculpture, innovation was key – scantily clad women, for instance, of old Indian art were ill-fitted for the Victorian age.[222] Besides, as the historian Priya Maholay-Jaradi writes, ruler and artist shared the conviction that 'national expression' was not about reviving the past. It was, on the contrary, 'a cosmopolitan assemblage' of old and new; of being able to match attractive Indian elements with modern methods and ideals. So, if 'Sayajirao's commissions to Varma' welded 'themes, styles, and techniques from diverse traditions', and became 'carriers of a graphic national imagination', they were also

Ravi Varma's Sita Bhumipravesh.

defined by newness.[223] It was, after all, a very *contemporary* detail that
Ravi Varma's goddesses were dressed in saris, and high-necked blouses.

Significantly, Sayaji Rao let Ravi Varma exhibit the Baroda series
in multiple cities. And their reception was proof that artist and patron
had set off something of immense cultural import. The public that came
to view the paintings was not all erudite. They were neither scholars,
nor familiar with the nuances of Sanskrit literature. But it would not
be an overstatement that they all knew stories of Rama and Sita, or
of Krishna and Kamsa. They adored the *devis* Lakshmi and Sarasvati,
now personified in a contemporary form. As Partha Mitter writes,
the paintings 'dazzled' ordinary people.[224] Indeed, it was the success of
these works that inspired Ravi Varma to invest in a lithographic press
(for which Naoroji is said to have helped obtain machines[225]) and
manufacture prints for mass consumption – a decision that imprinted
his visualization on several generations.[226] Gods and goddesses left

the temple for framed pictures in household corners. Wherever one lived, gods were slowly *imagined* as Ravi Varma saw them. Indeed, the prints were so popular that they began to feature on everything from matchboxes to baby food, as advertisers gave buyers an added incentive to consume their products.[227] It was something Madhava Rao – who viewed 'the broadcasting of Indian mythology' as 'a step towards . . . nation building' – foresaw.[228] Admittedly, this was all a Sanskritic and Victorian portrayal, brushing aside the local and subaltern, but at a time when elites set the agenda, it fit the mood of the hour. And as a British official put it, these pictures 'enjoyed a wide popularity, and gave much pleasure to all classes of Indians'.[229]

As far as Sayaji Rao went, of course, patronage of such art was only one of many innovations he attempted – a patronage which may have had a connection with the fact that as the ruler of feuding Gujaratis and Marathas, he had to find a common ground that transcended these rivalries. But even so, cultural experiments were easy to pull off compared to political ambitions, for in the latter space the Raj was touchy. The more the maharajah's name shone through the pens of native intellectuals, the more uncertain the British grew. His difficulties, in fact, began less than a decade into his rule, and one cause was the influence of his tutor, Elliot. This man, a Resident claimed in 1888, had been giving the ruler 'advice in direct opposition to [British] interests'.[230] As far as the establishment cared, Indian maharajahs needed white guidance, but *only* through official channels; by depending on a friend rather than Resident, the maharajah was flouting norms. Sayaji Rao also objected to the practice of the British agent collecting petitions from his subjects and serving as a court of appeal whenever his decisions did not go down well.[231] This, after all, had been one of the factors behind Malhar Rao's impotence, and his successor had no intention of allowing it to diminish his own strength. Naturally, successive colonial officers found they could not get along with the maharajah, with one going so far as to say that the ruler was 'disloyal both in thought and action'.[232] Indeed, to this Resident's mind, Sayaji Rao was the instrument of a larger conspiracy:

I cannot avoid the suspicion that there is a settled policy among the Poona Brahmins [i.e., Ranade, and other nationalists] to use Baroda as a focus of opposition to the British Government ... Their constant interference in Baroda affairs, the continual irritation kept up in the Gaekwad's mind against the Government of India ... the constant glorification of the Gaekwad by the Mahratta press, all point to a concerted object.[233]

Moreover, under Elliot's tutelage – proof of whose subversion amusingly included the fact that he presented the maharajah Machiavelli's *The Prince* – Sayaji Rao was assuming unbecoming airs. Not only did he have an 'unsatisfactory' attitude towards his imperial betters, he had been 'taught to believe that the Baroda state is practically equal with the British Government', which had as much right to interfere here as it had in 'Denmark or Portugal'.[234] This particular Resident, a Colonel Biddulph, went to the extent of suggesting that Indian clerks in Bombay's government offices were secret cheerleaders of the maharajah.[235] Biddulph's tirade must have registered, for Elliot was asked to revert to British service – an order particularly vindictive given that he had only months left for retirement and had now to spend them in the post of a district collector.[236] Ironically, even as Elliot was cast as a sinister power, his name was deployed to prevent Sayaji Rao from claiming any successes. By the late 1880s it was acknowledged that 'beneficial' changes had been made in Baroda, and that the ruler was all 'feverish activity'. Indeed, Sayaji Rao suffered from overwork and insomnia. And yet the Resident did not show sympathy; on the contrary, if the ruler was unwell, it was because he was of a 'very moderate mental capacity' and in his silly mission to make Baroda 'superior', had been 'overtaxing his powers'. In any case, because Elliot was the real author of the principality's gains, if applause was due, it was to the rogue Englishman rather than this native prince.[237]

It is no wonder, then, that the maharajah's animosity towards the colonial bureaucracy grew, finding an outlet in even more furious modernization, as if to prove a point. To begin with, he wished to end the feud between Gujarati and Maratha factions in the state, which played into the British policy of divide and rule. So, he made changes. In 1890, Baroda for the first time saw a Gujarati Dewan.[238] Indeed, where in 1875–76 there were twenty-four Gujaratis among the top 100 officials, as compared to sixty-four Marathas, Sayaji Rao would rectify this to sixty-seven and fourteen respectively by 1921. Under him, 'sons of the soil' obtained a stake in the system.[239] Education was another focus: where 1 per cent of revenue was channelled under this head in his year of enthronement, towards the end of his reign, the figure touched 17 per cent. As early as 1882 the state had a college, and ten years later, the ruler passed orders to 'maintain a schoolmaster' and open schools in 'all villages in which sixteen children were willing to attend'. In 1907, primary education would be declared free and compulsory, though, due to caste taboos, many children continued to be excluded.[240] The state's intention, however, was lauded. The maharajah also pushed for industrial activity: his government set up its own enterprises, from a sugar mill in 1884 to the Bank of Baroda in 1908, while also offering loans, tax concessions and other incentives to capitalists.[241] It was an uphill task and some of the early establishments had to shut down, but efforts continued till slowly there were triumphs.

To British discomfort, then, advances in Baroda installed it ahead of other territories. In 1910, it was possible, thus, for a journalist to inform American readers how, while in British India the government gave 'less than five dollars per one thousand of population for education, the Gaekwar of Baroda spends five dollars on every fifty-five of his subjects'. The state had a legislative council, rural self-government, and as Indians agitated for a greater power in running their country, it easily answered that old question on whether natives were ready. At a time when nationalist demands were no longer for 'good government' but for 'self-government', Baroda grew 'dear to the Indian heart'.[242] As early as 1894, in fact, Sayaji Rao himself had spoken of 'elective village councils'. 'I am deeply interested in that measure,' he wrote, 'and wish to extend it to all my state. It will be the keynote of what I wish to develop', for 'the policy of the curtailment of people's rights' was 'weakening the Rajas' – the very idea of 'people's rights' was novel coming from a hereditary prince.[243]

Sayaji Rao's grand Lakshmi Vilas Palace, as featured in Edward St Clair Weeden's A Year with the Gaekwar of Baroda *(1911).*

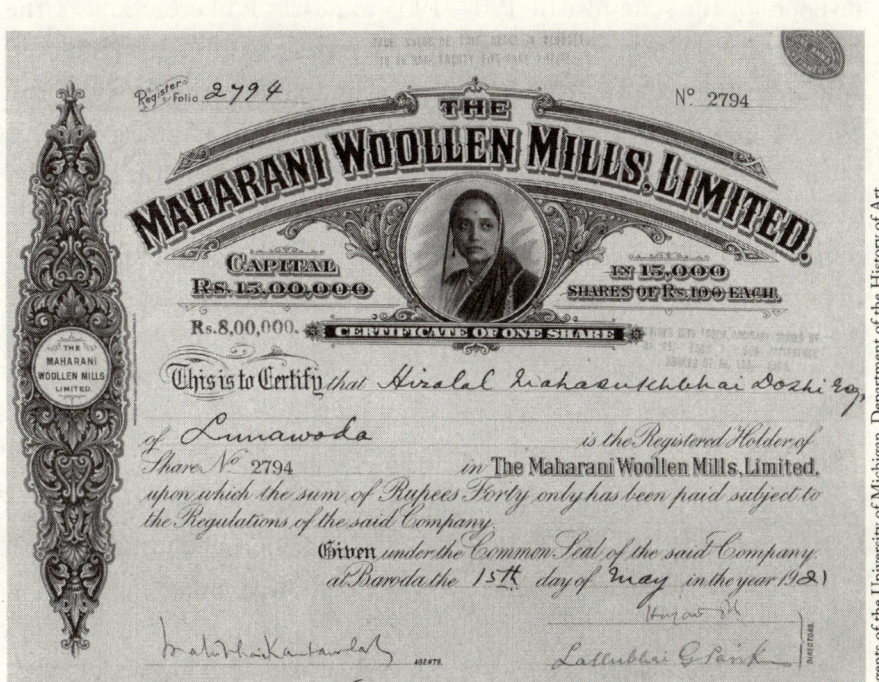

Share certificate from one of Baroda's industrial ventures, featuring a portrait of Sayaji Rao's second wife, Maharani Chimnabai II.

In the 1920s, in fact, another Gujarati Dewan, Manubhai Mehta, would even propose a plan for democracy, or rather a constitutional monarchy where 'the ultimate source of Power is . . . the Will or the Majesty of the People'.[244] While Sayaji Rao did not sanction the idea, the fact that such a plan could be pitched to him in the first place reflects a willingness to consider well-argued cases for progress.

Given that Mehta's plan was shelved, it could well be that, when it came to putting his money where his mouth was, Sayaji Rao was not keen to surrender power; that he preferred to remain an enlightened despot than voluntarily accept constitutional restraints. And most certainly he was capable of autocratic conduct: when G.S. Sardesai, who would achieve fame as a historian, put in his papers after thirty-seven years of service, a peeved Sayaji Rao was not above slashing his pension by 60 per cent. 'The root of the trouble,' the scholar complained, 'is that he is offended at my refusing to stay in Baroda and serve him all my life.'[245] So too while revenues of the state rose by 1904–1905 to nearly 1.14 crore rupees, the maharajah took as much as 23 per cent for his establishment.[246] But even admitting these flashes of imperiousness and an appetite for grandeur, Sayaji Rao was not unaware that these halcyon days had an expiry date. He understood that India's destiny lay in democracy and in the surrender of despotic power by men like him. His ability to contemplate a starkly different future went so far as to frankly admit the eventual termination of princely rule in India as a positive. In 1908 in a conversation with the Aga Khan he remarked how

> The first thing . . . to do when the English are gone, is to get rid of all these rubbishy states. I tell you there'll never be an Indian nation until this so-called Princely order disappears. Its disappearance will be the best thing that can happen to India – the best possible thing. There'll never be an Indian nation so long as there's a Princely order.[247]

Clearly, the maharajah had spent some time thinking about what point the princes served, half sedated by the Raj. To a British politician he wrote how they were denied a chance to wield power meaningfully.

Rajahs could be 'made and unmade' by imperial whims, their powers usurped by Residents. Even their own employees might defy them if they had British backing (an experience he had with his first Gujarati Dewan who became too pally with the Resident). Was it any surprise, then, that princes gave themselves up to meaningless diversions? Why, even when they *did* bring energy to their duties, there was 'the unsympathetic attitude of some Political Officers'. They would tolerate 'bad copies of British models', but 'even a slight departure from them' was 'an act of presumption'.[248] To the British, 'progress' was a stick to nanny Indian rulers with; but when the latter applied themselves innovatively, it was seen as arrogance. Princes were exotic props, occasionally dishing out a few colonial-style reforms, while never allowed to really succeed. Of course, Sayaji Rao did not include himself in this lament, for in his case, he put the Raj to shame. In 1908, in fact, a question was asked in the British parliament if the Baroda model could be exported to other states; the secretary of state for India mumbled that this would amount to 'interference'. After all, as the scholar Manu Bhagavan tells, any acknowledgement that Baroda had set higher standards 'would implicitly' mean having to 'accept [the] native ability to progress' – something that questioned the very basis of British rule.[249]

What Sayaji Rao stands out for, then, is his bold approach. Progress was not merely a defensive strategy, as in the days of Ayilyam Tirunal, but a proactive affair, infused with pride about the nation. In this, his field of inspiration lay not just in Europe, but also in America and Japan. India, he believed, could not achieve greatness through an overdependence on history: 'No reactionary sentiment of mere respect for the past will save India', the maharajah believed, and 'no amount of emotional patriotism will drag us out of our slough'. On the contrary, '[w]e must set our faces ... patiently to master [the very] modern methods and implements that have mastered us'. It was science and technology that aided Western domination; only equipped with the same tools could Indians fight. 'It is my profound conviction,' Sayaji Rao stated, that 'the progress of India . . . lies in the hard study and consistent application of the paraphernalia of industrialism to Indian conditions'. Only thus could 'we fit ourselves for the larger demands of statesmanship'; only 'this way can we as a people expect ever to enter the haven of economic independence'.[250] Of course, it would not be easy. In a speech at an industrial conference in Benares in 1905 he explained how '[w]e in our ignorance and poverty, have to compete with some of the richest, best trained and most skilful nations on earth'. But if India was to break its 'serfdom' and emancipate its people from 'economic slavery', it would *have* to learn.[251]

Naturally, with this talk of nationalism and slavery, of the rise of the East against the West, the British sensed danger. A clash with Sayaji Rao was inevitable. Things came perilously close in Curzon's viceregal tenure. As one who believed in Britain's duty to civilize the world, he could not brook an independent minded maharajah. In 1900, in fact, when Sayaji Rao left for one of his many European trips, Curzon issued a circular requiring all rulers to apply for permission in future. Generally seen as a rebuke to Baroda, the maharajah was tempted to register a protest, but his counsellors, including Naoroji in London – to whose historic election campaign he had donated years before – dissuaded him.[252] He did find an opportunity to pay Curzon back in kind, though. When Edward VII came to the throne after Victoria's death, the viceroy ordered a durbar, with a procession of princes. It was demeaning, for this was really a homage to Curzon than the sovereign. Sayaji Rao, therefore, tried to avoid it. 'I am afraid,' he wrote, 'it would seriously inconvenience me to join it.'[253] Not prepared to take this lying down, Curzon insisted: the maharajah would *have* to come. Sayaji Rao gave in, but not without stating that this was 'forced upon him'.[254] And in the last minute he absented himself anyway: an old widow had died in the palace, giving him an excuse to turn up several days late.[255] Naturally, Curzon was not pleased: in his eyes, Baroda was the 'sole important Prince' who was 'not loyal'.[256] Undefeated, when in 1905 the viceroy left, the maharajah is said to have sent him a telegram dripping with sarcasm: 'Bon Voyage,' it read, 'may India never see the like of you again.'[257]

In the final assessment, there have been mixed reviews about Sayaji Rao. To some, his fame is inflated, because – as the British suspected – the Indian press needed heroes and latched on to the first one they could find. And as soon as his power was threatened, as we shall see, the man sobered his rhetoric. To others, however, even if his forthrightness later petered out, for two decades the maharajah did challenge the British. His speeches certainly did not lack intensity. In 1902, for example, he declared that India's poverty was directly connected to colonialism. Only a 'great national movement in which each man will work for the nation and not for himself or for his caste' could reinvigorate the country. A nationalist culture would, he argued, birth a 'national art and a national literature and a flourishing commerce', which in turn would pave the way for 'national government'.[258] It is noteworthy that this speech was written by a Bengali aide: a firebrand who would later achieve fame as Sri Aurobindo.[259] So too one of the maharajah's Dewans, R.C. Dutt, was a Congress ex-president, whose economic criticisms had agitated even Curzon into personally writing a rejoinder.[260] When Dutt died in 1909, the ruler eulogized him as 'a great patriot' and a 'staunch and fearless supporter' of the rights of 'every Indian'.[261] So, while critics may say that the maharajah only 'dabbled with nationalism' and was never 'serious',[262] it would not be easy to find another major prince even using terms like 'nation' and 'national' half as often as Sayaji Rao did.

For its part, the Raj punished the maharajah. From the 1880s he had been ruffling feathers, so over time, elements for a showdown were in place. The dramatis personae on the British side had also changed. Between 1905 and 1910 Lord Minto, famous for the Morley–Minto reforms, which conceded a measure of power to Indians, was viceroy. Two years into his arrival, Sayaji Rao openly told him that 'whereas one would have expected the control of Native States to have been relaxed as the years went on', it had in fact 'become stricter', doing the princes a real injustice.[263] All along, revolutionary activity was gaining pace, and the maharajah's response was not unequivocal. For instance, while condemning violence in a speech in 1909, Sayaji Rao could not also help add that 'discontent [itself] is not an evil', and that to calm political agitation, its root causes would have to be addressed.[264] It did not take much to put two and two together in blaming the Raj for these causes. Later in the year, when the viceroy was on his way to Baroda, bombs were flung at his carriage. They did not go off, but the British were jolted. Minto had just announced that the princely states must 'bar the entrance of sedition' into their realms.[265] And yet, on arriving in Sayaji Rao's capital, he learnt of graffiti warning, 'You may bring as many British troops as you like . . . but they will not deter us from our purpose.'[266] By early 1910, in fact, pro-establishment newspapers began to warn that not only was Baroda a staging point for sedition, the maharajah was in cahoots with shady groups.[267]

When Lord Hardinge succeeded Minto, things got even worse. Grown angry on a diet of secret updates from the Resident, the viceroy believed that Baroda afforded 'direct support and encouragement' to anti-British forces. Sayaji Rao himself had, at different times, met all kinds of dangerous types: by now his ex-employee Aurobindo was a confirmed seditionist, and during trips overseas the ruler met the revolutionaries Tarak Nath Das in Vancouver, Madame Cama in Paris and Shyamji Krishna Varma in London. Varma, in particular, was notorious as the founder of India House, one of whose members carried out a high-profile assassination, while another, V.D. Savarkar, was convicted for conspiracy.[268] Questioned about his contacts with revolutionaries, Sayaji Rao 'provided innocent excuses', but also realized that he was under surveillance.[269] Then, to further aggravate matters, in the winter of 1911 two Baroda officials were implicated in sedition. Revolutionary propaganda was being published in areas under them, and at one site, hundreds of copies of a banned book were unearthed, camouflaged under the title *Vegetable Medicines*.[270] The officials, in British eyes, were suspect, but one of them, instead of showing contrition, asked the Bombay police on whose permission they had raided Baroda in the first place. This was too much for the viceroy: the ruler's man was talking jurisdiction instead of answering questions.[271] So, in the end Hardinge attacked Sayaji Rao all daggers drawn, sending to London a full indictment.

Alluding to his adoption, Hardinge marvelled at the 'exaggerated idea of his own importance' and the 'pretensions to equality' Sayaji Rao showed. This may yet have been forgiven were it not for the fact that he was now 'actively disloyal'. He had not sent in Baroda soldiers to the Imperial Service Troops, but, despite British objections, was raising the strength of his army. In his government, he hosted known critics of the Raj, and was too energetic a supporter of the Congress. On revolutionary activities, even the palace was not free from dangerous influences. Sayaji Rao's public statements, moreover, were often a 'thinly veiled disparagement of British rule', and during the viceroy's visit in 1909, he had had to be pressed by the Resident to even affirm loyalty – evidently, the ruler wished to pay homage to the *Crown*, not the government. The discovery of seditious material was only the last straw, for the fact was that of 167 books proscribed by the Raj, seventeen had emerged from Baroda. 'His Highness now stands,' the viceroy concluded, 'without excuse.' If indeed he was a loyal feudatory, and not a 'patron of sedition', he must prove it. Or as Hardinge proposed, he should do the following: deliver a pre-approved condemnation of revolutionaries; close all legal loopholes allowing the publication of seditious writing in Baroda; place his police under a British officer; and banish officials who did not enjoy imperial confidence. If, however, instead of obeying, Sayaji Rao threatened to abdicate, it should be allowed despite risk of 'hostile criticism'.[272]

While this letter was sent off to London in November 1911, the maharajah was in no mood to bend. For instance, the district officials who provoked the Bombay police were not banished, but only demoted; indeed, when one of them decided to resign, Sayaji Rao gave him a purse of 10,000 rupees.[273] Things were still bad and the viceroy's animosity an open secret when the maharajah went to Delhi for the famous 1911 durbar soon afterwards. Here, for the first and only time, the British monarch, George V, was personally present. As heir to the throne, he had visited India six years before – at that time, the maharajah had gone abroad, grumbling that he was not a 'servant' to cancel his plans for the prince.[274] Now, however, with this talk of sedition, a gesture of loyalty seemed wise. Except, however, that this is not what happened. On the morning of the durbar, Sayaji Rao was agitated for personal reasons.[275] Hours later, as rulers began paying homage to George V, the maharajah messed up. He was meant to go up to the enthroned king and his wife, bow separately and take seven steps back, before returning to his place. But as a newspaper put it, 'he walked up jauntily swinging a stick in his hand – in itself a gross breach of etiquette – and as he passed before their Majesties, he saluted in the most perfunctory manner' before showing them his back. That it was an innocent error would not fly, for earlier too, when the viceroy entered, apparently 'the Gaekwar rose from his seat for barely a moment . . . and then reseated himself, ostentatiously stretching out his legs'. Everyone else had remained standing till Hardinge took a seat.[276]

There were exaggerations in this account, but within days the episode was politicized. It was true that Sayaji Rao, having missed a rehearsal, was lost at the durbar, but he had not been swinging his stick. Nor did he turn his back discourteously – in his confusion, instead of going seven paces backwards, he turned too soon.[277] Even so, it did not strike him that anything was wrong, and indeed, in video footage of the event, other princes also pay homage in a manner not unlike Sayaji Rao.[278] The next day, however, the maharajah found that he was accused of insulting George V, writing at once to apologize. It was not an enviable place to be in, given how in Hardinge's eyes everything Sayaji Rao did was a slight. This combined with the pro-British press baying for blood meant that, in a rare display, the maharajah dished out loyalty in obsequious language. 'To the British Government the Baroda State owes everything, and to that Government my State and I myself personally will always be truly grateful and loyal,' he explained.[279] Gleeful, Hardinge released the letter to *The Times*, which while publishing it, also carried a column listing the maharajah's many sins. Another publication admonished this 'son of a small cultivator' for the 'gross insult' he gave 'his Suzerain before all India'.[280] Interestingly, one of the crimes the maharajah was guilty of was not appearing in state jewellery, or the sash, robes and other insignia of his British honours; he had presented himself in 'everyday dress'.[281] And amusingly enough, descriptions of his clothes match what Malhar Rao, decades before, had worn to the trial that ended in his deposition.[282] If these were omens, they were definitely not very encouraging.

At last, the British had Sayaji Rao where they wanted him, and the possibility of deposition was real. For once, it also did not help that

Sayaji Rao around the time of the notorious 'Durbar Incident', as featured in Edward St Clair Weeden's A Year with the Gaekwar of Baroda *(1911).*

nationalist editors turned Sayaji Rao into a hero for slighting the British king. In fact, the 'durbar incident' would feature in the press whenever the maharajah was mentioned for the next many years, a Sword of Damocles over his head. Not only did the ruler have to issue multiple clarifications, but letters were also sent out to everyone from the Resident upwards to conciliate them. This was why, early in 1912, Sayaji Rao issued orders that his officials and subjects must hereon view 'every misguided person who attempted to excite ill-will, hatred, or contempt against the British Government' as an enemy. In the same year, he also sacked a state servant who had seen Aurobindo recently.[283] On international trips in the aftermath, the Resident would hand the maharajah lists of people he absolutely could *not* meet, and Sayaji Rao accepted – unimaginable two years earlier. The whole experience – being watched by the police, the dressing-down, the denial of even a meeting with the viceroy until he apologized and slander in the press – led to a muted tone in the maharajah's remaining career. It also did not help that he was having family troubles during the same period: the death of his eldest son, the determination of his daughter to marry an unsuitable man and so on. As one of his early biographers wrote:

> There was no doubt that the Durbar affair and the subsequent charges made against his administration of Baroda had a lasting effect on the Maharaja's after-life; not, indeed, to lessen his loyalty to the Paramount Power, but to increase the self-repression . . . and to render him less confident in his attitude in face of the Western world. He felt that he had been, not only misunderstood, but unjustly treated. Nor does this view appear unreasonable. An unintentional breach of etiquette (by no means unparalleled in the West, it may be said) had been made the excuse for a calumnious attack on his past character . . . it was Maharaja Sayajirao's deep misfortune to lay himself open to accusations, however little grounded on fact, at such a time.[284]

What is ironic is that all these years, the maharajah had managed to say and, indeed, do things derogatory to the British and get away with it. But then, when he did *not* intend offence, that episode offered the means with which to threaten punishment for all his previous transgressions. In this circumstance, as Bhagavan notes, there was no need for the colonial establishment to depose him: he was 'embarrassed and significantly weakened'. The British, then, were happy to leave him in place 'with a tenuous grasp', and no more in a mood for battle.[285] This is not to say that Sayaji Rao sold his principles and became subservient; what did happen, however, was that he rarely again bared rhetorical fangs against the Raj, and even if he had a message to deliver, enlisted subordinates instead of putting his own head on the line. Thus, for example, in a 1926 publication, it was his Dewan who took the lead in criticizing dictatorial Residents.[286] At the end of the day, the maharajah calculated, there was no point being kicked off the throne and rendered unable to do anything; so, after years as a nationalist icon, the maharajah took a back seat. His attitude now resembled Ayilyam Tirunal's from the nineteenth century, who knew the perils of openly provoking the Raj and opted to be diplomatic. In other words, thirty years after Madhava Rao departed Baroda and long after that Dewan was dead, his ward did reluctantly embrace the teachings of his *Minor Hints*.

And yet, as late as April 1938, ten months before the boy from Kavalane went to the grave, he was still unable to wholly contain himself. Urging the Raj – from Naoroji's enduring platform of the East India Association in London – to do justice by India, he asked that the country be granted dominion status. The British had, three years before, passed reforms that led, for the first time, to the formation of provincial governments with Indian ministers. It had produced a system by which parties like the Congress were able to gain administrative experience, backed by the legitimizing force of elections. While pleased, the maharajah also reminded the imperial power that this was not adequate – India had to be granted the position white nations within the empire had long enjoyed. Or as Sayaji Rao said,

> My only hope is that the British will not be satisfied with what they have already done. There is a great deal more that they can do and I feel that it cannot be less than they have done for Canada and Australia. If they do follow that policy, you will find that India will progress apace, will have greater confidence in herself, and will create self-respect among her peoples. Failing that, you can hardly expect honesty in the administration. India needs freedom and that freedom should be wisely, properly and quickly given.[287]

Amusingly, the moderation that marked the final phase of the maharajah's career led to some strange consequences insofar as the world viewed him. When Sayaji Rao died in February 1939, old and wheelchair-bound, *The New York Times* lamented the loss of this 'ablest and most powerful of Indian princes'. He was, the paper explained, a 'poor shepherd boy' elevated to princely rank, and, more accurately, a ruler who had given his people a reign of prosperity and contentment. But then the paper delivered the coup de grâce: Sayaji Rao, one of the most difficult Indian rulers the Raj ever encountered, a veritable case study in disloyal conduct, was branded a 'strong supporter of British rule in India'![288] As for his links to the Congress: a few years later, as independence approached, his widow met a senior Raj official. And to him she couldn't help but chuckle how 'she was surprised to learn that [the British] were now proposing to hand over power in India to the [very] people her husband had been blamed for associating with'. In response the man had a single word: 'Touché!'[289]

Portrait of Ravi Varma by his son, Rama Varma.

We return to Travancore in this chapter and to Ravi Varma's personal life and complicated marriage. Though himself not royal, his granddaughters became the maharanis of the state, and their troubled relationship is the focus here, revealing the inner conflicts of royal courts and their ruling families.

5

Princesses and Consorts

On 4 August 1875, when Ravi Varma was still in Travancore, and Seshiah Sastri was Dewan to Ayilyam Tirunal, the streets of Trivandrum were witness to a strange sight: police descending on a royal abode to seize a poet for treason. A magistrate entered the Sarasvati Vilasam Palace to read out the warrant of arrest, and soon the poet was bundled into a carriage, silver shackles locked around his wrists. To everyone's astonishment, however, a princess ran out from the building, chasing after the officers and their prisoner. Her clothes in disarray, her hair flying behind her, this was a woman possessed. She was restrained quickly, collapsing in a heap on the street, while the poet was driven away.[1] The story goes that nobody came out of the nearby buildings to tend to the lady, dishevelled and humiliated in public; a woman they ordinarily viewed with reverence, now revealed as tragically human. Instead, all shut their doors and looked away, for any action to the contrary would be noticed. After all, the maharajah himself had ordered the poet's arrest; to show sympathy for the princess would be construed as taking sides in a feud that was toxic. And so it was that Lakshmi Bayi of Travancore (1848–1901) was left friendless and alone on the road. From now on, the poet – her husband – was no longer Valiya Koil Tampuran ('senior consort') to the princess. He had instead become simply Kerala Varma, state prisoner, convicted for sedition.[2]

In matrilineal Travancore, the ruling family did not comprise the maharajah, his wife and children; instead, it was the king's sisters and nieces who were royalty, succession devolving on *their* children. Descent in the *female* line from a common ancestress was the dynasty's organizing principle. Thus, Swathi Tirunal and Uthram Tirunal were sons of a queen called Gowri Lakshmi Bayi (1791–1814) – they were both maharajahs not because their father belonged to the royal lineage, but by virtue of their mother's membership in it. So too neither of their sons succeeded to their titles; instead, their sister's boys, Ayilyam Tirunal and Visakham Tirunal, held power. Which then caused a problem if there were no women. When Ayilyam Tirunal's sister passed away in 1857, leaving only sons, an adoption became necessary. And so, two girls from a collateral family were brought in as 'nieces'.[3] The older was Lakshmi Bayi, whose poet husband was arrested in 1875, and the younger, Parvathi Bayi (1850–93). In keeping with custom, both took aristocratic consorts, and it is in Parvathi Bayi's context that the story of Ravi Varma's rejection as a potential mate is told. Whatever its truth, the lady married a Kilimanoor cousin of his, with whom she had several children, including the tricycle-riding prince of our Introduction. And when her husband died of alcoholism, she replaced him with his brother in an arrangement called *kutu-irikkuka* ('giving company').[4] Unlike elsewhere, in Travancore self-denying widowhood was not a concept for royal women.

Interestingly, the ranis' husbands were not their equals. As an observer wrote, consorts 'though fed and kindly treated . . . have no authority, nor are they permitted to sit in the Ranee's presence in public. In addition to which, she may change them whenever she is tired of one, by sending him away, and selecting another.'[5] As late as the 1920s, a Resident recorded how the consorts, though 'highly educated, and of superior caste' were 'entitled only to a monthly allowance from the Durbar of Rs 200 per mensem with meals from the Palace, and the use of a brougham and pair of horses'. They were not permitted to travel in the same carriage as their wives, and if by some chance they did, it was essential they sat *opposite*, and not next to the ranis to avoid any appearance of equality.[6]

Rani Lakshmi Bayi (top) and Rani Parvathi Bayi (right) of Travancore, as featured in
M. Griffith's India's Princes *(1894).*

Rani Parvathi Bayi's first husband, a
cousin of Ravi Varma's from the Kilimanoor
family.

The custom was the same in Cochin: if in Travancore the consorts were Kshatriyas, termed Koil Tampurans, here the princesses took Brahmins. Called *irippukkar* (literally, those who 'sat' in their wives' homes), if they came from exalted lines, their pay was eight rupees a month, but for those of regular background, only six – that is till someone complained, it is said, that two rates for men working the same job was an injustice.[7] Understandably, to outsiders the whole system was puzzling, which explains why a visitor once sighed, 'The law of succession in Travancore is very difficult to understand, and I should be sorry to attempt to pass an examination in it.'[8]

In the late-nineteenth century, the senior female figure at court was the sociable and charming Lakshmi Bayi. On the one hand, she was curious enough to take Bible lessons twice a week from a missionary called Augusta Blandford.[9] Equally, she also upheld customary regulations, like her adoptive uncles. Once, for example, when reading with Blandford, she was 'seized with a violent fit of coughing'. Asked to have some water, she said, 'You forget that I must not take any till I have bathed because you have been near me.'[10] On another occasion when she shook hands with a European couple, though it was probably before her bath, the surprised visitors ascribed such an action from this 'pleasing person' to 'intercourse with a cultivated Christian lady'.[11] They had other grounds too for awe – if elsewhere, royal ladies lived in seclusion, Travancore's princesses had no such restrictions. Indeed, Lakshmi Bayi had a positive appetite for life: great was her excitement, for example, at her first railway journey to Madras in 1883. And once there, she dragged her sister to a fancy dress ball – 'an unheard-of event!'[12] In fact, in a splendid Ravi Varma portrait, Lakshmi Bayi appears in rather inventive clothes for a mid-thirties' Malayali queen from an orthodox state. For instead of traditional white garments, the rani wears a gold brocade skirt, draped around which is a red *dupatta*. Sporting heavy jewellery, her hand rests on books intended to impress Western viewers, including Favell Lee Mortimer's *Near Home or Europe Described* (1881).

In her day, Lakshmi Bayi was considered a beauty of talent and character. Blandford reported how she was 'fond of drawing', and 'having

succeeded well with flower painting' one year, had 'begun a new style –
heads in black and white crayons'.[13] Visitors noticed a studio in Sarasvati
Vilasam, and the rani's works were even exhibited in Bombay.[14] Music
was a passion shared with Ayilyam Tirunal, for whom she often played
the veena.[15] There was also something regal about the lady – Ravi Varma's
granddaughter would recall her palace, with 'huge halls and haunting
passages'. Up a 'picturesque staircase' lay Lakshmi Bayi's apartments,
where hung from the ceiling a wooden swing, with bolsters and cushions.
'This was used by the [rani], who sat in it and talked to her retainers
and gave her orders for the day.'[16] Meeting her when she was middle-
aged, the novelist Pierre Loti saw her as 'a charming personification
of India', with 'pure features', 'magnificent large eyes' and a mound of
gems decorating her 'statuesque form'. Indeed, 'her face does not seem
to belong to our times', the Frenchman rhapsodized, 'and it is only in
old Indian miniatures that I have had a glimpse of such princesses'.[17] As
with her Ravi Varma portrait, these accounts confirmed that mix the Raj
sought in Indian royalty: a colourful 'oriental' quality married to an ease
with colonial modernity. And where Janaki of Pudukkottai, for example,
represented decadent feminine influences, Lakshmi Bayi of Travancore
offered a 'healthier' alternative – one validated by Queen Victoria herself.

In general, British misgivings about female Indian royalty stemmed
from their difficulty in penetrating *zenanas*. After all, a ruler's court was
open to white men, who could participate in its rituals, and even amend
these for imperial purposes. *Women's* quarters, however, as a viceroy put
it, were 'shut to British influence', making them 'mischievous', 'powerful'
sites of politics.[18] Indeed, the very act of stereotyping royal ladies as
'idle intriguers' preoccupied 'with making trouble'[19] revealed the Raj's
immense paranoia; in presenting the harem as a debauched place, the
British were breaking its legitimacy as a *political* platform. And they
had good reasons. In Jaipur, for example, early in the nineteenth century
when the ruler was a minor, the regent queen used purdah as an excuse
to keep the Resident at bay.[20] Responding to such strategies, the Raj
developed a policy where Residents, rather than royal mothers, became
guardians to underage princes. Or as another viceroy explained, zenana

ladies gave 'an infinite amount of trouble'; the British object was to cut their influence.[21] Of course, it remained impossible for the Raj to wholly subdue the harem: a century later in Jaipur, a fully grown maharajah was decried for being under the influence of a 'female Rasputin'.[22] Not long after, in Cochin, its talented but ageing ruler was 'entirely swayed' by his consort.[23] In combating these unpoliced influences on native princes, then, the British publicised certain ideas on what kind of women royals were acceptable, and what were not. And here Lakshmi Bayi passed muster.

This validation had much to do with the rani's husband – our seditious poet of 1875 – and was linked not so much to breaking zenana cliches but rather to accepting certain patriarchal ideals in a matrilineal court. Like his wife, this man too was all charm and affability. Chosen for her in 1859,[24] Kerala Varma (1845–1914) was destined for more than a footnote in royal chronicles, despite being just a consort. For like Ravi Varma, he made ample use of the exposure court life provided. He learnt from eminent scholars, training also in music. English lessons were gained from a durbar physician and by tagging alongside Visakham Tirunal. Occult knowledge was also acquired from a traditional master, besides fashionable interests like shooting and riding, making Kerala Varma a well-rounded gentleman in Eastern and Western society both.[25] He became, as the *Times of India* noted, 'the favourite of the Royal household and the hero of the people'.[26] It helped that he was handsome, and had style: Loti noted his velvet *achkan* 'with diamond buttons', and a 'turban of white silk', which served his trademark look of expensive simplicity.[27] But what really set the rani's consort apart was literary talent. Within a decade of their marriage, he had begun producing what would in time become an impressive corpus of writing, including the *Tirunal Prabandham* (1861), a eulogy to Ayilyam Tirunal, the *Kamsavadha Champu* (1869) and the *Tulabharasatakam* (1870).

As a confirmed 'enlightened native', Kerala Varma soon rose to influence even where policy was concerned – an area in theory closed to royal spouses. For instance, he served as the ruler's go-between in dealings with the Resident.[28] As part of the state's modernization drive, in 1868 he

Varma's portraits of Rani Lakshmi Bayi and Kerala Varma from the 1890s, featuring their imperial medals of the Order of the Crown of India and the Order of the Star of India.

chaired a committee to develop school textbooks, personally authoring fifteen.[29] Blandford too thought highly of him – if Lakshmi Bayi came to her school to give out prizes, the Valiya Koil Tampuran conducted its examinations.[30] Helping the rani run her estate, he also acquired a capacity for extending patronage: in 1866 it was Kerala Varma who first gifted eighteen-year-old Ravi Varma 'fairly inaccessible' oil paints from Madras.[31] While not as well known today, in their time Kerala Varma was as much a celebrity as the artist. Reviewing the future Congress president R.C. Dutt's writing, thus, our Sanskrit scholar flaunted his knowledge of English literature: 'The honest boldness of your style often reminds me of Bulwer Lytton; your description of medieval manners . . . is not less thorough . . . than Scott's; your character-sketches compare favourably with Thackeray's and your narration of incidents has all the fertility and charm . . . of Alexander Dumas.'[32] Describing him as 'the greatest Indian statesman and writer of modern times', he added how it was men like Dutt and their work that was 'fast making us a nation, united within and respected without'.[33] Kerala Varma too, then, was part of that age of nationalism by stealth.

But the fairy tale wasn't without hiccups. In the 1870s, when ties between the maharajah and his brother, Visakham Tirunal, ruptured, the rani and her husband faced a crisis. Two factions formed, with Lakshmi Bayi and Kerala Varma struggling for a balance. Displeasing Ayilyam Tirunal was not an option, but equally, there was affection for his estranged brother. At first, Kerala Varma kept away, but it was not long before gossipmongers and partisans began to fan suspicion – even being seen with Visakham Tirunal was a risk. In the Valiya Koil Tampuran's case, though in 1872 the maharajah took him along on business to Bombay and Benares, after their return he was dropped.[34] Lakshmi Bayi and he began to see less and less of Ayilyam Tirunal, which was an ominous turn of events. Things were so bad in Trivandrum, in fact, that at one point Visakham Tirunal's followers set on fire the maharajah's beach house.[35] Indeed, in correspondence with the British, Kerala Varma claimed *he* was in danger, asking permission to move with his wife into the Residency a la Jamnabai of Baroda. As he wrote, 'We are not fighting against the Maha Raja when we say that you must give us British Protection. We live in the fear of life.'[36] In another baffling note he claimed that he had been asked to 'surrender'; that he would not 'take the drink & mixture' – possibly a reference to poison and a threat of suicide.[37]

But these were not an innocent man's expostulations. In June 1875, Dewan Sastri received a note signed 'Peter III', telling him to 'take care of your cooks' because the ruler was planning to poison him.[38] Infuriated, he took the note to the maharajah, with whom he was already on poor terms. In the course of events, Madras was informed, handwriting experts were consulted and suspicion landed on the rani's husband. He, of course, denied it all: 'I know nothing of the authorship of the anonymous letter.'[39] Apoplectic at this lie, and the fact that after all his efforts to demonstrate 'progress' a consort had made the durbar look like a hotbed of intrigue, the ruler decided to act. Hence was the Valiya Koil Tampuran expelled from the palace. As *The Pall Mall Gazette* told its London readers in a one-line update, 'The consort of the senior Ranee of Travancore has been arrested.'[40] Divested of titles and dignities,

Kerala Varma was packed off to jail. It was a colossal fall – yesterday the man was Lakshmi Bayi's beloved, spending his days writing poetry, and in the company of the who's who of the Raj. Now, aged thirty, he was bunking with criminals. For fifteen months the consort languished in horrific conditions, and no appeal was allowed – on the contrary, Kerala Varma's name was struck off even almanacs which listed him as the rani's husband.[41] But eventually, following his mother's pleas and a kind of hunger strike by Lakshmi Bayi, he was released and put under house arrest instead.[42]

Interestingly, the prisoner sent in a grovelling confession to the ruler, in which some of his 'sins' appear to have been just too much Westernization.[43] That is, while a degree of English influence was acceptable, the same substance could also become an indictment. Thus, in this letter, the man whom Malayalis remember as the Father of Modern Malayalam Prose and the Kalidas of Kerala, referred to himself as 'slave' (or *adiyan* in the lost Malayalam original). With 'the most sincere repentance and most contrite sorrow' he acknowledged his 'great treasonous acts': yes, he wrote 'letters against Your Highness'; indeed, he had written 'that anonymous letter to the Dewan'; why, he had even written to 'some of the Europeans' about his 'ungrounded suspicion' that the maharajah and his brother were possibly murderers. Worse, he was 'corresponding unnecessarily' with journalists and had 'somehow' grown fond of Christianity; despite his status, he had succumbed to that 'forbidden vice of drinking' and to the 'intemperate use' of narcotics. Sorry now for all these sins, he wanted nothing more than Ayilyam Tirunal's forgiveness. Even if the ruler commanded him to quit Travancore and 'rove as a Fakir' to 'perish in the snowy regions of the Himalayas', he would 'submit to it', without deviating 'a hair breadth'.[44] All he wanted was his freedom, and he would accept it at any price the ruler set.

The great irony, of course, is that while her husband drafted his mercy petition, Lakshmi Bayi – oblivious that he had offered to give her up and move on – was fighting Ayilyam Tirunal tooth and nail. The rani's loyalty to her consort was unshakeable: for five years, she defied the ruler, even as her income was slashed and her movements limited.[45] Visakham Tirunal was sympathetic, and his aide, Nilakantha Pillai, relayed news whenever possible. The maharajah, however, insisted she take a new husband – not an unusual proposal in the matrilineal system where consorts were expendable. But Lakshmi Bayi refused – indeed, when Ayilyam Tirunal sent a replacement, 'she had', as Blandford wrote, 'the firmness and strength of mind . . . to bid him depart'.[46] Indian ranis, seen generally as victims or scheming Jezebels by the Raj, now had a new example to offer: a stoic English-speaking princess, who consorted with missionaries and whites, was unburdened by purdah and was steadfastly loyal to her husband. Lakshmi Bayi became a symbol for new ideas of virtue. It was for this reason that in 1881 Queen Victoria would admit her into the Order of the Crown of India – an honour that, in Blandford's words, 'cannot fail to do good' for 'the news will spread throughout Travancore' and 'other women [would] be induced to try and tread' in the rani's footsteps.[47] Besides, it was proof, she added, that Lakshmi Bayi lived by the precepts of the Bible even if she did not officially embrace the faith;[48] she was, another observer noted, 'intellectually a believer'.[49]

The larger context in which the rani negotiated this crisis is telling. Missionaries like Blandford had been importing new notions of morality into the land, while growing interaction with other parts of India, where patriarchy was the norm, also put matrilineal institutions under duress. In fact, Blandford in a 1903 book described matrilineal marriage customs as 'very revolting'.[50] Even the *Travancore Census Report* of the year Kerala Varma was arrested was apologetic about the 'the unbinding nature of the marriage tie, which possesses such fascination for the majority of our population'.[51] The sexual autonomy women enjoyed, their access to divorce and even polyandry began to look embarrassing when 'progress' was defined in Victorian terms. Kerala men going out to new universities encountered others with different notions of marriage. 'The Malayalis as a class are the most idle and homesick of the whole Hindu community,' a newspaper offered, 'owing to the enervating influence exercised on their character by their peculiar system of inheritance and their obnoxious system of promiscuous marriage.'[52] Hitherto local practices struck no Malayali as odd. But now, under English education, he had to face derogatory remarks.[53] Suddenly, Kerala women were expected to be paragons of Victorian virtue, and monogamy became a strict new ideal.[54] Given the internalization of these norms, the rani's fight for her husband ceased to be a personal affair, cast instead into a call for matrilineal women in general to embrace patriarchal conventions. Colonialism, in that sense, was not about governments and politics alone; it also touched Indian minds and mindsets.

In any case, Ayilyam Tirunal's death liberated Lakshmi Bayi, transforming her into a heroine; in 1880, after Visakham Tirunal succeeded to the throne, he ordered Kerala Varma's release. In Blandford's words, 'My dear Ranee's husband has been brought back and restored to all his former honours . . . and the joy of seeing them together is very great.'[55] More significantly, life in prison also set the Valiya Koil Tampuran's head straight, refocusing his attention towards literature – of his thirty-one Sanskrit compositions, the most outstanding were born from the time of his confinement.[56] In 1878, for instance, he had sent Ayilyam Tirunal a thousand-stanza apology in Sanskrit, known as the *Kshamapanasahasra*.[57] Despite its beauty, the ruler ignored it. Then in 1880, in a rage, Kerala Varma wrote the *Yamapranamasataka*, in which the villain is a weakly disguised Ayilyam Tirunal.[58] And in the years ahead, not only did he translate works into Malayalam – famously Kalidas's *Abhijnana Sakuntalam* – but he also wrote a magnificent original, the *Mayurasandesam* (1894), conveying his angst on being separated from his wife.[59] The consequence of all this prodigious work was that in 1883 Kerala Varma was made a Fellow of the Madras University, and by 1895 a 'Companion of the Most Exalted Order of the Star of India (CSI)' by the Raj – to mark which distinction Ravi Varma executed a portrait. Besides, while Lakshmi Bayi went around placing pictures of Victoria all over her palace,[60] her husband thanked the British monarch through a panegyric in 1887. As he prefaced it in third person,

As [the author] was reading Mr Barnet's 'Life of Her Majesty Queen Victoria' . . . it occurred to him that the main features of so noble a

Ravi Varma's 1887 painting of an unidentified lady holding in her hand a casket featuring an address from the women of Travancore to Queen Victoria during her golden jubilee celebrations.

life, if embodied in Sanskrit stanzas of simple diction, might exert a beneficial influence on the minds of the girls of this Coast who generally study Sanskrit in their early years. His object, therefore, is not to excite admiration [for himself], but simply to serve the above purpose.[61]

In a sense this was not unlike sentiments Blandford expressed when enshrining Lakshmi Bayi as an icon for modern Malayali women. A Victorian vision of femininity was now embodied in Kerala Varma's wife, and here we have her husband too transmitting it in Sanskrit to 'girls of this coast' so they might emulate her. In a matrilineal world navigating colonial modernity, this is of great interest, as are details Kerala Varma highlights. Victoria's pledging of 'obedience' to her husband, despite being queen, is welcomed; the devotion of wife to husband, and husband to wife is celebrated; their moral conservatism is played up; the queen's resigned widowhood is admired; and so on.[62] Of course, insofar as obsequious writing goes, this was not the first time Kerala Varma produced some: released by the new maharajah, he composed the *Visakhavijaya* (Victory of Visakham Tirunal, 1881) in gratitude. In it not only is Ayilyam Tirunal grossly vilified, but his brother is cast as a wronged hero. Despite the literary quality of the work, it is a hagiography, intended simultaneously to clear Kerala Varma's own record. And if the ode to Victoria impressed the colonial establishment, with its chant of the imperial name more than a hundred times,[63] this other poem helped restore the Valiya Koil Tampuran to a lordly position in Trivandrum. Past sins were forgotten as literary verse became a stepping stone to renewed glory.

If as the twentieth century approached, the rani of Travancore was projected as the principal icon for girls in Kerala, among those who fell by the proverbial wayside was a relative who did not fit the new morality. In 1862, the year Ravi Varma landed in Trivandrum, Ayilyam Tirunal 'gave the cloth' (that is, married) a Nair lady from

Cochin. Kalyani Ammachi was the daughter of a former Dewan of that state,[64] and would for years stand out for her talent. Described as a woman of 'great beauty and intelligence',[65] she is believed to have been as instrumental in Ravi Varma's career as her husband – in 1870 it was their joint portrait that won the artist his first honour. Herself inclined towards the arts, Kalyani Ammachi produced compositions such as the *Parvathi Swayamvaram* and *Patrivritya Panchakam*, as well as collections to be danced to such as the *Rasakrida*, *Ambarishacharitam* and *Stavamalika* (the 'Ganasara' section alone of which had thirty-three songs).[66] That she was striking is clear – an 1868 photograph indicates that she was perhaps the first Malayali woman to wear the sari (the traditional dress being the *mundu*), while another shows her in a private setting with her spouse. While Ayilyam Tirunal is in glorious déshabillé, his wife appears in exquisite form, offering a glamorous contrast to her physically unimpressive husband. Ravi Varma, in fact, is believed to have done more than one portrait of the maharajah's wife, including an unsigned canvas often mistakenly described as featuring Rani Parvathi Bayi of Travancore.[67]

Kalyani Ammachi (1839–1909) was a well-educated woman, but in time her antecedents would be concealed and hidden away. For if Lakshmi Bayi symbolized fidelity and wifely deference, Kalyani Ammachi caused chagrin to architects of modern morality. And this was due to a single now-embarrassing detail – that when she first met the ruler, she was already married, making her an example of everything seen as wrong in matriliny. While it may seem odd today, at the time such a history was not at all bizarre. Thus, for example, more than one rajah of Cochin married a lady who already had a previous husband (and children),[68] while in Travancore in 1899, Ayilyam Tirunal's nephew would take as his consort the wife of a palace employee: a situation that led, years later, to that servant being described as 'the former husband of the Maharajah's present wife'.[69] Divorce was not scandalous – Ravi Varma's brother, Rajaraja, was husband to a lady who had had a failed relationship before, and who, after his death, would go on to marry the novelist C.V. Raman Pillai, whose own first marriage had culminated

Portrait, generally described as featuring Parvathi Bayi of Travancore, but which is more likely Kalyani Ammachi, wife of Ayilyam Tirunal (top).

1868 photograph of Kalyani Ammachi in a sari. She was probably the first Malayali woman to wear the modern sari (right).

in divorce.[70] Nor was polyandry embarrassing: a 'progressive', highly respected rajah of Cochin openly wrote how he became involved with the stepdaughter of one of his royal uncles, after her 'husband raised no objection'. 'This kind of things [sic],' he explained, 'was not considered improper at the time.'[71] In other words, princes could marry divorcees as well as widows, and it was 'normal' for a woman to have more than one partner if she chose.[72]

Given this context, the idea that Kalyani Ammachi was married when she met Ayilyam Tirunal is not as controversial as it would become later. Interestingly, her ex-husband was none other than Easwara Pillai, the Kathakali star from Uthram Tirunal's court. That later generations grew uncomfortable with this is clear from the convoluted stories that attempt to paper it over. One claims that Pillai visited Cochin on pilgrimage and stayed with its ex-Dewan. The old man spoke of his difficulties in finding his daughter a suitable boy, so rising manfully, Pillai offered to ensure Kalyani's marriage with Ayilyam Tirunal (whose first wife had died). And, thus, the lady left with him.[73] Oral histories, however, offer a different account, in which the Dewan's daughter elopes with the actor. This could be dismissed as gossip, were it not for tales that seek desperately to establish Kalyani's innocence. One anecdote has the maharajah, disturbed by talk of a relationship between his wife and the Kathakali master, carry out a test: in a room where the two are to meet, he places mirrors in strategic positions to spy on them. What he sees sets his mind at peace, for when the actor enters Kalyani Ammachi's presence, her demeanour is that of a disciple – no liberties that might betray him as a lover are taken.[74] So too in a character sketch written long after she was dead, we read how the maharajah's wife was 'a worshipper of the goddess Chastity' – again an effort to put to rest awkward talk around her.[75]

So, if a Lakshmi Bayi was glorified for wifely loyalty, here the maharajah's consort had to jump through proverbial hoops to fit a matching template. In the process a sense of shame veiled her history, which otherwise would not have merited special comment. Sadly, Kalyani Ammachi was also handicapped for one more reason –

that, ultimately, she was not herself royal. For in the matrilineal system, the ruler's wife did not join his family. By the same logic that determined succession in the royal house, her children too were commoners, inheriting their *mother's* rank and status. Thus, Visakham Tirunal's beloved firstborn had no claim to the throne – the closest he came to power was through a seat in the state assembly.[76] At best, secondary posts could be offered to descendants of male royals – during 1809–12, for example, the Dewan was a prince's grandson.[77] Others made a name through cultural pursuits, such as Irayimman Tampi (1782–1856), a poet known to the royals as Tampi Mama (Uncle Tampi).[78] But equally, over time these descendants could lapse into oblivion: a member of Irayimman Tampi's house worked as a clerk, and the poet himself in his last years pawned valuables to get by.[79] It was this that often startled colonial authorities and even Indians from elsewhere: the fact that a king's lineal heirs could fall on hard times; that a maharajah's son might enter a shop 'unnoticed', like a nobody.[80] Or as a rani sniffed in 1915 after encountering yet another bewildered party, 'They found it difficult to understand our . . . system.'[81]

There was, however, an arrangement in Travancore to ensure that descendants of assorted rulers lived in dignity at least for a few generations. Local custom required princes to take wives from a handful of families known as *ammaveedus* (literally, 'consort houses'),[82] setting them apart from ordinary Nairs.[83] These clans enjoyed many royal privileges – allowances, ritual honours, exemption from gun licences – but not royal power.[84] Often, maharajahs did take wives from outside, ensuring, however, to *adopt* their brides into an ammaveedu. Thus, Swathi Tirunal's wives became members of the Tiruvattar and Vadasseri ammaveedus, while Uthram Tirunal's lady was brought into the Nagercoil ammaveedu.[85] Shrewd rulers also orchestrated marriages between royal nephews and their daughters. So, Uthram Tirunal early on apprised the British of his intention to have Ayilyam Tirunal wed his English-speaking daughter.[86] Ayilyam Tirunal and Kalyani Ammachi, in turn, had *their* adopted daughter given in marriage to another junior prince. One maharajah's child, thus, became Ammachi to his successor, allowing their families to live in luxury. As for sons, extraordinary measures could be taken – a popular tale has it that an astrologer told Visakham Tirunal that his boy would die penniless; the maharajah at once ordered all feeding houses in the state that if a Sri Narayanan Tampi ever came to their doors, he was to be fed.[87]

However, as far as popular knowledge went, a maharajah's family did not command the same reverence as members of the royal matrilineage. As an observer put it, a prince's consort was 'not a member of the royal household, and is in nowise associated with the royal court. She has neither official nor social position at Court, and cannot even be seen in public with the ruler whose wife she is.'[88] While true, this should not be overstated, for the ammaveedus were rulers' cousins. Indeed, their menfolk's title, 'Tampi', translates as 'brother', indicating a relationship with the royal family. At durbars the Tampis stood close to the throne,[89] and weddings of the maharajahs' female issue were state events. Thus, fifteen years after Visakham Tirunal died, his heir celebrated the marriage of that ruler's granddaughters with enough fanfare for it to receive coverage in London.[90] When the British wished to flatter this other maharajah, all they had to do was give his daughter a medal.[91] So too the position of the Ammachi was of respect. Translated as 'the mother of His Highness's children', it was not the equivalent of 'rani'.[92] But this did not divest its holder of regard, even if such respect was limited to courtly circles. While missionary accounts reported that they were not meant to be seen with their husbands, the fact was that they stayed in palaces during the princes' lifetimes.[93] And between these morganatic wives and their royal husbands there was genuine love and affection.

Thus, with Uthram Tirunal, a British official found his wife, Madhavi Ammachi, living with him.[94] Indeed, in 1860, while duty required the maharajah to host a banquet to please the Raj, he rushed immediately after the celebrations to the side of his dying lady.[95] And when she was gone, the man was so crushed that he 'made a pilgrimage to several shrines, practicing great austerities and fastings' despite fragile health; where in May, Madhavi Ammachi died, three months later Uthram Tirunal followed.[96] In 1882, similarly, when Ayilyam Tirunal's daughter

Portrait of Lakshmi Ammachi by K. Padmanabhan Tampi, a royal descendant and a distant cousin of Ravi Varma's.

died in childbirth, his nephew, writing to a relation, cried, 'The loss is an irreparable one and it is more than I could bear with all my fortitude.' He spent years alone thereafter, 'bestowing all his affection on his motherless boy'.[97] So much for difference in status, and the fact that royal wives and children were not officially part of the dynasty, clearly, then, there was no shortage of a sense of duty. In fact, with Visakham Tirunal we have a record of his final days that conveys this poignantly:

> A short time before his death the Maharajah sent for all the members of the royal family, and took leave of them. To his son, the pride of his life, he sincerely hoped he would prove worthy of his father ... He was conscious till four o'clock in the evening, when he died. At the time of his death his Consort and his daughters were not near him, but only his son. Ten days before death he sent for his Consort and children, and they came before him in the evening very late. He beckoned his daughters to approach close to his cot, and the light not being very bright, he bade his Consort trim the flickering lamp, in order to enable him to see his daughters well, and he gazed on them for a while and wept. His Consort and children also wept; but he told them that God would protect and help them, and asked them to take leave. His Consort, his son, and daughters, prostrated themselves at his feet, according to oriental custom, and took their last farewell. On the same night his Consort and his eldest daughter took ill, being overcome with grief...[98]

Ammachis, in fact, even played a supporting act in dealings with the Raj. Visakham Tirunal's consort, Lakshmi Ammachi (1848–1914), not only travelled with him to places like Madras and Bombay (where she was mistaken for a rani),[99] but on visits by foreign grandees to the palace, was often present.[100] But *too much* influence could also attract trouble. In the early years of the nineteenth century, when a weak maharajah reigned and power lay with the Dewan, the ruler's wife not only supplied intelligence to the latter, but also helped manipulate her husband.[101] Furious, the British placed the lady in 'confinement at a distance of 40 Miles' from her spouse, on whom a fresh bride was forced against his will.[102] For long the expelled lady's ammaveedu was out of favour, and it was only when Visakham Tirunal married Lakshmi Ammachi from here that the relationship was mended.[103] Of course, though described as 'quite a love affair',[104] the marriage was not devoid of stress: given Ayilyam Tirunal's hostility towards her husband, Lakshmi Ammachi was dead against letting princes anywhere near her daughters. While the next maharajah was keen to marry one of them, the proposal went nowhere because of the Ammachi's objections.[105] The ruler, it is said, felt the rebuff but could do little – as the widow of a maharajah, Lakshmi Ammachi's opinions had force. Women of the ammaveedus were not concubines or at a level where they could be ordered around.

Thus, though Ammachis do not feature in official narratives, they were an integral part of the maharajahs' lives. Their neglect in durbar histories stems from multiple reasons. One was that while in the lifetime of a ruler his wife enjoyed prominence, after the man's death the limelight would move to the next ruler, *his* consort and a new ring of courtiers. Royal widows were well taken care of but were expected to spend the remainder of their days in pious withdrawal. Even the talented Kalyani Ammachi became a recluse after Ayilyam Tirunal's death: as Blandford recorded, 'Her eyes are beginning to fail her, though she is not an old woman . . . She is very thin and delicate looking, and has lost much of her beauty . . . She seems so friendless and lonely that I feel very sorry for her.'[106] Occasionally, Kalyani Ammachi did play a public role: in 1887, during Victoria's jubilee celebrations in Trivandrum – a necessarily extravagant affair to impress British superiors – she sent felicitations to be read, for instance.[107] In 1906, similarly, when the then rani married, the widow presented one of her final compositions, the *Vancheeswari Parinayam*, blessing the newly-weds. But in general she had become a minor figure. When she passed away in 1909, the rani recorded: 'The day before yesterday at 2 o'clock [Kalyani] Ammachi died. I do not know definitely what the cause was.'[108] Remembering her seventeen years later, a magazine pithily declared, 'She died in her 70th year without leaving any issue except her poetic works.'[109]

In other words, unlike the exaggerated idea that the Ammachis

cinquantaine de mètres, sur les herbes roussies de la plaine solitaire. Les trois compagnons, sans mot dire, bondissent vers le fouillis de l'enveloppe écroulée qui couvre la nacelle. Ils arrivent devant les sabords et regardent avidement l'intérieur de l'immense cavité.

Un cri de colère et de désappointement leur échappe. Ils viennent d'apercevoir miss Ellen renversée dans son léger fauteuil canné, l'ingénieur étendu sur le dos près de la soute, le reporter et Jean Renaud rigides.

« Malédiction !...

— Nous nous sommes trompés !

— *Il* n'est pas là ! »

Puis un des hommes reprend :

« Une affaire si bien combinée !

« *Il* devait partir lui-même à l'usine mise en révolte par nos gens... et tout cela se termine par un fiasco piteux !

— Oui ! piteux et terrible, ajoute son compagnon... car nous allons être pris... et ce sera pour nous la mort sans phrases, car il est implacable. Et puis, où fuir ?... où nous cacher ?... ils accourent et vont nous empoigner comme de vulgaires malfaiteurs. »

La voix féminine, aux vibrations ardentes et mélodieuses, répond, triomphante :

« Non ! car la délivrance nous arrive. »

Les yeux de l'énigmatique personnage qui luisent, à travers les trous du masque, viennent d'apercevoir une chose stupéfiante.

Au ras de la plaine et poussé par une brise légère, glisse lentement un magnifique ballon qui semble désemparé. Il s'avance par bonds successifs, très doux et très souple, touche à peine le sol qu'il effleure.

Toujours hypnotisés par l'aspect redoutable des croiseurs qui grossissent et se rapprochent avec rapidité, les deux hommes n'ont rien vu, rien soupçonné. Ils croient leur compagne frappée de folie quand elle leur crie :

« Regardez ! mais regardez donc ! »

Ils abaissent un moment leurs yeux et poussent un hurlement de joie. Ils voient à leur tour le ballon qui vient par l'arrière et passe à cinquante mètres.

Ils s'élancent vers lui, l'atteignent et leurs mains crispées saisissent la nacelle. Maintenu énergiquement, le dirigeable s'arrête. La nacelle est vide, mais de prime abord ses appareils sont en bon état.

« Personne ! Personne ! il est à nous !

— Et béni soit ce vagabond qui a cassé son amarre ! »

Sur le côté de l'enveloppe azurée flamboie en grosses lettres d'or un nom : *Instantaneous.*

Ainsi, le fugitif est le propre ballon du reporter ! Après s'être échappé de l'usine dans les circonstances que l'on sait, il a erré tout seul à travers les espaces... puis, comme si pareille succession d'incohérence était chose toute naturelle, il est venu s'échouer près de son légitime possesseur... pour assurer le salut du trio des forbans ! Les deux hommes s'engouffrent dans la nacelle.

« Embarquez ! embarquez ! crie l'un d'eux à la jeune femme.

— Pas encore ! deux minutes et je reviens...

« Vous, remettez en état les choses...

— Mais c'est de la folie ! »

(*À suivre.*) ☙ Louis Boussenard.

☙ **Altesses Indiennes** ☙

La Souveraine de Travancore

Bien qu'un lecteur du *Journal des Voyages* ne puisse décemment ignorer que le Travancore est un des principaux États indigènes de la péninsule hindoustanique, nous croyons devoir rafraîchir sa mémoire en lui résumant ici ce qu'il faut savoir sur cette principauté, avant de lui en présenter la souveraine.

Le Travancore est situé dans la région de Madras. Au dernier recensement, il comptait plus de trois millions d'habitants.

Et c'est indiquer déjà qu'à ne considérer que l'importance numérique de la population, le Travancore mériterait plus d'attention que bon nombre de républiques américaines.

Trois millions ! La Norvège est loin d'atteindre ce chiffre !

Cet État indien, gouverné depuis longtemps par la dynastie Kshatriya, qui a donné des chefs à cinq autres principautés, doit sa prospérité à l'intelligence de son souverain actuel, le maharajah de Travancore, qui a trouvé en son épouse une femme digne de ses hautes destinées.

La princesse Karchiayani, dont nous sommes heureux de publier le portrait, est une femme de grande valeur. Elle appartient d'ailleurs à la race *Inair* (ou malyali), réputée dans toutes les Indes pour ses dons intellectuels et artistiques.

Ne croyez pas que nous adressions ici un vain compliment à la princesse : notre opinion est basée sur des faits que tout le monde pourrait au besoin contrôler.

LA SOUVERAINE DE TRAVANCORE
Peintre habile et musicienne consommée, cette princesse hindoue possède une voix admirable et les rares Européens qui l'ont entendue chanter disent merveille de son talent de cantatrice.

Toute jeune, elle s'était signalée par ses dispositions musicales. Sa famille lui donna des maîtres européens qui développèrent ces heureuses dispositions.

Et quand elle se rendit en Angleterre, il y a quelques années, elle mit son amour-propre à suivre les cours du Collège de musique de Londres, établissement analogue au Conservatoire de musique de Paris.

À la fin de la première année scolaire, elle passait ses examens avec un brio qui lui valut les compliments de la presse londonienne, et elle rapportait dans son pays natal un diplôme de pianiste, récompense fort recherchée.

L'instrument favori de la princesse Karchiayani Amma n'est pourtant pas le piano : elle lui préfère

Karthyayani Ammachi, second wife of Ayilyam Tirunal's and Visakham Tirunal's nephew, Maharajah Mulam Tirunal, featured in a French publication.

had no status at court, the fact was that the state did, even after the death of its maharajahs, continue to honour their families. To those outside, however, all still looked wholly outlandish – the ruler's wife not enjoying a rani's rank, his sons denied power, and indeed, his family being inferior in caste, so that no ruler (a Kshatriya) could share a meal with his lady (a Sudra). In neighbouring Cochin, for example, a prince's son would tell how his father could not, even in the twentieth century, freely touch him. Physical contact was limited to mornings (before the bath), to late afternoons (after lunch), and then the night.[110] But these local conventions and usages fit the logic of matrilineal succession, and to Malayalis was the way things were. Slowly, however, the external gaze was here also internalized, and the ammaveedu as an institution went into decline. In the twentieth century, as matriliny broke down, Travancore's last maharajah would struggle with the idea of marriage. At one time, thus, there was a proposal for him to wed a granddaughter of Sayaji Rao of Baroda, but it fell through when the bride's family learnt she would never be a royal.[111] Eventually, it was noted, the ruler opted not to marry at all because he 'disliked' the matrilineal system. Though it was this very form of succession that brought him to power, yet 'the idea of his wife being only the consort and his children excluded' from the dynasty were 'most repugnant' to him. In the end, then, the last maharajah died a bachelor.[112]

Incidentally, this ruler was Ravi Varma's great-grandson.

In 1862, only weeks after Ravi Varma first arrived at its court, Travancore was gripped by a sensational murder. The scene of the crime was Mavelikara, a town far from the capital, but which held, nonetheless, a degree of importance. Once this had been the commercial headquarters for the state,[113] and in the nineteenth century remained a place of administrative significance. Its old fort had crumbled into a memory, but the temple to Krishnaswamy as well as the fact that it was home to the ruler's close relations invested Mavelikara with a regional consequence.

THE HOUSE OF TRAVANCORE

The Kolathiri Princes
Chathayam Tirunal
Mahaprabha

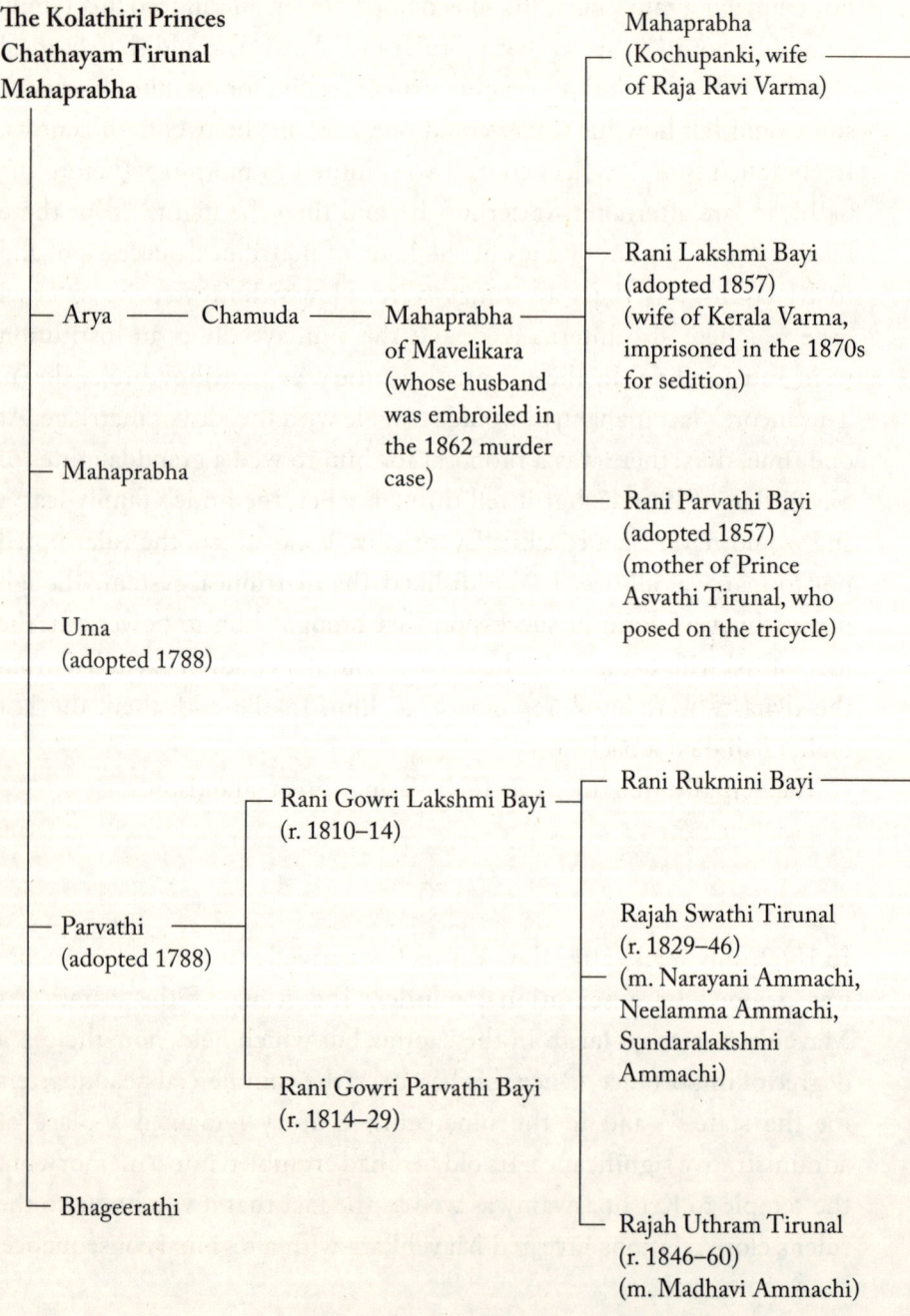

Mahaprabha
(Kochupanki, wife
of Raja Ravi Varma)

Arya ——— Chamuda ——— Mahaprabha
of Mavelikara
(whose husband
was embroiled in
the 1862 murder
case)

Mahaprabha

Rani Lakshmi Bayi
(adopted 1857)
(wife of Kerala Varma,
imprisoned in the 1870s
for sedition)

Rani Parvathi Bayi
(adopted 1857)
(mother of Prince
Asvathi Tirunal, who
posed on the tricycle)

Uma
(adopted 1788)

Rani Gowri Lakshmi Bayi
(r. 1810–14)

Rani Rukmini Bayi

Parvathi
(adopted 1788)

Rajah Swathi Tirunal
(r. 1829–46)
(m. Narayani Ammachi,
Neelamma Ammachi,
Sundaralakshmi
Ammachi)

Rani Gowri Parvathi Bayi
(r. 1814–29)

Bhageerathi

Rajah Uthram Tirunal
(r. 1846–60)
(m. Madhavi Ammachi)

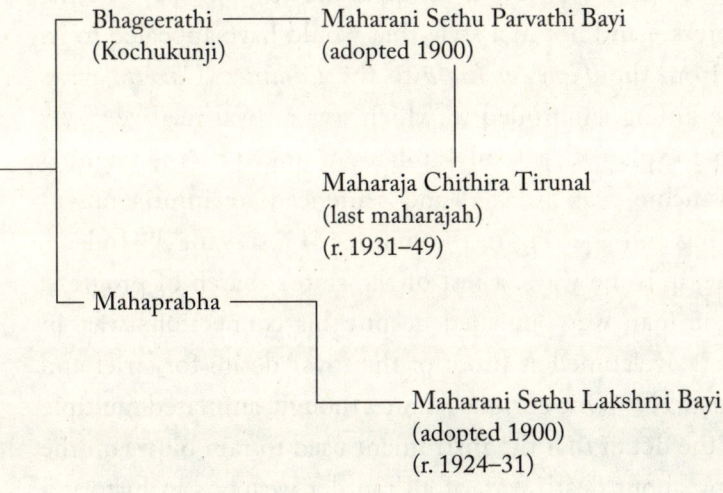

Bhageerathi
(Kochukunji) —————— Maharani Sethu Parvathi Bayi
(adopted 1900)

Maharaja Chithira Tirunal
(last maharajah)
(r. 1931–49)

Mahaprabha

Maharani Sethu Lakshmi Bayi
(adopted 1900)
(r. 1924–31)

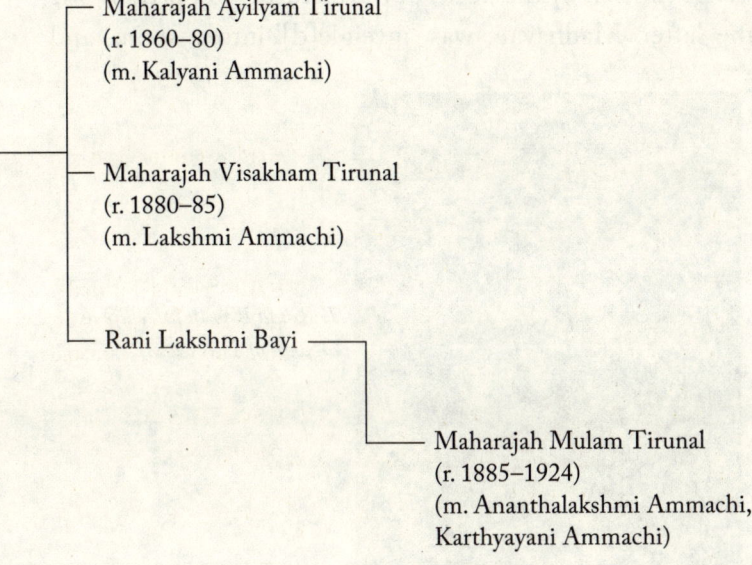

Maharajah Ayilyam Tirunal
(r. 1860–80)
(m. Kalyani Ammachi)

Maharajah Visakham Tirunal
(r. 1880–85)
(m. Lakshmi Ammachi)

Rani Lakshmi Bayi

Maharajah Mulam Tirunal
(r. 1885–1924)
(m. Ananthalakshmi Ammachi,
Karthyayani Ammachi)

The affair of 1862, however, brought upon the town the eye of the international press – and not in a style that would have appealed to its residents. For from the *Times of India* to the *Lancaster Gazette*, news travelled of the killing, embroiled in which was a royal relative.[114] As the second paper explained, a 'Coil Tambooran' linked to 'the reigning Prince of Travancore' was arrested and sentenced to 'imprisonment for life' for 'aiding and abetting in the murder of a servant'.[115] Indeed, this too became, in some ways, a test of the state's march of progress: the fact that the man was punished despite his connections was, in Western quarters, welcomed as proof of the royal 'desire for strict and even-handed justice'.[116] One curious feature, though, animated multiple news outlets – the detail that the instrument used to rain blows on the victim and bring about death was, of all murder weapons in history, a jackfruit.[117]

Two versions of the story emerged, the first of which caused understandable outrage. As the *Cochin Courier* alleged, and which in turn other papers parroted, a lady related to the maharajah was 'suspected' by her husband of 'illicit intercourse' with a servant.[118] The cuckolded man decided to 'revenge himself by the death of the disturber of his domestic felicity'. So the latter, Madhavan, was 'inveigle[d]' into a room, and

T. Rama Rao in later life as Dewan of Travancore.

Wikimedia Commons

beaten with that fruit-turned-torture instrument on 'the abdomen and vital parts', an attempt also being made to gouge out his eyes.[119] Quickly, this version was denied – while the murder was real, the *Times of India* amended its motivation, not least because it had 'traduced the character of a lady closely allied to the friendly and royal family of Travancore' and 'wound[ed] deeply' the feelings of many.[120] In reality, it was instead asserted that Madhavan was killed for theft.[121] But that 'torture' was attempted was not denied: indeed a knife had been taken to the man's left eye, and he was beaten 'in a manner too horrible to describe'. And when he died, his body was 'hung up' in order to 'produce the idea that the death was the result of suicide'.[122]

It appears that initially the local police – given the high-status persons entangled in it – tried to bury the crime. That is, till their superior got wind of things. T. Rama Rao (1831–95) was a cousin of the then Dewan Madhava Rao and would be described in time as 'well spoken of', 'able and upright'[123] and 'an excellent public officer.'[124] In fact, when the Dewan fell out with the maharajah and left, Rama Rao's name featured in a list of potential successors.[125] During the Mavelikara fiasco, as his biographer tells, 'without fear or favour of the powers that be' he went to the scene of the murder to ensure the investigation was not derailed by local officers' 'supineness'.[126] The sitting tehsildar was 'very lax' given that a 'Koil Tampuran was implicated in the case', so not only did Rama Rao instruct a more reliable man to join the inquiry, but by landing up personally, also prevented further bungling. To his horror he found that the police had omitted to inspect the murder scene and forgotten to examine witnesses, check for blood and other evidence on the clothes of the apprehended men and even to look for the knife that had wounded the victim.[127] Rao's resolve in correcting this impressed the Dewan, and at least some members of the royal family. As Visakham Tirunal wrote,

I regret much to hear of the occurrence of that murder at Mavelikarai. I trust this is the first instance in our memory of a man in the Koil Pandalay's [that is, Koil Tampuran's] rank having committed so heinous a crime and I hope the case will be dealt with as to make it the last.[128]

All along, meanwhile, the accused denied everything: he claimed that on the night of the crime it was so rainy he had not stirred at all from his room.[129] But this did not address the allegation that he was 'the chief instigator of the crime' and that 'the murder was planned and carried out . . . under his instructions'.[130] By the end of August it was reported, then, that the accessory who wielded the jackfruit was on death row, while his master was given twenty years of hard labour in prison.[131] The case passed through the court at Quilon, after which, on appeal, it was taken to Trivandrum. Here, in 1864, then, the sentence was modified: the husband of the Mavelikara lady would serve only simple imprisonment because 'a sentence of hard labour against a person of his position would be opposed to the usages of this state'.[132] Determined yet to clear his name, the Koil Tampuran next approached British higher-ups in Madras.[133] The case was laid before the advocate-general and a senior lawyer who decided, in a twist, that evidence categorically linking the maharajah's relative to the crime was inadequate; hereafter the man disappears from the record.[134] As for Rama Rao who had pursued the case, Visakham Tirunal (still heir apparent, and on poor terms with his brother, the maharajah) warned: 'Great intrigues are, I hear, going on here. The object of them is to get rid of you!'[135] While he survived, one wonders if the bureaucrat's all-too-keen effort to investigate a royal relative was a factor in delaying his rise to the Dewanship.

Notwithstanding coverage in the press, besides Rama Rao's biography, the whole episode is not mentioned in official histories. The reasons seem obvious. At first, during the investigation, *The Friend of India* noted, '[t]he Rajah's family' had stayed above board 'in spite of the disgrace they have suffered'.[136] Whether, as time passed, their attitude changed and the Dewan's influence with the Madras advocate-general – none other than his mentor J.B. Norton – played any role in easing the aristocrat's embarrassment is not known.[137] If something was done, it would not be wholly surprising, not just because of Visakham Tirunal's comment, but also due to the nature of the arrested man's relationship with the royal family: he was father to the two adopted ranis of the state, Lakshmi Bayi and Parvathi Bayi, and his wife who was slandered in the press, their mother.[138] In the future, their grandsons – including Asvathi Tirunal of our Introduction – would be in line to succeed as maharajahs, making it, arguably, in everyone's interest to forget the event altogether. Interestingly, this Mavelikara couple had a *third* daughter who would later herself wed a Koil Tampuran with a reputation; a painter from Kilimanoor who happened to carry the same name as her father. And so it was that Ravi Varma, the artist, became brother-in-law to the Travancore ranis – and son-in-law to the man held in the strange case of Mavelikara's jackfruit murder.

Ravi Varma was only in his teens when he married his adolescent wife. Her family too was of royal descent, though now in humbler circumstances. Their forebears were the Kolathiri rajahs of north Malabar – the house from which Travancore adopted girls whenever its matrilineage faced extinction. This was an ancient line, and all kinds of tales shroud its prehistory: in one story, the son of a legendary monarch called Cheraman Perumal by a north Indian princess is its founder, while another claims a pregnant queen, surviving a dreadful Puranic massacre, gave birth to the first Kolathiri prince in the dwelling of a cursed rat.[139] But origin myths aside, the fact is that the Kolathiris constituted an old lineage. North Malabar was their sovereign base, and a bond with Travancore was formed through the periodic supply of princesses into this southern line. Since then the families were closely allied, so that when Kolathiri possessions were seized by Hyder Ali and Tipu Sultan in the eighteenth century, it was to Travancore that they fled. And sanctuary was provided by the reigning maharajah, whose mother was herself a Kolathiri adoptee. After Tipu's defeat in 1792, while some of the family returned to Malabar, most elected to remain in Travancore as subjects of the maharajah. Here they were allotted pensions and other perquisites, making them first class dependants of the durbar.

Mavelikara was one of the residences allocated to these Kolathiri scions. Among these exiles, incidentally, was a princess who was mother to five girls. In 1788, when Travancore had no ranis to continue its royal line, it was her second and third daughters who were adopted. Indeed, all the nineteenth-century rulers of the state, including Ayilyam Tirunal and Visakham Tirunal, were descended from one of these princesses. Naturally, the mother and her three other girls stayed close to these neo-ranis: a circumstance that on the face of it was happy, but in actuality led to much intrigue. For as a Resident put it, the old lady was 'a woman of violent, profligate, and sordid character', with great ambition.[140] She allegedly resented her daughters who lived in state and pomp in Trivandrum; and becoming 'jealous of [their] superior dignity', launched a series of plots 'with a malignity and rancor that embittered her subsequent life'.[141] In the end, however, her intrigues failed: in the 1810s, when the British lieutenant B.S. Ward conducted a survey of Travancore, one of the highlights he recorded about Mavelikara was that it was home to this lady, who lived here as 'a prisoner in her own palace'.[142] And the person who kept her under restraint was her own grandchild, then head of the state.[143] When it came to power and politics, blood ties meant little – an attribute that was to affect the fortunes and lives of Ravi Varma's own descendants.

But despite their ancestress's misdeeds, the wider family did not suffer. On the contrary, when in 1857 adoption was necessitated again with the death of Ayilyam Tirunal's sister (who, as we saw, left no girl children), Lakshmi Bayi and her sibling – daughters of the alleged jackfruit murderer – were introduced into the dynasty. But when these ranis departed Mavelikara for the palace, they left behind a sister who would continue as non-royal: Kochupanki, a woman whose claim to fame is that she was Ravi Varma's wife.[144] It was in 1866, four years after the Mavelikara murder, that the artist married her and became brother-in-law to the Travancore ranis. But the union was unhappy and his long absences caused Kochupanki considerable distress. One anecdote encapsulates the turbulence in their marriage. Ravi Varma, sometime in the 1880s, by when he was famous, brought home a chandelier of Murano glass. 'When he arrived,' we read, 'he found that [Kochupanki] had gone to the temple. Wishing to give her a surprise, he had the

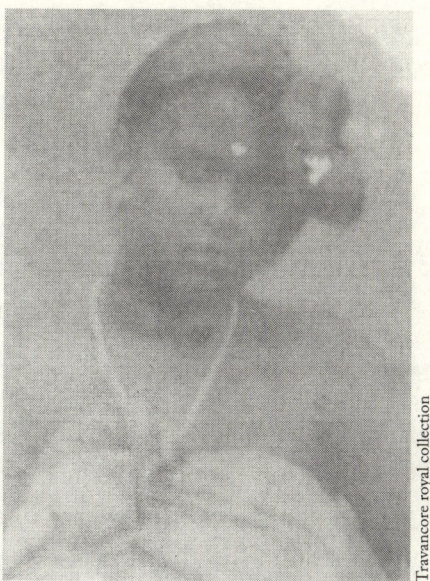

Travancore royal collection

Travancore royal collection

Ravi Varma's mother-in-law and his eldest daughter (left), and Ravi Varma's wife (right), Kochupanki. See plates section for their portraits by the artist.

chandelier hung and lit.' The attendants were told not to breathe a word, and the man went out, confident his wife would be delighted when she saw his gift. When she returned, however, '[a]ll her resentment welled up', and asking the servants to blow out the flames, she ordered the whole thing to be thrown out. Ravi Varma was furious and announced he would leave her. Hearing this, Kochupanki, the story goes, declared: 'All I want is you, not presents.'[145]

The reimagined dialogues aside, it was, simply put, a stormy marriage, and Kochupanki's was not a cheerful life. She lived not only in the shadow of her sisters, who had been exalted to royal status, but also a cloistered life in Mavelikara; her husband too, meanwhile, gravitated towards the court, in addition to which his unaristocratic vocation attracted comment.[146] Besides, as a descendant put it, Kochupanki was 'incompatible' with Ravi Varma, whose 'highly developed aesthetic sense and urges found no sympathy in her. She was exactly the opposite: a down-to-earth, plain, unimaginative woman while he took his sense of creativity to the heights of worship.' Where the 'play of light upon skin or leaf would send her husband into ecstasies', Kochupanki 'could not have cared less'.[147] While in the early years there was still hope, Ravi Varma's ambition and subcontinental peregrinations meant that his wife grew increasingly lonely: by the time she died in 1891, only in her thirties, she was, a nephew wrote, 'addicted to drink'.[148] Ravi Varma was remorseful on receiving news of her demise, but did not hasten back, leaving his children to turn their mother to ashes by themselves.

Ravi Varma did, however, commemorate his wife with his brush. Throughout his career, the artist produced many portraits of his relations. While his sisters-in-law were among his patrons, sketches, watercolours and oils were also executed of his wife and children. In Kochupanki's painting, for example, her features, curiously enough, acquire a gentle quality, for the woman we see in the odd photograph looks unlike this incarnation. The difference is less stark, however, in the magnificent painting Ravi Varma did of his mother-in-law, the woman at the centre of that 1862 scandal. For a man who would promote a new notion of feminine Indian beauty – with pale skin, docility and delicate features – Kochupanki's mother presents a contradiction. To begin with, she was so dark that he sat her against a white wall on a marble plinth for a manageable contrast. In the portrait her eyes are bloodshot, and she glares down a bulbous nose, her hair yellowy white and her shawl blazing red. For a woman defamed once, her face bears not even a hint of embarrassment: she is uncompromisingly herself, and issues, instead, a challenge to the viewer. In her hands are *rudraksha* beads, something of a standard prop for elders, but it does little to dim the power she radiates. Where her daughter, Rani Lakshmi Bayi, came to symbolize new ideals of virtue and femininity, as we saw, this lady is emblematic of the matrilineal system and the authority it could offer women.

This is especially interesting given that Ravi Varma generally presented matrilineal women in a softer tone, more pleasing to Victorian viewers. His own daughter, Mahaprabha (1872–1919), for example, features in a famous work, *There Comes Papa* (1892). Described as 'a high-spirited and dignified lady of remarkable personality',[149] she was a woman with a temper that even her husband took care not to offend. Photographs confirm a demeanour that was anything but sweet, Mahaprabha having inherited her grandmother's penetrating gaze. And yet in her father's depiction – shown in America and through countless prints since – she is more beauty and grace than strength and personality. The very title which has mother and child await the husband/father is telling, as the scholar G. Arunima has observed, of the shift in local society where the *patriarchal* family was now advertised as more modern. In welcoming this, Ravi Varma was not alone: three years before, O. Chandu Menon had published his iconic novel *Indulekha* in which the protagonist, Madhavi, stands up to an array of 'backward' matrilineal practices: she is devoted to one man, who becomes her husband; has the graces and cultivation of English ladies; does not talk politics; and her virtue is spotless by Victorian standards. Ravi Varma's *There Comes Papa* is in a way a visualization of *Indulekha*'s message: its Mahaprabha is not real, but an idea embodied.[150]

But while Ravi Varma painted away, his troubled marriage left repercussions on his children's lives, and on Travancore's history. To begin with, his sons did not live up to expectations. The older, Kerala Varma (1876–c.1912), 'belying much promise, turned a profligate' and simply disappeared in his thirties.[151] The younger, Rama Varma (1879–1970), went to art school in Bombay, hoping to carry on his father's legacy, but never managed to scale any heights.[152] The artist's *daughters*, however, attained a refracted eminence. Ravi Varma and Kochupanki had three girls, the first two of whom were spirited.[153] Following Kochupanki's untimely death, nineteen-year-old Mahaprabha assumed the role of family head. Imperious and beautiful, she was an object of awe: her father is said to have used Mahaprabha's face as a template for his goddesses. Meanwhile, the equally able second girl, Kochukunji (1878–1946),[154] seems to have been dissatisfied with her place. It also appears to have affected Kochukunji that she was not, like Mahaprabha, a looker. On the contrary, with a squint and increasingly unfashionable dark skin, she was deemed less attractive. The sisters also harboured an unspoken rivalry in the 1890s, for their aunts adopted into the royal family had no daughters: if these two nieces in Mavelikara

Mahaprabha (left) in a detail from There Comes Papa, *and Kochukunji (right, seen with her husband).*

produced girls, *those* babies could be parachuted as the next ranis of Travancore.

In fact, this rise of Ravi Varma's descendants to royal status is quite the story. In 1894, Rani Lakshmi Bayi took Mahaprabha and Kochukunji on a pilgrimage to Ramesvaram to wash off their sins and pray for girls. In one tale, she has a vision at the temple, while in a second, she is assured her wishes via a dream. Either way, she got what she wanted: in the winter of 1895 Mahaprabha gave birth to a female child, and a year later Kochukunji brought forth her own. Their adoption exercised minds even outside family circles: old Seshiah Sastri, writing from retirement, for example, told the rani of a dream he had, in which he saw 'two young angelic princesses'.[155] And once the girls grew a little, in 1899, the rani asked the ruler to proceed with their adoption. The children were 'old enough to be properly educated and trained to follow the royal etiquette', Lakshmi Bayi wrote, and so, '[t]o propagate your family, brother, we request you to get this thing done'.[156] Ravi Varma's granddaughters were on their way to becoming princesses; in the court which he entered as a country aristocrat, seeking colour and paint, girls of his blood would now sit at its head.

But if the maharajah personally was amenable, another individual objected, warning of discord. The heir apparent, who was Asvathi Tirunal's brother, not only highlighted Kochupanki's drinking habit as a point against the children, but also the existence of cancer in their family. But just as importantly, it was by now clear that there was no love lost between Ravi Varma's daughters; and given that the girls proposed for adoption were *their* children, he feared they would import ill-feeling with them. Or as the prince explained: 'These babies are the children of two mothers, and each will exert a most deleterious influence on the peace of the family.'[157] He preferred adopting natural sisters, writing officially to the Resident.[158] But Lakshmi Bayi, no novice at durbar politics, got her way: she persuaded the ruler, canvassed the clique that had influence over him and bore her nephew's insult. It is also said that Ravi Varma put in a word with the viceroy, using his own social capital.[159] Timing proved to be critical, for this – ensuring the future of the royal line – was to be the rani's final accomplishment. Shortly after the adoption in 1900, Asvathi Tirunal died,[160] months after which, the defiant (and diabetic) heir apparent passed away.[161] The shock of these tragedies was too much for a simultaneously ailing (and also diabetic) rani, and on 15 June 1901 Lakshmi Bayi followed. As her husband, the grieving Kerala Varma, diarized: 'My angel, my life, my darling, my all and all, my pride, my idol, my sweetheart – alas! and what not – expired quietly at 8 PM.'[162]

The result was that Ravi Varma's granddaughters were not only transformed into royalty, they also overnight became the only female members in the House of Travancore. While formally under Kerala Varma's guardianship, with the old rani gone, the chief female influences in their lives remained – as was forewarned – their mothers. And Mahaprabha and Kochukunji's quarrels meant that the young ranis never bonded as sisters; they remained *cousins* and at a distance. It did not help that they had no friends either, and only family networks to fall back on: as the older child would recount, 'It was a time of great intrigues and conspiracies and they feared the influence of other factions.'[163] Of course, a governess was appointed, they went out on drives, took music classes and toured the country together as senior and junior ranis. When a governor of Madras visited, they stood together and recited poetry praising the British king.[164] But looming in the background was that tension between their mothers and a variance of interests. After all, whichever one of them produced a male child first would give Travancore its next ruler. And so, friction between Ravi Varma's two daughters slowly aggravated into a political contest between *their* children; what began with family jealousies mutated into something that would have historical consequences.

The weddings of both ranis in 1906 and 1907 respectively added fresh flies to the ointment. In the elder rani Sethu Lakshmi Bayi's case, two nephews of Kerala Varma were shown. Everyone preferred the older boy, so handsome and well built that Ravi Varma had him pose for his *Sri Rama Vanquishing the Sea* (1904). But the senior rani chose the other. It was to be a long marriage, and her retiring personality allowed her husband tremendous ascendancy: by the 1910s, the maharajah was upset that he was 'advising his wife in all matters', besides doing such bad things as sitting down in her presence.[165] The senior rani, meanwhile, seemed to care more for her duty as a wife than pulling rank; she was, in some ways, torn between patriarchal expectations and her matrilineal position. Where her mother Mahaprabha posed for *There Comes Papa*, then, the daughter embraced its message.[166] In the 1920s, in fact, when Sethu Lakshmi Bayi was in power, even her Dewan grew frustrated. He complained that the consort prevented papers from reaching the rani,[167] and referred to him as the 'boudoir Dewan'.[168] While the British found claims of the rani being under her husband's thumb overstated,[169] his strong personality didn't help his own case: a British tutor compared him to a 'sly-faced babu in European dress'. 'I did not like him', the man wrote, though the rani was 'very striking', 'with a delicate, beautiful face, and shy manner'.[170]

Ravi Varma's younger granddaughter, Sethu Parvathi Bayi, meanwhile, selected one of five candidates sent her – sadly her pick was a dozen years older, this age gap unconducive to harmony. Where

Ravi Varma's granddaughters Sethu Lakshmi Bayi (left) and Sethu Parvathi Bayi (right), as children, and (below) after their marriages.

she was gregarious, unorthodox, dynamic and ambitious, her consort had, in a contemporary's words, 'no social graces and no wish to acquire them'.[171] He was so conservative that he would not shake hands with women at the fashionable parties she attended, and to a Resident had the personality of a 'worm'.[172] When he did show pluck, it could do damage: in the 1920s, there was a scandal after the man accused a musician of 'undue familiarity' with the junior rani.[173] Neither woman, arguably then, had peace thanks to her husband: where the senior's consort had such a high profile that it generated resentment, the junior's incompatibility with hers caused a different kind of pain.[174] Indeed, one of the reasons their own relations worsened was this issue of their men. As the British recorded, the senior rani's husband, early on, started avoiding the junior, 'as he was afraid she might treat him in the same casual manner as . . . her own husband', and keep him 'standing in her presence'.[175] As royalty she outranked him. However, being the *senior* rani's consort, he was unhappy bowing to the junior. These questions of protocol grew into major quarrels,[176] till a Resident observed: 'Nothing will terminate the feud' between senior consort and junior rani 'but the death of one of them'.[177]

The divide, in fact, had gathered steam from the ranis' teens. Though married at ten, the girls only met their husbands for games of hopscotch or to read fairy tales; only some years later were the unions consummated. This immediately triggered a race to produce the heir: the senior rani got pregnant first but lost the baby. In 1912, then, the junior rani gave birth to a prince – Ravi Varma's great-grandson, and Travancore's final maharajah – which at once raised her status. Hitherto as *junior* rani, she had been in her cousin's shadow. Now, however, her infant was the heir, which gave her access not only to a separate establishment, but also to greater public standing. Acolytes fanned hostility: the senior rani heard whispers that her miscarriages were of human design, while the junior rani was so protective of her baby that she policed all access to him.[178] Letters show Mahaprabha, whose pride was proverbial, facing barbs about her daughter's incapacity to deliver.[179] At the same time, Kochukunji began to shine: she was no longer Ravi Varma's cockeyed, neglected middle daughter but a future king's grandmother. In 1916, the junior rani gave birth to a female child and six years later a second boy, cementing her status. The senior rani, however, had to go through a variety of treatments before finally, approaching thirty, she gave birth to the first of two girls. By then, however, Mahaprabha was dead – the proud dame never got to see any royal grandchildren.

Soon the ranis were leading separate lives, Sethu Lakshmi Bayi and her husband marginalized at court as well. This was not only because of the senior rani's 'barren' phase, but also because of her disapproval of the maharajah's coterie. The ruler – Ayilyam Tirunal and Visakham Tirunal's nephew – was in the hands of his second wife's first husband. This favourite was not to be taken lightly: in Ravi Varma's brother's diaries, while there is carping about his reach,[180] the artist was also careful to present his work to him.[181] The man was too mighty, with the British noting his 'backdoor influence'.[182] So, when the senior rani and her consort rubbed him the wrong way, they were cornered. To the couple the royal henchman's corruption was abhorrent; but by snubbing him, they turned the most powerful man around into an enemy.[183] After Kerala Varma, their only sympathizer, died in 1914, the alienation was complete – the establishment limited Sethu Lakshmi Bayi's time with her natural family, inflicted harassment and made the rani unwelcome at court. A shrewder mind might have been more diplomatic, but the young woman would not relent. Sethu Parvathi Bayi, on the other hand, was a smarter politician – not only was the favourite carefully dealt with,[184] but the maharajah's daughter was also married to the junior rani's brother. If as heir apparent's mother Sethu Parvathi Bayi's future was secure, being sister-in-law to the Ammachi's daughter smoothed the present.[185]

But then, in 1924, the ruler died, and Sethu Parvathi Bayi's older son – Ravi Varma's great-grandson – was declared maharajah. However, given that the boy, Chithira Tirunal, was only twelve, he would have to wait some years to rule. And here, matriliny allowed Sethu Lakshmi Bayi a window of glory: as per custom, in the absence of an adult male, power vested in the dynasty's eldest *female* member. So, while the junior rani's son marked time, the senior became regent. Much was accomplished:

revenues rose, investment in infrastructure and education was widened to record highs and the rani impressed everyone from the viceroy, Lord Irwin, to Gandhi. Knowledge that her time at the helm was limited meant she exerted herself to an uncommon degree, to leave a mark. In this she succeeded: in 1929, she was made a member of the Order of the Crown of India, with the viceroy paying her rich tributes.[186] But politically Travancore was a tinderbox: the junior rani's partisans ran hostile press campaigns, quarrels broke out about money and there was even a bizarre episode where the junior rani's palace hosted black magicians – an event, featuring the sacrifice of rats, that shocked everyone up to the viceroy.[187] Outside too there was heat: where the old maharajah sided with the orthodox Hindu element, Sethu Lakshmi Bayi's regime came to be seen as pro-Christian.[188] So for all the encomiums she won, when the regency closed, the senior rani was again cornered.

Interestingly, one of the key witnesses to the feud between the two ranis was a British officer called G.T.B. Harvey.[189] Tutor to the boy maharajah, Harvey also maintained a diary where he minced no words about Travancore's royal drama. He was, of course, a white interloper, and his views are coloured; but insofar as the tension between Sethu Lakshmi Bayi and Sethu Parvathi Bayi is concerned, he offers an uncensored record of what was said and heard in high places, even attacking the Raj's blunders. To begin with, Harvey found that while the state was 'very rich', the ruling house, unlike opulent counterparts in the north, was 'd—d careful' about spending money. Society, meanwhile, was 'terribly religionized'.[190] At court, Harvey was enamoured of no one: if the senior rani's austerity impressed Gandhi, Harvey found it irritating. It was impossible, for instance, to obtain decent horses for his ward,[191] and even the Dewan complained of bad pay.[192] The regent herself, he observed, was 'charming' but 'utterly uninteresting',[193] while her consort was 'hated and feared'.[194] The consort's feud with the junior rani was also noted: Sethu Parvathi Bayi apparently told Harvey how she always kept an eye on her son's food, 'for fear of the other palace',[195] while he himself was amazed that in eighteen months Sethu Lakshmi Bayi and the maharajah saw each other only once.[196] For all practical

The 1924 durbar at which Sethu Lakshmi Bayi became regent of Travancore, while her minor nephew was installed as maharajah.

purposes, aunt and nephew were strangers; theirs was not one family but two feuding houses.

In what is amusing, this animosity was never openly exhibited. Once, the maharajah's mother ran into the regent in the temple – they 'smiled at each other and talked sweet nothings', as if all was well, with the senior rani offering her cousin a lift.[197] When the viceroy was to visit in 1929, there was a battle on whether the regent or the boy should have precedence; so much for seeking higher rank, in the end when the senior rani came to the banquet she was so shy she stood in the middle of the room, unable to talk to anyone.[198] So too when the regent won an imperial honour, the more socially active junior rani found people mistaking *her* as its recipient. At a party, 'half a dozen' people congratulated her, Harvey chuckled, while she 'thanked each of them, and never let on [that] it was her hated cousin' who had earned the distinction.[199] Indeed, the junior rani's yearning to shine offered some droll moments: Harvey wrote how her son, wishing to show himself to his people once, got out of their car. But the crowd, keen to look inside the limousine, 'missed the little Maharajah walking in front' while his mother, seated within, 'bowed and smiled graciously', enjoying the moment.[200] Gossip was coolly catalogued: the ranis' old governess told Harvey that 'in the Palace whenever the Regent wishes to . . . disagree with [her consort], the latter now says . . . he'll commit suicide'.[201] While it is difficult to picture the senior rani's husband threatening self-liquidation, the story hints at tensions.[202]

But Harvey's worst was reserved for Sethu Parvathi Bayi's mother, Kochukunji, in describing whom he descended to venomous name-calling. For many years, the lady had been a force in the royal household. The late Kerala Varma had spoken of her growing 'insolence',[203] and in the 1920s, fingers were pointed by others in the family too. The junior rani's husband blamed Kochukunji for his marital difficulties, thus, and after she was charged as prime instigator in the bizarre black magic incident, the viceroy banished her to Mavelikara.[204] Indeed, a British agent labelled Kochukunji and her children a 'thoroughly bad lot' who ought to be kept away for good.[205] In Harvey's mind, two brothers of

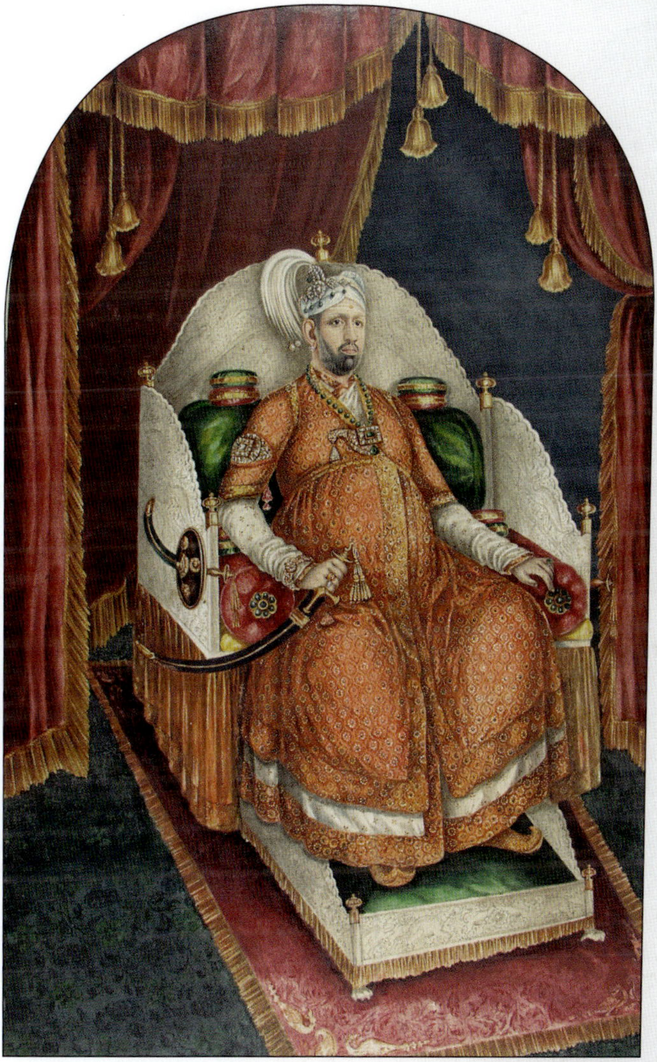

Harvard Art Museums / Arthur M. Sackler Museum, The Stuart Cary Welch Collection, Gift of Edith I. Welch in memory of Stuart Cary Welch. Photo © President and Fellows of Harvard College

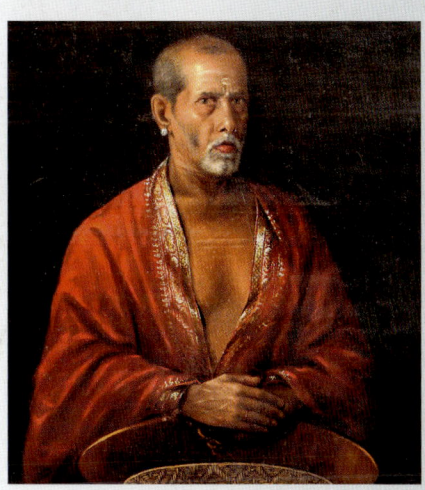

Uthram Tirunal of Travancore (1814–60) was an endearing, most colourful Anglophile prince, though wedded equally to traditional ideas of Hindu kingship. His struggle to manage these seemingly contradictory impulses would set off Travancore's proactive effort to 'modernize' in the colonial period and, by so doing, reduce imperial interference to a minimum – a strategy several maharajahs appropriated to survive British imperialism.

The Sree Chitra Art Gallery, Thiruvananthapuram

Rajaraja Varma of Kilimanoor (1813–84), Ravi Varma's maternal uncle, was a courtier to Uthram Tirunal and a talented artist who painted in traditional styles, including on ivory. It was through him that Ravi Varma obtained royal patronage at the Travancore durbar, and became the Ravi Varma we know – a visual chronicler of late Victorian India.

Ayilyam Tirunal of Travancore (1832–80) was Ravi Varma's first major patron, seen here in a state portrait by the artist. As ruler Ayilyam Tirunal proved an energetic modernizer and, joining forces with able, English-educated ministers, learnt to beat the British at their own game of 'progress'.

His nephew Mulam Tirunal (1857–1924) – a less enthusiastic supporter of Ravi Varma – was not quite as gifted, and his several weaknesses would open the door again for colonial interference. Interestingly, Mulam Tirunal was succeeded on his death by Ravi Varma's own granddaughter, Maharani Sethu Lakshmi Bayi of Travancore.

In 1870 Ravi Varma painted the family of a British-appointed judge in Calicut called Kizhakkepat Krishna Menon, in what was his first paid commission outside the Travancore court. Menon was father-in-law to the future Congress President Sir C. Sankaran Nair. By the end of his career, Ravi Varma would be on friendly terms with both 'moderate' Congress leaders like G.K. Gokhale and 'extremists' like B.G. Tilak.

Maharajah Visakham Tirunal of Travancore (1837–85), seen here receiving a British governor of Madras in 1880, was an amateur botanist, industrialist and writer. Popular with the Raj, he was held up as a positive example of the effect of Western education on otherwise backward Indian royalty, even if his zeal to 'reform' and leave a mark at times led to blunders. He was unfriendly towards Ravi Varma, who left the Travancore durbar in Visakham Tirunal's reign.

Its commercial value notwithstanding, this painting also fared badly. In The Pioneer dated 29 March 1881 one critic claimed that the only good thing about this 'gaudy', 'reprehensible' work was 'the cocoanut trees in the background'.

Ramachandra Tondaiman of Pudukkottai (1829–86) was the ruler of a small Tamil state, where Ravi Varma received a commission in the 1870s. The rajah was a misfit in late-nineteenth-century Indian politics – he spoke English with charm, but was unable to marshal up a formula for 'progress' unlike his peers in Travancore. The result was that the Raj drained away power from the palace, and appointed a minister of its liking. Tondaiman's caste background also meant, however, that, besides colonial pressures to transform and bureaucratize the administration, his family had to satisfy the expectations of an English-educated Indian minister to Sanskritize and Brahminize, at the cost of their own distinct identity and seemingly anachronistic political traditions.

Rani Janaki of Pudukkottai was a woman of tremendous spirit, and the second wife of Ramachandra Tondaiman. Not only did she resist colonial machinations, she also attempted (unsuccessfully) to thwart the Raj-appointed minister in his efforts to redefine kingship in the state.

In response, the British and the minister limited Janaki's influence over her husband's heir, Martanda Bhairava Tondaiman (1875–1928), instead placing him under a white tutor and encouraging an English education. The scheme backfired – when the boy grew up, he proved a bad ruler, married an Australian and eventually abandoned his state to seek his personal happiness. The British had turned him into a white man in all but complexion, and would rue the mistake.

In 1881 Ravi Varma travelled to Baroda in western India to paint its Maratha maharajah. Sayaji Rao Gaekwad (1863–1939) was, like many other princes, raised under the nose of the British, and carefully tutored to be loyal. But as it happened, he proved his own man, who cultivated contacts with nationalists, radical intellectuals and even revolutionaries. Among the most unpopular of Indian princes as far as the colonial establishment was concerned, he was a hero to the Congress (which he funded) and is proof of how maharajahs had enough power to actively subvert British interests. Incidentally, one of his granddaughters would in time be briefly considered as a wife for Ravi Varma's great-grandson – not something Sayaji Rao would have thought ever likely when he first met the painter.

During his stints in Baroda, Ravi Varma also painted women of that court, including Chimnabai I (right), Sayaji Rao's beloved first wife from Tanjore, and Tarabai, the maharajah's sister (below).

Though the Raj frowned on 'native' princesses exerting any influence over brown princes, as with Rani Janaki in Pudukkottai, in Baroda its maharanis were able and politically astute women. Tarabai's mother, Jamnabai, for example, was a force to reckon with, in the 1870s joining forces with the British to topple the then maharajah.

Raja Sir T. Madhava Rao was a Marathi Brahmin who served successively as Dewan (minister) of Travancore, Indore and Baroda. A lion's share of the success in making these principalities 'model states' – with sound financial management, infrastructure, modern bureaucracies and much else – rests with him, though his relations with his royal masters soured in direct proportion to his own growing prominence. Rao appears here in a posthumous painting by Ravi Varma, and was the most famous 'native statesman' of his time. Though a hero to many Victorian Indians, by the twentieth century Rao's legacy was challenged and, like the artist, he was relegated to a lower place in public esteem.

Chamarajendra Wadiyar (1863–94) was maharajah of Mysore, seen here in the mid–1880s as painted by Ravi Varma. Along with his minister, C.V. Rangacharlu, he would place Mysore on the path to administrative success, responding to the Raj's stereotypes about 'natives' by ambitiously seeking industrial glory. Mysore was almost annexed by the Raj in Chamarajendra's predecessor's reign, and his accession to its throne is a story that tells of complex, layered negotiations between princes and the British, treaty rights, law and legality, political lobbying and plain old-fashioned duplicity.

Ravi Varma was commissioned to paint for the Mysore durbar by two generations of its princes. Here he depicts Chamarajendra's son, Krishnaraja IV (1884–1940), with his Rajput wife – a union with its own interesting caste politics. The young maharajah reigned nearly forty years, and took Mysore to the heights of success, though ultimately political turmoil would convulse the state. In the photograph (right), the maharajah appears in the late 1920s, interacting with a teenaged ruler called Chithira Tirunal – Ravi Varma's great-grandson and the last maharajah of Travancore.

Maharana Fateh Singh of Mewar (Udaipur) (1849–1930) was one of the grandest, most old-world figures Ravi Varma painted in a princely universe dominated by 'progressive' rulers. Fateh Singh, who resisted everything from the English language to Western modes of governance, harnessed his status among Rajputs to keep the British at a distance. Indeed, he even dispensed with the services of his minister, Rai Pannalal Mehta (right), suspected of being too comfortable with Western modernity and more loyal to the Raj than to him. A shrewd ruler, Fateh Singh's charisma and aura worked wonders – until peasant and tribal resistance unsettled Mewar and ultimately divested him of authority.

The Sree Chitra Art Gallery, Thiruvananthapuram

Kerala Varma Valiya Koil Tampuran (1845–1914) was a Malayalam writer and Sanskrit scholar, popularly called the Kalidas of Kerala. Ravi Varma's brother-in-law, he maintained contacts not only with leading nationalist thinkers like R.C. Dutt, but also with the who's who of the Raj, besides suffering the consequences of his own misadventures. He appears below in a photograph from later years, posing with Ravi Varma's infant granddaughter – the future Maharani Sethu Lakshmi Bayi of Travancore (1895–1985).

The Sree Chitra Art Gallery, Thiruvananthapuram

Rani Lakshmi Bayi of Travancore (1848–1901) was Ravi Varma's sister-in-law and rani of Travancore in the late-nineteenth century. She was seen to embody Victorian ideals of femininity and virtue, and was decorated by Queen Victoria for fitting a new colonial template for royal women. She appears on the left in a photograph, posing with Ravi Varma's two granddaughters, who were adopted as her heirs into the matrilineal Travancore dynasty. It was through this adoption that the artist's descendants were themselves transformed into royalty, in a land where their grandfather had begun as a court painter and dependant.

Ravi Varma, besides his portraits of maharajahs, did a number of paintings of his family. The older lady here is his mother-in-law, Mahaprabha Tampuratti of Mavelikara. For a man who helped popularize fair skin and coy feminine beauty, this work stands out for its powerful contrast. Additionally, though unrecorded by all his biographers, Mahaprabha Tampuratti was embroiled in a scandal in 1862 when her husband – the artist's father-in-law – was named in a murder case. The couple's youngest daughter, Kochupanki (right), married Ravi Varma in 1866. It was not a happy marriage and would affect the lives of their children and, later, their royal grandchildren in the Travancore palace.

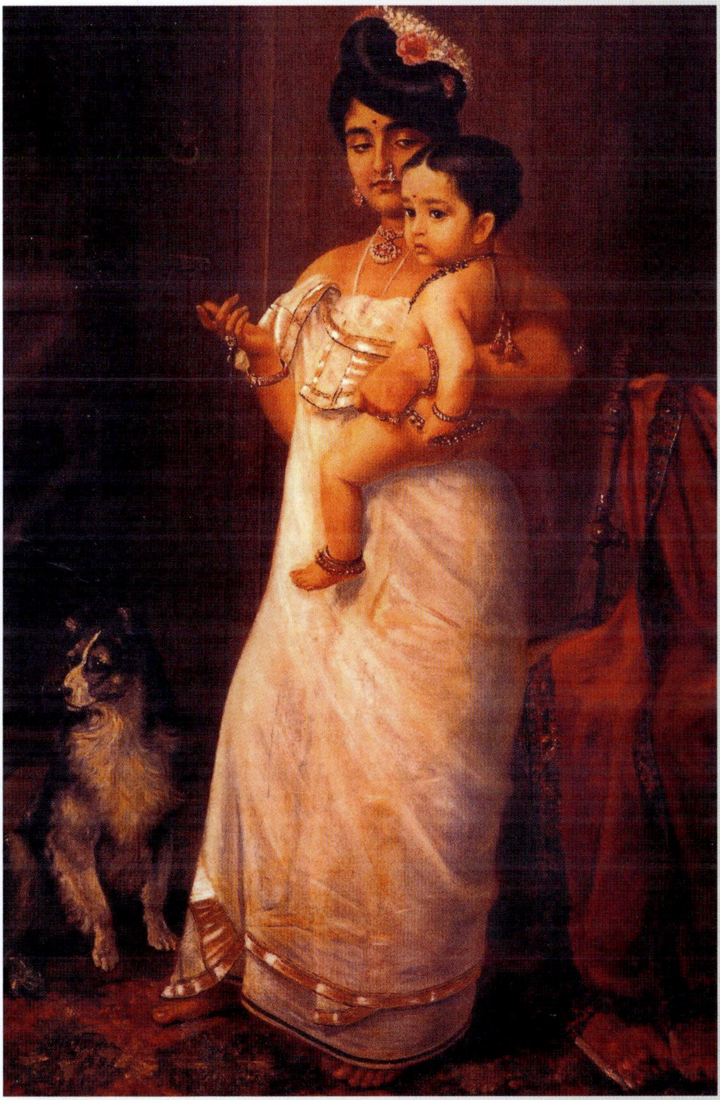

Currently in the Travancore royal collection

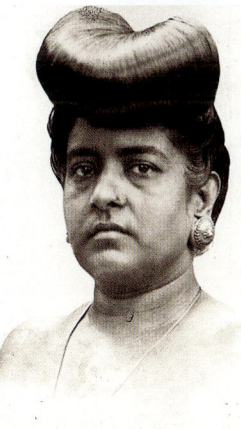

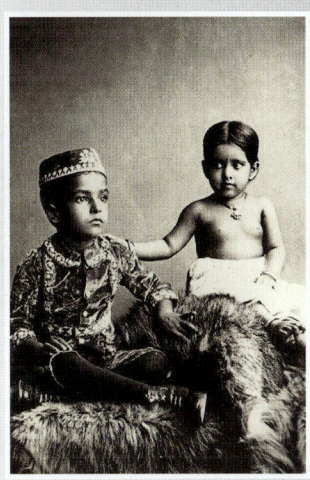

Ravi Varma's daughter, also named Mahaprabha, poses here in his famous There Comes Papa. *A celebrated beauty and a lady of personality, her face was often used by the artist for his goddesses and celestial beauties. In the photograph on the left, we see Mahaprabha approaching middle age, while on the right appear her two older children – R. Martanda Varma, the baby boy featured in* There Comes Papa, *and Maharani Sethu Lakshmi Bayi of Travancore.*

Ravi Varma's posthumous 1948 portrait by his son, Rama Varma. The artist had become, by the time of his death, key witness to a fascinating world, with its prominent princes, nascent nationalism and 'native statesmen'. Contemporaneous with his demise, however, this world began to make way for a new, more restless one – within decades the princes, once allies of the nationalists, came to be seen as villains, and princely India was denied legitimacy in the country's post-colonial, democratic future.

the junior rani in particular were 'budmashes', with one of them of such 'hopeless' morals that he had to formally ask the chap to leave the palace.[206] Allegedly, these uncles had 'a set policy of making themselves indispensable to H.H. [the maharajah] and of acquiring overpowering influence' for the future, but their mother was 'worse, in practically every respect'.[207] The 'old witch', meanwhile, returned the favour, wearing a 'diabolical and persistent scowl' whenever she set eyes on Harvey.[208] In the end, of course, Kochukunji would return after her grandson came of age, hovering in the background till her death in the 1940s. It was an eventful innings for Ravi Varma's second daughter: from being less than equal to her sister, the underdog ended her days in a palace, watching her line wield royal power.

To be clear, Harvey's railing against the maharajah's relatives' attempt to control him omits that the British were just as keen to 'shape' the boy. Indeed, the junior rani's descendants cast *Harvey* as a 'dangerous' enemy and 'harbinger of ill-fortune'. Evidently, he went so far as to threaten and beat the maharajah and plotted with the regent.[209] Harvey's diaries, however, suggest something different: his comments on the senior rani's husband are negative, and his interaction with them was minimal. In fact, both the junior rani and the maharajah are often praised, till Kochukunji's intrigues revised his opinion. Sethu Parvathi Bayi, thus, is described as 'extraordinarily well educated', 'capable', 'keen on [her son], and the place he holds in the hearts of Travancoreans' and 'broadminded'. Why, even her extravagance was forgivable given that she had taste.[210] When she did go overboard, Harvey thought it was because she was 'in the toils of her family'.[211] 'I personally think,' he wrote, 'she is only *evil* when they [Kochukunji and relatives] put her up to it.'[212] So too with the boy, the tutor saw much to admire: he was 'industrious and methodical', his general bearing was 'excellent'; he had 'good morals'; showed no excessive tastes like 'drinking, spending'; and, in what was a useful quality in princes, gave 'nothing away by expression'.[213] This was not to say he was perfect: he could lie 'glibly', was 'unforgiving over disproportionately small matters', 'suspicious' and blamed all 'ill fortune' on others, shirking responsibility for his own actions.[214] But these negatives were not exaggerated: Harvey seems only to suggest that the maharajah had a good side and bad, both.

Importantly, however, Harvey was aware that he was not entirely welcome in Travancore. In his diaries we often read about Brahmins scowling at him, unhappy at the Englishman's role in their semi-divine king's life. But they needn't have worried, for the junior rani's son was not entirely of plastic frame. While it is apparent that his mother had a powerful hold over him, what appears to have independently shaped him was religion. Twice, in fact, the maharajah rowed with his teacher, accusing him of trying to 'anglicise' him.[215] Harvey begged him to be frank whenever he had such concerns, but the would-be ruler remained suspicious. In fact, Harvey once wrote of his feeling that the maharajah was merely waiting 'till our control is out of the way' to be who he *wanted* to be, instead of what the Raj expected of him.[216] After the tutor alerted the authorities to such events as black magic in the palace, when the ruler was separated from his mother in the name of 'training' elsewhere, the maharajah shut himself off completely. Harvey wrote how the boy went through his routine, but without enthusiasm.[217] The only times he showed excitement was in the company of his staff – who were Malayalis – or when relating fantastic stories, such as of a powerful Brahmin who turned metal bullets into water.[218] While Harvey disapproved of both the menials and superstition, there was not much he could do: when his back was turned the maharajah did as he pleased.

It was also not like British efforts to end the junior rani's influence over her son paid dividends either. Yes, the maharajah took advantage of distance from his mother to defy some orders – like not cutting off that tuft of hair, the *kudumi*, worn by orthodox Hindus[219] – but despite official limits on her access to him, he managed to stay in touch. A family friend, for example, is said to have smuggled letters to the maharajah, unknown to the tutor, thus subverting the very point of placing him under Raj-approved influences.[220] Meanwhile, the junior rani was also making moves to be reunited with her son. When at first separated from him, Harvey found her in a gloomy state. 'We sat for a minute or so, saying nothing, while she began to weep silently'.[221] It was, if the recollection is accurate, a rare instance of the junior rani showing herself as vulnerable. But soon she resumed her fight. And assisting her was a gifted Madras lawyer, Sir C.P. Ramaswami Iyer, destined to become one of the most memorable Dewans of Travancore, and in Harvey's words, a 'clever snake'.[222] Where the authorities had been consistently hostile to the junior rani so far, this man would help her win the ear of the viceroy, reversing years of imperial policy to give her what she wanted.

Many of the junior rani's grievances against her cousin, the regent, had lacked substance, while her own doings, ranging from hiring lobbyists to seeking sympathy in the press, had provoked stern words from the Raj. Meanwhile, despite political agitation, the regency was popular, delivering material benefits to the people. In 1929 the viceroy paid it a compliment by stating that the senior rani had delivered 'the highest proportion of advancement' in all the state's history – and this just as the junior rani submitted another petition.[223] The modernization Ravi Varma's first patron, Ayilyam Tirunal, set off in the 1860s was taken, that is, to new highs by his granddaughter. For Sethu Parvathi Bayi, though, this was all trying: as a contemporary put it, 'that her quiet, retiring and orthodox cousin became Regent was a bitter blow to her; that she won the love and respect of her people was still more bitter'.[224] Successive Residents backed the senior rani: one went so far as to say that the junior's fear was that her son would recognize the 'greater virtues of his aunt', and relegate his mother to the background.[225] To top it, in 1927, the junior rani was told that, due to a new policy, her son would *not* come to power at eighteen but at nineteen and a half, thus extending the regency.[226] It was at this juncture that C.P. entered the picture as her latest promoter, who besides helping draft petitions, physically went to London. It did not work, and the Madras man may well have become the latest in a series of failed lobbyists. But then, in 1931, there was a change.

That summer, Irwin was replaced by Lord Willingdon as viceroy. The two could not have been more unlike each other, showing how much colonial policy depended on personalities. Irwin, for example, authoritatively declared that India would attain dominion status, that

Sethu Parvathi Bayi with her son in 1933.

Rama Varma, consort to the senior rani.

Maharajah Chithira Tirunal, Ravi Varma's great-grandson and the last ruler of Travancore.

Sethu Lakshmi Bayi with her daughter.

is, freedom within the empire, on the lines of Canada or Australia. Willingdon, a reactionary imperialist, was determined to reverse this. Irwin came to terms with Gandhi and signed a 'pact' to put the Raj and nationalists on the same page, only for Willingdon to tear it all up.[227] Travancore was among the apple carts the new viceroy turned over – and this at C.P.'s intervention. The two men were friends from Willingdon's time as governor of Madras years ago, and tales circulated about the lawyer's influence with the viceroy's wife.[228] In any case, C.P.'s access to the highest offices of the Raj aided the junior rani. Harvey was asked to bring up her son, and after an interview, the viceroy decided he could be given his powers without further ado, cutting the regency by nine months. The decision shocked his own officials: the Resident warned that the senior rani, who had 'given her best' would feel her 'face has been blackened'.[229] Meanwhile, the deputy political secretary told Harvey 'very bitterly' that C.P. had convinced Willingdon through the vicereine.[230] In succumbing, the deputy added, the viceroy had been 'disloyal' to his own officers.[231] The senior political secretary was 'just as hopeless',[232] and it was confirmed that 'from his first coming, [Willingdon] had intended to give' the maharajah his powers.[233] He had not read the files, and not obtained a briefing from his underlings.[234] C.P.'s influence had won the day.

In a fascinating way, this was a reversal of prejudices. In princely India, as stated before, the British made a great point of frowning on female influence. They often made clear 'the bad effects of yielding to the caprices of females' who claimed a 'right to interfere' in government; it was 'the duty of the paramount power to free' native princes from the 'thralldom' of royal women.[235] It is a funny little twist, then, that when Sethu Parvathi Bayi, through her agent, finally succeeded in pushing her agenda, it was not through petitions or formal mechanisms of the Raj, but by using her own 'backdoor' influence: the viceroy's wife. As she announced to Harvey, the whole episode would have 'far-reaching repercussions', giving the British pause in future while separating princes from their mothers.[236] The system had been against her, but thanks to Willingdon and his lady, victory was at hand.

Thus, in late 1931, Sethu Lakshmi Bayi's regency ended, leaving her, as the Resident reported, 'gravely hurt'.[237] Her future was dire, for till the state merged with the independent Indian Union, the junior rani and her son would dominate it, with C.P. their loyal servant. In fact, as early as 1924 a Resident had warned that the maharajah's mother was counting the days for 'la revanche' (revenge).[238] And after 1931 this was slowly dished out. To begin with, it took a Herculean effort to have the maharajah grant his aunt a dignified pension. After seven years of governing the state, the senior rani received 75,000 rupees a year. The sum comes into sharp relief when noted that C.P., newly appointed 'legal adviser', was given nearly the same figure,[239] while the maharajah's brother of nineteen received a whole lakh in allowances a few years later.[240] In the two decades that lay ahead, Sethu Lakshmi Bayi and her family retired to a private country house and avoided the capital; insulted when her status was lowered, the rani chose not to attend state events; and for all practical purposes she disappeared from the court.[241] Her children too were not treated well: where the maharajah's sister had an allowance in the 1940s of over 20,000 rupees, the senior rani's daughters had just over 8,000 a year.[242] Not only was her ancestral estate confiscated, even private property was seized; in the second instance, it was the government of independent India that returned this, aware that the senior rani had been unfairly treated.[243]

While Ravi Varma's eldest granddaughter was fast becoming a footnote, thus, Sethu Parvathi Bayi was coming into her own: she became the first Travancore royal to break orthodox taboos on foreign travel; she collected art in extraordinary quantities; she put her musical talent to use, reviving Swathi Tirunal's compositions; and generally, in the press, the junior rani became *the* maharani of Travancore. Her boldness was striking – in 1935 she jolted the pious old men of Trivandrum by inviting Margaret Sanger, the birth control crusader, to deliver a lecture, while an American diplomat a little later was astonished to find that, even as the maharajah led a temple procession, his mother had arranged for scotch whisky in their viewing pavilion.[244] Her desire for recognition was also satisfied: her son managed to get her the style of 'Her Highness' – till then only permitted to the senior rani – and the removal of the much-despised tag of 'junior' from her title. By 1941 a statue too was installed of the ruler's mother, making her the only rani to enjoy the honour.[245] Meanwhile, the privy purse touched new highs – in 1949 the maharajah would be among the wealthiest princes in India with well over two crore rupees in assets.[246] Gone was the regency-era austerity; in the last ruler's reign, the Travancore royal family acquired an air of glamour.

All along, the state sustained its name for modernization too: C.P., who was upgraded soon to Dewan, gave it everything from a university to a chemicals and fertilizer factory, scoring many a tactical and material victory over the Raj. Politically, however, neither he nor the junior rani were popular. As Lord Wavell, the viceroy, observed in the 1940s, the maharajah was 'entirely overshadowed by his mother' and the 'forcible Dewan'.[247] By 1938 it was also clear that the educated class had an 'intense, almost hysterical hatred' for the minister.[248] Nor did the junior rani enjoy approval, partly because of the 'feud which she carried on for years against the popular and respected' senior rani.[249] As was reconfirmed in 1944 by a Resident, while C.P.'s 'flair for publicity' kept the ruler and his mother in 'a dignified limelight', they were not 'in close enough contact and sympathy with their people'. The senior rani 'was very popular' but her cousin, he added, 'does not seem to appeal to the common herd'.[250] Why, as late as 1949, officials under Sardar Patel negotiating Travancore's integration with the Indian Union, noted this too. During discussions on the royal family's future, while the maharajah 'did not once refer even to the existence of' his aunt, the fact was that Sethu Lakshmi Bayi – eighteen years after her regency ended – was 'still regarded with very great respect', and 'with greater affection than either the [junior rani] or her son, by the people'.[251]

But what the junior rani, her son and the minister are most censured for is an ill-fated venture to keep Travancore independent in 1947. Where Sayaji Rao in Baroda had been among those princes who could sense the appeal of democracy, Travancore joined an ignoble category of states resisting this. In June that historic year, C.P. went on the radio and declared that on 15 August, 'Travancore will become an independent country'.

Days later the ruler also asserted that his kingdom would 'reassume its . . . sovereignty'. It does not seem to have been just a negotiating position: C.P. began trade talks with M.A. Jinnah of Pakistan, and at a meeting with the viceroy, brandished press cuttings to 'prove that Gandhi was a dangerous sex maniac', while Nehru would make India an 'unreliable' nation state.[252] In the end, the maharajah blinked after a physical attack on the Dewan – lights went off as C.P. was exiting a function and a man struck him with a sickle.[253] Even so, C.P. was sure that post-colonial India would not last. He warned that 'half a dozen' states would emerge 'as in the 18th century', and this after a 'massacre' of Congressmen; the junior rani and the maharajah could either 'fight it out' or accede like the other states.[254] As it happened, Sethu Parvathi Bayi and her son chose option two. Since then, some have sought to pin the blame for the attempt at independence on C.P. But as a historian wrote, the Dewan was 'only echoing His Masters' Voice' or 'that of Their Highnesses of Travancore, the son and the mother'.[255]

Incidentally, when Travancore merged with the Union, its senior rani also obtained her liberty. Hitherto her daughters and she had been at the maharajah's mercy; now their allowances came from the government, so they could hope, as Sethu Lakshmi Bayi wrote, to 'live the rest of our lives in peace and free from constant harassment'.[256] It was a little late, however. Though princesses, her daughters were locked in a gilded cage – in theory they had privilege, but in practice they had neither power nor equality in the family. So, when the opportunity presented itself, they left: in 1949 the senior rani's first daughter moved out, followed later by the second. In 1957 Sethu Lakshmi Bayi herself left the land she had ruled: she went to Bangalore, dying there in obscurity twenty-eight years later. It was in a bungalow that the ex-regent had lived; her palace was declared the maharajah's property,[257] and her self-acquired houses sold after her departure. In an auction, movable goods were also given up for financial liquidity, so that her royal status was by the end a hazy memory. The junior rani, on the other hand, continued in the palace, where to this day her line enjoys public regard as royalty. Unlike her cousin, whose remains in 1985 received all the honour that a local crematorium can

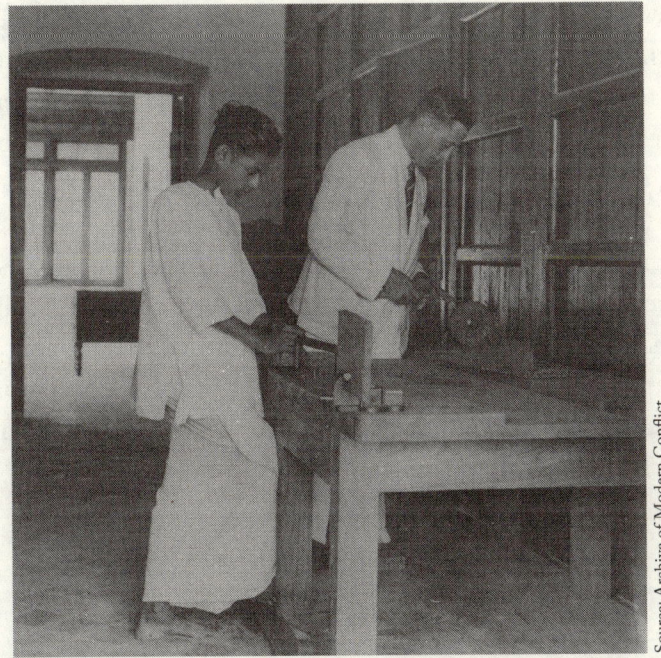

The adolescent Chithira Tirunal with his tutor G.T.B. Harvey, as photographed by the journalist St Nihal Singh.

supply, Sethu Parvathi Bayi's demise two years before had her lie in state. Before their deaths, however, the two did meet one last time – after the senior rani's eighty-fourth birthday, the junior came to visit. It was not a reconciliation for Ravi Varma's granddaughters, but in a photograph, Sethu Lakshmi Bayi beams. She had lost the war, and yet she seemed happier for it.

In some ways, the last maharajah, who would die in 1991, had much in common with his aunt, the senior rani. Though he barely knew her, both were, at their core, reserved individuals; both found themselves in seats of authority, pressed by forceful figures; both were conservative. If in the regent's case it was her consort, in the maharajah's life it was his mother who erected walls. While Sethu Lakshmi Bayi in the end gave up life in Trivandrum for peace in Bangalore, her nephew sought solace in the temple and in religion. Both had their strengths and weaknesses. It is a pity they never got to know one another, for without extraneous influences, as that Resident believed, it is possible the maharajah would have found much to admire in his aunt. But politics got in the way. If Ravi Varma's granddaughter and his great-grandson, both rulers of the kingdom where he had begun as a court dependant, were not sworn enemies, they were yet unable to become friends. As for old Harvey, for all his efforts with the maharajah, he had clearly failed. Indeed, his parting moment with Chithira Tirunal reveals the hopelessness of the enterprise. When Harvey went to say goodbye, the maharajah shook hands and bid him well, but said 'Not a word of thanks, appreciation, hope or regret – not a word!'[258] In a sense he may have been dominated by others: but he was still dominated by his Dewan and the junior rani, not by a British tutor or the Resident. And in that there was a small, quiet victory.[259]

Ravi Varma strikes a pose here with a parasol bearer, as he plans a mythological work for Mysore state. His relationship with Mysore began in the mid–1880s and continued till his death over twenty years later – this chapter tells the story of that principality and its quest for industrial glory as a means to make a mark, and stand up to the Raj.

6

The King as Bureaucrat

In July 1867, at an assembly in Mysore, an English civil servant scooped up a boy of four and transferred him to the lap of a seventy-three-year-old. And with that act the British inserted themselves between a dynast, who had begun life in the days of Tipu Sultan, and his adopted son, who would grow into a symbol of modern, 'reformed' kingship. One represented, in colonial eyes, a profligate history while the other would herald a future defined by the Raj's loftier standards. Either way, the introduction of an heir to its royal family brought jubilation to Mysore. As the elderly maharajah said, 'I was placed on the throne in the reign of his Majesty King George III, and fortune that then attended my house has now, through the beneficent will of his grand-daughter ... the Queen, been graciously continued to the son of my adoption.' He asked for his thanks to be conveyed to Victoria, adding that just as the British monarch had 'advanced my family, so may the family of her Majesty be advanced, and may I be long privileged to repose under her protection'. As usual, claims of loyalty were expressed, a ritual of state performed and the British agent welcomed the 'auspicious event', wishing the heir a career as a 'wise and successful ruler'. The little fellow, 'covered with precious stones', was then 'carried around to be salaamed to and shaken hands with a crowd of queer-looking, white-faced strangers': an exercise through which he held himself 'very creditably'. And so it was that Mysore's ruler acquired, with the blessings of the Raj, a successor who would carry forth the dynasty of the Wadiyars.[1]

For all the warm sentiments aired in public, though, the event had taken a Herculean effort to bring about, and while Krishnaraja Wadiyar III (1794–1868) emerged triumphant, there was still uncertainty in the air. Obtaining recognition of his adopted son had required, firstly, a large outlay of funds, embroiling the man in ever-swelling debt. It had also needed allies in England, who did everything from expostulating in newspapers to petitioning parliament so the ruler could have his way. So too a great deal depended on English-speaking natives, who called public meetings and urged the Raj to do justice by Mysore. Timing also mattered: after the rebellion of 1857, sympathy for brown royalty was at a high. As with the trial of Malhar Rao in Baroda, at stake were ideas of colonial morality, native rights and plain honesty. It became a tense dance between conflicting agendas – of a local maharajah to retain his family's hold over territory, and of the colonial bureaucracy determined to seize plum princely property. Under the veneer of solemn language, both parties had multiple strategies at play: Krishnaraja had to redefine his sovereignty in the face of foreign supremacy, just as the British sought to further imperial interests without betraying its crudeness. Where the ruler marshalled gods and religion in his fight, the Raj split legal hairs to justify its hypocrisy. For the fact was that though in 1858 the queen loudly disavowed annexation, her officers had no qualms in pursuing the exact opposite. Far from welcoming an adoption, what they truly hoped for was a loophole to take Mysore the moment Krishnaraja dropped dead.

The antecedents of the case are fascinating. The Wadiyars were a chiefly line originating in the fourteenth century, who, along the way, as they rose to kingly stature, constructed a grander genealogy. Multiple origin myths offer the same broad plot: of heroic Kshatriya warriors of the lunar race (*yaduvamsa*) coming down to Karnataka, where they save a helpless princess from the machinations of a villain. One of these figures then marries the lady, founding the dynasty.[2] In a more actual sense, though, the roots of the family appear to have been local, and after serving the Vijayanagara empire, when that power began to fragment in the sixteenth century, the Wadiyars ascended to royal status themselves. From being tributaries to the Vijayanagara viceroy at Srirangapattana, they first began defaulting on their dues, and finally, in the seventeenth century, seized that city; where earlier accounts recount an armed takeover, later sources refashioned the Wadiyars as liberators who saved Srirangapattana from invaders and were *invited* to assume government.[3] In any case, possession of a recognized seat of authority was key to transforming these country chieftains into legitimized kings. Down till the eighteenth century, the family presided over an expanding state, clashing with sultans in the north, conquering Tamil territory in the east, seeking to subdue coastal kingdoms in the west and even becoming tributaries to the Mughals while battling Maratha inroads into the south.[4] That is, till in the 1730s their hereditary *dalavoys* (ministers) became the real power in the land, and the Wadiyars were reduced to puppets.

The British would make much of this period of royal emasculation, especially after consigning to history the sultans who dominated Mysore in the second half of the eighteenth century. Theirs is one of the most memorable phases in the state's story, not least for their resounding clashes with the East India Company. Hyder Ali (1722–82) was the scion of a family with a history of service under various powers in the Deccan. His father having become a Mysore servant, Hyder pursued a career here, ascending to such military success that by 1761 he was able to topple the dalavoys and 'save' the Wadiyars. Of course, as far as the king was concerned, he merely found himself extricated from the hold of old ministers and placed in a cage by a new one. And while Hyder, now styled nawab, never cast aside the Hindu dynasty, in fresh territory he brought under his control, he assumed sovereign rights, becoming simultaneously Mysore's regent as well as monarch in its outer, newly annexed lands. The man also gave the British cause for concern, becoming one of their fiercest enemies, and on his death, his son, Tipu (1750–99) inherited this hatred of hat-wearers. Tipu, however, had no reservations formalizing what his father had achieved: the Wadiyars were retired and Hyder's son proclaimed himself sultan of Mysore as well. He gave the Company much more than a bloody nose, but from the late 1780s, began to suffer reversals: his invasion of Travancore fired off the Third Anglo-Mysore War, at the end of which territory was forfeited. Even so Tipu resisted, till death in 1799 put an end to his ambition to flush the Company out of India forever.[5]

It was at this stage that Krishnaraja III entered the picture. The Company entertained several options as far as Mysore was concerned. One was a division of its territory between themselves and their ally, the nizam of Hyderabad. But this risked provoking the Marathas, besides aggrandizing the nizam 'beyond all bounds of discretion'.[6] Since replacing Tipu with another potential enemy was not wise, a second option was proposed: a partition of the state three ways, with more modest shares for the nizam and the Company, while a sizeable landlocked segment would be retained under local rule. This opened the next question: which royal house would hold it? As the governor-general wrote, the Wadiyars were so enfeebled that they were used to the 'humility of their actual fortunes' despite a greater pedigree; whereas Tipu's parvenu dynasty had 'the most exalted expectations of sovereignty'.[7] Indeed, even the dead sultan's minister, a Marathi Brahmin called Purniah, was in favour of reinstating the Muslim family.[8] Again, then, strategic calculations carried the day: Tipu's sons, it was feared, would resent the Company for reducing them to vassalage. On the other hand, a 'restoration of the descendant of the ancient Rajahs' from 'degradation and misery' would 'excite a sentiment of gratitude', keeping future kings both loyal and open to manipulation.[9] And thus, Krishnaraja, son of the previous Wadiyar, was installed on the throne in June 1799.[10] The Company could (and would) now claim to have delivered a Hindu line from the clutches of Islamic usurpers, casting this as a moral victory as much as a political one.[11]

Conveniently enough, given that Krishnaraja was only five, his installation did not allow the Wadiyars any immediate taste of power. For twelve years, instead, Purniah stayed at the helm, having transferred his allegiance to the Company. His history with Tipu was no impediment.[12] For he was an 'extraordinary man' with a character 'far surpassing' expectations;[13] indeed, the governor-general's brother affirmed, 'Purneah's abilities have astonished me.'[14] Under him, by 1801 the

Dewan Purniah as painted by Thomas Hickey.

A young Krishnaraja Wadiyar III as depicted in The Indian Journal Of Lady Charlotte Florentia Clive.

(THE RAJAH OF MYSORE.)

country was 'in the most prosperous state' and 'in perfect tranquillity'.[15]
The Dewan so succeeded in winning colonial endorsement, in fact, that
long before Madhava Rao and his tribe of native statesmen emerged, this
man marked himself 'one of India's most successful administrators'.[16]
But Purniah's tenure had another familiar impact: as with Travancore
and Pudukkottai, in Mysore too Marathi Brahmins were installed in
high places.[17] The Dewan kept the British happy, while his caste men
acted as loyal subordinates, making him unassailable. So much so that
approaching adulthood, Krishnaraja began to resent Purniah. It was
alleged that the Dewan wished to keep him 'in a state of perpetual
tutelage',[18] and neglected to 'initiate the Rajah into a knowledge of
public affairs'.[19] Worse, Purniah proposed a hereditary family claim
over the Dewanship – something odious to the Wadiyars who had been
paralysed more than once by ambitious servants.[20]

After a struggle in 1810–11, then,[21] Purniah was shown the door and
Krishnaraja acquired control of his government; following generations
of political impotence, a Wadiyar was again in possession of power. The
Dewan was rewarded, of course, with twenty-five tax-free villages,[22] and
his reputation was at a high: at the time of his exit, the treasury was not
only able to service its tribute to the Company, but also had over two
crore rupees in cash.[23] This praise, however, must be qualified, for the
prime British concern was revenue management. So long as the account
books were balanced, they were glad, for it ensured they received their
dues. By this logic of extracting taxes with energy and precision, Purniah
was a success. Indeed, his flair for this pre-dated the British. After all,
Tipu too maintained a ravenous war chest; with 'the greatest dexterity'
it was Purniah who squeezed funds out of the people.[24] In fact, from the
seventeenth century, Mysore had had an increasingly centralized model
at work, Tipu taking this to its heights. Appointed officials answerable
to the capital were preferred to chiefs with strong cultural bases, for
example.[25] But this also birthed tensions – as a Company man recorded,
the kingdom was 'a combination of numerous turbulent principalities',
with a 'spirit of insurrection' 'inherent' in it.[26] In Tipu's day resistance
was firmly dealt with, and Purniah too had the advantage of Company

boots behind him. But keeping a lid on the problem did not remove it; centrifugal forces were 'subdued', not 'extinguished'.[27] And, ironically, it was Krishnaraja who would foot the bill for innovations set off long before he was born.

For the time being, though, with Purniah's departure, the maharajah gladly slid into the saddle. From the start, however, he was handicapped. To begin with, the many units of the Company army that were posted across Mysore after Tipu's fall had withdrawn. While it did not loosen the capital's hold over the provinces immediately, in due course the absence of awe-inspiring visible strength emboldened regional political loyalties and aspirations. That is, strong impulses on the ground kept in check by Tipu and Purniah found room to breathe again. Then there was the fact that while the old Dewan was toppled, the bureaucracy was dominated by as many as 5,500 Brahmins – by bringing in royal kinsmen and non-Brahmins, the young maharajah launched clashes.[28] To this was combined the ruler's outlook, shaped by grand ideals of Hindu sovereignty, that did not sit comfortably with the colonial political economy. Understandably, Krishnaraja thought not like a civil servant but a *king*, inspired by traditional notions of a monarch's duties. Indeed, given how the Wadiyars had been eclipsed for generations, the new maharajah had an especial desire to shine,[29] compensating for historical embarrassments with grandeur.[30] Secure in his possessions, he showered largesse and patronage, sponsored temples and generally followed a familiar orthodox pattern. To his own peril, however, he was also determined to maintain control on the nitty-gritties of administration: something that might have worked for a seasoned autocrat, but in a sixteen-year-old's untested hands carried risks.

That Krishnaraja proved a jealous prince is not surprising. Given Purniah's dominating style, the ruler had a 'fear of supercession [sic] in power' and distrusted strong ministers – none of them was given 'authority necessary to make them useful instruments', and even the Resident's 'counsel' was viewed as 'an encroachment on his sovereignty'.[31] But this was not irrational, for the maharajah was also being undermined from within. For instance, alarmed by the Wadiyar preference for non-Brahmin aides, the Marathi Brahmins had coalesced around the Resident.[32] This British officer, in turn, keen to pose as a hero, urged his superiors to let him interfere.[33] As early as 1813, he complained that though Krishnaraja lacked training, he refused to delegate authority. Not only did he 'disregard' advice, he was also 'prone to dissimulation' and an 'anxiety to conceal' the accounts of his government. His suspicious nature meant that only those in a closed circle were trusted: people described as 'wretches who pandered to his pleasures even by the prostitution of their wives'.[34] Even the dispensing of justice was affected: it was alleged that 'in the same suit, as many as four or five contradictory decrees' might be passed, depending on which party had royal favour.[35] While the Resident's complaints saw his higher-ups ask Krishnaraja to 'banish … all evil counsellors, profligate companions, and low minded parasites', the Resident too was told not to get nosy. Their view was that the British agent should advise 'in a private and conciliatory form', not harangue the ruler.[36] The imperial mood, in other words, was of minimal intervention, showing again flip-flops in colonial policy.

That said, the Company's willingness to give Krishnaraja a chance is not surprising, for he was an intelligent man. Well before the colonial establishment admitted it, he pointed out how his lauded ex-Dewan's 'talents lay only in the collection of the revenues'; Purniah's chief intent was not to make Mysore thrive but to display his prowess. Yes, he had left an overflowing treasury, but that was easy when the government was not run in the 'interests of his people'. In fact, if revenues were falling now, it was precisely because the maharajah wished to 'show indulgence of the people, and to be moderate'.[37] Implicit in this is a larger point: that Krishnaraja was not seeking popularity with the British but to show his *subjects* that he was a good king. So too in keeping at bay the Resident, he was indicating that he was his own man and not a cipher for the white man's rule. Indeed, this was admitted as much by a governor of Madras a decade after Krishnaraja came to power: the prevailing attitude in Mysore, he rued, was that once tribute was paid, the Company had no business in the state.[38] But while the maharajah's resistance is in some ways admirable, internal politics did mar his reputation – the Marathi

Krishnaraja Wadiyar III as an adult ruler, in an engraving by S.W. Reynolds, based on a painting by A. Stuart.

Brahmins' machinations with the Resident produced the impression that Krishnaraja simply could not manage his state.[39] Or as one governor noted, Mysore would do wonderfully 'under almost any other Prince than the present one; a weaker one would be more easily guided, an abler one would act more prudently for his own sake'.[40]

Meanwhile, as players at the high table were caught in their own games, there was a growing alienation of the court from the people. One element lay, for example, in the fact that the chief beneficiaries of royal patronage were priests, courtiers, temples and the wider capital.[41] While Purniah too had increased expenditure on traditional charities, in less than two decades after coming to power, Krishnaraja upped it from 7 per cent of revenue to as much as 14. When questioned, the maharajah argued that this was imperative for 'the dignity of the State' and for the 'reputation of my [fore]fathers'.[42] The British were never convinced: in 1814 the Resident claimed that the ruler 'dissipated on worthless persons' obscene amounts, while the pay of his troops was in arrears.[43] Three years later, another official lamented how Krishnaraja was 'indolent and prodigal' and had somehow managed to spend 'about sixty lacs of pagodas [that is, over a crore and a half rupees] of the treasure' amassed by his ex-Dewan. Furthermore, though still in his early years, he was allegedly 'detested by his subjects'.[44] This last remark was not just the bleating of a crusty Englishman: when sometime later it was suggested to a Mysore officer that his king's charitable expenses were intended to enrich the country – by circulating cash and an economic stimulus – the man said, 'What have the [peasants] got by the Rajahs [sic] expenditures?'[45] All that Krishnaraja accomplished, it appeared, was a reputation for spending; and while intended to burnish the Wadiyar name, it allegedly only produced a pomp disconnected from reality. And as a result, to quote a colonial official, 'the vessel of the state' would soon be 'hopelessly shattered on the rock of extravagance'.[46]

But a king with loose financial morals was hardly unusual, whether in India or elsewhere. What truly infringed on the lives of ordinary subjects was Krishnaraja's administrative system, which was almost designed to spark discontent. The government was in the habit of farming out its districts to contractors to collect revenue. The arrangement was simple: the assigned party committed to depositing a fixed sum in the treasury, and if there was a shortfall, pledged to make up for it from their pocket.[47] Various candidates bid for these revenue allotments, and as an official remarked, it was from 'this plan of [giving] the land to the highest bidder that the country' was ruined.[48] For in general, revenue farmers while doing all they could to meet targets, also worked to earn a private profit. A recession in southern India and a steady decline in agricultural prices also led to a fall in revenue. Though pledged against exploiting cultivators, in reality contractors could reduce people to misery, employing every instrument from flogging to detaining peasants' wives to exact payments.[49] To this disastrous system was added a second layer of damage: the Marathi Brahmins' influence. Though aliens, they had 'engrossed almost all offices of any importance' and inserted themselves everywhere.[50] Unsurprisingly, most of the revenue contractors were also from this class, with no cultural ties to the land, going about their business with ruthless efficiency.[51] Their determination to extract taxes had such hellish results that harassed cultivators would later declare that they far preferred Tipu's government over the supposedly more legitimate Wadiyars.[52]

In 1830–31, then, there was a revolt. It began in Nagara district – an area the Wadiyars had never ruled in the past, and which was conquered by the late sultans. Not only were its warlike people poorly incorporated, they also had enduring memories of their previous rulers, deposed in 1763. Located in the highlands, the dominant groups here were of tribal origin, and a large portion were Virasaivas (later called Lingayats) who rejected caste and had an intellectual history of anti-Brahminism.[53] It is not surprising, therefore, that Brahmin interlopers from the capital were unpopular.[54] Two sparks, however, allowed simmering discontent to bubble into rebellion. After Purniah left, a subordinate, Rama Rao, had grown in influence.[55] Several of his acolytes were granted government offices, particularly in Nagara, and to maintain their influence from royal encroachments, this Marathi Brahmin network actively worked with the Resident. Then, in the 1820s, the maharajah tried to dislodge them by sending to Nagara his own man. Provoked, Rao's partisans prodded peasant leaders into revolt.[56] While this was intended to get rid of the royal nominee, a second, unforeseen spark arrived from a different direction. A petty criminal had chanced on heirlooms belonging to the last independent Nagara king; claiming to be a descendant, this pretender now called on the people to shake off Mysore's yoke, also throwing in the promise of a lower tax rate.[57] A bad economy, the exactions of the Brahmins and the freak coincidence of a would-be prince set the district on fire. Even local law enforcement officers joined the revolt, thanks to their kinship with the rebels.[58] And to make things worse for the capital, Virasaiva networks saw the rebellion flare out from Nagara to other parts of Mysore. Krishnaraja had never known such a crisis.

What is telling here is that the Wadiyar court – not the Company or any foreign power – was being held to account. In Nagara especially, it was this Hindu dynasty, with its Brahminical ideology and Marathi civil servants, who were seen as colonizers. As a British major would report from the ground (albeit with some exaggeration), the Nagara people might even accept the white man's rule but 'never will quietly submit to the raja's government'.[59] That is, they saw little in common between themselves and the Wadiyar kingdom. Virasaivism supplied them ideological meaning, while economic woes electrified the wider peasantry.[60] To make the political nature of the rebellion clear, the pretender-rajah's supporters even seized eighty forts.[61] In Bednore, twenty Brahmin officials were brutally killed,[62] while messengers sent out with conciliatory terms were found dead on the road, 'the proclamations placed open by their side, as if to express . . . defiance'.[63] Meanwhile, as the revolt spread, by mid-December 1830, the maharajah himself set out to soothe the people. While on the way to the unsettled districts Krishnaraja did punish a few corrupt officials and make amends, midway to Nagara he found 'the shops shut up, and the necessary supplies for his retinue refused', as thousands stood before him 'beating their drums and blowing their horns – acts indicative of gross disrespect'.[64] The result was that the ruler's troops – urged by the Resident – hanged peasant leaders,[65] while the maharajah turned back to return to his capital. In the end, the Company army stepped in in the summer of 1831 to break the revolt, though bands of rebels were still active two years later.

But if the rebellion was crushed, it also brought the Company to the palace gates. Even when the state was created in its present form, the British had asserted a right to check Wadiyar excesses – it was hoped that threat of intervention would moderate royal conduct.[66] In practice, however, the Company – unlike in states like Travancore, and again showing the absence of a standard policy – did not intervene up until now. So divorced had they seemed, in fact, that after the rebellion, an inquiry noted 'the prevalence of the belief' that Company troops would *not* aid the maharajah, leaving him to face the people's wrath; this had emboldened resistance.[67] In any case, having handled the rebels, the British turned next to Krishnaraja: in September 1831, he was temporarily divested of power. Charges against him were many: the ruler had squandered Purniah's hoard, alienated assets, piled up debt, ignored 'every symptom of maladministration', let 'improper' officers into service, sold revenue positions to 'greedy adventurers' and, in the end, incited revolt.[68] A subsequent inquiry committee was a little more sympathetic: while the maharajah's administration was certainly 'venal and corrupt', much of the discontent was due to extraneous economic trends. Mysore had been a conquest state, its military–industrial complex an engine of growth as much as a glue to keep it together; now, in its straitjacketed, truncated form, decline was inevitable, as was the mass frustration it carried in its wake.[69] The ruler's chief fault was that he had failed to see the sands under his feet shifting. Even so, what was done was done; after a stint in the limelight, then, the Wadiyars were suspended once again, as the Company assumed the reins of state.

Writing over thirty-five years after surrendering power, the man the British installed as a child on Mysore's throne and then cast aside sought to exhibit his new knowledge of 'enlightened' government. In an

1866 letter to the viceroy, a greyer, more shrivelled Krishnaraja sounded different from the king he was prior to Nagara. Or as he admitted, in his 'long retirement', he had had a chance to learn one or two things. For instance, 'I have learned', he wrote, 'that the possession of absolute power is a dangerous and undesirable' thing. And this wisdom had dawned the hard way: through his 'unskilful use of absolute power', he had made mistakes, and knew now why the British never allowed their own servants untrammelled influence. From 'highest to the lowest', from magistrate to monarch, everyone was 'ruled and guided by Law'. Describing this as a 'great method', the maharajah – now in his seventies – got to the point: he wished to be restored to the throne. If this application were admitted, he promised, not only would he conform to Western models of governance, but the Wadiyars would also be 'willing to bind' themselves to 'rule in obedience to such regulations' as would please the Raj.[70] In other words, having been reduced to a titular prince, Krishnaraja realized that to pull on in colonial India he would have to adapt. In his youth, he exalted Brahminical ideals of kingship. But bitter experience generated a readiness now, the scholar Janaki Nair writes, to transform into 'a *legal* king instead of [just] a *divinely ordained* one'. That is, to allow the Wadiyars a shot at surviving the imperial age, Krishnaraja was willing to have the monarchy 'reconstituted' for Western eyes.[71]

In many ways, the maharajah inspired sympathy in British minds, including in the governor-general who had attached his state. Lord Bentinck would regret the haste with which he decided the Wadiyars' fate in 1831, for it soon became clear that while misrule was a factor, 'agrarian depression' had been an equally strong trigger.[72] Indeed, shortly after his removal, Krishnaraja too warned that Bentinck was 'in ignorance of the true merits of the case'.[73] The new Resident, appointed after the ruler's suspension, backed this line: the maharajah had flaws but was not a bad man, and there was no justification for such an extreme measure as the assumption of his government. After all, if the ruler were at fault, the Resident argued, the Company could hardly be absolved. For despite enjoying the legal and moral right to intervene in Mysore,[74] instead of insisting on a 'vigorous correction' when Krishnaraja first

Wikimedia Commons

Krishnaraja Wadiyar III in 1867 as featured in The Illustrated London News.

went astray, they had settled for 'palliative admonitions'. So much so that it was 'a matter of much surprise to [the maharajah himself] . . . that he had been so long allowed a loose rein'. What the authorities ought to have done *before* the rebellion – and which could now be arranged instead – was to give the ruler a generous purse to satisfy his 'love of pleasure' and keep up a 'pageant', while making use of his dislike of 'application to business' to govern through a Dewan.[75] That is, the Company's man on the ground regretted how for decades his bosses had not interfered where they *should* have interfered. It was, after all, they who created the state and put a teenager on its throne – it was hardly fair that when a price had to be paid he alone was blamed.[76]

Besides, Bentinck himself feared, as he wrote in 1834, that the 'legality and the justice' of what was done was questionable. By treaty the British could assume *parts* of the state if tribute were endangered; in Mysore, they had taken the whole, despite the fact that the maharajah had, in advance, deposited lakhs of rupees with the Resident.[77] A proportionate response to the Nagara crisis, then, would have been to give Krishnaraja a 'more distinct' warning to get his house in order, not to remove him altogether.[78] Moreover, after a visit, Bentinck found that the ruler was in 'the highest degree intelligent' and the 'reverse of tyrannical'; having received a jolt, he would 'not neglect to bring his good qualities into active operation'.[79] To assuage anti-Mysore elements in his own establishment, the governor–general suggested a compromise: that the state temporarily surrender certain districts, including Nagara, to the Company, with the remainder restored to the Wadiyars. Bentinck's superiors, however, rejected the idea.[80] Already while approving the 'temporary assumption' in 1831, some in London had suggested that the arrangement be made permanent. The only reason they did not prevail was that 'the faith of treaties' did not allow this, unless the maharajah relinquished his rights. That pending, given Mysore's 'lamentable state', and the fact that this could be ascribed to the 'want of vigilance and efficient superintendence' by its British overlords, its rule for now would vest with the latter.[81] To correct their own mistake of not having intervened in time, they would temporarily shelve Krishnaraja, and shower compensatory good governance on the state.

Of course, if the durbar was riven by factions, neither was the Company free of such dynamics. For the first four years, given that there was a Resident as well as two commissioners in Mysore, the British were mired in quarrels. Then, in 1834, full charge of the administration was handed to a sole commissioner: the celebrated Mark Cubbon (1775–1861), who would reign for over a quarter century. In that period of direct rule, as an admirer wrote, the story of Mysore became one 'of a people made happy by release from serfdom, and of a ruined state restored to financial prosperity'.[82] Cubbon modified the revenue system, abolished 769 petty taxes,[83] built roads connecting the state to British districts and new markets[84] and much else. But it wasn't all as it should have been. The original idea was to preserve the native system and avoid importing white officials; in practice the reverse occurred, with positions cornered by Company servants.[85] For years, moreover, not only did the commissioner spar with the Resident, but the maharajah was also suspicious. Or as a supporter wrote, 'Every innovation appeared to [the court] to be a new turn of the screw, securing the English occupation, and making the restoration of the Rajah's authority more difficult.'[86] Besides, for all the trumpeting of progress, 'improvements', as Nair tells, were slow to appear: Cubbon took twenty-five years just 'to reach the annual gross revenue of 1799–1810 [that is, Purniah era] Mysore'.[87] Still, on the whole, by establishing new systems, the man fixed an infrastructure that would allow Mysore too, in time, to become a 'model state'.[88] Colonial intervention created a steel frame for the state, destined to last the rest of its existence.

In the meantime, the maharajah was not twiddling his thumbs. On the contrary, Krishnaraja continued to cultivate respect, not least by redefining the very concept of sovereignty. As Caleb Simmons observes, shorn of administrative power, Krishnaraja transported the idea of the king to the one space the British could not control: that of the divine.[89] Though it is tempting to see loss of control as emasculating the ruler, this one survived by transcending the problem. He had a generous allowance, including a fifth of the state's revenue, and put these resources to brilliant use.[90] For instance, images were commissioned, showing the king not on the throne, but in a host of religious postures. These, emphasizing a *sacred* kingship, were distributed across the principality, so that, in miniature form, the maharajah continued to survey land physically lost to him, like a divine icon. So too Krishnaraja deployed his 'devotional sovereignty' to woo hostile groups. In some portraits, Simmons notes, the ruler appears with Virasaiva *ishtalingams* – an effort to conciliate a community that had grievances against him.[91] Similarly, in major temples, the maharajah installed sculptures of himself, like older images of prominent ancestors. And by placing himself alongside these remarkable predecessors – such as the kingdom's founder, Srirangapattana's conqueror and others – he signalled continuity as well as his own greatness.[92] Crucially, their positioning in temples was also a reminder to the people that the maharajahs were, political vicissitudes aside, 'long-standing royal patrons and devotees'.[93] The British might have appropriated the right to govern, but in serving god and in Mysore's *spiritual* landscape, a Cubbon could never replace a Wadiyar.

Indeed, through courtly productions, the maharajah was able to flex both creative and political muscles, reminding his elites that kingship was more than just administration. On the one hand, Krishnaraja's own dozens of literary compositions, coupled with his patronage of some of the great poets and artists of the day, earned him a reputation as a scholar-king.[94] But there was a clear attempt to also magnify the royal principle as opposed to impersonal Company rule. For example, the ruler built the Jaganmohan Palace, with the Rangamahal (Hall of Colours). And in the murals on its walls, we find 'a counternarrative to the military and administrative power of the British'.[95] One painting, on the face of it, is genealogical. It depicts Krishnaraja's dynasty from its Puranic ancestors, such as Lord Krishna, down to historical kings. But beyond flaunting a fancy family tree, by so highlighting descent from mythic lines, the maharajah was also telling that the Wadiyars' story was 'inseparable from the history of the gods'.[96] Additionally, flanking this work are portraits of various princely contemporaries, as well as kings long dead and gone. Everyone from Akbar and Aurangzeb to the Sikh emperor Ranjit Singh, as well as great Hindu rulers, finds a place in this space.[97] Conspicuously, however, as Simmons notes, it is the *British* who are absent, when even Hyder and Tipu are honoured.[98] Through art, then, the maharajah was showing himself as part of the same kingly dominion as these great sovereigns; in this symbolic universe, he denied Victoria and her agents influence.[99] They certainly had the power to dislodge him, but his legitimacy was rooted in something greater.

But while these strategies were aimed at local audiences, Krishnaraja's resistance assumed more direct forms when dealing with the imperial power itself. While at first the maharajah feuded with the commissioner, in time he realized the value of advocacy in a British legal language.[100] To begin with, he never let the Company forget that his state's takeover was temporary; as early as 1836 he had inquired as to 'who was to be the judge' of when Mysore was sufficiently settled for it to be handed back.[101]

Eight years later, he reiterated that while 'evil counsels' had marred his previous innings, the British 'interposed, not to wrest the country from my hands, but to heal it . . . and return it to me in a healthy state'.[102] In these exchanges, the maharajah see-sawed between diplomatic obsequity and forthrightness. In 1846, for example, he expressed how, after over a decade in the 'school of adversity', he had learnt 'lessons of true wisdom'. And having emerged, he looked to the governor-general to restore the kingdom.[103] On the other hand, a little later he was cold in pointing out the impropriety of a prolonged colonial presence in Mysore. 'Disturbances there were in some districts,' he agreed, 'but do not disturbances occur in portions of the Company's country . . .?' Yes, he had debts, but 'have not the best and most upright Governments in the world debts?'[104] For all the petitioning, though, the ruler did not obtain results; in fact, the British often delayed replying, and when they did, it was in the negative. The key argument that the treaty did not allow them to keep Mysore indefinitely was ignored: in 1847, for instance, London held that since Krishnaraja was 'incompetent', they could not allow his subjects to suffer him – an altruistic line, but of doubtful legal substance.[105] Put frankly, the Company had grown used to holding Mysore, and was determined to keep it.

From here on, in fact, British falsity was on full display. At first the Company never denied the legal eventuality of returning Mysore to its rulers: this was repeated in 1835 and 1839 by London,[106] in 1840 by Calcutta (which described the British as 'trustees' for the maharajah)[107] and even in 1858 when the principality was officially referred to as 'foreign territory'.[108] It was the notorious annexationist, Lord Dalhousie, who turned things over. Restoration, he argued, was out of the question, given how Krishnaraja was 'scandalously and hopelessly bad' at his job. The issue then was about returning the state to a successor. Here too, the governor-general claimed, the *British* were his natural heirs. The existing treaties, Dalhousie felt, were 'silent as to heirs'; they pertained to the maharajah as an *individual*, not the Wadiyars as a dynasty. And so, the ruler's title was not heritable. Besides, given that the man's life would not be 'much further prolonged', and since he had no legitimate sons, annexation was inevitable. In other words, the British would keep Mysore in Krishnaraja's name, and after he died, formally take it, allowing their 'good work' to continue.[109] While Dalhousie's professional record renders this self-serving approach unsurprising, what stands out is how his successor, Lord Canning, upheld the fiction that Krishnaraja would 'bequeath his kingdom' to the Raj. While he admitted that there was no 'official evidence' to back this bold assumption, it was claimed the maharajah, through a 'private channel', had expressed such a wish himself.[110] In any case, whether or not the ruler made the suggestion, a 'private' remark was treated with all the force of irreversible policy. That is, no matter the letter and spirit of the treaties, the British were pushing a paper-thin argument simply because they had the power to do it.

Unfortunately for the viceroy, Victoria's proclamation after the Great Rebellion, which abjured annexation, inspired hope in the palace. In 1861, Krishnaraja wrote to Canning, soliciting the return of his kingdom, and *officially* clarifying that he had no intention of allowing the Raj to keep it.[111] Thirteen months later, Calcutta wrote back with unfriendly words. Asserting that Wadiyar claims rested solely on the British victory over Tipu, the viceroy told the ruler that 'supreme sovereignty' belonged to the Raj. Krishnaraja had had a chance to rule, but having squandered it, he and his rights were 'cancelled'. Yes, Bentinck did intend to restore 'native government', but nobody had said that this meant 'specifically [the government] of your Highness'. That shifty line about British duties 'towards the people', and of preserving them from 'oppression', was also trotted out. In sum, the Wadiyars could stop praying: Mysore was lost.[112] It was the first time the maharajah was categorically denied the legality of his claim, and startled, he sent in a more pointed representation. In this he admitted the Company's right of conquest from defeating Tipu, but shrewdly pointed out a detail: that this conquest was made with the nizam of Hyderabad. That is, if Mysore were swallowed up, the Raj would have to share it with an Indian prince – a point to which the nizam latched on, opening a separate legal headache for the Raj.[113] Krishnaraja also excoriated all the moral gymnastics: the official claim, for instance, that a treaty, with a declared validity of 'as long as the sun and the moon shall endure' was only contingent on one man's lifetime.[114] Indeed, so obscene was the British case that at one point London went so far as to state that the treaty only covered circumstances under which Mysore could be assumed; because it said nothing explicitly about how to restore, it never contemplated a restoration at all![115]

It may have been the end of the matter, but for sheer embarrassment even within the British establishment. The scheme to take Mysore, despite the queen's promises, left some members of the India Council in London aghast. One, for example, asserted that the 1831 assumption itself was 'not warranted' – the treaty allowed the British to seize parts of its territory, not the state in toto.[116] A colleague, meanwhile, challenged the projection of the 1799 agreement as a personal one for not mentioning heirs; by this standard, he scoffed, 'half the princes of India' would be on the streets. As for the pretence of saving Mysore's people from an atrocious ruler, it was a sham argument because the Company had just presented British territory as a reward for loyalty during 1857 to princes 'more corrupt and tyrannical'.[117] More generally, a third councillor added how there was proof that 'a large portion' of the people *preferred* 'native to British rule'. To annex the state would be 'a repudiation of all the pledges and assurances' so 'lavishly bestowed' when the Crown took over from the Company; they would be afflicted by the charge that, like the Company, the queen too was 'lying in wait' for 'absorbing territory'.[118] Besides, this dissenting minority felt the maharajah had atoned enough; the treaty only allowed for 'occupation' to safeguard tribute, and so 'we are bound to restore'.[119] The elephant in the room was too large to ignore, and as a critic wrote, imperial claims over Mysore clearly came from avarice.[120] Furthermore, by the 1860s, several native states – Travancore for example – were doing very well under their rulers, so that even racial prejudice could not fly.[121] It was all so dishonourable that pressure mounted in London. Why, even the queen thought her government was being 'very shabby' with the Wadiyars.[122]

Meanwhile, alongside restoration, a new front was opened on adoption. For years Krishnaraja had dilly-dallied, but in 1864 when

Krishnaraja Wadiyar III as featured in J. Forbes Watson and John William Kaye's The People of India *(1897, Volume 8).*

he decided in the affirmative, he was told any adoptee would only have rights over his 'private property'; he had 'no authority' to pass on his throne.[123] Again a band of dissenters in the India Council recorded objections, calling this move not only 'illegal and unjust' but also a 'violation of the treaties'.[124] Krishnaraja himself defiantly went ahead, adopting a 'successor to all my rights and privileges'.[125] The press was electrified. One paper in 1863 had dismissed the ruler as a 'tottering old man' with a 'foot in the grave'.[126] Now, however, the mood turned: Mysore, *The Homeward Mail* argued, had put British honour on 'trial'.[127] *The Daily News* warned that India's princes were 'capable of becoming dangerous enemies' if their rights were trampled upon, and that the Raj had better think again.[128] *The Pall Mall Gazette* reminded the authorities that the outcry was 'as much on the score of policy as on the score of justice'.[129] 'We had hoped – and, indeed, for some time we had believed – that the British Government in India had ceased to lie in wait for pretexts for annexing the native states,' another editorial read. But the 'refusal of the paramount state to recognise the adoption' was evidence that the 'practice of taking all that we can take by virtue of our superior strength . . . has not . . . been in anywise abandoned'.[130] The moral upper ground the Raj claimed was slipping away even in the eyes of the British commentariat.

With the publication of internal correspondence on Mysore in parliament, things only got more heated. In 1866 a petition by the philosopher John Stuart Mill with various British officers and the scholar Max Müller was tendered to the House of Commons, expressing 'grief and alarm' that the queen's proclamation was being so brazenly violated. They were 'firmly convinced' that while British supremacy was good for India, it *had* to be based 'upon moral influence' – a sophistic defiance of treaties was abhorrent.[131] While Krishnaraja's British allies kept up their agitation, what ultimately aided the Wadiyar monarchy, though, was democracy. In June 1866 the British government fell and the incoming cabinet installed fresh officials in the India Office. Seven months later, the new regime affirmed that it was *against* destroying Indian principalities. These, it was declared, raised 'the self-respect of the natives' and, therefore, it was no longer 'the intention of her Majesty's government . . . that the state of Mysore should be annexed'.[132] The secretary of state also privately admitted that the agenda pursued by his predecessors had been not only 'unsound' but also 'unworthy of a great Power' like Britain.[133] There was no doubt that in 1799 the Company wished to create a 'separate Hindoo State' and that this 'was in no sense a temporary' arrangement; the British had no 'reversionary right' over Mysore.[134] But even this new government insisted that the treaty was limited to just Krishnaraja, which meant his successor would have to 'come to some new' terms.[135] In that sense, the Raj left the door open for interference, even while, at long last, conceding Mysore's claims.[136]

But that was enough for the maharajah. In June 1867 he was informed that his adoption was formally recognized: the new heir would succeed him in a personal as well as political capacity, and the Wadiyar dynasty would be sustained. Krishnaraja was thrilled. He had had to concede one or two things, but as far as claims of moral superiority went, this brown native had come out firmly on top, with much of the colonial

officialdom left red-faced by their public shaming in Britain. Or as one of
the maharajah's legal assistants had written, 'Truth is always truth, on the
banks of the Ganges, as well as on those of the Thames.'[137] And having
proved this point and achieved victory, within months, old Krishnaraja
was dead.[138]

In 1875, among the princes and potentates Queen Victoria's heir met
on his tour of India was the new maharajah of Mysore. Chamarajendra
Wadiyar (1863–94) had arrived in Bombay looking fittingly exotic,
weighed down in luxurious robes and jewels, while literally holding
the hand of an English guardian.[139] That he was of thoroughly princely
bearing enhanced his appeal; one commentator had early on, noting his
'rich olive complexion' and 'splendid eyes', described the boy as 'a born
king'. Even at his installation in 1868, he made an impression. Through
the ceremonies of the day, the five-year-old held himself with 'astonishing
coolness', 'chewing a betel-nut' like a grand old man of the court.[140] The
public loved him: on travelling with the maharajah, his tutor was amazed
to see villagers 'drop on the ground' at his sight, showing a 'religious
veneration' for the Wadiyar prince.[141] In report cards, his intelligence
and charm were also praised: by his teens, we read, the maharajah was
demonstrating 'caution and prudence in an unusual degree' – qualities
not associated with his predecessor.[142] He enjoyed 'manly' exercises –
riding, cricket, etc. – conveying with enthusiasm the count of tigers and
porcupines he shot.[143] All in all, Chamarajendra embodied the vision of
Indian royalty the Raj promoted: an ancient (-looking) symbol of kingly
power with (guided) modern impulses. Which also perhaps explains
why, where his adoptive father was a patron of traditional styles of art,
this maharajah quite connected with the hybrid format of a Ravi Varma:
like him, both Indian as well as touched by the Raj.

Of course, much time and thought had gone into moulding
Krishnaraja's heir to take precisely this avatar, his amiable character
making things easier. No sooner had the old maharajah died than

A young Chamarajendra Wadiyar.

everyone from the secretary of state in London to the ranis in Mysore got involved in the details of his successor's upbringing. Was he to be raised in the palace, 'near the influences of the zenana', or should he be placed with the commissioner in Bangalore, with British troops in the background?[144] In the event, it was decided to keep the boy in Mysore till he was older, while ensuring that those likely to gain 'undue influence' or urge 'demoralising' pastimes were kept away.[145] But what was to be done with the last maharajah's establishment? Not only had Krishnaraja left a collection of cows, he also had 619 relatives and 9,687 servants, including many 'so-called learned men' and 'lazy Mussulmans'.[146] It took months of plodding to work out how many of these to retain. And what of the administration? To the commissioner it was obvious that while endorsing native royalty was all good, Mysore had to 'assimilate' with the British model.[147] Chamarajendra, then, was to be educated to avoid the mistake his adoptive father made by attempting originality; he was to learn to *operate* a pre-engineered system, not question its wisdom. From the start, the ruler was groomed for a defined purpose. And unlike his contemporary Sayaji Rao, Mysore's maharajah never would assume a defiant posture, constrained as he was within clear limits.

Indeed, where in Baroda attempts to tie the ruler down met with resistance, in Mysore, because the Raj was rendering the state to the Wadiyars as an imperial gift, it was able to gain the upper hand. Having governed for decades, when transferring the 'rich and civilised' results of their work, the British demanded guarantees.[148] Mysore was projected as an 'experiment' – a term repeated often – in constitutional government; what Madhava Rao had hoped for Baroda, was executed here.[149] The imperial logic was that they could not risk 'chronic misrule' in case Chamarajendra became a new Krishnaraja. So, 'fundamental principles' were contemplated, including a system where the ruler worked with and would be moderated by a council. While he retained the power to override everyone (except, of course, the Resident), by getting him to share authority the Raj hoped to establish 'the groundwork' for a pan-Indian policy. Mysore, they hoped, would set a 'valuable precedent' in the imperial relationship with the states,[150] by adopting this rudimentary 'constitution'.[151] Chamarajendra's job was simple: to 'take a lively interest' in government without meddling in its details; to 'exercise a healthy influence' from a distance; and to appoint 'proper men' for all heavy lifting.[152] This constitution, predictably, was arrived at without consulting the boy himself; it was assumed he would take an 'intelligent view' and not object.[153] By all means, he was to be the master of his house; it was just that the institutional shape of the edifice was non-negotiable.

Thus, Chamarajendra's right to govern was construed as *not* derived from any treaties but from an 1881 Instrument of Transfer, after he came of age. In fact, 'unnecessary reference' to treaties would no longer be entertained.[154] That the new terms were one-sided is clear. For instance, the agreement required Mysore to surrender land to the Raj for telegraphs and railways; it divested the maharajah of jurisdiction over white residents of the state; opium and salt production was regulated; the imperial army had the right to occupy whichever areas it liked, whenever it liked; and more in this vein.[155] Besides, Calcutta would have 'practically unlimited' powers to interfere: a necessary condition to avoid quibbling as with Krishnaraja.[156] Of course, given the grand declarations about their work in Mysore, and the pontification around barring the ruler from jeopardizing what was achieved, one would think the Raj was giving the maharajah a state in immaculate condition. The facts, however, are otherwise. While Cubbon, when he ended his term in 1860, left a heap of money,[157] this had dwindled over time. Famine in 1877 demanded not only spending the balance, but also for sums to be borrowed. Yes, the British built 3,750 miles of new roads and set up 886 schools, but they were also saddling Chamarajendra with a debt of 80 lakh rupees.[158] Furthermore, Mysore's gold mines were leased to a foreign company *before* the transfer, leaving the ruler unable to amend this. And finally, so much for negating previous treaties, the authorities fell back on those very papers to justify an exorbitant tribute: the already large figure of twenty-four and a half lakh was raised to thirty-five lakh rupees, the highest in India.[159]

And so in 1881, a young prince was parked on the throne of an altered, colonially reinvented Mysore. In his people's eyes, he would remain a magnificent maharajah, but in action the Raj expected him to behave as chief executive of a de facto British province. It did not make the man despondent; it was clear that 'royalty could survive in India only in the highly institutionalised form' the British endorsed, and so, despite limits, Chamarajendra embraced the system.[160] Krishnaraja had resisted this in his day, bypassing hard limits on his position with tradition, art and literature.[161] Chamarajendra, on the other hand, does not seem to have been vexed; he was reared in the new framework, happy to excel on its terms. Given the British stranglehold on Mysore, perhaps there was no option,[162] and in time the principality developed a 'Janus-faced' image, as 'both a puppet and, at the same time, a model state'. Its rulers neither took on the Raj like Baroda, nor did they allow the stereotype of backwardness.[163] They managed to keep a footing in both tradition and modernity for different audiences, reflected in how Mysore city now became just the maharajah's abode ('a museumized royal landscape'[164]), while his self-consciously modern government was conducted from Bangalore, as under the old British commissioners. Where king and state were traditionally inseparable, now they occupied designated spaces.[165] The *state* was what mattered, and the ruler served as a hands-on executive, rather than a monarch of prior imagination: a policy that satisfied the Raj but would ultimately dilute what power remained with the Wadiyars.

For instance, the maharajah was taken on tours of the land as a child and continued this on a pan-Indian scale now. At first, Krishnaraja's widows were against allowing him even to leave Mysore fort, while crossing the Kaveri for trips outside the state was sacrilege.[166] In their view, the maharajah was a sacred being, enshrined in the palace 'like a god's idol in a temple'; he could not be carted around unceremoniously as if a mortal.[167] To represent functional elements there were ministers: the *ruler* stood higher. Sadly for court patricians, this approach was past its use-by date in the 1880s. The only time the old conception reared its head was at dasara, where too the British intervened. As a Resident complained, the festival had the ruler sit 'as a God to be worshipped', assuming a 'kingly divinity'. And alongside his subjects, a 'procession of

Europeans' also filed past, with even the British representative made to stand in the royal presence. While in Krishnaraja's day this was tolerated, now that Wadiyar power stemmed fully from Calcutta, the Resident opposed any such 'divine right' even in ritual form.[168] The maharajah gave way and allowed the man to sit.[169] But then again, Chamarajendra did not see such innovations as painful – to give a 'useful' modern gloss to an old kingly tradition, in 1888 he himself inaugurated an industrial exhibition to occur simultaneously with the festival. Dasara was no longer only about magnifying the monarch and his divinity, or reinforcing ritual bonds with the people; like the king, the festival too acquired a 'practical' quality.[170]

Indeed, this businessman's air appears even in Chamarajendra's portraits by Ravi Varma. In 1885, *The Pioneer* announced how 'Ravi Vurmah of Travancore' was 'now in Mysore' to paint its twenty-two-year-old ruler.[171] And the maharajah we see in two frames from this time is a man with a plan. In one, he stands bearing a sword. His neck and turban are ornamented, as befitting an 'oriental' prince, but his resolute gaze and the hand he places on his hip produce the impression of a man ready to attend to business as soon as done posing. The second picture features Chamarajendra in a chair, this time with a pocket watch and stick. Here his oblique gaze shows a mind reflecting on greater things, but again, the way his hand grasps the armrest, as though he is about to rise, suggests imminent activity. Compared, for instance, to Sayaji Rao's portrait, the contrast is clear. Baroda's maharajah is more 'present'; the ruler of Mysore is anxious to prove something. The irony, of course, is that while Sayaji Rao, who patiently endured his guardians' lectures, formed a dramatically rebellious character, it was the sprightly Chamarajendra who became a more compliant vassal of the Raj.[172] Unlike his predecessor, achievement would not take the form of temple donations, but of showing that the king could adhere to a work ethic. The maharajah had both a symbolic purpose, and a *job* behind a desk – which led a Resident to declare that without losing 'an atom' of his nativeness, the ruler behaved 'as if he were one of ourselves' (that is, an Englishman).[173] This rebranding was, in fact, internalized to such a

Ravi Varma's state portrait of Chamarajendra Wadiyar.

degree that when Chamarajendra's son succeeded him, a commentator wrote how that maharajah handled 900 files in his very first year.[174] Gone was the warrior, the conqueror and even the divine ruler; this was the age of the bureaucrat king.[175]

The transformation paid systemic dividends, for the nearly seventy years of Wadiyar rule ahead are deemed Mysore's golden age. On the face of it, the state got everything right: as far as the British cared, it followed 'practically the same' system as them, and Mysore would be grandly described by the 1930s as not just an Indian success story, but as a 'pattern for the world'.[176] Its triumphs were prominently advertised: hundreds of miles of railways; tens of thousands of irrigation tanks, not to speak of a monumental dam project; 8,000 educational institutions; a university; everything from a sandalwood oil factory to iron and steel works; and revenue, at three and a half crore rupees, which ranked the state among the wealthiest.[177] If Krishnaraja III had come back to life, he would have been astonished by what his heirs pulled off. For after the Wadiyar restoration, development became the state creed. In 1881, for example, Dewan C.V. Rangacharlu (1831–83) – Madhava Rao's junior at school – gave Mysore, for the first time in India, a representative assembly, albeit filled by nomination. When critics remarked that the people were not qualified for democratic experiments, the Dewan retorted that 'common sense and practical views' was all they needed.[178] A decade later, elections were introduced, and though few were eligible to vote, it caused enough sensation for an activist called M.K. Gandhi to cite this native 'parliament' when taking a political stand in South Africa.[179] Into the twentieth century, the state's success also made it a training ground for other princes, including Ravi Varma's great-grandson from Travancore. But what distinguished Mysore even among model states was its *industrial* prowess – a principle adopted in Chamarajendra's day and given force by his son.

At one level, Chamarajendra's personal temperament was conducive to this. As a boy, while cheerfully attending all classes, the maharajah evidently showed 'the most interest' in physics. Indeed, to his teachers, he seemed 'a different person' when 'dealing with concrete facts' as opposed

to abstract topics.[180] Rangacharlu encouraged this – he was on the ruler's
tutorial team prior to becoming Dewan and shared an enthusiasm for the
technical. As minister too, he supported students with scholarships to
study subjects like engineering; even when selecting a college principal, a
background in science was preferred to the humanities.[181] To the Dewan,
'machinery and capital' were imperative to agriculture also,[182] and in 1882
after telling the state assembly about government mills, Rangacharlu
delivered a sermon of national resonance. 'When all the world around
is working marvellous progress,' he declared, 'the 200 millions of people
in this country cannot . . . continue in their long sleep, simply following
the traditions of their ancestors.' A century before, India 'used to export
cloths', till technology revolutionized Western industry and turned the
tables. Mechanical strength was key to 'wealth and general prosperity',
and it fell upon Mysore to 'rouse' 'industrial enterprise' among natives.
By so doing, the state would 'infuse new life into the nation', becoming a
nursery for India's technological ambitions.[183] While Rangacharlu died
too soon, in the decades ahead his views were reiterated, not only because
they provided direction, but also for prestige. After all, when Bangalore
was 'illuminated by electric lights *before* Bombay, Calcutta and Madras',
it was not just about street lamps but also native pride.[184]

Here again we see a kind of nationalism that did not take to the
streets or quarrel head-on with the Raj. Instead, it sought to inspire
certain values in the people aimed at making them efficient, strong
and capable of holding their own. To be clear, in lecturing the masses,
Mysore's elite were viewing the people much as the Raj viewed them;
just as princes adapted to compensate for inadequacies exaggerated
by the British, they too expected their subjects to shed 'backward'
characteristics and to be shepherded. The elite had seen the light, as
it were, and preached their wisdom now. So, when Rangacharlu urged
Mysoreans on a 'career of progress' and to 'aggregate' their capacities for
the state,[185] he was asking them to become 'useful' for a higher purpose.
As Chandan Gowda observes, the people became 'assets' in a Mission
Mysore; they had to become a part of its 'productive powers', 'weaned'
from their complacency.[186] Indeed, one minister would demand that every

Wikimedia Commons

J.D. Rees's *The Duke of Clarence & Avondale in Southern India* (1891)

Dewan C.V. Rangacharlu, who set Mysore on the path to industrialization.

Chamarajendra Wadiyar shortly before his death.

subject 'adopt a policy of hustle and action' and 'change [his] psychology' even.[187] Another required that the people conjure up a 'burning desire' for advancement.[188] In other words, as the king had become 'useful', 'the masses' too were seen now as a *resource* for the state; their leaders had set a goal, and society had to climb into the bus. These periodic declarations from Mysore's rulers and Dewans were publicized widely too: after all, the imperial assault on India was also a battle of perceptions. The very picture of natives giving speeches on modern ideas was a retort to imperialism and its stereotypes.[189] Mysore also had an advantage in that Chamarajendra had inherited from the British commissioners a basic infrastructure; so, his idea of 'progress' moved beyond roads and schools, aspiring to that holy grail of Western superiority: industrialization.

Indeed, 'progress' under the Wadiyars wasn't just about keeping the British at a distance: there was an angst to set an example for India. And to be sure, as with many things driven by zeal, the state also ended up with some half-baked goods: glamorous policies, such as of compulsory education, won excellent press (not least for being passed soon after the British rejected the idea) but existed chiefly on paper. There were other risks also. Ninety per cent of the state's subjects were villagers, but money was channelled disproportionately towards stylish industrial schemes to fulfil official ambitions. It was not immediate mass welfare that mattered but the great *journey* Mysore was on, led by its English-educated elites.[190] For example, when the government set up its iron and steel plant it was aware that profits were unlikely; why, for fifteen years it ended up losing crores of rupees, which might have been invested elsewhere. But the intent was never monetary to start with; the whole thing was a powerful 'symbolic asset'.[191] The perils, everyone knew, were myriad, but the maharajah dove in anyway to make a point.[192] While there were critics – one lamented that the authorities devoured ideas from Canada to Japan but somehow skipped local needs – there was also patriotic support.[193] A newspaper reminded naysayers that Mysore was building a 'national asset' with 'noble' goals. Another spoke of 'unseen' benefits in inspiring Indians and paving the way to scientific greatness.[194] The real question was simple: could princely states only build schools and bridges, or were they entitled to bigger dreams? Could an Indian principality earn global respect and admiration?

While Mysoreans sought to realize its official dreams, outside, the state became a darling project even for nationalists. In 1894 when Chamarajendra died, at just over thirty, the news was so depressing that Ranade thought India's progress as a whole was 'thrown back a decade or two'.[195] The maharajah was not particularly bold insofar as challenging British dictates went, but because of what Mysore represented, even Ravi Varma's brother noted a 'deep gloom' among the native intelligentsia.[196] For seven years the state was under a regency, after which the late ruler's son, Krishnaraja IV (1884–1940), held power for four decades: a reign when industrial glory was sought with vigour. Indeed, Gandhi too, no friend of machines, respected the mission: in 1927, he would express admiration for Mysore's 'scientific spirit', seeing it as evidence against talk that Indians had 'no practical genius'.[197] In fact, successful states like this stumped the Congress somewhat in its attempts to frame a policy towards the princes: at once Mysore seemed joined to the imperial hip,

REGISTERED No. 664   RAVI VARMA PRESS PICTURE DEPOT.   H. H. Sir Krishna Raja   BOMBAY   RAVI VARMA PRESS. MALAVLI-LONAVLA.
Wadiyar Bahadur G. C. S. J. Ruler of Mysore

Krishnaraja Wadiyar IV in a chromolithograph print from the Ravi Varma press.

but it was also a fount of native achievement.[198] So even though in 1921 the Congress agreed, in principle, that states' issues could be discussed on its platform, prevailing wisdom was to avoid attacking maharajahs.[199] In fact, as late as 1934, Gandhi would respect this boundary: Congress, he wrote, had 'no more power to shape the policy of the States than' it had of working in 'Afghanistan or Ceylon'[200] – an attitude that would recede only in the twilight of the Raj, under pressure from a younger, socialist set. Until then, it was praise for enclaves like Mysore. Even into the twentieth century, that is, while Congress agitated against colonial rule, many British vassals remained examples of *Indian* rule.

Interestingly, this ambiguity existed on the royal side also, with the Wadiyars making sure to court nationalist praise alongside imperial approval. For example, the new Krishnaraja was a 'gentle', 'reflective man', evincing a 'prim sense of propriety'.[201] Under him, kingship, his Dewan confirmed, became even more about 'neutrality', 'restraint' and 'impartiality' – all to British liking.[202] Where Sayaji Rao was accused of sponsoring sedition, Krishnaraja went out of his way to assuage colonial fears.[203] And if Baroda was reprimanded, its southern counterpart was favoured: in 1913 the new ruler got the Raj to sign a fresh, less demeaning treaty,[204] and by 1927 tribute was negotiated to pre-1881 figures.[205] Mysore's nationalism too was for the most part limited to a 'safe' scientific space, never taking on Baroda-style adventurism. Which is not to say other strategies were completely absent. The press, for example, would be taken to the cleaners if it criticized the royal family; but when the same papers attacked the British, the government often looked away.[206] Colonial pressure led to stringent legislation, but even so, as late as 1922 the British complained that Mysore's papers would anywhere else have been long ago prosecuted into oblivion.[207] If and when the state tilted too much towards Congress – as in 1933 when its Dewan praised Gandhi[208] – there were rebukes, and the ruler would pull back. But soon, a coy flirtation would resume.[209] The nationalists reciprocated: they celebrated the state as an exemplar of good governance and discouraged anti-royal agitation. In 1929, in fact, Sardar Patel proclaimed Mysoreans lucky to have such a good ruler, adding that if they were still unhappy, the fault was probably theirs.[210]

In the realm of high politics, then, the Wadiyars got a few things right: industrialization brought home praise, and relationships with both the Raj and their increasingly strong opponents in the Congress were cordial. Underneath, however, unsettling dynamics were bubbling up, as Mysore's *people* revealed an appetite for politics. Technocratic visions of the future aside, the present still involved a society rooted in caste and older institutions. Demographic math holds some clues. The royal family and aristocracy at the time of the Wadiyar restoration in 1881 made up about 5,000 individuals. But this tiny sliver governed 4,70,000-Lingayat and 8,60,000-odd Vokkaliga cultivators with whom it had no kinship links.[211] So even as the state went ahead with new schemes, rural interests of a less 'progressive' type, James Manor notes, were left alone, to avoid unnecessary conflict.[212] Civil servants went out from the capital to collect taxes and inspect village accounts, for example, but so long as nothing egregious appeared, they 'rubber-stamped' whatever the Lingayat or Vokkaliga headmen presented.[213] Indeed, even the state's 'preference for prestige projects over village development', it is argued, was partly born from its risk aversion: 'improving' villages entailed dismantling socio-political structures, and after Nagara, the Wadiyars did not wish to unsettle the people.[214] So in the cities, urban hubs and on English-speaking platforms, the state tailored grand 'progressive schemes', while as far as possible avoiding stepping on rural toes. Of course, this was easier said than done, and as inevitable overlaps occurred, room was created for mass agitation.

The origins of the impending crisis lay in caste rivalry. Like other states, Mysore drew senior talent from a pool in British India. Rangacharlu was a Tamil Brahmin, and his protégé-turned-successor in office was of similar background. The latter, in an eighteen-year Dewanship (1883–1901), personally imported another 100 officials from Madras. In time this birthed that familiar lament against 'foreigners', by which critics did not mean the British.[215] While Chamarajendra had been happy to let his Dewans take the lead, his death saw his widow – the regent Kempa Nanjammani (1866–1934) – initiate a shift. Sympathetic to local aspirations, she disliked the Dewan's 'autocracy', and disapproved of his 'exclusion of her own countrymen' in favour of the 'Madras Brahmin element'.[216] Asserting royal prerogative, then, she, not the minister, chose members to the ruler's council, setting a precedent by introducing a Christian, a *local* Brahmin and a Muslim.[217] When the Dewan retired, the regent put a Mysorean in office (interestingly, Purniah's descendant).[218] Though from now on the Mysore Brahmin began to hold his own against the shipped-in Madras version, by 1918 this led to a fresh problem: despite being 3.8 per cent of the population, Brahmins held 65 per cent of higher appointments, and 69 per cent of the lower.[219] Their early investment in English education explains this dominance, but as non-Brahmin officials – a slice of the Lingayat and Vokkaliga groupings – slowly entered the fray, they appealed to the ruler for fairer shares of posts in government. And as with his mother, Krishnaraja IV was sympathetic; conciliating these powerful segments was critical to prevent resentment welling up against the royal family.

Such changes were, however, to the umbrage of the engineer-Dewan, Sir M. Visvesvaraya (in office from 1912 to 1919). To him, merit was the sole criterion for government appointments: a problematic line when 'merit' was measured against English qualifications, where Brahmins dominated.[220] In his mind, there was nothing wrong with the existing arrangements, and the people were not *really* dissatisfied; only a loud minority had started manufacturing grievances.[221] The Dewan's fear was also that if 'efficiency' and 'merit and capacity' were subordinated to social pressures, Mission Mysore would be jeopardized. So, while he was willing to grant more scholarships and so on to non-Brahmins, he would go no further.[222] This, however, was where the palace came in: non-Brahmins had the maharajah's ear, and when he ordered a detailed study of the issue, the Dewan resigned. In 1921, then, the Wadiyars pushed mild reforms in the teeth of official (Brahmin) opposition.[223] While it did not birth any dramatic results, the non-Brahmins' success catalysed a political awakening – it was clear that pressing the government delivered results.[224] By the 1930s, then, two groups formed: non-Brahmins with rural roots, and a largely Brahmin urban set. One flashed hinterland dominance and strength in numbers; the other, resentful of competition

Krishnaraja Wadiyar IV in a portrait by K. Keshavayya.

Dewan Sir Mirza Ismail.

and the new royal policy, picked up nationalism as its weapon.[225] It was not that the Congress's anti-colonialism suddenly acquired a magical hold; it simply offered an otherwise small group a disproportionately long stick to wield in local battles.

A century after Nagara, then, the political chessboard was again uncertain. The ruling elite's goal in the 1880s was to show that 'the interests of the government' were 'identical with those of the people'; now, however, doubts emerged that the two were at variance.[226] Over time, for all its excellent press, Mysore's money-guzzling industrial projects had required cuts in other areas, ranging from schools to health. Funds were pulled from rural areas to power big schemes, which also accumulated debt.[227] If earlier rural populations were content with being left alone in their preserves, with time, exposure, and the new education system, they wondered aloud why they were subsidizing grand enterprises, all decisions for which were taken by a Brahmin-led bureaucracy. All at once, thus, the powerful Brahmin element felt let down by the Wadiyars' non-Brahmin turn, while the non-Brahmins

began to grumble about the state's priorities. Animosity was also born
of the latest's Dewan's personality. By the late 1920s the maharajah was
dismayed by his ministers' inability to rein in factionalism and the threat
this posed to Mission Mysore; so, he placed in office Mirza Ismail, a
trusted friend. Ismail was devoted to the ruler but proved also a dictator.
Or, as Manor tells, just as the British were readying, in *their* territories, to
share more power with Indians, Mysore fell into the lap of a Dewan with
no corresponding intentions.[228] Instead of coming to an arrangement
with progressively more frustrated parties on either side, Ismail clamped
down. By doing so he moved politics into a much wider, less governable
space inspired by that dreaded word: democracy.

The result was that the chief forces in the state would soon combine.
The sequence, in fact, also reveals how local politics and the national
at last began to overlap. The Congress's state wing – dominated by
Brahmins – derived its appeal from the prestige of its parent body.
But in 1936 when it contested elections,[229] its fears were confirmed:
Congress's nationalism, for all the respect it commanded in theory, did
not have reach on the ground with princely subjects.[230] Instead, it was
the non-Brahmin People's Federation that did an excellent job, given
its rural networks, playing on *local* issues.[231] But instead of retreating
into their tents, the rivals reassessed each other, their shared dislike for
the Dewan serving as a bridge. On the one hand, to be taken seriously
by their own national leadership, the local Congress needed to win; as
mentioned before, princely states were not a nationalist priority, and if
this attitude were to change, state units would have to make a mark.
But then again, to win in Mysore, non-Brahmins were key.[232] The non-
Brahmins, in turn, had the capacity to win, but the legislature was,
by design, dominated by officials who thwarted all anti-government
moves. From the non-Brahmins' perspective, only extraneous pressure
could move the Dewan – and Congress, whose praise the government
valued, and whose criticism would, by that yardstick, sting, suddenly
looked useful. Soon, a marriage was in the works. A force emerged that
was both local as well as enmeshed with the nationalist movement. Its
goals were also unprecedented: instead of simply seeking to manipulate

the system for a better share of government posts, this new united front wished to transform that system and give Mysore representative government.[233]

Thus, in 1937 the two groups – hitherto enemies – united into a single entity, which, after a few hiccups,[234] was incarnated as the Mysore State Congress (MSC). Its call for democracy may yet have failed were it not, as with Nagara long ago, for a violent event. In preparation for a royal wedding in 1938, the state banned political agitation. The MSC was amenable – dislike of the Dewan did not mean royalty was disrespected – but information about the ban did not circulate. In April, then, at Viduraswatha in rural Mysore there was a tragedy. Local MSC members had called a meeting on the margins of a festival attended by tens of thousands of people. Though most of the crowd had nothing to do with politics, a nervous police squad fired, killing dozens: a circumstance that has led to the event being termed south India's Jallianwala Bagh.[235] Details were disseminated across the country.[236] Indeed, Gandhi, who had hitherto censured younger Congressmen for encouraging agitation against maharajahs and been less than warm towards the MSC, reversed his stand. Referring to it as an 'awakening', he gave the party his endorsement.[237] Where so far it was the *government* that had sought nationalist praise, now that prestigious commodity legitimized its dissenters. Additionally, as Manor tells, most Mysoreans had been 'largely apolitical': they loved their ruler, enjoyed the attention the state received, and kept faith in the order. But after Viduraswatha, politicians, who had so far looked like a 'collection of eccentrics', now seemed to have a point.[238] And when Ismail haughtily described all this as less 'awakening', more 'hooliganism', he made himself and the system he represented lose even more sympathy.[239]

To Krishnaraja's credit, however, he was responsive. In 1938 a committee was organized to recommend reforms, leading to the promulgation of a fresh constitution in Mysore.[240] The old representative assembly was expanded; in the legislature, for the first time, the majority of seats were reserved for elected members, ending the government's capacity to smash inconvenient proposals; and at least two ministers

would be people's representatives, not royal appointees.[241] The Dewan
would, of course, remain powerful, but the carrot of future changes
was dangled. Again, however, paper pledges did not translate neatly
into action. While conceding a limited democracy, Ismail was bent on
keeping the MSC out: in the 1941 elections, the first under the new
constitution, many MSC candidates were declared ineligible on spurious
pretexts, and their candidates accepted only in twenty-one of forty-four
seats. But even so, the party won seventeen.[242] Meanwhile, there was
also drama in the palace. In June 1940, two months after promulgating
the constitution, Krishnaraja IV died, and was succeeded by his nephew
– the son of a brother, who had never got along with Ismail.[243] The new
ruler thus had little fondness for the Dewan, so after the 1941 election,
Ismail's fate was sealed: the maharajah informed the Resident that his
minister's hands were 'not clean'.[244] Interestingly, the young prince was
also against 'running Mysore by over-industrialisation': to the horror
of his technocrats, he rejected an automobile manufacturing scheme.[245]
Industrialization for the sake of industrialization did not appeal to him;
it had in some ways even hurt the state and its internal peace.

But if there was hope attached to the new ruler – who attended
college like an ordinary student and reportedly sympathized with the
MSC – it was soon dashed. Having succeeded to the Wadiyar state,
with its many balances and calculations, this scion proved no radical.
Agitation continued as a result. In 1947 the maharajah acceded to the
Indian Union, but still resisted full representative government. (It is
generally assumed that with Independence, royalty lost all its powers; in
reality rulers retained a great measure of authority until the states were
integrated with the Union in 1949.) An effort was made to maintain
the old system, with a cabinet dominated by royal officials, whereas the
MSC insisted that elected representatives hold the balance of power. An
impasse having been reached, in September 1947, there were protests
on a historic scale. Students walked out of school, workers abandoned
Mysore's factories and a crowd of 1,50,000 descended on Bangalore to
stand before their ruler.[246] It was an interesting parallel to the Nagara
rebellion, when too thousands had banded together, blowing horns

and defying royal authority before Krishnaraja III. At that time, the maharajah turned his back, and British troops broke the revolt. This time, however, there was no Raj. The writing on the wall was clear, with some papers even carrying extreme headlines calling for a 'Destruction of the Maharajahs', and cartoons where the Wadiyar was depicted as a donkey.[247] And so, finally, on 12 October 1947, the ruler gave in: Mysore would have democracy. Two years later, when the state was merged into the Indian Union, he was given a ceremonial post, till eventually the royal family was left with no role at all in government.

But for all this radical change, in one area, the dynasty retained its kingly identity: to this day, the head of the house appears on the old throne at the dasara festival, representing a sovereignty that once was. And as if hedging bets, the last maharajah's son would join the Congress and win parliamentary elections, reconstituting the Wadiyar image yet again in the eyes of a new, democratic public.

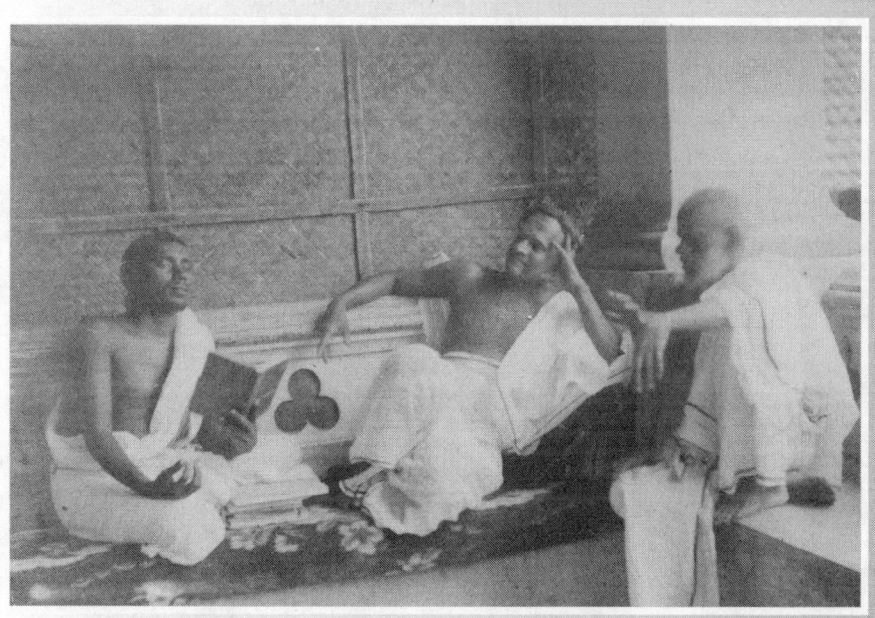

Ravi Varma, seen here listening to Puranic tales, remained a fairly conservative man all his life. In 1901 the artist went to Mewar (Udaipur), a most orthodox state, whose ruler impressed him with his old-world charm and bearing. This chapter tells the tale of this Rajput kingdom, and of a prince who resisted British ideas of modernization — and nearly got away with it, but for conflict emerging within his realm.

7

The Rana Who Would Not Reform

Not long before Ravi Varma's death in 1906, the Wadiyars of Mysore commissioned him to do a fresh set of paintings. By now he was known to more than one generation of maharajahs, who recognized his stature by bestowing hefty fees as well as gifts of prestige. On one occasion this included an elephant, for example, while another present was an exquisite length of Mysore silk – when the artist produced a final Puranic series, he showed the fabric draped around the deity Krishna, subtly thanking his patrons for having given him something worthy of the gods.[1] Ravi Varma then had the gift repurposed, surrendering it to his ten-year-old granddaughter to make into a skirt and blouse; it was wearing these that Sethu Lakshmi Bayi entered her wedding *mandapam* in Travancore in 1906. But if the shawl went from Krishna's shoulders to a Malayali rani's waist, another Ravi Varma frame – also featuring silk brocade – tells a more fascinating tale. For after Krishnaraja IV was married, the artist was asked to do a portrait of the couple.[2] At a glance, the result is wooden: despite splendid clothes and an opulent background, there is a listlessness in the faces. The lady leans on a chair while her husband rests his hand on a table on the other side, lending to the picture not regal formality but an undertone of awkwardness. It could be written off as a natural lack of ease between two people put together in an arranged marriage, were there not as much awkwardness in the *political* context behind this union. For although the bride is dressed entirely in the

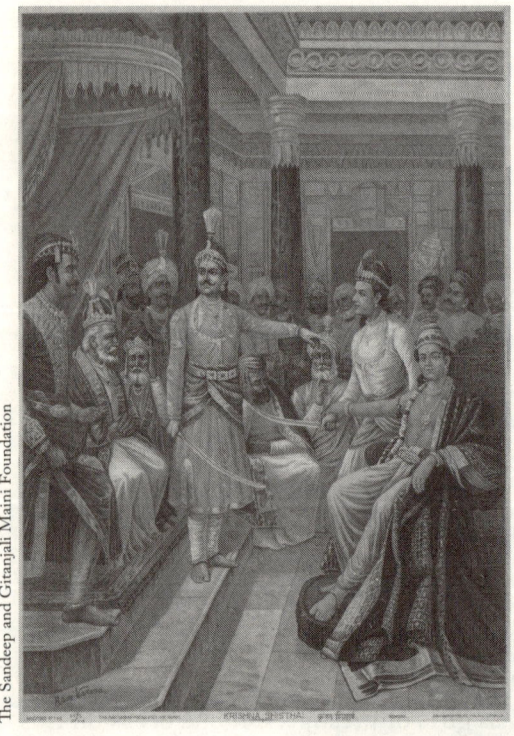

Chromolithograph print of the painting featuring Lord Krishna wearing the Mysore silk shawl gifted to Ravi Varma.

Sethu Lakshmi Bayi and her husband in her wedding portrait by N.N. Nambiyar.

Chromolithograph print of Ravi Varma's portrait of Krishnaraja Wadiyar IV with his Rajput wife.

Mysore style, she was an imported Rajput princess, lost in the world of her southern husband.

The Wadiyar obsession with Rajputs began in Chamarajendra's day. Typically, royal spouses were drawn from the ruling dynasty's own Arasu caste, while concubines and junior wives came from other regional groups. But with the royal family's gaze moving from a local horizon to a pan-Indian colonial landscape in the late nineteenth century, a desire emerged to associate with dynasties elsewhere. And Rajputs, valorized by the Raj and respected by Indians, were the very cream on the spousal menu. The first moves were engineered by Chamarajendra's guardians: on a trip north in 1876–77, the then British commissioner and the future Dewan Rangacharlu attempted to pick the maharajah a bride from the Rajput house of Rewa. Sadly for them, the queens at home were against bringing in a girl from a 'strange family' and, in keeping with custom, demanded an Arasu.[3] The guardians conceded, though as mentors of a 'modern' maharajah, there was no question of allowing him polygamy – where his adoptive father had twenty ladies, Chamarajendra took only one wife. She was given an education, and in the 1890s their English-speaking daughter invited appreciative remarks for spurning purdah.[4] But the impulse to forge a new tradition and cast a wider marriage net did not disappear; and though Chamarajendra married locally, he revived his guardians' plan by seeking options for his *children* from outside Mysore's limited buffet of mates.

It was, however, an ambition easier dreamed up than achieved. To begin with, the maharajah died before his offspring were wed. Imperial officials-turned-marriage brokers reported to his widow that Rajputana's aristocracy 'did not recognise the Mysore family'; before they could be persuaded to give a daughter, perhaps a foot could be got in the door by marrying a Wadiyar princess to a Rajput ruler. Though it meant admitting inferiority, an alliance with Kota was considered, but its prince wanted a dowry so unprecedented in size that the proposal failed.[5] But for Krishnaraja IV, his mother was determined, having the Dewan fuse old narratives with these new dynastic needs. Mysore's maharajahs, he thus claimed, were also Rajputs, only that having migrated south centuries ago, 'distance, difficulty of communication etc.' had cut them off. Happily, however, the 'railways and telegraphs' had made the world flatter, and so a 'more intimate intercourse' was feasible again with their northern kin.[6] The argument, in other words, was that the Wadiyar anxiety for Rajput blood was not an innovation, but a revival of custom. Of course, none of the chief Rajput maharajahs bought the tale, and Mysore's claims to matching status remained in the realm of theory for some more years.[7]

After great effort, however, Chamarajendra's son did find a Rajput bride: the girl in that Ravi Varma portrait. For all its grandeur, though, the scene masks a compromise. Krishnaraja IV was a prince entitled to a twenty-one-gun salute, ruling over millions and master of one of India's richest states. His wife, however, came from a family that governed a microscopic dot in Kathiawar, with no salute, 3,000 subjects and less than 40,000 rupees in revenue. That is, when premier Rajputs declined Mysore's overtures, its royal house had to fish beneath its political status.[8] It was not a popular decision. Arasus did not take kindly to being bypassed, and a critic warned of 'evils'. Rajputs were 'flesh-eaters'; would the bride adapt in a vegetarian palace? What language would the dowager maharani speak with the mother of her future grandson?[9] But it was all a fuss about nothing, for ultimately the union failed. Five years after marriage, the viceroy was told that it remained unconsummated, and that the 'poor sweet' girl, unable to fit in, was suicidal.[10] Calcutta was asked to intervene, because Krishnaraja had 'forbidden even his mother and sister' to speak to him on the matter.[11] It all went nowhere: the Rajput princess never had children, and Mysore's next (and last) maharajah was Krishnaraja's brother's son – a Wadiyar born, as before, to an Arasu mother.[12]

By the time Mysore's rulers began these matrimonial quests, a romance around Rajputs was well established in the Raj and among India's English-speaking intelligentsia. This had much to do with the Rajput self-image, defined by valour and a martial spirit. For instance, it was a source of awe that when faced with defeat, Rajput communities once embraced mass suicide (*jauhar* and *saka*), with women burning themselves, while men, high on opium and 'insensible of danger', charged towards death at the hands of their enemies.[13] Poetic embellishments birthed songs of resistance – the tale of Padmavati of Chittor, for example, has inspired multiple retellings, even as historians quibble over its veracity.[14] By the late nineteenth century, jauhar, with its heroic figures resisting subjugation, animated nationalists, Ravi Varma catering to the mood by painting a scene.[15] The Rajput lionizing of honour – and their vaunted preference for death over disgrace – touched living memory too. In 1810, for instance, a Mewar princess gave her life to terminate a military stand-off. Krishna Kumari was promised to a Marwar prince. But when he died, her father betrothed her to another suitor. This agitated the Marwars, who claimed the alliance was dynastic, not specific to the dead man, till things escalated into armed conflict. Years passed, and neither party could be satisfied without dishonouring the other; so, for peace, the princess took poison: an event that not only amazed the British,[16] but led even a Travancore Dewan in the south to dramatize it in his *Kishun Koovur: A Tragedy in Five Acts* (1840), among the earliest English plays by an Indian.[17]

That said, the romanticization of Rajputs owes as much to imperialism as it does to tradition. Though incarnated later as a closed, proud community, there is evidence that Rajput identity was more porous, based first on a warrior ethos before it evolved into a caste. That is, as mobile, warlike classes achieved landed status through military success, they slowly constituted a sealed ethnic group. While some Rajput clans trace back their history into the medieval period, it was under Islamic rule that the identity solidified. Combining Sanskritic modes of legitimization – involving claims of descent from gods and Puranic heroes – with bardic lore and an emphasis on genealogy, the Rajputs slowly became the community we know today. While several groups around upper and western India claimed the label, Rajputana became the focus of 'purer' lines, with others often deemed spurious.[18] Either way, by the seventeenth century, Rajputs enjoyed widespread recognition as authentic Kshatriyas, reflected also, for instance, in how the ascendant Marathas sometimes claimed Rajput descent.[19] The Mughals not only won them over, but also deployed them across the subcontinent in their expansionist ventures – it was a Rajput, thus, who led a major campaign against the Deccan's warrior-king Shivaji. By the time the British replaced Timur's heirs as the land's dominant force, then, Rajput society had established practices, including 'ancient' ideals of kingship, and an image that would appeal to their new (white) interlocutors – besides, evidently, English-speaking Mysorean princes.

In what sits inconveniently with India's nationalist narratives, however, the Company's arrival in their dominions was welcomed by several Rajput powers. Once, during the high noon of the Mughals, these kings were treated with respect, united through marital ties with the emperors, and benefited materially from the alliance.[20] But Mughal decline in the

'Rajpoots' by Francis Frith.

Elisha Whittelsey collection, the Elisha Whittelsey Fund, 1972, via the Metropolitan Museum of Art, New York

eighteenth century saw the Marathas burst forth from the Deccan to subjugate Rajputana. This had interesting results. For instance, Jai Singh II of Dhundar (founder of Jaipur city) first used this time of flux to widen his territorial influence; but on his death, his conquests fell under Maratha hegemony, which so embarrassed his successors that as late as the 1940s, a historical treatise was barred from publication for describing their vassalage too transparently.[21] Rajputs, with a sophisticated court culture, also tended to look down on the Marathas as upstarts, which made their political emasculation extra humiliating. As James Tod (1782–1835), the celebrated colonial-era writer, argued, the Maratha period was 'surcharged with evil', as these 'vampires' drained the Rajputs' 'life-blood'.[22] There was only partial truth to his claim, however, because not all suffered. Kota, for example, prospered by provisioning the very Maratha armies that tormented Rajputana.[23] But Deccani dominion did cause instability, so that when the Company arrived as victors of the Anglo-Maratha War in 1817–18, many rajahs felt genuine relief.

It is no wonder, then, that Tod, appointed colonial agent in western Rajputana soon afterwards, would cast the British as saviours of noble Rajputs – a formula in which the local kings became legitimate rulers, Muslims and Marathas illegitimate interlopers and the Company restorers of order.[24] Tod's *Annals and Antiquities of Rajast'han* (1829, 1832) would in fact become *the* textbook on Rajput history, including for Rajputs themselves.[25] The man was certainly special: wedded to romanticism, he was keen to demonstrate that India had natural leaders. To Tod, these kings only needed to be restored – they would shine without imperial interference. Rajputs were not savages: they had a powerful history and constituted a 'nation' which had endured dramatic tribulations.[26] Though, for instance, jauhar and saka occurred in intra-Rajput conflicts also,[27] hereafter they were cast as proof of Hindu resilience against Islamic invaders. Or as Tod wrote, these were the 'struggles of a brave people for independence' and for 'the maintenance of the religion of their forefathers'; what they had been 'sturdily defending' was 'national liberty'.[28] To be clear, the Scotsman was not pulling theories out of the air: seated 'amidst the ruins of ancient cities' he listened to songs of bravery, picking up from local bards what he would rehash (uncritically) in English.[29] If, he further believed, the Company did well by Rajputs, they would win not only submission, but also India's finest warriors to 'die in our defence'.[30] In glorifying Rajputs, that is, the imperial official saw profit for his own side also.

Interestingly, many of Tod's beliefs stemmed from a passion for Mewar's Sisodias, deemed the most important of all royal Rajputs – and the focus of this chapter. Ruling from Chittor and then Udaipur, Mewar's kings were styled 'maharanas'. That their dynasty was notable is clear: where other Rajputs bent the knee to the Mughals early on, the maharanas held out. So defiantly, in fact, that even Emperor Akbar ordered a massacre in their capital in 1568 – and still, the rulers would not submit. It was in Jahangir's reign that the family surrendered, but on unique terms: no maharana would appear at the imperial court, sending his heir instead, and Mewar was exempted from military service. That is, in an early form of 'indirect rule', Mewar was promised it would be left alone if it accepted nominal suzerainty. This, in fact, became something of a calling card for the Sisodias: that they never gave daughters to the imperial harem was worn as a distinction, while heirs apparent, disgraced by dancing attendance on the Mughals, were at home ranked below some of their own nobles.[31] Jahangir himself played up Mewar's eminence: before him, he declared, they had 'bowed in submission to no sultan'. Though intended to parade how the emperor had outdone his 'exalted father',[32] it was also a backhanded compliment to Mewar. The maharanas, meanwhile, cast themselves as upholders of Hindu honour.[33] If other houses challenged these claims – especially Dhundar (Jaipur) and Marwar (Jodhpur), which thrived under Mughal patronage – Tod's bias for the maharanas meant that *their* view was amplified into a general truth.[34]

But for all his glorification of Rajput yesterdays, the living horizon before Tod during his 1818–23 tenure was uncertain. Rajputana's states were born of complex dynamics of conquest and expansion, with lasting structural effects.[35] So much for 'ancient' legitimacy, these kingdoms were historically established on land seized from others – Bundi, for instance, had been under nomadic Meena tribes till the Chauhans took it, as was Dhundar before it was conquered by the Kachwahas.[36] Mewar was dominated by Bhils, an echo of which was visible at every royal coronation, where a Bhil tribesman had ritual duties.[37] Many of these tribes continued restlessly on the peripheries, so the Rajput order stayed highly militaristic. Moreover, the king was not master of all: his clansmen who had enabled the first conquest received land (*thikanas*) to govern autonomously. So autonomously, in fact, that even royal troops did not ordinarily transgress.[38] Similarly, junior sons with no prospects of the throne had an incentive in conquering virgin territory – if in subordination to their fathers or brothers these would become fresh thikanas, but could also serve as nuclei for future kingdoms. Bikaner, thus, was established by a Marwar prince, Kota by a breakaway member of the Bundi family, while in the eighteenth century a Dhundar relative carved out Alwar.[39] Recognition could be purchased in defiance of the parent state – both Kota and Alwar obtained *Mughal* certification of their independence.[40] The Rajput system, then, was a balance of power between kings and *thikanedars* (chieftains) and royalty was always tested by subordinates, waiting to transition to princely rank themselves.[41]

It was precisely this fluidity that led a colonial official to describe the Rajput order as made of 'septs', unable by design to become bureaucratic states. Great swathes of Rajputana, he noted, existed in this 'molecular condition' – there were vassals, and then more vassals, down to the village level.[42] Holding it all together, then, depended on the king's ability: if he were weak, he would find his nobles trying on big boots, but if strong, he could keep them in check. This also explains why at the height of Maratha power Rajput rulers found themselves under siege outside as well as within – a king weakened by external enemies would find his underlings trying to realize their own political ambitions.[43] Why, an ineffective royal centre could provoke even seemingly non-political institutions to flex their muscles: in Mewar a prominent temple began to assert control over its surroundings, becoming 'a kingdom within a kingdom complete with military levies'.[44] Ministers too could reduce weak rulers into marionettes. Kota, for example, was for fifty years, in the late-Maratha and early-British period, under a regent. He kept the king grandly but cornered power, raised a loyal army, took up patronage of royal shrines, stabilized the economy and orchestrated a 'slow conquest' from within.[45] In the end, seventeen Kota districts had to be carved out as an independent state for the regent's heirs – the creation of yet another Rajput principality at the cost of an older one, this time in the nineteenth century.[46]

It is not surprising, therefore, that in framing policy for Rajputana, the British were determined to place its shifting polities into a more concrete grid. Though the place was shaped intimately by Mughal imperialism as much as by these internal dynamics, Tod was convinced there was an 'original' system that had worked in a 'degree of perfection'.[47] In this imagined past, the Rajput order functioned like a well-oiled machine, where chiefs quietly served the king, whose authority was sacrosanct. If evidence contradicted this, it was blamed wholly on Maratha and Mughal intrusions. Armed with this outlook, Tod and his fellows set out to restore substance to princes, nearly everywhere in enervation – Mewar's maharana, for example, despite claims of primacy, was in such dire straits that he lived off a pension Kota's regent sent him.[48] To correct things, Tod retrieved the *khalsa* – that is, the territorial segment under direct royal control, most of which had been usurped by thikanedars; with British guns, he now commanded their return. Or to quote from an announcement in Dhundar, 'friends of the Maharaja were the friends of the British' while his enemies would be deemed 'their enemies'.[49] Soon Tod had thirty-three Mewar chiefs sign an agreement with the maharana, by which the nobles gave up encroached khalsa lands and promised to obey their king.[50] With Company soldiers backing the throne, the thikanedars had no option, but even so they retained formidable influence.[51]

Of course, the British incentive in reinforcing royalty is familiar to us from other cases: only an empowered king could collect revenue. Or as a local minister put it, 'What is chiefly wanted by your [people] is our money.'[52] But even so, the centralizing policies espoused in Mysore, Travancore and Pudukkottai were absent; in Rajputana the British were less keen to do away with the chiefs. Indeed, it was stated later that helping maharajahs 'break' the 'turbulent and reactionary nobles' and establish 'uniform administration' might appear 'an obvious duty' to British civil servants. But they were to 'abstain' and keep 'the equilibrium of weight' between king and lords instead.[53] The Mughals too had followed this pattern, using thikanedars as a check on Rajput princes, to ensure the rajahs never got *so* secure as to challenge the emperor.[54] In copying this attitude, the British added their own interests and explanations. For instance, in the 1830s, Tod would argue that in the event of a Russian invasion, unlike perfidious Marathas and Muslims, Rajputs would fight for the empire, given how the Company had liberated them from their spoliators.[55] But for this it was essential to preserve their moral and physical vigour – and this was best guaranteed by leaving them alone. Unlike, say, a Pudukkottai in the south where the British had no interest in local Kallar chiefs, Rajputana's nearness to international frontiers and the Rajputs' history of fighting across India provided the Company a military impetus to try and respect their political traditions.

But if these were colonial calculations, the maharana and his courtiers also tried to manipulate the British. When the nobles attended Tod's call in 1818 to do homage to their ruler, it was British arms that persuaded them, not a call of duty. Wisely, the maharana too did not gloat. In a later literary rendition, Tod is presented as declaring, 'Point out to me those who would wish ill of you, Maharana Sahib; the English Government is prepared to deliver punishment.' It is the *king* who excuses 'previous offences', with the soft warning that if anyone misbehaves again, 'Sahib will be notified immediately.'[56] In other words, though restored to vitality, the ruler wished to stress power on *his* terms; by showing himself as kind, he was reminding errant nobles that he was his own man, and imperial action depended on *his* word. Subtle reminders could be circulated, as in 1849 when Mewar's coins were minted with the inscription 'dosti landan' ('friendship with London').[57] But the nobles too knew tricks. In 1821, thus, Tod was sent a representation by Marwar's chieftains, which would have resonated in Mewar also. The thikanedars agreed they were 'servants' of the maharajah but pointed out that just as the king's

Wikimedia Commons

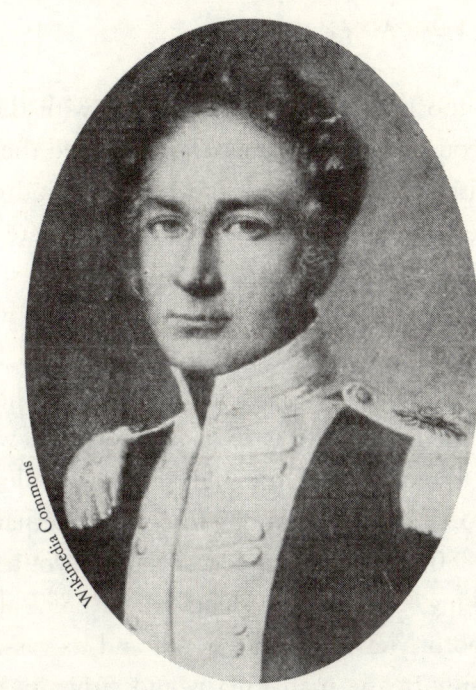

James Tod, British political officer and influential colonial-era historian of Rajputana.

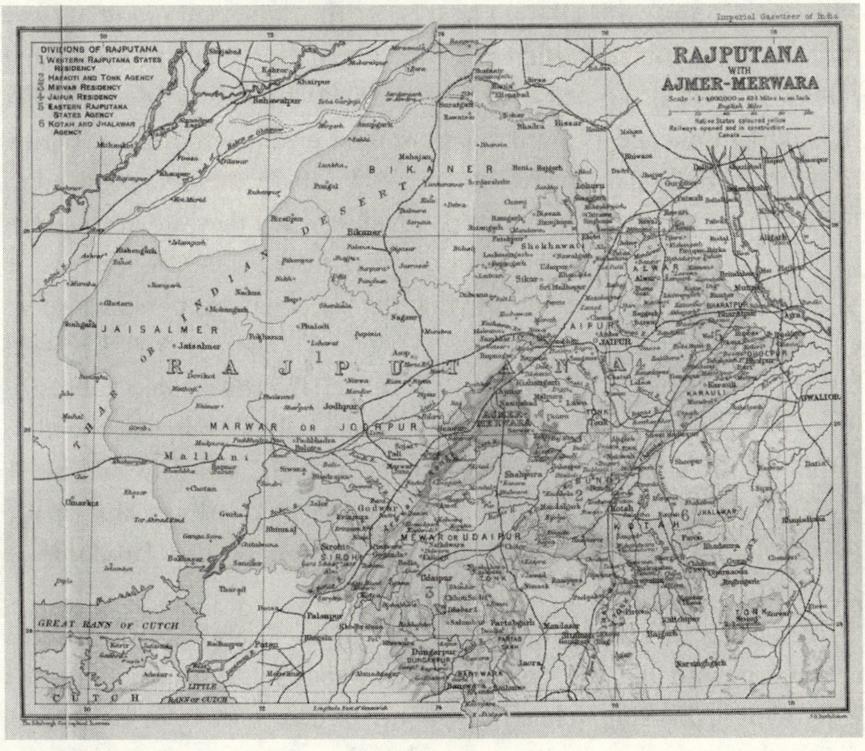

Wikimedia Commons

Map of Rajputana.

ancestors had reigned, theirs too had 'made the state', and 'with their lives preserved the land'. Of course, when the maharajah needed them, they would come; but otherwise, 'we are again his brothers and kindred, claimants and laying claim to the land'.[58] That is, their rights were as sacred as those of the royal line.[59]

In Mewar, this volatility between nobles and the throne was embarrassingly obvious, well into the British period. In 1855, for instance, the maharana's soldiers would be chased out of a thikana where they had gone to inflict punishment.[60] As late as 1876 a Mewar chief was trying to persuade the British to recognize him as independent, while in 1884 royal troops again had to attack a defiant chiefdom.[61] Underhand tactics were also at play: in 1880 certain thikanedars would encourage a peasant revolt against the king.[62] The Great Rebellion of 1857 also revealed divergent interests: both Mewar's ruling house and its vassals knew that without British support, the maharana would struggle. So, when the Company faced its gravest crisis, the ruler went out of his way to support it, while powerful nobles advocated for the rebels.[63] Financial subversion was also possible. As late as the 1930s it was admitted that though the thikanedars owed a sixth of their revenues in tribute, '[t]ruly speaking' nobody 'pays the full amount'.[64] Formally they were obliged to place armed men at the king's disposal – but when they did, it was with bad horses 'and men who were not of the right type', such as 'barbers' or 'sickly people'.[65] It was also found that the big chieftains possessed more villages than on the record, paying no tribute for these; so too they used bribery to manipulate royal servants.[66] In fact, the thikanedars' influence was so deep-rooted that even in the 1940s, wholesale bureaucratization stayed off the table: British officials knew that the vassals would never give up those judicial, economic and political privileges that made them little rajahs in their own right, and simply become landlords or pensioners.[67]

This sense of autonomy extended to protocol also. Just as princes negotiated with the Raj on points of ceremonial, thikanedars did so with rulers across Rajputana. The distance of their seats from the throne, the thickness of the cushions on which they rested, the colour of the cloth draped over it, all signalled status and were carefully managed; for some vassals the king might rise only on their arrival but for others, on their departure also, confirming difference in prestige.[68] In Mewar, particularly, some nobles were entitled to be received at the palace door by the ruler, as opposed to others who met him in the durbar.[69] Why, some of them were important enough to even mint coins.[70] In this ritualized setting, nobles could also pose as sticklers for tradition to humiliate the ruler or show themselves as better. For example, when the Company banned sati, the maharana took an age to pass corresponding orders. It was frustrating for the British who did not, however, realize that if the ruler accepted Calcutta's policies without a fight, his own thikanedars would loudly accuse him of 'ingratiating himself' with foreigners and dishonouring their ancestors.[71] Mewar, for all practical purposes, was a state with smaller states within it; the maharana had not only to manage the Raj but also shrewd vassals. Or as was noted in 1880:

> The chiefs of Meywar enjoy rights and privileges which do not obtain in any other part of Rajputana. The court maintained at their own estates is almost an exact counterpart of that of their prince, and they exhibit few of the marks of vassalage observable at other courts; and only on particular festivals and solemnities do they join the prince's cavalcade. In durbar they take rank above the heir-apparent . . . [and when] a [senior] chief enters the presence, the entire court rises, and the ceremonial is most intricate.[72]

In fact, serious political interests were at stake in the management of durbar rituals – something the British understood. Practically speaking, in the early colonial phase it was their agent, Tod, who was really in control in Mewar – under him khalsa territory was recovered, and from fifty thousand rupees in 1818, the maharana received about ten lakh four years later.[73] And yet, when it came to displays, Tod kept the king supreme: he even sat barefoot on the ground like everyone else.[74] While sadly the man's career ended under suspicion that he had become 'too much of a Rajpoot himself',[75] his approach was essential to fortifying royal authority. Only by showing that the British too respected kingly rituals would the king be able to assert himself over *his* subordinates. Which for superiors in Calcutta opened other problems: if the colonial state got too accommodating, what about its own prestige? For instance, Mewar's rulers tried to absent themselves from the Raj's pageants on the count that they had never appeared even before the Mughals. The viceroy would not allow it, given that it would make the British look weak. So, he offered a compromise: at an imperial durbar in 1870, the viceroy went to the door to welcome the maharana, while others had to show themselves in.[76] But the issue of ritual remained prickly. In 1875, compelled to go to Bombay to receive Victoria's son, the maharana was aghast at having to walk behind Sayaji Rao of Baroda.[77] And in 1903 a successor went to Delhi, only to turn back on discovering he would not rank first in Curzon's durbar.[78] This was not whimsy or petulance, but knowledge that inferiority before the British would affect how the maharana was perceived by testy *Indian* subordinates.[79]

To be clear, not all Rajput princes behaved the same way. For example, when the maharana was made a member of the Order of the Star of India in 1871, far from rousing affection for Victoria, it left him horrified – the Sisodia king was styled 'Sun of the Hindus' ('Hindu Suraj') and could hardly accept the inferior tag of a regular 'star'.[80] On the other hand, Ram Singh II of Dhundar (Jaipur) (1833–80) relished imperial titles: in *his* situation, they were useful to brandish as marks of British support, helping assert control over his nobles.[81] Ram Singh, in fact, played both the British and his thikanedars. He knew the authorities liked schools, but when he established one for his nobility, it was to mould minor thikanedars to his liking.[82] He developed a bureaucracy, but limited its scope: for instance, revenue collection was *not* modernized to avoid giving anyone 'detailed knowledge' of state accounts.[83] The books were coolly fudged – in 1871 Ram Singh claimed revenue of under forty lakh when it was between fifty and sixty, by so doing paying a lower tribute.[84] He welcomed British railway and irrigation schemes, but limited these to khalsa lands: thikanedars were content that their autonomy was respected, but in the long run lost out as the king enriched himself.[85] In

Rijksmuseum, Amsterdam

Ram Singh II of Jaipur.

all, as an official noted in 1907, the state presented a 'strange combination of conservatism and progress' – Dhundar's rulers knew what to conserve and where to progress, serving themselves against the Raj and their nobles both.[86]

But in a monarchical system so dependent on the king and his capacity to hold the reins firmly, what if he were a minor? Rajput elders typically saw minorities as dangerous; as was remarked, child rulers brought 'evil'.[87] In the 1890s, a Bikaner prince on his accession after a regency also began by announcing how 'if the people' – by which he meant thikanedars – 'have no strong hand over them they go wrong'.[88] In Mewar's experience, minorities allowed not only the British a greater say, it emboldened the nobility too. In 1861, for example, a regency council was formed for a boy king: colonial officials used it to introduce 'reforms', while thikanedars got away with reducing dues to the durbar as well as reclaiming territory.[89] When in 1874 again there was no heir, the British banished an older claimant and adopted a minor for the 'ample powers' it gave them;[90] yet again the throne lost strength. But then Mewar had a stroke of luck: in 1884 the sitting maharana died, and his place had to be filled by adoption. As such, many royal cadet lines existed – Chundawats, born of a fourteenth-century prince; Shaktawats from a brother of the iconic Maharana Pratap – but recent adoptions were made from one of three houses sprung from an eighteenth-century king. So together the nobles chose their next ruler, this time a man of thirty-five, who had been running his own thikana, and would perhaps be sympathetic to thikanedars' rights. It certainly gave the state stability, but the latest Sun of the Hindus would neither satisfy his vassals nor dance to the Raj's tune. The reign had begun of a maharana who would not reform – and who would diminish his thikanedars further still.

In 1901, Ravi Varma came to Udaipur – Mewar's capital – to do a portrait of its ruler. It was not the kind of place he was used to. Rudyard Kipling had noted its 'swaggering gentlemen' so 'lavishly adorned with arms',[91] and a second visitor also observed how practically everybody was 'bristling with weapons'.[92] Unlike the great cities of the Raj, it was only recently that the place even became easily accessible, for earlier the nearest rail station was seventy miles away. Naturally, then, Udaipur retained a quaint magic, its life dominated by the court, rather than the commercial hustle and bustle of a Bombay or Madras.[93] The maharana himself was unlike the 'enlightened princes' the artist knew, and surprisingly for a major ruler, spoke no English: when Ravi Varma and his brother went to the palace, they were received 'in the old style', with everyone squatting on a carpet, speaking Hindi.[94] While the visitors were state guests,[95] it was weeks before the ruler deigned to pose for them. Even when he did, he betrayed little interest. Or, as Ravi Varma's sibling diarized: 'The Maharana is too shrewd a man to express his opinion on any thing off hand. We shall know what he thinks of [our work] by and by.' In fact, even when he *seemed* pleased, 'he did not express any opinion'.[96] His satisfaction was only patent right at the end, when in addition to fees, the painters were honoured with ceremonial robes, Ravi Varma personally also receiving a necklace of pearls.[97]

Maharana Fateh Singh of Mewar (see plates section for his portrait by Ravi Varma).

In the principal portrait that came of these brief sittings, Maharana Fateh Singh (1849–1930) is a stately being. Unlike Ravi Varma's typical compositions, this canvas is not crowded: there are no distant hills, marble pillars, carved armchairs, or English books. The maharana stands against a pale green curtain; there is a handsome carpet beneath his feet; and his robes are silky white. In contrast to Ravi Varma's other maharajahs, he also does not appear in trousers and achkan – the uniform of the new, business-oriented prince – nor does he wear imperial medals. Instead, it is an *angarkha* we see, from under which emerge two feet, encased in blue slippers.[98] Ornaments, of course, are visible, but the real highlight is the sword in Fateh Singh's right hand, and the shield tucked under his left. Indeed, the impression the portrait creates is not of a twentieth-century ruler – certainly not a bureaucrat king – but of a warrior about to mount a horse and ride into the distance. The most powerful features, however, are Fateh Singh's eyes: regal and unapologetic. This, in some ways, was a one-man answer to the cliché of Asiatic effeminacy; and if there was 'backwardness' in the maharana's un-Westernised look, he wore it with pride.[99] To those prone to romance, here was a living embodiment of all that was glorified in Rajputs. In fact, with Fateh Singh the stereotype fit the man, for the maharana had a deep consciousness of legacy – of

Ravi Varma's Udaipur paintings, only two were focused on the ruler; the remainder were recreations from older works showing four of Mewar's greatest kings.[100]

Fateh Singh, as alluded to before, had landed on the throne by accident in 1884. It was lifestyle choices that killed the previous occupant – he had an opium addiction, and as the British noted, lacked the 'moral courage' to exercise 'abstention from excitement' even when unwell.[101] As soon as the man passed, the nobles were gathered, and royal widows consulted. Their finger fell on Fateh Singh, who not only came from one of the eligible families, but also had a son to cement his succession. The chief reason for electing an adult, though, was that the thikanedars 'avoided what [they all] dread [namely] a long minority' – under British-controlled regencies, they too had lost some rights.[102] In fact, the maharana was enthroned the same night, annoying Calcutta – in installing a ruler without imperial consent, the court was perpetuating 'mistaken ideas' as to its power.[103] Still, what was done was done, but since Fateh Singh lacked 'training', the Raj tied his hands with 'stipulations'.[104] From the start, it was clear that 'progress' would be rewarded.[105] Fateh Singh played along till the stipulations were waived: he pledged loyalty, put up Victoria's statue, and named buildings after imperial figures. Meanwhile, the British approved of his character: unlike his predecessor, this maharana rose at four every morning and was at work by six.[106] Instead of erotic poetry, his favourite readings were from the Sanskrit law books.[107] Unusually, Fateh Singh was also a monogamist.[108] His only overwhelming passion was for the hunt, and any time news arrived of a worthy animal, off he would go, throwing state business to the wind.[109]

However, over time it became clear that the maharana was pointedly conservative, and that tradition to him was an article of faith. Where in the 1860s his forebear spoke English,[110] and there was even a thikanedar who drank sherry and smoked cigars,[111] the current ruler showed not the remotest inclination to anglicize himself. Yes, externalities were welcome: Western art attracted him, 'so long as [it] served to glorify the Sisodia tradition'.[112] So too with sport, Fateh Singh was open to European influence – a Resident would remember how his retinue

Clockwise, Maharana Pratap Singh I (r. 1572–97 CE), Maharana Amar Singh I (r. 1597–20 CE), Maharana Raj Singh I (r. 1652–80 CE) and Maharana Jai Singh (r. 1680–98 CE), all painted by Ravi Varma for Fateh Singh in 1901.

and he, 'depositing their swords on a table and kilting up their skirts', played tennis.[113] But when it came to *kingly* duties, the maharana was less interested in 'enlightened' ideas: if his predecessors established schools, constructed roads and brought in the railways, Fateh Singh only half-heartedly kept these up. In fact, under him, Mewar's 270 miles of metalled roads actually fell to 257 miles due to neglect.[114] It was not as though the ruler was incapable: projects that appealed to him, such as restoring old forts, went excellently well; he simply refused to buy into the cult of 'improvement'. The political philosophies of his ancestors were adequate, and he saw no reason to join a race with 'model states' – the Sisodias existed above such fashionable trends. This attitude baffled outsiders. As a Resident reported, Fateh Singh was 'extremely pleasant' but 'narrow minded, very suspicious and sensitive as regards his dignity', and in what was a handicap for a modern prince, knew 'nothing of the world.'[115] As he had governed his thikana prior to adoption, so, it seemed, he would rule Mewar as maharana.

While some thought it was lack of exposure that gave Fateh Singh this anachronistic vision of kingship, this was only partially true. An early visitor, for example, thought him 'a shrewd, careful statesman', perfectly abreast of Britain's latest troubles in Ireland.[116] So too a la Ram Singh, he allowed calculated doses of 'progress' if he saw gain. Railways, for example, had years ago come to Chittor – Mewar's old capital – but expansion to Udaipur was pending. The maharana simply would not move. It was a decade before Fateh Singh accepted British urgings, after extracting something in return. His minister Pannalal Mehta (1843–1919) – also painted by Ravi Varma – had become something of a pain. Mewar's own 'native statesman', Mehta's force of personality made him enemies while his ease with the British allowed detractors to brand him an imperial cat's paw. While the fact that the two previous rulers were young (both died in their twenties) and, thus, amenable to guidance made him a fixture in the system; now, however, the man had to deal with a dominating maharana. After ten years of putting up with Mehta, then, the railway question gave Fateh Singh a window: he would, he told the Resident, sanction the project if the Raj let him dump the minister.[117]

And because, as the maharana understood, imperial interests trumped sentiment, the British agreed. They got their railway, but Fateh Singh won the better bargain. For never again would he appoint a Dewan, leaving the British to rue the day they dismissed their friend.[118]

Unsurprisingly, Fateh Singh's rule was beset with problems – one viceroy described Udaipur as 'most beautiful' but also 'capital of the most backward state in India'.[119] The maharana did not care, for he was not in the business of seeking imperial approval: Mewar had survived centuries, and it would last into the future also. Besides, all this song and dance about progress perplexed him: he could not, for example, understand the obsession with good roads when cart tracks had worked perfectly well for a thousand years. Indeed, when managers of a pilgrim town appealed for better connectivity, Fateh Singh asked *them* to foot the bill; after all, it was their temple that stood to benefit.[120] Resistance to modernization touched even administrative structures – in 1903, thus, the officer in charge of Rajput states admitted the 'difficulty of inducing

Private collection, New Delhi

Ravi Varma's 1901 portrait of Rai Pannalal Mehta. On meeting him Marianne North wrote, 'He had an emerald necklace that I longed to command possession of immediately, or loot.'

[Fateh Singh] to move in the direction of modern progress', for he was too jealous of 'his hereditary rights'; the smallest reforms entailed giving up some control, and here was a man who would not even appoint a Dewan.[121] Two decades later, the grievance was repeated: Mewar was 'one of the worst' states, and a key factor was that the maharana would 'grant no delegation of his powers'.[122] Instead, he maintained secretaries, and to sustain his hold, played one against the other.[123] So bad was Mewar's appearance, in fact, that even nationalists – otherwise defensive of princely autonomy – were alarmed. Gokhale, for instance, asked the British to do something, leaving an official chuckling that amidst cries of 'India for Indians', here was a patriot endorsing colonial interference.[124]

What is interesting, however, is that the authorities were constrained when it came to coercing the maharana. In 1893, for example, the Resident observed how just as Mewar was once 'the only Rajput state that refused to give daughters to Delhi', now it was the 'only large state that refuses to [maintain] Imperial Troops' for the empire.[125] Successive viceroys nagged Fateh Singh, but it took him decades to raise a single cavalry squadron.[126] The governance pattern was similar. Though in 1905 he agreed to develop three irrigation projects, as late as 1921 little was done.[127] Still, generally speaking, Calcutta had 'no intention of pressing reforms' on Fateh Singh 'against his will'.[128] Why, even one as hostile as Curzon was gentle: when he came to Udaipur, he praised Fateh Singh as a 'hard-working ruler, who lives a simple and exemplary life' and worked 'assiduously'. Only in the mildest terms was the maharana asked to reform, when the viceroy feigned concern that 'His Highness takes himself too severely' and should 'allow himself a little respite and . . . outside assistance', to take some weight off.[129] But there was logic behind treating Mewar with kid gloves. To begin with, the maharana was 'personally upright, just, and sincere' and his 'private character' was 'above reproach' – he was not squandering money or whiling away his time in European tours.[130] Secondly, Mewar was not in the red: interference was easier if there were a financial crisis. All that could be said was that were not enough roads and canals, but that was ultimately Fateh Singh's internal business. So, as a Resident reminisced, the system could be 'hopelessly clogged', with even death sentences pending twelve years – but there was little anyone could do other than cajole and hope.[131]

Personally too Fateh Singh was grand and not the type a civil servant could berate. One visitor thought 'this marvellous Maharana, so stern, so bearded, and so brilliantly turbaned' every bit 'the direct descendant of the sun'.[132] Another felt Fateh Singh 'needed no jewels' to lend him majesty, for he was 'the natural embodiment of royalty'.[133] Indeed, it was added, 'if this was the result of nearly two thousand years of breeding and generations of personal rule, there was clearly something to be said for *preserving* such qualities'.[134] Even Residents were seduced. One reported how he had 'never seen a finer or more dignified countenance', and that for all of Mewar's flaws, in 'no State were the relations between the Ruler and the Resident so generally happy'.[135] Another described Fateh Singh, as 'one of the finest characters I have ever met'; he was 'constitutionally incapable of deviating from the truth' – it just happened to be the truth 'as he conceives it', disinterested in moving with the times.[136] On visits to discuss state matters with the Resident, the maharana's conduct was

A view of Udaipur from M. Griffith's India's Princes *(1894).*

such that the former 'learned to respect and venerate' him – language imperial officials were unaccustomed to employing for native princes.[137] There was also an old-world charm to the man: he often tucked notes in his turban and waistband, which could lead to amusing moments when the wind sent official secrets flying around. At such times, the Sun of the Hindus and the viceroy's agent, 'dodging amongst the chimneys and ventilators', would run about to retrieve the papers.[138]

To British officials, in fact, though the administration looked prehistoric, they could also see that Fateh Singh worked extremely hard. As we read from one account:

> I had an insight into the methods of a lonely, deeply conscientious man, whose conception of his duties involved the responsibility of coming to a decision independently of any possibility of outside influence by interested parties. He kept all the records of important questions under his own lock and key in small tin trunks. Every memo relating to a case was known to him and to him alone. And we would, on such occasions, sit side by side, with the yellow tin trunks on the ground beside His Highness, who, with meticulous care, producing at each step the relevant paper, would give an outline of the matter in dispute. I would give much to be able to present . . . a portrait of this splendid old man, bearded and robed in the long coat of the Sesodia tradition, bending the whole of his mind and soul to the service of his State and ancestry. Never, in the unravelling of the many problems we discussed, did a consideration of self enter into the matter.[139]

Clearly, then, the British were in awe of this vassal. The press played up his significance – Fateh Singh was, one paper wrote, 'a demigod' and 'an object of worship' to Rajputs.[140] Officials agreed, with even an unfriendly Resident warning that the maharana's status could in future make Udaipur a Hindu 'rallying point' in a Great Rebellion–style anti-colonial movement.[141] Even when Fateh Singh did naughty things – such as avoid functions at the 1911 Delhi Durbar claiming ill health[142] – it was not easy to admonish him. For whatever 'punishment' was imposed, 'we [the British] can never dethrone [the maharana] from his position in the hearts of the Rajput people'. An insult to him would, in fact, put the Raj 'in collision with the Rajputs, the most loyal of all Indian communities'.[143] So where a Sayaji Rao was harassed, this ruler had too much cultural capital to be dealt with roughly.[144] Besides, did they *really* want to force 'progress' on him? Many believed – thanks to Tod's romanticizations – that 'patriarchal' government was 'suited' to Rajputana; the 'poorest Rajput', it was observed, 'has a pride in ancestry which is a shield against Western modes of thought'. The maharana was merely a manifestation of this trait – if he kept modern schemes 'under consideration' for decades, it was perhaps because his people did not need them.[145] In 1906 the Resident agreed that local 'conditions and customs should be scrupulously respected and no change should be introduced merely because it coincides with some preconceived idea'. It would, he warned, 'be a great mistake' to 'attempt to transform an essentially Rajput state into a model British province'.[146]

Interestingly, while the colonial attitude towards Fateh Singh bordered on reverence, among Rajputs he had a reputation as a difficult, overbearing man. One of his daughters, for example, was betrothed to Bikaner's maharajah – but when the latter came of age, he backed out because 'he felt that the ultra-conservative Maharana' would be 'troublesome' as a father-in-law.[147] He had a point: when the maharana gave a daughter to Kishangarh, he treated his son-in-law hideously. On arriving in Udaipur, thus, the wedding party found that not only had Fateh Singh not come to receive them, but he also forgot to send anyone of any standing.[148] Though the guests were unhappy – 'If Odeypore is so big,' one wrote, 'why the devil does he give his daughter to Kishengarh' – they had to swallow the insult.[149] Things got worse: the maharana did not visit his son-in-law's camp, arranged no entertainments, and, to add injury to insult, delivered such a colossal dowry that his superiority was reinforced.[150] Elaborate protocol was also on display to demonstrate that Mewar was in a different league: each time the maharana took a sip from his wine glass, for instance, a fresh handkerchief would be presented for him to wipe his mouth. Rumours circulated that every time he picked something off his plate, 'a servant . . . carefully wipes off every finger', again and again till the dinner's end.[151] Monotonous as it seems, for Fateh Singh it achieved his goal of flaunting status. Venting against him, then, was done in private: a visiting nobleman, thus, wrote that though the maharana was fond of riding, his stables were 'not worth much', his horses 'fat as bulls'.[152] If ever the maharana read this rant, he would have curled his lip.

Given that this is how even fellow princes fared, it is hardly astonishing that Fateh Singh was 'uncompromising in his attitude towards' Mewar's thikanedars.[153] As one commentator wrote, these lords were 'as proud as [the ruler], and every one is rigorously tenacious of his hereditary rights'.[154] Their autonomy is also clear in that in 1880 their combined income came close to the royal khalsa revenue.[155] In other words, they were a powerful group if they banded together. For this reason, recent maharanas had cultivated loyalty, in general using more carrots than sticks. Fateh Singh, however, began to intrude even in the thikanas' internal matters, and areas essential to his vassals' dignity. That is, while he was particular about protecting his own rights and the aura of his position vis-à-vis the Raj, *within* Mewar, he was prepared to ride roughshod over rights claimed by his nobles. Less than fifteen years into his rule, thus, the chiefs sent the British a diary of grievances: the king was, they complained, forcing his laws into the thikanas; their right to use emblems and marks of status were being denied; the maharana was interfering in economic affairs; minority rule in the chiefdoms was being exploited; and so on.[156] Fateh Singh, of course, sent in a rejoinder – the chiefs were idlers and steeped in luxury; they did not show respect; tributes were measly; and more along these lines.[157] While the British tried to mediate, fifteen years later relations between the maharana and his lords were still frosty. And since the Raj would not categorically reprimand the ruler, it only made him bolder.

Indeed, the maharana's confrontations with his nobility, some of them with roots going back generations, reveal a form of centralization after all. The rajadhiraj of Shahpura, for example, was practically independent – his seat was a Mughal grant (hence its name, honouring Emperor

Fateh Singh and his entourage, by the Udaipur painter Liladhar.

Shahjahan), but as a Sisodia clansman, he also held titles and lands from Mewar. So, while the British had separate dealings with him, the maharana also levied tribute.[158] In recent years, Shahpura had tried to break loose of Mewar, provoking Fateh Singh to assert rights even more strongly. The rajadhiraj, for example, was asked, like other nobles, to come to Udaipur and wait on the ruler. And when he declined, territory was seized. It led to a decade-long legal wrangle, but in the end, Shahpura had to bend.[159] In another estate, when the chief died, Fateh Singh announced an adoption without hearing the family's wishes. There was a will favouring another man, with the Resident agreeing that his claim was stronger. But the maharana fixed his nominee – it was alleged that he preferred a child to an adult, for the same reason the Raj preferred minorities: it offered a chance to interfere. And besides, the family's candidate had received a Western education, which to Fateh Singh was a disqualification.[160] In a third thikana, where the chief and his heir died in the 1918 influenza pandemic, the ruler denied adoption altogether: the dead thikanedar had not been loyal, he argued, so, with his death, his territory was escheated. It was, curiously, a Rajput prince applying the notorious Doctrine of Lapse *within* his state, and when alarmed nobles appealed against this, Fateh Singh rejected their pleas, acting like a Rajput Dalhousie.[161]

In sum, then, the maharana's vision of kingship was simple: to avoid modernization as well as instruction from his colonial superiors; to rule autocratically, even if it created a mountain of problems; to cut to size his thikanedars and leave them shorn of any capacity to challenge the royal centre; and, thus, to focus all authority in the person of the king. Given the British regard for him, Fateh Singh's policy may even have worked – as it indeed did for decades – but for the fact that it was impossible in the twentieth century to remain an island amidst changes in the larger context. With the First World War, the colonial framework itself underwent convulsions, and Indian nationalism was beginning to disrupt the status quo; in these circumstances, even relatively recent promises grew outdated. For instance, in 1909 at a speech in Udaipur the viceroy had declared that the Raj would not interfere in any state, unless things got so bad as to make it seem an 'instrument of misrule'. Each principality, Lord Minto added, was free to be governed by its internal balances, and any reforms 'should emanate from the Darbars themselves, and grow up in harmony with' local culture. Instead of the British ramming ideas, 'methods sanctioned by tradition', he believed, were better.[162] By this yardstick, the maharana had no cause to worry – his rule was traditional, his subjects did not complain, even if nobles did, and he was respected by the Raj. But by the fourth decade of his reign, something shifted: suddenly the bonds that held Mewar were imperilled. And in the end, though left alone by the British, the maharana's rule – with what an American called its 'senile medievalism' – was terminated by resentment bubbling up from the ground.[163]

One of the side effects of Fateh Singh's resistance to material modernization was that his people had increasingly to pay a price – and if they did not earlier realize it, with time things became starkly obvious. For example, even if the maharana's refusal to build roads and allow railways was a sign of resistance to colonial penetration, when Rajputana suffered a famine in 1899, it proved a rather costly way of marking defiance. News circulated of people feeding on human flesh, but when the British recommended that loans be given to thikanedars for relief, the maharana spent months arguing about the terms, instead of acting.[164] Combined with a cholera epidemic, nearly a million people died in Mewar, with Calcutta noting that much of this could have been avoided had Fateh Singh made even the slightest investment towards an efficient administrative mechanism.[165] Similarly, at a later period, it was found that though a cess was collected to set up modern medical facilities, these taxes, accumulated into a grand sum, were lying unused simply because the maharana had not sanctioned any spending.[166] There was no Dewan, no qualified man to seriously guide the government, and so matters of general public welfare were hanging fire. As noted before, Fateh Singh was still too grand a personage to be reprimanded, but with time, his suspicion of change would cost him gravely – and not because of the Raj, but because his *people* refused to put up with it.

For example, the maharana's intransigent attitude towards his thikanedars indirectly sparked peasant resentment. The royal policy of extracting as much financial heft and power as possible from the nobles meant that within their domains thikanedars acted in the same cavalier fashion towards the people. That is, if Udaipur highlighted royal prerogatives and put pressure on the chiefdoms, the lords became just as jealous of *their* feudal privileges vis-à-vis their subjects. Many traditional levies the thikanedars claimed, for example, had made sense in earlier days when they protected peasants from threats; but by the end of the nineteenth century, with overall political stability, it was patent that these taxes had become anachronistic. All the same, there was no room for the people to convey disillusionment, for any challenge to the thikanedars' right might open the door to retaliation, including in the form of torture. As we read of one technique:

> A common form of physical torture, practiced more often in the thikanas, was the device of putting the male members of the kisans' [peasants'] families in *kathi*. Kathi was a medieval instrument of torture. It was made of two parallel wooden bars, with a third piece of wood going only halfway up the middle. The legs of the person . . . were tied down to the parallel bars while the middle bar was fixed between the legs so that he could neither sit, nor bend, nor move around. Normally, a person was put in kathi for 5 to 6 hours at a stretch.[167]

Historically, this was not always how things were. Given that density of population was low in Rajputana, the ruling class could not afford peasants abandoning the fields. So, in general, if oppressed, farmers were able to petition their lords or the maharana for redress. With the sitting ruler, however, because he was doggedly against tampering with the feudal system, the people had few options. For instance, in 1897 in Bijolia, peasants were unhappy with their thikanedar. Their tax was nearly half the yield, to which was added many dozens of cesses and an obligation to provide corvee labour.[168] When representatives were sent to the capital for relief, it took half a year to obtain an audience with Fateh Singh; he in turn gave the Bijolia chief little more than a warning. Famine made things worse: the thikanedar launched a dam project to employ and feed people, but also used their desperation to break peasant unity. Four years later, he imposed a fresh tax: no marriage was allowed without paying a fee. It was such an unpopular move that the peasants 'in protest stopped marrying their daughters, and in 1905 took two hundred marriageable' girls in a march to the thikana headquarters.[169] This forced the thikanedar to rescind the tax, but respite was brief. When the man died, his heir had to pay Fateh Singh a succession fee. To find the money, the new thikanedar raised taxes again, and this time the peasants threatened an exodus out of Bijolia. If there were hopes that Fateh Singh might mollify them, they were dashed: instead, their leaders were arrested.[170]

What nobody at the time realized, though, was that Bijolia would become the nucleus of a wider movement. Spread over 260 square kilometres, this was a major thikana, with eighty-three villages and thirteen junior lords within its bounds.[171] All too clearly structural defects in the Rajput system were visible here. The peasants were Dhakar Jat, and not direct beneficiaries of the Rajput order.[172] These Jats were also connected through caste networks with Jats in British territory; and as they felt increasingly unheard in Mewar, winds of resistance blowing in from outside acquired meaning. In fact, a Bijolia resident, Sadhu Sitaramdas, in 1905 formed an association to disseminate nationalist news in the thikana, and by the end of the decade, was urging peasants to stand up for their rights. 'How long will you keep on giving away 40 per cent ... to the [thikanedar]?' he thundered. 'How long will you accept the position of slaves?'[173] In 1913, he launched an agitation which saw Jats refuse to touch the plough for three seasons. Soon after, Sitaramdas invited a revolutionary, Vijay Singh Pathik, to lead the movement.[174] The result was that in one of Mewar's principal thikanas, an organic protest was streamlined and sharpened by experienced leadership and a nationalist vocabulary, including the cry of 'Vande Mataram'. By 1919

Gandhi had learnt of Bijolia, while Pathik began attending Congress sessions.[175] He went so far as to challenge Rajput legitimacy, in an effort to rouse the people:

> [The] majority of the rulers of Rajasthan brutally crushed the republics of Bhils, Minas, Yaudheyas and Jats by the might of their swords but their own pride could not stand before the Mughal Emperors, the Maratha Generals, and the English merchants.[176]

This, in fact, troubled the Raj more than Fateh Singh's administrative obstructionism. To begin with, contacts with nationalists were worrying. But, more ominously, by banding together the peasants of Bijolia emasculated the thikana administration. Under Pathik, they constituted an elected board, raised a volunteer police force, set up courts, a school and a parallel power structure.[177] It was 'a revolutionary repudiation of all that the feudal polity of Rajasthan stood for', as Pathik trained farmers to 'run a civil institution', bypassing existing systems.[178] Indeed, Bijolia inspired copycat efforts, as in princely Sirohi; soon a local affair was metamorphosing into a wider movement, provoking colonial paranoia. In fact, songs critical of the maharana too were being sung in Bijolia. Hitherto his officials and the thikanedars might be attacked, but the royal name was above reproach; now, however, Fateh Singh was *personally* targeted, in what was an unusual development. The Sun of the Hindus – the Rajput leader whom even the Raj hesitated to admonish – was losing the ground on which he stood. Though there was outside influence in giving the resistance strategy and leadership, at the end of the day the grievances were local; even without the nationalists, a people's movement would have expressed itself one way or another. Alarm bells also rang given global events, and there was, as an official remembered, a real fear 'that Rajputana was going Bolshevik'.[179] This was not unjustified. One song, for instance, warned:

Listen, O Rana of Mewar!
Your subjects are crying for your attention,

Pay heed to their cries
The ryots of Bijolia are tired of writing about their woes to you
There is little time left to waste . . .

There is no trace left of the Russian Tsar
Listen Fateh Mal
Be true to your religion
Your Upparmal [that is, the Bijolia region] is in a deep sea of sorrow . . . [180]

Even as peasants reminded Fateh Singh of the Russian emperor's fate, a second crisis arose in the form of tribal agitation. This had its own history. Late in the nineteenth century, a British politician had during a visit noticed 'occasional companies of fierce' Bhils who made up 'a large section of [Mewar's] population'. Noting how they were 'armed with bows and arrows', to him it appeared as if these 'aborigines' were 'untamed' even under the Raj.[181] He was not the first to detect their

Purchase, Cynthia Hazen Polsky Gift, 1992. Metropolitan Museum of Art, New York

Fateh Singh hunting female bears, by Udaipur painter Pannalal.

restive shadow.[182] In the 1860s, the Frenchman Louis Rousselet wrote of these one-time masters of Mewar, forced uphill as the plains were conquered by the Sisodias. Like Pudukkottai's Kallars, Bhils were cast as 'thieves' who went on 'marauding expeditions' into Rajput areas. Though to an extent incorporated into the system,[183] the greater portion of Bhils lived in 'almost perfect independence' in the south-western hill tracts, 'scattering terror amongst merchants and agriculturists'.[184] Nearby villages paid the tribes tribute as did passing caravans, failing which they would attack and plunder. Or as was noted in 1841:

> When their dues are paid the Bheels seldom commit depredations; [but] when withheld, no native power has yet been able to coerce them; travellers and merchants pass through their hills without molestation or interference after paying the usual tax, and property under their charge is rarely plundered or touched; on the other hand if any attempt be rashly made by travellers to force a passage without paying these dues, they are certain to be pillaged: thousands of these wild and lawless spirits, as their war scream is re-echoed from hill to hill, will immediately collect from every hamlet in the neighbourhood to resist this or any other innovation.[185]

That is, though outside the mainstream shaped by so-called civilized classes, these beef eaters were not to be trifled with. While clashes with the Rajput rulers and their satellites was endemic, the entry of the British worsened things. In fact, from the 1820s the latter deployed arms against the Bhils, intending to cut off their traditional levies, and tame them into a sedate existence.[186] Of course, this was quicker hoped for than achieved, because Bhils resisted with all their might. Thus, for instance, despite the maharana's loyalty to the Company during the Great Rebellion, when rebel troops entered Mewar, 4,000 of his Bhil subjects aided *them* instead of upholding the ruler's stand.[187] A decade later, Bhils again 'indulged into lawless activities', and military retaliation was ordered in 1868.[188] In 1876, guns were used for the first time against them,[189] and even then they did not give up – because, what to the Raj and court seemed like refractory behaviour, was to Bhils a defence of their way of life. They had their own gods and institutions and tested royal authority constantly; just as thikanedars were protective of their autonomy, Bhils too had rights they viewed as inviolable. In other words, besides the struggle between king and nobles, or nobles and peasants, Mewar also saw tension between the state and tribal groups.

This tribal question, in fact, traditionally aggravated the Raj. For 'unsteadiness' with Bhils in Mewar could and did provoke 'turbulent and audacious behaviour' in Bhils in *British* territory also.[190] Tribal networks criss-crossed large swathes of upper India, and unrest in one corner could easily threaten imperial security. In 1881, for instance, this was visible during a rebellion in the maharana's lands, triggered by colonial-style 'reforms'. The state had opened customs posts at the borders, depriving Bhils of their dues. Around the same time, pressed by the Raj, the maharana banned salt production: this led to inflation, hurting all poor groups, Bhils included.[191] Cultural prerogatives, such as the right to brew mahua liquor, were ended so as to be commercialized by outsiders,[192] while unfamiliar activities like the census sparked fears.[193] The Bhils felt as if under siege, and a small fracas set the region on fire.[194] Government officials were murdered,[195] and soldiers had to be sent in yet again. Eventually diplomacy placed a bandage over the issue, but the problem itself festered.[196] Concessions made were whittled down slowly, and in Fateh Singh's reign, cultural and economic space for the Bhils continued to shrink – as their population grew, there wasn't even enough land to graze cattle, with large areas reserved as royal hunting grounds.[197] More and more Bhils were forced to move out of their hill zones, seeking work from thikanedars. And if these men made exploitative demands of Jat peasants, towards the tribes they also showed that contempt for 'savages'.

The situation had all the ingredients for another flare-up of resentment and revolt. And as with Bijolia, what catalysed things was external assistance, and changes wrought in the twentieth century. A man called Motilal Tejawat, a thikana employee grown disgusted by the treatment meted out to Bhils, began to organize them in protest.[198] As in the Jat movement, nationalist language was seized on, and Gandhi presented as a semi-divine symbolic focus instead of the king.[199] That is, a loyalty higher than to the throne was constructed, with a figure superior to Fateh Singh. An alliance too was struck with the Jats, and in June 1921 a Bhil delegation joined meetings in Udaipur to negotiate with the maharana. But Fateh Singh was against the drastic changes demanded, fearing it would topple the Rajput balance of power. In a dramatic move, then, at a gathering Tejawat got the Bhils to swear oaths on unsheathed swords not to pay taxes, to deny the lords all say in civil matters and even appoint a military leader. That is, as in Bijolia, the Bhils began setting up a parallel state and engaging in active disobedience.[200] Petitions were submitted to the British, while thikanas were warned that if they did not act with justice, the Bhils would come to an independent arrangement with the Raj.[201] The threat, simply put, was that the tribes would no longer treat the maharana and his subordinates even as parties at the negotiating table.

As with the Jats of Bijolia, then, the Bhil agitation quickly became a threat to Mewar's ruler – and given Bhil networks in other geographies, to the empire itself. At a meeting at the end of 1921, for instance, Tejawat addressed 9,000 Bhils, many of them armed, while as far away as Gujarat, Bhils rose against local authorities.[202] Early in 1922, Tejawat began to move around, clashing with the police and government authorities, galvanizing a wider territory.[203] Furious, the British sent in troops and at a meeting of Bhils in Idar state, opened fire, killing twenty-two in the official record, though locally it was claimed that at least 1,000 had died.[204] Propaganda was unleashed on both sides: at one point, Tejawat sent bangles to Bhil villages, his emissaries telling tribesmen that they could either fight or stay home with women.[205] The English press meanwhile parroted lines about the tribes' barbarity, an official describing them as 'ignorant and inflammable' and 'little removed from savagery'.[206] In the end, though, for obvious reasons, the Raj was to win. A major offensive was unleashed, and not just in Mewar – in Sirohi, for example, guns were fired and 600 Bhil houses burned in a single military encounter.[207] This turning up of the heat meant that by the end of 1922, the movement was crushed. As for Tejawat: he disappeared, and was arrested seven years later.[208]

But the twin problems of the peasant agitation and the Bhil revolt scarred the palace too. Fateh Singh was an important symbolic asset for the Raj in keeping the loyalty of the Rajputs; but at a time when the Rajput order was under siege, his value depreciated. Grievances from the past thirty-six years were now funnelled as proof of his incapacity. Or as the Resident wrote: 'All powers are merged in one man, who by want of education, narrowness of outlook, slavish adherence to precedent, suspicion, niggardliness with regard to public improvement, fear of opposition, and inability to grasp the situation or to come to decisions is unfitted to rule.'[209] Unless a public example was made of Fateh Singh, the risk of agitation remained high. Mewar, after all, had become 'a hotbed of lawlessness' and '[s]editionist emissaries' from British India were 'teaching the people that all men are equal'; that land belonged to them, not their lords; and that the maharana would go the way of the Russian emperor.[210] At the imperial level, Bhil agitation and the peasant revolt were seen as lessons in also reconsidering the policy of non-interference in princely territory. As an official noted, Mewar's government went on a 'steep downward curve' ever since Residents were told to 'leave the Darbars to their own devices'. This meant that 'nobles and cultivators alike lost their only hope of protection' while the masses – unable to seek redress via a strong Resident – were forced towards drastic steps.[211] Even in the present crisis, in the end it was the British who in 1922 negotiated an agreement to end the Bijolia peasant movement.[212]

Fateh Singh's fate was sealed. Already in his seventies, he was told that 'it is highly desirable that Your Highness should for the future resign active participation in the administration' given the 'very serious state of affairs now existing in Mewar'.[213] The order came as a bolt from the blue, for the maharana always assumed that the difficulties were not as complex as made out to be; and certainly he never imagined he would be asked to effectively abdicate. Even now, of course, the Raj was not crude in its words. 'The Government,' it was written, 'are fully aware that Your Highness's labours on behalf of your people . . . have been inspired

Fateh Singh in later years.

by an earnest desire for justice, and that you have performed the duties of your high office with unselfish and unremitting zeal.' However, because 'the whole of the administrative arrangements have been concentrated in Your Highness's hands', his own lofty goals were rendered 'impossible of achievement'.[214] To be clear, while misgovernment was the ostensible reason, the British had other complaints too against Fateh Singh, one being that Mewar's contribution to the First World War effort had been less than generous. In fact, while he was given an imperial honour for the help he *did* provide, his attitude was irreverent. One story has it that when asked why he had received a distinction for doing nothing, Fateh Singh laughed. 'Because I rendered the British the highest service. While the British were away fighting the war in Europe I didn't take Delhi. Isn't that a big enough service?'[215] It was a clever joke, till the Raj turned the tables.

Told to resign, the maharana first resisted. He asked for a list of grievances against him, which when submitted seemed vague. On the recent disturbances, his instinct was to blame his thikanedars as well as wicked outside forces for unsettling his otherwise loyal subjects. He was also unhappy that the Raj did not lend him troops – troops for which Mewar paid – to make a show of strength and calm the air early on, as had been done in 1881. But it was a bit late for all this. The British gave him two options: either to step down or face an inquiry. The second would have caused a loss of prestige, whereas the first came with a face-saving option, in that the maharana would only be 'delegating' powers to his heir.[216] It was not an easy choice to make. Fateh Singh had hitherto denied his successor participation in government, and on his death in 1930 was discovered to have been paying for 'propaganda' against the prince in the press.[217] While he would launch a doomed correspondence with London, and even try to bribe a senior official,[218] soon enough the maharana had to swallow the pill. In theory, he remained king, sat on the throne and judicial matters needed his approval, but in practice it was his paraplegic son, Bhupal Singh, who now ruled Mewar, while the father spent his time hunting. It probably gave him some joy in an otherwise gloomy final years of existence, for as a friend would remember, 'He was at his best and happiest in these conditions; and no news was at any time more welcome than that a tiger had entered some accessible jungle.'[219]

Indeed, late in the 1920s a visitor would find the 'erect and stately' Fateh Singh hunting 'boar and wild elephant', living the 'life of a feudal, sportsman King'.[220] One day he saw the maharana descend to his boat, recording:

> At the foot of the hill, he swung from his horse with the vigor of a young man. A splendid figure, he led the way through banks of salaaming nobility, under the arches, out across the marble steps to the canopied crimson throne, which had been placed high in the stern of the royal barge. His nobles gathered about him. A group of dancing girls made a vivid splash of color in the prow. Low in the center of the galley, a long bank of pale blue oars stirred the waters, and the barge swung away.[221]

It was almost a metaphor for princely India itself – a splash of outward glory before fading into the proverbial twilight of history.

Fateh Singh prepares to be photographed by E.O. Hoppe.

Epilogue

In 1906, when Ravi Varma was back at his ancestral home, working on a final commission from Mysore, his diabetes took a turn for the worse. A carbuncle appeared on his body but the surgical operation that followed led to complications: at two o'clock on 2 October, the artist passed away. He was already by then no longer up to the mark emotionally. As his obituary in *The Hindu* reported, 'By his brother's untimely death [in 1905], Mr Ravi Varma sustained a heavy and irreparable loss', from which he 'never wholly recovered'.[1] So too in a letter written in the same phase, Ravi Varma revealed his vulnerability when he termed himself a *paapi* (sinner).[2] Besides, as with most human beings, life had brought its disappointments: if he saved his father's family from financial ruin,[3] he also failed to prevent his older son from going astray. He had succeeded as feudal head of the Kilimanoor clan, but there were private debts to pay. His granddaughters were princesses, but his marriage had been a turbulent affair. Indeed, another regret was also that though he had painted the who's who of the day, he had not thought to do a portrait of his own mother before her death.[4] And now, just short of sixty, the artist's story came to a sudden end. He might have been consoled to know that his passing was widely lamented: as a former governor of Madras wrote, 'When I think I would not see Ravi Varma in this world anymore, my heart is filled with sorrow.'[5]

Ironically, however, soon after his demise, Ravi Varma's legacy was challenged – the man held to be 'unrivalled among Indian Artists' was by 1911 coolly dismissed as 'a once famous native artist'.[6] The reasons were

345

largely political. This was a time when nationalism was acquiring a more forthright tone; in the age of *swadeshi*, anything foreign was suspicious. Ravi Varma may have painted Hindu gods and scenes, but his use of a Western style meant he was no longer worthy of esteem. He was accused of participating in an 'orgy of foreignism' and had apparently 'swallowed with open mouth' un-Indian inspirations.[7] Aurobindo proclaimed him the 'grand debaser of Indian taste'.[8] Sister Nivedita decried Ravi Varma's Shakuntala, who, to her, was wholly 'ill-bred': 'Every home,' she cried, 'contains a picture of a fat young woman lying full length on the floor writing a letter on a lotus leaf.' Abanindranath Tagore's *Bharat Mata* 'in her homespun sari' as a 'virgin mother rather than a temptress', she argued, conveyed a more respectable ideal.[9] The critic, Ananda Coomaraswamy, meanwhile, decided that Ravi Varma was not just 'vulgar' but 'ten thousand times more so than Raphael'. His art was 'not national art' and while he had had an opportunity to inspire a pan-Indian aesthetic, he had regrettably missed the bus.[10]

Viewed in isolation, the artist's fall appears dramatic. But the fact is that it was a generational affair. As we saw earlier, Madhava Rao and Seshiah Sastri too – for all their achievements and reputation – fared poorly in the eyes of their younger countrymen. At one time they were icons, but as colonialism was delegitimized, the fact that they had worked within its rules saw them consigned to the proverbial dustbin. Indeed, older Congressmen too were paid in the same coin – men who, like the native statesmen of the day, advocated moderation and saw little contradiction between nationalism and pledging allegiance to the queen. Indeed, much of the stigma comes precisely from the lack of vigour in their tone; from the fact that they played it safe by shrouding subversion in coy words of loyalism. Their world was, moreover, dominated by elites, with the larger public excluded, and the fact that these early Congressmen showed faith in princes too became jarring. By the mid-twentieth century Nehru, for example, would describe the states as 'sinks of reaction and incompetence' and the '[o]ffspring of the British power in India, suckled by imperialism'. To his peers, the compact their predecessors forged with the maharajahs was embarrassing.[11] But as

B.R. Nanda observes, the fury this generation faced is explained by the 'conscious superiority and almost contempt with which each generation tends to judge its predecessor'.[12] After all, there are those today who feel *Nehru* was deracinated and not in tune with India's cultural realities.

But as always, viewed in context, much of what Ravi Varma's generation did – and in the way they did it – makes sense. Perhaps this can be put in perspective by studying the Congress itself. For instance, the early nationalists' conciliatory language towards the Raj is easily explained. Many Congress founders were born before 1857. Wounds from the Great Rebellion were too fresh for revolt to hold appeal. So also mass awakening, premised on the existence of an overarching Indian identity, in their day was at a discount. People still thought of themselves as Banias and Brahmins, Marathas and Mewaris, and through prisms emphasizing difference, not oneness. A peasant in Gorakhpur had little contact with or knowledge of peasant life in Malabar, let alone the capacity to march together for change. Nationalism was not a given – it had to be slowly constructed. And this was no easy task, even at elite levels. Why, there wasn't even a common mother tongue in which to formulate a political vocabulary: the circular inviting delegates to the first Congress aspired to a 'Native Parliament' and yet required them to be 'well acquainted with the *English* language'. For otherwise there could be no exchange.[13] Even the Congress's nationalism, that is, was for a long time a work in progress – and while its success was limited, its leaders were originators of an important historical process. They may have played by rules set by foreigners, but passive they were not, finding their own creative responses.

The task of the first generation of Indian nationalists was made doubly tough given how critics accentuated every contradiction. When the first seventy-two Congress attendees met in 1885, one paper – studying the bewildering array of complexions and costumes gathered – sniggered that this effort at national integration resembled an evening of fancy dress.[14] The very thesis that Indians, divided by caste, religion, food and even bathing styles,[15] constituted a nation was a newfangled position. So uphill was the nationalist task, in fact, that as late as 1903 an 'Indian' cricket team failed to materialize because nobody could agree as to how many social groups in what proportion might claim that label.[16] Besides, enough Indians were anti-Congress. One north Indian critic, for example, declared it as ruled by eastern Indians, and refused to 'lick the Bengali shoes'.[17] The *Times of India* lampooned the party as a 'suburban literary society at whose meetings a number of earnest people read elaborate essays'.[18] Nationalists were told they were not representative of India: *real* India lay with the poor. The poor did not ask for democracy – why should men in coats seek it? The United Indian Patriotic Association claimed the Congress wanted 'misrule and anarchy'.[19] Amusingly, the nationalists were derided for their moderation even then: 'Those who wish to dictate how India shall be governed, ought to talk at the head of an army.'[20] If they could not marshal troops, they had better keep spines flexible.

In other words, even creating a limited anglicized nationalism was a formidable task. There was no pre-existing national energy that could be harnessed: it had to be carved out, developed and nourished through an elite consensus. This too was why early Congressmen empathized with the princes and borrowed their technique of couching anti-colonial feelings in flowery language. They could not afford to be shut down: singing 'God Save the Queen' screened them from charges of disloyalty while granting access to political principles borrowed from British democracy. Indeed, at the first Congress, delegates went out of their way to proclaim loyalty: 'Had it not been for English education and Western civilisation,' one declared, 'persons inhabiting different parts of this vast country . . . could not have this day met together.'[21] A fellow participant agreed that a 'desire to be governed according to the ideas of Government prevalent in Europe was in no way incompatible' with 'thorough loyalty' to the Raj. All they wished was that 'the people' should have their 'legitimate share' of power.[22] While this choice of tone made later Congressmen recoil, contemporary critics saw through what the nationalists were doing. As one remarked, 'the speeches of the agitators abound in loyal protestations' and 'cheers for the Queen-Empress'. 'But the whole thing is obviously forced and artificial.'[23] Which then raises the question: if we can sympathize with the moderation of the early

Congress, might we also extend that courtesy to contemporary princes and their ministers?[24]

Solidarity, in fact, came easily to brown royalty and early progressives under colonial authority, for both had incentives in smashing imperial claims about native incapacity for government: the princes to deter interference and educated Indians to win power. For all its supposed sins – the glorifying of princes who would eventually get on the wrong side of the nationalist cause, and the dominance of an anglicized class – *at that time* when options were fewer, and nationalism was an elite coalition, these figures made a profound difference. To diminish that phase omits how, if nothing else, they built the intellectual foundations upon which taller efforts could be imagined. It is, in other words, easy to criticize the output by subsequent preoccupations. Only when viewed in context can each be understood in the right perspective. That Congressmen like Gokhale and Ranade served the colonial state in official capacities does not diminish their patriotism. So too that the maharajah of Mysore did not join street agitation, but inspired Indians by showcasing bold industrial experiments is a valid part of anti-colonial resistance. Madhava Rao may have been cautious about upsetting the British regime, but he demonstrated admirably that a capacity for governing well had nothing to do with the colour of one's skin. Against what, for example, a Gandhi achieved later, these may seem like small victories. But it was, arguably, the coming together of several such small streams that later allowed nationalism to grow into a great and powerful force, capable of breaking the empire.

There was also another reason why both the early Congressmen and those in princely territory worked within the Raj's conceptual frame. While colonial injustice was real, it had critics even on the British side. In 1853 an India Reform Society was founded in London, criticizing Company rule.[25] John Bruce Norton's analysis of the Great Rebellion of 1857 excoriated his countrymen: 'We have governed too much for ourselves, too little for the people,' he argued, simply 'to extract revenue'.[26] Lord Ripon, the liberal viceroy, advocated Indian participation in administration, believing this essential for the moral and political justification of the empire.[27] Many of his efforts, as we saw, were thwarted, but Indian regard showed itself in the thousands of people who lined the roads to bid him farewell.[28] Even in the year of the Congress's founding, the journalist William Digby published his *India for Indians* in which he called on the British public to demand better treatment for the queen's Eastern subjects.[29] Given all this – the existence of British voices in favour, the toughness of even constructing a common ground among native elites – Indian politicians and thinkers of the age were quite willing to give the politics of negotiation a chance. Besides, by engaging with the Raj, they were also able to expose the Raj; by mastering its terms, they were able to highlight British hypocrisy too.

Of course, it was only natural that moderate methods would lose their utility with time; that political maturity would require new strategies. The early nationalists, like the native statesmen who served princes, hoped the Raj would live up to its declared ideals. Instead, they received insincerity and betrayal. It was no wonder, then, that the mood began to shift. By the dawn of the twentieth century the queen died and was replaced by Edward VII; British promises were proved largely noise; and Curzon, even as he feuded with princes, held an open ambition to 'assist' Congress to its 'demise'.[30] An angrier band of nationalists appeared, led by B.G. Tilak's cry of 'Militancy – not mendicancy'.[31] There was no disagreement on goals: it was the means that provoked differences. For years 'we have been shouting ourselves hoarse', Tilak argued, 'but our shouting has no more affected the Government than the sound of a gnat'.[32] In 1902 Lajpat Rai, another firebrand, wrote how 'no nation is worthy of any political status if it could not distinguish between begging political rights and claiming them'.[33] While more energetic, this approach did not lead to transformation: Indian society's divisive nature, for example, meant a Tilak had little appeal outside his core Marathi zone. If the moderates had been too rational in their patriotic scheme, the extremist dependence on emotion in a culturally diverse country also had limits.[34] It was only the rise of Gandhi that bridged the gap. By now, however, the princes were becoming enemies, and the moderates a minority.

Interestingly, Ravi Varma's death in 1906 coincided with this change in nationalist winds – the next year the Congress split between moderates and the so-called extremists. The artist himself had cultivated contacts with both sides. In the 1890s, thus, Ravi Varma requested Gokhale to use his influence *within* the system for pushing legislative business dear to creative professionals like him, while helping burnish his rival Tilak's image by printing popular lithograph portraits of the man.[35] Tilak was impressed by Ravi Varma's portrayal of the Maratha hero Chhatrapati Shivaji, in whose name he launched an annual festival for mass galvanization.[36] Through his affordable prints, as is well acknowledged now, Ravi Varma created a visual imagery for India's masses across divides of region and language. He even 'presented his goddesses . . . to convey their pan-national identity'. In an age when costume was linked to caste, he depicted Lakshmi, for example, in a 'sari [that] did not belong to any particular region'. Instead, it was in a style that surmounted provincial limitations. 'At a time that India was seeking its national identity,' writes Rupika Chawla, 'this was a very powerful message . . . replete with patriotic significance.'[37] So too in his *Galaxy of Musicians* (1889), by featuring women from across the subcontinent, Ravi Varma conveyed that though all different, they yet belonged on a single canvas. Funded by maharajahs, admired by moderates while also welcoming the extremist vision, in his domain Ravi Varma manifested a quiet patriotism of his own.[38]

The odium the man later attracted – for being seduced by a foreign style at the expense of the native and 'authentic' – is also unkind. Nationalist fervour explains this, but objectively, what Ravi Varma attempted was quite natural. After all, art in India has been nourished by myriad influences, responding constantly to external stimulation. One of the great examples of Deccan art, for instance, features the Hindu goddess Sarasvati in a Persianate style.[39] Done by Farukh Husain in the seventeenth century, it features the Hindu iconography associated conventionally with the goddess: a peacock, a veena, a lotus and a conch. And yet it reinvents her, projecting Sarasvati not in any consciously 'authentic' Hindu style, but in an Islamicate setting, marrying two traditions. So too in the Vijayanagara empire, sculpture, mural paintings and architectural styles welcomed innovation from across the land, and even overseas from Persia. The painters of Tanjore in the early-nineteenth century were inspired not only by indigenous schools but also by European practices.[40] Viewed by these precedents, then, Ravi Varma's love of oil painting, realism and its application to indigenous subjects sat in harmony with 'tradition'. In drawing from European masters to recreate Puranic scenes, in combining his exposure to Kathakali with a Western technique and in using the camera to plot poses and frames, Ravi Varma was not renouncing Indian art but opening a new path.

Like their favourite artist, however, his patrons – the princes – too were unfairly dismissed. If at all discussed, they are usually treated in a negative light or reduced to cliché. Indeed, a 2021 book repeats the trope that India's maharajahs were 'resistant to political and cultural change, except in its more gimcrack and superficial forms, such as French jewellery or Rolls Royce cars'.[41] Without denying that there were indeed princes who had a disproportionate taste for luxury, generalizations like this do not serve the study of history. Sayaji Rao II of Baroda owned limousines, but to brand him anti-change is a falsehood. Ayilyam Tirunal in Travancore was nervous about cultural transformation, but himself proved its catalyst through administrative and political reforms. Men like Rao and Sastri did not toil in multiple states to keep them 'traditional' in some stereotypical sense: they were hired precisely to help those principalities negotiate change, despite Raj-imposed political limitations. Even in Mewar, where Fateh Singh despised Western modes of government, he used colonial dynamics to try and amend the state's internal structure by diminishing his vassals; 'traditional' Mewar too was no unchanging place. Besides, the idea that loving jewellery and cars was solely an Indian princely preoccupation is disingenuous: Western history has its share of luxury-loving spendthrift rulers, and its dynasties too have their share of scandal and intrigue.

One hopes, then, this book might allow us to look at India's princes a *little* more seriously. They were not unchanging relics of some ancient past, out of place in modern India's evolution: they were part of the process themselves, even if, ultimately, they lost out. Their states were not old-fashioned islands where time stood still and society decayed: they had their own politics and internal dynamics, which are also part of this country's tale.

Ravi Varma's Galaxy of Musicians *(1889).*

Notes

Archival Sources

National Archives of India, New Delhi (NAI)
India Office Records at the British Library, London (IOR)
Private Papers at the British Library (MSS) (including Curzon Papers)
National Library of Scotland, Edinburgh (NLS) (Minto Papers)
Archive of Modern Conflict, London (AMC)

Newspaper Sources

The Pioneer
The Times of India
The Madras Mail
The Bombay Gazette
The Homeward Mail
The Madras Weekly Mail
The Lady
The Englishman's Overland Mail
The Central Somerset Gazette
The Pall Mall Gazette
The Sphere
The Friend of India
The Lancaster Gazette
The Bombay Gazette Overland Summary

The Hitechhu
The Evening Mail
The New York Times
The Cork Examiner
The Daily News
The Bombay Chronicle
The Englishman
The Queen, The Lady's Newspaper
The Times Weekly Edition
The Scotsman
The Indian Spectator

Introduction

1.   *The Pioneer* dated 6 October 1887.
2.   The prince's given name was Martanda Varma. Asvathi Tirunal, literally 'His Highness born on Asvathi day', was the deferential Kerala style of referring to royalty using Hindu birth stars (*nakshatras*) instead of names.
3.   John Woodforde, *The Story of the Bicycle* (London: Routledge and Kegan Paul, 1970), pp. 67, 78, 80.
4.   Robert Needham Cust, *Pictures of Indian Life: Sketched with the Pen from 1852 to 1881* (London: Trubner and Co., 1881), pp. 91, 95. Cust was writing of interactions from over twenty years ago, but given his general attitude and the fact that he published these without qualms later, it would appear his views had not changed.
5.   Ibid., p. 95.
6.   Ibid., p. 94.
7.   Ibid., p. 96.
8.   Ibid., p. 93.
9.   This painting also marks an interesting contrast with an 1833 portrait of Raja Rammohun Roy's son by John King in which he holds a map. Whereas in that early-nineteenth-century portrait the boy is pointing out Bengal in India to his Western audience, in this later one, Indian subjects are exploring the world.
10. Visakham Tirunal, 'A Native Statesman', p. 251 in *The Calcutta Review*, Vol. LV, No. CX (1872), pp. 225–63.
11. Extract from the *Times of India* in the *Madras Mail* dated 21 January 1874. Asvathi Tirunal's uncle, the ruling maharajah, despite 'a sound English education' was 'determined to maintain cherished customs', for instance. Doctors could not

touch his person without violating his caste purity – the man eventually died of septicaemia after he refused to let dentists extract an infected tooth from his royal jaw fearing ritual contamination. See J.D. Rees, 'The Daily Life of an Indian Prince' in *Macmillan's Magazine*, Vol. 1, No. 9 (1906), pp. 711–20, and Manu S. Pillai, *The Ivory Throne: Chronicles of the House of Travancore* (Noida: HarperCollins, 2015), p. 129.

12.   Quoted in Robin Jeffrey, *The Decline of Nair Dominance: Society and Politics in Travancore, 1857–1908* (New Delhi: Manohar, 2014), p. 66.

13.   The tulabharam was conducted by almost every maharajah once during his reign as an essential ritual and ceremonial act of sovereignty. A brief description of the 1892 tulabharam of Maharajah Mulam Tirunal appears in the *Nottingham Evening Post* dated 25 May 1892. A more detailed version features in T. Padmanabha Row, *Thulapurushadanom: A Brief Sketch of Travancore of To-Day with a Short Memoir of His Highness Sir Rama Varma Maha Rajah of Travancore* (Trivandrum: Keralodayam Press, 1892), pp. 50–76.

14.   K. Sundarama Iyer in *Reminiscences of Swami Vivekananda* at https://www.ramakrishnavivekananda.info/reminiscences/057_ksi.htm. Iyer was tutor to Asvathi Tirunal, at this time helping him study for a master of arts degree – a course the prince decided to discontinue after some time.

15.   C. Rajaraja Varma, *A Narrative of the Tour in Upper India of His Highness Prince Martanda Varma of Travancore* (Bombay: Education Society's Steam Press, 1896), p. 27. Ravi Varma was with him on this trip.

16.   George N. Curzon, *Speeches by Lord Curzon of Kedleston, Viceroy and Governor-General of India, 1898–1901* (Calcutta: Thacker, Spink and Co., 1901), p. 364.

17.   Cust, *Pictures of Indian Life*, pp. 92–93.

18.   Letter dated 12 December 1899 from the resident to the chief secretary, Government of Madras, in IOR/R/2/892/278.

19.   Cust, *Pictures of Indian Life*, pp. 97–98.

20.   Sunil Khilnani, *The Idea of India* (London: Hamish Hamilton, 1997), p. 25.

21.   Kanhayalal Gauba, *His Highness: Or the Pathology of Princes* (Lahore: The Times Publishing Company, 1931), p. 45.

22.   Larry Collins and Dominique Lapierre, *Freedom at Midnight* (New York: Simon and Schuster, 1975), pp. 175–79.

23.   Cited in Edward S. Haynes, 'The Political Role of the Armed Forces of the Indian States after World War I', p. 41 in *Journal of Asian History*, Vol. 24, No. 1 (1990), pp. 30–56. Haynes does not, however, give the exact source for this or the name of the prince accused, stating that it would amount to defamation.

24.   Quoted in Barbara N. Ramusack, *The Indian Princes and Their States* (The New Cambridge History of India, 3:6) (Cambridge: Cambridge University Press, 2004), pp. 166–67.

25. This topic is covered in Manu Bhagavan, 'Princely States and the Hindu Imaginary: Exploring the Cartography of Hindu Nationalism in Colonial India', in *The Journal of Asian Studies*, Vol. 67, No. 3 (2008), pp. 881–915. For B.S. Moonje's 1944 quote, see ibid., p. 887. V.D. Savarkar, the father of Hindutva, also published in the 1940s an 'academical' view that envisioned India as a coalition of princely states, with the king of Nepal as its emperor. Published in *The Khyber Mail* on 17 November 1940, the article also appears in Savarkar's *Swatantrya Veer Savarkar, Hindu Sanghatan: Its Ideology and Immediate Programme: A Collection of His Three Presidential Speeches at Karnavati (Ahmadabad), Nagpur and Calcutta* (N.V. Damle: Bombay, 1940), pp. 213–18.

26. I refer here to the leadership, that is, Nehru and his socialist colleagues, for there were many other Congressmen who were sympathizers of the Mahasabha to varying degrees, and Mahasabha members, for many years, could also be Congressmen.

27. See Ramusack, *Indian Princes*, p. 53, and Waltraud Ernst and Biswamoy Pati, 'People, Princes and Colonialism', p. 1, in Ernst and Pati eds, *India's Princely States: People, Princes and Colonialism* (Abingdon: Routledge, 2007), pp. 1–14.

28. See André Béteille's Foreword in Hira Singh, *Colonial Hegemony and Popular Resistance: Princes, Peasants, and Paramount Power* (New Delhi: Sage, 1998).

29. James Manor's study of Mysore, for example, is a good example of how caste rivalries and highly localized politics later merged with the nationalist movement, with a give and take for both parties. See Manor, *Political Change in an Indian State: Mysore, 1917–1955* (New Delhi: Manohar, 1977). Robin Jeffrey, similarly, studies the emergence of mass politics in Travancore in the nineteenth century along communal lines, which in the 1930s linked itself to the national agitation against colonialism. See Jeffrey, *Decline*.

30. Ramusack, *Indian Princes*, p. 187.

31. See Singh, *Colonial Hegemony*, pp. 33–36, for a discussion on this.

32. In the early decades of the nineteenth century, the nizam was still addressed in obsequious language by the governor-general, suggesting implicit superiority. See K.M. Panikkar, *Indian States and the Government of India* (London: Martin Hopkinson, 1932), p. 13. On the 1903 reference, see Stephen Ashton, 'British Policy Towards the Indian States, 1905–1939', PhD thesis, School of Oriental and African Studies, University of London (1977), p. 159.

33. See *Report of the Indian States Committee, 1928–1929* (London: Secretary of State for India, 1929), p. 10.

34. Benjamin B. Cohen, *Kingship and Colonialism in India's Deccan, 1850–1948* (New York: Palgrave Macmillan, 2007), p. 2. Cohen discusses Hyderabad's vassal states in rich detail.

35. Susanne Hoeber Rudolph and Lloyd I. Rudolph, 'Rajputana Under British

Paramountcy: The Failure of Indirect Rule', pp. 10–11, in Rudolph and Rudolph, *Essays on Rajputana: Reflections on History, Culture and Administration* (New Delhi: Concept Publishing Company, 1984), pp. 3–37. Rajat K. Ray, 'Mewar: The Breakdown of the Princely Order' in Robin Jeffrey ed., *People, Princes and Paramount Power*, pp. 205–39, covers the case of Udaipur and the breakdown of the old arrangement in the twentieth century in this premier Rajput state. See also Susanne Hoeber Rudolph, Lloyd I. Rudolph and Mohan Singh, 'A Bureaucratic Lineage in Princely India: Elite Formation and Conflict in a Patrimonial System' in *The Journal of Asian Studies*, Vol. 34, No. 3 (1975), pp. 717–53, for a sense of the internal operation of power and patronage in a Rajput state.

36. David Hardiman, 'Baroda: The Structure of a "Progressive" State', p. 123 in Jeffrey ed., *People, Princes and Paramount Power*, pp. 107–35.

37. Ibid., p. 131.

38. Razak Khan, 'Local Pasts: Space, Emotions and Identities in Vernacular Histories of Princely Rampur' in *Journal of the Economic and Social History of the Orient*, Vol. 58, No. 5 (2015), pp. 693–731.

39. Note dated 2 April 1948 by 'N.N.' in File No. 4(24), Political, Ministry of States, NAI.

40. Memorial of the Members of the Legislative Council of the Pudukkottai State in ibid.

41. This is not to say that meanings associated with rulers did not change. Nandini Sundar shows, for instance, how the people of Bastar denied their king's legitimacy and construed him as part of the colonial apparatus in 1910, only, in 1966, in independent India, to rally behind a royal descendant, in their fight against the *Indian* state. See Sundar, *Subalterns and Sovereigns: An Anthropological History of Bastar, 1854–1996* (Delhi: Oxford University Press, 1997).

42. Robert Grenville Wallace, *Fifteen Years in India; or, Sketches of a Soldier's Life* (London: Longman, Hurst, Rees, Orme, and Brown, 1823), p. 207.

43. Quoted in C.U. Aitchison, *The Native States of India: An Attempt to Elucidate a Few of the Principles Which Underlie Their Relations with the British Government* (Calcutta: Government Printing, 1881), p. 41.

44. Quoted in Jeffrey ed., 'Introduction', in *People, Princes and Paramount Power*, pp. 1–2.

45. Ibid., pp. 11–12.

46. Describing an early Company encounter with the Mughal governor of Orissa, William Bruton wrote: 'Then the Noble-man (Mersimomein) presented our Merchant (Mr Ralph Cartwright) to the King [i.e. the nawab/subedar of Orissa] ... and the King very affably bended forward (in manner of a Curtsie or respect) and withal leaned his Armes on two mens shoulders, and slipped off his Sandall from his foote (for he was bare-legged) and presented his foot to our Merchant to

kisse, which hee twice did refuse to doe, but at the last hee was faine to doe it.' See Bruton, 'Newes from the East Indies or A Voyage to Bengalla' (London: J. Okes, 1638), p. 263, in *A Selection of Curious, Rare, and Early Voyages and Histories of Interesting Discoveries, Chiefly Published by Hakluyt* (London: R.H. Evans, 1812).

47.   Or as Hira Singh put it, the Raj was 'socializing [itself] into Indian tradition'. Singh, *Colonial Hegemony*, p. 34. See also Max-Jean Zins, 'Invented and Imported Traditions: Some Reflections on the Policy of Protocol during the British Raj' in *Proceedings of the Indian History Congress*, Vol. 57 (1996), pp. 659–79.

48.   Betty Balfour ed., *The History of Lord Lytton's Indian Administration, 1876 to 1880: Compiled from Letters and Official Papers* (London: Longmans, Green and Co., 1899), p. 109.

49.   Quoted in David Gilmour, *Curzon: Imperial Statesman* (London: Penguin, 2019, 1994 original), p. 167. A predecessor, Lord Lytton, made a similar point when he said, 'Politically speaking, the Indian peasantry is an inert mass. If it ever moves at all, it will move in obedience, not to its British benefactors, but to its native chiefs and princes, however tyrannical they may be.'

50.   Quoted in Walter Sichel, *Disraeli: A Study in Personality and Ideas* (New York: Funk and Wagnalls Company, 1904), pp. 218–20.

51.   Priya Atwal cites a historical account from the Sikh court of Punjab which notes, for example, how neighbouring princes were quite aware that signing treaties with the Company was akin to 'consumption' and that the British would eat up the 'vital parts' of power. But those rulers signed anyway because they calculated it as a better option than 'sudden death' at the hands of Ranjit Singh of Punjab. That is, they were not naive in engaging with the British and knew they would have to pay a price. See Atwal, *Royals and Rebels: The Rise and Fall of the Sikh Empire* (Noida: HarperCollins Publishers, 2021), p. 95.

52.   Bhupan Qanungo, 'A Study of British Relations with the Native States of India, 1858–62', p. 252 in *The Journal of Asian Studies*, Vol. 26, No. 2 (1967), pp. 251–65.

53.   Quoted in Balfour, *History of Lord Lytton's Indian Administration*, p. 123.

54.   See letter dated 10 October 1881 from the maharajah of Indore to Lord Ripon and H.M. Durand's note dated 28 October 1881 in File No. 221–33, Pros. Foreign Dep. (Political A), April 1882, NAI.

55.   Lord Reading to the nizam in J. Coatman, *Report of the Administration of Lord Reading, Viceroy and Governor-General of India, 1921–1926: General Summary* (Simla: Government of India Press, 1927), p. 60. This was addressed to the nizam who was demanding back territory under British control but given that the viceroy had the whole correspondence published, it was intended also as a notice to princes in general. The viceroy's stand was, of course, challenged, including by British commentators.

56.   Thomas Munro (A.J. Arbuthnot ed.), *Major-General Sir Thomas Munro, Governor*

of Madras: Selections from His Minutes and Other Official Writings, Vol. 2 (London: C. Kegan Paul, 1882), p. 87.

57. Quoted in Michael H. Fisher, 'The Resident in Court Ritual, 1764–1858', p. 432 in *Modern Asian Studies*, Vol. 24, No. 3 (1990), pp. 419–58.

58. Michael H. Fisher, *Indirect Rule in India: Residents and the Residency System, 1764–1858* (New Delhi: Oxford University Press, 1991), p. 256. In a related instance in an Indian court, Priya Atwal notes how when the Sikh king Ranjit Singh received his uncle – ruler of an independent state – in Lahore, he showered the man with presents and a landed estate. The uncle tried to avoid accepting them but was essentially made to, this simple act marking a public statement of inferiority. See Atwal, *Royals and Rebels*, p. 97.

59. See a few instances in Fisher, *Indirect Rule*, p. 185.

60. The British awareness of symbolic power is clear also in Ellenborough's retrieval of supposedly long-lost Hindu relics from Afghanistan. He believed these to have been plundered from the famous shrine at Somnath by invaders centuries ago, grandly telling Indians, 'You see how worthy [the British government] proves itself of your love, when regarding your honour as its own, it exerts the power of its arms to restore to you the gates of the temple.' Quoted in Richard H. Davis, *Lives of Indian Images* (Princeton: Princeton University Press, 1997), p. 202. Edward Law (Lord Colchester ed.), *History of the Indian Administration of Lord Ellenborough in His Correspondence with the Duke of Wellington, to Which Is Prefixed, by Permission of Her Majesty, Lord Ellenborough's Letters to the Queen During that Period* (London: Richard Bentley and Son, 1874), pp. 64–65.

61. Bakhtiar K. Dadabhoy, *The Magnificent Diwan: The Life and Times of Sir Salar Jung I* (Gurugram: Vintage, 2020), pp. 90–91.

62. Quoted in Caroline Keen, *Princely India and the British: Political Development and the Operation of Empire* (New Delhi: Viva Books, 2013), p. 184.

63. See C.L. Tupper, *Indian Political Practice: A Collection of the Decisions of the Government of India in Political Cases*, Vol. 1 (Delhi: B.R. Publishing Corporation, 1974), p. 131.

64. See Joanne Punzo Waghorne, *The Raja's Magic Clothes: Re-Visioning Kingship and Divinity in England's India* (Pennsylvania: The Pennsylvania State University Press, 1994), p. 68, for an instance of the Pudukkottai minister being pulled up for using the term 'royal', and note dated 04/10/1876 by 'F.H.' in File Nos. 832–38, Foreign Dep. (Political B), March 1877, NAI, where the minister of Baroda is criticized for this 'trick' which was 'objectionable' because 'this English word is inapplicable to the case of the Feudatory Chiefs'.

65. John McLeod, *Sovereignty, Power, Control: Politics in the States of Western India (1916–1947)* (New Delhi: Decent Books, 2007) (First Edition, Leiden, 1999), p. 8.

66.   Quoted in Fisher, *Indirect Rule*, pp. 293–94.

67.   Ashton, 'British Policy', p. 116.

68.   As early as 1779, Residents were told by the Company of 'The utility of collecting every possible information respecting the disposition, genius, talents, character, connections, views, interests, revenues, military strength, and even domestic history of those Princes or people, with whose affairs our own happens to be interwoven or related, either immediately or remotely'. Quoted in Fisher, *Indirect Rule*, pp. 130–31.

69.   Fisher, *Indirect Rule*, pp. 300–301. In the case of the Ramnad zamindari, thus, we have a British collector in 1842 complain: 'I have proof . . . that hardly a servant of my office . . . ever accompanied me through the Zamindary without finding provisions, etc., cost free. I have reason to believe all are in some degree implicated in the corruptions so widely and distantly spread by [the zamindari manager], and I have strong reason to fear one of my best accountants . . . was only using his ability with a view to falsify them and deceive me.' See Pamela G. Price, *Kingship and Political Practice in Colonial India* (Cambridge: Cambridge University Press, 1996), p. 84.

70.   Conrad Corfield, *The Princely India I Knew: From Reading to Mountbatten* (Madras: Indo British Historical Society, 1975), p. 81. The sender was a maharani who was then in power.

71.   Fisher, 'The Resident in Court Ritual', p. 435.

72.   Fisher, *Indirect Rule*, p. 225.

73.   Quoted in Robert W. Stern, *The Cat and the Lion: Jaipur State in the British Raj* (Ahmedabad: Allied Publishers, 1988), p. 185. In Hyderabad, with the company watching the government treasury, the nizams secreted wealth in the palace. See Fisher, *Indirect Rule*, p. 294.

74.   Quoted in Stern, *The Cat and the Lion*, p. 215. Such tactics worked. As late as 1928, one of Curzon's former aides would note how 'very little is known about the Indian States' despite the surplus of reports and official documents – the states were 'a *terra incognita*'. See Walter Roper Lawrence, *The India We Served* (London: Cassell and Co., 1928), p. 182. Lawrence also notes (p. 188) how the British occasionally did tap into the secret reserves of maharajahs: when Kashmir's ruler was deposed in 1889, his state was bankrupt, so 'the Government of India decided to explore the resources of one of the distant forts in the Dogra hills. There were gold and silver, gold coins which would have made the numismatist tremble with excitement, and in a corner, in muddy sacks, were loads of sapphires which a great English jeweller pronounced to be the finest stones.' They knew, however, that their action was controversial – the local people saw this 'violation' of the fort as 'an act of sacrilege'.

75.   Callie Wilkinson, 'The Residents of the British East India Company at Indian royal courts, c. 1798–1818', PhD thesis, University of Cambridge (2017), p. 38.

76. Dadabhoy, *Magnificent Diwan*, pp. 150–51.

77. Wilkinson, 'Residents of the British East India Company', p. 109.

78. Ibid., p. 110. Even so, Hastings sent the emperor a present ('a gaudy state chariot') to make up for any slight in not personally appearing before him.

79. Reference is to the Ramnad rajah. See Maria Misra, 'Indian Aristocrats, British Imperialists and "Conservative Modernization" After the Great Rebellion', pp. 65–66, in Uyama Tomohiko ed., *Comparing Modern Empires: Imperial Rule and Decolonization in the Changing World Order* (Sapporo: Slavic-Eurasian Research Centre, Hokkaido University, 2018), pp. 65–98.

80. Waghorne, *Raja's Magic Clothes*, p. 21.

81. Ramusack, *Indian Princes*, p. 2.

82. The idea of a divided sovereignty with a specific discussion on the states receives attention in Lauren Benton, *A Search for Sovereignty: Law and Geography in European Empires, 1400–1900* (New York: Cambridge University Press, 2010), pp. 236–64.

83. Quoted in Ashton, 'British Policy', p. 28. See Miles Taylor, *The English Maharani: Queen Victoria and India* (Gurgaon: Penguin Viking, 2018), for a more detailed discussion on how the empress used her connection with India to assert more power and meaning at home. Waghorne also makes this point on Victoria's 'pageant rule' in Waghorne, *Raja's Magic Clothes*, p. 21.

84. The total number (9,390 artillerymen, 2,41,036 infantry, and 64,172 cavalry, coming to 3,14,598) is taken from Appendix C, p. 51 in C.U. Aitchison's *The Native States of India*.

85. Barbara Ramusack, *The Princes of India in the Twilight of Empire: Dissolution of a Patron–Client System, 1914–1939* (Columbus: University of Cincinnati/Ohio State University Press, 1978), p. 38.

86. Haynes, 'Political Role', pp. 30–56.

87. Samiksha Sehrawat, '"Hostages in Our Camp": Military Collaboration Between Princely India and the British Raj, c. 1880–1920', p. 125, in Ernst and Pati eds, *India's Princely States*, pp. 118–38.

88. Ibid., p. 126. The latter's state forces departed India in 1914 and did not return for five whole years, making a real contribution on international soil. Additionally, as Tony McClenaghan notes, the 'total manpower contribution from the Princely States was of about 140,000' men, and the states won 'a total of 689 decorations for gallantry … and a total of 132 Battle Honours'. See McLenaghan, 'The Maharajas' Contribution to the First World War: An Overview', p. 80 in Ashutosh Kumar and Claude Markovits eds, *Indian Soldiers in the First World War: Re-visiting a Global Conflict* (Abingdon: Routledge, 2021), pp. 63–88.

89. Quoted in Ramusack, *Twilight*, p. 80.

90. Quoted in ibid., p. 49.

91. Ibid., p. 45.

92. Ibid., p. 58.

93. Ibid., p. 46.

94. Quoted in D.R. Mankekar, *Accession to Extinction: The Story of Indian Princes* (Delhi: Vikas, 1974), p. 12.

95. Ashton, 'British Policy', p. 58.

96. Quoted in Ramusack, *Twilight*, p. 80.

97. Years later, in fact, it was the support a large number of wealthy princes gave the opposition parties in independent India that provoked Indira Gandhi to put an end to the privy purses paid them.

98. Ramusack, *Twilight*, pp. 47–48.

99. Ashton, 'British Policy', p. 124.

100. Ibid., pp. 114, 123.

101. Quoted in Ramusack, *Twilight*, p. 53. On the reluctance to interfere too much, this was observed in the case of this nizam's father too, whom Curzon wanted to depose. Curzon's boss, the secretary of state in London, however, vetoed the proposal calling it 'so serious a matter that I would tolerate a good deal of oppression and maladministration' before even considering such an idea. See Ashton, 'British Policy', p. 114. In 1947 Muhammad Ali Jinnah would also take a similar (somewhat exaggerated) line when he told the viceroy that 'every Muslim throughout the whole of India, yes, all the hundred million Muslims, would rise as one man to defend the oldest Muslim dynasty in India'. Quoted in Sunil Purushotham, 'Internal Violence: The "Police Action" in Hyderabad', p. 439, in *Comparative Studies in Society and History*, Vol. 57, No. 2 (2015), pp. 435–66.

102. Quoted in Ashton, 'British Policy', p. 174.

103. As Patiala remarked, if power was surrendered into 'the hands of the people', the Raj had also to assuage princes 'who do not desire to be handed over to the British Indian democracy'. Quoted in ibid., p. 150.

104. Quoted in ibid., p. 166.

105. See Pillai, *Ivory Throne*, p. 156.

106. Y. Vaikuntham, *People's Movements in the Princely States* (New Delhi: Manohar, 2004), p. 121.

107. Ramusack, *Indian Princes*, p. 245.

108. Quoted in Ashton, 'British Policy', p. 125.

109. Francis Wylie quoted in Ramusack, *Indian Princes*, p. 266.

110. The Pandit Sunderlal Report on Hyderabad and a detailed study of its annexation appears in A.G. Noorani, *The Destruction of Hyderabad* (New Delhi: Tulika Books, 2013). For the bombing and other details, see Purushotham, 'Internal Violence', p. 440 and further, including for numbers of the dead. See also Purushotham, *From Raj to Republic: Sovereignty, Violence and Democracy in India* (Stanford: Stanford

University Press, 2021), pp. 11–12, where he notes that the 'police action' occurred just as the nizam's appeal to be heard at the United Nations was being discussed. See also ibid., pp. 82–83, for the Indian leadership's rejection of the Sunderlal Report figures, though even the government acknowledged that at least 3,375 Muslims had been killed during the 'police action', giving pensions to their wives.

111. Vallabhbhai Patel (P.N. Chopra ed.), *The Collected Works of Sardar Vallabhbhai Patel: 1 January 1948–31 December 1948* (Delhi: Konark, 1998), p. 270. One biographer went a step further in describing the states as 'chronic ulcers' – Patel 'cured' and 'eliminated' these. See P.D. Saggi ed., *A Nation's Homage: Life and Work of Sardar Vallabhbhai Patel* (Bombay: Overseas Publishing House, 1949), p. xi.

112. Though there are Ravi Varma paintings in Britain, including in the royal collection, this portrait of the king was evidently for someone in India. See Erwin Neumayer and Christine Schelberger eds, *Raja Ravi Varma, Portrait of an Artist: The Diary of C. Raja Raja Varma* (New Delhi: Oxford University Press, 2005), p. 184.

113. Quoted in ibid., p. 210.

114. Twice in his brother's diary we see references to casual racism. In 1903 there is reference to an 'Englishman [who] came into our [railway] compartment and behaved rudely' while earlier, in 1899 we read about another journey when 'one Mr Joseph I.C.S.... seemed not to like our presence in a first class compartment' and was 'in a rage with everybody'. See Neumayer and Schelberger eds, *The Diary*, pp. 74, 192. Ravi Varma and his brother were at the Madras Congress in 1903, and judged the Fine Arts section of the parallel industrial exhibition. See ibid., p. 193.

115. Reference is to Rupika Chawla's *Raja Ravi Varma: Painter of Colonial India* (Ahmedabad: Mapin, 2010).

116. Lawrence, *India*, p. 203.

117. Ibid., pp. 182–83.

118. Harcourt Butler quoted in Ian Copland, *The Princes of India in the Endgame of Empire, 1917–1947* (Cambridge: Cambridge University Press, 1997), p. 25.

119. Unnamed official quoted in Ashton, 'British Policy', p. 25.

120. John R. McLane, *Indian Nationalism and the Early Congress* (Princeton: Princeton University Press, 1977), p. 144.

121. Ibid., p. 141. See also Dinyar Patel, *Naoroji: Pioneer of Indian Nationalism* (Cambridge: Harvard University Press, 2020), p. 183, for more details on these princes and their secret contributions to Naoroji's election.

122. 'The conduct of the association of the Deccan landholders called the "Surva-Janik Sabha",' wrote Sir Richard Temple, 'has long been . . . regarded with suspicion – which suspicion continues . . . its wires are believed to be pulled by men with tainted views.' Quoted in B.R. Nanda, *Gokhale: The Indian Moderates and the British Raj* (Princeton: Princeton University Press, 1977), p. 41.

123. Richard I. Cashman, *The Myth of the Lokamanya: Tilak and Mass Politics in Maharashtra* (Berkeley: University of California Press, 1975), p. 100.

124. Haynes, 'Political Role', p. 52.

125. George Nathaniel Curzon, *British Government in India: The Story of the Viceroys and Government Houses*, Vol. 2 (London: Cassell and Company, 1925), pp.133–34.

126. See, for instance, an excerpt from Lal Mohan Ghose's presidential address to the Congress in 1903 in A.C. Banerjee ed., *Indian Constitutional Documents, 1757–1947: Vol. II 1958–1917* (Calcutta: A. Mukherjee and Co., 1961 edn), pp. 349–50.

127. McLane, *Indian Nationalism*, p. 192.

128. Barbara Ramusack, 'Congress and the People's Movement in Princely India: Ambivalence in Strategy and Organization', p. 379, in Richard Sisson and Stanley Wolpert eds, *Congress and Indian Nationalism: The Pre-Independence Phase* (Berkeley: University of California Press, 1988), pp. 377–404.

129. T.V. Parvate, *Mahadev Govind Ranade: A Biography* (New York: Asia Publishing House, 1963), p. 91. Ranade's writings on the states have been compiled by V.W. Thakur in *Select Writings of the Late Hon'ble Mr Justice M.G. Ranade on Indian States* (Indore: V.W. Thakur, 1942).

130. Ramusack, 'Congress', p. 380.

131. Quoted in Mark Bence-Jones, *The Viceroys of India* (New York: St Martin's Press, 1982), p. 187.

132. Quoted in Cashman, *Myth*, p. 63.

133. Panikkar, *Indian States*, pp. xvi–vii.

1. The Rajah in a Suit

1. Like Asvathi Tirunal, his given name was also Martanda Varma.

2. James Welsh, *Military Reminiscences: Extracted from a Journal of Nearly Forty Years' Active Service in the East Indies*, Vol. 2 (London: Smith, Elder and Co., 1830), p. 146. Sometime later, even aged nine, Uthram Tirunal again during a meeting parked himself on a colonel's lap and 'retained his place nearly all the time' of the event.

3. John Abbs, *Twenty-Two Years' Missionary Experience in Travancore* (London: John Snow and Co., 1870), p. 88.

4. P. Shungoonny Menon, *A History of Travancore from the Earliest Times* (Madras: Higginbotham and Co., 1878), p. 444. Menon was a senior courtier whose name came up briefly in consideration for ministership of the state in the 1870s. He served multiple rulers and put down a lot of his personal memories in this book. His son, K.P. Sankara Menon, appears repeatedly in the diary of Ravi Varma's brother, Rajaraja Varma, and was a friend of theirs.

5. Ibid., p. 445.

6. Ibid., p. 446.

7.   Ibid., p. 447.

8.   The skeleton now is on display in the Napier Museum in Thiruvananthapuram.

9.   Heber Drury, *Reminiscences of Life and Sport in Southern India* (London: W.H. Allen and Co., 1890), p. 111.

10.   Ibid., p. 164.

11.   Drury also tells the story, possibly exaggerated, of an Indian prince who placed an order for 'fine perukes' not knowing what these were. When the wigs arrived, there was a minor fright because it was thought someone had delivered to the palace a box full of human scalps.

12.   Wilkinson, 'Residents of the British East India Company', pp. 101–102 discusses this in a general sense.

13.   Menon, *History of Travancore*, p. 447.

14.   Alexey Saltykov quoted in Richard R. Walding, Helen Stone and Achuthsankar S. Nair, 'The Russian Prince and the Maharajah of Travancore', p. 52, in *Journal of Kerala Studies*, Vol. 36 (2009), pp. 10–87.

15.   This picture is reminiscent of the 'Portrait of Thakur Raja Bakhtawar Singh, standing in a European-style interior' c. 1800 at the Victoria and Albert Museum. See http://collections.vam.ac.uk/item/O17904/portrait-of-thakur-raja-bakhtawar-painting-unknown/

16.   V. Nagam Aiya, *The Travancore State Manual*, Vol. 1 (Trivandrum: Government of Travancore, 1906), pp. 505, 525. In 1838, similarly, while riding near the beach, he saw a ship in the distance with a signal of distress visible through his telescope. After help was sent, Uthram Tirunal made a four-hour-long personal visit to the frigate. Delighted by the experience, the next day he went again, asking the soldiers aboard to entertain him with a drill. See Menon, *History of Travancore*, pp. 448–49.

17.   Ibid., p. 451. Alexey Saltykov wrote how Uthram Tirunal went 'along to European dinners with his entourage of naked followers, not trying any food at all and continually chewing on betel nut which he does to excess'. See Walding, Stone and Nair, 'Russian Prince', pp. 52–53. Drury also recorded this latter 'disagreeable habit'. See Drury, *Reminiscences of Life*, p. 165. On the subject of food, there is also a hilarious story about how Uthram Tirunal, who was fond of eating bonbons and jujubes, once saw an advertisement for 'jubons' in a Madras paper. Assuming them to be part of the same sugary category of foodstuff, he placed a large order only to find himself the owner of crinolines (stiffened European women's petticoats, to give their dresses that distinct puffy shape). See Francis Day, *The Land of the Perumauls, or Cochin, Its Past and Its Present* (Madras: Gantz Brothers, 1863), p. 407.

18.   Drury, *Reminiscences of Life*, pp. 166–67.

19.   Abbs, *Twenty-Two Years' Missionary Experience*, p. 88.

20.   Menon, *History of Travancore*, p. 452.

21.   Drury, *Reminiscences of Life,* pp. 189–90.

22.   K.P. Padmanabhan Tampy, *Kathakali: An Indigenous Art-Form of Kerala* (Calcutta: Indian Publications, 1963), p. 27.

23.   Raman Unni was generally called Nalan Unni for his fame in playing the character Nala.

24.   See P.K. Parameswaran Nair (E.M.J. Venniyoor trans.), *History of Malayalam Literature* (New Delhi: Sahitya Akademi, 1967), p. 116. Pillai was appointed *vicharippukar* in the palace, and documents in Sharat Sunder Rajeev's possession show his family continuing to receive pensions long after he was dead. When in 1859 Uthram Tirunal's niece was wed, the London papers reported how 'Eshnera Pillay, the principal servant of the palace' and an 'intelligent' man was one of its organizers. See, for example, *The Homeward Mail from India, China and the East* for 9 June 1859. Uthram Tirunal also got his son Padmanabhan Tampi married to Pillai's daughter. Pillai, who came from south Travancore and poverty, was first noticed as an adolescent by Vilayikottu Namboodiri, who installed him in the palace troupe. See Kottarathil Sankunni (Sreekumari Ramachandran trans.), *Aitihyamaala: The Great Legends of Kerala*, Vol. 2 (Kozhikode: Mathrubhumi Books, 2010), pp. 197–99, for more.

25.   Welsh, *Military Reminiscences*, p. 144.

26.   By the second half of the eighteenth century, it was increasingly standard for Indian rulers – in a changing political environment – to employ white mercenaries. S. Inayet A. Zaidi finds, for example, 179 clearly identifiable senior mercenaries in this period across India, a large number of them French. Awadh had seven, Jaipur had four, while the Marathas had as many as 107. See Zaidi, 'European Mercenaries in the Indian Armies: AD 1750–1803' in *Studies in History*, Vol. 27, No. 1 (2011), pp. 55–83.

27.   A.P. Ibrahim Kunju, *Rise of Travancore: A Study of the Life and Times of Martanda Varma* (Trivandrum: Kerala Historical Society, 1976), p. 62.

28.   See Mark de Lannoy, *The Kulasekhara Perumals of Travancore: History and State Formation in Travancore, 1671 to 1758* (Leiden: CNWS, 1997), p. 123.

29.   From the *Tampimar Kathai Villupattu* (bow song) translated by Stuart H. Blackburn in *Singing of Birth and Death: Texts in Performance* (Philadelphia: University of Philadelphia Press, 1988), p. 137.

30.   In a Sanskrit poem, *Balamartandavijaya*, produced some years later, in fact, Martanda Varma's actions are given a retrospective legitimacy by having his dynastic deity appear in a dream before him, asking him to reconstruct his temple. But because the deity knew the king was poor, he was given permission to defeat his neighbouring princes, seize their wealth, and master the land. See K. Sambasiva Sastri ed., *Balamartandavijayam Devarajakavivirchitam* (*Devaraja Kavi's Balamartandavijaya*) (Trivandrum: Government Press, 1930).

31. Commenting on Shungoonny Menon's history, the Dewan of Cochin T. Sankunni Menon in fact wrote in 1875: 'Sankunni Menon Peishkar [that is, Shungoonny] paid me a visit, and showed me the first chapter of his History of Travancore. It is a crude production, and his whole aim seems to be to show that the Royal family is very ancient, and belongs not to the Samanta caste, as is generally believed, but to the Kshatriya caste.' See C. Achyuta Menon, *The Life of T. Sankunni Menon: Diwan of Cochin, 1860–79* (Trichur: V. Sundra Iyer and Sons, 1923), pp. 226–27.

32. Aiya, *Travancore State Manual*, p. 362.

33. Menon, *History of Travancore*, p. 289.

34. Samuel Mateer, *Native Life in Travancore* (London: W.H. Allen, 1883), p. 129.

35. It continues to this day, in fact, where the head of the Travancore family remains in charge of the temple.

36. Menon, *History of Travancore*, p. 175.

37. See the treaty in *A Collection of Treaties and Engagements with the Native Princes and States of Asia Concluded on Behalf of the East India Company by the British Governments in India* (London: East India Company, 1812), pp. 170–76.

38. See the correspondence and treaty in Menon, *History of Travancore*, pp. 310–17.

39. Translation of the Memorial from His Highness the Rajah of Travancore in Pros., Fort William, dated 16 August 1807, in MS 11571, Minto Papers, NLS. It was to become a standard approach. Criticizing the annexation of Awadh much later, Malcolm Lewis wrote how 'A threat to take possession of the country has always been found capable of extorting the sums required for the exigencies of the Indian Government'. See Lewis, *Has Oude Been Worse Governed by Its Native Princes than Our Indian Territories by Leadenhall Street?* (London: James Ridgway, 1857), p. 5.

40. Lord Hastings quoted in Fisher, *Indirect Rule*, p. 212. See also p. 227. In time, with the advent of the telegraph it became easier for Company bosses to keep an eye, but in the early nineteenth century, the British agent had room to become a tyrant.

41. See Wilkinson, 'Residents of the British East India Company', pp. 21–22, for a comparison between the Nagpur and Delhi Residencies for instance, as well as for a splendid general study of the Residency system.

42. A famous case being James Kirkpatrick whom the nizam titled 'Hushmat Jung' ('Valiant in Battle') and 'nawab'. His relationship with Khair-un-Nissa and conversion to Islam is the subject of William Dalrymple's *White Mughals: Love and Betrayal in Eighteenth-Century India* (London: HarperCollins, 2002).

43. See Robin Jeffrey, 'The Politics of "Indirect Rule": Types of Relationship Among Rulers, Ministers and Residents in a "Native State"' in *Journal of the Commonwealth and Comparative Politics*, Vol. 13, No. 3 (1975), pp. 261–81, for his classification of Residents into four types.

44. Quoted in Amar Farooqui, *Sindias and the Raj: Princely Gwalior, c. 1800–1850* (Delhi: Primus Books, 2011), pp. 53–54.

45. Which is what happened to Baizabai, who, thanks to British machinations with another faction at court, was toppled and forced into exile.

46. Abbs, *Twenty-Two Years' Missionary Experience*, p. 87. His full name was Swathi Tirunal Rama Varma.

47. Welsh, *Military Reminiscences*, pp. 145–46.

48. Saltykov quoted in Walding, Stone and Nair, 'Russian Prince', p. 52.

49. S. Balachander, for instance, went even to the extent of doubting if Swathi Tirunal even existed.

50. R.P. Raja, *New Light on Swathi Tirunal* (Thiruvananthapuram: INDIS, 2006), p. 55.

51. Amanda J. Weidman, *Singing the Classical, Voicing the Modern: The Postcolonial Politics of Music in South India* (Durham and London: Duke University Press, 2006), pp. 64–65.

52. Jeffrey, *Decline*, p. 261. The *Bombay Gazette* dated 6 December 1853 also carries a traveller's account where we read that the Resident was referred to as 'Buffaloe-gal-loving General [Cullen]'. Of course, Cullen's supporters deny stories of his roving eye.

53. Menon, *History of Travancore*, p. 425.

54. Ibid., p. 427.

55. Raja, *New Light*, p. 218.

56. Ibid., p. 224.

57. Menon, *History of Travancore*, pp. 430–31.

58. Sixty-five of such compositions have been translated into English by Uthradam Tirunal Martanda Varma, the last Elayarajah (heir apparent) of Travancore, and published posthumously in Uma Maheswari S. ed., *Navaratri* (Thiruvananthapuram: Sri Uthradom Tirunal Marthanda Varma Literary and Charitable Trust, 2020), pp. 39–130.

59. Drury, *Reminiscences of Life*, p. 188.

60. T.E. Colebrooke, *Life of the Honourable Mountstuart Elphinstone*, Vol. 2 (London: John Murray, 1884), pp. 187–88. Elphinstone also noted his wonder at seeing this 'descendant of Sivajee' sitting at a desk doing his correspondence, asking what 'his ancestor would think of so peaceful a descendant'.

61. *Gazetteer of the Bombay Presidency, Volume XIX: Satara* (Bombay: Government Central Press, 1885), pp. 310–11.

62. Anonymous, *Indian Annexations: British Treatment of Native Princes* (London: Trubner and Co., 1863), p. 11.

63. On the British side too this was well known. Henry Russell, who served in Poona and Hyderabad as Resident, told parliament in 1832 how 'the habit of [the

states] relying on foreign support gradually paralyses its own faculties, and in the end it loses the form as well as the substance of independence. If it is galled by its trammels, and makes an effort to shake them off as the Peshwa did, it only precipitates its own destruction; if it submits, it declines, by degrees, from one stage of weakness to another, until, like the Nizam and the Rajah of Mysore, it expires from exhaustion. The choice is between a violent and a lingering death.' Quoted in Fisher, *Indirect Rule*, p. 17.

64. Menon, *History of Travancore*, p. 453.

65. Ibid.

66. Quoted in Walding, Stone and Nair, 'Russian Prince', p. 55.

67. Menon, *History of Travancore*, p. 456.

68. For more on the throne, see Deepthi Murali, 'Producing a Throne Fit for a Queen: Travancore's Contribution to the Great Exhibition in Crystal Palace, 1851', at http://www.deepthimurali.com/publications/2016/8/producing-a-throne-fit-for-a-queen-travancores-contribution-to-the-great-exhibition-in-crystal-palace-1851

69. Quoted in Menon, *History of Travancore*, p. 469.

70. Quoted in Taylor, *English Maharani*, p. 29.

71. Ibid., pp. 82–83.

72. Ibid., pp. 183–84.

73. J.M. Ludlow quoted in ibid., p. 87. Long after Uthram Tirunal was dead, when Curzon became viceroy, an elderly Victoria urged even him (unsuccessfully) to eschew the 'snobbish and vulgar, overbearing and offensive' style associated with her officials. He was to 'hear for himself what the feelings of the Natives really are', taking care not to 'trample on' their aspirations or 'make them feel that they are a conquered people'. Gilmour, *Curzon*, p. 137.

74. In Swathi Tirunal's time the total number of people who came to the capital for this *murajapom* ceremony was estimated at 60,000. See *Memoir of Travancore, Historical and Statistical, Compiled from Various Authentic Records and Personal Observation by W.H. Horsley (for J.S. Fraser Resident)*, p. 14, in Heber Drury ed., *Selections from the Records of Travancore* (Trevandrum: 1860, Press of His Highness the Rajah).

75. Menon, *History of Travancore*, p. 473.

76. Wilkinson, 'Residents of the British East India Company', p. 31.

77. All the previous quotes are taken from John Cox, *Travancore: Its Present Ruin Shown and the Remedy Sought in a Correspondence with the Government of Madras in the Years 1855–1857* (Nagercoil: London Mission Press, 1857).

78. Drury, *Reminiscences of Life*, p. 212.

79. Dalhousie was a devout Christian. When Duleep Singh of Punjab wished to convert to Christianity, Dalhousie was thrilled at his moving from 'darkness to

light', and it was 'in every way gratifying' to him personally. See J.G.A. Baird ed., *Private Letters of the Marquess of Dalhousie* (Edinburgh and London: William Blackwood and Sons, 1910), pp. 248–49, 307. Charles Wood, president of the Board of Control in London, similarly expressed hope for 'a civilized and Christian empire in India', and was 'much satisfied' when he learnt about Singh. Wood quoted in *The Bombay Guardian*, 8 July 1853. On Resident Cullen, as the man on the ground showing less sympathy for missionaries, see Dick Kooiman, *Conversion and Social Equality in India: The London Missionary Society in South Travancore in the 19th Century* (Columbia: South Asia Publications, 1989), p. 154.

80. Drury, *Reminiscences of Life*, p. 187.

81. An account and criticism of the 'misery' it caused appears in *The Bombay Gazette* and *Daily News* dated 14 March 1851, though it also added that were the ruler made aware of this, he would redress grievances. It was noted that even the surplus from the marriage feast was such that people had to be forced to cart it away, and the market was glutted with leftover provisions.

82. Madhava Rao quoted in Ranade, *Select Writings*, p. 339.

83. Quoted in Abbs, *Twenty-Two Years' Missionary Experience*, p. 89. We find a similar sentiment in A. Hawksworth's *Day Dawn in Travancore: A Brief Account of the Manners and Customs of the People and the Efforts that Are Being Made for Their Improvement* (Cottayam: C.M. Press, 1860), pp. 2–3, where, in a fictional dialogue, Uthram Tirunal is discussed as follows: 'It is true, I have read he is a most enlightened Prince; he has received an English education himself, and encourages learning in others, and for this purpose has established a good school at Trevandrum; where many of the highest caste native youths are being educated, and what is more he not only allows the Bible to be taught in the school, but he has read it himself, and formerly his children were also instructed in its contents. Yet notwithstanding all this, it is still a melancholy fact, that he remains a heathen.'

84. Abbs, *Twenty-Two Years' Missionary Experience*, p. 90.

85. There is a funny epilogue to this connection. In 1949 when the Travancore minister said to Sardar Patel that the state could not merge with the Indian Union since it belonged to the deity, the latter asked: 'Is that so? Then please tell me how could Travancore's rulers allow Lord Padmanabha to become subservient to the British Crown.' Quoted in S.N. Sahu, 'A Secularist, Sardar Patel Had United India in Spite of Travancore's "Hindu God" Excuse' in the Wire at https://thewire.in/history/sardar-vallabhbhai-patel-national-unity-day-travancore-secular

86. Ramusack, *Indian Princes*, p. 82.

87. *Indian Annexations*, pp. 20–21.

88. Menon, *History of Travancore*, p. 482.

89. 'Missionaries in Travancore, General Petition' in *Parliamentary Papers, Accounts and Papers, East India: Session 2* (31 May–13 August 1859), Vol. 25, pp. 29–

31, in 'Official Papers Sent from India, Touching the Recent Disturbances in Travancore', pp. 353–400 (hereafter *Parliamentary Papers*).

90. Visakham Tirunal, 'A Native Statesman', p. 235. The full letter may be read in Aiya, *Travancore State Manual*, pp. 513–15.

91. *Parliamentary Papers*, p. 32.

92. As Fisher observes in his *Indirect Rule*, p. 208, the standard method by which annexation could be justified was by claiming to do it for the good of the people – even if the people did not demand it. In this context, missionary polemics about misgovernment and suffering in Travancore was a very useful premise for action.

93. *Parliamentary Papers*, p. 32.

94. The British acknowledged this: As the chief secretary in Madras wrote in Note dated 12 March 1859 in ibid., 'The degree of interference which for many years past has been exercised by the representative of the British Government in the affairs of Travancore, is so large, and his intervention so general, that the credit or discredit of the administration greatly rests with the British Government, and it has thereby become their duty to insist upon the observance of a system of toleration, in a more decided manner than they would be at liberty to adopt, if they had merely to bring their influence to bear on an independent State.'

95. See Tirunal, 'Native Statesman', p. 235. He adds that instead of being used to address urgent financial commitments, the corrupt Dewan foisted on the rajah by the Resident kept most of it. As for the transaction itself, the maharajah paid back with interest.

96. Quoted in letter dated 23 March 1859 from the chief secretary of Madras to the secretary, Foreign Dep., in Calcutta in *Parliamentary Papers*, pp. 37–38.

97. *Parliamentary Papers*, p. 36.

98. See Misra, 'Indian Aristocrats'.

99. W.W. Hunter, *A Life of the Earl of Mayo: Fourth Viceroy of India*, Vol. 1 (Second Edition) (London: Smith, Elder and Co., 1876), pp. 207–209.

100. This comes across in Dewan Krishna Rao's 1844 administrative report on Travancore in the reign of Swathi Tirunal, where much of the attention is on temples, the qualities expected of priests, the Brahmin feeding houses, the quality of meals provided there and so on. See V. Kristno Row, *A Description of the Administrative System of Travancore in the Year 1844* in Drury ed., *Selections*.

101. Author's interview with Rukmini Varma.

102. In this story, declaring that while she had been a *balabhakshini* (devourer of children) so far, the yakshi now became a *balarakshini* (protector of the young). Author's interview with Prasanna Varma.

103. Author's interview with Rukmini Varma.

104. P.K. Parameswaran Nair (translated by E.M.J. Venniyoor), *History of Malayalam Literature* (New Delhi: Sahitya Akademi, 1967), p. 100. Also Raja, *New Light*, p. 211.

105. Sharat Sunder Rajeev, 'The Durbar Artists of Travancore' at https://tinpahar. com/?p=1928

106. Serfoji is dealt with in detail by Savithri Preetha Nair in her *Raja Serfoji II: Science, Medicine and Enlightenment in Tanjore* (New Delhi: Routledge, 2012) as well as by Indira Viswanathan Peterson in multiple essays as well as a forthcoming biography.

107. Sharat Sunder Rajeev, 'Durbar Artists'.

108. The durbar painting is on display at the Kuthiramalika Museum in Trivandrum; the portrait showing Uthram Tirunal's sons does not appear to have ever been displayed, but those of his nephews were used in 1878 by Shungoonny Menon to illustrate his history of Travancore. The originals remain in the palace collection.

109. Mentioned as Motookistnah in Drury, *Reminiscences of Life*, p. 197.

110. Author's interview with Rukmini Varma, whose grandmother Maharani Sethu Lakshmi Bayi had described these ivory works by Rajaraja Varma to her, having personally seen them.

111. See Arthur Lewis, *George Maxwell Gordon; The Pilgrim Missionary of the Punjab: A History of His Life and Work, 1839–1880* (London: Seeley and Co., 1889), p. 130. Though the artist is not named here, I make the connection with Rajaraja Varma on the basis of the fact that the portrait was recorded as having been made 'by one of the family, who executed it himself'. The only male relation of the royal family who, at that time, painted in this traditional style was Rajaraja Varma. He was, admittedly, a relative and not 'one of the family', but it is possible the missionary was oblivious to these nuances. R. Kulathu Iyer in an article in *The Madras Weekly Mail* dated 8 August 1907 also mentions Rajaraja Varma as teaching the art of painting on ivory.

112. I take the traditional ingredients from Venniyoor, *Raja Ravi Varma*, p. 3. Tradition has it that in 1805 two princes related to the Pazhassi Rajah of Malabar, who fought and was killed by the British, sought refuge in Kilimanoor. They were disguised as Brahmins, but the women of the house shrewdly noticed that their manners betrayed warriors, not priests. Interestingly, the men were painters too, and imparted lessons to two sisters in Kilimanoor during their stay. One of these two was Rajaraja Varma's mother. Author's interview with Rukmini Varma and Sharat Sunder Rajeev.

113. V. Nagam Aiya, *The Travancore State Manual*, Vol. I (Trivandrum: Government of Travancore, 1906).

114. George Joseph, 'Great Indian Artist', p. 907.

115. See Venniyoor, *History of Malayalam Literature*, p. 4, for the story. See also Chawla, *Raja Ravi Varma*, p. 34. Rukmini Varma, however, believes that Ravi Varma's first visit to Thiruvananthapuram was not in 1862 – he was indeed brought here once in 1861 and rejected as consort to the junior rani. It may also be, considering that

the princess did marry a Kilimanoor boy, that Ravi Varma's name came up when the search for a bridegroom began, and that his dark skin was a factor. This story may later have been combined with his subsequent appearance at court the next year, aged fourteen.

116. Martanda Varma (r. 1729–58), Karthika Tirunal Dharmarajah (r. 1758–98), Avittom Tirunal Balarama Varma (r. 1798–1810), Gowri Lakshmi Bayi (r. 1810–14) and Gowri Parvathi Bayi (r. 1814–29) were the rulers of Travancore fathered by great-uncles of Ravi Varma from the Kilimanoor family. Gowri Parvathi Bayi did not have children but both her husbands were men from Kilimanoor.

117. While the *tali* or wedding locket of the Zamorin princesses was tied ritually by a member of the Kodungallur rajah's family, as K.V. Krishna Ayyar notes in *The Zamorins of Calicut* (Calicut: Norman Printing Bureau, 1938), pp. 7–8, the actual husbands who lived with the princesses came from several families, including Beypore, that is, Ravi Varma's ancestral line. The Beypore family, meanwhile, sent men to tie talis for the women of the family of the Kadathanad rajahs, who in turn were later actually married by Namboothiri Brahmins. The tying of the tali in matrilineal communities in Kerala was less marriage and more a rite of passage: the actual marriage was a later ceremony largely described just as *sambandham* or 'relationship'. It was such a sambandham that united Ravi Varma's own parents, Umamba (1832–87) of Kilimanoor and Neelakandan Bhattathiri (1826–98), a Brahmin of the Ezhumavil family in Cochin.

118. There are, however, those who question the claim that the family had Rajput links. The other line that is held to be connected to the Rajputs are the Kottayam rajahs, who were known as Puranattu Swaroopam. 'Puranattu' means 'those of a foreign land'. According to R.P. Raja, who gave this writer an interview for his first book, *The Ivory Throne*, however, Ravi Varma's ancestors, who belonged to Parappur Swaroopam, are indeed said to be of Rajput origin.

119. The Zamorins, for instance, were Samantas, which is a ritually superior class of Nairs, who in turn were officially deemed Sudras since they did not wear the sacred thread like the Kshatriyas. Travancore's rajahs acquired the sacred thread in the eighteenth century but were still not equal in status to older thread-wearing lines. As A. Aiyappan writes in *The Personality of Kerala* (Trivandrum: University of Kerala, 1982), p. 153, the foremost Kshatriya houses of Kerala were Kottayam, Kurumbranad, Parappanad, Beypore, Cochin and Kodungallur.

120. E.M.J. Venniyoor, *Raja Ravi Varma* (Trivandrum: Government of Kerala, 1981), p. 2.

121. Ibid.

122. In the 1795 treaty signed by the maharajah with the East India Company he is referred to in Article 9 as a 'tributary' of the nawab of the Carnatic. See C.U. Aitchison ed., *A Collection of Treaties, Engagements, and Sunnuds, Relating*

to India and Neighbouring Countries, Vol. 5 (Calcutta: J.L. Kingham, Foreign Dep., 1864), p. 306. The tribute was Rs 6,000 a year and every few years, a fixed number of elephants. After the nawab's state was annexed, this amount was fully transferred to the Company. When Uthram Tirunal succeeded to the throne, he sent a customary letter to the nawab in which he referred formally to how his accession was 'by Your Highness' favour' and declared himself as 'one of the most faithful allies and dependents of Your Highness'. See Aiya, Travancore State Manual, pp. 517–18.

123. Menon, History of Travancore, p. 267.

124. Ibid. The visitor also described this ruler, Karthika Tirunal, as follows: 'The military forces of the present king of Travancor (sic) consists of 50,000 men, disciplined according to the European manner; and 100,000 Malabar Nayris and Cegos, armed with bows and arrows, spears, swords, and battle-axes . . . After deducting the expenses of Government, his yearly income may amount to half a million of rupees, arising from trade, duties, and various kinds of fines . . . He generally wears a turban of dark blue silk; a long white robe, fastened at the breast with a string of diamonds; long wide drawers of red silk; and shoes, the points of which are bent backwards like those of the Chinese. A sabre is suspended from his shoulders; and in the blue girdle bound round his loins is stuck a poniard, or Persian dagger, which can be used either for attack or defence. When he shows himself to the people in full State, he is attended by 5,000 or 6,000 men, together with a great number of palanquins and elephants . . . In my time he was very much attached to the Catholic missionaries. As often as he passed by the parsonage house at Angenga, where I resided two years, he always sent two of the gentlemen of his bedchamber to enquire after my health . . . He is an affable, polite, contented, prudent, and friendly man.' Quoted in ibid., pp. 262–64.

125. The dead Uthram Tirunal had four nephews, and as per the matrilineal system of succession, the oldest of them should have followed him on the throne. Sadly, this candidate was in a 'state of hopeless imbecility', so the next in line, Ayilyam Tirunal, was instead recognized. Again, the third of the siblings was also considered mentally incapable of ruling, making the youngest, Visakham Tirunal, successor to Ayilyam Tirunal. During Ayilyam Tirunal's reign, his immediate younger sibling as always honoured as the Elayarajah, but this was just a titular dignity, making the 'First Prince' Visakham Tirunal the actual heir apparent. See Statement Exhibiting the Moral and Material Progress and Condition of India During the Year 1860–61 (London: George Edward Eyre and William Spottiswoode, 1862), p. 275.

126. Tapati Guha Thakurta, 'Westernisation and Tradition in South Indian Painting in the Nineteenth Century: The Case of Raja Ravi Varma (1848–1906)', p. 177, in Studies in History, Vol. 2, No. 2 (1986), pp. 165–95.

127. Venniyoor, *Raja Ravi Varma*, p. 5. These were illustrations of Indian paintings, bronzes and other artefacts.

128. This fascination was not entirely new. Emperor Akbar's chronicler, Abul Fazl, centuries before had remarked how 'painters, especially those of Europe, succeed in drawing figures expressive of the conceptions which the artist has of the mental states, so much so that people may mistake a picture for reality'. Quoted in Crispin Branfoot, 'Introduction: Portraiture in South Asia', p. 7, in Branfoot ed., *Portraiture in South Asia Since the Mughals: Art, Representation and History* (London: I.B. Tauris, 2018), pp. 1–22.

129. He is also often called Ramaswamy Naicker.

130. Stella Kramrisch, J.H. Cousins and R. Vasudeva Poduval, *The Arts and Crafts of Travancore* (London: The Royal India Society, 1948), p. 136.

131. Partha Mitter, *Art and Nationalism in Colonial India, 1850–1922: Occidental Orientations* (Cambridge: Cambridge University Press, 1994), p. 184. Details on Jensen's visit and the four paintings he made appear in the *Times of India* dated 23 September 1868.

132. Venniyoor, *Raja Ravi Varma*, p. 5.

133. Geeta Kapur, *When Was Modernism: Essays on Contemporary Cultural Practice in India* (New Delhi: Tulika Books, 2000), p. 149.

134. Neumayer and Schelberger in Ramanthan ed., *Pages of a Mind*, p. 23.

135. Venniyoor, *Raja Ravi Varma*, p. 6.

136. Ibid., p. 8.

137. Author's interview with Rukmini Varma, who states that it was always his secretary who handled money.

138. This frowning on art continued long after his death. His great-great-granddaughter Rukmini Varma recalls having to sketch in the privacy of the bathroom in the palace in Trivandrum, since it would not be allowed outside as she grew up – it was not a suitable pursuit for a young girl.

139. Venniyoor, *Raja Ravi Varma*, p. 11.

140. Indira Varma, 'Artist of the People and of the Gods' in the *Illustrated Weekly of India*, Vol. 97, No. 22 (1976), p. 23. Ravi Varma does appear to have consulted astrologers occasionally. In October 1903, for instance, his brother recorded in his diary how they met with an astrologer 'who is said to be doing wonders in the way of prophesy'. Rajaraja Varma was quick to add that he personally had no belief in astrology, for 'God has not given men the power to pierce into … the dark future'. See Neumayer and Schelberger eds, *The Diary*, p. 179.

141. Author's interview with Jay Varma. Indira Varma's article cited above (she was Ravi Varma's great-granddaughter) speaks of a similar episode, except it involved the daughter of an unnamed 'North Indian Maharaja'.

142. Venniyoor, *Raja Ravi Varma*, p. 11.

143. The judge was Kizhakkepat Krishna Menon and his daughter was the wife of Sir C. Sankaran Nair, who became a Congress president.

144. Venniyoor, *Raja Ravi Varma*, p. 12. As Menon, *History of Travancore*, p. 520, wrote, the *veerasrinkhala* or *veerachangala* was 'considered to be the greatest mark of distinction'.

145. This was Robert Chisholm who is better known as an architect. See Joseph, 'Great Indian Artist', p. 907. Joseph does make an error, however, in stating that Ravi Varma's first appearance hereafter in Madras was in 1874.

146. Venniyoor, *Raja Ravi Varma*, pp. 15–16. This is seemingly incorrect because we find Ravi Varma winning a medal in 1881.

147. Quoted in Christopher Hibbert, *Edward VII: The Last Victorian King* (New York: Palgrave Macmillan, 2007), p. 135.

148. The *Veltikodegone* dated 18 December 1875, in William Howard Russell, *The Prince of Wales' Tour: A Diary in India* (New York: R. Worthington, 1878), p. 544.

149. Hibbert, p. 136. In Madras alone, while the prince received presents valued at £20,000, his own gifts cost only £8,000. Indeed, the received goods were so impressive that they were put up for exhibition in Britain, France and Denmark after the prince's return. Between 1876 and 1883 an estimated 2.5 million people would visit the exhibitions in Britain alone, generating so much revenue that a new art gallery was commissioned at one location, and the Indian Museum in London was able to substantially expand its collection. See the relevant statistics at https://www.rct.uk/about/press-office/press-releases/dazzling-works-of-art-from-the-indian-subcontinent-go-on-display#/

150. Russell, *Prince of Wales' Tour*, p. 277. See also Kajal Meghani, *Splendours of the Subcontinent: A Prince's Tour of India, 1875–6* (London: Royal Collection Trust, 2017). See also https://www.rct.uk/about/news-and-features/dazzling-works-of-art-from-the-indian-subcontinent-go-on-display-at-the#/

151. See *The Homeward Mail from India, China and the East* dated 6 May 1876 and *The Madras Weekly Mail* dated 12 February 1876. We know this artist was Ravi Varma because it is described as an oil painting done by a 'Coil Tambooran', that is, Koil Tampuran, Ravi Varma's title.

2. The Brahmin Who Knew English

1. Lewis, *George Maxwell Gordon*, p. 121.

2. Quoted in Aiya, *Travancore State Manual*, p. 547.

3. Ibid., p. 555. Of course, their man on the ground, the Resident, at the opening of the secretariat building had caused offence by showing up in checked trousers and a hunting coat. See the *Times of India* dated 6 January 1870 for a scathing review in which the insult is called out. When he retired, the *Friend of India* dated 24

April 1875 welcomed the departure of this 'personally distasteful and obnoxious' Resident who 'tyrannized' over the ruler. The same paper on 13 March 1873 had also noted his 'want of courtesy and rough bearing'.

4. Or as P. Ramakrishna Pillai in *Visakhavijaya: A Study* (Thiruvananthapuram: Anitha Publications, 1990), p. 63, put it, 'If Martanda Varma was the maker of the modern state of Travancore, Ayilyam Tirunal had the honour of being the maker of the model State of Travancore.' As for interference, of course the British always made attempts to meddle in the state's internal matters and even the royal household's affairs.

5. Drury, *Reminiscences of Life*, p. 168.

6. F.N. Maltby quoted in Loke Nath Ghose, *The Modern History of the Indian Chiefs, Rajas, Zamindars and c., Part II: The Native Aristocracy and Gentry, comprising Historical, Political, Social and Other Accounts of Several Ancient Families, Noblemen, and Eminent Men* (Calcutta: J.N. Ghose and Co., 1881), p. 537. In fact, Maltby added, nothing made him 'more hopeful of the effect which English influence and English education are producing on the Native mind, than my intercourse' with this unusual gentleman.

7. Letter dated 23 July 1866 from Madhava Rao to the Secretary of the Most Exalted Order of the Star of India in File No. G.O. 193, Madras (Pol. Dep.) dated 21 August 1866, NAI.

8. See Urmila Rau Lal, *Diwan Sir Thanjavur Madhava Row: Statesman, Administrator Extraordinaire* (Mumbai: Bharatiya Vidya Bhavan, 2015), pp. 16–17, for an account of Rao's ancestors and their earlier home in Bijapur.

9. See David Washbrook, 'The Maratha Brahmin Model in South India: An Afterword' in *The Indian Economic and Social History Review*, Vol. 47, No. 4 (2010), pp. 597–615, for a brief study of the transition of Marathi Brahmins from religious to secular purposes under various rulers, including the Company.

10. Macaulay's Minute dated 2 February 1835, Law Member, General Dep., p. 171, in Lynn Zastoupil and Martin Moir eds, *The Great Indian Education Debate: Documents Relating to the Orientalist–Anglicist Controversy, 1781–1843* (Routledge: New York, 2016), pp. 161–73. Robert E. Frykenberg in the context of Guntur district refers to how Marathi Brahmins 'carved out, secretly and silently, a state within a state'. See Frykenberg, *Guntur District, 1788–1848: A History of Local Influence and Central Authority in South India* (Oxford: Clarendon Press, 1965), p. 233.

11. Quoted in Wilkinson, 'Residents of the British East India Company', p. 145.

12. Aiya, *Travancore State Manual*, pp. 471–72.

13. Ibid., p. 474.

14. Ibid., pp. 476, 483. Subba Rao would return for another stint between 1839 and 1842 during which time he also wrote a literary work called *Kishun Kovur: A Tragedy in Five Acts* (Trivandrum: Government Press, 1840).

15. It took him some time, during which gap his brother warmed the seat.

16. The Marathi Brahmins were certainly grateful for the avenues Travancore provided them. In 1888 a caste association in Madras would formally thank the maharajah for drawing Dewans from among them, while in response the maharajah himself thanked 'your intellectual race for some of the best Dewans' his state had had. See *The Madras Weekly Mail* dated 14 March 1888.

17. This idea of the 'foreigner' appears in other princely states also. For Hyderabad, for example, see K.V. Narayana Rao, *Internal Migration Policies in an Indian State: A Case Study of the Mulki Rules in Hyderabad and Andhra* (Cambridge, Massachusetts: Centre for International Studies, 1977). In Travancore, as late as 1947, the state's just-retired Dewan Sir C.P. Ramaswamy Iyer would write how people were 'prepared to go to any length to get rid of a so-called foreigner' like him. So too when a Congress politician was disallowed in the state on grounds of her being an outsider, Mahatma Gandhi asked what locus standi the Dewan had in the matter, since he was 'himself a foreigner'. See A. Sreedhara Menon, *Triumph and Tragedy in Travancore: Annals of Sir CP's Sixteen Years* (Kottayam: Current Books, 2001), pp. 20, 164–65.

18. He features prominently in an 1858 'List of the Proficients' of the institution. John Bruce Norton (G.R. Norton ed.), *Topics for Indian Statesmen* (London: Richardson Brothers, 1858), Appendix B, No. 1, p. 399.

19. John Bruce Norton, *The Rebellion in India: How to Prevent Another* (London: Richardson Brothers, 1857), p. 59.

20. John Bruce Norton, *The Educational Speeches of the Hon'ble John Bruce Norton* (Madras: Advertising and Printing Company, 1870), p. 31. Norton recounted this episode in a speech he gave in 1855.

21. Ibid.

22. Ibid., p. 61.

23. Note cited in Norton, *Topics*, pp. 361–62.

24. Menon, *History of Travancore*, p. 458.

25. Norton, *Topics*, p. 361.

26. Aiya, *Travancore State Manual*, p. 561.

27. Norton, *Topics*, pp. 361–62. See also Aiya, *Travancore State Manual*, p. 561.

28. Norton, *Topics*, pp. 361–62.

29. Quoted in B.V. Kamesvara Aiyar, *Sir A. Sashiah Sastri: An Indian Statesman* (Madras: Srinivasa, Varadachari and Co., 1902), p. 87.

30. Norton, *Topics*, Appendix B, No. 1, p. 399, provides a table with their salaries.

31. Chief Secretary's Minute dated 17 June 1863 in File No. G.O. 175, Pros. Madras (Pol. Dep.) dated 22 June 1863, NAI.

32. The idea that tutors could influence their royal wards was something that did eventually cause discomfort in Travancore, after Rao fell out with Ayilyam

Tirunal in the 1870s. As we saw, Swathi Tirunal had made his tutor Dewan, and Rao's own rise owed a great deal to his closeness with the royal family. In the 1890s, Ravi Varma's brother recorded how the then heir apparent, Chathayam Tirunal, was alienated from his parents, having become 'only a tool' in the hands of his tutor (see Neumayer and Schelberger eds, *The Diary*, pp. 100–101). And in the 1920s, Ravi Varma's granddaughter, as maharani of Travancore, wrote to the British how she would prefer an older man as tutor for her nephew, the minor maharajah, so that the tutor would be 'uninfluenced by considerations of self-advancement' and hopes of 'any fat employment in the state' by reason of his advanced years (see Pillai, *Ivory Throne*, p. 323). The irony, of course, was that the maharani herself to a great extent was led by the advice of her husband, who in turn had given his own former tutor a post as 'Palace Special Officer'.

33. M.G. Ranade made this point when he wrote, thus: 'It is a sad reflection on British rule in India that Sir Madhav Rao found his career, not in British India, but in Indian States. If the red line in the map of India had not been here and there interrupted, would young Madhav, serving in the Accountant-General's office at Madras in 1847, have died Raja Sir T. Madhav Rao, the administrator, the politician, and the statesman? Would he not have been one of those many flowers that are, "born to blush unseen"? And yet "Annex Indian States" is the cry of Civilians of the imperialist school ... There is no chance for an Indian of Sir T. Madhav Rao's talents to develop and display his powers and be useful alike to the rulers and the ruled. The life of Sir T. Madhav Rao, we repeat, is a sad commentary on the British Indian Administration.' See Ranade, *Select Writings*, p. 343.

34. Note dated 10 December 1880 by Secretary H.M. Durand in File Nos. 57–63, Pros. Foreign Dep. (Political A) July 1881, NAI.

35. Quoted in Aiya, *Travancore State Manual*, p. 546.

36. Cited in Tirunal, 'Native Statesman', p. 245.

37. Quoted in Aiya, *Travancore State Manual*, p. 547.

38. As an official wrote, the Dewan was 'always ready to bring his influence and authority as Prime Minister to bear upon any matter conducive to the interests and welfare of the country'. See Drury, *Reminiscences of Life*, p. 217. And in many ways, he was willing to learn from India's self-appointed colonial supervisors, opening him up to the charge of being a bit too deferential to the British. In the world of the 1850s and 1860s, however, his attitude was in order, and he acknowledged frankly the role the British had played in his rapid growth. In 1866 he wrote in a letter how it was the Residency's positive review of his term as royal tutor many years ago that delivered him greater roles. 'Ever since that time my position and opportunities have been improving.' See letter dated 27 June 1866 from Rao to Drury quoted in full in Drury, *Reminiscences of Life*, p. 169.

39. Undated letter in ibid., p. 220

40. Quoted in Loke Nath Ghose, *Modern History*, p. 538, and Aiya, *Travancore State Manual*, p. 555.

41. Quoted in Aiya, *Travancore State Manual*, p. 591. The addressee is Nanoo Pillai, Dewan between 1877 and 1880.

42. Rao also explained – seemingly oblivious to how his own family rose through the same formula – how influence with white officials aggrandized subordinate Indians: 'A Tahsildar who happens to be any relation of the Sheristadar, or had been the butler of the Collector, and as such enjoying the favour of his lady' was bound to rise more easily, and prone to 'astonishing' corruption.

43. Quoted in John Bruce Norton, *A Letter to Robert Lowe, Joint Secretary of the Board of Control, on the Condition and Requirements of the Presidency of Madras* (London: Richardson Brothers, 1854), pp. 152–53.

44. In Malcolm Lewis's pamphlet on Oude cited before too there is a 'native gentleman' from Madras whose note to Lewis is printed. Excoriating the British policy of annexation and 'convenient absorption' of princely states so as to cause the 'general extinction' of the princes, the unnamed author cites Travancore as a 'favourable contrast' to British-ruled territories. 'In spite of a subsidiary force and other subsidies paid to the British Government, its treasury is well-stocked,' he wrote, adding sarcastically, 'what more heinous crime in the eyes of an Indian Government'. See Lewis, *George Maxwell Gordon*, pp. 19, 25. One suspects this may have been Rao, given the positive emphasis Travancore receives. His preference to stay anonymous can be explained by his now senior post in the state – direct criticism when annexation fever raged could have been risky and embarrassed not just Rao but also his employer.

45. It does, however, appear that senior officials of the government did correspond with newspaper editors. In 1870, for instance, letters from Vedadridasa Mudaliar, a judge, and Shungoonny Menon to the editor of the *Western Star* fell into the wrong hands and resulted in their blackmail. See Menon, *Life of T. Sankunni Menon*, p. 234. Mudaliar is supposed to have been a permanent opponent of Rao's, and a favourite of Ayilyam Tirunal.

46. Meanwhile, the Dewan of Cochin in 1874 was receiving only 1,300 rupees. See Menon, *Life of T. Sankunni Menon*, p. 177.

47. Letter dated 25 April 1863 and letter dated 5 May 1863 from the maharajah to the Resident in File No. G.O. 175, Pros. Madras (Pol. Dep.) dated 22 June 1863, NAI.

48. Letter dated 12 June 1863 from the Resident to the chief secretary in Madras in ibid.

49. Chief Secretary's Minute dated 17 June 1863 in ibid. As the chief secretary in Madras noted with 'much regret', not only did Rao enjoy a handsome salary, he had received a house from the ruler and land valued at 50,000 rupees, on a token

tax rate. So too when the Dewan's daughter was married, Ayilyam Tirunal gave him 3,000 rupees in cash, besides 10,000 to build himself another house. All in all, 'in the brief space of less than three years the Dewan had obtained from [the maharajah] land and money to the amount of 63,000 Rupees, besides getting his salary increased 25 per cent' through means of a 'pension' for his twelve- and eight-year-old boys. This, a self-righteous British establishment felt, could not be swallowed: the maharajah was told that no matter what 'kindly feeling' he entertained for his minister, it had 'been carried beyond what the occasion demanded'. Charges of nepotism would reappear. See *The Friend of India* dated 7 January 1869.

50. Ibid.

51. Governor's Minute dated 18 June 1863 in ibid.

52. Letter dated 25 August 1863 from the Resident to the chief secretary in Madras in File No. G.O. 287, Pros. Madras (Pol. Dep.) dated 24 September 1863, NAI. The relatives mentioned were Rama Rao (at Rs 350 in salary), Lakshman Rao (at Rs 80), Annaji Rao (Rs 70), Jagannath Rao (Rs 25), another Annaji Rao (Rs 21) and finally Srinivas Rao (Rs 10).

53. Norton, *Educational Speeches*, p. 113. This was, he added, somewhat predictably, 'the effect produced by Madava Row's labours' as their teacher. Visakham Tirunal agreed that the 'talented, distinguished, and successful' Rao 'accomplished with the greatest skill' the 'extremely delicate and responsible task' of preparing them for the world; he had 'exceeded the most ardent expectations' of the late Uthram Tirunal. Quoted in Norton, *Topics*, pp. 361–62.

54. Letter dated 5 February 1869 from the Resident to the chief secretary in Madras in File No. G.O. 166, Pros. Madras (Pol. Dep.) dated 13 May 1869, NAI.

55. As early as 1862 it was noted that he looked older than his thirty-two years and was stout with a 'comfortable-looking face'. See William Denison, *Varieties of Vice-Regal Life*, Vol. 2 (London: Longmans, Green and Co., 1970), pp. 208–209. The comment on the maharajah looking older would be made again in 1875 during the Prince of Wales's tour, when it was noted that though in his forties, he looked 'nearly sixty'. See Russell, *Prince of Wales' Tour*, p. 285.

56. Menon, *History of Travancore*, p. 482.

57. Tirunal, 'Native Statesman', p. 239.

58. Menon, *History of Travancore*, p. 491. The senior official, Raman Menon, resigned and departed with a pension of Rs 175.

59. Ibid., p. 493.

60. Jeffrey, *Decline*, p. 84.

61. Shaji A., *Politicisation of Caste Relations in a Princely State: Communal Politics in Modern Travancore (1891–1947)* (Gurugram: Zorba Books, 2017), p. 44. A related matter that reveals the tightrope the ruler had to walk features in *The*

Friend of India dated 5 March 1874. A Tamil Brahmin in Travancore called Sesha Iyengar had got his widowed daughter – who was widowed a 'virgin', that is, as a child bride – remarried. His reformist act was allowed by the state in that the local officials gave his family and him protection. However, when pressure was placed on the maharajah in terms of caste matters, the latter gave way: Iyengar and his kin were barred from temples and subject to social deprivations.

62.   See Menon, *Life of T. Sankunni Menon*, p. 36.

63.   Lewis, *George Maxwell Gordon*, p. 123. This response is not surprising and would spread across states. As Fisher notes in his *Indirect Rule*, p. 251: 'When addressing European audiences in India or Britain, the British symbolically contrasted their honest, plain black frock coats or formal uniforms with the pretentious glitter and clashing colours of the pageant of the "oriental" courts they controlled.' It was only natural that rulers too would formulate a response.

64.   See Dick Kooiman, 'The Guns of Travancore or How Much Powder May a Maharaja Blaze Away?' in *Indian Economic Social History Review*, Vol. 43, No. 3 (2006), pp. 301–22. It may also, however, be noted here that in 1858 after the Great Rebellion, the East India Company lost power to the British Crown, and hereafter the approach to Indian princes was much more conciliatory. On the matter of Travancore's gun salute: while nineteen guns was what the British recognized, locally Travancore always maintained a twenty-one-gun salute for its ruler.

65.   Lewis, *George Maxwell Gordon*, p. 123.

66.   Besides, early appointments 'would naturally be an economy of soap and water' given that multiple dips in the pond could be avoided. Ibid. As late as the 1920s, the rulers were still receiving Europeans at seven in the morning so that, as a commentator put it in the case of Ravi Varma's granddaughter – the state's future maharani – 'Her Highness can wash off the contamination of shaking hands with an outcaste before proceeding to other business.' See letter dated 28 June 1929 from Louise Ouwerkerk, a European lecturer at the Women's College in Thiruvananthapuram, to her mother in MSS EUR F232/60, IOR. Indeed, English tutors, particularly on auspicious days, could not even stand on the same carpet as members of the royal house. See letter dated 22 February 1929 from the British Resident to the political secretary, G.O.I., in IOR/R/1/1/1849. And at banquets, the maharajah's family sat with lemons in their hands, which were believed to absorb the impurities of being around beastly meat dishes.

67.   Jeffrey, *Decline*, p. 78.

68.   Lal, *Diwan Sir Thanjavur Madhava Row*, p. 64.

69.   Denison, *Varieties of Vice-Regal Life*, pp. 210–11.

70.   For the estimate from 1936, see letter dated 6 December 1936 from A.C. Lothian to the political secretary, G.O.I., in IOR/L/PS/13/750.

71. Letter dated 5 February 1869 from the Resident to the chief secretary, Madras, in File No. 166, Pros. Madras (Pol. Dep.) dated 13 May 1869, NAI.

72. A.J. Arbuthnot's Minute dated 28 January 1871 in IOR/R/2/891/251.

73. Ibid.

74. Ibid. Newill's personality is discussed in an extract from the *Madras Mail* published in the *Times of India* dated 6 May 1869 where he is described as among the mistakes of the British government. 'Feeble where he should have been strong, and stubborn where he should have been pliant', Newill was the wrong man for a 'post that calls for the exhibition of habitual tact, energy, and breadth of view'.

75. Letter dated 11 November 1871 from the Resident to the chief secretary in Madras.

76. Letter dated 26 March 1872 from the Resident to the chief secretary in Madras, File No. 148, Pros. Madras (Pol. Dep.) dated 15 March 1872, NAI.

77. Letter dated 23 January 1871 from Madhava Rao to Ayilyam Tirunal in ibid.

78. Letter dated 11 November 1871 from the Resident to the chief secretary in Madras in IOR/R/2/891/250.

79. Letter dated 11 May 1872 from Acting Governor Arbuthnot to the secretary of state in File No 7–11, Pros. Madras (Pol. Dep.) dated 11 May 1872, NAI. Rao, of course, defended himself: he did not want the details to be secret and had advised the maharajah to involve the Resident; and the sinecure was only to avoid setting a precedent with a Rs 1000 pension. See letter dated 12 February 1872 from Madhava Rao to the Resident in G.O. No 106 (II), Pros. Madras (Pol. Dep.) dated 20 March 1872, NAI.

80. See File No. 148, Pros. Madras (Pol. Dep.) dated 15 April 1872 and File No. 190, Pros. Madras (Pol. Dep.) dated 8 May 1872, NAI.

81. Letter dated 1 April 1872 from the Resident to the chief secretary in Madras in File No. 148, Pros. Madras (Pol. Dep.) dated 15 April 1872, NAI.

82. G. Paramaswaran Pillai, *Representative Indians* (London: George Routledge and Sons, 1897), p. 105.

83. For an essay on Pillai see Usha Sahana, 'G. Parameswaran Pillai: Early Indian-English Writer' in *Indian Literature*, Vol. 47, No. 6 (2003), pp. 155–57. Pillai also appears in Rajaraja Varma's diary in January 1901 requesting 'a short life of Brother with photographs of some of his Puranic Pictures for publication in some magazine in England'. See Neumayer and Schelberger eds, *The Diary*, p. 80. Pillai was also the author of an 1887 pamphlet called *An Open Letter to Lord Connemara, Governor of Madras*, under the pseudonym 'Pro Patria', which was one of the strongest attacks on a Travancore ruler. See T.P. Sankarankutty Nair, 'Govindan Parameswaran Pillai: The Father of Political Agitation in Travancore' in *Proceedings of the Indian History Congress*, Vol. 37 (1976), pp. 354–60.

84. Pillai, *Visakhavijaya*, p. 149. This is quite in contrast to a remark a missionary

made in 1860 when Ayilyam Tirunal first came to power of his reputation: 'The present Rajah is a young man . . . who has kept himself much aloof, it is said, from the usual vices . . . of an Eastern Court.' Quoted in Waghorne, *Raja's Magic Clothes*, p. 61.

85.   Pillai, *Visakhavijaya*, p. 149.

86.   Letter dated 11 May 1872 from the acting governor to the secretary of state in File Nos. 7–11, Pros. Madras (Pol. Dep.) dated 11 May 1872, NAI.

87.   Letter dated 01 April 1872 from the Resident to the chief secretary in Madras in File No. 148, Pros. Madras (Pol. Dep.) dated 15 April 1872, NAI.

88.   These names included Shungoonny Menon, our court historian, who was described as 'a fine old man of good family, position, and address' but 'old, very conservative, narrow, and a hot partisan'. See letter dated 7 February 1872 from the Resident to the chief secretary in Madras in File No. 106 (2), Pros. Madras (Pol. Dep.), NAI. A feeler also seems to have been sent to the Dewan of Cochin, T. Sankunni Menon. See Menon, *Life of T. Sankunni Menon*, p. 173.

89.   Augusta Blandford in *India's Women: The Magazine of the Church of England Zenana Missionary Society*, Vol. 1 (London: James Nisbet and Co., 1881), p. 24. Ravi Varma's brother also notes the story of one such scapegoat and the charitable public works he undertook. See Rajaraja Varma, *A Narrative*, p. 8.

90.   Venniyoor, *Raja Ravi Varma*, p. 6. In fact, it took 'a good deal of perseverance' on Visakham Tirunal's part for Ayilyam Tirunal to see him even as he lay dying. See Aiya, *Travancore State Manual*, pp. 585–86.

91.   See Tirunal, 'Native Statesman', p. 240 which praises Rao for his 'zeal, earnestness, noble ambition, and honesty of purpose unrivalled among the natives of India'. So too in that 1868–69 dispute on military honours to the Dewan, Visakham Tirunal sided with the Dewan. In a letter he wrote: 'I feel that you have just grounds to complain.' The 'discontinuance of any of these [honours] can only be regarded as so much of clear diminution of the marks of honour enjoyed by all the Dewans . . . If you deserve any difference of treatment from your predecessors . . . that difference should certainly be on the side of increase, and not of decrease of honours.' See letter dated 6 April 1868 from Visakham Tirunal to the Dewan in File No. 227, Pros. Madras (Pol. Dep.) dated 9 July 1869. Elsewhere he wrote of Rao as follows: 'What Pericles did for Athens, what Cromwell did for England, that Madava Row did for Travancore.' See Aiya, *Travancore State Manual*, p. 556. Finally, Visakham Tirunal and Madhava Rao had joint investments in coffee. See letter dated 11 December 1874 from the Resident to the acting chief secretary in Madras in IOR/R/2/891/253.

92.   Quoted in Aiyar, *Sir A. Sashiah Sastri*, p. 228.

93.   See 'C.K.', *A Biographical Sketch of Dewan Bahadur V. Nagam Aiya* (Madras: Law Printing House, 1913), p. 14. Visakham Tirunal also kept detailed diaries, which

are said to have been destroyed by his nephew, Mulam Tirunal, precisely because they contained potentially embarrassing material on the feud with Ayilyam Tirunal. A fragment from 1870 was published in Mountstuart E. Grant Duff, *Notes from a Diary: Kept Chiefly in Southern India, 1881–1886*, Vol. 1 (London: John Murray, 1899), pp. 343–44.

94.   This evidently affected the two brothers of Ayilyam Tirunal and Visakham Tirunal who were barred from succession due to 'imbecility' also. When Ayilyam Tirunal died and Visakham Tirunal was to be enthroned, it was reported that the new ruler's immediate senior brother – the younger of the two 'imbecile' princes – was urged by a servant called Pappu to park himself physically on the throne and claim his right. The prince evidently did as told, till informed by Visakham Tirunal that though 'he had personally no objection' to his brother succeeding, it would entail serious responsibilities for which he would have to answer to Madras. At this the would-be ruler got off the seat and went away. 'We are told,' the report dated 30 June 1880 in *The Englishman's Overland Mail* concludes, 'that the conspiring Puppoo received his desserts for the part he took in the affair.' (This report was reproduced from the *Western Star*.)

95.   Menon, *History of Travancore*, pp. 178–79. Reference is to the terms 'Tirumeni' and 'Adiyan'.

96.   In 1859, for example, aged twenty-two, he chose his bride unilaterally, against the express wishes of the then maharajah. Pillai, *Visakhavijaya*, p. 148. Ayilyam Tirunal, meanwhile, was married to Uthram Tirunal's daughter, which was another reason for his closeness to the latter.

97.   Aiyar, *Sir A. Sashiah Sastri*, p. 153. Sastri himself would concede this: 'V. Ramiengar ought to have got it before me and was very near it in the race. But God then willed it otherwise.'

98.   Mitter's foreword in Neumayer and Schelberger eds, *The Diary*, p. ix.

99.   Venniyoor, *Raja Ravi Varma*, p. 21. This departure of court artists is not unusual with a change in ruler. Decades later, in 1931, a similar story would play out. Mukundan Tampi, whose work was much admired by Ravi Varma, had been chief court painter to Senior Maharani Sethu Lakshmi Bayi during her rule as regent. But given her bad relations with Junior Maharani Sethu Parvathi Bayi, when the latter's son came to power, Tampi was no longer in a position of privilege: he retired to Mavelikkara and lived there the rest of his time, it is said, unless he was specifically invited to visit the capital.

100.   Funnily enough, despite getting on the wrong side of the maharajah, Ravi Varma, who participated in the Madras Fine Arts Exhibition the next year, ended up winning the official prize instituted by the Travancore ruler. See the *Times of India* dated 8 March 1881. On Visakham Tirunal's temper, Robin Jeffrey shared with me his notes from an interview with archaeologist R. Vasudeva Poduval in

1971. According to Poduval, Visakham Tirunal had careless servants beaten up, and sometimes smacked them himself – apparently he had large hands, which served this purpose well! More broadly, that a maharajah could be so touchy may be surprising, but then as today pettiness was an all-consuming force. In Travancore, successive rulers' personal lives were marked by quarrels and intrigue. In public imagination, the maharajah was 'Ponnu Tampuran' (the golden king) beyond human weakness, fortified by devotion to his deity and driven by a sense of duty. In the official theory of kingship, the ruler was a sacerdotal figure, surrounded by a family basking in the aura of the great temple. Even into the 1940s, when communism reared its head in Travancore, in fact, there remained many wedded to this royal narrative; men and women who looked upon the king as *pratyaksha* Padmanabha, or god incarnate. But peeling back the layers, even a cursory appraisal of the dynasty's inner workings reveals poisonous feuds and jealousies. It was a vitiated world where mothers might plot against daughters, brothers could seek to thwart one another and bonds of kinship meant little when the prize was power. Of course, nobody rowed in public, so ritual slights were served. For example, the Onam festival saw the family feast together, allowing the ruler an excellent opportunity to insult his juniors. Thus, cheap presents were a sign that all was not well, though ignoring people outright was better – the tricycle-riding Asvathi Tirunal's brother complained once, for example, that the then maharajah, had after a ceremony not given him the traditional presents, just as during a feast he was demoted from his seat. Of course, this junior prince retaliated in his own way: where the ruler was clean-shaven, his nephew sported a defiantly twirled moustache. These were small quibbles but had stinging effects on the target's dignity at court. On the term 'Ponnu Tampuran': while 'ponnu' can also be read as 'beloved' officially 'Ponnu Tampuran' in Travancore was linked to one of the state rituals called *padmagarbham*, which had the maharajah 'reborn' from a golden womb in the form of a giant, gold vessel ('in the shape of a lotus flower ten feet high and eight feet in circumference . . . with a cover in the form of a crown'), as opposed to the golden cow. It was on completion of this that the ruler became 'Ponnu Tampuran'. See T.K. Velu Pillai, *The Travancore State Manual*, Vol. 4 (Trivandrum: Government of Travancore, 1940), p. 571. On the idea of the pratyaksha Padmanabha, this is how Chithira Tirunal Balarama Varma, the last maharajah, is regarded by many. See Gouri Lakshmi Bayi, *Sree Padmanabhaswamy Temple* (Bombay: Bharatiya Vidya Bhavan, 1995), p. 162. Of course, as Menon wrote in *Triumph and Tragedy*, pp. 340–41, while royalty was respected, post-independence things were taken to 'ridiculous lengths' by their descendants who transformed the last ruler into a 'sage' and a 'cult figure' – this must be borne in mind. On bad Onam presents, Kerala Varma Valiya Koil Tampuran referred to Mulam Tirunal's Onam gifts as 'paltry' once, for example. See Lakshmi Raghunandan,

At the Turn of the Tide: The Life and Times of Maharani Setu Lakshmi Bayi, the Last Queen of Travancore (Bangalore: Maharani Setu Lakshmi Bayi Memorial Charitable Trust, 1995), p. 43. And for the matter of the prince being demoted from his seat, see letter dated 18 December 1899 from the Elayarajah to the Resident in IOR/R/2/892/278.

101. His full name was Visakham Tirunal Rama Varma.

102. Tirunal, 'Native Statesman', p. 230.

103. V. Ramiengar, 'A Sketch of the Late Maharajah of Travancore', pp. 189–90, in *The Indian Magazine* (issued by the National Indian Association in Aid of Social Progress and Education in India) (London: C. Kegan Paul, Trench and Co., 1886), pp. 189–95. Nagam Aiya gives the year as 1849, which would make him twelve.

104. Ibid., p. 190. His first writing was on 'The Horrors of War and Benefits of Peace' in 1855. The first article mentioned here was written subsequently and sent unsuccessfully to be published.

105. Ibid., p. 191.

106. Tirunal, 'Native Statesman', p. 251.

107. Quoted in Pillai, *Representative Indians*, p. 99. See also 'C.K.', *Nagam Aiya*, p. 24, for a letter Visakham Tirunal wrote where he refers to the tulabharam as 'one of the greatest religious dues of my reign', the organization of which by Aiya was 'a source of true gratification'. A little observation by an external party adds an amusing element to this: when the maharajah performed the tulabharam, evidently the Brahmins 'wished to defer the ceremony, in the hope that the Maharajah', who weighed nine stone might increase his weight to 14¾ like his uncle. Noted by T.B. Birchall, 'The Weight in Gold of the Maharajah Given to the Poor' in *The Folklore Journal*, Vol. 3, No. 3 (1885), pp. 278–84.

108. Quoted in Aiya, *Travancore State Manual*, p. 589.

109. Quoted in Ramiengar, 'A Sketch', p. 191.

110. See *The Athenaeum* dated 8 January 1876 in *The Athenaeum Journal of Literature, Science, the Fine Arts, Music, and the Drama* (January to June) (London: The Athenaeum, 1876), p. 55.

111. See Visakham Tirunal, *Observations on Higher Education and the Education of the Masses in India: A Letter Addressed to H.E. the Right Honorable M.E. Grant Duff, Governor of Madras by the Maharaja of Travancore* (Madras: Addison and Co., 1882), pp. 10–11.

112. Pillai, *Representative Indians*, p. 88.

113. See Tirunal, 'Native Statesman', pp. 225–26.

114. See letter dated 11 December 1874 from the Resident to the acting chief secretary in Madras in IOR/R/2/891/253. This plantation used to belong to the controversial Resident Cullen earlier.

115. Ramiengar, 'A Sketch', p. 191.

116. Pillai, *Representative Indians*, p. 89.

117. *The Globe* extracted in *The Central Somerset Gazette* dated 12 August 1876.

118. Indeed, some would go to the extent of declaring that 'there is no poor man in the land who eats [tapioca] without silently blessing the memory of Visakham Rajah'. Quoted in Aiya, *Travancore State Manual*, p. 589.

119. *The Central Somerset Gazette* dated 12 August 1876.

120. Pillai, *Representative Indians*, p. 91.

121. Ibid., p. 98. See also *Proceedings of the Linnean Society of London* (from November 1883 to June 1886) (London: The Linnean Society, 1886), p. 148.

122. See Visakham Tirunal, 'Suka-sandesah: A Sanskrit Poem by Lakshmi-dasa' in *The Journal of the Royal Asiatic Society of Great Britain and Ireland*, New Series, Vol. 16, No. 4 (1884), pp. 401–52. See also Chinmay Tumbe, *The Age of Pandemics, 1817– 1920: How They Shaped India and the World* (Noida: HarperCollins Publishers, 2020), p. 59, for an account of how the maharajah was among the first to value M.C. Furnell's research on the spread of cholera through water, having some of this translated into Malayalam and published.

123. Aiya, *Travancore State Manual*, p. 589.

124. Visakham Tirunal's speech at his investiture quoted in full in Blandford, *India's Women*, Vol. 1, pp. 28–29.

125. Visakham Tirunal's speech at the C.M.S. College on 11 August 1880 quoted in ibid., p. 30.

126. Quoted in Aiya, *Travancore State Manual*, p. 587.

127. Quoted in ibid., p. 594. Rao was, in fact, even criticized in the press for continuing to 'interfere' in Travancore. See *The Madras Weekly Mail* dated 11 June 1881.

128. Ramiengar, 'A Sketch', p. 193.

129. Aiya, *Travancore State Manual*, pp. 594–95.

130. See Pillai, *Representative Indians*, pp. 85–100.

131. As the Resident put it, 'I feel that by the death of His Highness the State of Travancore has met with a great misfortune. His entire abilities and energies were devoted with a single eye to the welfare of his country. To this end he personally worked vigorously and unselfishly . . . He lived not for himself but for his people and has conscientiously performed the promise he made in his inaugural speech, to endeavour to secure good government and progressive happiness to his subjects.' Quoted in Aiya, *Travancore State Manual*, p. 601.

132. In 1887 there was a scandal when the heir apparent, Revathi Tirunal, reportedly tried to bribe the Resident. In the course of what followed, the fact that the then favourite 'Saravanai' (pet name of Anantha Rama Iyer) had 'widened' the rupture between ruler and heir was noted. See the *Times of India* dated 23 December 1887. The same paper dated 13 January 1888 tells that Revathi Tirunal went to Madras to see the governor and consult the law firm Norton and Grant, evidently

'determined not to return to his country' till Saravanai was removed. According to *The Madras Mail* dated 30 April 1888, a reconciliation was arranged through Madhava Rao's intercession. The next year, quoting the *Madras Standard*, *The Civil and Military Gazette* dated 28 February 1889 in Lahore reported that the favourite was even said to have assaulted the maharajah himself, though the allegation was officially denied by the palace secretary. *The Bangalore Spectator* for 19 January 1887 also, in a piece on how Travancore needed a strong Dewan, noted Saravanai's 'evil genius'. See also P.K.K. Menon, *The History of the Freedom Struggle in Kerala*, Vol. 2 (Trivandrum: Government of Kerala, 1972), pp. 4–6, for more on this.

133. Quoted in Row, *Thulapurushadanom*, p. 22. A later commentator would diplomatically write that 'His Highness had no attraction for the glamour of spectacular policies or the transient popularity of political booms. With a lively suspicion of leaps in the dark' he presided over a 'noiseless rule' that served his kingdom well even if it 'did not boost his kingdom into the limelight'. 'A more steady-going monarch in India ... was seldom known.' See N.K. Venkateswaran, *Glimpses of Travancore* (Trivandrum: S. Gnanaskanda Iyer, 1926), pp. 24–25.

134. Row, *Thulapurushadanom*, p. 70.

135. *Report on the Administration of Travancore for the Year 1066 ME/1890–91 AD* (Trevandrum: Travancore Government Press, 1892), p. 135.

136. Robin Jeffrey, 'The Politics of "Indirect Rule"', pp. 273–74. Of course, this minister did not last, and while the new maharajah, Mulam Tirunal, was of tepid make, the strong structural and institutional changes his uncles had made meant that Travancore did continue to 'progress' under reasonably efficient Dewans. See S. Parameswara Aiyar, *Progress of Travancore Under Sree Moolam Tirunal* (Thiruvananthapuram: Government of Kerala, 1998 edn), which lists all the reforms of this long but uninspired reign.

3. Of Robber Kings and Civil Servants

1. In fact, Ravi Varma had paid for the tour, with the Travancore maharajah reimbursing him later. See Venniyoor, *Raja Ravi Varma*, p. 34.

2. Neumayer and Schelberger eds, *The Diary*, p. 16. In 1876 a native high school was founded here by three English-educated Brahmins, which was both a prestige project for Indians as well as an institutional success.

3. It may be worth noting that for the first half of his career he was called Amaravati Seshiah. It was around 1859 due to a bureaucratic error that his name was recorded in the government gazette as Seshiah Sastri. But he liked the change and retained it for the rest of his life.

4. Neumayer and Schelberger eds, *The Diary*, p. 16.

5. Sastri's name appears in Rajaraja Varma's diary in a list of 'native gentlemen' whose

portraits the artist and his brother had done. See Neumayer and Schelberger eds, *The Diary*, p. 78.

6.   Quoted in Chawla, *Raja Ravi Varma*, p. 81. A few decades after Sastri died, a descendant sold six paintings from his collection by Ravi Varma for Rs 1,000 apiece.

7.   Sastri's great-grandfather is supposed to have been a celebrity scholar, honoured at the court of the Peshwa in Pune. See C. Karunakara Menon, *A Critical Essay on Sir A. Seshia Sastri* (Madras: Thompson and Co., 1903), p. 3. When first brought to Madras, Sastri was in a Christian mission school, but when some boys converted, his alarmed family moved him to the government's high school.

8.   *Indian Statesmen: Dewans and Prime Ministers of Native States* (Madras: G.A. Natesan and Co., 1927), p. 275.

9.   Ibid., p. 274.

10.   Quoted in ibid., p. 276.

11.   Aiyar, *Sir A. Sashiah Sastri*, p. 16.

12.   Ibid., p. 19. Sastri would years later write to Alexander Arbuthnot how the latter was the junior official at the time before whom these fees were deposited by each student. In 1871, Arbuthnot was also the man who came from Madras to reconcile Madhava Rao with Ayilyam Tirunal, which having failed paved the way for Sastri's succession as Dewan of Travancore. On Powell's views on why he was moulding his students the way he did, see N.S. Chandrasekhara, *Dewan Rangacharlu* (Delhi: Publications Division, G.O.I., 1968), p. 144, where he states: 'The advance of a Hindu to a prominent position amongst statesmen necessarily raises the whole country, and is an incentive to his countrymen to persevere in well-doing.'

13.   See C.J. Fuller and Haripriya Narasimhan, *Tamil Brahmans: The Making of a Middle-Class Caste* (Chicago: The University of Chicago Press, 2014), specifically chapter 2, for an analysis of the slow rise of Tamil Brahmins as rivals and ultimately replacements to Marathi Deshastha Brahmins, who had joined the secular employment game a few generations earlier.

14.   Aiyar, *Sir A. Sashiah Sastri*, pp. 20–31.

15.   Ibid., p. 32.

16.   Ibid., p. 3.

17.   Ibid., p. 4.

18.   Ibid., p. 6.

19.   Madhava Rao was Dewan from 1857 until 1872; Seshiah Sastri from 1872 until 1877; and V. Ramiengar from 1880 until 1887. The contemporary Trivandrum resident and missionary Augusta Blandford had good things to say about the first two; Ramiengar, however, she dismissed as a 'bigoted Hindu'. See Blandford, *The*

Land of the Conch Shell: A Short History of Travancore and CEZ Mission Work There (London: Church of England Zenana Missionary Society, 1903), p. 60.

20. Quoted in Aiyar, *Sir A. Sashiah Sastri*, p. 29. Rao himself was at that time uncertain about his future.

21. See Note 5 above.

22. Aiyar, *Sir A. Sashiah Sastri*, p. 36.

23. Ibid., p. 35.

24. Ibid., p. 42, where Madhava Rao sees this as a great object of desire for Sastri and their like.

25. Quoted in ibid., p. 41.

26. Quoted in ibid., p. 43.

27. Quoted in ibid., p. 54. Among the many who sent congratulations was John Bruce Norton, familiar to us as Rao's friend with Indian sympathies.

28. Others too saw this: as a friend reported, even superiors were aware that 'you accepted the present post not from the love of lucre or the emoluments of the office, but to show what great improvements could be effected by an intelligent and honest Tahsildar'. Quoted in ibid., p. 56.

29. Ibid., p. 57.

30. C. Sankaran Nair, *Autobiography of Sir C. Sankaran Nair* (Madras: Lady Madhavan Nair, 1966), p. 8.

31. Quoted in C.K., *Nagam Aiya*, p. 12.

32. Natesan, *Indian Statesmen*, p. 278.

33. Aiyar, *Sir A. Sashiah Sastri*, p. 86. Emphasis added.

34. Natesan, *Indian Statesmen*, p. 279.

35. Aiyar, *Sir A. Sashiah Sastri*, p. 88.

36. Ibid., pp. 108–109.

37. Ibid., p. 117.

38. J. Hope quoted in *Reports on the Settlement of the Land Revenue of the Provinces Under the Madras Presidency for Fusly 1276 (1866–67)* (Madras: Board of Revenue, 1869), p. 15.

39. Aiyar, *Sir A. Sashiah Sastri*, pp. 150–51.

40. Letter dated 11 May 1872 from the acting governor to the secretary of state in File Nos. 7–11, Pros. Madras (Pol. Dep.) dated 11 May 1872, NAI.

41. Quoted in Aiyar, *Sir A. Sashiah Sastri*, p. 154.

42. Ibid., p. 155.

43. Letter dated 25 March 1873 from the Resident to the chief secretary in File No. 149, Pros. Madras (Pol. Dep.) dated 5 April 1873, NAI.

44. Quoted in Aiyar, *Sir A. Sashiah Sastri*, p. 164.

45. Quoted in ibid., p. 160.

46. Quoted in ibid., p. 158.

47. Quoted in Waghorne, *Raja's Magic Clothes*, p. 65.

48. Aiyar, *Sir A. Sashiah Sastri*, p. 198. It was Sastri who fixed gold finials atop the tower, no doubt feeling religious merit in this. This finishing of the *gopuram* had been pending since the eighteenth century.

49. Ibid., p. 200.

50. Ibid., p. 209.

51. As he wrote, this 'would amount to serious interference with customs, rules and practices, which unfortunately are so closely interwoven with the religious rites and beliefs of the Hindu nation . . . however unreasonable or even irrational they may seem in the eyes of Englishmen brought up in beliefs, notions and feelings, the effect of a different education and of the teachings of a different religion and in some measure the resultants of a different climate'. See ibid., pp. 280–81.

52. Quoted in Menon, *Life of T. Sankunni Menon*, p. 65.

53. Aiyar, *Sir A. Sashiah Sastri*, p. 205. In fact, after retirement too, he kept up this battle. 'In matters criminal,' Sastri wrote, 'the present position of the Englishman . . . is almost one of impunity . . . It is a notorious fact that in remote and unpeopled parts of the country, whither British enterprise and capital take them, they not unoften take the law into their own hands, and frustrate all attempts to bring them to punishment.' 'Why should,' asked Sastri, 'he shrink from the manly test of submitting to it himself when it comes to the native's turn to take the law of him?' See letter dated 1 June 1883 from Seshiah Sastri to the chief secretary, Madras, in *Further Papers on the Subject of the Proposed Alteration of the Provisions of the Indian Code of Criminal Procedure, 1882, with respect to Jurisdiction over European British Subjects Comprising Opinions of Local Governments, Officials, and Others, with Memorials from Non-Official Residents &c.* (London: Eyre and Spottiswoode, 1883), p. 23.

54. Aiyar, *Sir A. Sashiah Sastri*, pp. 182–83.

55. Quoted in ibid., pp. 254–56. Sastri later (see p. 260) apologized for using the phrase 'penniless patriots' which had caused umbrage among young students and others.

56. Letter dated 9 April 1883 from Rao to the chief secretary, Madras, in *Further Papers*, pp. 2–3.

57. Sastri in *Further Papers*, p. 23.

58. Ibid.

59. Ibid., p. 24.

60. Aiyar, *Sir A. Sashiah Sastri*, p. 221. This was some years ahead; as noted below, Sastri was originally panned by the Congress for failing to show public support when it was founded.

61. Ibid., pp. 175–78. As Sastri would write, 'Low salaries, engendered by a false

sense of economy, are the bane of native states and a stumbling block to reform and good administration.' Good and honest men could not be found 'at a rate of remuneration in which they could not live decently'. See ibid., p. 341.

62. Ibid., p. 190. These 'attaches' seem to have become standard in subsequent Dewans' offices too. Years later, a young man called K. Narayanan Pandalai would begin his career thus in the minister's office, before becoming a clerk and rising to chief-secretaryship of Travancore. Upon retirement in 1926, then, he became private secretary to Maharani Sethu Lakshmi Bayi, Ravi Varma's granddaughter.

63. Ibid., p. 202.

64. Ibid., p. 170. These were linked not only to the state temple, but also more than one diplomatic visit Ayilyam Tirunal made to Madras and Calcutta.

65. Nagam Aiya quoted in C.K., *Nagam Aiya*, p. 150.

66. Aiyar, *Sir A. Sashiah Sastri*, p. 224.

67. Ibid., p. 222.

68. Ibid., p. 224.

69. A little less than Rao though – as with everything else, Sastri never quite beat his schoolmate.

70. Aiyar, *Sir A. Sashiah Sastri*, p. 227.

71. Sastri, whose wife's name was Sundari, given their childlessness adopted his brother's son, who in turn had two boys of his own named Kalyanasundara and Rajagopalan. They seem to have inherited most of Sastri's wealth and property and owned a great deal of land in Kumbakonam.

72. Aiyar, *Sir A. Sashiah Sastri*, p. 251.

73. Quoted in ibid., p. 295. See also p. 298 where Madhava Rao is quoted speaking of 'saving' the state.

74. Quoted in Aiyar, *Sir A. Sashiah Sastri*, p. 296.

75. Rao was thrilled that he had helped persuade his friend, telling the rajah he could count on happy days now, for with Sastri at the helm, the British would 'have no need to interfere much' in his affairs. Quoted in ibid., p. 299.

76. The rajah's son and heir under patriarchal succession had died over a decade ago.

77. Quoted in Aiyar, *A. Sashiah Sastri*, p. 294.

78. Frederick S. Mullaly, *Notes on Criminal Classes of the Madras Presidency* (Madras: Government of Madras, 1892), p. 82.

79. Venkat Row (N. Thiagarajan ed.), *Manual of the Pudukkottai State* (Pudukkottai: Sri Brihadamba State Press, 1921), p. 26.

80. Kallars had parallels in other parts also, such as the Ramoshis in Maharashtra.

81. Quoted in Stuart H. Blackburn, 'The Kallars: A Tamil "Criminal Tribe" Reconsidered', p. 47 in *Journal of South Asian Studies*, Vol. 1, No. 1 (1978), pp. 38–51.

82. Row, *Pudukkottai State*, p. 20.

83. The well-known Ramayana episode where Indra seduces Ahalya, wife to Gautama, the sage, was given a friendly twist in which sons are born of the liaison: the ancestor of the Kallars was one of these divine offspring. The others were Maravars, Akampatiyars and Vellalars. Leaving the high-caste Vellalars aside, the others were referred to sometimes as *muventira kulam* ('the three families of Indra'). All at once it acknowledged the group as outside the pale by giving them an unorthodox origin, while yet granting status and an official history that linked them to divine forces. See David Dean Shulman, *The King and the Clown in South Indian Myth and Poetry* (Princeton: Princeton University Press, 1985), p. 349. See also Nicholas B. Dirks, *The Hollow Crown: Ethnohistory of an Indian Kingdom* (Cambridge: Cambridge University Press, 1987), p. 156. Indra features also in the narrative of the Shanar community, where he begets seven sons from seven celestial women, who are then raised by the goddess Bhadrakali. See Robert L. Hardgrave, *The Nadars of Tamilnad: The Political Culture of a Community in Change* (Berkeley: University of California Press, 1969), pp. 19–20.

84. In the 1907 ballad 'Santhana Thevan Sinthu' we read of its protagonist thus: 'He would walk through jungles, in the company of bears, tigers, and elephants – He would grasp and cast away jungle ghosts and goblins, as if they were nothing – Those of the country would flee at the sight of his terrible form, for fear of what might happen.' Quoted in Anand Pandian, 'Securing the Rural Citizen: The Anti-Kallar Movement of 1896', p. 25, in *The Indian Economic and Social History Review*, Vol. 42, No. 1 (2005), pp. 1–39.

85. Pandian, 'Securing the Rural Citizen', p. 7.

86. Thus in 1811, we have the Madurai collector Rous Peter write of the role of a hereditary watchman (*kavalkar*): 'The duties of a Cawolgar have always been considered, to watch over the Crops on the Ground, to ground them when reaped, and when thrashed, the produce is measured in his presence, and delivered over to his charge entirely; after which whatever loss is sustained, he is considered the accountable person for it. To protect the Village to which he belongs, and should any of the Inhabitants be robbed, he is obliged to make good from his own Mauniam Lands, the value of whatever Articles may have been stolen unless he can deliver up the offenders to Justice, and in that case he is absolved from all responsibility. This method in the first instance compels him to guard the Village with the utmost caution and in the latter occasions his being alert in the apprehension of the people who have been guilty of the Theft. He is also to watch over the Circar Grain wherever it may be deposited within the range of his Cawol, to be a guide to Detachments passing through the Country if required, and to protect all Travelers as long as they continue within his Village. These are considered the principal duties of a Cawolgar . . .' Ibid., pp. 6–7.

87. Blackburn, 'The Kallars', p. 42.

88. Pandian, 'Securing the Rural Citizen', pp. 9, 20.

89. Quoted in ibid., p. 27.

90. Dirks, *Hollow Crown*, p. 158. See also Waghorne, *Raja's Magic Clothes*, p. 176.

91. Dirks, *Hollow Crown*, p. 50. Here, for their services, they were counted among the *kumaravarga*, that is, honorary sons of the ruler.

92. Row, *Pudukkottai State*, p. 31.

93. As the nawab grandiloquently expressed in 1752, for instance, 'I should necessarily fill up sheets of paper were I (at least briefly) to write to you the favorable light your attachment to us has often been represented in, the numerous instances of your good wishes, and the nature of the assistance you rendered us.' Full letter in T. Rungasamy Naidoo, *Translations, Copies and Extracts of the Several Letters in Which the Services of the Ancestors of His Excellency the Maha Rajah of Poodoocottah Are Particularly Acknowledged and Approved by the Governors and Other Public Officers of the Honourable E.I. Company and the Nabob of the Carnatic* (Puducota: Sree Brehademba Press, 1874), p. 2.

94. As Nicholas Dirks writes, there was that reigning 'world view which [insisted] on the centrality of Brahmanical learning, of ritual performance, and of royal support for the worship of temples'. See Dirks, *Hollow Crown*, p. 123.

95. Ibid., pp. 166, 196.

96. Ibid., p. 167.

97. Ibid., p. 387.

98. Orme quoted in ibid., p. 193. A British official would recall how 'a contingent of Kallar matchlockmen and spearsmen was by no means to be despised'. D.F. Carmichael, chief secretary to the government of Madras, quoted in Aiyar, *Sir A. Sashiah Sastri*, p. 297.

99. Naidoo, *Translations*, p. iv.

100. As the rajah reported, he 'stationed guards in different places to seize Cataboma Naig' and having discovered his location, sent men in to seize him. The warrior would have liked to commit suicide, 'but my people having bound his hands [and] kept him in confinement', this was foiled.

101. Letter dated 24 September 1799 from the rajah in Naidoo, *Translations*, pp. 24–25.

102. Letter dated 14 September 1799 from the rajah in ibid., pp. 44–45.

103. For a short account of Ramnad kingship and challenges born because of their loss of power in the colonial period, see Carol Appadurai Breckenridge, 'From Protector to Litigant – Changing Relations Between Hindu Temples and the Raja of Ramnad' in *The Indian Economic and Social History Review*, Vol. 14, No. 1, (1977), pp. 75–106.

104. Dirks, *Hollow Crown*, pp. 116, 196–97. The British, after helping the rajahs gain some territory in 1803 from Tanjore, attempted to introduce a nominal tribute

of one elephant a year, but even this was never actually paid, and in 1836 was officially waived. As was explained in 1822 to another prince who was puzzled by Pudukkottai's status: 'A Zemindar is a landholder, paying rent to the Government, but possessing neither Military nor Civil authority over the land of which he is the protector. He and all his dependents being amenable to the British Courts of Justice, Civil and Criminal. Rajah Tondiman Behauder [on the other hand] is a native hereditary Chief, the Prince and ruler of an extensive Province. He is a dependent Chief, in regard to all matters of a political nature, on the British Government, to whom as his liege lord he owes allegiance and Military service. In the internal arrangement of his Province he is absolute. He has the power of life and death. He enacts laws, appoints Courts of Justice, Civil and Criminal, maintains a considerable Military force, collects his revenues, and disposes of them at pleasure, paying no tribute even directly or indirectly through the well deserved kindness and favor of the British Government. All his subjects are expressly exempted from the jurisdiction of the British Courts.' See letter dated 31 December 1822 from the Resident at Tanjore to Rajah Serfoji of Tanjore in Naidoo, *Translations*, pp. 123–24.

105. Row, *Pudukkottai State*, p. 89. Indeed, in the next generation the man's sibling, who would hold the same office as Resident, was on that account treated as an 'uncle' to the king. See Waghorne, *Raja's Magic Clothes*, p. 48. It was the younger prince's son who called the Resident's brother, who also in time became Resident 'uncle'.

106. Once, for example, Blackburne wrote to the rajah to 'Protect all your subjects from oppression and extortion. This is the most sacred duty of a king.' Violence against his people was tantamount to 'an injury to you' and nothing 'should induce you . . . to acquiesce in an injury to a poor man'. If the rajah dedicated himself to his people like a 'tender parent', 'the blessings of the great Judge of kings [that is, god]' would be showered upon him. Quoted in Row, *Pudukkottai State*, pp. 88–89.

107. Quoted in ibid., p. 89.

108. Ibid., pp. 89–90.

109. Dirks, *Hollow Crown*, p. 122. A similar state of affairs prevailed in Ramnad also, where by the end of the eighteenth century, of 2,167 villages, its rulers had given away 865 to Brahmins and religious institutions. See Price, *Kingship*, p. 110.

110. Dirks, *Hollow Crown*, p. 117.

111. Row, *Pudukkottai State*, p. 93.

112. Quoted in ibid., p. 105. This was not limited to any one part. In 1845 it was found that in Guntur district in the Madras Presidency, a powerful Brahmin called Sashagiri Rao had installed as many as seventy-four relatives and dependants in positions of influence. See Frykenberg, *Guntur*, p. 164.

113. Row, *Pudukkottai State*, p. 93.

114. Thus, the authorities were pleased with these English-speaking, exotic 'robber

caste' princes, and the state too did not suffer convulsions. As was written in 1837 about the younger ruler, 'The Rajah Tondiman is indeed all that you could have wished him to be, and he possesses [the Resident's] entire confidence and friendship.' See letter dated 3 June 1837 from the Resident to William Blackburne in Naidoo, *Translations*, pp. 144–45. When the man died two years later, to his son the governor of Madras wrote a note expecting the new rajah to also follow in his predecessor's malleable and loyal footsteps. See letter dated 30 July 1839 from Lord Elphinstone to the rajah in ibid., pp. 154–55.

115. Dirks, *Hollow Crown*, pp. 314, 318–19.

116. See Extract from Minute dated 23 May 1854 in Naidoo, *Translations*, pp. 159–60.

117. Dirks, *Hollow Crown*, p. 319.

118. Ibid., p. 317. The death of the senior rani is noted in passing in *The Hindoo Patriot* dated 9 July 1888.

119. Quoted in ibid., p. 318.

120. Quoted in ibid., p. 309.

121. Quoted in ibid., p. 316.

122. Waghorne, *Raja's Magic Clothes*, p. 46, and Row, *Pudukkottai State*, pp. 104–105.

123. Madhava Rao quoted in Aiyar, *Sir A. Sashiah Sastri*, p. 291.

124. Waghorne, *Raja's Magic Clothes*, p. 46.

125. Quoted in ibid., p. 45.

126. Row, *Pudukkottai State*, p. 103.

127. Quoted in Denison, *Varieties of Vice-Regal Life*, p. 192. In 1887, after the rajah died, the *Times of India* dated 3 January carried an amusing snippet about a creditor writing to Dewan Sastri asking if the state had a fund to settle the dead ruler's debts. Evidently Sastri wrote back saying, 'Not to make you wait for an answer, I write to say that there is not a farthing.'

128. Percy Macqueen, *The Pudukotah Portraits* (Pudukotah: Sri Brihadamba State Press, 1926), p. 11.

129. Quoted in Waghorne, *Raja's Magic Clothes*, p. 55. One of the triggers for the aborted 1854 rebellion had been 'disturbances' by her brother, for example. See Venkat Row, *Pudukkottai State*, p. 103.

130. Waghorne, *Raja's Magic Clothes*, p. 61.

131. Quoted in Dirks, *Hollow Crown*, p. 317.

132. Waghorne, *Raja's Magic Clothes*, p. 61.

133. See letter dated 2 March 1877 from the rajah to the viceroy in Naidoo, *Translations*, pp. 163–64.

134. See C.L. Tupper, *Indian Political Practice: A Collection of the Decisions of the Government of India in Political Cases*, Vol. 2 (Delhi: B.R. Publishing Corporation, 1974 edn, 1895 original), pp. 107–109 for more on this. The local authorities were inclined to reject the adoption, which claimed legitimacy on the basis of the

government's 1862 guarantee that royal adoptions would be recognized. Their argument was that adoptions could only be carried out on the failure of natural heirs (in this case, the rajah's nephews). There was some debate, however, on whether 'natural heirs' meant lineal descendants or also collaterals. The secretary of state in London was inclined to support the view that it was restricted to lineal heirs alone. So the rajah was free to adopt. Besides, and perhaps more importantly, the London authorities were keen to avoid creating doubt among other princes on the issue of adoption by meddling too much in what was already done here. So, over the head of Madras and despite their objections, Ramachandra's grandson was recognized. See also Naidoo, *Translations*, p. 168, for the official recognition sent by the British authorities in January 1878. See also correspondence on this matter in File No. 175/176, Pros. Madras (Pol. Dep.) dated 30 April 1872, NAI.

135. Quoted in Dirks, *Hollow Crown*, p. 347.

136. Ibid., p. 348. When, however, the minister called the dispossessed lord's junior wife 'illegitimate', the latter hit back. Polygamy, he reminded the sirkele, was recognized practice, and did not make younger consorts anything less than legal partners. Ibid., p. 347. Sastri's moralistic crusade against Kallar custom even outlasted him: in a few years, taking his lead, bureaucrats would ban widow remarriage in state-run temples, though it was standard practice for non-Brahmins. Ibid., p. 360.

137. Row, *Pudukkottai State*, p. 119.

138. Dirks, *Hollow Crown*, pp. 335, 352.

139. Quoted in Row, *Pudukkottai State*, p. 112.

140. Aiyar, *Sir A. Sashiah Sastri*, pp. 302–14.

141. Ibid., p. 315.

142. Quoted in ibid., p. 326.

143. Row, *Pudukkottai State*, p. 121. See also Aiyar, *Sir A. Sashiah Sastri*, pp. 350–51.

144. Quoted in Aiyar, *Sir A. Sashiah Sastri*, p. 361.

145. As Dirks observes, perhaps unkindly, 'the historical record leaves little doubt that he bankrupted the state with an ambitious building program' that was really about his ego than 'the needs of state citizens'. Dirks, *Hollow Crown*, p. 389.

146. Aiyar, *Sir A. Sashiah Sastri*, p. 356. Aiyar, a sympathetic biographer, tries and justifies the spending of 'a great part of the savings of the state' on these projects by noting that the money spent 'went to the poor workmen – almost all of them natives of the state'. See ibid., p. 361.

147. This was reported in *The Pioneer* dated 26 February 1879.

148. Quoted in Aiyar, *Sir A. Sashiah Sastri*, p. 379.

149. Quoted in ibid., p. 380.

150. Some of Sastri's worries may also have come from British pressure. As soon as Ramachandra died in 1886, in fact, the colonial state, while confirming him as Dewan-Regent, noted that 'for a variety of reasons' it was not 'desirable that

he should be vested with practically uncontrolled authority. The right of the Political Agent . . . to supervise and control the Dewan's proceedings' was to be maintained. Naturally, then, if the Resident gave advice, 'the Dewan must accept it'. See Tupper, *Indian Political Practice*, p. 185. So too for example, even though Sastri's reforms were increasing revenue from earth salt, objections from the Madras authorities that Pudukkottai salt, thanks to smugglers, was eating into *their* market led to 'proposals' to suppress and end salt manufacturing in the principality altogether. Sastri tried to resist but in the end had to give way – salt production in Pudukkottai was terminated, for a measly compensation of 38,000 rupees a year. See Row, *Pudukkottai State*, p. 118, and Aiyar, *Sir A. Sashiah Sastri*, pp. 331–36. He was aware this would make him look bad in the state, writing to the British how the 'measure created great unpopularity' (quoted in Aiyar, *Sir A. Sashiah Sastri*, p. 337), which in turn added to resentment against a 'foreign' Dewan.

151. Quoted in Aiyar, *Sir A. Sashiah Sastri*, p. 386.

152. Aiyar, his biographer, writes, for example in ibid., p. 378: 'He succeeded in all he undertook; but his successes were often won against heavy odds. His all-canopying personality had cast into the shadow those who had enjoyed almost unbounded influence and power and created for him enemies in high circles; and when the time came for fight he stood his ground boldly and cared not to hide his iron hand under velvet gloves. He was at once the envy and despair of his opponents. The more difficulties there were, the more pleased he seemed to be. His spirit rose with obstacles and he was never so sure to excel himself as when he was confronted with difficulties that would have crushed a weaker man.'

153. Quoted in ibid., p. 386. Sastri seems to have liked the prickly pear analogy. Elsewhere he wrote, ostensibly in a physical sense about Pudukkottai: 'The prickly pears, grown into enormous bushes sheltering venomous reptiles . . . were flourishing' when he came to Pudukkottai 'in close vicinity of the villages all over the State and threatened to swallow up the habitations . . . The climatic conditions of the State unfortunately seemed too favourable for it.' A cynic would read into this a subtle critique of the royal family and palace too. Quoted in Waghorne, *Raja's Magic Clothes*, p. 55

154. Quoted in ibid., p. 65.

155. Mountstuart E. Grant Duff, *Notes from a Diary: Kept Chiefly in Southern India, 1881–1886*, Vol. 2 (London: John Murray, 1899), p. 172. The governor noted also a funny incident which reveals something about Sastri. 'The most amusing incident of my journey occurred at Pudukota. The Rajah is the head of the great Kullar or Robber Caste of South India. His Dewan Sashiah Shastri, who speaks excellent English, but stammers a good deal, was standing by my chair, as their chiefs of the clans came up to pay me their homage. "These," he observed, "are

the Ca, Ca, Campbells, and so forth, of this part of the country!'" The Dewan was comparing the Kallar grandees to Scottish nobility and clans, evidently in an effort to make it easier for the governor to relate. Ibid., p. 173.

156. Waghorne, *Raja's Magic Clothes*, p. 63.

157. Ibid.

158. Ibid., pp. 59–61.

159. Quoted in ibid., p. 61.

160. Quoted in ibid., pp. 40–41.

161. Ibid., p. 72. The title was used in 1869 before Sastri too but it was under Sastri that it became permanently attached to the royal name. The British even objected at first to this imitation of the Travancore tradition.

162. Quoted in Aiyar, *Sir A. Sashiah Sastri*, p. 387.

163. Quoted in ibid., p. 291.

164. Row, *Pudukkottai State*, pp. 114–15. Sastri was not terribly pleased with this, writing to the maharajah of Travancore: 'I am most anxious of what the outcome of this kind of education will be, and I am simply watching the results since it is useless to run counter to the Political Agent's opinion.' See Waghorne, *Raja's Magic Clothes*, p. 75.

165. Quoted in ibid., p. 74.

166. Quoted in Row, *Pudukkottai State*, p. 115.

167. Waghorne, *Raja's Magic Clothes*, p. 81.

168. Quoted in Row, *Pudukkottai State*, p. 116.

169. Quoted in Aiyar, *Sir A. Sashiah Sastri*, p. 390.

170. Ibid., p. 392.

171. Quoted in ibid., pp. 386–87.

172. Quoted in ibid., p. 390. Sastri had also, in 1887, during Queen Victoria's jubilee celebrations organized prayers in 'all the temples and mosques' in Pudukkottai. See Charles Lawson, *Narrative of the Celebration of the Jubilee of Her Most Gracious Majesty, Queen Victoria, Empress of India, in the Presidency of Madras* (London: Macmillan and Co., 1887), p. 224. Menon, *Critical Essay*, p. 28, also observes that when in 1887 the Indian National Congress met in Madras, while Madhava Rao participated and the princely governments of Mysore, Travancore and Cochin contributed money, Sastri who was Dewan 'paid not a pie'.

173. Menon, *Critical Essay*, pp. 29–30.

174. Dirks, *Hollow Crown*, p. 391.

175. Ibid.

176. Letter dated 22 June 1908 from the acting chief secretary of Madras to the secretary, G.O.I., in IOR/R/1/1/1019.

177. Quoted in Dirks, *Hollow Crown*, p. 395.

178. Quoted in Row, *Pudukkottai State*, p. 141.

179. Dirks, *Hollow Crown*, p. 392. Apparently there was an effort to poison Maharani Molly.

180. Quoted in Angma Dey Jhala, *Courtly Indian Women in Late Imperial India* (London: Pickering and Chatto, 2008), p. 64.

181. Quoted in Dirks, *Hollow Crown*, p. 392.

182. G.T.B. Harvey's letter dated 7 April 1948 to the chief secretary in Madras, File No. 4 (24) (Pol.), Ministry of States, NAI. It may be of interest to note that Martanda Bhairava's half-Australian son was briefly considered for succession. The deputy president of the Legislative Council of Pudukkottai in 1927, for example, believed that if the boy could be 'converted' to Hinduism by the Arya Samaj, objections on the count of race might be waived. Another person to whom the Resident spoke also felt that if the boy were more visible in Pudukkottai, the masses would be loyal. See Resident's Report for the Second Half of September 1927 in File No. 32/27 (Pol.), Home Dep., NAI. A 'People's Conference' of politicians in 1926 also saw one member try (and fail) to introduce a resolution that Martanda Bhairava's mixed-race son be made to practise Hinduism and then recognized as heir. See Resident's Report for the First Half of December 1926 in File No. 112-IV (Pol.), Home Dep., NAI.

183. See note dated 11 September 1948 by V.P. Menon and note dated 2 April 1948 by 'N.N.' in ibid.

184. Letter dated 18 March 1948 from K. Ramunni Menon, chief secretary of Madras, and letter dated 1 April 1948 from the rajah of Pudukkottai in ibid.

4. A Patron of Sedition

1. Phayre's testimony before the 1875 Baroda Commission, in *The Trial and Deposition of Mulhar Rao Gaekwar of Baroda* (Bombay: Bombay Gazette Steam Press, 1875), pp. 41–42.

2. Telegram dated 9 November 1874 in ibid., p. 43.

3. Durbar *yad* dated 14 November 1874 in ibid., p. 45.

4. Fatesinghrao P. Gaekwad, *Sayajirao of Baroda: The Prince and the Man* (Bombay: Popular Prakashan, 1997 edn), p. 34.

5. *Trial and Deposition*, p. ix.

6. Ibid., p. 4.

7. Ibid., p. 3, and *The Hitechhu* dated 19 August 1873 in *The Gaikwari Raj: Being a Reprint of the Notices Which Appeared in the Hitechhu of Ahmedabad* (Ahmedabad: Pitramberdas Tribhowandas Mehta, 1875), p. 20.

8. Judith Rowbotham, 'Miscarriage of Justice? Postcolonial Reflections on the Trial of the Maharajah of Baroda, 1875', p. 387, in the *Liverpool Law Review*, Vol. 28

(2007), pp. 377–403. See also the original correspondence in 'Correspondence Connected with the Marriage of the Gaekwar of Baroda' in *Accounts and Papers of the House of Commons* (East India: Baroda), Vol. 56 (London: House of Commons, 1875). Hereafter 'Gaekwar Marriage'.

9. *The Hitechhu* dated 11 June 1874 in *Gaikwari Raj*, p. 92.

10. *Report on the Administration of the Baroda State for 1875–76* (Calcutta: Foreign Department Press, 1876), p. 14.

11. Baroda was immediately below the nizam of Hyderabad, who was the premier native prince.

12. T.H. Thornton, *General Sir Richard Meade and the Feudatory States of Central and Southern India: A Record of Forty-Three Years' Service as Soldier, Political Officer and Administrator* (London: Longmans, Green and Co., 1898), p. 161.

13. Philip W. Sergeant, *The Ruler of Baroda: An Account of the Life and Work of the Maharaja Gaekwar* (London: John Murray, 1928), pp. 9–10.

14. See letter dated 25 March 1873 from the Resident to the President in Council, Bombay in 'Report of the Commission Appointed to Inquire into the Administration of the Baroda State' in *Accounts and Papers*, Vol. 56. Hereafter 'Baroda Administration Commission'.

15. To be fair to the British authorities, decades before when in 1817 a Resident in Hyderabad called Henry Russell flogged two Indians to death, the Resident was condemned for his behaviour and giving the public a poor impression of British justice. Cited in Wilkinson, 'Residents of the British East India Company', p. 88.

16. Letter dated 29 August 1873 from the secretary, G.O.B., to the secretary, Foreign Dep., G.O.I., in 'Baroda Administration Commission', pp. 16–19.

17. Interestingly, the viceroy did not wish to 'unnecessarily interfere with the details' of *how* Malhar Rao ruled or encourage 'frivolous or vexatious complaints'. Letter dated 19 September 1873 from the secretary, Foreign Dep., G.O.I., to the secretary, G.O.B., in ibid., pp. 30–32.

18. Letter dated 10 October 1873 from the secretary, Foreign Dep., G.O.I., to the secretary, G.O.B., in ibid., pp. 35–56.

19. 'Report of the Baroda Commission of 1873' in ibid., pp. 81–104.

20. In fact, Phayre's appointment as political agent had not been received well in Calcutta, where he was seen as 'not very conciliatory in his style', and where bureaucrats predicted that he would make things worse in Baroda. See I.F.S. Copland, 'The Baroda Crisis of 1873–77: A Study in Governmental Rivalry', pp. 103–105, *in Modern Asian Studies*, Vol. 2, No. 2 (1968), pp. 97–123.

21. See, for example, M.G. Ranade's 'A Constitution for Native (Indian) States' in Ranade, *Select Writings*, pp. 175–195, for very similar views.

22. Tucker's Minute in 'Baroda Administration Commission', pp. 65–71.

23. M.G. Ranade also alludes to this 'weak side of the old order of things' for with

the 'gradual growth of absolute power in the hands of the reigning Gaykawad, the removal of all the old checks on this power caused by the weakening of the military classes, the entire dependence of the nobles on his pleasure' and much else, the state structure began to break down. See 'The Rulers of Baroda', p. 64, in M.G. Ranade (Ramabai Ranade ed.), *The Miscellaneous Writings of the Late Hon'ble Mr Justice M.G. Ranade* (Bombay: Manoranjan Press, 1915), pp. 60–65. Nearly a century later, this position was articulated by the maharajah of Dewas (Senior) when he noted that 'the degeneration of the Princes of India' was due to British protection which ended accountability to the people. See A.C. Mayer, 'Perceptions of Princely Rule: Perspectives from a Biography', p. 138, in T.N. Madan ed., *Way of Life: King, Householder, Renouncer – Essays in Honour of Louis Dumont* (Delhi: Motilal Banarsidass Publishers, 1988 edn), pp. 127–54.

24. In Bengal in 1783, for example, a British collector learnt this from a peasant delegation. 'You are the head of one country,' their petition declared, 'we have a thousand countries to go to, You are Chief, we are Ryotts (subjects), you will therefore order us Justice.' Quoted in Jon E. Wilson, *The Domination of Strangers: Modern Governance in Eastern India, 1780–1835* (Basingstoke: Palgrave Macmillan, 2008), p. 26.

25. Quoted in ibid. This happened in Rajputana also. See Norbert Peabody, *Hindu Kingship and Polity in Precolonial India* (New Delhi: Foundation Books, 2006), p. 95.

26. The great eighteenth-century banking firm of Bengal, the Jagat Seths, for instance, sided with the British before the Battle of Plassey of 1757. See G.J. Bryant, *The Emergence of British Power in India, 1600–1784: A Grand Strategic Interpretation* (Woodbridge: Boydell and Brewer, 2013), p. 111, and C.A. Bayly, *Indian Society and the Making of the British Empire* (Cambridge: Cambridge University Press, 1988), pp. 49–50.

27. Gaekwad, *Sayajirao of Baroda*, p. 35.

28. His colleague, A. Rogers, also noted that a system where people were 'arbitrarily taxed at the pleasure of a selfish man, surrounded by courtiers . . . eager to amass riches', was not tenable. The British were 'morally responsible' for their actions. See his minute in 'Baroda Administration Commission', pp. 79–80. The Bombay authorities even in May 1874 sent in a minute from James Gibbs, a judge who sat on the council temporarily, who did not think a constitution would help, but recommended something like a regency. See ibid., pp. 348–51.

29. Letter dated 25 July 1874 from the secretary, G.O.I., to the secretary, G.O.B., in ibid., pp. 353–55.

30. Viceroy's letter dated 25 July 1874 to the maharajah in ibid., pp. 355–57.

31. Letter dated 15 August 1874 from the Resident to the secretary, G.O.B., in 'Correspondence with Respect to Proposed Reforms in the Administration of Baroda' in *Accounts and Papers*, Vol. 56, pp. 31–32. Hereafter 'Proposed Reforms'.

32. Ibid.

33. Letter dated 24 August 1874 from the secretary, G.O.B., to the Resident in ibid., pp. 35–36.

34. Patel, *Naoroji*, p. 5. This was before Gandhi himself was given these appellations, of course.

35. Ibid., p. 71.

36. Ibid., p. 74.

37. Quoted in ibid., p. 76.

38. Quoted n ibid., p. 54.

39. Ibid., p. 74. So, for instance, in 1872 when donating 25,000 rupees, the Indore maharajah lauded the association's 'patriotic exertions' and reiterated 'the utmost importance that the true state of India be correctly known to the public and Parliament of England' so as to make 'the British rule in India a just and beneficent one'. See letter dated 23 September 1872 from the Dewan of Indore to Naoroji in *Journal of the East India Association, London*, Vol. 5 (1871), pp. 223–24.

40. In his election campaign, for example, though derided as a 'black man', he was endorsed by the likes of William Gladstone and Florence Nightingale. Patel, *Naoroji*, pp. 166, 187.

41. Letter dated 9 May 1874 from the Resident to the secretary, G.O.B., in 'Gaekwar Marriage', pp. 9–16. But there was history here: in 1872, Naoroji had helped the maharajah in a dispute on durbar ceremonial with Bombay. It was a question of whether British representatives should be seated on the left or right side of the throne; the Raj demanded the exalted right, while the ruler insisted they stay on the left. It was Naoroji who drafted a memorandum for Malhar Rao, for which the maharajah gifted him 50,000 rupees in trust. Patel, *Naoroji*, p. 75. The beneficiaries of the trust were Naoroji's children. This is also discussed in Dick Kooiman, 'Meeting at the Threshold, at the Edge of the Carpet, or Somewhere in Between? Questions of Ceremonial in Princely India' in *The Indian Economic and Social History Review*, Vol. 40, No. 3 (2003), pp. 311–33. Phayre construed such financial arrangements as shady. In his opinion, 'under various pretences' Naoroji had got Malhar Rao to 'appoint him his Agent in England' to argue all kinds of 'imaginary cases' and turn a profit. Letter dated 15 August 1874 from the Resident to the secretary, G.O.B., in 'Proposed Reforms', pp. 31–32.

42. Letter dated 9 May 1874 from the maharajah to the viceroy in 'Gaekwar Marriage', pp. 16–17.

43. Letter dated 9 May 1874 from the Resident to the secretary, G.O.B., in ibid., pp. 9–16.

44. Patel, *Naoroji*, p. 76.

45. A short profile appears in Natesan, *Indian Statesmen*, pp. 225–32.

46. Quoted in Patel, *Naoroji*, p. 77.

47. See ibid. And also letter dated 29 September 1875 from Madhava Rao to the Resident in Pros. Foreign Dep. File Nos. 356–59 dated December 1875, NAI, where Rao acknowledges Naoroji's reforms in the state.

48. Of course, Phayre wrote off Naoroji's fervour to the salary of 1,00,000 rupees he was receiving a year. Naoroji later corrected this: he was paid 53,000 rupees.

49. Letter dated 11 August 1874 from the Resident to the secretary, G.O.B., in 'Proposed Reforms', pp. 23–24. Naoroji would later, in a publication, wonder 'where on earth had the Colonel's common sense fled when he seriously wrote all this stuff'.

50. *The Hitechhu* dated 2 July 1874 in *Gaikwari Raj*, p. 95. It also added how 'It was not a wise plan for Mr Dadabhai to connect his fortunes with such a barbarous and savage prince.' *The Hitechhu* dated 11 June 1874 in *Gaikwari Raj*, p. 89. The article goes on to say: 'It ought to have been anticipated by him that he was not called at Baroda to improve the state but to lend his influence to the continuance and support of the wicked course which Mulhar Rao was following.'

51. Letter dated 16 August 1874 from the secretary, G.O.B., to the Resident in 'Proposed Reforms', pp. 24–25.

52. Letter dated 29 October 1874 from the secretary, G.O.B., to the secretary, G.O.I., in 'Gaekwar Marriage', pp. 24–25.

53. See Resident's progress report dated 2 November 1874 in 'Proposed Reforms', pp. 43–63.

54. Letter dated 2 November 1874 from the governor of Bombay to the viceroy in ibid., p. 76.

55. Letter dated 2 November 1874 from the maharajah to the viceroy in ibid., pp. 78–79.

56. In a letter dated 15 April 1875 from the viceroy to the secretary of state in London the viceroy observed how he had shown 'more zeal than discretion' and that he was 'wanting in consideration' in his dealings with the maharajah and Naoroji – indeed, sometimes he also acted 'contrary to his instructions'. When the 2 November 1874 complaint from Malhar Rao was received, Phayre proved his obstinacy again: offered the opportunity to resign, he declined and had to be sacked. See 'Correspondence on the Deposition of Mulhar Rao', pp. 3–8, in *Accounts and Papers*, Vol. 56. Hereafter 'Deposition'.

57. Interestingly, these secret communications were apparently first discovered 'from the driver of a hack bullock shigram in the Camp Bazaar' who was heard saying that he had once 'driven an ayah from the Residency to the Gaekwar's Palace in the city at a late hour'. See *Trial and Deposition*, p. xiii.

58. Letter dated 15 April 1875 from the viceroy to the secretary of state in 'Deposition', pp. 3–8.

59. *The Hitechhu* dated 26 November 1874 in *Gaikwari Raj*, p. 116.

60. It was this panic in princely circles, in fact, that caused the government later in the year to orchestrate that high-profile visit of Prince Edward, to 'soothe the feelings' of native royalty. Matthew Glencross, *The State Visits of Edward VII: Reinventing Royal Diplomacy for the Twentieth Century* (Basingstoke: Palgrave Macmillan, 2015), p. 33.

61. *Trial and Deposition*, p. xv.

62. Nanda, *Gokhale*, p. 41.

63. Rowbotham, 'Miscarriage of Justice?', p. 382.

64. Ibid., p. 391.

65. William Ballantine, *Some Experiences of a Barrister's Life* (New York: Henry Holt and Co., 1882), p. 451.

66. Having arrived, for example, he observed that 'there was an utter absence of all joyousness'. Everybody 'scowled' and 'certainly the impression made upon me was that the Europeans were most thoroughly hated'. Ibid., p. 456.

67. Rowbotham, 'Miscarriage of Justice?', p. 393.

68. Advocate-general's opening speech in the *Times of India* dated 24 February 1875.

69. Rowbotham, 'Miscarriage of Justice?', p. 395.

70. *Trial and Deposition*, p. 51.

71. Ballantine, *Barrister's Life*, p. 467.

72. *Trial and Deposition*, p. 51.

73. Ballantine, *Barrister's Life*, p. 467.

74. Ibid., p. 468.

75. Rowbotham, 'Miscarriage of Justice?', p. 394, and ibid, p. 473. For the complete record of the trial, see also *Proceedings of the Baroda Commission Appointed to Inquire into the Charges Against H.H. Malharrow Gaekwar of Baroda of Instigating an Attempt to Poison the British Resident* (Bombay: Times of India Steam Press, 1875).

76. Quoted in Rowbotham, 'Miscarriage of Justice?', p. 396.

77. Ibid., p. 398.

78. Ballantine, *Barrister's Life*, p. 471.

79. Rowbotham, 'Miscarriage of Justice?', p. 383. In this context see Price, *Kingship*, pp. 58–70, for how perjury was in fact used consciously by Indians in colonial courts to manipulate things to their advantage, exploit judges' lack of clarity on caste usage, customs and so on. By this they revealed that they saw the colonial courts with their new lawbooks and methods not as dispensing noble justice but as a realm for politics.

80. Letter dated 15 April 1875 from the viceroy to the secretary of state in 'Deposition', pp. 3–8.

81. Letter dated 22 April 1875 from the viceroy to the secretary of state in ibid., pp. 29–31.

82. Summary of the telegraph received from London explaining this is given in ibid.

83. See proclamation dated 19 April 1874 in ibid., pp. 31–32.

84. *Trial and Deposition*, p. xix.

85. Patel, *Naoroji*, pp. 79, 82. And, during the trial, while not directly present, he did manage to indict the ex-Resident in public, enjoying a moment of revenge via the press. See Naoroji's letter to the editor of the *Times of India* in *Proceedings of the Baroda Commission*, p. 197. Naoroji also published 'The Baroda Administration in 1874', where he wrote of his difficulties with Phayre who always took a 'jaundiced view' of things. See Chunilal Lallubhai Parekh ed., *Essays, Speeches, Addresses and Writings of the Hon'ble Dadabhai Naoroji* (Bombay: Caxton Printing Works, 1887), pp. 382–413.

86. *Trial and Deposition*, p. xix. Sergeant, *Ruler of Baroda*, p. 21, mentions Malhar Rao's senior wife, Mahalsabai, as the instigator of this foiled installation of the prince.

87. See *Report on the Administration of the Baroda State for 1881–82* (Bombay: Education Society's Press, 1883), pp. 7–8. The passing of his son in 1880 is reported in Thornton, *General Sir Richard Meade*, p. 201. The ex-ruler died at a place called Doveton House in Madras. His older wife, Mahalsabai, retired to Dabhol, while the scandalous Lakshmibai returned to Baroda.

88. *Trial and Deposition*, p. xix.

89. Gaekwad, *Sayajirao of Baroda*, pp. 33–34.

90. Viceroy's proclamation dated 19 April 1874 in 'Deposition', pp. 31–32.

91. Behramji M. Malabari, *Gujarat and the Gujaratis: Pictures of Men and Manners Taken from Life* (London: W.H. Allen and Co., 1882).

92. All biographical details on Jamnabai are taken from Nageshrao Bapat's *Shrimant Maharani Jamnabai Saheb Yanche Charitra* (1900, publisher unknown). Rising to prominence under the Bijapur sultanate, briefly serving the Mughals thereafter, the Manes later tied their destinies to the Maratha cause. The family is repeatedly discussed in Stewart Gordon's *The New Cambridge History of India: The Marathas, 1600–1818* (Cambridge: Cambridge University Press, 1993). While over time their line was divided into many branches with reduced fortunes, their bloodline remained an asset. In caste prestige, in fact, the Manes claimed superiority over the Gaekwads, who, despite their wealth and power, were of recent vintage. Where the Manes were associated with the illustrious house of Shivaji – the Maratha royal family – the Gaekwads rose to glory in service of the Peshwas, who were the Maratha state's hereditary *ministers*, and thus, officially, only employees. Simply put, the Manes were among a higher class of nobility. During formal durbars, in fact, the Peshwa's warriors – the Gaekwads, Scindias, Holkars – were not even admitted into the Maratha king's court. See André Wink, *Land and Sovereignty in India: Agrarian Society and Politics under the Eighteenth-Century*

Maratha Svarajya (Cambridge: Cambridge University Press, 1986), pp. 81–82. Interestingly, these distinctions did not preclude intermarriage: the formidable Gwalior queen, Baizabai, was chosen for the Scindia maharajah precisely because she brought status to the table, while her husband delivered power. See Elissa Vann Struth, 'Splitting the Stereotype: Reading Women in Colonial Texts' (unpublished thesis, University of British Columbia, 2001), p. 31. See also N.K. Wagle, 'Ritual and Change in Early Nineteenth Century Society in Maharashtra: Vedokta Disputes in Baroda, Pune and Satara, 1824–38', p. 165, in Milton Israel and N.K. Wagle eds, *Religion and Society in Maharashtra* (Toronto: Centre for South Asian Studies, 1987), pp. 145–81, for a discussion on how, in the 1830s, when high-status Maratha families began to marry into the Gaekwad's clan, the Chhatrapati in Satara objected to this as illegal.

93. This was the Kale family. Her sister too had a Baroda connection – she was married to the Harpale sirdar.

94. Bapat, *Shrimant Maharani*, pp. 16–17.

95. For instance, Jamnabai loved wood apples. One day, when a basket arrived, a servant thought the fruits looked odd – they had been injected, it turned out, with an extraneous substance. Ibid., p. 26.

96. Gaekwad, *Sayajirao of Baroda*, p. 33. His suspicion was not unreasonable. A British officer wrote how in Rajputana also 'an ambitious widow has at her peculiar command one resource for creating political dilemmas, that of declaring herself enceinte immediately after the death of her husband'. See Alfred C. Lyall, *Asiatic Studies: Religious and Social* (London: John Murray, 1884), p. 202.

97. Gaekwad, *Sayajirao of Baroda*, p. 33.

98. Bapat, *Shrimant Maharani*, p. 27. She was later granted an allowance. An offer by the maharajah to give her a lump sum of 1,00,000 rupees was turned down.

99. Russell, *Prince of Wales' Tour*, pp. 177, 192.

100. Ibid., p. 176. Like Uthram Tirunal in Travancore, Khande Rao also was an amateur doctor. As Malabari, *Gujarat and the Gujaratis*, pp. 55–56, wrote, 'He had a remedy for all disease, known and unknown, and used to physic everyone about him. He used to experiment on a large scale. The shortest way to his favour was to go and say you had the belly-ache . . . His Highness would straightaway repair to the dispensary and return with a large bowl containing some vile mixture.' When the photographer Louis Rousselet visited him in the 1860s, the maharajah amused himself by getting the Frenchman to wear one of his robes and state jewels. See Louis Rousselet (C.R. Buckle ed.), *India and Its Native Princes: Travels in Central India and in the Presidencies of Bombay and Bengal* (London: Bickers and Son, 1882 edn), pp. 100–101.

101. See Russell, *Prince of Wales' Tour*, pp. 189–90, for the royal entourage's comment on this.

102. Durand's note dated 15 May 1875 in Pros. Foreign (Pol. Dep. A), File Nos. 297–381, G.O.I., NAI.

103. Talk existed, though, that this adoption had been on the condition that it did *not* grant its beneficiaries rights to the throne. Ibid.

104. Hoping to impress the British, he wrote how he was 'actuated not only by a belief that he is merely asking for his rights, but by an earnest desire to do whatever in him lies for the happiness and prosperity of the people'. He knew also, evidently, that Baroda could become 'a wealthy and prosperous State' only if it had a proper ruler – the very fact that he was conscious of this, it was hinted, demonstrated a desire to reign with 'wisdom, justice, and moderation' while preserving 'friendly relations' with the country's imperial comptrollers. Memorial dated 9 February 1875 from Sadasheo Rao in ibid.

105. Memorial by Gubajirao, Baburao, Kashirao, Okhajirao and Sucaramrao bin Bhicajirao Guicowad, residents of Kavalane, Taluka Malegaum, in the Nassik District in ibid. This petition is opposed to Sayaji Rao Gaekwad's biography by Sergeant, *Ruler of Baroda*, p. 4, which claims: 'It is uncertain who first suggested to the British authorities that the humble Kavalana brothers' be considered. The suggestion, as archival evidence shows, came from the family itself, that is, Sayaji Rao's father and his uncles.

106. See telegram dated 5 May 1875 from the Resident to the foreign secretary, G.O.I., in ibid.

107. Letter dated 19 May 1875 from the foreign secretary, G.O.I., to the Resident in ibid.

108. Telegram dated 20 May 1875 from the foreign secretary, G.O.I., to the Resident in ibid.

109. Telegram dated 27 May 1875 from the viceroy to the secretary of state in ibid.

110. Telegram dated 21 May 1875 from the Resident to the foreign secretary, G.O.I., in ibid.

111. Sergeant, *Ruler of Baroda*, p. 24.

112. Ibid., p. 27.

113. Extract from letter dated 28 May 1875 from the Resident to the foreign secretary, G.O.I., in Pros. Foreign Dep. (Pol. A) File Nos. 280–311, April 1882, NAI.

114. Baroda Administration Report, 1875–76, p. 21.

115. Quoted in Gaekwad, *Sayajirao of Baroda*, p. 152.

116. Sergeant, *Ruler of Baroda*, p. 3. Sayaji Rao's only visit after his adoption occurred in 1926.

117. Russell, *Prince of Wales' Tour*, p. 177.

118. Ibid., p. 129.

119. Edward St Clair Weeden, *A Year with the Gaekwar of Baroda* (London: Hutchinson and Co., 1911), pp. 1–2.

120. See Charles W. Nuckolls, 'The Durbar Incident', p. 551, in *Modern Asian Studies*, Vol. 24, No. 3 (1990), pp. 529–59.

121. Sergeant, *Ruler of Baroda*, p. 23.

122. As the viceroy wrote to the secretary of state, though they would be justified in 'imposing some penalty' on the state for Malhar Rao's misdeeds, by 'revising and re-adjusting our relations with the State', due to the divided report on whether he was guilty, this could not be done. See telegram dated 13 April 1875 in Pros. Foreign Dep. (Pol. A) dated April 1882, NAI.

123. Viceroy's proclamation dated 19 April 1874 in 'Deposition', pp. 31–32.

124. Tukoji Holkar II quoted in Article 5, p. 228, in *The London Quarterly Review*, Vol. 145, January–April 1878 (New York: The Leonard Scott Publishing Company, 1878), pp. 221–37. The irony, of course, is that the house of Indore too had, some years before, suffered similar problems, where in 1834 a legitimately adopted heir was put aside for a maharajah of illegitimate birth for the reason that the adoption was not conducted with the Resident's approval. See Hira Lal Gupta, 'Indore Successions, 1833–34 & 1843' in *Proceedings of the Indian History Congress*, Vol. 18 (1955), pp. 243–51.

125. See Henry Tucker's Minute in 'Baroda Administration Commission', pp. 65–71.

126. Rahul Sagar, *The Dewan* (forthcoming). See also 'How, and Why, the First Constitution in Modern India Was Written, 75 Years Before the One We Follow' at https://scroll.in/article/950118/how-and-why-the-first-constitution-in-modern-india-was-written-75-years-before-the-one-we-follow. Tucker too gives clues when he states that the native statesman had served as Dewan in two different parts of the country – only Rao fits the description.

127. For Dinkar Rao, see *Memorandum of Observations on the Administration of India by The Hon'ble Rao Raja Dinker Rao Rughoonath, Moontazim Bahadoor, of Gwalior for Making Laws and Regulations* (Agra: Delhi Gazette Press, 1876 edn). Rao, most certainly, had been thinking about these subjects too. In respect of Visakham Tirunal of Travancore, for example, he later published a list of twenty-five good qualities in that ruler, which communicate his vision of an ideal autocrat. Thus, besides truisms on the 'good of his subjects' being the object of the maharajah's life, Rao highlighted the attention Visakham Tirunal gave to 'judicial purity and independence', public education, 'moderation in public taxation', lack of extravagance and the restraint with which he prevented his 'reforming zeal' from riding roughshod over tradition. See the full list in Aiya, *Travancore State Manual*, Vol. 1, pp. 602–603.

128. Madhava Rao's memorandum in 'Baroda Administration Commission', pp 71–73.

129. Ibid.

130. Ibid.

131. See Rao's 'Charter or Constitution' in ibid., pp. 73–79.

132. For instance, to enforce discipline, only orders channelled through the Dewan were to have legal force; private allowances of the royal family were to be fixed, within the bounds of which the maharajah was free to shower largesse on whom he liked; laws ought to be respected; and so on. Why, the Parsi Dewan had even discussed this with the Indore maharajah, when the latter was in negotiations with Rao about bringing him on as Dewan. Naoroji, 'The Baroda Administration', pp. 403–406. Rao's defence of princely states also aligns a great deal with Naoroji. In a lecture he noted how in native-ruled territory, 'revenues are chiefly spent in the country itself'; taxes were 'levied with less rigorous exactitude, and remissions are granted with more freedom'; there was 'more elasticity and less cast-iron adherence to rule'; 'less litigation' because it was easier to make grievances heard; more native education and better management of religious shrines, etc.; all of which produced a 'quiet' contentment among the people. To him, the disappearance of the states would be a sad occurrence. See Rao quoted in J.D. Rees, *The Duke of Clarence & Avondale in Southern India (With a Narrative of Elephant-Catching in Mysore by G.P. Sanderson)* (London: Kegan Paul, Trench, Trubner and Co. Ltd, 1891), pp. 7–8.

133. Ranade in his 'A Constitution' cited before, however, noted that Rao was limited when the ruler he worked with was strong-willed. This, Ranade added, was why his Indore term was not as significant as Travancore.

134. Rao was once quoted as saying that 'left to themselves, they [that is, native rulers] will wipe themselves out'. Quoted in *The London Quarterly Review*, p. 228. He also is alleged to have said that if the Raj ended any time soon, 'it would be like loosing the bars of the cages of the Zoological Gardens and letting out the animals, that very soon they would all be dead except the tiger', this tiger being 'the warlike people of Northern India'. Quoted in McLane, *Indian Nationalism*, p. 68. He saw himself very much as a saviour of Indian-ruled territories, and a man making history. The British too noted this: when in 1876, for example, he sent them a report on Baroda, an official thought this 'dissertation' an 'interesting document', not least because Rao was keen to 'reconcile modern ideas with the time-honored customs of Native society.' Note by F. Henvey dated 4 October 1876 in Pros. Foreign Dep. (Pol. B), File Nos. 832–38, March 1877, NAI.

135. Resident's letter dated 24 August 1876 in Baroda Administration Report, 1875–76, p. 3.

136. Letter dated 16 September 1875 from the Resident to the foreign secretary, G.O.I., in Pros. Foreign Dep. (Pol. A), File Nos. 345–55, December 1875, NAI.

137. To be clear, the support Rao received was no accident – for as with Naoroji, Bombay was keen to promote the Resident over the Dewan. Though the proclamation had promised that Baroda would continue under native rule, the governor advised a

'rigid interpretation' of that term, and to allow the Resident to veto every action of the Dewan if he so saw fit. (See letter dated March 1875 from the secretary, G.O.B., to the foreign secretary, G.O.I., in ibid.) Calcutta, however, nipped this mischief, which would 'keep the administration practically in its own hands' – their man was *only* to step in during emergencies and otherwise to 'carefully abstain from putting himself forward'. (See foreign secretary's notes dated 25 March and 1 May 1875 in ibid.) Anything but a 'purely Native administration' would be a 'breach of faith', and it was 'of the greatest importance' to avoid all action which could justify complaints that 'under the pretence of maintaining a Native Administration' the British were 'introducing our own system'. (See 'A.E.''s note dated 11 May 1875 in ibid.) It was easier too for the viceroy to be lenient, given that Rao, thanks to a towering reputation, commanded respect. For his part, meanwhile, the Dewan came to a diplomatic understanding with all parties involved. To ensure, for instance, that Jamnabai did not present a hurdle, it was agreed that every fortnight he would brief her, ensuring her position as 'head of the family' was respected. (See Resident's note dated 15 September 1875 in ibid.)

138. Malabari, *Gujarat and the Gujaratis*, p. 70.

139. See Pros. Foreign Dep. (Pol. B), File Nos. 84–92, May 1876, NAI, for Kamabai Shirke's grievances.

140. See Pros. Foreign Dep. (Pol. A), File Nos. 87–96, August 1879, NAI, for their representation and the British response. Of the forty-five nobles, fourteen were significant. Rao defended his actions stating that most of their grievances pertained to the previous ruler's time – and that many of the signatories were 'mere boys' and not men of consequence.

141. Baroda Administration Report, 1875–76, p. 22.

142. Ibid., p. 20.

143. Ibid., p. 38.

144. Letter dated 29 September 1875 from the Dewan to the Resident in Pros. Foreign Dep. (Pol. A), File Nos. 356–59, December 1875, NAI. See also Baroda Administration Report, 1875–76, p. 23. As David Hardiman writes, the Gaekwads originally came to power by winning over local Gujarati powers and these bankers, who became extremely powerful by funding their campaigns. In 1825, five of the state bankers alone were owed some 1.3 crore rupees by the royal family. Local Gujaratis were also sold revenue farming rights. All of these were now reversed. See Hardiman, 'Baroda: The Structure of a "Progressive" State', pp. 110–11, in Robin Jeffrey ed., *People, Princes and Paramount Power: Society and Politics in the Indian Princely States* (Delhi: Oxford University Press, 1978), pp. 107–35.

145. Baroda Administration Report, 1875–76, p. 5.

146. Ibid., pp. 28–29.

147. Malabari, *Gujarat and the Gujaratis*, p. 77.

148. Ibid., pp. 49–50.

149. Ibid., p. 78.

150. Natesan, *Indian Statesmen*, p. 212.

151. Gaekwad, *Sayajirao of Baroda*, p. 62.

152. Ibid., p. 73.

153. Ibid., pp. 67–68,

154. Quoted in ibid., p. 67.

155. Note dated 12 April 1883 by 'J.A.C.' in Pros. Foreign Dep. (A-Pol.-I), File Nos. 129–33, May 1883, NAI.

156. Quoted in Gaekwad, *Sayajirao of Baroda*, p. 66.

157. See Ranade, *Select Writings*, pp. 329–34.

158. Quoted in Gaekwad, *Sayajirao of Baroda*, p. 64.

159. Ibid.

160. Baroda Administration Report, 1875–76, p. 41.

161. Reference is to F.A.H. Elliot's *The Rulers of Baroda* (Bombay: Education Society's Press, 1879). He would continue in service of the state for a decade and a half after Sayaji Rao came to power.

162. Quoted in Caroline Keen, *Princely India and the British: Political Development and the Operation of Empire* (New Delhi: Viva Books, 2013), p. 37.

163. P.S. Melvill's memorandum in letter dated 28 September 1880 from the Resident to the foreign secretary, G.O.I., in Foreign Dep. (Pol. A), File Nos. 57–63, July 1881, NAI.

164. Madhava Rao's memorandum dated 27 September 1880 in ibid.

165. 'J.W.R.'s note dated 5 November 1880 in ibid.

166. H.M. Durand's note dated 10 December 1880 in ibid.

167. Ibid.

168. Note by A.C. Lyall appended to H.M. Durand's note in ibid.

169. A.C. Lyall's note dated 14 December 1880 in ibid.

170. Letter dated 12 February 1881 from the foreign secretary, G.O.I., to the Resident in ibid.

171. Sergeant, *Ruler of Baroda*, p. 46, records that twenty-three lectures were delivered by Rao, twenty-seven by Kazi Shahabuddin, eighteen by the chief justice, seven by another judge, six by an officer on police matters, nine by another on various departments and others on law and accounts by two more officials.

172. T. Madhava Rao, *Minor Hints: Lectures Delivered to H.H. the Maharaja Gaekwar, Sayaji Rao III by Raja Sir T. Madhava Rao, K.C.S.I.* (Bombay: British India Press, 1881), p. 37.

173. Ibid., p. 38.

174. Ibid., p. 98.

175. Ibid., p. 109.

176. Rao quoted in John Hurd and Ian J. Kerr, *India's Railway History: A Research Handbook* (Leiden: Brill, 2012), p. 114. He was not alone in holding such views. An editorial in *The Hindu* dated 18 April 1887 also noted that the Raj had in some ways been a 'unifying force', waking Indians to the fact that they were a 'common nation'.

177. The claim was not without logic. As the scholar Maria Misra writes, the journey from Calcutta to the Puri temple went from twenty-six days to twelve hours, generating a boom in pilgrims, and boosting the revenues of that shrine – the railways did not speed the march of rationalism as much as give wings to tradition. Maria Misra, *Vishnu's Crowded Temple: India Since the Great Rebellion* (London: Allen Lane, 2007), p. 23.

178. Quoted in Chawla, *Raja Ravi Varma*, p. 61.

179. Naoroji's speech in *Addresses and Writings*, pp. 332–33.

180. Rao quoted in Robert Spence Watson, 'Indian National Congresses', p. 103 in *The Contemporary Review*, Vol. 54 (London: Isbister and Company, 1888), pp. 89–104.

181. In that short time, he does not seem to have revised this view, unlike Naoroji who shed parts of his earlier avatar, opting for a more aggressive tone. In fact, Rao remained convinced that the British would ultimately do good by India, even while *older* contemporaries felt otherwise. Dinkar Rao, for example, described as 'one of the saviours of the British Empire' for his loyalty during the Great Rebellion (see Mukund W. Burway, *Life of the Honourable Rajah Sir Dinkar Rao* [Bombay: M.W. Burway, 1907], p. 184) is a case in point. He believed the British 'had not kept faith with India'. 'You are not now,' he remarked in the 1870s, 'true to your word. Once your word was as if it were written on a stone tablet ... Now I speak of it as a promissory note. You promise and do not fulfil.' It looked like the British had forgotten their 'duty of looking to the happiness of the people placed under her protection by the Almighty God'. Instead, while their island home grew rich, the subcontinent 'was yearly becoming poorer, and under the Queen's government had lost many of the advantages' it had enjoyed even under the Company. See James Routledge, *English Rule and Native Opinion in India: From Notes Taken, 1870–74* (London: Trubner and Co., 1878), pp. 86–89.

182. Letter dated 18 June 1881 from the Resident to the foreign secretary, G.O.I., in Pros. Foreign Dep. (Pol. A), File Nos. 280–311, April 1882, NAI.

183. Memorandum dated 20 September 1881 by A.C. Lyall in Pros. Foreign Dep. (Pol. A), File Nos. 221–33, April 1882, NAI.

184. Ibid. The maharajah's determination to restrict limitations is noteworthy when viewed against the fact that in 1898, when the prince of Bikaner accepted similar limitations, they ended up lasting a decade.

185. H.M. Durand's note dated 28 October 1881 in Pros. Foreign Dep. (Pol. A), File Nos. 221–33, April 1882, NAI. The maharajah's background would in fact lead to

all kinds of tales; one recorded by a member of the Prince of Wales's party in the 1870s claimed that even on the morning before his installation on the throne of Baroda, Sayaji Rao was seen 'playing in the streets naked, with the exception of a cloth around his body'. See George Wheeler, *India in 1875–76: The Visit of the Prince of Wales – A Chronicle of His Royal Highness's Journeyings in India, Ceylon, Spain and Portugal* (London: Chapman and Hall, 1876), p. 44.

186. Letter dated 7 October 1881 from the Resident to the foreign secretary in Pros. Foreign Dep. (Pol. A), File Nos. 221–33, April 1882, NAI.

187. Melvill's speech at the installation banquet in Pros. Foreign Dep. (Pol. A), File Nos. 280–311, April 1882, NAI.

188. *The Bombay Gazette* dated 6 April 1891. Ranade did, however, try to articulate a defence. See his *Select Writings*, pp. 295–96. Interestingly, among those who disagreed with Rao's moderate stance in the years prior to his death was the son of his mentor John Bruce Norton, Eardley. For more on Rao's bitter fallout with younger Congressmen, see Ramanathan Suntharalingam, 'Politics and Change in the Madras Presidency, 1884–1894: A Regional Study of Indian Nationalism', unpublished PhD thesis, School of Oriental and African Studies (1966), pp. 270–76.

189. Quoted in Thornton, *General Sir Richard Meade*, p. 240.

190. Chawla, *Raja Ravi Varma*, p. 49.

191. Ibid., p. 84.

192. Ibid.

193. Priya Maholay-Jaradi, *Fashioning a National Art: Baroda's Royal Collection and Art Institutions* (1875–1924) (New Delhi: Oxford University Press, 2016), p. 69.

194. One should not underrate what the villager-turned-prince had already achieved, for he could easily have buckled under the pressures of his position. This, in fact, is what happened to a contemporary, with a near-exact background. Like Baroda, Kolhapur had adopted an heir of the same age as Sayaji Rao. But if the latter embraced his new identity, even standing up to the British, the former's tale culminated in tragedy. Separated from his family and thrust into an unsolicited limelight, the Kolhapur prince grew depressed. In court he was 'shy and reserved' and only the company of menials gave him the freedom to be himself. Scandalized, the British purged all Indian influence around him, including that of his wife and parents; besides cooks, few natives were permitted on his staff, the idea being that in white company he might grow more manly. Instead, the maharajah's mental state deteriorated, till he tried to run away disguised as a bullock-cart driver. And in 1883, two years after Sayaji Rao launched what would become a glorious career in Baroda, the Kolhapur rajah was killed in a scuffle with his de facto British jailer. The story of Maharaja Shivaji IV receives attention in Shruti Kapila, 'Masculinity and Madness: Princely Personhood and Colonial Sciences

of the Mind in Western India, 1871–1940' in *Past and Present*, No. 187 (2005), pp. 121–156, and Avanish Patil, 'Public Opinion in Colonial India: The "Kesari" and the Kolhapur Affair, 1881–1883' in *Proceedings of the Indian History Congress*, Vol. 67 (2006–2007), pp. 711–24.

195. Rao quoted in Bapat, *Shrimant Maharani*, pp. 16–17, in an English extract. He was, of course, being diplomatic because Jamnabai did try to limit Rao's influence.

196. Memorial dated 28 November 1883 from Jamnabai to the Resident in Pros. Foreign Dep. (Secret I), File Nos. 1–6, February 1884, NAI.

197. Letter dated 4 December 1883 from Jamnabai to the Resident in ibid.

198. Ibid.

199. Secretary, Foreign Dep.'s note dated 7 January 1884 in ibid.

200. Resident's undated letter from December 1883 to the secretary, Foreign Dep. in ibid.

201. Letter dated 28 December 1883 from the Resident to the secretary, Foreign Dep. in ibid.

202. See correspondence in Pros. Foreign Dep. (Pol. B), File No. 113, June 1876, NAI.

203. V.C. Prinsep, *Imperial India: An Artist's Journals* (London: Chapman and Hall, 1879), p. 324.

204. Once, at a function, the girl 'slipped away from [her mother's] couch' and 'screwed herself into the corner of the Gaekwar's arm chair'. It was a tiny bit of furniture and 'there was some difficulty in her getting in, but the Gaekwar made as much room for her as he could'. Letter dated 2 January 1882 from the Resident to the viceroy in Pros. Foreign Dep. (Pol. A), File Nos. 280–311, April 1882, NAI. Tarabai would marry and become the rani of Sawantwadi.

205. Rao quoted in Bapat, *Shrimant Maharani*, p. 17.

206. Ibid., p. 89.

207. *Times of India* dated 1 December 1898.

208. Gaekwad, *Sayajirao of Baroda*, p. 62.

209. Sergeant, *Ruler of Baroda*, p. 58.

210. Ibid., p. 59.

211. Gaekwad, *Sayajirao of Baroda*, p. 105.

212. Dhananjay Keer, *Mahatma Jotirao Phooley: Father of the Indian Social Revolution* (Bombay: Popular Prakashan), p. 181.

213. See letter to the maharajah in P.G. Patil (trans.), *Selections: Collected Works of Mahatma Jotirao Phule*, Vol. 2 (Bombay: Education Department, Government of Maharashtra, 1991), pp. 81–82.

214. Baroda Administration Report, 1875–76, p. 10.

215. See Keer, *Phooley*, pp. 212–13, and also the maharajah's own reference to this in a 1926 speech in A.G. Widgery ed., *Speeches and Addresses of His Highness Sayaji Rao III, Maharaja of Baroda*, Vol. 2 (Cambridge: Cambridge University Press, 1927), pp. 509–10.

216. Gaekwad, *Sayajirao of Baroda*, pp. 307–308. Indeed, Sayaji Rao was to have several run-ins with the Brahmin orthodoxy. In 1887, he went to Europe despite religious objections about overseas travel. The one Maratha who ventured out before – a Kolhapur rajah – had died in Italy, worsening the superstition. (See Edward W. West ed., *Diary of the Late Rajah of Kolhapoor During His Visit to Europe in 1870* [London: Smith, Elder and Co., 1872] for more on this.) For the generality of Hindu princes, caste and ritual purity precluded such adventurism. Sayaji Rao, however, was too curious; he first sent a brother to test the waters, and then decided to take the plunge himself. It was a productive, if expensive, trip, setting off a lifelong love of Europe. However, as a concession to the orthodoxy, the ruler agreed to perform purificatory rituals on his return. (See Gaekwad, *Sayajirao of Baroda*, p. 121. These cost a good 27,000 rupees.) More trips followed, till there was a rupture on this ceremonial question with the Brahmins. It turned out that religious rites were performed in the Puranic, not Vedic, mode. The former was deemed appropriate for Sudras, with only Kshatriyas entitled to the latter. Things had been this way for generations, and indeed a Gaekwad prince himself had referred to the dynasty as Sudra as late as the 1870s. (See Telegram dated 13 May 1875 from Sadasheo Rao Gaekwad to the viceroy in Pros. Foreign (Pol. Dep. A), File Nos. 297–381, NAI.) In 1896, however, a Brahmin from Rajasthan asked Sayaji Rao why he did not assert the right to Vedic ceremonies. When the idea was broached, the family preceptor refused, which provoked the ruler; Sayaji Rao coolly asked his Rajasthani guest and Gujarati priests to execute his orders instead, over screeching objections in the Marathi press. (See Dhananjay Keer, *Shahu Chhatrapati: A Royal Revolutionary* [Bombay: Popular Prakashan, 1976], pp. 82–83.) While this might be read as princely vanity, the maharajah's response appears in a somewhat different light when viewed alongside the general anti-Brahmin assertion in this period in Maharashtra, which would also envelop Kolhapur in a few years. (Maratha grandees in general had also been fighting Brahmins on this count. See Wagle, 'Ritual and Change'. In Kolhapur, Maharajah Shahu would also show an anti-Congress attitude because he regarded it, especially in western India, as Brahmin dominated. See Ramusack, *Twilight*, p. 113.) Declaring that the Brahmins had been duping people, Sayaji Rao promptly also began Sanskrit lessons. (See Gaekwad, *Sayajirao of Baroda*, p. 177.)

217. Gaekwar's speech read out by Sampatrao Gaikwad in the *Journal of the Society for Arts*, Vol. 41, No. 2106 (1893), p. 472.

218. Quoted in Gaekwad, *Sayajirao of Baroda*, pp. 136–37.

219. Quoted in Mason Olcott, *Village Schools in India: An Investigation with Suggestions* (Calcutta: Association Press, 1926), pp. 59–60.

220. Lord Napier quoted in Mitter, *Art and Nationalism*, p. 64.

221. Ibid., p. 201.

222. Ibid.

223. Maholay-Jaradi, *Fashioning a National Art*, p. 92.

224. Ibid., p. 204.

225. Neumayer and Schelberger eds, *The Diary*, p. 3.

226. Lina Vincent Sunish, 'From Maharajas to the Masses: Ravi Varma (1848–1906), the Maker of Multiples', p. 41, in Vaishnavi Ramanathan ed., *Pages of a Mind: Raja Ravi Varma – Life and Expressions* (Mumbai: Piramal Art Foundation, 2016), pp. 38–53. Of course, as one critic wrote in *The Indian Review* in 1911, the press was also 'the only artistic blunder of his life' because though popular, the prints were 'executed by unperfected mechanism and soulless mechanics' with colours in 'the worst possible taste'. See G. Joseph, 'A Great Indian Artist' in *The Indian Review*, November–December 1911, pp. 905–909.

227. Mitter, *Art and Nationalism*, p. 215.

228. Neumayer and Schelberger eds, *The Diary*, p. 7.

229. Evan Maconochie, *Life in the Indian Civil Service* (London: Chapman and Hall, 1926), p. 154.

230. Quoted in Gaekwad, *Sayajirao of Baroda*, p. 128.

231. Ibid., p. 130.

232. Ibid., p. 160.

233. Quoted in ibid., pp. 169–70.

234. Ibid., p. 171.

235. Ibid., p. 173.

236. Ibid., pp. 174–75. It was also made clear that the government would not look favourably at any post-retirement office being granted to the man by the maharajah.

237. Quoted in ibid., p. 156.

238. The Gujarati Manibhai Jassabhai was loaned from the British service to Baroda. By 1888, he had a salary so generous that it 'qualified him for a pension five times higher' than he would have received had he continued in colonial offices, showing the disparity between princely and British service. Hardiman, 'Baroda', p. 119.

239. Ibid., p. 134.

240. Ibid., pp. 117–18.

241. Ibid., p. 121.

242. See Saint Nihal Singh in *The North American Review*, Vol. 192, No. 658 (1910), pp. 369–78. The Calcutta authorities, interestingly, saw Singh as anti-British.

243. Quoted in Gaekwad, *Sayajirao of Baroda*, p. 162.

244. Dewan Manubhai Mehta quoted in Manu Bhagavan, 'The Rebel Academy: Modernity and the Movement for a University in Princely Baroda, 1908–49', p. 926, in *The Journal of Asian Studies*, Vol. 61, No. 3 (2002), pp. 919–47.

245. Quoted in T.C.A. Raghavan, *History Men: Jadunath Sarkar, G.S. Sardesai, Raghubir Sinh and Their Quest for India's Past* (Noida: HarperCollins, 2020), p. 52.

246. See R.C. Dutt, *Baroda Administration Report, 1904–05* (Bombay: The British India Printing Works, 1906), pp. 203–204, for the revenue and its disbursement for that year.

247. Quoted in Sultan Mahomed Shah, *The Memoirs of Aga Khan: World Enough and Time* (London: Cassell and Co., 1954), p. 301. The Aga Khan described the maharajah as a man for whom 'India always came first'.

248. Quoted in Maholay-Jaradi, *Fashioning a National Art*, p. 51.

249. Manu Bhagavan, 'Demystifying the "Ideal Progressive": Resistance Through Mimicked Modernity in Princely Baroda, 1900–1913', pp. 393–94 in *Modern Asian Studies*, Vol. 35, No. 2 (2001), pp. 385–409. See also Manu Bhagavan, *Sovereign Spheres: Princes, Education and Empire in Colonial India* (New Delhi: Oxford University Press, 2003), p. 54.

250. See speech dated 9 July 1908 in A.G. Widgery ed., *Speeches and Addresses of His Highness Sayaji Rao III, Maharaja of Baroda*, Vol. 1 (Cambridge: Cambridge University Press, 1927), pp. 221–30.

251. See speech in *The Indian Nation Builders*, Part 1 (Madras: Ganesh and Co., c. 1910), pp. 232–67.

252. See Gaekwad, *Sayajirao of Baroda*, pp. 188–89, and Patel, *Naoroji*, pp. 183, 188. Of course, the maharajah found informal methods to let the government know his views. As he wrote to Sir John Pulestan, 'It is cruel and humiliating treatment we Indian Rajas are put to by the Government of India. I consider in many respects we are worse dealt with than servants and labourers . . . A Raja, if found troublesome, may be deposed or punished without any public inquiry. A Raja is asked to produce a medical certificate if he desires to visit Europe for his health, a treatment which is inconsistent with his dignity . . . The result of this treatment will, in my opinion, be that the Rajas will be so disgusted as to prefer to be treated as pensioners, and to give up the fictitious, evanescent of an Indian Chief.' See Bhagavan, *Sovereign Spheres*, p. 48.

253. Quoted in Gaekwad, *Sayajirao of Baroda*, p. 195.

254. Quoted in Bhagavan, *Sovereign Spheres*, p. 49.

255. See Stephen Wheeler, *History of the Delhi Coronation Durbar: Held on the First of January 1903 to Celebrate the Coronation of His Majesty King Edward VII, Emperor of India* (London: John Murray, 1904), p. 30. Bhagavan notes that the lady who died was Jamnabai, but it was really Radhabai, the widow of the maharajah who ruled before even old Khande Rao.

256. Quoted in Cashman, *Myth*, p. 110.

257. Quoted in Bhagavan, 'Demystifying', p. 388. The maharajah would also in 1911 complain that Curzon had treated him 'like a servant'. See Gaekwad, *Sayajirao of Baroda*, p. 228.

258. See *Speeches and Addresses*, Vol. 1, pp. 83–117.

259. Peter Heehs, *The Lives of Sri Aurobindo* (New York: Columbia University Press, 2008), p. 68. Aurobindo had, as early as 1893, when already in service of Baroda, started publishing in the press. 'We must no longer hold out supplicating hands to the English Parliament, like an infant crying to its nurse for a toy,' he had advised the Moderates in an 1893 article, 'but must recognise the hard truth that every nation must beat out its own path to salvation with pain and difficulty . . . (not) the tutelage of another.' See ibid., p. 38.

260. Gilmour, *Curzon*, pp. 174–75.

261. See speech dated 30 November 1909 in *Speeches and Addresses*, Vol. 1, pp. 353–57. Sayaji Rao had sought Dutt's services first in 1895. He was Revenue Minister in Baroda between 1904 and 1907 and then Dewan in 1909.

262. Hardiman, 'Baroda', p. 124.

263. Quoted in Mary Minto, *India: Minto and Morley, 1905–1910, Compiled from the Correspondence Between the Viceroy and the Secretary of State* (London: Macmillan and Co., 1934), p. 72.

264. *The Evening Mail* dated 17 September 1909 and *The Pioneer* dated 16 September 1909. His 'coolness' is also mentioned in Valentine Chirol, *Indian Unrest* (London: Macmillan and Co., 1910), p. 193. See also Bhagavan, *Sovereign Spheres*, p. 56.

265. Quoted in Mary Minto, *India*, pp. 343–44.

266. Ibid., p. 350.

267. Bhagavan, 'Demystifying', p. 396.

268. Ibid., pp. 223, 396.

269. Ibid., pp. 396–97.

270. Ibid., p. 399.

271. Jurisdiction had caused trouble in Malhar Rao's reign also. One of Baroda's four territorial segments featured a hilly area wherefrom raiders evidently entered and attacked British territory before retreating into their princely base, where the Raj had no jurisdiction. This is discussed in Benton, *Search for Sovereignty*, pp. 254–55.

272. The viceroy's letter dated November 1911 to the secretary of state in *Source Material for a History of the Freedom Movement in India*, Vol. 2 (Bombay: Government Central Press, 1958), pp. 570–86.

273. Gaekwad, *Sayajirao of Baroda*, p. 236.

274. The Dewan's note dated 27 March 1905 on the maharajah's meeting with the Resident in ibid., pp. 558–60.

275. News had reached him that he was being sued in London for apparently seducing a married woman. This was the famous *Statham vs Statham* case.

276. Quoted in Nuckolls, 'Durbar Incident', p. 543.

277. Sergeant, *Ruler of Baroda*, pp. 131–32.

278. Nuckolls, 'Durbar Incident', p. 548.

279. Sergeant, *Ruler of Baroda*, p. 132.

280. Nuckolls, 'Durbar Incident', pp. 537, 541.

281. Charles Hardinge, *My Indian Years: 1910–1916* (London: John Murray, 1948), p. 51.

282. See *Proceedings of the Baroda Commission*, p. 1. Ravi Varma's brother also described this 'plain' everyday costume of the ruler in 1894–95. See Neumayer and Schelberger eds, *The Diary*, p. 31.

283. Sergeant, *Ruler of Baroda*, pp. 139–40.

284. Ibid., pp. 141–42.

285. Bhagavan, 'Demystifying', p. 408.

286. See the Dewan's foreword, pp. v–viii, in Krishnarao N. Panemanglor, *The Viceregal Visit to Baroda, 1926* (Baroda, 1927).

287. Speech dated 11 April 1938 in *Speeches and Addresses of His Highness Sayaji Rao III, Maharaja of Baroda*, Vol. 4 (Cambridge: Cambridge University Press, 1938), pp. 889–90.

288. *The New York Times* dated 7 February 1939.

289. Corfield, *Princely India*, p. 168.

5. Princesses and Consorts

1. Pillai, *Visakhavijaya*, p. 93. This 'heartrending scene' where the rani was 'torn' from her husband is also mentioned in *The Friend of India* dated 28 August 1875. *The Madras Mail*, years later, on 17 March 1883, however, simply stated that the rani held on to the carriage and would not let it move till the maharajah sent word that 'physical force' would be used. Either way, some form of obstruction on her part is evident. See also *The Indian Statesman* dated 21 August 1875.

2. This is how Kerala Varma was mentioned in an 1877 letter he wrote the maharajah. See G.O. No. 62, Pros. Madras (Pol. Dep.) dated 26 January 1877 in IOR/R/2/891/260.

3. It was Uthram Tirunal who, before his death, performed the adoption, and the ranis were his 'grand-nieces'. They are here referred to as Ayilyam Tirunal's nieces because that is how they appear in state papers.

4. On the alcoholism, see Pillai, *Visakhavijaya*, p. 150. On 'giving company' see V. Nagam Aiya, *The Travancore State Manual*, Vol. 2 (Trivandrum: Government of Travancore, 1906), p. 324. This rani was a homely type: a missionary recorded her as spending her time in such activities as knitting woollen antimacassars. See Augusta Blandford in *India's Women: The Magazine of the Church of England Zenana Missionary Society*, Vol. 2 (London: James Nisbet and Co., 1882), pp. 33–34. She was a woman of 'great amiability' and a devoted mother, 'anxious that her sons should grow up to be good, wise men. See Augusta Blandford, 'Mission Work Amongst High Caste Hindu Women in Trevandrum', p. 174, in *The Missionary*

Conference: South India and Ceylon, 1879, Vol. 1 (Madras: Addison and Co., 1880), pp. 172–74. A visiting party made similar observations, noting that while Parvathi Bayi was not particularly interesting, she did line up her boys and make them read in English, give an impromptu music recital and then distribute their pictures. See Maria Hay Flyter Mitchell (Mrs Murray Mitchell), *Scenes in Southern India* (New York: American Tract Society, 1886), p. 240. Parvathi Bayi, besides the death of her first husband, had also suffered the loss of an infant daughter, and then in 1875 a son, Adithya Varma. According to the *Times of India* dated 29 May 1875, the ten-year-old had had a fatal fall.

5.   Welsh, *Military Reminiscences*, p. 145.

6.   Letter dated 19 September 1924 from the Resident to the secretary, Foreign and Pol. Dep., G.O.I., in IOR/R/1/1/1530 (2).

7.   Author's interview with Paliath Ravi Achan. The nonagenarian Achan lives in Tripunithura, the seat of the Cochin royal family, and his father was a prince of that house. This was also confirmed with Sethu Tampuratti, the eldest female member of the Kilimanoor family, married to a Cochin prince.

8.   Lewis, *George Maxwell Gordon*, p. 129.

9.   Blandford, *India's Women*, Vol. 1, pp. 291, 293. Blandford called her 'the most diligent' of her pupils. She was less ecstatic on meeting the rani's grandmother who, on learning that the missionary was unmarried, 'seemed sorry for me, as if, under these mournful conditions, life was not worth having'. See Blandford in *India's Women*, Vol. 2, p. 34.

10. Quoted in Blandford, *India's Women*, Vol. 1, p. 294. She did add that these rules were 'troublesome'.

11. Mitchell, *Scenes in Southern India*, pp. 236–37.

12. See Mountstuart E. Grant Duff, *Notes from a Diary: Kept Chiefly in Southern India, 1881–1886*, Vol. 1 (London: John Murray, 1899), pp. 94–95.

13. Blandford, *India's Women*, Vol. 2, p. 33.

14. Mitchell, *Scenes in Southern India*, p. 237. On the exhibition, see Henry M. Vibart, *The Life of General Sir Harry N.D. Prendergast* (London: Eveleigh Nash, 1914), p. 318.

15. Narayana Pillai, *Kerala Varma* (Delhi: Sahitya Akademi, 1988), p. 20.

16. Sethu Lakshmi Bayi quoted in Charles Allen and Sharada Dwivedi, *Lives of the Indian Princes* (London: Century Publishing, 1984), p. 31. This was of course a contrast from her early years. In 1862 the Madras governor's wife wrote: 'In they came presently . . . two girls, one not quite fifteen, the other eleven; both small of their age, and so cumbered with their dress and ornaments that it seemed almost difficult to them to walk. They had only a petticoat on by way of lower dress, but were muffled up in great red shawls; they had jewels in their noses, and such

enormous ear-rings that they quite drag the ears down, and make large holes in them; broad, heavy gold necklaces and anklets, and each one ring on their second toe. They came up and shook hands with us, and just said "Good morning"… and this was the extent of our communication; for, though I spoke once to the eldest, the Rajah answered for her, as if conscious that she would not be able to do so, though they have both been … learning a little English. They are both married! But their husbands did not appear.' See Denison, *Varieties of Vice-Regal Life*, pp. 212–13.

17. Pierre Loti (George A.F. Inman trans.), *India* (London: T. Werner Laurie Ltd, 1928 edn), pp. 55–56.

18. Keen, *Princely India*, p. 107. For another detailed study, see Jhala, *Courtly Indian Women*.

19. Price, *Kingship and Political Practice*, p. 75.

20. Stern, *The Cat and the Lion*, pp. 70–78.

21. Lord Lansdowne quoted in Keen, *Princely India*, p. 117.

22. John Zubrzycki, *The House of Jaipur: The Inside Story of India's Most Glamorous Royal Family* (New Delhi: Juggernaut Books, 2020), p. 25.

23. Resident's Report for the Second Half of July 1928 in File No. 1/28 (Pol.), Home Dep., NAI. See also Report for the First Half of May 1928 in ibid., and for the First Half of May 1929 in File No. F-17 (Pol.), Home Dep., NAI, and for the First Half of April 1929 in File No. 17/29 (Pol.), Home Dep., NAI, for the ways in which the consort was attempting to influence government appointments. For more, see also https://www.cochinroyalhistory.org/pages.php?menu_id=2&submenu_id=5&submenu2_id=18.

24. His uncle was married to Ayilyam Tirunal and Visakham Tirunal's only sister. On his deathbed, he requested that his nephew Kerala Varma (son of his sister Deviamba) be married to the freshly adopted Lakshmi Bayi. See Pillai, *Visakhavijaya*, pp. 9–10, and Pillai, *Kerala Varma*, p. 30.

25. Ibid., pp. 19–23.

26. See the *Times of India* dated 23 August 1875.

27. Loti, *India*, p. 55.

28. Pillai, *Kerala Varma*, pp. 18, 30. See also Minute dated 28 January 1871 by A.J. Arbuthnot in IOR/R/2/891/251. At one point, when the British agent alluded to that old treaty by which the ruler was always to accept 'advice', the Valiya Koil Tampuran immediately made it known that bringing up the treaty was quite 'out of place'.

29. A full list is available in Sreekala M., 'Yamapranamasataka: A Critical Study', PhD thesis (University of Kerala, 1999), p. 38.

30. Blandford, *India's Women*, Vol. 1, p. 291.

31. Chawla, *Raja Ravi Varma*, p. 34.

32. Quoted in J.N. Gupta, *Life and Work of Romesh Chunder Dutt* (London: J.M. Dent and Sons, 1911), pp. 76–77.

33. Quoted in ibid., pp. 435–36.

34. Pillai, *Kerala Varma*, pp. 32–33.

35. Pillai, *Visakhavijaya*, p. 156.

36. Undated letter (A) from 1875 from the Valiya Koil Tampuran to the Acting Resident in IOR/R/891/256.

37. Undated letter (B) from 1875 in ibid.

38. Letter from 'Peter III' to the Dewan in IOR/R/891/256.

39. Letter dated 7 July 1875 from the Valiya Koil Tampuran to the Resident in IOR/R/891/256.

40. *The Pall Mall Gazette* dated 6 September 1875. See also the *Times of India* dated 23 August 1875 for a longer contemporary account of how 'he grew ungrateful, disloyal and impertinent'. See also *The Friend of India* dated 21 August 1875 which mentions another letter Kerala Varma allegedly wrote to the Madras authorities, stating that the maharajah intended to poison his brother also.

41. See, for instance, *Travancore Almanac* (Trivandrum: Government of Travancore, 1878).

42. Pillai, *Kerala Varma*, p. 35. *The Madras Weekly Mail* dated 22 March 1881, in recollecting the event, reported that Lakshmi Bayi went on some kind of a fast till the maharajah released Kerala Varma from jail.

43. Kerala Varma's letter from prison to Ayilyam Tirunal in IOR/R/2/891/260.

44. Ibid. The point on an attraction to Christianity is interesting. It was mentioned by *The Friend of India* dated 28 August 1875 as having seriously affected the palace, adding that both the ranis also wished to convert. A Miss Ballard was mentioned as 'an accomplice' to this plan – she was the Resident's sister and one wonders if there is something to the story. Augusta Blandford speaks of the Malayalam lessons the lady took and her 'self-denying labours' including in the palace in *India's Women: The Magazine of the Church of England Zenana Missionary Society*, Vol. 3 (London: James Nisbet and Co., 1883), p. 317.

45. Pillai, *Kerala Varma*, p. 36.

46. Blandford, *Conch Shell*, p. 57.

47. Blandford, *India's Women*, Vol. 1, p. 293.

48. Blandford, *Conch Shell*, p. 57.

49. Mitchell, *Scenes in Southern India*, p. 238.

50. Blandford, *Conch Shell*, p. 39.

51. Quoted in Pillai, *Ivory Throne*, p. 183.

52. Jeffrey, *Decline*, p. 157.

53. As the scholar K. Saradamoni tells, matrilineal unions were 'equated to concubinage and the women to mistresses and the children called bastards'. See K. Saradamoni, *Matriliny Transformed: Family, Law and Ideology in Twentieth Century Travancore* (New Delhi: Sage Publications, 1999), p. 65.

54. Even Ravi Varma's brother, when urged in 1903 to take a 'beautiful and accomplished' new wife, declared how he 'could take no second wife without lowering my self in the estimate of people'. Neumayer and Schelberger eds, *The Diary*, p. 177. Polygamy was also possible in Kerala, which is what Rajaraja condemns.

55. Blandford, *India's Women*, Vol. 1, p. 23.

56. Amaresh Datta ed., *Encyclopaedia of Indian Literature*, Vol. 3 (New Delhi: Sahitya Akademi, 1949), p. 2056. Between 1861 and 1875 he composed nine works of poetry; in his imprisonment eleven; and in subsequent years another eleven.

57. For details, see Sreekala, 'Yamapranamasataka', pp. 67–71.

58. There is an enduring story that the day Kerala Varma finished this work coincided with the maharajah's death. Besides the 'Yamapranamasataka', two other works calling for the annihilation of his enemies are the 'Satrusamharaprarthanasataka' and the 'Lalitambastotra', also composed during his imprisonment. The latter, for instance, assumes the voice of Krishna's father Vasudeva when imprisoned by Kamsa. For details on the Yamapranamasataka, see Sreekala, 'Yamapranamasataka', pp. 74–100.

59. Datta, *Indian Literature*, p. 2056. There is a play here on the word 'Nilakantha': it refers both to the peacock as messenger, but also to Visakham Tirunal's secretary, Nilakantha Pillai.

60. Mitchell, *Scenes in Southern India*, p. 237, where she notes how 'in every apartment almost' in the palace 'there hung a portrait of Her Majesty the Queen, of whom Her Highness speaks with the greatest reverence'.

61. See the preface in Kerala Varma, *A Jubilee Tribute to Her Most Gracious Majesty Victoria: The Queen Empress* (Bombay: Nirnayasagara Press, 1887). *The Illustrated London News* on 26 September 1891, in a follow-up, reported how 'a conclave of eleven Malayalam poets' had recently been formed to translate Kerala Varma's Sanskrit verses on Victoria into Malayalam as well.

62. Varma, *Jubilee Tribute*. The poet A.R. Rajaraja Varma also contributed a poem to the book in which he wished to 'show his deep loyalty and deference to the great Heroine'.

63. This detail was approvingly picked up in a small review. See *The Orientalist: A Journal of Oriental Literature, Arts and Sciences, Folklore and C.*, Vol. 3, Parts 1 and 2 (Bombay: The Education Society's Press, 1887), p. 64.

64. The father's name was Kunjukrishna Menon of Cheruparambath house. The detail that he had four wives appears in Anonymous ('A Travancore Lady'), 'Literary Women of Kerala', p. 140, in A.C. Sarkar ed., *Welfare* magazine for March 1926, pp. 137–41. Kalyani Ammachi's mother was this fourth wife. See also R. Narayana Panikkar, *Kerala Bhasa Sahitya Charitram*, Vol. 4 (Trivandrum: V.V. Book Depot, 1944), p. 817, for more details on her family. She was born under the Mulam star, and her brothers were Krishna Menon and Madhava Menon. Her mother's name was Lakshmi, daughter of Kunjikutty. Her family name was Mathripillil.

65. Blandford, *Conch Shell*, p. 58.

66. Panikkar, *Kerala Bhasa*, pp. 817–18. See also S. Venkitasubramonia Iyer, 'Some Less Known Composers of Kerala', p. 102, in the *Journal of the Music Academy*, Vol. 40, Nos. 1–4, 1969 (Madras: The Music Academy, 1970), pp. 98–106.

67. A major clue as to the misappropriation is not only that the features of the woman in the painting align better with Kalyani Ammachi's but also the clothes: unlike the *methukettu* worn by Travancore's royalty – that is, a mundu wrapped around the torso – the lady in the portrait appears in the Cochin style, with a cloth held loosely against her breasts. The only important Cochin woman in Trivandrum and whom Ravi Varma was likely to paint in such dress was the maharajah's consort. We should not underestimate costume as a clue. The way individuals wore their hair, their ornaments, the length of the mundu: all these indicated region, class, caste and more. On a related note, since this painting is unsigned, there is a possibility that it was done by Sekhara Warrier, who painted several Cochin women, and that this may be an unidentified lady, and not Kalyani Ammachi at all. For now, the consensus, however, is that the painting is by Ravi Varma. Warrier, however, was no mean painter: *The Madras Mail* dated 14 January 1885 described him as 'an accomplished pupil of the world-renowned Travancore Artist Coil Tamburan', that is, Ravi Varma.

68. See, for instance, Pillai, *Ivory Throne*, p. 182. See also http://www.cochinroyal history.org/pages.php?menu_id=2&submenu_id=5&submenu2_id=11, which quotes from a Cochin rajah's letter, noting how his uncle's wife was first married to a Nair, then to a Tamil Brahmin and finally to the previous rajah, who also took in her son by the Brahmin.

69. A. Sreedhara Menon, *Triumph and Tragedy in Travancore*, p. 333. Ravi Varma's brother, Rajaraja Varma, in his diary also refers to a newspaper extract 'criticizing the Maharaja of Travancore's proposed marriage' in January 1899. See Neumayer and Schelberger eds, *The Diary*, p. 64. See also p. 177 for a reference where Rajaraja Varma speaks of a painting to be presented to Sankaran Tampi, the maharajah's wife's ex-husband.

70. Saradamoni, *Matriliny Transformed*, p. 10. C.V. Raman Pillai's first marriage ended in divorce and the second was with Rajaraja Varma's widow's sister, who died.

71.   Quoted in I.K.K. Menon ed., *The Rajarshi of Cochin: Autobiography and Biography of Maharaja Sir Sri Rama Varma* (Trivandrum: Kerala State Archives, 1994), p. 18. In addition to being 'paramour' to the lady referred to here, this rajah married the niece of a former Dewan, on whose death, after a space of twelve years, he married a lady who had already been married before; her daughter from the earlier relationship was wed to one of her new husband's royal nephews, Parikshit Tampuran. See V. Remadevi, 'Sri Rama Varma Vijaya Mahakavyam of M. Kunjan Varier: A Critical Study', PhD thesis (Kottayam: M.G. University, 1998), pp. 283–84.

72.   What *could* be scandalous, however, was an alleged murder attempt by a rajah of Cochin on his Dewan Sankunni Variyar because the latter was apparently having an affair with his consort. The episode is mentioned in Pillai, *Visakhavijaya*, p. 150.

73.   Related in Pratap Kizhakkemadom, *Pattum Parivattavum: Thiruvithamkur Rajapathnimarude Ithihasam* (Kollam: Saindhava Books, 2018), p. 73.

74.   Ibid., p. 75.

75.   'A Travancore Lady', p. 140. Even the dates of the royal wedding offer clues that Kalyani Ammachi was already involved with Pillai. When the maharajah married her, Kalyani Ammachi was twenty-three years old – this in a day and age where most women were wedded in their teens.

76.   When he was elected to the Sri Mulam Popular Assembly, he was described in the press as 'an elder brother of the Maharaja of Travancore' (that is, his father's nephew, Mulam Tirunal, who had inherited the throne from Visakham Tirunal). *The Morning Post* dated 7 February 1906 also noted how 'under a different law of succession' Tampi 'might have been Maharaja'.

77.   Reference is to Ummini Tampi (aka Tampi Martandan Iravi) who was the grandson of Prince Makayiram Tirunal, brother of Maharajah Karthika Tirunal. T.K. Vijayamohan in his 'Ummini Tampi, The Dewan of Travancore (1809–1812), p. 261, in the *Journal of Kerala Studies*, Vol. 5, Part 1 (Trivandrum: Kerala University, 1978), pp. 261–69, states that Tampi was Karthika Tirunal's son, which is an error.

78.   His daughter was also a composer, while her son – Padmanabhan Tampi – was Ravi Varma's contemporary and a talented painter.

79.   These details are all extracted from R. Sreelekha, 'Ravi Varman Tampi and His Contributions to Karnatak Music', PhD thesis (University of Kerala, 1998), pp. 10–27.

80.   Henry Bruce, *Letters from Malabar and on the Way* (London: G. Routledge and Sons, 1909), p. 79.

81.   Quoted in Raghunandan, *Turn of the Tide*, p. 96. The visitors were Sayaji Rao of Baroda and his wife.

82. The main ammaveedus were Arumana, Nagercoil, Thiruvattar, and Vadasseri. These were all the names of the towns or villages from which the first of the consorts were chosen. Sometimes, 'unofficial' ammaveedus would also emerge. Asvathi Tirunal, from our Introduction, for instance, married an outside lady; her house came to be called 'Bungalow ammaveedu'.

83. This would, as the Nair community consolidated itself in the twentieth century and united sub-castes, lead to complications. Thus, in February 1909 at a funerary feast following the death of Ayilyam Tirunal's wife, many Nairs demanded that the Tampis eat with them. The latter, however, claimed that 'being a connection of the reigning house, there were certain forms and ceremonies which had to be followed, and they could not divest themselves of their privileges without the sanction of the Maharaja'. The result was that the Nairs left and the affair received coverage in *The Homeward Mail* dated 27 February 1909.

84. In fact, if such dues were denied, it was only to spouses who came from *outside* ammaveedus. Thus, one late-nineteenth-century prince was furious with his uncle for failing to give his daughter an opulent wedding. The ruler, however, retorted that he was 'not bound' to go out of his way, since the prince's wife was not from an ammaveedu. Quoted in Raghunandan, *Turn of the Tide*, pp. 23–24.

85. Ramakrishna Pillai states that Uthram Tirunal's wife and daughter belonged to Tiruvattar ammaveedu, but Sharat Sunder Rajeev's research shows that they were from Nagercoil ammaveedu.

86. See Pillai, *Visakhavijaya*, p. 60, for the year of the wedding. The discussion with the British official appears in Drury, *Reminiscences*, pp. 167–68.

87. Ayilam Tirunal did something much more tangible: he allocated well over half a million rupees to his wife and dependants. Letter dated 11/12/1874 from the British Resident to the chief secretary in Madras in IOR/R/2/891/253.

88. Quoted in Mateer, *Native Life*, p. 118.

89. See Walter Hamilton, *A Geographical, Statistical, and Historical Description of Hindostan and the Adjacent Countries*, Vol. 2 (London: John Murray, 1820), p. 319, for an instance in 1813 when Gowri Lakshmi Bayi introduced the infant Swathi Tirunal to court. The painting of Uthram Tirunal's court done by F.C. Lewis, Jr, now at the Kuthiramalika Palace Museum, also depicts his sons in attendance, as do photographs from Mulam Tirunal's time in Aiya, *Travancore State Manual*, Vol. 1.

90. See *The Sphere* dated 3 November 1900: 'The marriage of four of the granddaughters of the late Sir Rama Varma G.C.S.I. [that is, Visakham Tirunal], Maharajah of Travancore, was celebrated in Trivandrum recently in great style . . . The brides, whose ages ranged between ten and six, naturally had no voice in the matter, and direction of all affairs in connection with the marriage rested with their grandmother, the Maharajah's widow. The bridegrooms on the present

occasion were scions of some of the aristocratic families in Travancore . . . the celebration of the marriage was kept up for four days . . . There were several grand processions of the married couples through the principal thoroughfares in Trivandrum. The brides and bridegrooms were carried on the backs of elephants, specially caparisoned for the occasion. Some of the most famous musicians in the capital . . . led the processions. Almost all State officials accompanied it . . . All the poor in the town were sumptuously fed . . .' See also Edward Balfour, *The Cyclopaedia of India and of Eastern and Southern Asia: Commercial, Industrial, and Scientific*, Vol. 3 (London: Bernard Quaritch, 1885), p. 247 for a description of the 1883 wedding of Visakham Tirunal's daughters, where too we read of elephants, nautch girls and the participation of 'all the great officers of the State'. *The Homeward Mail* for 26 June 1883 also covered the wedding, and its estimated expense of 3,00,000 rupees. *The Bombay Gazette and Indian Daily News* dated 14 March 1851 records details of Uthram Tirunal's daughter's wedding. See also *The Amrita Bazar Patrika* dated 26 January 1905 for details of the wedding of Mulam Tirunal's son with a granddaughter of Visakham Tirunal, a ceremony attended by the Dewan and other dignitaries.

91. Shortly before Mulam Tirunal Maharajah died in 1924, his daughter, Karthyayani Pillai of the Vadasseri ammaveedu, was honoured with the Kaiser-i-Hind medal. The maharajah was delighted, sending his 'profound and humble respects' to the British. See File H151 in IOR/L/PS/15/60. The next year, in September, the medal was presented to the lady in a public durbar. See the *Times of India* dated 22 September 1925.

92. *The Lady* dated 11 January 1912.

93. They were also often photographed and painted together with their wives. However, there does appear to have been some hesitation in revealing such material to third parties: Visakham Tirunal's wife is said to have kept hidden a painting that showed her with her husband.

94. His residence was Bhajanappura Palace, and his wife was known as Bhajanappura Ammachi. See Drury, *Reminiscences*, p. 165.

95. Menon, *History of Travancore*, p. 514.

96. Balfour, *Cyclopaedia of India*, p. 247.

97. Mulam Tirunal quoted in Pillai, *Ivory Throne*, p. 106. The second quote is from an official who wrote in 1892: 'His Highness was deeply afflicted by this sore calamity and so much was his love for his departed wife that he has not up to this (now nearly 10 years) married again, bestowing all his affection on his motherless boy.' See Row, *Thulapurushadanom*, p. 11.

98. Anonymous, 'The Late Maharajah of Travancore', in *Journal of the National Indian Association in Aid of Social Progress and Education in India* (London: C. Kegan Paul, Trench and Co., 1885), p. 559.

99.   Lakshmi Ammachi is mistakenly called a maharani in the *Times of India* dated
      13 February 1882 in Bombay, when she arrived at the railway station 'in a closed
      carriage'. 'A purdah,' we read, 'was then spread, when she entered a palanquin and
      was conveyed in it to her saloon.' See also the *Times of India* dated 27 January
      1882 which refers to the couple going to Madras – Lakshmi Ammachi is here
      correctly described as 'His Highness's consort'. A Spanish missionary also noted
      that 'no woman ever trod the palace except his spouse' in Visakham Tirunal's day
      and that the maharajah 'never left the fort without taking [his wife] with himself'.
      Quoted in Samuel Mateer, 'A Romish View of the British Indian Government',
      pp. 591–92, in *The Missionary Review of the World*, Vol. 16, No. 8 (1888),
      pp. 589–95.

100. Thus when the governor came calling in 1884, on his list of notables to visit
      was the ruler's wife. *Minute of His Excellency the Right Hon. the Governor, 5th
      November 1884* (Madras: Government Press, 1884), p. 28. See also *Report of the
      Political Administration of the Territories Within the Central India Agency for 1881–
      82* (Calcutta: Government Printing, 1883), p. 99, for a report on the maharajah's
      trip to Indore where he was accompanied by his son.

101. See Aiya, *Travancore State Manual*, Vol. 1, p. 431.

102. 'Representation from the Vakeels of the Travancore Maha Rajah to the governor-
      general' dated 21 December 1809 in MS 11582, Minto Papers, NLS. The woman
      they wanted the ruler to marry was the sister of Ummini Tampi, from the
      Puthumana ammaveedu.

103. The story of their first meeting is interesting: once, when out riding, the prince
      saw a group of girls. Just for kicks, he rode into their midst. Most fled, but eleven-
      year-old Lakshmi stood her ground, impressing the prince.

104. See *The Englishman's Overland Mail* dated 15 August 1885. An unnamed 'native
      correspondent' who claimed an intimate acquaintance with Visakham Tirunal
      sent in a letter that ran over a page of the newspaper, with details about the ruler's
      youth and marriage.

105. Author's interview with Sharat Sunder Rajeev. This was after Mulam Tirunal lost
      his first wife in 1882.

106. Blandford in *India's Women*, Vol. 2, p. 34. Blandford, in fact, had a close relationship
      with both Ayilyam Tirunal's and Visakham Tirunal's wives. 'The first palace to
      open its doors' to her was that of Lakshmi Ammachi, she wrote in *Conch Shell*,
      p. 57. She read the Bible with Visakham Tirunal's lady, hoping to pull off a
      high-profile conversion. But while Lakshmi Ammachi engaged with Christian
      scripture, she did not give up her religion. Twenty years later, Blandford was
      still complaining that though the lady read St Matthew, she was simultaneously
      planning a pilgrimage to Benares. See Blandford, *India's Women*, Vol. 2, pp. 31–
      36. The closest she came to conversion, in her own view, was with the wife of

Uthradam Tirunal Ravi Varma (1835–89), the mentally unstable middle brother between Ayilyam Tirunal and Visakham Tirunal. As she wrote in *Conch Shell*, p. 59, 'This young girl . . . studied the New Testament by herself, she made great progress in Divine knowledge. She was anxious to be taught, drinking in like a thirsty soul the waters of life. Four years passed away, and she not only confessed to me that she was a believer, but in my presence used to talk to her mother and brother about the Christian faith . . . [S]he promised me that when the child she was expecting was born she would declare herself boldly to be on the Lord's side. One day to my great grief I learned that all was over – that she had died in her confinement.' It ought not to have surprised her, for as early as the 1850s, as a colonial official noted, the Bible was viewed by Travancore's Hindu elites as a textbook rather than a means to salvation. So, the sight of 'a Christian and a Brahmin standing side by side in the same class reciting the "Crucifixion"' had less to do with faith and more with an aspiration to master English. See Drury, *Reminiscences*, p. 210.

107. Here she is described as 'Panappillai Lekshmy Kallyani Pillai (Lady of His Highness the late Rama Varma Maharajah, G.C.S.I., C.I.E.)'. See Lawson, *Narrative*, p. 213.

108. Letter dated 20 January 1909 from Sethu Lakshmi Bayi to her father, courtesy of Lakshmi Raghunandan, her granddaughter.

109. 'A Travancore Lady', p. 140. If, however, as happened occasionally, the women were not from any of the lordly consort-supplying lineages, more complete obscurity was their fate. For instance, Asvathi Tirunal, whom we met in the Introduction, died aged only thirty; his childless non-ammaveedu widow received an allowance, but was practically unknown for the rest of her life. His brother, Chathayam Tirunal, who died in 1901, also left behind a young wife and three daughters (see *The Pioneer* dated 7 June 1901). As late as 1934, she featured in the list of distinguished guests for a royal wedding; but beyond these occasions, she had little to do with the court. I am grateful to Sharat Sunder Rajeev for showing me the list of invitees for the wedding. The lady mentioned is Lakshmi Ammachi of the Kuruppath Menon family of Thrissur; her wedding to the prince was recorded in the *Times of India* dated 12 April 1887. A third brother of this generation, Revathi Tirunal, is reported in *The Madras Weekly Mail* dated 7 April 1886 as marrying one of Blandford's students, namely, Narayani Pillai Kartyayani Pillai of Attur, a town near Neyyattinkara. After Revathi Tirunal's death in 1895, we hear nothing about her.

110. Author's interview with Paliath Ravi Achan.

111. Reference is to Ila Devi of Cooch Behar, sister of Maharani Gayatri Devi of Jaipur and daughter of the maharajah of Cooch Behar and granddaughter of Sayaji Rao of Baroda. See letter dated 29 November 1932 from the Resident to the undersecretary, G.O.I., in IOR/L/PS/13/1283.

112. See letter dated 24 April 1944 from the Resident to the political secretary in IOR/L/PS/13/1285.

113. Menon, *History of Travancore*, p. 168.

114. See the *Times of India* dated 22 August 1862.

115. *Lancaster Gazette* dated 27 September 1862.

116. *The Homeward Mail* dated 13 September 1862.

117. See ibid., *The Dundee Courier and Argus* dated 18 September 1862, *The Homeward Mail* dated 11 October 1864, *The Bombay Gazette* dated 14 August 1862, *The Bombay Gazette Overland Summary* dated 27 August 1862, *The Friend of India* dated 28 August 1862 and so on. See also *The Bombay Miscellany*, Vol. 4 (May–October 1862) (Bombay: Chesson and Woodhall, 1862), pp. 805–806.

118. The *Cochin Courier* dated 2 August 1862 extracted in *The Friend of India* dated 28 August 1862. The same paper was also cited by *The Bombay Gazette* dated 14 August 1862. Madhavan was evidently employed by a brother of the lady called Punartham Nal Tampuran.

119. *The Bombay Gazette* dated 14 August 1862.

120. The *Times of India* dated 22 August 1862.

121. '[T]welve gold ornaments for the waist, and a pair of diamond earrings' went missing, and he was responsible. See *The Homeward Mail* dated 11 October 1864.

122. Reportedly, this sequence of events was confirmed by two accomplices turned approvers. See ibid.

123. Letter dated 25 August 1863 from the Resident to the chief secretary in Madras, Pol. Dep., File No. G.O. 287, dated 24 September 1863, NAI.

124. Aiya, *Travancore State Manual*, Vol. 1, p. 624. It was also under Rao that the famous outlaw Kayamkulam Kochunni was apprehended. Rama Rao's daughter would also marry Madhava Rao's son, T. Ananda Rao.

125. Letter dated 7 February 1872 from the Resident to the chief secretary in Pros. Madras, Pol. Dep., File No. 106 (2), NAI. At that time, he did not gain the office, but years later, between 1887 and 1892, he finally did obtain the Dewan's seat. See Aiya, *Travancore State Manual*, Vol. 1, pp. 623–28. The maharajah who gave him the Dewanship, judging by his words in a speech in 1888, liked him too. See *The Madras Weekly Mail* dated 14 March 1888.

126. S. Ramanatha Aiyar, *Diwan T. Rama Row* (Trivandrum: Anantha Rama Varma Press, 1926), p. 15. Aiyar was also the author of *A Brief Sketch of Travancore: The Model State of India – The Country, Its People and Its Progress Under the Maharajah* (Trevandrum: Western Star Press, 1903).

127. Madhava Rao quoted in Aiyar, *Diwan T. Rama Row*, p. 18.

128. Visakham Tirunal quoted in ibid., pp. 20–21.

129. *The Bombay Gazette Overland Summary* dated 27 August 1862. The date of the crime we find in Aiyar's biography of Rao is 22 Edavom 1037 of the Malayalam calendar.

130. Ibid.

131. *The Friend of India* dated 28 August 1862.

132. *The Friend of India* dated 1 September 1864. The sentencing itself two years before made it even to rather obscure papers in Britain. See the *Rochdale Observer* dated 27 September 1862.

133. See the summary in *The Bombay Gazette* dated 28 December 1864.

134. See *The Homeward Mail* dated 17 October 1864. Besides Norton, the other legal mind was J.D. Mayne, who also himself later became advocate-general of Madras. See also *The Bombay Gazette* dated 28 December 1864, which states that the case was being 'reopened'.

135. Aiyar, *Diwan T. Rama Row*, p. 22. See also p. 37 where we read Visakham Tirunal's desire to float away on a 'celestial balloon' with Rao to an 'island in the Pacific ocean' where they could rule as maharajah and Dewan. He was obviously referring also to Ayilyam Tirunal not giving Rao his due.

136. *The Friend of India* dated 28 August 1862.

137. A report in *The Friend of India* dated 1 September 1864 certainly suggests there were voices urging the maharajah to pardon the ranis' father.

138. The name of the father was Tiruvonam Nal Ravi Varma Koil Tampuran of the Pallom family. His wife was Mahaprabha Tampuratti of Mavelikara. We know it was this couple embroiled in the affair because every report constantly referred to the man as the father of the Travancore ranis adopted in 1857–58. That the ranis' father was indeed a Ravi Varma of Pallom is also affirmed by Ulloor S. Parameswara Iyer in his *Kerala Sahitya Charithram*, Vol. 4 (Trivandrum: University of Travancore, 1957), p. 433.

139. N.P. Unni, *A History of Mushika Vamsa* (Trivandrum: Kerala Historical Society, 1980), pp. 18–19, 24.

140. Letter dated 24 March 1818 from the British Resident to the chief secretary in Madras in IOR/R/1/1/1532 (2).

141. Ibid.

142. B.S. Ward, *Memoir of the Survey of Travancore and Cochin: 1816–1820* (Madras: Government of Madras, 1891), p. 47.

143. Reference is to Uttrittadhi Tirunal Gowri Parvathi Bayi, aunt to Swathi Tirunal and Uthram Tirunal.

144. Her full name was Pururuttathi Nal Mahaprabha Tampuratti.

145. Indira Varma, 'Artist of the People and of the Gods', p. 23, in the *Illustrated Weekly of India*, Vol. 97, No. 22 (1976), pp. 20–27. Interestingly, this is in contrast to the marriage of Ravi Varma's brother, Rajaraja Varma, to a lady known as Janaki Amma. Though she too missed him, and he is said, on his deathbed, to have regretted not taking better care of her, there seems to have been no animosity between them on account of their long separations.

146. Years later, in fact, when their son took up art, relatives would admonish him – no matter how much fame Ravi Varma acquired, his choice of profession was no replacement for a proper education. See Neumayer and Schelberger eds, *The Diary*, p. 68.

147. Rukmini Varma quoted in Pillai, *Ivory Throne*, p. 41.

148. Letter dated 18 December 1899 from the Elayarajah of Travancore to the Resident in IOR/R/2/892/278. On 13 September 1881, Kochupanki and the ranis' brother, Kerala Varma, also died aged thirty-seven. It was, according to a notice in *The Englishman's Overland Mail* of 26 September 1881, brought on by 'inflammation of the liver'. Augusta Blandford separately in 1882 noted the man's 'intemperance'. See Blandford, *India's Women*, Vol. 2, pp. 33–34.

149. R. Kulathu Iyer, *Her Highness Sethu Lakshmi Bayi, Senior Ranee of Travancore: A Short Life Sketch* (Madras: Methodist Publishing House, 1916), p. 2.

150. G. Arunima also notes a third portrait by Ravi Varma of his relatives featuring a grandmother and granddaughter; where the former has the confident, dominant gaze, the latter is gentler and calmer. See Arunima, 'Face Value: Ravi Varma's Portraiture and the Project of Colonial Modernity', in *The Indian Economic and Social History Review*, Vol. 40, No. 1 (2003), pp. 57–79. See also Niharika Dinkar, 'Private Lives and Interior Spaces: Raja Ravi Varma's Scholar Paintings' in *Art History*, Vol. 37, No. 3 (2014), pp. 510–35. The European influence in this also appears in novels about India authored by Europeans. Richard Garbe's *The Redemption of the Brahman* (1894), while identifying much that was 'wrong' in Hindu culture, casts a female protagonist in a Western frame. Gopa was beautiful with 'nobly chiseled' features, intelligent and not 'overladen with jewels' as was apparently the wont of Indian women. As one scholar notes, Garbe's Indian heroine 'seemed to be more of a Renaissance Venus than an Indian beauty'. See Kaushik Bagchi, 'An Orientalist in the Orient: Richard Garbe's Indian Journey, 1885–1886', p. 313, in *Journal of World History*, Vol. 14, No. 3 (2003), pp. 281–325.

151. Venniyoor, *Raja Ravi Varma*, p. 29. He was evidently talented, but succumbing to a platter of vices, simply disappeared in his thirties: his wife, a lady from Cochin, is said to have spent the rest of her life praying for his return. This was Kanavalli Ammalukutty Amma (aka Lakshmi Amma), and they had a daughter by the name of Meenakshikutty Amma. The daughter married her cousin (Ravi Varma's grandson by his second daughter) and had two sons and a daughter. Author's exchange with Gokul Varma, who is descended from one of the sons. It is interesting, however, that the lady chose a life of self-denial instead of marrying again: perhaps another example of patriarchal ideas of virtue and widowhood affecting matrilineal women.

152. He did, however, marry well. Rama Varma's wife, Gowri Kunjamma, came from

a prominent family in Mavelikara, and her brother, P.G.N. Unnithan, would serve as Dewan of the state. Rama Varma and Gowri Kunjamma's daughter, Manorama, would marry a cousin – another of Ravi Varma's grandchildren – namely, R. Martanda Varma, the baby boy in *There Comes Papa*.

153. The youngest lived quietly in Mavelikara. Officially called Uma Tampuratti, she was known as Kochomana.

154. Her official name was Tiruvathira Nal Bhageerathi Tampuratti.

155. Quoted in Raghunandan, *Turn of the Tide*, pp. 9–10. Sastri also wrote to her husband, Kerala Varma, asking that he put his 'ability and tact' to the 'satisfactory settlement of this national matter'. Ibid., p. 12.

156. Ibid., p. 14.

157. Letter dated 18 December 1899 from the Elayarajah to the Resident in IOR/R/2/892/278.

158. His objections appear to have been public knowledge, considering they are mentioned in a later report in *The Madras Weekly Mail* dated 27 June 1901. The newspaper speculated that the prince's desire to also adopt older girls may have had to do with his own ill health: girls who could have children sooner than later were preferable because he was concerned he may not live to succeed his uncle.

159. Venniyoor, *Raja Ravi Varma*, p. 46.

160. The obituary in the *Times of India* dated 12 October 1900 also refers to the unexpected nature of the death 'from the effects of recent attacks of remittent fever'. He was described as 'universally loved and respected' and a 'polished gentleman, and a generous patron to poor students'.

161. Or as Ravi Varma's brother recorded, 'The immediate cause of death was the passing of an unusual quantity of urine which was followed by prostration and death.' He also added: 'What a pity that not one of the four princes – the sons of the late Junior Rani – lives to rule over Travancore.' See Neumayer and Schelberger eds, *The Diary*, p. 101.

162. Quoted in Raghunandan, *Turn of the Tide*, p. 54. See also the rani's obituaries in *The Madras Weekly Mail* dated 20 June 1901 and 27 June 1901.

163. Quoted in Charles Allen and Sharada Dwivedi, *Lives of the Indian Princes* (London: Century, 1984), p. 113.

164. The episode (and verses recited) appears in *The Madras Weekly Mail* dated 14 February 1907.

165. Quoted in Raghunandan, *Turn of the Tide*, p. 84. See also Pillai, *Ivory Throne*, p. 276.

166. This is attested to in the junior rani's granddaughter's memoirs. See Asvathi Thirunal Gouri Lakshmi Bayi, *History Liberated: The Sree Chithira Saga* (New Delhi: Konark Publishers, 2021), pp. 24, 33–35, 38–39.

167. Unpublished diary of G.T.B. Harvey, Vol. 1, p. 38, AMC. Hereafter 'Harvey's diary'.

168. Pillai, *Ivory Throne*, p. 270. In Harvey's diary, Vol. 2, p. 9, Watts also warns that the rani's husband would appoint a 'figure head Dewan' to 'run the country' himself after Watts resigned.

169. Pillai, *Ivory Throne*, pp. 157, 223.

170. Harvey's diary, Vol. 1, pp. 17–18.

171. Louise Ouwerkerk (Dick Kooiman ed.), *No Elephants for the Maharaja: Social and Political Change in the Princely State of Travancore (1921–1947)* (Delhi: Manohar, 1994), p. 74.

172. Letter dated 19 September 1924 from the Resident to the political secretary, G.O.I., in IOR/R/1/1/1530 (2).

173. Pillai, *Ivory Throne*, pp. 192–95.

174. See Lakshmi Bayi, *History Liberated*, pp. 24, 58.

175. Letter dated 27 October 1929 from the Resident to the political secretary, G.O.I., in IOR/R/2/885/175.

176. Sethu Parvathi Bayi retaliated in her own way: when invitations for birthday celebrations were sent out one year, her brother-in-law was omitted. Pillai, *Ivory Throne*, pp. 282–83.

177. Quoted in ibid., p. 205.

178. See Lakshmi Bayi, *History Liberated*, p. 34, where we read how at the *adima kidathal* ceremony where the infant is presented to the deity, the junior rani would not let even the priest pick up her baby.

179. See Raghunandan, *Turn of the Tide*, p. 78 for example.

180. See Neumayer and Schelberger eds, *The Diary*, p. 160.

181. Ibid., p. 177.

182. Quoted in Pillai, *Ivory Throne*, p. 107.

183. Pillai, *Ivory Throne*, pp. 111–12.

184. See Lakshmi Bayi, *History Liberated*, p. 38.

185. The maharajah also had an incentive in marrying his daughter to his heir's uncle: it offered a degree of security after his time.

186. See the official notification dated 3 June 1929 in File No. 113-H, Pros. Foreign and Pol. Dep., 1929, NAI.

187. See Pillai, *Ivory Throne*, for detailed accounts.

188. The junior rani's granddaughter states there were fears that if the regency continued, 'Travancore would have become totally Christian dominated!' See Lakshmi Bayi, *History Liberated*, p. 85.

189. His full name was Godfrey Thomas Benedict Harvey and he was a Cambridge graduate.

190. Ibid., Vol. 1, p. 6.

191. Ibid., pp. 44–45.

192. Ibid., p. 38.

193. Ibid., Vol. 2, p. 72.

194. Ibid., p. 82.

195. Ibid., p. 41.

196. Ibid., p. 98.

197. Ibid., p. 92.

198. Ibid., p. 98.

199. Ibid., p. 41.

200. Ibid., Vol. 3, p. 3. He was less amused, of course, when he was told off for allowing the ruler to drive in a new car before astrologers had determined an auspicious time for it. See ibid., p. 36.

201. Ibid., Vol. 2, p. 12.

202. Harvey sympathized. At the viceroy's visit, the question arose of whether her consort should receive a higher status at the table. The rani was in a tough spot, because her husband would 'play hell if he is treated as the nonentity he is', while showing any special favour would infuriate everyone else. Ibid., p. 88.

203. Quoted from his diary in Raghunandan, *Turn of the Tide*, pp. 81–82.

204. See Pillai, *Ivory Throne*, pp. 97, 196, and letter dated 22 February 1929 from the Resident to the political secretary, G.O.I., in IOR/R/1/1/1849. In Harvey's diary, Vol. 2, p. 10, we read how, after Kochukunji was expelled from the palace, her son-in-law, 'the poor fish' was 'rejuvenated' and talking 'excitedly to everyone, even to his son and wife'. While he was not yet living again with the junior rani, he hoped to return. As Harvey wrote, 'the joy of the dismissal of his wife's family, to whom he attributes all his misfortunes, seems to have sent him further off his rocker, but he's certainly happier for it'.

205. Pillai, *Ivory Throne*, pp. 284–87.

206. Harvey's diary, Vol. 1, p. 44.

207. Ibid., pp. 86–87.

208. Ibid., pp. 85–86.

209. Lakshmi Bayi, *History Liberated*, pp. 64–65, 68.

210. Harvey's diary, Vol. 1, pp. 3, 8, 12, 35.

211. Ibid., pp. 86–87.

212. Ibid., Vol. 2, p. 8.

213. See the tabular report card in ibid., Vol. 3, pp. 84–87.

214. Ibid.

215. Ibid., pp. 37, 58–59.

216. Ibid., p. 40.

217. Ibid., p. 22.

218. Ibid., Vol. 1, pp. 93–94.

219. Ibid., Vol. 3, p. 21. Harvey was not the only one to note some changes in the maharajah when his mother was away. A lecturer in Trivandrum, who sometimes played tennis with the maharajah, would write how the boy had two sides. With his mother around, she was the force in the room; but 'when Mama is not about' he was able to 'come out of his shell' and become 'quite a different person, a lively little cricket'. Louise Ouwerkerk quoted in Pillai, *Ivory Throne*, p. 326.

220. Lakshmi Bayi, *History Liberated*, p. 78.

221. Harvey's diary, Vol. 3, p. 17.

222. Ibid., Vol. 2, p. 90.

223. Quoted in Pillai, *Ivory Throne*, p. 300.

224. Ouwerkerk, *No Elephants*, p. 74.

225. Quoted in Pillai, *Ivory Throne*, p. 291.

226. Ibid., p. 303. See also viceroy's note on meeting with the junior rani dated 3 August 1927 in IOR/R/2/886/177, Vol. 1. Amusingly, the junior rani's granddaughter spins a conspiratorial narrative that has the regency being extended suddenly in 1930. The black magic incident in 1929 was invented, she suggests, to extend the regency. See Lakshmi Bayi, *History Liberated*, pp. 66, 75–76. This is untrue: the regency was already extended in 1927 and nobody had any incentive to invent a story to discredit the junior rani in 1929.

227. See Pillai, *Ivory Throne*, pp. 330–31.

228. Ibid., pp. 335–36. See also Menon, *Triumph and Tragedy*, pp. 322–23, where C.P. himself is quoted from a letter in which he complains how a later viceroy was unfavourable to him because 'I was supposed to be a favourite of Lord Willingdon'.

229. Pillai, *Ivory Throne*, pp. 336–37.

230. Harvey's diary, Vol. 3, pp. 73–74.

231. Ibid., p. 79.

232. Ibid., p. 73.

233. Ibid., p. 76.

234. Harvey was apoplectic. As he wrote in his diary in frustration, 'Someone must explain why the Boy was taken away from his mother, what he was like before with the wicked uncles, and the witch-grandmother, and the sorcerers, etc., how much had been done for him, in the State, outside the State, in his general happiness, his physique, and his savoir-faire. Someone also must tell him what trouble it's going to make in the State – this total capitulation to the trouble-makers – the blow to the Regent – the let-down of the British Government.' Ibid., p. 75.

235. Quoted in Stern, *The Cat and the Lion*, pp. 82–83.

236. Harvey's diary, Vol. 3, p. 77.

237. Pillai, *Ivory Throne*, p. 340.

238. Ibid., p. 354.

239. Ibid., pp. 348, 388.

240. Copy of letter dated 10 September 1941 from the Financial Secretary to the Accountant-General of Travancore in File No. 17 (20)-P/49, Pros. 1–53, Ministry of States (Pol.), 1949, NAI. For comparison, the heir presumptive of the Mysore maharajah – ruler of a wealthier state – when he came of age in 1937 received an allowance of 36,000 rupees. See Fortnightly Report by the Resident (Mysore) dated 2 July 1937 in File No. 18/6/37-Poll, Home Dep. (Pol.), NAI.

241. In a letter her brother R.K. Varma wrote to States Ministry officials on 4 August 1949 in File No. 17 (20)-P/49, Pros. 1–53, Ministry of States (Pol.), 1949, NAI, he noted how 'glad' his sister felt that their representative, M.K. Vellodi, had called on her. 'This was one of the rare occasions when a person of status from outside the State called on her after the Regency days.'

242. List of present, proposed and revised allowances in 1949 in ibid. When V.P. Menon had this raised to 19,000 for the senior rani's daughters, even though the maharajah's sister still had 3,000 more, Sethu Lakshmi Bayi wrote to him in a letter dated 23 October 1950 with her 'sincere gratitude for the sympathy and understanding' he brought to bear on 'the peculiar conditions prevailing' in the family.

243. In Pillai, *Ivory Throne*, p. 474, I make a mistake in stating that the Resident had foiled the maharajah's attempt to confiscate the rani's estate in Peermade. In reality it was indeed taken over, and it was in 1949 in negotiations with the States Ministry of free India that Sethu Lakshmi Bayi appealed for its return. See note by M.M. Thomas dated 7 July 1949 and Confidential Note appended to R.K. Varma's letter dated 3 June 1949 to M.K. Vellodi in File No. 17 (20)-P/49, Pros. 1–53, Ministry of States (Pol.), 1949, NAI.

244. John Paton Davies, *China Hand: An Autobiography* (Philadelphia: University of Pennsylvania Press, 2012), pp. 82–83.

245. Pillai, *Ivory Throne*, pp. 88, 456.

246. See 'Statement of Cash and Securities as on 30-6-1949' in File No. 17 (20)-P/49, Pros. 1–53, Ministry of States (Pol.), 1949, NAI.

247. Penderel Moon, *Wavell: The Viceroy's Journal* (London: Oxford University Press, 1973), p. 112.

248. Pillai, *Ivory Throne*, p. 453. The minister, in fact, assumed near-royal airs: his sixtieth birthday saw prayers in temples and churches in Travancore, and a three-day holiday. See A. Raghu, *CP: A Short Biography of C.P. Ramaswami Aiyar* (New Delhi: Prestige Books, 1998), p. 34. He also didn't bother much with outward deference to the ruler. The maharajah's brother, for instance, would recollect how C.P. walked in furious once about something, and flung a file at his royal master. 'My brother,' he wrote, 'was a perfect gentleman and instead of reacting, silently ignored and swallowed this affront. But I could not take it' – the junior rani's younger son picked up the file and flung it right back at the Dewan. See Marthanda

Varma (with Uma Maheswari), *Travancore: The Footprints of Destiny: My Life and Times Under the Grace of Lord Padmanabha – As Told to Uma Maheswari* (New Delhi: Konark, 2010), p. 135. See also Menon, *Triumph and Tragedy*, p. 88.

249. Quoted in Pillai, *Ivory Throne*, p. 454.

250. Quoted in ibid., p. 457.

251. Note dated 30 October 1949 by M.K. Vellodi in File No. 17 (20)-P/49, Pros. 1–53, Ministry of States (Pol.), 1949, NAI. Vellodi also noted that the maharajah was 'under the influence of his mother' and that they might try to 'perpetuate the difference in the status and in material advantages' their branch enjoyed over the senior rani. In sending in the proposed list of allowances, the maharajah had 'completely omitted to mention the case of the Senior Maharani'.

252. See Pillai, *Ivory Throne*, pp. 468–70. Even allowing for exaggeration on Mountbatten's part here, C.P. in his own writings while expressing respect for Gandhi's contribution 'in rousing the self-respect of Indians' still asserted that his philosophy was not truly grounded in Hindu civilization and was a mish-mash, and that his 'impractical and unhistorical ideal of non-violence' had actually led to 'discord, disunion and violence'. Quoted in Menon, *Triumph and Tragedy*, p. 324. Meanwhile, Nehru himself wrote in 1936 of how C.P. thought him 'dangerous', a man who had succumbed to 'self-hypnotisation' in getting carried away by his convictions, and as unrepresentative of mass sentiment. Nehru, of course, also paid back in kind by describing C.P. as 'a shining ornament of autocracy in an Indian State', 'a full-blooded apologist of British rule in India', and 'an admirer of dictatorship'. See Jawaharlal Nehru, *An Autobiography* (New Delhi: Jawaharlal Nehru Memorial Fund/Oxford University Press, 1982 edn), p. 596.

253. See Menon, *Triumph and Tragedy*, pp. 249–52, for details.

254. Quoted in ibid., pp. 388–89.

255. Ibid., p. 261.

256. Letter dated 9 May 1950 from the senior maharani to V.P. Menon in File No. 17 (20)-P/49, Pros. 1–53, Ministry of States (Pol.), 1949, NAI.

257. This was upheld by the Supreme Court of India when it became a matter of litigation. The rani had asked V.P. Menon (letter dated 5 March 1951) for a clear statement confirming that her palace be hers alone, since its listing as the maharajah's property was 'likely to lead to misunderstandings and trouble later on'. Menon wrote (10 April 1951) to the maharajah on this account but in his reply (15 April 1951) the latter said: 'I do not see the necessity for giving a formal assurance to Her Highness the Senior Maharani.' Menon (on 1 May 1951) apprised the senior rani of this but assured her that 'Your Highness' rights and those of your children to stay at Satelmond palace so long as you desire will be respected and safeguarded'. In an internal note dated 24 April 1951 we read how the officialdom was sure that the maharajah was not 'likely' to prevent his aunt

from enjoying occupation of the palace, but it was placed on the record that 'in the unlikely event' of this happening, 'we should take a firm attitude' and ensure the senior rani's rights were respected. See the correspondence in File No. 17 (20)-P/49, Pros. 1–53, Ministry of States (Pol.), 1949, NAI.

258. Harvey's diary, Vol. 3, p. 82.

259. For a recent celebration of his life and collection of eulogies by relatives and admirers, see S. Uma Maheswari ed., *Sree Chithira Tirunal: Life and Times* (Thiruvananthapuram: Sri Uthradom Tirunal Marthanda Varma Literary and Charitable Trust, 2015).

6. The King as Bureaucrat

1. Though the durbar occurred in June, a detailed account appears in *The Cork Examiner* dated 7 October 1867, wherefrom these quotes have been extracted. The maharajah gave his speech in Hindustani, which was translated into English.

2. Aya Ikegame, *Princely India Re-imagined: A Historical Anthropology of Mysore from 1799 to the Present* (New York: Routledge, 2013), pp. 80–82. As Ikegame notes, this combination of a pristine Sanskritized identity through the foreign Kshatriya and the local roots of the indigenous princess also answer the 'inconsistency' of the Wadiyars becoming Sri Vaishnavas while continuing to worship a goddess from outside the Sanskritic pale.

3. Caleb Simmons, *Devotional Sovereignty: Kingship and Religion in India* (New Delhi: Oxford University Press, 2020), pp. 6, 113.

4. For a succinct history of this period, see Sanjay Subrahmanyam, 'Warfare and State Finance in Wadiyar Mysore, 1724–25: A Missionary Perspective' in *The Indian Economic and Social History Review*, Vol. 26, No. 2 (1989), pp. 203–33. Interestingly, the throne used by the maharajahs was sent by the Mughal emperor to Chikkadevaraja in Hijri 1126 (1714–15). Or so claimed the future Mysore Commissioner L. Bowring in a letter dated 28 September 1868 to sec., G.O.I., in *Return: East India (Mysore Government) (385)* (London: House of Commons, 1878), p. 21 (hereafter '1878 Papers'). A signet ring is also said to have been sent, while the throne was modified over time so that 'little remains', Bowring wrote, 'of the original structure'.

5. Tipu famously commissioned a magnificent tiger throne for himself, but is said to have never mounted it, claiming he would do so only after defeating the Company for good. After his death, the British dismantled it.

6. Letter dated 3 August 1799 from the governor-general to the Court of Directors in Richard Wellesley (Montgomery Martin ed.), *The Despatches, Minutes, and Correspondence of the Marquess Wellesley During His Administration in India*, Vol. 2 (London: W.H. Allen, 1836), p. 74.

7. Ibid., p. 78.

8. Letter dated 13 May 1799 from Lt General Harris to the governor-general in ibid., p. 7.

9. Letter dated 3 August 1799 from the governor-general to the Court of Directors in Wellesley, *Despatches*, p. 81.

10. As we saw with Sayaji Rao in Baroda, the adoption of this ruler, Khasa Chamaraja Wadiyar (r. 1776–96) has its own interesting stories supposed to communicate the innate worth of the chosen prince. One tells that when the old Wadiyar died, Hyder collected all the eligible male children and sent them into a hall 'strewed with fruits, sweetmeats and toys, telling them to help themselves'. While all the other children went 'scrambling', one of them 'took up a dagger in one hand and a lime in the other'. 'That is the Raja', Hyder declared, for 'his first care is military protection, his second to realise the produce of his dominions.' So it was that Krishnaraja III's father was installed. See Lewis Rice, *Mysore and Coorg: A Gazetteer Compiled for the Government of India*, Vol. 1 (Bangalore: Mysore Government Press, 1877), pp. 267–68.

11. Or as the governor-general wrote, 'The establishment of an Hindoo State in Mysore, with the restoration of the temples and endowments of that religion, must be grateful to the [Maratha] Government of Poonah, independently of the advantages arising from the substitution of a power of the same religion, and of pacific views, in the place of an odious Mahommedan usurpation, scarcely less hostile to the Mahratta than to the British nation.' See letter dated 3 August 1799 from the governor-general to the Court of Directors in Richard Wellesley, *Despatches*, p. 99. This view would catch on in historiography, down to this day, though as Simmons shows, Tipu Sultan had often projected himself as a protector of dharma, supporting temples, having Hindu ceremonies performed for himself, etc. See Simmons, *Devotional Sovereignty*, pp. 68–76.

12. This is not to say he was disloyal to his previous masters: as we saw, he had advocated for Tipu's son to be put on the throne, besides which, years before when Hyder died, it was Purniah who kept the news from breaking out, giving Tipu time to arrive and take control. See Rice, *Gazetteer*, p. 276.

13. M. Wilks, *Report on the Interior Administration, Resources, and Expenditure of the Government of Mysore Under the System Prescribed by the Orders of the Governor General in Council Dated 4th September 1799* (Bangalore: Mysore Government Press, 1864 edn), p. 25, in *Selections from the Records of the Mysore Commissioner's Office* (Bangalore: Mysore Government Press, 1864). People, of course, could still be racist. Arthur Wellesley, brother of the governor-general, warned not to include him in 1799 in finalizing the future of Mysore, 'until the whole [plan] is ready for execution' because 'if one black man ever hears of your plan, it may well be published in the bazaar'. See *Supplementary Despatches and Memoranda of*

Field Marshal Arthur Duke of Wellington: India 1797–1805, Vol. 1 (London: John Murray, 1858), p. 228.

14. See *Supplementary Despatches*, p. 90.

15. See ibid., pp. 410–11.

16. Charles Irving Smith, *Statistical Report on the Mysore* (Edinburgh: Robert Hardie and Co., 1854), p. 3.

17. See Sebastian Joseph, 'A Service Elite Against the Peasants: Encounter and Collision (Mysore 1799–1831)' in *Proceedings of the Indian History Congress*, Vol. 41 (1980), pp. 670–81, for more on this.

18. T. Hawker, W. Morison, J.M. Macleod, and M. Cubbon, *Report on the Insurrection in Mysore (December 1833)* (Bangalore: Mysore Government Press, 1858), p. 6 (hereafter *Insurrection Report*), and Anonymous ('A Native of Mysore'), *The British Administration of Mysore, Part 1* (London: Longmans, Green and Co., 1874), p. 2.

19. *Insurrection Report*, p. 6.

20. Ibid.

21. See Nigel Hugh Mosman Chancellor, 'Mysore: The Making and Unmaking of a Model State, c. 1799–1834', unpublished PhD thesis (2002), University of Cambridge, pp. 92–93, 96, 98–99, 142, 187, for more on this. Purniah was not only paid handsomely, including receiving 1 per cent of revenues as a bonus each year, but also, when asked to involve the ruler in government, dismissed the latter as a 'foolish child'. His power and confidence, despite humble beginnings, was such that in open court too he insulted the ruler. In 1811, his son and brother-in-law were caught trying to make off with valuables from the state treasury, and eventually the Resident concluded that 'old age and imbecility' had caused the once-respected Dewan to cling to power, and that he maintained a 'a systematic violence to his Prince' and 'determined opposition to his authority'. Even so, of course, the Dewan remained popular – an oil painting of his by Thomas Hickey used to hang in the Residency: a reminder, perhaps, of his true loyalties.

22. See Sanjay Subrahmanyam, 'A Note on Some Early Nineteenth Century Inam Records in the Karnataka State Archives', p. 441, in *The Indian Economic and Social History Review*, Vol. 28, No. 4 (1991), pp. 435–43.

23. Rice, *Gazetteer*, pp. 297–98. Interestingly, Purniah had kept this treasure a secret till 1809, when a mutiny by white Company officers stationed in Srirangapattana forced him to reveal its existence. See Chancellor, 'Mysore', p. 70.

24. 'Indicus' (Evans Bell), *The Rajah and Principality of Mysore with a Letter to the Right Hon. Lord Stanley, MP* (London: Thomas Richards, 1865), p. 15. Scholars call this process 'military fiscalism', that is, a tax system that delivered enough for the state's expansionist wars to be financed.

25. See Burton Stein, 'State Formation and Economy Reconsidered: Part One', in *Modern Asian Studies*, Vol. 19, No. 3 (1985), pp. 387–413, for a detailed essay on this.

26. Quoted in *Insurrection Report*, p. 5.

27. Ibid.

28. Chancellor, 'Mysore', p. 165. See also p. 124 where we read that as late as 1834, thirty-seven relatives of Purniah were still in the administrative system, and p. 235 for how in 1823, Purniah's nephew was put forth by the Resident as a candidate for the Dewanship.

29. Francis Buchanan travelling in Mysore in 1800 found that even in a temple town like Melkote, where the Wadiyars had, in earlier times, been great benefactors, loyalty was at a low. The Brahmins there seemed 'not at all interested about their young Raja', he wrote, because his 'family has been so long in obscurity, that it is no longer looked up to with awe'. See Buchanan, *A Journey from Madras Through the Countries of Mysore, Canara, and Malabar*, Vol. 2 (London: T. Cadell, W. Davies, Black, Parry and Kingsbury, 1807), pp. 72–73.

30. Janaki Nair, *Mysore Modern: Rethinking the Region Under Princely Rule* (Minneapolis: University of Minnesota Press, 2011), p. 6.

31. *Insurrection Report*, pp. 6–7.

32. Chancellor, 'Mysore', pp. 143, 190.

33. Ibid., p. 47. See also p. 189 where we find the Resident complaining of his inability to influence the king.

34. Resident's 1813 report quoted in *Insurrection Report*, pp. 7–8.

35. Mark Cubbon, *Report on the Civil and Criminal Judicature in Mysore, 26th April 1838* (Bangalore: Mysore Government Press, 1858), p. 8.

36. *Insurrection Report*, pp. 9–10.

37. Ibid., p. 11.

38. Quoted in ibid., p. 13.

39. This became a particularly dominant line of imperial thinking in the 1820s. The most powerful Marathi Brahmin, Rama Rao, who also controlled the Mysore Silahdar cavalry corps, was accused of fraud during the corps' involvement in the 1817–18 Anglo-Maratha War. He was guilty, but during the inquiry between 1822 and 1827 diverted attention to the maharajah's supposed inadequacies and weaknesses. Besides, the governor of Madras also believed that the buck for Rama Rao's crimes stopped at the royal door – by failing to rein him in, the ruler proved that his hold over Mysore was weak. See Chancellor, 'Mysore', pp. 207–50, for details of this episode. The Resident's complicity is not to be played down either: in 1825, by which time the maharajah officially complained against him and the Resident's stock was falling even on the British side, the man tried to argue that

Krishnaraja had conspired with the Marathas against the Company in 1817–18. See ibid., p. 245. It did not work, and when in the same year the governor visited the state, he publicly rebuked the Resident by refusing to stay with him. Interestingly, while this Resident, Arthur Cole, did much damage in Mysore, on his return to Britain he became a parliamentarian.

40. Quoted in Rice, *Gazetteer*, p. 299.

41. Janaki Nair, *Mysore Modern*, p. 133. It was found, years later, that nearly a fifth of Mysore city's population, at 10,000 souls, were palace dependants. An inquiry later found that even what was spent by the maharajah on luxuries was paid to foreign merchants who took the money out of the state, with the result that it did not boost local networks of production. See *Insurrection Report*, p. 64.

42. Subrahmanyam, 'A Note', p. 439. It also did not help when British inquiries found that Purniah too had been spending a lot more than he admitted in his reports. See ibid., p. 438.

43. Rice, *Gazetteer*, p. 298.

44. Munro quoted in G.R. Gleig, *The Life of Major-General Sir Thomas Munro: Late Governor of Madras with Extracts from His Correspondence and Private Papers*, Vol. 2 (London: Henry Colburn and Richard Bentley, 1831), p. 8. The man was making a larger point of how British support to Indian princes tended to make the latter despotic, as they had no fear of their subjects and of pressures from below, protected as they were by Company arms.

45. Quoted in Kyrre Magnus Lind, 'The Nagar Rebellion 1830–31: Administration and Rule in an Indian Native State', unpublished dissertation, University of Oslo (2004), p. 26.

46. Letter dated 23 January 1868 from the Mysore commissioner to the secretary, Foreign Dep., in 1878 Papers, p. 21.

47. In fact, besides district headships (Foujdaris) sold at 10,000 rupees, even small posts worth 100 rupees were sold by the maharajah. See Joseph, 'A Service', p. 675.

48. Quoted in Magnus Lind, 'Nagar Rebellion', p. 32. Something similar happened in Bastar a few decades later, with matching results. See Sundar, *Subalterns and Sovereigns*, pp. 96–97.

49. Ibid., pp. 41, 78.

50. Quoted in *Insurrection Report*, p. 71. Thus, all 125 talukas in the state were under Brahmin officials. See Chancellor, 'Mysore', p. 261.

51. Decades before, in fact, the risk of exactly this happening was noted by Company official Mark Wilks when he wrote how 'The exercise of power by the Native Officers of the Government, doubtlessly requires the most vigilant control. The Subadars of the Provinces, though men of respectability, may not always watch the civil rights of the people with sufficient jealousy.' See Wilks, *Report*, p. 24.

52. Janaki Nair, *Mysore Modern*, p. 6.

53. On the political history of Virasaivism and the rise of the modern Lingayat collective identity, see Prithvi Datta Chandra Shobhi, 'Pre-Modern Communities and Modern Histories: Narrating Virasaiva and Lingayat Selves', PhD thesis, University of Chicago (2005). The Wadiyars, once themselves Saivites, had recognized the power of this community. Krishnaraja, thus, accorded the same privileges and honours the Brahmins of Sringeri received to the chief Lingayat gurus in Mysore. See Chancellor, 'Mysore', pp. 177–78.

54. Brahmins were 7 per cent of the population in Nagara but only a third of this were locals; the rest were Marathi Brahmins. See Burton Stein, 'Notes on "Peasant Insurgency" in Colonial Mysore: Event and Process', p. 17, in *South Asia Research*, Vol. 5, No. 1 (1985), pp. 11–27. See also *Insurrection Report*, p. 71, and H. Stokes, *Report on the Nugur Division of Mysore* in *Selections from the Records of the Mysore Commissioner's Office*, pp. 3, 13 (for a breakdown of castes), 27 (on the Lingayat–Brahmin feud). See also Janaki Nair, 'Modernity and "Publicness": The Career of the Mysore Matha, 1880–1940', p. 7, in *The Indian Economic and Social History Review*, Vol. 57, No. 1 (2020), pp. 5–29, for an instance of conflict between the Sringeri Matha and a Lingayat guru in 1836 over the use of certain honours and privileges.

55. This included being granted ritual honours and privileges. In Purniah's day itself, Rama Rao had received a generous pension, while Krishnaraja gave him the right to ride in a howdah atop an elephant, of his portrait being placed in the palace and so on. See Chancellor, 'Mysore', p. 169.

56. For instance, one of his acolytes, Gopal Rao, in Chinnagery told the peasants not to return to their lands even if the maharajah ordered them. Magnus Lind, 'Nagar Rebellion', p. 44. Rao's man had remitted lakhs of rupees in revenue, which decision the new man tried to overturn, not only for giving the state its dues but because Rao had apparently secretly been taking bribes for granting the remissions. See also *Insurrection Report*, pp. 15–22.

57. Ibid., p. 23. As a group of peasants would tell the Resident in 1831: 'The petitioners state, that when Tippoo Sultan was sovereign of the country, they all lived in peace and prosperity . . . That the oppressions and cruelties unceasingly practised by the officers of [the maharajah's] government were such that they had become unable to endure them any longer.' They had decided to leave the district and settle elsewhere 'when the Killade Padshah of Nugur, the descendant of Sevappah Naik, having heard of it, collected a body of troops, and placed garrisons in the different towns and forts . . .' asked them to stay. Ibid., p. 56. See also Chancellor, 'Mysore', pp. 307–308, where we find that Rama Rao's people helped this would-be ruler of Keladi, sponsoring his wedding and an enthronement of sorts.

58. *Insurrection Report*, pp. 52–53. Reference is to the Kandachar peons who were akin to local police.

59. Letter dated 11 October 1833 from Major J.P. James to Maj. General Hawker, in C.H. Philips ed., *The Correspondence of Lord William Cavendish Bentinck: Governor General of India, 1828–1835*, Vol. 2 (Oxford: Oxford University Press, 1977), pp. 1123–24 (hereafter 'Bentinck Correspondence').

60. For instance, the famous Lingayat Murugha Matha supplied the rebels with grain and resources, and the institution was attacked by royal forces as a result. See Chancellor, 'Mysore', p. 326.

61. Stein, 'Notes on "Peasant Insurgency"', p. 18.

62. *Insurrection Report*, p. 50.

63. Ibid., p. 58.

64. Ibid., pp. 33–34.

65. Chancellor, 'Mysore', p. 316.

66. Wilks, *Report*, p. 24.

67. *Insurrection Report*, pp. 62, 69.

68. Letter dated 7 September 1831 from the governor-general to the maharajah in Evans Bell, *The Mysore Reversion, 'An Exceptional Case'* (London: Trubner and Co., 1866), pp. 278–82.

69. *Insurrection Report*, pp. 62–64.

70. Quoted in M. Shama Rao, *Modern Mysore: From the Beginning to 1868* (Vol. 1) (Bangalore: Higginbothams, 1936), p. 586.

71. Janaki Nair, *Mysore Modern*, p. 10. However, for Indian eyes, a local idiom, as Simmons argues, did matter and also remained in play.

72. John Rosselli, *Lord William Bentinck: The Making of a Liberal Imperialist, 1744–1839* (Delhi: Thomson Press, 1974), p. 229.

73. Letter dated 3 January 1832 from the Resident to the governor-general in Bentinck Correspondence, p. 747. Incidentally, the Madras authorities were happy to restore Mysore into the hands of a nominee of theirs as Dewan, controlled by the Resident. But Bentinck did not like this two-faced policy, and preferred transparent control to a facade of native rule. For more on the Madras governor Stephen Lushington's personal interest in bringing Mysore under British control, see Chancellor, 'Mysore', p. 300.

74. Indeed, Lord Wellesley had written in 1799 then: 'I resolved to reserve to the Company the most extensive and indisputable powers of interposition in the internal affairs of Mysore, as well as an unlimited right of assuming the direct management of the country (whenever such a step might appear necessary for the security of the funds designed to the subsidy), and of requiring extraordinary aid beyond the amount of the fixed subsidy, either in time of war, or of preparations for hostility.'

75. Letter dated 4 October 1832 from the Resident to the governor-general in Bentinck Correspondence, pp. 904–908.

76. This argument was repeated by the governor of Madras in a minute dated 27 September 1831 where he wrote: 'Our departure from the spirit and intentions of the original treaty, and not wholly the personal defects of the Rajah himself, are responsible for the vices prevailing in Mysore.' Quoted in K.N. Venkatasubba Sastri, *The Administration of Mysore Under Sir Mark Cubbon (1834–1861)* (London: George Allen and Unwin, 1932), p. 21.

77. 'Indicus', *The Rajah*, p. 23. See also Chancellor, 'Mysore', p. 338.

78. Bentinck's despatch dated 14 April 1834 quoted in Bell, *Mysore Reversion*, p. 22.

79. Ibid.

80. Letter dated 17 July 1863 from the secretary of state to the viceroy in *Parliamentary Papers, Accounts and Papers, East India: Session* (1 February–10 August 1866), Vol. 52, pp. 15–16 (hereafter 'Mysore Papers'). See also Rao, *Modern Mysore*, p. 457.

81. Letter dated 12 January 1833 from Company secretary Peter Auber to the governor-general in Bentinck Correspondence, pp. 992–93.

82. Rice, *Gazetteer*, p. 304.

83. Ibid.

84. 'Indicus', *The Rajah*, p. 20.

85. Bell, *Mysore Reversion*, p. 30. There were fifty-seven Europeans heading the most important departments, with seventeen native assistants in the 1860s. See letter dated 23 January 1868 from the Mysore commissioner to the secretary, Foreign Dep., G.O.I., in 1878 Papers, p. 29.

86. Ibid.

87. Nair, *Mysore Modern*, p. 10. Cubbon's administration's limitations would also be admitted by his successor as commissioner in the 1860s. See letter dated 23 January 1868 from the Mysore commissioner to the secretary, Foreign Dep., G.O.I., in 1878 Papers, pp. 21–29.

88. Incidentally, one of his assistants was Venkata Rao, uncle to the famous Madhava Rao. See Sastri, *Administration of Mysore*, p. 203.

89. Simmons, *Devotional Sovereignty*, p. 108.

90. The stipend was three and a half lakh rupees, while his share of revenue in 1865–66 came to over ten lakh rupees. See 1878 Papers, p. 7.

91. Simmons, *Devotional Sovereignty*, pp. 138–40.

92. Ibid., p. 143.

93. Ibid., p. 144.

94. For a study of painting in his reign, see Robert J. Del Bonta, 'See Krsna Run: Narrative Painting for Mummadi Krsnaraja Wadiyar' in *Ars Orientalis*, Vol. 30, Supplementary 1 (Chachaji: Professor Walter M. Spink Felicitation Volume, 2000), pp. 99–113.

95. Simmons, *Devotional Sovereignty*, p. 170.

96. Caleb Simmons, 'The King and the Yadu Line: Performing Lineage through Dasara in Nineteenth-Century Mysore', p. 69, in Caleb Simmons, Moumita Sen and Hillary Rodrigues eds, *Nine Nights of the Goddess: The Navaratri Festival in South Asia* (Albany: State University of New York Press, 2018), pp. 63–82.

97. Nair, *Mysore Modern*, p. 86.

98. Unsurprisingly, even Krishnaraja's successor early on informed the British that maintaining Hyder's and Tipu's mausoleums was 'a point of honour'. See letter dated 17 December 1880 from the commissioner's secretary to the secretary, Foreign Dep., G.O.I., in *Further Papers Relating to the Transfer of the Province of Mysore to Native Rule* (Presented to both Houses of Parliament by Command of Her Majesty) (London: Her Majesty's Stationery Office, 1881) (hereafter 1881 Papers), p. 187.

99. For more on the Rangamahal murals, see Simmons, 'The King and the Yadu Line'.

100. As his supporter Evans Bell wrote in general about Indians: 'The working of British institutions is much more clearly understood and appreciated now-a-days in India, than was the case twenty years ago. Newspapers and Blue-books are not only read by natives of English education, but are also transmitted and translated to the dependent Sovereigns . . . The names of our leading Statesmen and their avowed or supposed views on Indian subjects, are known and canvassed in the Durbar and the closet of every Native Prince.' See 'Indicus', *The Rajah*, pp. 4–5.

101. Quoted in Bell, *Mysore Reversion*, p. 36.

102. Quoted in ibid., p. 32.

103. Quoted in ibid.

104. Quoted in ibid., p. 33.

105. Quoted in ibid., p. 36.

106. 'Indicus', *The Rajah*, p. 27, and John P. Willoughby's dissent dated 18 August 1863 in Mysore Papers.

107. Willoughby's dissent note, ibid.

108. Quoted in ibid.

109. Quoted in Bell, *Mysore Reversion*, p. 41. See also Willoughby's dissent, p. 31.

110. See ibid.

111. Letter dated 23 February 1861 from the maharajah to the viceroy, Mysore Papers, pp. 1–3.

112. Letter dated 11 March 1862 from the viceroy to the maharajah, Mysore Papers, pp. 4–7.

113. See Dadabhoy, *Magnificent Diwan*, p. 142. Sir Salar Jung of Hyderabad wished to use the state's claim over Mysore as a negotiatory carrot to obtain the territory of Berar, which the Company had taken from the nizam.

114. Letter dated 20 April 1862 from the maharajah to the viceroy, Mysore Papers,

pp. 8–12. The maharajah had two illegitimate sons, Nanjaraja and Chamaraja, both of whom were dead by now. Talk of heirs here was in the context of adoption. He also had four illegitimate grandsons, of whom Deva Parthiva, son of Nanjaraja, was a favourite. The other three – sons of the aforementioned Chamaraja – were Nanjaraja, Deoraja and Chamaraja.

115. Letter dated 17 July 1863 from the secretary of state to the viceroy in ibid., pp. 13–18.

116. Henry Montgomery's dissent dated 13 July 1863 in ibid., pp. 18–22.

117. Frederick Currie's dissent dated 17 July 1863 in ibid., pp. 22–25.

118. This second part ('lying in wait') are Canning's words quoted by the member. Another noteworthy point made by this member was that 'particularly the higher classes' preferred native rule – an important detail, for even in retirement Krishnaraja's largesse had benefited chiefly these higher classes and elites.

119. John P. Willoughby's dissent dated 18 August 1863 in Mysore Papers, pp. 25–34.

120. 'Indicus', The Rajah, p. 28.

121. Bell, Mysore Reversion, p. x.

122. Taylor, English Maharani, p. 110.

123. Letter dated 29 March 1864 from the secretary, Foreign Dep., G.O.I., to the Mysore commissioner in Mysore Papers, pp. 39–42.

124. Frederick Currie's dissent dated 9 August 1864 in Mysore Papers, pp. 45–47.

125. Letter dated 18 June 1865 from the maharajah to the viceroy in ibid., pp. 91–92.

126. The Friend of India dated 19 February 1863.

127. The Homeward Mail dated 23 August 1865.

128. The Daily News dated 8 August 1866 in Mysore Papers, pp. 14–15.

129. The Pall Mall Gazette dated 26 September 1866.

130. The Homeward Mail dated 23 April 1866.

131. See the petition in Opinions of the Press on the Annexation of Mysore (London: John Camden Hotten, 1866), pp. 1–13.

132. See the debate on 22 February 1867 at https://hansard.parliament.uk/Commons/1867-02-22/debates/ae0ebea5-18df-4d3e-a839-2777f6595211/India%E2%80%94TheMaharajahOfMysore

133. Quoted in Andrew Land, Life, Letters and Diaries of Sir Stafford Northcote, First Earl of Iddesleigh (Edinburgh and London: William Blackwood and Sons, 1891), pp. 188–89. The secretary of state who made the February 1867 announcement in parliament was Lord Cranborne, replaced a few months later by Northcote. Cranborne had stated that the partition treaty was restricted to the life of the maharajah, and his decision not to annex despite this was a political choice; Northcote, however, as quoted, believed the partition and Mysore's statehood to be permanent, with only the subsidiary treaty with Krishnaraja being temporary.

134. Ibid.

135. Ibid., p. 189.

136. See letter dated 16 April 1867 from the secretary of state to the viceroy in 1878 Papers, p. 46, which simply states that the family was to be allowed to keep Mysore mainly due to the queen's desire to let native states continue, '[w]ithout entering upon any minute examination' of the treaties as the source of the retention.

137. Vishwanath Narayan Mandlik, *Adoption Versus Annexation: With Remarks on the Mysore Question* (London: Smith, Elder and Co., 1866), p. 7.

138. In the commissioner's report the day after the maharajah passed away, we read that he suffered from 'a repeated and violent vomiting and purging' which weakened him greatly. See letter dated 28 March 1868 from the commissioner to the secretary, Foreign Dep., G.O.I., in 1878 Papers, pp. 37–38. The proclamation the commissioner put out immediately recognized his son as the new maharajah. See ibid., pp. 38–39.

139. Wheeler, *India in 1875–76*, p. 43.

140. Mrs Bowring quoted in M. Shama Rao, *Modern Mysore: From the Coronation of Chamaraja Wadiyar X in 1868 to the Present Time* (Vol. 2) (Bangalore: Higginbothams, 1936), p. 7.

141. Quoted in letter dated 15 September 1879 from the maharajah's tutor to the commissioner in 1881 Papers, p. 126.

142. Ibid., p. 125.

143. Ibid. See also Rao, *Modern Mysore*, Vol. 2, p. 31.

144. Letter dated 2 July 1868 from the officiating commissioner to the foreign secretary in 1878 Papers, p. 16.

145. Letter dated 12 December 1868 from the foreign secretary to the commissioner in ibid., p. 82.

146. Letter dated 5 September 1868 from the commissioner to the foreign secretary in ibid., p. 57.

147. Letter dated 23 January 1868 from the commissioner to the foreign secretary in ibid., p. 21.

148. Letter dated 22 May 1879 from the Foreign Dep. to the secretary of state in 1881 Papers, p. 9.

149. Incidentally, his son would later be Dewan of Mysore. T. Ananda Rao, who was in office between 1909 and 1912, was, however, criticized for being lacklustre. Towards the end of his term, *The Madras Standard* dated 29 October 1912 described his administration as a 'weak and aimless one beginning to end'. On the question of a constitution, besides Rao, Ranade was also quite happy with the idea of a constitution even if imposed by the Raj. See his *Select Writings*, p. 340.

150. Letter dated 22 May 1879 from the Foreign Dep. to the secretary of state in 1881 Papers, p. 13.

151. Letter dated 9 November 1878 from the foreign secretary to the commissioner

in ibid., p. 88. And it did: in the 1890s, for example, Cambay State was made to adopt certain principles on the Mysore model. See Tupper, *Indian Political Practice*, Vol. 1, p. 71.

152. Commissioner's minute dated 10 February 1879 in 1881 Papers, p. 93.

153. Letter dated 7 August 1879 from the secretary of state to the viceroy in ibid., p. 107.

154. Letter dated 12 August 1880 from the secretary of state to the viceroy in 1881 Papers, p. 138.

155. Instrument of Transfer appended to letter dated 24 January 1881 from the foreign secretary to the commissioner in ibid., pp. 193–95.

156. Letter dated 3 March 1880 from the Foreign Dep. to the secretary of state in ibid., p. 132.

157. Chiefly because under Company rule, spending to 'improve' the territory was not much of a factor.

158. Rao, *Modern Mysore*, Vol. 2, pp. 24, 28, 134.

159. Letter dated 3 March 1880 from the Foreign Dep. to the secretary of state in ibid., p. 128. Due to the famine, this higher rate was deferred for a time – first for five years till 1886, and then again for ten years till 1896 – but the number itself was not open to revision for a long time.

160. Nair, *Mysore Modern*, p. 93.

161. For instance, while adoption was routine in India, the British emphasis on biological succession, and Dalhousie's annexations wherever this was lacking, puzzled Krishnaraja. So, at the time when he began negotiations for adopting an heir himself, he also produced a literary work highlighting *non-biological* succession in Mysore as not only the norm, but also as positively ordained by god. A story about a curse on the Wadiyars was for the first time formally brought to the centre of the royal tradition: it was this, a power even greater than the British, that prevented biological continuity and required Mysore's kings to periodically adopt. See Simmons, *Devotional Sovereignty*, pp. 115–20.

162. After all, the proclamation even recognizing the adoption made it clear that Chamarajendra would only be allowed to rule if at eighteen he was 'found qualified'. See Rice, *Gazetteer*, p. 307.

163. Ikegame, *Princely India Re-imagined*, p. 10.

164. Janaki Nair, 'Mysore's Wembley? The Dasara Exhibition's Imagined Economies', p. 1550, in *Modern Asian Studies*, Vol. 5, No. 47 (2013), pp. 1549–87.

165. As Nair tells, Mysore went from being the 'realm of a ruling dynasty' to a territorial unit of which royalty 'was only a symbol'. Nair, *Mysore Modern*, p. 11.

166. Ikegame, *Princely India Re-imagined*, pp. 28, 59, 101.

167. Ibid., p. 59. This was no overstatement. In 1804 when visiting the boy Krishnaraja

III, an Englishman found that while he seemed a 'lively' and 'intelligent' child, so solemn was he expected to be that it 'would have been indecorous' to smile. When he did once, he was 'immediately checked by a person who stood by him'. Quoted in Geoffrey C. Ward, *The Maharajas* (Illinois: Stonehenge Press, 1983) p. 81.

168. Ikegame, *Princely India Re-imagined*, p. 153.

169. This was unlike in the Ramnad zamindari, for example, where the same festival also saw English presence, but at 'no point in the ritual' was the impression allowed that the rajah's power was 'derived from the imperial system'. It was the deity who was the source of legitimacy, and the British were only 'guests'. See Breckenridge, 'From Protector', p. 87.

170. Nair, *Mysore Modern*, pp. 134–35, and Rao, *Modern Mysore*, Vol. 2, p. 123. See also Nair, 'Mysore's Wembley', p. 1552. This extended even to religious institutions: by 1917 the head of the Muzrai Department which superintended temples and religious establishments urged the government to include this too under 'Progressive Departments' since it aimed at 'advance' in social practices. See Nair, 'Modernity and Publicness', pp. 10–11.

171. *The Pioneer* dated 7 December 1885, which adds that the pictures were to be exhibited in London. The story goes that the painter had done a royal secretary's portrait, which so impressed the maharajah that he invited him to the palace. See Joseph, 'Great Indian Artist', p. 908.

172. Or as one commentator put it later, 'The Maharaja . . . had been taught not to imitate the conduct which had necessitated [his predecessor's] deposition. And he showed that the lesson had not been wasted.' See G.F. Abbott, *Through India with the Prince* (London: Edward Arnold, 1906), p. 249.

173. Without 'abating one jot of his dignity, without, in the smallest degree, denationalizing himself, and without forfeiting one atom of the reverence and regard of his people', the maharajah behaved 'almost as if he were one of ourselves'. Quoted in *The Bangalore Spectator* dated 6 October 1887.

174. Rao, *Modern Mysore*, Vol. 2, p. 200.

175. This was something abhorrent to Krishnaraja's contemporaries like Evans Bell who wrote: 'There cannot be a greater mistake than to set up that invidious comparison, which is so often made, between a British Commissioner and a Hindoo Sovereign.' See 'Indicus', *The Rajah*, p. 49.

176. Lord Sankey quoted in Mankekar, *Accession to Extinction*, p. 33.

177. See *Memoranda on the Indian States: 1932* (Calcutta: Government of India, 1933), pp. 92–95. Rao, *Modern Mysore*, Vol. 2, p. i, also quips that if the old British commissioners 'came back to life' they would 'find the Mysore Administration developed more largely on the British model' they established.

178. See the Dewan's speech dated 26 October 1882 in *Addresses of the Dewans of*

Mysore to the Dasara Representative Assembly: From 1881 to 1899, Vol. 1 (Bangalore: Government Press, 1914), p. 11. See also D.V. Gundappa, *Dewan C. Rangacharlu: A Sketch of His Life and Career* (Madras: G.A. Natesan and Co., date unknown), p. 52 (reprinted from Gundappa's original publication in *Supplement to The Indian Review*, August 1912, pp. 657–64). See also ibid., p. 44, for Rangacharlu's remarks on another occasion when he called for women legislators, noting: 'We cannot altogether trust in the legislation of men for the softer sex, any more than in the legislation of one class for another. Such legislation is often apt to err as much on the side of extravagance, as on that of despotism, indulging in imaginary ideas of women's rights and other extravagant notions. The happy means will be arrived at, if we leave to women all that concerns themselves to be judged and determined by the standards of their feelings and ideas on the subject.' Rangacharlu was also no mindless admirer of the British. His anonymously published *The British Administration of Mysore: Fifty Years of Administration* (By a Native of Mysore) (London: Longmans, Green and Co., 1874) was the first of two parts. The publication of part one caused enough scandal that having been identified, Rangacharlu had no option but to suppress part two.

179. B.M. Chandana Gowda, 'Development, Elite Agency and the Politics of Recognition in Mysore State, 1881–1947', PhD thesis, University of Michigan (2007), p. 25. Interestingly, M. Veeraraghavachariar, one of the founders of *The Hindu*, published a pamphlet around this time where, in a dialogue, praise is heaped on the Mysore representative assembly against the 'gilded shams' that were British legislative councils. See M. Viraraghava Chari, *The Mysore Representative Assembly and the Indian National Congress: A Dialogue* (Madras: National Press, 1891). The British, on the other hand, said the opposite: for instance, in 1895 an imperial figure called the state assembly 'the shrewdest bit of Constitution mongering' he knew; it played up the principle of elections – and won laurels – while delegating no actual power to the winners of those elections. Manor, *Political Change*, p. 24. In 1906 a companion in the party of a visiting British prince was also told by the Resident how Assembly members 'have no power to do anything but ask questions; that if a member ventures to display any morbid tendency to criticism, he can be summarily dismissed . . . and that, in brief, the Mysorean Constitution is a great sham.' See Abbott, *Through India*, p. 250.

180. Letter dated 15 September 1879 from the tutor to the commissioner in 1881 Papers, p. 125.

181. Chandrasekhara, *Dewan Rangacharlu*, pp. 108–109. One of these scholarship winners for engineering was Sir M. Vivesvaraya, who later became Dewan.

182. The Dewan's speech dated 26 October 1882 in *Addresses of the Dewans*, p. 9.

183. Ibid., p. 20.

184. Manor, *Political Change*, p. 12. Emphasis added. States, in fact, also gave each other's industrial ventures support. When in the 1940s Travancore set up a fertilizer factory, among the investors were the governments of Cochin, Mysore, Pudukkottai, Morvi, Nawanagar and even Nepal. See Menon, *Triumph and Tragedy*, pp. 93–94.

185. The Dewan's speech dated 26 October 1882 in *Addresses of the Dewans*, p. 20.

186. Gowda, 'Development', pp. 71–78.

187. Quoted in ibid., p. 93.

188. Quoted in ibid., p. 99.

189. One is reminded here, of course, of Ashis Nandy's argument on how 'the ultimate violence which colonialism does to its victims' is that 'it creates a culture in which the ruled are constantly tempted to fight their rulers within the psychological limits set by the latter'. See Nandy, *The Intimate Enemy: Loss and Recovery of Self Under Colonialism* (Delhi: Oxford University Press, 1989), p. 3.

190. Of course, other states like Baroda, Cochin and Travancore also had industrial ambitions, but as Vanaja Rangaswami writes, these were 'not in such a spectacular manner' as Mysore, which was in its own league. See Rangaswami, *The Story of Integration: A New Interpretation in the Context of the Democratic Movements in the Princely States of Mysore, Travancore and Cochin: 1900–1947* (Delhi: Manohar, 1981), p. 9.

191. Chandan Gowda, '"Advance Mysore!": The Cultural Logic of a Developmental State', pp. 91–93 (quote from p. 93), in *Economic and Political Weekly*, Vol. 45, No. 29 (2010), pp. 88–95.

192. In 1924, for example, the Dewan would tell the Resident that the state had 'suffered to the extent of over 75 lakhs' in 'the experiment of operating' the iron works. The same record also states that the previous Dewan had spent four and a half crore on 'schemes which he left half-developed' and which now needed loans to continue. See Fortnightly Report from the Resident (Mysore) dated 15 December 1924 in File No. 25 (Pol.) (1924), Home Dep., G.O.I., NAI. In 1937, a profit was reported of 50,000 rupees only, while the total capital expenditure 'after writing off a sum of Rs. 90 lakhs' was 156 lakh rupees. See Fortnightly Report from the Resident (Mysore) dated 2 July 1937 in File No. 18/6/37-Poll, Home Dep. (Pol.), NAI. In 1935, Mysore's trade commissioner in London again repeated that though the pig iron produced could not be sold (given that supply was ten times the demand in India), and though the venture had cost the state in 'one form or the other' some 400 lakh rupees, it was not a 'mistake' because 'experience teaches'. Quoting a British paper's reference to another plant as 'a symbol of enterprise, high courage and progress', he added that this was exactly what 'the Mysore people' felt about their own iron and steel works. See C. Ranganatha Rao, 'The Recent Industrial

Progress of Mysore', pp. 384–85, in *Journal of the Royal Society of Arts*, Vol. 83, No. 4294 (1935), pp. 372–94.

193. See Gowda, 'Development', p. 146.

194. Ibid., pp. 151–53.

195. Ranade quoted in ibid., p. 43.

196. Quoted in Chawla, *Raja Ravi Varma*, p. 109.

197. Quoted in Gowda, 'Development', p. 171.

198. Besides, somewhat embarrassingly, the states' people showed little interest in nationalism. In 1930, for instance, even the Mahatma's famous Salt March generated barely a ripple in highly literate Travancore. Rangaswami, *Story of Integration*, p. 116.

199. As Pattabhi Sitaramayya wrote, 'the local vagaries and idiosyncrasies' of the states put them 'obviously beyond the pale of the practical politics of Congress'.

200. See letter dated 2 July 1934 from Gandhi to the president, All-Indian States' People's Conference, in the *Collected Works of Mahatma Gandhi*, Vol. 64, pp. 121–22 at https://www.gandhiashramsevagram.org/gandhi-literature/mahatma-gandhi-collected-works-volume-64.pdf. Gandhi's colleague and the future president of India, Rajendra Prasad, would later, somewhat disingenuously, write that Gandhi's policy was to get states' people to 'stand on their own feet'. See Rajendra Prasad, *Autobiography* (New Delhi: Penguin, 2010), pp. 396–97.

201. Manor, *Political Change*, p. 14.

202. Quoted in Rao, *Modern Mysore*, Vol. 2, p. 347.

203. Rangaswami, *Story of Integration*, pp. 54–55.

204. Rao, *Modern Mysore*, Vol. 2, p. 248.

205. Ibid., p. 346. Evidently, the original plan was to give him a new title – a military one – and flatter him, but the maharajah suggested that the best way to honour him would be to reduce the heavy burden on the state's finances. See Mirza Ismail, *My Public Life: Recollections and Reflections of Sir Mirza Ismail* (London: George Allen and Unwin, 1954), p. 60. In 1932 Ismail also, in a speech, argued that while originally tributes might have been imposed as war indemnities, their continued extraction was a 'source of humiliation'. Gowda, 'Development', p. 51, also notes how one-third of the total value of tribute received by the Raj came from Mysore, and that from 1799 until 1934 the state lost over 33 crore rupees.

206. In 1906, thus, a Resident grumbled that Mysore's 'mischievous' newspapers had such a long leash as was 'unparalleled' in other states. Quoted in Rangaswami, *Story of Integration*, p. 34.

207. Manor, *Political Change*, pp. 13, 49.

208. Quoted in K. Veerathappa, 'Dewan Mirza Ismail and Mysore Congress', p. 653, in *Proceedings of the Indian History Congress*, Vol. 40 (1979), pp. 653–61.

209. Rangaswami, *Story of Integration*, p. 106.

210. Ibid., p. 105.

211. Lewis Rice, *Report on the Mysore Census of 1881* (Bangalore: Mysore Government Press, 1884), pp. 62–65. Both of these identities included diverse, endogamous groups but were now, in keeping with a colonial pattern, boxed into castes, which even as it in some ways removed them from their own local understandings of self, helped create new public personalities and, eventually, political blocs as the state began to recognize and thus legitimize these new boxes and categories.

212. Manor, *Political Change*, p. 11.

213. Ibid., p. 17. Gowda 'Development', pp. 184–243, nuances this by stating that the authorities did intervene in rural life insofar as pushing farmers to adopt technologically sounder means and implements went, or in adopting cash crops, though the results were mixed, and there was resistance.

214. Manor, *Political Change*, p. 20. Gowda, 'Development', p. 114, also notes how this was also why the state avoided interference in social matters, so as not to provoke anger in sensitive areas.

215. Ramusack, *Indian Princes*, p. 183. He also rendered the ruler's council, which had local officers, powerless. As early as 1886 there were complaints from its members that they barely had a role. See Rao, *Modern Mysore*, Vol. 2 p. 173. This Dewan, Seshadri Iyer, was a friend of Ranade.

216. Quoted from an 1895 letter by her brother in Lelah Dushkin, 'The NonBrahman Movement in Princely Mysore', PhD thesis, University of Pennsylvania (1974), p. 81. The maharani was an astute politician. Shortly after her husband died in Calcutta, when a senior Raj representative offered his condolences, she remarked that to her it appeared 'as if the Maharaja had proceeded to Calcutta to personally entrust his family and his State to the care of the Paramount Power' before departing the world. See Rao, *Modern Mysore*, Vol. 2, p. 172.

217. Dushkin, 'NonBrahman Movement', p. 81. See also S. Chandrasekhar, *Dimensions of Socio-Political Change in Mysore, 1918–40* (New Delhi: Ashish Publishing House, 1985), pp. 25–26.

218. Ibid., pp. 28–29. Though of Maharashtrian origin, having been naturalized over generations, Purniah's kin were seen very much as 'local' Brahmins by now.

219. Manor, *Political Change*, pp. 31–32. As early as 1892 the Dewan had, in fact, admitted that Brahmins were 'already too well represented' in the state services.

220. In 1884, thus, the governor of Madras noted how of 1,346 graduates from Madras University, as many as 899 were Brahmins. See Grant Duff, *Notes from a Diary*, Vol. 1, p. 264. See also Rangaswami, *Story of Integration*, p. 41, which notes the parallel argument made in Mysore that while land revenue and even excise revenue were drawn from non-Brahmins, it was Brahmins who monopolized government posts. See also Dushkin, 'NonBrahman Movement', pp. 53–57 and pp. 96–97, where she notes how when an inquiry was opened, 'backwardness' was measured by the access to and literacy in English that each community possessed.

221. They were, he held, misguided by events in Madras, where the Brahmin–non-Brahmin rivalry had teeth. Dushkin, 'NonBrahman Movement', p. 82. See also p. 90 where she writes: 'Even without a shred of responsible government, official decisions were the product of interactions with various publics – within the administration, between it and articulate nonofficials, and between those in Mysore and events and opinion in Madras.'

222. M. Vivesvaraya, *Memoirs of My Working Life* (Bangalore: M. Visvesvaraya, 1951), pp. 86–87. As Dushkin, 'NonBrahman Movement', pp. 85–86, points out, however, some thought the non-Brahmin movement began in *Mysore* and travelled to Madras. She herself argues that they sprang simultaneously and overlapped.

223. This was the Miller Committee of 1918. Its report is available online at https://roundtableindia.co.in/index.php?option=com_content&view=article&id=8894:miller-committee-report-1919&catid=115&Itemid=127. The non-Brahmins were also inspired and to an extent supported by the Justice Party in Madras, though unlike the Justice Party, the Mysore non-Brahmins did not have a pointed anti-Brahmin cultural agenda. See Dushkin, 'NonBrahman Movement', for more on this.

224. Nair, *Mysore Modern*, p. 20. See also Dushkin, 'NonBrahman Movement', p. 13.

225. Ibid., p. 157. See also p. 168 where Dushkin tells how there was 'no inconsistency in being a Brahman communalist and an anti-government nationalist'.

226. Rao, *Modern Mysore*, Vol. 2, p. 75.

227. James Manor, 'Princely Mysore before the Storm: The State-Level Political System of India's Model State, 1920–1936', p. 46, in *Modern Asian Studies*, Vol. 9, No. 1 (1975), pp. 31–58. See also Dushkin, 'NonBrahman Movement', pp. 237–38.

228. Manor, *Political Change*, pp. 14–15. See also Manor, 'Princely Mysore', for a brief account of how Mysore's lower-level legislative bodies and political platforms were lethargic, powerless and lagged seriously – sometimes by decades – behind comparable institutions in Madras. See also Ramusack, *Twilight*, p. 43. See also Ismail, *My Public Life*, p. 132 where he, interestingly, attempts to pass on the blame to the Raj stating that it encouraged autocratic rule, and 'discouraged any attempt to associate the people in the administration'.

229. This was for the legislature, separate from the assembly mentioned before. The legislature was established in 1907, with power even to vote on the budget. K. Veerathappa, 'Mysore Legislative Council (1907–1947), in *Proceedings of the Indian History Congress*, Vol. 48 (1987), pp. 404–10.

230. Dushkin, 'NonBrahman Movement', p. 274, notes that 'As late as 1935' Congress 'recruited only 101 new members', half of them students, and all from Bangalore and Mysore cities.

231. This was a combination of older, smaller 'groups' such as the Praja Mitra Mandali, People's Party, etc.

232. For instance, in September 1926 when the Bangalore District Committee of the Congress met, only about thirty people were present, and the secretary informed them that 'finances were low and membership poor'. See Fortnightly Report from the Resident (Mysore) dated 1 October 1926 in File No. F-112-IV-26 (Pol.), Home Dep., G.O.I., NAI.

233. Dushkin, 'NonBrahman Movement', pp. 20, 233.

234. For instance, Gandhi dissociated the Congress from these Congressmen who had to, thus, fight alone.

235. Government claimed between ten and twelve deaths, while MSC members said thirty-two were killed and another forty-eight injured. See H. Raghunath, 'Viduraswatha Tragedy and Its Aftermath: 1938' in *Proceedings of the Indian History Congress*, Vol. 38 (1977), pp. 452–59. See also Rangaswami, *Story of Integration*, p. 169.

236. The press communique said that despite being asked to disperse, the crowd showed 'an attitude of defiance' and engaged in 'hooting and jeering . . . and speaking contemptuously of the Government'. 'No amount of persuasion and advice' seemed to work, since the crowed had come 'determined to give trouble'. Having behaved 'riotously', the police had no option but to attack. See Publicity Officer's press communique dated 28 April 1938 in Fortnightly Report by the Resident (Mysore) dated 1 May 1938 in File No. 18/4/38-Poll, Home Dep. (Pol.), NAI. On international reportage, see *The New York Times* dated 27 April 1938.

237. See Manor, *Political Change*, pp. 96–110. This is not altogether surprising. Gandhi had stated how non-intervention was 'a perfect piece of statesmanship' given that the 'people of the States were not awakened'. But now that there was 'all-round awakening', it would be 'cowardice' to stand aside. So, whenever 'the Congress thinks it can usefully intervene, it must intervene'. Quoted in M.K. Gandhi, *The Indian States' Problem* (Ahmedabad: Navajivan Press, 1941), p. 132. See also *The Bombay Chronicle* dated 3 May 1938 which reported how Minoo Masani, at a local meeting in Poona described the policy of non-intervention in the state as 'nauseating and reactionary', comparing Mysore to chaotic Spain. Another headline in the same paper asked: 'Will Viduraswatham Massacre Bring Doom of Autocracy in Mysore State?'

238. Manor, *Political Change*, p. 111.

239. Quoted in Chandrasekhar, *Dimensions*, p. 161. What is interesting is that a century before, Krishnaraja III's crisis in Nagara also featured a massacre that added fat to the flames. Though it was done by the Marathi Brahmin Rama Rao's faction, the king was held responsible when at Hole Honnur a large crowd of peasants gathered for redress. Not only were 100 killed, those who were wounded were allegedly sown into jute bags and thrown into a river. See Chancellor, 'Mysore', p. 312.

240. A brief summary of the arrangement reached with the Congress can be seen in *The Bombay Chronicle* dated 9 May 1938. The same paper on 6 May 1938 carried a front page headline that read: 'Maharaja Concerned Over Recent Firing'.

241. K.R. Srinivasiengar, 'The Mysore Constitution' in *Current Science*, Vol. 9 (1940), pp. xxxv–vii.

242. Chandrasekhar, *Dimensions*, p. 160. This was not the first time the government tried to thwart candidates it did not like. Around 1908 also when two known critics were elected, the maharajah used his prerogative to cancel their elections. See Rangaswami, *Story of Integration*, p. 36.

243. In the pre-Ismail years, the brother had been a member of the council, and at one time was granted precedence over the Dewan through an extra vote. See Rangaswami, *Story of Integration*, p. 43.

244. Quoted in M.B. Gayathri, 'The Development of Mysore State from 1940 to 1956', PhD thesis, University of Mysore (1980), p. 51. See also Manor, *Political Change*, p. 133. The new maharajah posed as a people's champion by asking Ismail to give more seats on his cabinet than the intended three (health, education, and local self-government) to elected men. Ismail refused and left, and this goal having been achieved, the maharajah abandoned his proposal, which had been designed precisely to orchestrate the Dewan's departure!

245. Ismail and Visvesvaraya quoted in Gayathri, 'Development of Mysore State', pp. 52–53.

246. Manor, *Political Change*, p. 156.

247. See the cartoon and more in M. Kumaraswamy, 'The Role of Underground Press in Mysore Chalo Movement in 1947' in *Proceedings of the Indian History Congress*, Vol. 67 (2006–2007), pp. 725–29.

7. The Rana Who Would Not Reform

1. Chawla, *Raja Ravi Varma*, p. 123. This Mysore commission also involved a few informal paintings. For instance, Ravi Varma did a portrait of Krishnaraja IV's English secretary's little boy. See Maconochie, *Indian Civil Service*, p. 155.

2. This painting was done from a photograph.

3. G.R. Josyer, *History of Mysore and the Yadava Dynasty* (Mysore: Coronation Press, date unclear), p. 205.

4. Rao, *Modern Mysore*, Vol. 2, pp. 154, 167. His wife was a descendant of the family of those eighteenth-century dalavoys who had all but replaced the Wadiyars. She, unlike her daughter, did keep purdah; when she needed a dentist once, the operation had to be carried out through a slit in a purdah screen. Ward, *The Maharajas*, p. 83.

5.   Ikegame, *Princely India Re-imagined*, p. 102. Besides, the princess does not seem to have liked the idea of becoming a purdah wife in an alien culture. As her mother wrote, she refused 'to go out at all'. Ibid., p. 103.

6.   Ibid.

7.   Or as John McLeod wrote, Mysore was 'premier' only to the British; 'the heads of the ancient Rajput lineages saw it as an upstart [house] of questionable antecedents'. See McLeod, 'Towards the Analysis of Hindu Princely Genealogy in the British Period, 1850–1950', p. 88, in *South Asia Research*, Vol. 6, No. 2 (1986), pp. 181–93. For the Wadiyars, a bond with this romanticized group was also to confirm their own claims to Kshatriyahood. Historical antecedents did not favour them, for it was only in the seventeenth century that the ruling line, with a heterogeneous band of supporters, sealed itself into the Arasu community. Thirteen clans adopted Kshatriya rites, asserting that 'out of ignorance' they had hitherto been living as Sudras, and were now rectifying this to go back to their so-called original status. See Nair, *Mysore Modern*, p. 129. Still, enough people deemed them Sudras, and it took till 1928 for the Raj to cease classing the dynasty under that tag. See ibid., p. 12. This was also framed as a Vaishnava–Saiva issue, that is, they had been practising Saiva devotions like Sudras and now switched to Vaishnavism. This was not long after they took Srirangapattana, a noted Vaishnava site. Just as the city gave the Wadiyars kingly legitimacy, the family also had to adapt to the city's religious identity. The British authorities were aware of this. As the commissioner wrote to the foreign secretary in a letter dated 4 November 1868, 'the Mysore family, though originally Vaishnavs, followed for several generations the tenets of the Saivas, and it was quite recently, comparatively, that the Rajahs reverted to their former faith, while some of the branches still continue followers of Siva (sic)'. See 1878 Papers, p. 77. On caste, Nair quotes from the *Sriman Maharajara Vamshavali*, which has thirteen Arasu families adopt Vaishnava practices and the rites of Kshatriyas, and state: '(Although we had) taken birth among the loftiest of kshatriyas … without understanding this faith, and out of ignorance abandoning our caste traditions, and in violation of the four varnashrama acharas (observance of caste customs), (we) became adherents of the religion of the Sudras, Saivism, (and) gave and took women in violation of caste norms.' See also Ikegame, *Princely India Re-imagined*, pp. 77, 101. There were, other than these thirteen, eighteen inferior clans of Arasus.

8.   Ikegame, *Princely India Re-imagined*, p. 105.

9.   Quoted in Keen, *Princely India*, p. 98.

10.   Letter dated 19 January 1905 from the viceroy to Lady Curzon in the Alexandra Metcalfe Papers. I am grateful to David Gilmour for making this available to me. See also Gilmour, *Curzon*, pp. 189–90.

11. Letter dated 3 February 1905 from the governor of Madras to the viceroy in MSS EUR F111/210, British Library. See also letter dated 19 January 1905 from the maharajah's secretary to the viceroy's secretary in ibid. on the subject of the maharajah going to Calcutta to discuss the matter with Curzon. The meeting never took place: the maharajah had an attack of chronic laryngitis and was advised not to travel. See letter dated 2 February from the maharajah to the viceroy in ibid.

12. The brother's *daughters* did, however, marry Rajputs. The brother's son, the last Mysore maharajah, married a Rajput as well, but the union did not last, and it was his local second wife who gave him his children. Their only son died childless in 2013, and his widow adopted a boy. This young man, Yaduveer Wadiyar, married from the Rajput family of Dungarpur. The birth of a son to him means that finally the Wadiyars have an heir with north Indian blood. Meanwhile by 1915 at least in some Rajput circles Mysore's claims were admitted. Jessrajsinghji Seesodia in his *The Rajputs: A Fighting Race* (London: East and West, 1915) lists the Wadiyars as Rajputs.

13. Francois Bernier (A. Constable ed.), *Travels in the Mogul Empire: AD 1656–1668* (Westminster: Archibald Constable and Co., 1891), pp. 39–40.

14. For more on the many mutations of the Padmavati story, see Ramya Sreenivasan, *The Many Lives of a Rajput Queen: Heroic Pasts in India, c. 1500–1900* (Seattle: University of Washington Press, 2007).

15. This painting, *Johar*, sits in the Sree Chitra Gallery, Thiruvananthapuram.

16. See John Malcolm's *A Memoir of Central India, Including Malwa, and Adjoining Provinces with the History, and Copious Illustrations, of the Past and Present Condition of that Country*, Vol. 1 (London: Kingsbury, Parbury and Allen, 1824), pp. 330–40. A later functionary also noted that though the event was 'perfectly authentic' it was 'the kind which some future mythologist will prove to be an obvious solar myth'. See Alfred C. Lyall, *Asiatic Studies*, p. 192.

17. Soobrow, *Kishun Koovur: A Tragedy in Five Acts* (Trevandrum: Government Press, 1840). This was Subba Rao who was tutor and then minister to Swathi Tirunal who, he writes, urged him to publish the play.

18. For more on this formation of the Rajputs, see Dirk H.A. Kolff's *Naukar, Rajput and Sepoy: The Ethnohistory of the Military Labour Market in Hindustan, 1450–1850* (Cambridge: Cambridge University Press, 1990). See also Brajadulal Chattopadhyaya, *The Making of Early Medieval India* (Second Edition) (New Delhi: Oxford University Press, 2012 edn), pp. 59–92.

19. Chhatrapati Shivaji's family, thus, claimed descent from the Sisodias of Mewar. In the late nineteenth and early twentieth centuries, the powerful Rana family of Nepal also claimed descent from a Sisodia who had fled to the Himalayas centuries before. Curzon got the maharana to recognize the claim, thus certifying the family's status as 'good' Rajputs. See Stefanie Lotter, 'Continuity and Change

as Two Identifying Principles', pp. 84–85, in Jon Abbink and Tijo Salverda eds, *The Anthropology of Elites: Power, Culture, and the Complexities of Distinction* (New York: Palgrave Macmillan, 2013), pp. 71–94. However, this recognition was not without challenges. See Monika Horstmann, *Jaipur 1778: The Making of a King* (Wiesbaden: Harrassowitz Verlag, 2013), pp. 61–62, where we read of a denial of Kshatriya status as late as the eighteenth century.

20. For instance, booty from imperial wars enriched Rajput rajahs. Sometimes, new kingdoms were established: Sitamau, for instance, was granted as jagir to a Ratlam prince and continued till 1949 as a princely state.

21. See more on this in T.C.A. Raghavan, *History Men: Jadunath Sarkar, G.S. Sardesai, Raghubir Sinh and Their Quest for India's Past* (Noida: HarperCollins, 2020), p. 345. The book, by Sarkar, was published in the 1980s.

22. James Tod, *Annals and Antiquities of Rajast'han, or the Central and Western Rajpoot States of India*, Vol. 1, (London: Smith, Elder and Co., 1829), pp. 406, 438.

23. Peabody, *Hindu Kingship*, pp. 126–30.

24. Thus, for instance, he wrote: 'Till this period, not a chief present had throughout his life ever laid his head upon his pillow without being prepared to be roused from his sleep by the cry of "the enemy is at the gate": some ancient foeman [sic], who had come to "balance the feud", or marauding mountaineer or forest Bhil, who had emptied his cow-pens. All these sources of anxiety were now at an end . . .' See James Tod, *Travels in Western India Embracing a Visit to the Sacred Mounts of the Jains and the Most Celebrated Shrines of Hindu Faith Between Rajpootana and the Indus* (London: W.H. Allen and Co., 1839), p. 3.

25. Jason Freitag, *Serving Empire, Serving Nation: James Tod and the Rajputs of Rajasthan* (Leiden and Boston: Brill, 2009), pp. 10, 14.

26. Florence D'Souza, *Knowledge, Mediation and Empire: James Tod's Journeys Among the Rajputs* (Manchester: Manchester University Press, 2015), pp. 48–49.

27. See Rima Hooja, *A History of Rajasthan* (New Delhi: Rupa and Co., 2006), pp. 246–47, 551, for examples.

28. Tod, *Annals*, Vol. 1, p. xvii.

29. Ibid.

30. Freitag, *Serving Empire*, pp. 85–90, 99. Quote from p. 90.

31. Fateh Lal Mehta, *Handbook of Meywar and Guide to Its Principal Objects of Interest* (Bombay: Times of India Steam Press, 1888), pp. 49–50, and *The Rajputana Gazetteer*, Vol. 3 (Gazetteer of Meywar by C.E. Yate) (Simla: Government Central Branch Press, 1880), p. 23. It is, however, likely that this was a later interpretation to play down the autonomy of the nobles, who as coparceners in the realm, claimed a status higher than the heir, rather than due to anything to do with the Mughals.

32. See Jahangir (Wheeler M. Thackston ed.), *The Jahangirnama: Memoirs of Jahangir, Emperor of India* (New York, Oxford and Washington, DC: The Smithsonian Institution with Oxford University Press, 1999), p. 149.

33. See Sreenivasan, *Many Lives*, p. 76, for a discussion on how, in fact, Raj Singh I of Mewar is even supposed to have taken a princess from a Marwar chieftain's house who was meant to be married to Aurangzeb. It was also in Mewar that such actions were cast as a defence of religion. That said, as Melia Belli Bose notes, spared future attacks by the Mughals, Mewar's court was able to dedicate resources to patronizing art and architecture, and amplify its royal identity, while its princes – though exempt – *did* serve in Mughal armies. See Bose, *Royal Umbrellas of Stone: Memory, Politics, and Public Identity in Rajput Funerary Art* (Leiden: Brill, 2015), pp. 251–56. See also Ulrike Teuscher, 'Changing Eklingji: A Holy Place as a Source of Royal Legitimation' in *Studies in History*, Vol. 21, No. 1 (2005), pp. 1–16, for a brief account of the different branches of the clan that held Mewar over a thousand-year period, and shifting strategies of legitimization.

34. Mewar's supremacy was challenged as late as 1870 by a Marwar maharajah at the viceroy Lord Mayo's durbar in Ajmer, where Marwar claimed 'perfect equality'. The British denied this, and the maharajah absented himself from the event, for which he was punished. See *The Homeward Mail* dated 3 December 1870. All the same, by the seventeenth century local chroniclers like Nainsi (1610–70) had acknowledged Mewar's priority, even when patronized by other families. See Tanuja Kothiyal, *Nomadic Narratives: A History of Mobility and Identity in the Great Indian Desert* (Delhi: Cambridge University Press, 2016), p. 54.

35. The account here, given lack of space, is necessarily simplified. For a detailed account of Rajput state formation, see Nandini Sinha Kapur, *State Formation in Rajasthan: Mewar During the Seventh–Fifteenth Centuries* (New Delhi: Manohar, 2002).

36. An interesting detail in the Rajput suppression of powerful tribes was their better access to horses. In Bundi, myths tell how a single horse was enough to subjugate a large number of Meenas. See Yashaswini Chandra, *The Tale of the Horse: A History of India on Horseback* (New Delhi: Picador India, 2021), p. 140. See also Kothiyal, *Nomadic Narratives*, pp. 64–120.

37. See Hooja, *History of Rajasthan*, p. 418; Peabody, *Hindu Kingship*, pp. 86–88; and Tod, *Annals*, Vol. 1, p. 224. It was ironically into Bhil areas that the maharanas disappeared whenever the Mughals made life difficult. See K.S. Saxena, *The Political Movements and Awakening in Rajasthan (1847 to 1947)* (New Delhi: S. Chand and Co., 1971), p. 164. In Dhundar, meanwhile, it was a Meena who performed the ritual, besides which they guarded the royal treasury.

38. Singh, *Colonial Hegemony*, pp. 64–66, 77–78. This meant that a criminal could seek refuge in a thikana and shake off the police. See also Ramya Sreenivasan,

'Rethinking Kingship and Authority in South Asia: Amber (Rajasthan), ca, 1560–1615', in *Journal of the Economic and Social History of the Orient,* Vol. 57, No. 4 (2014), pp. 549–86, for a brief description of the emergence of Dhundar (Amber was its old capital) as the premier kingdom among several Kachwaha chiefdoms, and a discussion on constructing kingship for different audiences.

39. See Edward S. Haynes, 'Imperial Impact on Rajputana: The Case of Alwar, 1775–1850', in *Modern Asian Studies,* Vol. 12, No. 3 (1978), pp. 419–53. In Jodhpur, thus the royal clan was of Rathores, in Mewar of Sisodias, in Karauli of Jadauns and in Jaisalmer of Bhatis.

40. See Haynes, 'Imperial Impact' for Alwar, and Peabody, *Hindu Kingship,* pp. 12, 22, for Kota, including an instance where the Mughals helped it assert *superiority* over its parent state, Bundi.

41. As one scholar put it, the chiefs were both royal supporters as well as rivals, and power was 'diffused throughout a community of potential rulers'. Edward S. Haynes, 'Rajput Ceremonial Interactions as a Mirror of a Dying Indian State System, 1820–1947', pp. 464, 468, 471, in *Modern Asian Studies,* Vol. 24, No. 3 (1990), pp. 459–92. See also Kapur, *State Formation,* pp. 102–105.

42. Lyall, *Asiatic Studies,* pp. 218–19.

43. In Mewar under the Marathas, thus, a maharana saw some nobles band around a rival, with the result that he had to make concessions to another faction to keep them on his side. Tej Kumar Mathur, *Feudal Polity in Mewar (1750–1850)* (Jaipur: Publication Scheme, 1987), pp. 24–48.

44. Peabody, *Hindu Kingship,* p. 71. Reference is to the Shrinathji temple in Nathdwara.

45. Norbert Peabody, 'Tod's *Rajast'han* and the Boundaries of Imperial Rule in Nineteenth-Century India', p. 213, in *Modern Asian Studies,* Vol. 30, No. 1 (1996), pp. 185–220.

46. This was Jhalawar state. For this, and more on Zalim Singh, the regent, see Peabody, *Hindu Kingship,* pp. 112–55. Interestingly, this state was not acknowledged by other Rajput rulers. In 1870, at a durbar in Ajmer, it was the viceroy who got the Mewar maharana to publicly receive Zalim Singh's descendant, thus giving him legitimacy. See D.L. Paliwal, *Mewar and the British: A History of the Relations of the Mewar State with the British Government of India from 1857 to 1921 AD* (Jaipur: Bafna Prakashan, 1971), pp. 111–12. See also Stern, *The Cat and the Lion,* pp. 88–98, for how, in Dhundar, a thikanedar family, the Nathawats, manipulated the Company.

47. Tod, *Annals,* Vol. 1, p. 129. 'Original' is my emphasis and not from Tod's quote.

48. *Memoranda on the Indian States: 1935* (New Delhi: Manager of Publications, 1936), p. 209.

49. D. Ochterlony quoted in H.C. Batra, *The Relations of Jaipur State with East India Company (1803–1858),* p. 52.

50. See the agreement in Rajat K. Ray, 'Mewar: The Breakdown of the Princely

Order', pp. 212–13, in Jeffrey ed., *People, Princes and Paramount Power,* pp. 205–39. See also Tod's agreement in Paliwal, *Mewar,* pp. 281–82 (Appendix 2).

51. Paliwal, *Mewar,* pp. 7–8. Even the tribute was based on the extent of land under *royal* control, not sums receivable by the king from his vassals. This too indicates that the British alliance was not with the state as much as with its ruling family. See Appendix 13, Tod's letter, pp. 123–24, in *Minutes of Evidence Taken Before the Select Committee on the Affairs of the East India Company and also an Appendix and Index (VI: Political or Foreign)* (London: House of Commons, 1832) at https:// books.google.co.in/books?id=lGtbAAAAQAAJ

52. Quoted in Stern, *The Cat and the Lion,* p. 71.

53. Lyall, *Asiatic Studies,* pp. 225–26.

54. See Stern, *The Cat and the Lion,* pp. 8–10.

55. Tod's letter in *Minutes of Evidence,* pp. 128–29.

56. Quoted from Shyamaldas's *Vir Vinod* in ibid., p. 72.

57. Andrew Topsfield, *Court Painting at Udaipur: Art Under the Patronage of the Maharanas of Mewar* (Zurich: Museum Rietberg and Artibus Asiae Publishers, 2001), p. 254.

58. Letter from the Marwar chiefs in Tod, *Annals,* Vol. 1, pp. 197–98.

59. For more on Marwar and the rivalry between the maharajah and his chiefs, see P.R. Shah, *Raj Marwar During British Paramountcy: A Study in Problems and Policies up to 1923* (Jodhpur: Sharda Publishing House, 1982), pp. 14–16. See also Singh, *Colonial Hegemony,* p. 87, where he notes that just as royal dynasties had bards commemorate their heroic deeds, bards also sang of thikanedars' sacrifices. See also Stern, *The Cat and the Lion,* pp. 60–62, where he notes ideological claims by nobles against the king.

60. Paliwal, *Mewar,* p. 22.

61. Ibid., pp. 169–71.

62. Saxena, *Political Movements,* p. 88.

63. See K.S. Gupta, 'A Study of the Revolt of 1857: On the Basis of Regional Records' in *Proceedings of the Indian History Congress,* Vol. 49 (1988), pp. 360–63. See also Ray, 'Mewar', p. 214, and Paliwal, *Mewar,* p. 52, where the maharana is quoted as hoping after Victoria's reign is proclaimed that 'the auspicious change in the Government now inaugurated may prove to India, still smouldering from the recent conflagration, like rain from heaven at once quenching the fire and renovating the soil . . .' A similar pattern was visible in Marwar and Dhundar also, where influential lords showed themselves sympathetic to the Company's enemies, while the rulers were less keen. See Stern, *The Cat and the Lion,* p. 64, and Shah, *Raj Marwar,* pp. 25–26. Luckily, much of the rebel leadership was Maratha – Rajputs, it was explained, had little love for these fellow Indians, which strengthened the rulers' hands. See John Kaye and George Bruce Malleson,

Kaye's and Malleson's History of the Indian Mutiny of 1857–8, Vol. 4 (Cambridge: Cambridge University Press, 2010 edn), pp. 403–404. See also Paliwal, *Mewar*, pp. 20, 39, where the maharana writes to a fellow prince: 'The advent of the British power has proved beneficial to all Rajwara and has been the means of restoring tranquility to the chiefs in the country. On this account, we earnestly wish and pray . . . for the stability of the British power.'

64. Sukhdeo Prasad Kak, *Mewar Under Maharana Bhupal Singhji* (Allahabad: Leader Press, 1935), p. 27.

65. Ibid., p. 28.

66. Ibid., p. 45.

67. Singh, *Colonial Hegemony*, p. 55. In Marwar it was warned that 'there would be bloodshed' if the thikanas were meddled with. Ibid., p. 209. And when in Dhundar an attempt was made in this direction in the 1930s, it was met with armed retaliation. Reference is to the durbar's action against the ruler of Sikar in the late 1930s. For a history of Sikar, see *Rajasthan District Gazetteers: Sikar* (Jaipur: Directorate of District Gazetteers, 1974), pp. 23–44. For the Shekhawati lords more generally, of whom Sikar was one, and who controlled a third of Dhundar's territory, see Stern, *The Cat and the Lion*, pp. 41–44.

68. Horstmann, *Jaipur 1778*, pp. 5, 17.

69. For instance, senior nobles, such as the Rao of Bedla, were received at the 'entrance of the palace'. See Louis Rousselet (C.R. Buckle ed.), *India and Its Native Princes: Travels in Central India and in the Presidencies of Bombay and Bengal* (London: Bickers and Son, 1882 edn), p. 160.

70. Hooja, *History of Rajasthan*, p. 820.

71. Quoted in Monika Horstmann, 'The Sati Debate in the Rajputana Agency', p. 87, in Jamal Malik ed., *Perspectives of Mutual Encounters in South Asian History: 1760–1860* (Leiden: Brill, 2000), pp. 79–96. This particular maharana had bad relations with his nobles. See Paliwal, *Mewar*, p. 13.

72. *Rajputana Gazetteer*, p. 23. See also W.S. Caine, *Picturesque India: A Handbook for European Travellers* (London: George Routledge and Sons, 1891), p. 92. Tod in his *Travels*, p. 32, also noted how the rana of Panarwa, a subordinate chief, with 1,200 villages and towns, kept court 'in imitation' of the maharana, and that 'the greatest etiquette prevails' with the chief exacting 'as much deference' from *his* vassals as his master extracted from him.

73. Paliwal, *Mewar*, p. 10.

74. Ramusack, *Indian Princes*, p. 151. This would cause great umbrage to a later Resident who was expected to follow this protocol. See K.N. Panikkar, 'Shoe Question', p. 27.

75. Quoted in Sukumar Bhattacharya, *The Rajput States and the East India Company: From the Close of the 18th Century to 1820* (New Delhi: Munshiram Manoharlal, 1972), p. 260. In one way the man was not wrong, in that the rani of Bundi

had tied a rakhi around Tod's wrist, making him a 'brother' and de facto Rajput. He also began his letters to the maharana of Udaipur with such salutations as 'Praise to Shree Ramji' and 'Shree Nathji be praised'. See D'Souza, *Knowledge*, pp. 209–12. See also James Tod, *Annals and Antiquities of Rajast'han, or the Central and Western Rajpoot States of India*, Vol. 2 (London: Smith, Elder and Co., 1832), p. vii, for Tod's reference to his 'sacred obligation' to Rajputs. His influence is clear also in how he was the first to use the word 'Rajasthan', today used to denote the region. See Kothiyal, *Nomadic Narratives*, p. 3.

76. Paliwal, *Mewar*, pp. 108–10. The 1870 meeting with the viceroy was not the first – a similarly awkward durbar had been held in 1832 with Lord Bentinck, with a lot of negotiation on protocol.

77. Ibid., pp. 132–33.

78. Ibid., p. 203. What is interesting is that this went beyond royal pride and had wider support. Kesari Singh Barahath composed at this time his *Chetavani-ra-Chungatiya* where he called on the maharana to recall the bravery of his ancestors who preferred wandering in the forest to subjugation by an imperial power, telling him not to be 'frightened by the orders of the British Government'. Where great kings, he added, bowed before Udaipur's throne, how could its ruler go and 'stand in line to salute the British throne'? See the full song in Paliwal, *Mewar*, pp. 294–95. See also Madhu Sethia, 'British Paramountcy: Reaction and Response by the Nineteenth Century Poets of Rajasthan' in *Social Scientist*, Vol. 33, Nos. 11–12 (2005), pp. 14–28, for more on how local bards often made political points to Rajput rulers.

79. We see something similar in Bastar in 1876 where, even as the rajah was on his way to an imperial event, his own porters blocked him. One of the fears was that if he left the state, he might not return and British-appointed non-local bureaucrats would rule instead. See Sundar, *Subalterns and Sovereigns*, pp. 79–85.

80. Paliwal, *Mewar*, p. 121.

81. Stern, *The Cat and the Lion*, p. 122.

82. Ibid., p. 124.

83. Ibid., p. 127.

84. Ibid., p. 142.

85. Ibid., pp. 140, 143–44.

86. Quoted in ibid., p. 185. For similar rulers and their policies in Marwar and Bikaner, see R.B. Van Wart, *The Life of Lieut-General HH Sir Pratap Singh* (London: Humphrey Milford, Oxford University Press, 1926), and Hugh Purcell, *The Maharaja of Bikaner* (New Delhi: Rupa Publications, 2013).

87. Quoted in Lyall, *Asiatic Studies*, p. 206.

88. Quoted in Purcell, *Maharaja of Bikaner*, p. 16.

89. Paliwal, *Mewar*, pp. 61–62, 65–66.

90. Paliwal, *Mewar*, pp. 125–28, and *Rajputana Gazetteer*, p. 23. The older claimant was exiled to Benares. He would be permitted to return in 1880 after waiving his claims, with a pension settled instead.

91. Rudyard Kipling, *Letters of Marque* (New York and Boston: H.M. Caldwell Company, 1899), p. 59. He added (pp. 67–68): 'Each man who has any claims to respectability walks armed, carrying his tulwar sheathed ... Now it is possible to carry any number of lethal weapons without being actually dangerous ... But the Rajput's weapons are not meant for display.'

92. W.S. Caine in *The Pall Mall Gazette* dated 20 February 1891.

93. Mehta, *Handbook of Meywar*, pp. i, 8.

94. Neumayer and Schelberger eds, *The Diary*, pp. 87–88. Ravi Varma was also accompanied by his younger son on this trip.

95. This sparked the envy of a local painter, Kundanlal, who lacked their status. Kundanlal was trained in Bombay and at London's Slade School of Art but with a thirty-rupee stipend, remained at the level of the ordinary durbar painters. Chawla, *Raja Ravi Varma*, p. 132.

96. Neumayer and Schelberger eds, *The Diary*, pp. 97–98.

97. Ibid., p. 104. Their fee was 5,500 rupees.

98. This is unlike Ram Singh II of Dhundar who belonged to a previous generation but wore glasses and trousers and posed with books on a table when he sat for the camera. He was himself also a photographer.

99. One suspects that the art critic who disliked Asvathi Tirunal's portrait from 1887 would approve of this one.

100. To execute these, the maharana not only made antique armour available, but also gave details on the heights and complexions of his ancestors. Amazed, the artist's brother diarized: 'I think very few in Travancore will be able to say as much' about some of their own principality's prominent rulers. Neumayer and Schelberger eds, *The Diary*, pp. 92–93, 95.

101. Letter dated 26 December 1884 from the Resident to the Agent to the Governor-General (A.G.G.) for Rajputana in File No. 210 (Udaipur, 1884), Rajputana Agency Office, Political Branch, NAI.

102. Ibid. The three families were Bagore, Kirjali and Sheorati, and Fateh Singh was from the last.

103. Letter dated 27 January 1885 from the officiating secretary, G.O.I., to the A.G.G. in ibid. The Resident was reprimanded for allowing the enthronement, showing again that the attitude of the man on the ground often made a great difference.

104. Letter dated 29 December 1884 from the Resident to the A.G.G. in ibid. Attached is also a letter signed by sixty-eight nobles and officials confirming Fateh Singh's adoption.

105. For instance, when the two previous maharanas died, seven lakh rupees was spent

on ceremonial expenses; now half that figure was sanctioned for Fateh Singh's predecessor, and even of this a substantial portion was set aside to maintain schools and hospitals in his name. Letter dated 31 December 1884 from the Resident to the A.G.G. in ibid.

106. Kipling, *Letters of Marque*, p. 89. See also *The Pioneer* dated 11 March 1885 which features a report on the maharana's installation, with a lot of praise for his character, 'perfect dignity and tact' and 'fair promise'.

107. Topsfield, *Court Painting*, p. 285.

108. Paliwal, *Mewar*, p. 262. See also A.P. Nicholson, *Scraps of Paper: India's Broken Treaties, Her Princes, and the Problem* (London: Ernest Benn Ltd, 1930), p. 244.

109. The maharana's love for hunting is also reflected in the large number of paintings on this theme, showing him in all kinds of forest settings. It should be noted, however, that while the hunt appeared irrational to outsiders, to Fateh Singh it was an essential attribute of kingship. For a full study, see Julie Elaine Hughes, 'Animal Kingdoms: Princely Power, the Environment, and the Hunt in Colonial India', unpublished PhD thesis (2009), University of Texas at Austin. As she notes (pp. 191–92), expertise in pig-sticking and recommendations to visiting British grandees not to risk attempting it were moments for Rajput princes to subtly project superiority in a recognizably manly sport.

110. Topsfield, *Court Painting*, pp. 275, 280. The biologist Marianne North recorded also how this ruler was building an 'English palace'. As with Uthram Tirunal in chapter 1, this too was full of 'clocks in every room, all telling different time', while in the drawing room, 'two carriage-lamps were hung on each side of the door'. See North, *Recollections of a Happy Life: Being the Autobiography of Marianne North*, Vol. 2 (London: Macmillan and Co., 1893), p. 67.

111. Rousselet, *India and Its Native Princes*, p. 161. This was the Rao of Bedla. When he met Rousselet, he 'wished to examine all our luggage, down to the articles of our toilet, and went into prolonged ecstasies over a stereoscope containing coloured views of the Tuileries and Versailles . . . To show us that he was a perfect master of civilized habits, he took a glass of sherry and asked me for a cigar. This astonished me more than I can express, having never seen any Indian, especially one of high caste, thus openly adopt our customs.'

112. Topsfield, *Court Painting*, p. 287. Thus, even Ravi Varma's portrait has a near exact, *older* counterpart on cloth done by a durbar artist, Sivalal. See ibid., p. 286. Sivalal was the son of an earlier court artist called Tarachund. The latter was exposed to European painting from the 1850s, when William Carpenter came to Udaipur, while the former modified the traditional style based on his exposure to photography.

113. Arthur Cunningham Lothian, *Kingdoms of Yesterday* (London: John Murray, 1951), p. 105.

114. Paliwal, *Mewar*, p. 202.

115. Quoted in ibid., p. 199.

116. W.S. Caine in *The Pall Mall Gazette* dated 20 February 1891.

117. Pannalal's control also extended through his son, Fatehlal (Ravi Varma's intermediary at court), who was the maharana's English secretary. When Kipling visited, this son was twenty but had 'won a fair insight into State affairs, and [knew] generally what [was] going forward' because his services were essential to the ruler.

118. Paliwal, *Mewar*, pp. 190–99. He was not alone. Ganga Singh of Bikaner also avoided hiring ministers for years.

119. Lord Hardinge quoted in Topsfield, *Court Painting*, p. 285.

120. Claude H. Hill, *India – Stepmother* (London: William Blackwood and Sons, 1929), p. 91.

121. Quoted in Ashton, 'British Policy', pp. 96–97.

122. Quoted in ibid., p. 97.

123. Paliwal, *Mewar*, p. 204. Once, when a Resident advised that 'an exceedingly attractive and able' assistant be given more responsibility, Fateh Singh retorted that if so singled out, the man would crack under the pressure – the maharana justified one-man rule as necessary for his secretary's well-being! See Hill, *India – Stepmother*, p. 161. Fateh Singh did briefly appoint Shyamji Krishnavarma as secretary with nearly all the powers of a Dewan, but the arrangement did not last. It did, however, influence the nationalist's views on the states and help him critique the Raj. See Ganeshi Lal Varma, *Shyamji Krishna Varma: The Unknown Patriot* (New Delhi: Publications Division, 1993), pp. 15–22.

124. Hill, *India – Stepmother*, p. 92. Bureaucratization was also difficult for, as an official wrote in 1867, the chiefs 'as a rule, consider reading and writing beneath their dignity' and as something paid servants could do. Education in the Western sense that churned out clerks was seen as inappropriate for Rajputs. See Stern, *The Cat and the Lion*, p. 158.

125. Paliwal, *Mewar*, p. 197. The Resident was not entirely correct, however, in that the Hadas of Kota and Bundi also, it is believed, never gave daughters to the Mughals.

126. Ibid., p. 240.

127. Ibid., pp. 212, 254.

128. Keen, *Princely India*, p. 156.

129. Curzon's speech quoted in *The Englishman* dated 20 November 1902.

130. Narratives of Native States and Chiefships in Rajputana (Udaipur) in File Nos. 301–303, Pros. Foreign Dep. (Internal-B), 1902, NAI.

131. Lothian, *Kingdoms*, pp. 103–104.

132. Abbott, *Through India*, pp. 46–47. Corfield, *Princely India*, p. 166, also wrote how 'I could almost believe that he *was* the direct descendant of the Sun'.

133. Corfield, *Princely India*, pp. 166–67.

134. Conrad Corfield quoted in Topsfield, *Court Painting*, p. 285. Emphasis added.

135. Lothian, *Kingdoms*, pp. 103–105.

136. Hill, *India – Stepmother*, p. 78.

137. Ibid., p. 80.

138. Ibid., p. 162.

139. Ibid., p. 163.

140. *The Pall Mall Gazette* dated 20 February 1891. See also *The Queen, The Lady's Newspaper* dated 18 November 1905 where we read: 'In the Hindu Pantheon every Maharana of Udaipur is a sacred personage, and is an object of worship.'

141. Quoted in Paliwal, *Mewar*, p. 197. An anecdote from the previous maharana's reign similarly has it that in 1875 when waiting for Victoria's son to arrive in Bombay, Alfred Lyall, the British civil servant, said to Salar Jung of Hyderabad: 'It must interest you to see the future king of England.' To this the nizam's Dewan replied: 'More than I can say there is one other here to-night whom I long wished to see, to an Indian, the greatest of Indians, the Maharana of Udaipur.' See Kak, *Mewar Under Maharana Bhupal Singhji*, p. 1.

142. See *The Historical Record of the Imperial Visit to India (1911): Compiled from the Official Records Under the Orders of the Viceroy and Governor-General of India* (London: John Murray for the Government of India, 1914), pp. 77, 160. See also Paliwal, *Mewar*, p. 235, where we read how the maharana's 'illness' had much to do with hearing that his elephant in the state procession would be behind that of Baroda's Maratha ruler.

143. Quoted in Paliwal, *Mewar*, p. 235.

144. Not least because over 300 Indian states had Rajput heads. Haynes, 'Rajput Ceremonial Interactions', p. 467. This, of course, includes states outside Rajputana.

145. Nicholson, *Scraps of Paper*, pp. 243–45.

146. Resident's Note dated 8 March 1906 in IOR/R/2/147/97. The maharana himself would also make a similar point years later. See K.M. Panikkar, *Indian States*, pp. 66–67.

147. Keen, *Princely India*, p. 99.

148. Susanne Hoeber Rudolph and Lloyd I. Rudolph eds, with Mohan Singh Kanota, *Reversing the Gaze: Amar Singh's Diary, A Colonial Subject's Narrative of Imperial India* (Boulder: Westview Press, 2002), pp. 455–56.

149. Ibid., p. 465.

150. Ibid., p. 466.

151. Ibid., p. 462.

152. Ibid.

153. Resident's note dated 7 March 1901 in IOR/R/2/147/97.

154. Hill, *India – Stepmother*, p. 79.

155. *Rajputana Gazetteer*, pp. 25–26, 32. The thikanas paid a tribute of 91,000 rupees against a total income of ten lakh rupees, while the ruler had twelve lakh from his khalsa. The maharana did, of course, have other sources of income from customs, etc. making his total revenue over twenty-three lakh rupees. But it is also possible the thikanedars played down their revenues just as Ram Singh concealed his income from the British in Dhundar. See also Ray, 'Mewar', p. 209, where we find that even in 1941, of 5,582 villages in Mewar, the nobles controlled 3,546 and the king 1,553.

156. Paliwal, *Mewar*, pp. 215–16.

157. Ibid.

158. Ibid., pp. 95–97.

159. Ibid., pp. 220–22.

160. Ibid., pp. 223–24. See also p. 213 where we read that Fateh Singh was against the idea of a European tutor for his son. See also Rudolph and Rudolph eds, with Singh, *Reversing the Gaze*, p. 461, to read how the maharana told off a visiting party for its men dressed in the Western style and for eating prohibited food items.

161. Ibid., pp. 225–26. This (*murisala*) was even translated in English by state authorities as the Doctrine of Lapse. In the early years of the maharana's son's reign, thus, 114 villages were resumed into the khalsa. See Kak, *Mewar Under Maharana Bhupal Singhji*, p. 57.

162. Viceroy's speech dated 3 November 1909 in *Selections from the Records of the Government of India, Foreign Department, No. 443: Correspondence Between His Excellency Lord Minto and Certain Ruling Chiefs Regarding Measures to Be Taken for the Suppression of Sedition, and Extracts from Speeches During His Excellency's Recent Tour* (Calcutta: Superintendent Government Printing, 1910), pp. 45–47. The ruler of Dewas (Senior) also made similar remarks when he recounted a conversation with the British agent: 'As far as you are the Political Agent concerned, I want to know, you are concerned whether my State is ruled well and my people are contented or not. The method is immaterial as far as you are concerned?' When the man replied in the affirmative, the maharajah said: 'That's the thermometer I use, the contentment of my people. Don't ask me the Constitution [sic] ... ask the common man if he is happy under my rule. If he is, I see no reason why I should give a Constitution.' See A.C. Mayer, 'Perceptions of Princely Rule', p. 138.

163. Quoted from Fred L. Gray, *Zigzagging in the Orient, 1921–22* (Minneapolis: Byron and Learned, 1922), p. 92.

164. Paliwal, *Mewar*, p. 207.

165. Ibid., p. 209. To be clear, the Raj's own record with famines and saving lives is controversial. In Rajputana, famine was not an infrequent occurrence, its earliest record dating to 1309–13, and some twenty famines noted between

the seventeenth and nineteenth centuries. See Kothiyal, *Nomadic Narratives*, pp. 38–39.

166. Paliwal, *Mewar*, p. 255.

167. Singh, *Colonial Hegemony*, p. 107.

168. Hooja, *History of Rajasthan*, pp. 818–19. This was usually during marriages in the thikanedar's family, festivals and celebrations, on visits of officials from Udaipur etc.

169. Ray, 'Mewar', pp. 218–19.

170. Ibid.

171. David Hardiman, *The Nonviolent Struggle for Indian Freedom: 1905–19* (New York: Oxford University Press, 2018), p. 116.

172. In general, the Jats had been able to stand up to the state – around the same time as the Bhil agitation in 1881, they had gathered at a common festival and decided to strike work in response to certain reforms ordered by the government. As many as 250 cultivators personally came to Udaipur where they were assured that their rights would not be trampled on. See Saxena, *Political Movements* p. 90.

173. Hardiman, *Nonviolent Struggle*, p. 118.

174. Originally Bhoop Singh, he assumed a new identity to evade arrest.

175. Hardiman, *Nonviolent Struggle*, pp. 123–24.

176. Quoted in R.S. Darda, *From Feudalism to Democracy: A Study in the Growth of Representative Institutions in Rajasthan, 1908–1948* (New Delhi: S. Chand and Co., 1971), p. x.

177. Saxena, *Political Movements*, p. 152; Ray, 'Mewar', p. 227; and Hardiman, *Nonviolent Struggle*, p. 121.

178. Hardiman, *Nonviolent Struggle*, p. 126.

179. Nicholson, *Scraps of Paper*, p. 248. See also Paliwal, *Mewar*, p. 240, and Saxena, *Political Movements*, p. 152.

180. Quoted in Singh, *Colonial Hegemony*, p. 151.

181. W.S. Caine in *The Pall Mall Gazette* dated 20 February 1891.

182. Erstwhile Bhil influence comes across in the fact that towns like Dungarpur, Banswara and Deolia are named after Bhil chieftains. See Saxena, *Political Movements*, p. 163. For the strength of the Bhils as late as the fourteenth and fifteenth centuries in neighbouring Gujarat, see Sameera Shaikh, *Forging a Region: Sultans, Traders and Pilgrims in Gujarat, 1200–1500* (New Delhi: Oxford University Press, 2010), pp. 68–72.

183. The rana of Panarwa was himself of Bhil descent. Such families were called Bhilalas, that is, sons of Rajput fathers and Bhil mothers. See Kapur, *State Formation*, pp. 127–33.

184. Rousselet, *India and Its Native Princes*, pp. 142–43. See also Malcolm, *Memoir of Central India*, pp. 520–22, where he describes Bhils in Malwa and central India, driven there by Rajput conquests of their original homes.

185. William Hunter, *Report on Some of the Rights, Privileges and Usages of the Grasseea Chiefs, and Hill Population of Meywar* (London: Acton Griffith, 1856), p. 11. Herbert Risley also recorded some proverbs on the Bhils. 'The Bhil is the king of the jungle; his arrow flies straight. The Bhil is always ready for the prey. With a Bhil for escort your life is safe. If you please him he is a Bhil; if not, he is the son of a dog.' See Herbert Risley, *The People of India* (Second Edition, edited by W. Crooke) (Calcutta and Simla: Thacker, Spink and Co., 1915), p. 323. And Tod in his *Travels*, p. 35, spoke of the Bhil as one likely to 'sacrifice his life to redeem his word'.

186. Paliwal, *Mewar*, p. 8. Thus, for instance, in 1825 Bhils were made to sign an agreement by which they agreed to surrender weapons, return plunder, never to attack villages, obey the Company, not give refuge to enemies, pay tribute, etc. See Saxena, *Political Movements*, p. 165.

187. Paliwal, *Mewar*, p. 47.

188. Ibid., p. 103.

189. Ibid., p. 143.

190. A.C. Lyall's note dated 24 June 1881 in File Nos. 313–34, Pros. Foreign Dep. (Political A), August 1881, NAI.

191. Hari Sen, 'The Bhil Rebellion of 1881', pp. 77, 83–84, in Biswamoy Pati ed., *Issues in Modern Indian History: For Sumit Sarkar* (Mumbai: Popular Prakashan, 2000), pp. 75–99. See also Paliwal, *Mewar*, p. 154, where we read that forty-three chiefs had salt works in Mewar, which had to be closed causing nobles also losses.

192. Sen, 'Bhil Rebellion', p. 79.

193. Worse, anthropometric data sought on height, weight, etc. led to talk of government meddling in Bhil society to 'force fat men to marry fat women, thin men to marry thin women' and so on. Ibid., p. 81. See also Paliwal, *Mewar*, p. 157.

194. See A. Wingate's note dated 26 April 1881 in File Nos. 313–34, Pros. Foreign Dep. (Political A), August 1881, NAI. Sen, 'Bhil Rebellion', p. 76, notes also that a thikanedar claimed land under Bhil control and that the man was summoned in this regard; when he refused to go, in the ensuing fracas, the escort sent to fetch him was killed.

195. The brutality of these murders was shocking. While the men were found with their bodies chopped up, the corpse of a female relation was found with the 'vagina pierced by a bamboo'. See Sen, 'Bhil Rebellion', p. 76.

196. In 1881 the matter had been closed through negotiation with the durbar: the then maharana knew that if the rebellion went out of hand, the colonial government might take over the hill tracts. Paliwal, *Mewar*, p. 161. In fact, while the durbar's representative talked with the Bhils, a British officer also went in. They confirmed that though the census was a trigger, the 'real complaint' was that the Bhils' customary rights were being torn up, and that state officials, who saw them as

'savages and cow-eaters', showed no respect for their ways. A. Wingate's note dated 26 April 1881. And it was also not as if the tribes were unaware of larger political dynamics: during negotiations, they asked the British official to advocate for them, while simultaneously telling the maharana's man that they would help 'drive the foreigners out' if their demands were met. Sen, 'Bhil Rebellion', p. 89. See also A. Wingate's note dated 26 April 1881. See the 21 Articles of Agreement in File Nos. 313–34, Pros. Foreign Dep. (Political A), August 1881, NAI. The maharana was at this stage not directly attacked. A similar situation some years later in the Garhwal kingdom has been studied by Ramachandra Guha, where again we see peasants reluctant to blame the king, seeing wicked officials as the root of their troubles. See Guha, *The Unquiet Woods: Ecological Change and Peasant Resistance in the Himalaya* (Delhi: Oxford University Press, 1989), pp. 62–70. In any case, by closing the matter themselves, and showing that the royal government could handle a crisis, Mewar's ruler strengthened his hand against the Raj. See Alf Gunvald Nilsen, 'Subalterns and the State in the Longue Durée: Notes from "The Rebellious Century" in the Bhil Heartland', pp. 581–82, in *Journal of Contemporary Asia*, Vol. 45, No. 4 (2015), pp. 574–95.

197. Ibid., p. 150.

198. For more on Tejawat's background, see Prakash Chandra Jain, *Tribal Agrarian Movement: A Case Study of the Bhil Movement of Rajasthan* (Udaipur: Himanshu Publications, 1989), pp. 68–72.

199. Gandhi, though, would deny connection with it. He wrote in the *Harijan* dated 10 February 1922: 'I hear that a gentleman by name Moti Lal Pancholi hailing from Udaipur claims to be my disciple and preaches temperance and what not among the rustics of the Rajputana states. He is reported to be surrounded by an armed crowd of admirers and is establishing his kingdom or some other dome wherever he goes. He claims miraculous powers. He or his admirers are reported to have done some destructive work. I wish that people will, once for all, understand that I have no disciples.' See also Hari Sen, 'The Maharana and the Bhils: The "Eki" Movement in Mewar, 1921–22', pp. 158–59, in Ernst and Pati eds, *India's Princely States*, pp. 157–72. The Bhils were not alone in envisioning Gandhi as a miraculous being. Peasants in Gorakhpur also believed he had supernatural powers and was something of a divine avatar. See Shahid Amin, 'Gandhi as Mahatma: Gorakhpur District, Eastern UP, 1921–2', in Ranajit Guha ed., *Subaltern Studies III: Writings on South Asian History and Society* (Delhi: Oxford University Press, 1984), pp. 1–61.

200. Sen, 'The Maharana and the Bhils', p. 159. In neighbouring Sirohi, meanwhile, Bhils later said that they had 'tried to establish a new kingdom of their own . . . that they were going to live in the (maharaja's) palace . . . and carry on the

administration . . . and . . . were going to marry the daughters of Brahmins and Mahajans.' Quoted in ibid., p. 165.

201. Ibid., p. 160.

202. Ibid., pp. 161–62.

203. At one point, they ran into revenue officials of a thikana, who were not only assaulted, but the money they had collected was also snatched. See Jain, *Tribal Agrarian Movement*, p. 89.

204. Hardiman, *Nonviolent Struggle*, pp. 140–41.

205. Hari Sen, 'Maharana and the Bhils', p. 161.

206. Quoted in Hardiman, *Nonviolent Struggle*, p. 141. This kind of criticism did hurt, in the sense that not only was the massacre covered up, Tejawat himself also organized a social reform movement among Bhils, urging them to give up alcohol, not plunder, transition to vegetarianism, etc.

207. Hari Sen, 'Maharana and the Bhils', p. 165.

208. Saxena, *Political Movements*, p. 182. Hari Sen in 'Maharana and the Bhils', p. 159, notes Bhil ballads in which Tejawat is treated as 'their unifier and guru'.

209. Quoted in Hardiman, *Nonviolent Struggle*, p. 126. What is interesting is that the Resident who so criticized the maharana also noted that his 'strength and personality are so striking that who knows him or has even once come into contact with him can not but feel a deep veneration for him'. Quoted in Paliwal, *Mewar*, p. 262. Note also that Fateh Singh was not alone in this crisis. Peasant unrest was spreading throughout Rajputana and in states like Bundi and Alwar also the British made drastic interventions.

210. Quoted in Paliwal, *Mewar*, p. 255. See also Singh, *Colonial Hegemony*, p. 188. For the eventual growth of movements for greater democratization in Rajputana, see Darda, *From Feudalism to Democracy*.

211. Quoted in Ashton, 'British Policy', p. 99.

212. Hardiman, *Nonviolent Struggle*, p. 125.

213. Quoted in Nicholson, *Scraps of Paper*, p. 249.

214. Ibid., p. 250.

215. Quoted in Allen and Dwivedi, *Lives of the Indian Princes*, pp. 96–97.

216. As the *Times of India* dated 19 August 1921 reported, 'His Highness, having reached the ripe old age of seventy five (sic), feels entitled to spend the evening of his life in greater leisure than bearing unaided the burden of administration.' The viceroy, for his part, sent 'cordial wishes that His Highness will now spend his remaining years in the enjoyment of good health, peace and happiness'.

217. Lothian, *Kingdoms*, p. 104.

218. Paliwal, *Mewar*, p. 259, and Saxena, *Political Movements* p. 158.

219. Hill, *India – Stepmother*, p. 87. When he died in 1930, *The Times Weekly Edition*

dated 29 May 1930 wrote how even at eighty, when 'blinded in the right eye by cataract' and with vision impaired in the left also, the maharana 'still brought down tiger, shooting from the left shoulder'.

220. Gertrude Marvin Williams, *Understanding India* (New York: Coward-McCann, 1928), pp. 117–18. He is said to have shot 375 tigers, nearly 1,000 leopards and over 1,200 boar. See Hughes, 'Animal Kingdoms', p. 104.

221. Williams, *Understanding India*, p. 119.

Epilogue

1. Chawla, *Raja Ravi Varma*, p. 118.

2. I am grateful to the Raja Ravi Varma Heritage Foundation for making this letter available to me.

3. R. Kulathu Iyer in *The Madras Weekly Mail* dated 8 August 1907 quotes a sizeable chunk from Ravi Varma's brother's diary. Rajaraja recorded how their father's nephew had squandered his family's wealth and it was Ravi Varma who not only paid for the dowry of an unmarried daughter in that Brahmin house, but also settled debts and reacquired lost property. 'Our father,' Rajaraja wrote, 'used to express his gratitude with tears of joy.'

4. Rajaraja Varma quoted in ibid: 'We regretted very much that we neither painted her portrait nor even photographed her while she lived.'

5. Lord Ampthill quoted in Mitter, *Art and Nationalism*, p. 180.

6. See *The Madras Weekly Mail* dated 11 October 1906 and *The Scotsman* dated 11 December 1911.

7. Sudha Bose, 'Raja Ravi Varma: A Centenary Tribute', in *Modern Review*, Vol. 84 (1948), pp. 124–28. Some did, of course, rise to Ravi Varma's defence. An anonymous writer in *The Indian Spectator* dated 12 September 1908 argued, for example, that the younger generation's idealism would bar many things other than Varma's art. The same paper also observed on 6 August 1910 that Ravi Varma's work was not 'faultless' but 'he has perhaps had too many critics'. To say he was un-Indian was unfair because he was 'an Indian to the back-bone'. The writer particularly addresses Coomaraswamy's and Sister Nivedita's complaints.

8. *The Complete Works of Sri Aurobindo*, Vol. 1 (*Early Cultural Writings*) (Pondicherry: Sri Aurobindo Ashram Publication Department, 2003), pp. 468–69.

9. Quoted in Nigel Leask, 'On Partha Mitter's Art and Nationalism in India', pp. 295–314, in E.S. Shaffer ed., *Comparative Criticism: Philosophical Dialogues*, Vol. XX (Cambridge: Cambridge University Press, 1998), p. 308.

10. Nalini Bhushan and Jay L. Garfield, *Minds Without Fear: Philosophy in the Indian Renaissance* (New York: Oxford University Press, 2017), p. 308.

11.   Quoted in Dorothy Norman ed., *Nehru: The First Sixty Years*, Vol. 1 (Bombay: Asia Publishing House, 1964), p. 610.

12.   B.R. Nanda, *The Moderate Era in Indian Politics* (Oxford: Oxford University Press, 1983), p. 5.

13.   *Proceedings of the First Indian National Congress Held at Bombay on the 28th, 29th, and 30th December 1885* (Madras: Swadesamitran Press, 1905), p. 5. Emphasis added.

14.   *The Bombay Gazette* quoted in ibid., p. 7.

15.   This comes across in Ramabai Ranade's memoirs. In 1886, when in Amritsar during a tour, she went to bathe. Local Punjabi women were struck that she bathed with her sari on. One of them asked: 'Do you always bathe like this in your country?' that is, the Deccan, to which Mrs Ranade replied, 'Yes, we are not at all used to bathing in the way you do.' See McLane, *Indian Nationalism*, p. 103, for the full extract.

16.   See Prashant Kidambi, *Cricket Country: The Untold History of the First All India Team* (Gurugram: Penguin Viking, 2019), pp. 101–107.

17.   McLane, *Indian Nationalism*, p. 107.

18.   Quoted in B.R. Nanda, *Gokhale*, p. 122. Lord Dufferin, viceroy between 1884 and 1888, was even more uncharitable. To him the 'Babu Congress' was comparable to 'an Eton or Harrow Debating Society rather than with the Oxford or Cambridge Union'. Of course, while publicly he demonstrated contempt for the Congress, his private expostulations against the 'bastard disloyalty' of these 'enemies of the British' reveal he saw them as a very real threat.

19.   'Democracy Not Suited to India' in United Indian Patriotic Association, *The Seditious Character of the Indian National Congress and the Opinions held by Eminent Natives of India Who Are Opposed to the Movement* (Allahabad: The Pioneer Press, 1888), pp. 1–2.

20.   Syed Hosain Bilgrami in ibid., pp. 57–58.

21.   *Proceedings of the First Indian National Congress*, p. 53.

22.   Ibid., p. 9.

23.   'Democracy Not Suited to India', pp. 1–2.

24.   This ought not to be surprising given that even in Britain in the eighteenth century, radicals like John Wilkes were able to attack the government by 'cloaking . . . in patriotic slogans and gestures' their criticism, and by suggesting that it was not they but the state that was 'deviating from right, constitutional behaviour'. See Linda Colley, *Britons: Forging the Nation, 1707–1837* (London: Pimlico, 2003), p. 110.

25.   See C.S. Srinivasachari, 'The India Reform Society and Its Impact on the Indian Administration in the Decade 1853–62' in *The Indian Journal of Political Science*,

Vol. 8, No. 1 (1946), pp. 648–61. See also the Society's founder John Dickinson's *The Government of India Under a Bureaucracy* (London: Saunders and Stanford, 1853).

26. J.B. Norton, *The Rebellion in India: How to Prevent Another* (London: Richardson Brothers, 1857), p. 59.

27. S. Gopal, *British Policy in India: 1858–1905* (Cambridge: Cambridge University Press, 1965), p. 147.

28. Quoted in Mark Bence-Jones, *The Viceroys of India* (New York: St Martin's Press, 1982), pp. 126–28. This was a contrast from the treatment Curzon received. Entering a city once, he passed a banner that read 'God Bles our Horrable Lout'. It was a typographical error for 'Honourable Lord' but in some respects quite captures Indian feelings towards this viceroy.

29. William Digby, *India for the Indians – And for England* (London: Talbot Brothers, 1885), p. xxvi.

30. Quoted in Nayana Goradia, *Lord Curzon: The Last of the British Moghuls* (Delhi: Oxford University Press, 1993), p. 213.

31. Quoted in Rachel Fell McDermott, Leonard A. Gordon, Ainslie T. Embree, Frances W. Pritchett and Dennis Dalton eds, *Sources of Indian Traditions, Vol. 2: Modern India, Pakistan, and Bangladesh* (Gurgaon: Penguin Books, 2014), p. 263.

32. Quoted in Cashman, *Myth*, p. 46.

33. Quoted in Purushottam Nagar, *Lala Lajpat Rai: The Man and His Ideas* (New Delhi: Manohar, 1977), p. 15.

34. In fact, Cashman, *Myth*, p. 192, argues that when Tilak did surmount regional limitations after 1914, it was by *moderating* his conduct and abandoning earlier tactics.

35. See Thakurta, 'Westernisation', pp. 188. Ravi Varma had long petitioned the British authorities on the matter of the copyright. In 1892 he wrote how 'There are several chromo-litho concerns started in India and some of them turn out tolerably good work, but they have unfortunately been exposed to foreign competition, inasmuch as their pictures and designs are copied outright in foreign countries and cheap reprints imported for sale into this country.' In 1895 he again wrote to the government, and then for a third time in 1902. See File Nos. 118–19 (June 1902), Pros. Home Dep., NAI. He was not exaggerating. In Bombay, for example, there was a 'Ravi-Udaya Press' that seems to have cashed in on his name, while the Chitrashala Press in Pune and the Bhau Bul Co. in London openly plagiarized his work. See Kajri Jain, *Gods in the Bazaar: The Economies of Indian Calendar Art* (Durham and London: Duke University Press, 2007), Notes to Chapter Two, p. 386.

36. Nair, *Raja Ravi Varma*, p. 90.

37. Chawla, *Raja Ravi Varma*, p. 94.

38. See the essay on Ravi Varma in Kapur, *When Was Modernism*. Nor was Ravi Varma unaware of the wider sentiment of Eastern awakening. Towards the end of his life he apparently produced a 'small, delicate study' of the Russo-Japanese War, which played a major role in invigorating Asian nationalists. This is mentioned in George Joseph, 'A Great Indian Artist', in *Indian Review* (November and December 1911), pp. 905–909.

39. See Navina Najat Haidar, 'The Kitab-i Nauras: Key to Bijapur's Golden Age' in Navina Najat Haidar and Marika Sardar eds, *Sultans of the South: Art of India's Deccan Courts, 1323–1687* (New York: Metropolitan Museum of Art, 2011), for more on this.

40. Nair, *Raja Serfoji*, p. xxxii.

41. Roderick Matthews, *Peace, Poverty and Betrayal: A New History of British India* (Noida: HarperCollins Publishers, 2021), p. 35.

Bibliography

Published Reports and Papers

A Collection of Treaties and Engagements with the Native Princes and States of Asia Concluded on Behalf of the East India Company by the British Governments in India. London: East India Company, 1812.

Accounts and Papers of the House of Commons (East India: Baroda), Vol. 56. London: House of Commons, 1875.

Addresses of the Dewans of Mysore to the Dasara Representative Assembly: From 1881 to 1899, Vol. 1. Bangalore: Government Press, 1914.

Baroda Administration Report, 1904–05. Bombay: The British India Printing Works, 1906.

Further Papers on the Subject of the Proposed Alteration of the Provisions of the Indian Code of Criminal Procedure, 1882, with respect to Jurisdiction over European British Subjects Comprising Opinions of Local Governments, Officials, and Others, with Memorials from Non–Official Residents &c. London: Eyre and Spottiswoode, 1883.

Further Papers Relating to the Transfer of the Province of Mysore to Native Rule. London: Her Majesty's Stationery Office, 1881.

Gazetteer of the Bombay Presidency, Volume XIX: Satara. Bombay: Government Central Press, 1885.

Memoranda on the Indian States: 1932. Calcutta: Government of India, 1933.

Memoranda on the Indian States: 1935. New Delhi: Manager of Publications, 1936.

Minutes of Evidence Taken Before the Select Committee on the Affairs of the East India Company and also an Appendix and Index (VI: Political or Foreign). London: House of Commons, 1832.

Minute of His Excellency the Right Hon. the Governor, 5th November 1884. Madras: Government Press, 1884.

Opinions of the Press on the Annexation of Mysore. London: John Camden Hotten, 1866.

Parliamentary Papers, Accounts and Papers, East India: Session 2 (31 May–13 August 1859), Vol. 25. London: House of Commons, 1859.

Parliamentary Papers, Accounts and Papers, East India: Session (1 February–10 August 1866), Vol. 52 (1866). London: House of Commons, 1866.

Parliamentary Papers, Accounts and Papers of the House of Commons (East India: Baroda), Vol. 56. London: House of Commons, 1875.

Proceedings of the Baroda Commission Appointed to Inquire into the Charges Against H.H. Malharrow Gaekwar of Baroda of Instigating an Attempt to Poison the British Resident. Bombay: Times of India Steam Press, 1875.

Proceedings of the First Indian National Congress Held at Bombay on the 28th, 29th, and 30th December 1885. Madras: Swadesamitran Press, 1905.

Rajasthan District Gazetteers: Sikar. Jaipur: Directorate of District Gazetteers, 1974.

Report on the Insurrection in Mysore (December 1833). Bangalore: Mysore Government Press, 1858.

Reports on the Settlement of the Land Revenue of the Provinces Under the Madras Presidency for Fusly 1276 (1866–67). Madras: Board of Revenue, 1869.

Report on the Administration of the Baroda State for 1875–76. Calcutta: Foreign Department Press, 1876.

Report on the Administration of the Baroda State for 1881–82. Bombay: Education Society's Press, 1883.

Report of the Political Administration of the Territories Within the Central India Agency for 1881–82. Calcutta: Government Printing, 1883.

Report on the Administration of Travancore for the Year 1066 ME/1890–91 AD. Trevandrum: Travancore Government Press, 1892.

Report of the Indian States Committee, 1928–1929. London: Secretary of State for India, 1929.

Return. East India (Mysore Government) (385). London: House of Commons, 1878.

Selections from the Records of the Mysore Commissioner's Office. Bangalore: Mysore Government Press, 1864.
  a) Wilks, M. 'Report on the Interior Administration, Resources, and Expenditure of the Government of Mysore Under the System Prescribed by the Orders of the Governor General in Council Dated 4th September 1799'.
  b) Stokes, H. 'Report on the Nugur Division of Mysore'.

Selections from the Records of the Government of India, Foreign Department, No. 443: Correspondence Between His Excellency Lord Minto and Certain Ruling Chiefs Regarding Measures to Be Taken for the Suppression of Sedition, and Extracts from Speeches During His Excellency's Recent Tour. Calcutta: Superintendent Government Printing, 1910.

Letter dated 17 July 1863 from the Secretary of State to the Viceroy, pp. 15–16, in *Parliamentary Papers, Accounts and Papers, East India: Session* (1 February–10 August 1866), Vol. 52 (1866) (hereafter 'Mysore Papers').

Source Material for a History of the Freedom Movement in India, Vol. 2. Bombay: Government Central Press, 1958.

Statement Exhibiting the Moral and Material Progress and Condition of India During the Year 1860–61. London: George Edward Eyre and William Spottiswoode, 1862.

Supplementary Despatches and Memoranda of Field Marshal Arthur Duke of Wellington: India 1797–1805, Vol. 1. London: John Murray, 1858.

The Trial and Deposition of Mulhar Rao Gaekwar of Baroda. Bombay: Bombay Gazette Steam Press, 1875.

The Gaikwari Raj: Being a Reprint of the Notices Which Appeared in the Hitechhu of Ahmedabad. Ahmedabad: Pitramberdas Tribhowandas Meheta, 1875.

The Seditious Character of the Indian National Congress and the Opinions held by Eminent Natives of India Who Are Opposed to the Movement. Allahabad: The Pioneer Press, 1888.

The Historical Record of the Imperial Visit to India (1911): Compiled from the Official Records Under the Orders of the Viceroy and Governor-General of India. London: John Murray for the Government of India, 1914.

The Rajputana Gazetteer, Vol. 3 ('Gazetteer of Meywar' by C.E. Yate). Simla: Government Central Branch Press, 1880.

Travancore Almanac. Trivandrum: Government of Travancore, 1878.

Unpublished PhD Theses

Ashton, Stephen. 'British Policy Towards the Indian States, 1905–1939', PhD thesis, School of Oriental and African Studies, University of London (1977).

Chancellor, Nigel Hugh Mosman. 'Mysore: The Making and Unmaking of a Model State, c. 1799–1834', PhD thesis, University of Cambridge (2002).

Dushkin, Lelah. 'The NonBrahman Movement in Princely Mysore', PhD thesis, University of Pennsylvania (1974).

Gayathri, M.B. 'The Development of Mysore State from 1940 to 1956', PhD thesis, University of Mysore (1980).

Gowda, B.M. Chandana. 'Development, Elite Agency and the Politics of Recognition in Mysore State, 1881–1947', PhD thesis, University of Michigan (2007).

Lind, Kyrre Magnus. 'The Nagar Rebellion, 1830–31: Administration and Rule in an Indian Native State', dissertation, University of Oslo (2004).

Remadevi, 'Sri Rama Varma Vijaya Mahakavyam of M. Kunjan Varier: A Critical Study', PhD thesis, M.G. University (1998).

Shobhi, Prithvi Datta Chandra. 'Pre-Modern Communities and Modern Histories: Narrating Virasaiva and Lingayat Selves', PhD thesis, University of Chicago (2005).

Sreekala, M. 'Yamapranamasataka: A Critical Study', PhD thesis, University of Kerala (1999).

Sreelekha, R. 'Ravi Varman Tampi and His Contributions to Karnatak Music', PhD thesis, University of Kerala (1998).

Suntharalingam, Ramanathan. 'Politics and Change in the Madras Presidency, 1884–1894: A Regional Study of Indian Nationalism', PhD thesis, School of Oriental and African Studies (1966).

Wilkinson, Callie. 'The Residents of the British East India Company at Indian Royal Courts, c. 1798–1818', PhD thesis, University of Cambridge (2017).

Books

Abbott, G.F. *Through India with the Prince*. London: Edward Arnold, 1906.

Abbink, Jon, and Tijo Salverda eds. *The Anthropology of Elites: Power, Culture, and the Complexities of Distinction*. New York: Palgrave Macmillan, 2013.
   a) Lotter, Stefanie. 'Continuity and Change as Two Identifying Principles': 71–94.

Abbs, John. *Twenty-Two Years' Missionary Experience in Travancore*. London: John Snow and Co., 1870.

Aitchison, C.U. ed. *A Collection of Treaties, Engagements, and Sunnuds, Relating to India and Neighbouring Countries*, Vol. 5. Calcutta: J.L. Kingham, Foreign Department, 1864.

Aitchison, C.U. *The Native States of India: An Attempt to Elucidate a Few of the Principles Which Underlie Their Relations with the British Government*. Calcutta: Government Printing, 1881.

Aiya, V. Nagam. *The Travancore State Manual*, Vols. 1 and 2. Trivandrum: Government of Travancore, 1906.

Aiyappan, A. *The Personality of Kerala*. Trivandrum: University of Kerala, 1982.

Aiyar, B.V. Kamesvara. *Sir A. Sashiah Sastri: An Indian Statesman*. Madras: Srinivasa, Varadachari and Co., 1902.

Aiyar, S. Parameswara, *Kerala Sahitya Charithram*, Vol. 4. Trivandrum: University of Travancore, 1957.

Aiyar, S. Parameswara. *Progress of Travancore Under Sree Moolam Tirunal*. Thiruvananthapuram: Government of Kerala, 1998 edn.

Aiyar, S. Ramanatha. *Diwan T. Rama Row*. Trivandrum: Anantha Rama Varma Press, 1926.

Aiyar, S. Ramanatha. *A Brief Sketch of Travancore: The Model State of India – The Country, Its People and Its Progress Under the Maharajah*. Trevandrum: Western Star Press, 1903.

Allen, Charles, and Sharada Dwivedi. *Lives of the Indian Princes*. London: Century Publishing, 1984.

Anonymous. *Indian Annexations: British Treatment of Native Princes*. London: Trubner and Co., 1863.

Atwal, Priya. *Royals and Rebels: The Rise and Fall of the Sikh Empire*. Noida: HarperCollins Publishers, 2021.

Ayyar, K.V. Krishna. *The Zamorins of Calicut*. Calicut: Norman Printing Bureau, 1938.

Aurobindo, Sri. *The Complete Works of Sri Aurobindo*, Vol. 1 (*Early Cultural Writings*). Pondicherry: Sri Aurobindo Ashram Publication Department, 2003.

Baird, J.G.A. ed. *Private Letters of the Marquess of Dalhousie*. Edinburgh and London: William Blackwood and Sons, 1910.

Balfour, Betty ed. *The History of Lord Lytton's Indian Administration, 1876 to 1880: Compiled from Letters and Official Papers*. London: Longmans, Green and Co., 1899.

Balfour, Edward. *The Cyclopaedia of India and of Eastern and Southern Asia: Commercial, Industrial, and Scientific*, Vol. 3. London: Bernard Quaritch, 1885.

Banerjee, A.C. ed. *Indian Constitutional Documents, 1757–1947: Vol. II 1958–1917*. Calcutta: A. Mukherjee and Co., 1961 edn.

Bapat, Nageshrao. *Shrimant Maharani Jamnabai Saheb Yanche Charitra*. 1900, publisher unknown.

Batra, H.C. *The Relations of Jaipur State with East India Company (1803–1858)*. Delhi: S. Chand, 1958.

Bayi, Gouri Lakshmi. *Sree Padmanabhaswamy Temple*. Bombay: Bharatiya Vidya Bhavan, 1995.

Bayi, Aswathi Thirunal Gouri Lakshmi. *History Liberated: The Sree Chithira Saga*. New Delhi: Konark Publishers, 2021.

Bayly, C.A. *Indian Society and the Making of the British Empire*. Cambridge: Cambridge University Press, 1988.

Bell, Evans. *The Rajah and Principality of Mysore with a Letter to the Right Hon. Lord Stanley, MP*. London: Thomas Richards, 1865.

Bell, Evans. *The Mysore Reversion, 'An Exceptional Case'*. London: Trubner and Co., 1866.

Bence-Jones, Mark. *The Viceroys of India*. New York: St Martin's Press, 1982.

Benton, Lauren. *A Search for Sovereignty: Law and Geography in European Empires, 1400–1900*. New York: Cambridge University Press, 2010.

Bernier, Francois (A. Constable ed.). *Travels in the Mogul Empire: AD 1656–1668*. Westminster: Archibald Constable and Co., 1891.

Bhagavan, Manu. *Sovereign Spheres: Princes, Education and Empire in Colonial India*. New Delhi: Oxford University Press, 2003.

Bhattacharya, Sukumar. *The Rajput States and the East India Company: From the Close of the 18th Century to 1820*. New Delhi: Munshiram Manoharlal, 1972.

Bhushan, Nalini, and Jay L. Garfield. *Minds Without Fear: Philosophy in the Indian Renaissance*. New York: Oxford University Press, 2017.

Blackburn, Stuart H. *Singing of Birth and Death: Texts in Performance*. Philadelphia: University of Philadelphia Press, 1988.

Blandford, Augusta. *The Land of the Conch Shell: A Short History of Travancore and CEZ Mission Work There*. London: Church of England Zenana Missionary Society, 1903.

Bose, Melia Belli. *Royal Umbrellas of Stone: Memory, Politics, and Public Identity in Rajput Funerary Art*. Leiden: Brill, 2015.

Branfoot, Crispin ed. *Portraiture in South Asia Since the Mughals: Art, Representation and History*. London: I.B. Tauris, 2018.

a) Branfoot, Crispin. 'Introduction: Portraiture in South Asia': 1–22.

Bruce, Henry. *Letters from Malabar and on the Way*. London: G. Routledge and Sons, 1909.

Bryant, G.J. *The Emergence of British Power in India, 1600–1784: A Grand Strategic Interpretation*. Woodbridge: Boydell and Brewer, 2013.

Buchanan, Francis. *A Journey from Madras Through the Countries of Mysore,*

Canara, and Malabar, Vol. 2. London: T. Cadell, W. Davies, Black, Parry and Kingsbury, 1807.

Burway, Mukund W. *Life of the Honourable Rajah Sir Dinkar Rao*. Bombay: M.W. Burway, 1907.

Caine, W.S. *Picturesque India: A Handbook for European Travellers*. London: George Routledge and Sons, 1891.

Cashman, Richard I. *The Myth of the Lokamanya: Tilak and Mass Politics in Maharashtra*. Berkeley: University of California Press, 1975.

Chawla, Rupika. *Raja Ravi Varma: Painter of Colonial India*. Ahmedabad: Mapin, 2010.

Chandra, Yashwasini. *The Tale of the Horse: A History of India on Horseback*. New Delhi: Picador India, 2021.

Chandrasekhara, N.S. *Dewan Rangacharlu*. Delhi: Publications Division, Government of India, 1968.

Chandrasekhar, S. *Dimensions of Socio-Political Change in Mysore, 1918–40*. New Delhi: Ashish Publishing House, 1985.

Chari, M. Viraraghava. *The Mysore Representative Assembly and the Indian National Congress: A Dialogue*. Madras: National Press, 1891.

Chattopadhyaya, Brajadulal. *The Making of Early Medieval India*. New Delhi: Oxford University Press, 2012 edn.

Chirol, Valentine. *Indian Unrest*. London: Macmillan and Co., 1910.

Church of England Zenana Missionary Society, *India's Women: The Magazine of the Church of England Zenana Missionary Society*, Vols. 1 and 2. London: James Nisbet and Co., 1881, 1882.

'C.K.' *A Biographical Sketch of Dewan Bahadur V. Nagam Aiya*. Madras: Law Printing House, 1913.

Coatman, J. *Report of the Administration of Lord Reading, Viceroy and Governor-General of India, 1921–1926: General Summary*. Simla: Government of India Press, 1927.

Cohen, Benjamin B. *Kingship and Colonialism in India's Deccan, 1850–1948*. New York: Palgrave Macmillan, 2007.

Colebrooke, T.E. *Life of the Honourable Mountstuart Elphinstone*, Vol. 2. London: John Murray, 1884.

Colley, Linda. *Britons: Forging the Nation, 1707–1837*. London: Pimlico, 2003.

Collins, Larry, and Dominique Lapierre. *Freedom at Midnight*. New York: Simon and Schuster, 1975.

Copland, Ian. *The Princes of India in the Endgame of Empire, 1917–1947*. Cambridge: Cambridge University Press, 1997.

Corfield, Conrad. *The Princely India I Knew: From Reading to Mountbatten.* Madras: Indo British Historical Society, 1975.

Cox, John. *Travancore: Its Present Ruin Shown and the Remedy Sought in a Correspondence with the Government of Madras in the Years 1855–1857.* Nagercoil: London Mission Press, 1857.

Cubbon, Mark. *Report on the Civil and Criminal Judicature in Mysore, 26th April 1838.* Bangalore: Mysore Government Press, 1858.

Curzon, George N. *Speeches by Lord Curzon of Kedleston, Viceroy and Governor-General of India, 1898–1901.* Calcutta: Thacker, Spink and Co., 1901.

Curzon, George Nathaniel. *British Government in India: The Story of the Viceroys and Government Houses,* Vol. 2. London: Cassell and Company, 1925.

Cust, Robert Needham. *Pictures of Indian Life: Sketched with the Pen from 1852 to 1881.* London: Trubner and Co., 1881.

D'Souza, Florence. *Knowledge, Mediation and Empire: James Tod's Journeys Among the Rajputs.* Manchester: Manchester University Press, 2015.

Dadabhoy, Bakhtiar K. *The Magnificent Diwan: The Life and Times of Sir Salar Jung I.* Gurugram: Vintage, 2020.

Darda, R.S. *From Feudalism to Democracy: A Study in the Growth of Representative Institutions in Rajasthan, 1908–1948.* New Delhi: S. Chand and Co., 1971.

Datta, Amaresh ed. *Encyclopaedia of Indian Literature,* Vol. 3. New Delhi: Sahitya Akademi, 1949.

Davies, John Paton. *China Hand: An Autobiography.* Philadelphia: University of Pennsylvania Press, 2012.

Davis, Richard H. *Lives of Indian Images.* Princeton: Princeton University Press, 1997.

Day, Francis. *The Land of the Perumauls, or Cochin, Its Past and Its Present.* Madras: Gantz Brothers, 1863.

De Lannoy, Mark. *The Kulasekhara Perumals of Travancore: History and State Formation in Travancore, 1671 to 1758.* Leiden: CNWS, 1997.

Denison, William. *Varieties of Vice-Regal Life,* Vol. 2. London: Longmans, Green and Co., 1970.

Dey Jhala, Angma. *Courtly Indian Women in Late Imperial India.* London: Pickering and Chatto, 2008.

Dickinson, John. *The Government of India Under a Bureaucracy.* London: Saunders and Stanford, 1853.

Dirks, Nicholas B. *The Hollow Crown: Ethnohistory of an Indian Kingdom.* Cambridge: Cambridge University Pres, 1987.

Drury, Heber ed. *Selections from the Records of Travancore*. Trevandrum: Press of His Highness the Rajah, 1860.

  a) Row, V. Kristno. *A Description of the Administrative System of Travancore in the Year 1844.*

  b) Horsley, W.H. *Memoir of Travancore, Historical and Statistical, Compiled from Various Authentic Records and Personal Observation.*

Drury, Heber. *Reminiscences of Life and Sport in Southern India*. London: W.H. Allen and Co., 1890.

Elliot, F.A.H. *The Rulers of Baroda*. Bombay: Education Society's Press, 1879.

Ernst, Waltraud, and Biswamoy Pati eds. *India's Princely States: People, Princes and Colonialism*. Abingdon: Routledge, 2007.

  a) Ernst, Waltraud, and Biswamoy Pati. 'People, Princes and Colonialism': 1–14.

  b) Sehrawat, Samiksha. '"Hostages in Our Camp": Military Collaboration Between Princely India and the British Raj, c. 1880–1920': 118–38.

  c) Sen, Hari. 'The Maharana and the Bhils: The "Eki" Movement in Mewar, 1921–22': 157–72.

Farooqui, Amar. *Sindias and the Raj: Princely Gwalior c. 1800–1850*. Delhi: Primus Books, 2011.

Fisher, Michael H. *Indirect Rule in India: Residents and the Residency System, 1764–1858*. New Delhi: Oxford University Press, 1991.

Freitag, Jason. *Serving Empire, Serving Nation: James Tod and the Rajputs of Rajasthan*. Leiden and Boston: Brill, 2009.

Frykenberg, Robert E. *Guntur District, 1788–1848: A History of Local Influence and Central Authority in South India*. Oxford: Clarendon Press, 1965.

Fuller, C.J., and Haripriya Narasimhan. *Tamil Brahmans: The Making of a Middle-Class Caste*. Chicago: University of Chicago Press, 2014.

Gaekwad, Fatesinghrao P. *Sayajirao of Baroda: The Prince and the Man*. Bombay: Popular Prakashan, 1997 edn.

Ganesh and Co. *The Indian Nation Builders*, Part 1. Madras: Ganesh and Co., c.1910.

Gandhi, M.K. *The Indian States' Problem*. Ahmedabad: Navajivan Press, 1941.

Gauba, Kanhayalal. *His Highness: Or the Pathology of Princes*. Lahore: The Times Publishing Company, 1931.

Ghose, Loke Nath. *The Modern History of the Indian Chiefs, Rajas, Zamindars and c., Part II: The Native Aristocracy and Gentry, comprising Historical, Political, Social and Other Accounts of Several Ancient Families, Noblemen, and Eminent Men*. Calcutta: J.N. Ghose and Co., 1881.

Gilmour, David. *Curzon: Imperial Statesman*. London: Penguin, 2019 edn.

Gleig, G.R. *The Life of Major-General Sir Thomas Munro: Late Governor of Madras with Extracts from His Correspondence and Private Papers*, Vol. 2. London: Henry Colburn and Richard Bentley, 1831.

Glencross, Matthew. *The State Visits of Edward VII: Reinventing Royal Diplomacy for the Twentieth Century*. Basingstoke: Palgrave Macmillan, 2015.

Gopal, S. *British Policy in India: 1858–1905*. Cambridge: Cambridge University Press, 1965.

Goradia, Nayana. *Lord Curzon: The Last of the British Moghuls*. Delhi: Oxford University Press, 1993.

Gordon, Stewart. *The New Cambridge History of India: The Marathas, 1600–1818*. Cambridge: Cambridge University Press, 1993.

Grant Duff, Mountstuart E. *Notes from a Diary: Kept Chiefly in Southern India, 1881–1886*, Vols. 1 and 2. London: John Murray, 1899.

Gray, Fred L. *Zigzagging in the Orient, 1921–22*. Minneapolis: Byron and Learned, 1922.

Guha, Ramachandra. *The Unquiet Woods: Ecological Change and Peasant Resistance in the Himalaya*. Delhi: Oxford University Press, 1989.

Guha, Ranajit ed. *Subaltern Studies III: Writings on South Asian History and Society*. Delhi: Oxford University Press, 1984.

    a) Amin, Shahid. 'Gandhi as Mahatma: Gorakhpur District, Eastern UP, 1921–2': 1–61.

Gundappa, D.V. *Dewan C. Rangacharlu: A Sketch of His Life and Career*. Madras: G.A. Natesan and Co., date unknown.

Gupta, J.N. *Life and Work of Romesh Chunder Dutt*. London: J.M. Dent and Sons, 1911.

Haidar, Navina Najat, and Marika Sardar eds. *Sultans of the South: Art of India's Deccan Courts, 1323–1687*. New York: The Metropolitan Museum of Art, 2011.

    a) Haidar, Navina Najat. 'The Kitab-i Nauras: Key to Bijapur's Golden Age'.

Hakluyt, Richard. *A Selection of Curious, Rare, and Early Voyages and Histories of Interesting Discoveries, Chiefly Published by Hakluyt*. London: R.H. Evans, 1812 edn.

Hamilton, Walter. *A Geographical, Statistical, and Historical Description of Hindostan and the Adjacent Countries*, Vol. 2. London: John Murray, 1820.

Hawksworth, A. *Day Dawn in Travancore: A Brief Account of the Manners and Customs of the People and the Efforts that Are Being Made for Their Improvement*. Cottayam: C.M. Press, 1860.

Hardgrave, Robert L. *The Nadars of Tamilnad: The Political Culture of a Community in Change*. Berkeley: University of California Press, 1969.

Hardiman, David. *The Nonviolent Struggle for Indian Freedom: 1905–19*. New York: Oxford University Press, 2018.

Hardinge, Charles. *My Indian Years: 1910–1916*. London: John Murray, 1948.

Heehs, Peter. *The Lives of Sri Aurobindo*. New York: Columbia University Press, 2008.

Hibbert, Christopher. *Edward VII: The Last Victorian King*. New York: Palgrave Macmillan, 2007.

Hill, Claude H. *India – Stepmother*. London: William Blackwood and Sons, 1929.

Hooja, Rima. *A History of Rajasthan*. New Delhi: Rupa and Co., 2006.

Horstmann, Monika. *Jaipur 1778: The Making of a King*. Wiesbaden: Harrassowitz Verlag, 2013.

Hunter, William. *Report on Some of the Rights, Privileges and Usages of the Grasseea Chiefs, and Hill Population of Meywar*. London: Acton Griffith, 1856.

Hunter, W.W. *A Life of the Earl of Mayo: Fourth Viceroy of India*, Vol. 1 (Second Edition). London: Smith, Elder and Co., 1876.

Hurd, John, and Ian J. Kerr. *India's Railway History: A Research Handbook*. Leiden: Brill, 2012.

Ikegame, Aya. *Princely India Re-imagined: A Historical Anthropology of Mysore from 1799 to the Present*. New York: Routledge, 2013.

Ismail, Mirza. *My Public Life: Recollections and Reflections of Sir Mirza Ismail*. London: George Allen and Unwin, 1954.

Israel, Milton, and N.K. Wagle eds. *Religion and Society in Maharashtra*. Toronto: Centre for South Asian Studies, 1987.

    a) Wagle, N.K. 'Ritual and Change in Early Nineteenth Century Society in Maharashtra: Vedokta Disputes in Baroda, Pune and Satara, 1824–38': 145–81.

Iyer, R. Kulathu. *Her Highness Sethu Lakshmi Bayi, Senior Ranee of Travancore: A Short Life Sketch*. Madras: Methodist Publishing House, 1916.

Jahangir (Wheeler M. Thackston ed.). *The Jahangirnama: Memoirs of Jahangir, Emperor of India*. New York, Oxford and Washington, DC: Smithsonian Institution with Oxford University Press, 1999.

Jain, Kajri. *Gods in the Bazaar: The Economies of Indian Calendar Art*. Durham and London: Duke University Press, 2007.

Jain, Prakash Chandra. *Tribal Agrarian Movement: A Case Study of the Bhil Movement of Rajasthan*. Udaipur: Himanshu Publications, 1989.

Jeffrey, Robin ed. *People, Princes and Paramount Power: Society and Politics in the Indian Princely States*. Delhi: Oxford University Press, 1978.

    a) Hardiman, David. 'Baroda: The Structure of a "Progressive" State': 107–35.

    b) Ray, Rajat K. 'Mewar: The Breakdown of the Princely Order': 205–39.

Jeffrey, Robin. *The Decline of Nair Dominance: Society and Politics in Travancore, 1857–1908*. New Delhi: Manohar, 2014 edn.

Josyer, G.R. *History of Mysore and the Yadava Dynasty*. Mysore: Coronation Press, date unclear.

Kak, Sukhdeo Prasad. *Mewar Under Maharana Bhupal Singhji*. Allahabad: Leader Press, 1935.

Kapur, Geeta. *When Was Modernism: Essays on Contemporary Cultural Practice in India*. New Delhi: Tulika Books, 2000.

Kaye, John, and George Bruce Malleson. *Kaye's and Malleson's History of the Indian Mutiny of 1857–8*, Vol. 4. Cambridge: Cambridge University Press, 2010 edn.

Keen, Caroline. *Princely India and the British: Political Development and the Operation of Empire*. New Delhi: Viva Books, 2013.

Keer, Dhananjay. *Mahatma Jotirao Phooley: Father of the Indian Social Revolution*. Bombay: Popular Prakashan, 1964.

Keer, Dhananjay. *Shahu Chhatrapati: A Royal Revolutionary*. Bombay: Popular Prakashan, 1976.

Khilnani, Sunil. *The Idea of India*. London: Hamish Hamilton, 1997.

Kidambi, Prashant. *Cricket Country: The Untold History of the First All India Team*. Gurugram: Penguin Viking, 2019.

Kipling, Rudyard. *Letters of Marque*. New York and Boston: H.M. Caldwell Company, 1899.

Kizhakkemadom, Pratap. *Pattum Parivattavum: Thiruvithamkur Rajapathnimarude Ithihasam*. Kollam: Saindhava Books, 2018.

Kolff, Dirk H.A. *Naukar, Rajput and Sepoy: The Ethnohistory of the Military Labour Market in Hindustan, 1450–1850*. Cambridge: Cambridge University Press, 1990.

Kooiman, Dick. *Conversion and Social Equality in India: The London Missionary Society in South Travancore in the 19th Century*. Columbia: South Asia Publications, 1989.

Kothiyal, Tanuja. *Nomadic Narratives: A History of Mobility and Identity in the Great Indian Desert*. Delhi: Cambridge University Press, 2016.

Kramrisch, Stella, J.H. Cousins, and R. Vasudeva Poduval. *The Arts and Crafts of Travancore*. London: The Royal India Society, 1948.

Kumar, Ashutosh, and Claude Markovits eds. *Indian Soldiers in the First World War: Re-visiting a Global Conflict*. Abingdon: Routledge, 2021.

a) McClenaghan, Tony. 'The Maharajas' Contribution to the First World War: An Overview': 63–88.

Kunju, A.P. Ibrahim. *Rise of Travancore: A Study of the Life and Times of Martanda Varma*. Trivandrum: Kerala Historical Society, 1976.

Land, Andrew. *Life, Letters and Diaries of Sir Stafford Northcote, First Earl of Iddesleigh*. Edinburgh and London: William Blackwood and Sons, 1891.

Law, Edward (Lord Colchester ed.). *History of the Indian Administration of Lord Ellenborough in His Correspondence with the Duke of Wellington, to Which Is Prefixed, by Permission of Her Majesty, Lord Ellenborough's Letters to the Queen During that Period*. London: Richard Bentley and Son, 1874.

Lawrence, Walter Roper. *The India We Served*. London: Cassell and Co., 1928.

Lawson, Charles. *Narrative of the Celebration of the Jubilee of Her Most Gracious Majesty, Queen Victoria, Empress of India, in the Presidency of Madras*. London: Macmillan and Co., 1887.

Lewis, Arthur. *George Maxwell Gordon: The Pilgrim Missionary of the Punjab: A History of His Life and Work, 1839–1880*. London: Seeley and Co., 1889.

Lothian, Arthur Cunningham. *Kingdoms of Yesterday*. London: John Murray, 1951.

Loti, Pierre (George A.F. Inman trans.). *India*. London: T. Werner Laurie Ltd, 1928 edn.

Lewis, Malcolm. *Has Oude Been Worse Governed by Its Native Princes than Our Indian Territories by Leadenhall Street?* London: James Ridgway, 1857.

Lyall, Alfred C. *Asiatic Studies: Religious and Social*. London: John Murray, 1884.

Maconochie, Evan. *Life in the Indian Civil Service*. London: Chapman and Hall, 1926.

Macqueen, Percy. *The Pudukotah Portraits*. Pudukotah: Sri Brihadamba State Press, 1926.

Madan, T.N. ed. *Way of Life: King, Householder, Renouncer – Essays in Honour of Louis Dumont*. Delhi: Motilal Banarsidass Publishers, 1988 edn.

a) Mayer, A.C. 'Perceptions of Princely Rule: Perspectives from a Biography': 127–54.

Maholay-Jaradi, Priya. *Fashioning a National Art: Baroda's Royal Collection and Art Institutions (1875–1924)*. New Delhi: Oxford University Press, 2016.

Malabari, Behramji M. *Gujarat and the Gujaratis: Pictures of Men and Manners Taken from Life*. London: W.H. Allen and Co., 1882.

Malcolm, John. *A Memoir of Central India, Including Malwa, and Adjoining Provinces with the History, and Copious Illustrations, of the Past and Present Condition of that Country*, Vol. 1. London: Kingsbury, Parbury and Allen, 1824.

Malik, Jamal ed. *Perspectives of Mutual Encounters in South Asian History: 1760–1860*. Leiden: Brill, 2000.

   a) Horstmann, Monika. 'The Sati Debate in the Rajputana Agency': 79–96.

Mandlik, Vishwanath Narayan. *Adoption Versus Annexation: With Remarks on the Mysore Question*. London: Smith, Elder and Co., 1866.

Mankekar, D.R. *Accession to Extinction: The Story of Indian Princes*. Delhi: Vikas, 1974.

Manor, James. *Political Change in an Indian State: Mysore, 1917–1955*. New Delhi: Manohar, 1977.

Mateer, Samuel. *Native Life in Travancore*. London: W.H. Allen, 1883.

Mathur, Tej Kumar. *Feudal Polity in Mewar (1750–1850)*. Jaipur: Publication Scheme, 1987.

Matthews, Roderick. *Peace, Poverty and Betrayal: A New History of British India*. Noida: HarperCollins Publishers, 2021.

McDermott, Rachell Fell, Leonard A. Gordon, Ainslie T. Embree, Frances W. Pritchett, and Dennis Dalton eds. *Sources of Indian Traditions, Vol. 2: Modern India, Pakistan, and Bangladesh*. Gurgaon: Penguin Books, 2014.

McLane, John R. *Indian Nationalism and the Early Congress*. Princeton: Princeton University Press, 1977.

McLeod, John. *Sovereignty, Power, Control: Politics in the States of Western India (1916–1947)*. New Delhi: Decent Books, 2007 edn.

Mehta, Fateh Lal. *Handbook of Meywar and Guide to Its Principal Objects of Interest*. Bombay: Times of India Steam Press, 1888.

Menon, A. Sreedhara. *Triumph and Tragedy in Travancore: Annals of Sir CP's Sixteen Years*. Kottayam: Current Books, 2001.

Menon, C. Achyuta. *The Life of T. Sankunni Menon: Diwan of Cochin, 1860–79*. Trichur: V. Sundra Iyer and Sons, 1923.

Menon, C. Karunakara. *A Critical Essay on Sir A. Seshia Sastri*. Madras: Thompson and Co., 1903.

Menon, I.K.K. ed. *The Rajarshi of Cochin: Autobiography and Biography of Maharaja Sir Sri Rama Varma*. Trivandrum: Kerala State Archives, 1994.

Menon, P.K.K. *The History of the Freedom Struggle in Kerala*, Vol. 2. Trivandrum: Government of Kerala, 1972.

Menon, P. Shungoonny. *A History of Travancore from the Earliest Times*. Madras: Higginbotham and Co., 1878.

Minto, Mary. *India: Minto and Morley, 1905–1910, Compiled from the Correspondence Between the Viceroy and the Secretary of State*. London: Macmillan and Co., 1934.

Misra, Maria. *Vishnu's Crowded Temple: India Since the Great Rebellion*. London: Allen Lane, 2007.

Mitchell, Maria Hay Flyter. *Scenes in Southern India*. New York: American Tract Society, 1886.

Mitter, Partha. *Art and Nationalism in Colonial India, 1850–1922: Occidental Orientations*. Cambridge: Cambridge University Press, 1994.

Moon, Penderel. *Wavell: The Viceroy's Journal*. London: Oxford University Press, 1973.

Mullaly, Frederick S. *Notes on Criminal Classes of the Madras Presidency*. Madras: Government of Madras, 1892.

Munro, Thomas (A.J. Arbuthnot ed.). *Major-General Sir Thomas Munro, Governor of Madras: Selections from His Minutes and Other Official Writings*, Vol. 2. London: C. Kegan Paul, 1882.

Naidoo, T. Rungasamy. *Translations, Copies and Extracts of the Several Letters in Which the Services of the Ancestors of His Excellency the Maha Rajah of Poodoocottah Are Particularly Acknowledged and Approved by the Governors and Other Public Officers of the Honourable E.I. Company and the Nabob of the Carnatic*. Puducota: Sree Brehademba Press, 1874.

Nair, C. Sankaran. *Autobiography of Sir C. Sankaran Nair*. Madras: Lady Madhavan Nair, 1966.

Nair, Janaki. *Mysore Modern: Rethinking the Region Under Princely Rule*. Minneapolis: University of Minnesota Press, 2011.

Nair, P.K. Parameswaran (E.M.J. Venniyoor trans.). *History of Malayalam Literature*. New Delhi: Sahitya Akademi, 1967.

Nair, Savithri Preetha. *Raja Serfoji II: Science, Medicine and Enlightenment in Tanjore*. New Delhi: Routledge, 2012.

Nagar, Purushottam. *Lala Lajpat Rai: The Man and His Ideas*. New Delhi: Manohar, 1977.

Nanda, B.R. *Gokhale: The Indian Moderates and the British Raj*. Princeton: Princeton University Press, 1977.

Nanda, B.R. *The Moderate Era in Indian Politics*. Oxford: Oxford University Press, 1983.

Nandy, Ashis. *The Intimate Enemy: Loss and Recovery of Self Under Colonialism*. Delhi: Oxford University Press, 1989.

Naoroji, Dadabhai (Chunilal Lallubhai Parekh ed.). *Essays, Speeches, Addresses and Writings of the Hon'ble Dadabhai Naoroji*. Bombay: Caxton Printing Works, 1887.

Natesan, G.A., and Co. *Indian Statesmen: Dewans and Prime Ministers of Native States*. Madras: G.A. Natesan and Co., 1927.

Nehru, Jawaharlal. *An Autobiography*. New Delhi: Jawaharlal Nehru Memorial Fund/Oxford University Press, 1982 edn.

Neumayer, Erwin, and Christine Schelberger eds. *Raja Ravi Varma: Portrait of an Artist: The Diary of C. Raja Raja Varma*. New Delhi: Oxford University Press, 2005.

Nicholson, A.P. *Scraps of Paper: India's Broken Treaties, Her Princes, and the Problem*. London: Ernest Benn Ltd, 1930.

Noorani, A.G. *The Destruction of Hyderabad*. New Delhi: Tulika Books, 2013.

Norman, Dorothy ed. *Nehru: The First Sixty Years*, Vol. 1. Bombay: Asia Publishing House, 1964.

North, Marianne. *Recollections of a Happy Life: Being the Autobiography of Marianne North*, Vol. 2. London: Macmillan and Co., 1893.

Norton, John Bruce. *A Letter to Robert Lowe, Joint Secretary of the Board of Control, on the Condition and Requirements of the Presidency of Madras*. London: Richardson Brothers, 1854.

Norton, John Bruce. *The Rebellion in India: How to Prevent Another*. London: Richardson Brothers, 1857.

Norton, John Bruce (G.R. Norton ed.). *Topics for Indian Statesmen*. London: Richardson Brothers, 1858.

Norton, John Bruce. *The Educational Speeches of the Hon'ble John Bruce Norton*. Madras: Advertising and Printing Company, 1870.

Olcott, Mason. *Village Schools in India: An Investigation with Suggestions*. Calcutta: Association Press, 1926.

Ouwerkerk, Louise (Dick Kooiman ed.). *No Elephants for the Maharaja: Social and Political Change in the Princely State of Travancore (1921–1947)*. New Delhi: Manohar, 1994.

Paliwal, D.L. *Mewar and the British: A History of the Relations of the Mewar State with the British Government of India from 1857 to 1921 AD*. Jaipur: Bafna Prakashan, 1971.

Panemanglor, Krishnarao N. *The Viceregal Visit to Baroda, 1926*. Baroda, 1927.

Panikkar, K.M. *Indian States and the Government of India*. London: Martin Hopkinson, 1932.

Panikkar, R. Narayana. *Kerala Bhasa Sahitya Charitram*, Vol. 4. Trivandrum: V.V. Book Depot, 1944.

Parvate, T.V. *Mahadev Govind Ranade: A Biography*. New York: Asia Publishing House, 1963.

Patel, Dinyar. *Naoroji: Pioneer of Indian Nationalism*. Cambridge: Harvard University Press, 2020.

Patel, Vallabhbhai (P.N. Chopra ed.). *The Collected Works of Sardar Vallabhbhai Patel: 1 January 1948–31 December 1948*. Delhi: Konark, 1998.

Pati, Biswamoy ed. *Issues in Modern Indian History: For Sumit Sarkar*. Mumbai: Popular Prakashan, 2000.

a) Sen, Hari. 'The Bhil Rebellion of 1881': 75–99.

Peabody, Norbert. *Hindu Kingship and Polity in Precolonial India*. New Delhi: Foundation Books, 2006.

Philips, C.H. ed. *The Correspondence of Lord William Cavendish Bentinck: Governor General of India, 1828–1835*, Vol. 2. Oxford: Oxford University Press, 1977.

Pillai, G. Paramaswaran. *Representative Indians*. London: George Routledge and Sons, 1897.

Pillai, Manu S. *The Ivory Throne: Chronicles of the House of Travancore*. Noida: HarperCollins, 2015.

Pillai, P. Ramakrishna. *Visakhavijaya: A Study*. Thiruvananthapuram: Anitha Publications, 1990.

Pillai, T.K. Velu. *The Travancore State Manual*, Vol. 4. Trivandrum: Government of Travancore, 1940.

Prasad, Rajendra. *Autobiography*. New Delhi: Penguin, 2010 edn.

Price, Pamela G. *Kingship and Political Practice in Colonial India*. Cambridge: Cambridge University Press, 1996.

Prinsep, V.C. *Imperial India: An Artist's Journals*. London: Chapman and Hall, 1879.

Purcell, Hugh. *The Maharaja of Bikaner*. New Delhi: Rupa Publications, 2013.

Purushotham, Sunil. *From Raj to Republic: Sovereignty, Violence and Democracy in India*. Stanford: Stanford University Press, 2021.

Raghavan, T.C.A. *History Men: Jadunath Sarkar, G.S. Sardesai, Raghubir Sinh and Their Quest for India's Past*. Noida: HarperCollins, 2020.

Raghu, A. *CP: A Short Biography of C.P. Ramaswami Aiyar*. New Delhi: Prestige Books, 1998.

Raghunandan, Lakshmi. *At the Turn of the Tide: The Life and Times of Maharani Setu Lakshmi Bayi, the Last Queen of Travancore*. Bangalore: Maharani Setu Lakshmi Bayi Memorial Charitable Trust, 1995.

Raja, R.P. *New Light on Swathi Tirunal*. Thiruvananthapuram: INDIS, 2006.

Ramanathan, Vaishnavi ed. *Pages of a Mind: Raja Ravi Varma – Life and Expressions*. Mumbai: Piramal Art Foundation, 2016.
   a) Sunish, Lina Vincent. 'From Maharajas to the Masses: Ravi Varma (1848–1906), the Maker of Multiples': 38–53.

Ramusack, Barbara. *The Princes of India in the Twilight of Empire: Dissolution of a Patron–Client System, 1914–1939*. Columbus: University of Cincinnati/Ohio State University Press, 1978.

Ramusack, Barbara N. *The Indian Princes and Their States* (The New Cambridge History of India, 3:6). Cambridge: Cambridge University Press, 2004.

Ranade, M.G. (Ramabai Ranade ed.). *The Miscellaneous Writings of the Late Hon'ble Mr Justice M.G. Ranade*. Bombay: Manoranjan Press, 1915.

Ranade, M.G. (V.W. Thakur ed.). *Select Writings of the Late Hon'ble Mr Justice M.G. Ranade on Indian States*. Indore: V.W. Thakur, 1942.

Rangacharlu, C.V. *The British Administration of Mysore, Part 1*. London: Longmans, Green and Co., 1874.

Rangaswami, Vanaja. *The Story of Integration: A New Interpretation in the Context of the Democratic Movements in the Princely States of Mysore, Travancore and Cochin: 1900–1947*. New Delhi: Manohar, 1981.

Rao, Dinkar. *Memorandum of Observations on the Administration of India by the Hon'ble Rao Raja Dinker Rao Rughoonath, Moontazim Bahadoor, of Gwalior for Making Laws and Regulations*. Agra: Delhi Gazette Press, 1876 edn.

Rao, K.V. Narayana. *Internal Migration Policies in an Indian State: A Case Study of the Mulki Rules in Hyderabad and Andhra*. Cambridge, Massachusetts: Centre for International Studies, 1977.

Rao, M. Shama. *Modern Mysore: From the Beginning to 1868*, Vol. 1. Bangalore: Higginbothams, 1936.

Rao, M. Shama. *Modern Mysore: From the Coronation of Chamaraja Wadiyar X in 1868 to the Present Time*, Vol. 2. Bangalore: Higginbothams, 1936.

Rao, T. Madhava. *Minor Hints: Lectures Delivered to H.H. the Maharaja Gaekwar, Sayaji Rao III by Raja Sir T. Madhava Rao, K.C.S.I.* Bombay: British India Press, 1881.

Rau Lal, Urmila. *Diwan Sir Thanjavur Madhava Row: Statesman, Administrator Extraordinaire*. Mumbai: Bharatiya Vidya Bhavan, 2015.

Rees, J.D. *The Duke of Clarence & Avondale in Southern India (With a Narrative of Elephant-Catching in Mysore by G.P. Sanderson)*. London: Kegan Paul, Trench, Trubner and Co. Ltd, 1891.

Rice, Lewis. *Mysore and Coorg: A Gazetteer Compiled for the Government of India*, Vol. 1. Bangalore: Mysore Government Press, 1877.

Rice, Lewis. *Report on the Mysore Census of 1881*. Bangalore: Mysore Government Press, 1884.

Risley, Herbert. *The People of India* (Second Edition, edited by W. Crooke). Calcutta and Simla: Thacker, Spink and Co., 1915.

Rosselli, John. *Lord William Bentinck: The Making of a Liberal Imperialist, 1744–1839*. Delhi: Thomson Press, 1974.

Routledge, James. *English Rule and Native Opinion in India: From Notes Taken, 1870–74*. London: Trubner and Co., 1878.

Row, T. Padmanabha. *Thulapurushadanom: A Brief Sketch of Travancore of To-Day with a Short Memoir of His Highness Sir Rama Varma Maha Rajah of Travancore*. Trivandrum: Keralodayam Press, 1892.

Row, Venkat (N. Thiagarajan ed.). *Manual of the Pudukkottai State*. Pudukkottai: Sri Brihadamba State Press, 1921.

Rousselet, Louis (C.R. Buckle ed.). *India and Its Native Princes: Travels in Central India and in the Presidencies of Bombay and Bengal*. London: Bickers and Son, 1882 edn.

Rudolph, Susanne Hoeber, and Lloyd I. Rudolph. *Essays on Rajputana: Reflections on History, Culture and Administration*. New Delhi: Concept Publishing Company, 1984.

Rudolph, Susanne Hoeber, and Lloyd I. Rudolph eds, with Mohan Singh Kanota. *Reversing the Gaze: Amar Singh's Diary, A Colonial Subject's Narrative of Imperial India*. Boulder: Westview Press, 2002.

Russell, William Howard. *The Prince of Wales' Tour: A Diary in India*. New York: R. Worthington, 1878.

S., Uma Maheswari ed. *Sree Chithira Tirunal: Life and Times*. Thiruvananthapuram: Sri Uthradom Tirunal Marthanda Varma Literary and Charitable Trust, 2015.

S., Uma Maheswari ed. *Navaratri*. Thiruvananthapuram: Sri Uthradom Tirunal Marthanda Varma Literary and Charitable Trust, 2020.

Saggi, P.D. ed. *A Nation's Homage: Life and Work of Sardar Vallabhbhai Patel*. Bombay: Overseas Publishing House, 1949.

Sankunni, Kottarathil (Sreekumari Ramachandran trans.). *Aitihihyamaala: The Great Legends of Kerala*, Vol. 2. Kozhikode: Mathrubhumi Books, 2010.

Saradamoni, K. *Matriliny Transformed: Family, Law and Ideology in Twentieth Century Travancore*. New Delhi: Sage Publications, 1999.

Savarkar, V.D. *Swatantrya Veer Savarkar, Hindu Sanghatan: Its Ideology and Immediate Programme: A Collection of His Three Presidential Speeches at Karnavati (Ahmadabad), Nagpur and Calcutta*. N.V. Damle: Bombay, 1940.

Sastri, K. Sambasiva ed. *Balamartandavijayam Devarajakavivirchitam* (*Devaraja Kavi's Balamartandavijaya*). Trivandrum: Government Press, 1930.

Sastri, K.N. Venkatasubba. *The Administration of Mysore Under Sir Mark Cubbon (1834–1861)*. London: George Allen and Unwin, 1932.

Saxena, K.S. *The Political Movements and Awakening in Rajasthan (1847 to 1947)*. New Delhi: S. Chand and Co., 1971.

Sergeant, Philip W. *The Ruler of Baroda: An Account of the Life and Work of the Maharaja Gaekwar*. London: John Murray, 1928.

Seesodia, Jessrajsinghji. *The Rajputs: A Fighting Race*. London: East and West, 1915.

Shah, P.R. *Raj Marwar During British Paramountcy: A Study in Problems and Policies up to 1923*. Jodhpur: Sharda Publishing House, 1982.

Shah, Sultan Mahomed. *The Memoirs of Aga Khan: World Enough and Time*. London: Cassell and Co., 1954.

Shaikh, Sameera. *Forging a Region: Sultans, Traders and Pilgrims in Gujarat, 1200–1500*. New Delhi: Oxford University Press, 2010.

Shaji, A. *Politicisation of Caste Relations in a Princely State: Communal Politics in Modern Travancore (1891–1947)*. Gurugram: Zorba Books, 2017.

Sichel, Walter. *Disraeli: A Study in Personality and Ideas*. New York: Funk and Wagnalls Company, 1904.

Simmons, Caleb, Moumita Sen, and Hillary Rodrigues eds. *Nine Nights of the Goddess: The Navaratri Festival in South Asia*. Albany: State University of New York Press, 2018.

   a) Simmons, Caleb. 'The King and the Yadu Line: Performing Lineage Through Dasara in Nineteenth-Century Mysore': 63–82.

Simmons, Caleb. *Devotional Sovereignty: Kingship and Religion in India*. New Delhi: Oxford University Press, 2020.

Singh, Hira. *Colonial Hegemony and Popular Resistance: Princes, Peasants, and Paramount Power*. New Delhi: Sage, 1998.

Sinha Kapur, Nandini. *State Formation in Rajasthan: Mewar During the Seventh–Fifteenth Centuries*. New Delhi: Manohar, 2002.

Sisson, Richard, and Stanley Wolpert eds. *Congress and Indian Nationalism: The Pre-Independence Phase*. Berkeley: University of California Press, 1988.

   a) Ramusack, Barbara. 'Congress and the People's Movement in Princely India: Ambivalence in Strategy and Organization': 377–404.

Soobrow. *Kishun Kovur: A Tragedy in Five Acts*. Trivandrum: Government Press, 1840.

Smith, Charles Irving. *Statistical Report on the Mysore*. Edinburgh: Robert Hardie and Co., 1854.

Sreenivasan, Ramya. *The Many Lives of a Rajput Queen: Heroic Pasts in India, c. 1500–1900*. Seattle: University of Washington Press, 2007.

St Clair Weeden, Edward. *A Year with the Gaekwar of Baroda*. London: Hutchinson and Co., 1911.

Stern, Robert W. *The Cat and the Lion: Jaipur State in the British Raj*. Ahmedabad: Allied Publishers, 1988.

Sundar, Nandini. *Subalterns and Sovereigns: An Anthropological History of Bastar, 1854–1996*. Delhi: Oxford University Press, 1997.

Tampy, K.P. Padmanabhan. *Kathakali: An Indigenous Art-Form of Kerala*. Calcutta: Indian Publications, 1963.

Taylor, Miles. *The English Maharani: Queen Victoria and India*. Gurgaon: Penguin Viking, 2018.

Thornton, T.H. *General Sir Richard Meade and the Feudatory States of Central and Southern India: A Record of Forty-Three Years' Service as Soldier, Political Officer and Administrator*. London: Longmans, Green and Co., 1898.

Tod, James. *Annals and Antiquities of Rajast'han, or the Central and Western Rajpoot States of India*, Vols. 1 and 2. London: Smith, Elder and Co., 1829, 1832.

Tod, James. *Travels in Western India Embracing a Visit to the Sacred Mounts of the Jains and the Most Celebrated Shrines of Hindu Faith Between Rajpootana and the Indus*. London: W.H. Allen and Co., 1839.

Tomohiko, Uyama ed. *Comparing Modern Empires: Imperial Rule and Decolonization in the Changing World Order*. Sapporo: Slavic-Eurasian Research Centre, Hokkaido University, 2018.

    a) Misra, Maria. 'Indian Aristocrats, British Imperialists and "Conservative Modernization" After the Great Rebellion': 65–98.

Topsfield, Andrew. *Court Painting at Udaipur: Art Under the Patronage of the Maharanas of Mewar*. Zurich: Museum Rietberg and Artibus Asiae Publishers, 2001.

Tumbe, Chinmay. *The Age of Pandemics, 1817–1920: How They Shaped India and the World*. Noida: HarperCollins Publishers, 2020.

Tupper, C.L. *Indian Political Practice: A Collection of the Decisions of the Government of India in Political Cases*, Vols. 1 and 2. Delhi: B.R. Publishing Corporation, 1974 edn.

Unni, N.P. *A History of Mushika Vamsa*. Trivandrum: Kerala Historical Society, 1980.

Vaikuntham, Y. *People's Movements in the Princely States*. New Delhi: Manohar, 2004.

Van Wart, R.B. *The Life of Lieut-General HH Sir Pratap Singh*. London: Humphrey Milford Oxford University Press, 1926.

Varma, C. Raja Raja. *A Narrative of the Tour in Upper India of His Highness Prince Martanda Varma of Travancore*. Bombay: Education Society's Steam Press, 1896.

Varma, Ganeshi Lal. *Shyamji Krishna Varma: The Unknown Patriot*. New Delhi: Publications Division, 1993.

Varma, Kerala. *A Jubilee Tribute to Her Most Gracious Majesty Victoria: The Queen Empress*. Bombay: Nirnayasagara Press, 1887.

Varma, Marthanda, with Uma Maheswari. *Travancore: The Footprints of Destiny: My Life and Times Under the Grace of Lord Padmanabha – As Told to Uma Maheswari*. New Delhi: Konark, 2010.

Varma, Rama Varma (Visakham Tirunal). *Observations on Higher Education and the Education of the Masses in India: A Letter Addressed to H.E. the Right Honorable M.E. Grant Duff, Governor of Madras by the Maharaja of Travancore*. Madras: Addison and Co., 1882.

Venkateswaran, N.K. *Glimpses of Travancore*. Trivandrum: S. Gnanaskanda Iyer, 1926.

Venniyoor, E.M.J. *Raja Ravi Varma*. Trivandrum: Government of Kerala, 1981.

Vibart, Henry M. *The Life of General Sir Harry N.D. Prendergast*. London: Eveleigh Nash, 1914.

Vivesvaraya, M. *Memoirs of My Working Life*. Bangalore: M. Visvesvaraya, 1951.

Waghorne, Joanne Punzo. *The Raja's Magic Clothes: Re-Visioning Kingship and Divinity in England's India*. Pennsylvania: The Pennsylvania State University Press, 1994.

Wallace, Robert Grenville. *Fifteen Years in India; or, Sketches of a Soldier's Life*. London: Longman, Hurst, Rees, Orme, and Brown, 1823.

Ward, B.S. *Memoir of the Survey of Travancore and Cochin: 1816–1820*. Madras: Government of Madras, 1891.

Ward, Geoffrey C. *The Maharajas*. Illinois: Stonehenge Press, 1983.

Weidman, Amanda J. *Singing the Classical, Voicing the Modern: The Postcolonial Politics of Music in South India*. Durham and London: Duke University Press, 2006.

Wellesley, Richard (Montgomery Martin ed.). *The Despatches, Minutes, and Correspondence of the Marquess Wellesley During His Administration in India*, Vol. 2. London: W.H. Allen, 1836.

Welsh, James. *Military Reminiscences: Extracted from a Journal of Nearly Forty Years' Active Service in the East Indies*, Vol. 2. London: Smith, Elder and Co., 1830.

West, Edward W. ed. *Diary of the Late Rajah of Kolhapoor During His Visit to Europe in 1870*. London: Smith, Elder and Co., 1872.

Wheeler, George. *India in 1875–76: The Visit of the Prince of Wales – A Chronicle of His Royal Highness's Journeyings in India, Ceylon, Spain and Portugal*. London: Chapman and Hall, 1876.

Wheeler, Stephen. *History of the Delhi Coronation Durbar: Held on the First of January 1903 to Celebrate the Coronation of His Majesty King Edward VII, Emperor of India*. London: John Murray, 1904.

Widgery, A. G. ed. *Speeches and Addresses of His Highness Sayaji Rao III, Maharaja of Baroda*, Vols. 1, 2 and 4. Cambridge: Cambridge University Press, 1927.

Williams, Gertrude Marvin. *Understanding India*. New York: Coward-McCann, 1928.

Wilson, Jon E. *The Domination of Strangers: Modern Governance in Eastern India, 1780–1835*. Basingstoke: Palgrave Macmillan, 2008.

Wink, André. *Land and Sovereignty in India: Agrarian Society and Politics under the Eighteenth-Century Maratha Svarajya*. Cambridge: Cambridge University Press, 1986.

Woodforde, John. *The Story of the Bicycle*. London: Routledge and Kegan Paul, 1970.

Zastoupil, Lynn, and Martin Moir eds. *The Great Indian Education Debate: Documents Relating to the Orientalist–Anglicist Controversy, 1781–1843*. Routledge: New York, 2016.

Zubrzycki, John. *The House of Jaipur: The Inside Story of India's Most Glamorous Royal Family*. New Delhi: Juggernaut Books, 2020.

Journals and Articles

Arunima, G. 'Face Value: Ravi Varma's Portraiture and the Project of Colonial Modernity'. *The Indian Economic and Social History Review*, 40, no. 1 (2003): 57–79.

Bagchi, Kaushik. 'An Orientalist in the Orient: Richard Garbe's Indian Journey, 1885–1886'. *Journal of World History* 14, no. 3 (2003): 281–325.

Bhagavan, Manu. 'Demystifying the "Ideal Progressive": Resistance Through Mimicked Modernity in Princely Baroda, 1900–1913'. *Modern Asian Studies* 35, no. 2 (2001): 385–409.

Bhagavan, Manu. 'The Rebel Academy: Modernity and the Movement for a University in Princely Baroda, 1908–49'. *The Journal of Asian Studies* 61, no. 3 (2002): 919–47.

Bhagavan, Manu. 'Princely States and the Hindu Imaginary: Exploring the Cartography of Hindu Nationalism in Colonial India'. *The Journal of Asian Studies* 67, no. 3 (2008): 881–915.

Birchall, T.B. 'The Weight in Gold of the Maharajah Given to the Poor'. *The Folklore Journal* 3, no. 3 (1885): 278–84.

Blackburn, Stuart H. 'The Kallars: A Tamil "Criminal Tribe" Reconsidered'. *Journal of South Asian Studies* 1, no. 1 (1978): 38–51.

Blandford, Augusta. 'Mission Work Amongst High Caste Hindu Women in Trevandrum'. *The Missionary Conference: South India and Ceylon, 1879*, Vol. 1 (Madras: Addison and Co., 1880), pp. 172–74.

Bose, Sudha. 'Raja Ravi Varma: A Centenary Tribute'. *Modern Review* 84 (1948): 124–28.

Breckenridge, Carol Appadurai. 'From Protector to Litigant – Changing Relations Between Hindu Temples and the Raja of Ramnad'. *The Indian Economic and Social History Review* 14, no. 1 (1977): 75–106.

Copland, I.F.S. 'The Baroda Crisis of 1873–77: A Study in Governmental Rivalry'. *Modern Asian Studies* 2, no. 2 (1968): 97–123.

Del Bonta, Robert J. 'See Krsna Run: Narrative Painting for Mummadi Krsnaraja Wadiyar'. *Ars Orientalis* 30, supplementary 1 (Chachaji: Professor Walter M. Spink Felicitation Volume, 2000): 99–113.

Dinkar, Niharika. 'Private Lives and Interior Spaces: Raja Ravi Varma's Scholar Paintings'. *Art History* 37, no. 3 (2014): 510–35.

Fisher, Michael H. 'The Resident in Court Ritual, 1764–1858'. *Modern Asian Studies* 24, no. 3 (1990): 419–58.

Gowda, Chandan. '"Advance Mysore!": The Cultural Logic of a Developmental State'. *Economic and Political Weekly* 45, no. 29 (2010): 88–95.

Guha Thakurta, Tapati. 'Westernisation and Tradition in South Indian Painting in the Nineteenth Century: The Case of Raja Ravi Varma (1848–1906)'. *Studies in History* 2, no. 2 (1986): 165–95.

Gupta, Hira Lal. 'Indore Successions, 1833–34 & 1843'. *Proceedings of the Indian History Congress* 18 (1955): 243–51.

Gupta, K.S. 'A Study of the Revolt of 1857: On the Basis of Regional Records'. *Proceedings of the Indian History Congress* 49 (1988): 360–63.

Haynes, Edward S. 'Imperial Impact on Rajputana: The Case of Alwar, 1775–1850'. *Modern Asian Studies* 12, no. 3 (1978): 419–53.

Haynes, Edward S. 'The Political Role of the Armed Forces of the Indian States after World War I'. *Journal of Asian History* 24, no. 1 (1990): 30–56.

Haynes, Edward S. 'Rajput Ceremonial Interactions as a Mirror of a Dying Indian State System, 1820–1947'. *Modern Asian Studies* 24, no. 3 (1990): 459–92.

Iyer, S. Venkitasubramonia. 'Some Less Known Composers of Kerala'. *The Journal of the Music Academy* 40, nos. 1–4 (1969): 98–106.

Jeffrey, Robin. 'The Politics of "Indirect Rule": Types of Relationship Among Rulers, Ministers and Residents in a "Native State"'. *Journal of the Commonwealth and Comparative Politics* 13, no. 3 (1975): 261–81.

Joseph, G. 'A Great Indian Artist'. *The Indian Review,* November–December 1911.

Joseph, Sebastian. 'A Service Elite Against the Peasants: Encounter and Collision (Mysore 1799–1831)'. *Proceedings of the Indian History Congress* 41 (1980): 670–81.

Journal of the East India Association, London 5 (1871).

Journal of the Society for Arts 41, no. 2106 (1893).

Kapila, Shruti. 'Masculinity and Madness: Princely Personhood and Colonial Sciences of the Mind in Western India, 1871–1940'. *Past and Present,* no. 187 (2005): 121–56.

Khan, Razak. 'Local Pasts: Space, Emotions and Identities in Vernacular Histories of Princely Rampur'. *Journal of the Economic and Social History of the Orient* 58, no. 5 (2015): 693–731.

Kooiman, Dick. 'Meeting at the Threshold, at the Edge of the Carpet, or Somewhere in Between? Questions of Ceremonial in Princely India'. *The Indian Economic and Social History Review* 40, no. 3 (2003): 311–33.

Kooiman, Dick. 'The Guns of Travancore or How Much Powder May a Maharaja Blaze Away?' *The Indian Economic and Social History Review* 43, no. 3 (2006): 301–22.

Kumaraswamy, M. 'The Role of Underground Press in Mysore Chalo Movement in 1947'. *Proceedings of the Indian History Congress* 67 (2006–2007): 725–29.

Leask, Nigel. 'On Partha Mitter's Art and Nationalism in India'. *Comparative Criticism: Philosophical Dialogues*, Vol. XX (Cambridge: Cambridge University Press, 1998), pp. 295–314.

Manor, James. 'Princely Mysore before the Storm: The State-Level Political System of India's Model State, 1920–1936'. *Modern Asian Studies* 9, no. 1 (1975): 31–58.

Mateer, Samuel. 'A Romish View of the British Indian Government'. *The Missionary Review of the World* 16, no. 8 (1888): 589–95.

McLeod, John. 'Towards the Analysis of Hindu Princely Genealogy in the British Period, 1850–1950'. *South Asia Research* 6, no. 2 (1986): 181–93.

Murali, Deepthi. 'Producing a Throne Fit for a Queen: Travancore's Contribution to the Great Exhibition in Crystal Palace, 1851' at http://www.deepthimurali.com/publications/2016/8/producing-a-throne-fit-for-a-queen-travancores-contribution-to-the-great-exhibition-in-crystal-palace-1851

Nair, Janaki. 'Mysore's Wembley? The Dasara Exhibition's Imagined Economies'. *Modern Asian Studies* 5, no. 47 (2013): 1549–87.

Nair, Janaki. 'Modernity and "Publicness": The Career of the Mysore Matha, 1880–1940'. *The Indian Economic and Social History Review* 57, no. 1 (2020): 5–29.

Nair, T.P. Sankarankutty. 'Govindan Parameswaran Pillai: The Father of Political Agitation in Travancore'. *Proceedings of the Indian History Congress* 37 (1976): 354–60.

Nilsen, Alf Gunvald. 'Subalterns and the State in the Longue Durée: Notes from "The Rebellious Century" in the Bhil Heartland'. *Journal of Contemporary Asia* 45, no. 4 (2015): 574–95.

Nuckolls, Charles W. 'The Durbar Incident'. *Modern Asian Studies* 24, no. 3 (1990): 529–59.

Pandian, Anand. 'Securing the Rural Citizen: The Anti-Kallar Movement of 1896'. *The Indian Economic and Social History Review* 42, no. 1 (2005): 1–39.

Patil, Avanish. 'Public Opinion in Colonial India: The "Kesari" and the Kolhapur Affair, 1881–1883'. *Proceedings of the Indian History Congress* 67 (2006–2007): 711–24.

Peabody, Norbert. 'Tod's *Rajast'han* and the Boundaries of Imperial Rule in Nineteenth-Century India'. *Modern Asian Studies* 30, no. 1 (1996): 185–220.

Proceedings of the Linnean Society of London (From November 1883 to June 1886). London: The Linnean Society, 1886.

Purushotham, Sunil. 'Internal Violence: The "Police Action" in Hyderabad'. *Comparative Studies in Society and History* 57, no. 2 (2015): 435–66.

Qanungo, Bhupan. 'A Study of British Relations with the Native States of India, 1858–62'. *The Journal of Asian Studies* 26, no. 2 (1967): 251–65.

Raghunath, H. 'Viduraswatha Tragedy and Its Aftermath: 1938'. *Proceedings of the Indian History Congress*, 38 (1977): 452–59.

Rajeev, Sharat Sunder. 'The Durbar Artists of Travancore', originally at https://tinpahar.com/?p=1928

Ramiengar, V. 'A Sketch of the Late Maharajah of Travancore'. *The Indian Magazine* (issued by the National Indian Association in Aid of Social Progress and Education in India) (London: C. Kegan Paul, Trench and Co., 1886): 189–95.

Rao, C. Ranganatha. 'The Recent Industrial Progress of Mysore'. *Journal of the Royal Society of Arts* 83, no. 4294 (1935): 372–94.

Rees, J.D. 'The Daily Life of an Indian Prince'. *Macmillan's Magazine* 1, no. 9 (1906): 711–20.

Rowbotham, Judith. 'Miscarriage of Justice? Postcolonial Reflections on the Trial of the Maharajah of Baroda, 1875'. *Liverpool Law Review* 28 (2007): 377–403.

Rudolph, Susanne Hoeber, Lloyd I. Rudolph, and Mohan Singh. 'A Bureaucratic Lineage in Princely India: Elite Formation and Conflict in a Patrimonial System'. *The Journal of Asian Studies* 34, no. 3 (1975): 717–53.

Sahana, Usha. 'G. Parameswaran Pillai: Early Indian-English Writer'. *Indian Literature* 47, no. 6 (2003): 155–57.

Sahu, S.N. 'A Secularist, Sardar Patel Had United India In Spite of Travancore's "Hindu God" Excuse'. The Wire at https://thewire.in/history/sardar-vallabhbhai-patel-national-unity-day-travancore-secular

Sethia, Madhu. 'British Paramountcy: Reaction and Response by the Nineteenth Century Poets of Rajasthan'. *Social Scientist* 33, nos. 11–12 (2005): 14–28.

Singh, Saint Nihal. 'Just What Does India Want Politically?' *The North American Review* 192, no. 658 (1910): 369–78.

Sreenivasan, Ramya. 'Rethinking Kingship and Authority in South Asia: Amber (Rajasthan), ca. 1560–1615'. *Journal of the Economic and Social History of the Orient* 57, no. 4 (2014): 549–86.

Srinivasachari, C.S. 'The India Reform Society and Its Impact on the Indian Administration in the Decade 1853–62'. *The Indian Journal of Political Science* 8, no. 1 (1946): 648–61.

Srinivasiengar, K.R. 'The Mysore Constitution'. *Current Science* 9 (1940): xxxv–vii.

Stein, Burton. 'State Formation and Economy Reconsidered: Part One'. *Modern Asian Studies* 19, no. 3 (1985): 387–413.

Stein, Burton. 'Notes on "Peasant Insurgency" in Colonial Mysore: Event and Process'. *South Asia Research* 5, no. 1 (1985): 11–27.

Subrahmanyam, Sanjay. 'Warfare and State Finance in Wadiyar Mysore, 1724–25: A Missionary Perspective'. *The Indian Economic and Social History Review* 26, no. 2 (1989): 203–33.

Subrahmanyam, Sanjay. 'A Note on Some Early Nineteenth Century Inam Records in the Karnataka State Archives'. *The Indian Economic and Social History Review* 28, no. 4 (1991): 435–43.

Teuscher, Ulrike. 'Changing Eklingji: A Holy Place as a Source of Royal Legitimation'. *Studies in History* 21, no. 1 (2005): 1–16.

The Athenaeum Journal of Literature, Science, the Fine Arts, Music, and the Drama (January to June). London: The Athenaeum, 1876.

The London Quarterly Review 145, January–April 1878 (New York: The Leonard Scott Publishing Company, 1878).

The Orientalist: A Journal of Oriental Literature, Arts and Sciences, Folklore &c. 3, parts 1 and 2 (Bombay: The Education Society's Press, 1887).

Varma, Indira. 'Artist of the People and of the Gods'. *The Illustrated Weekly of India* 97, no. 22 (1976): 20–27.

Varma, Rama (Visakham Tirunal). 'A Native Statesman'. *The Calcutta Review* 55, no. 110 (1872): 225–63.

Varma, Rama (Visakham Tirunal). 'Suka-sandesah: A Sanskrit Poem by Lakshmi-dasa'. *The Journal of the Royal Asiatic Society of Great Britain and Ireland*, New Series 16, no. 4 (1884): 401–52.

Veerathappa, K. 'Dewan Mirza Ismail and Mysore Congress'. *Proceedings of the Indian History Congress* 40 (1979): 653–61.

Veerathappa, K. 'Mysore Legislative Council (1907–1947)'. *Proceedings of the Indian History Congress* 48 (1987): 404–10.

Vijayamohan, T.K. 'Ummini Tampi, The Dewan of Travancore (1809–1812). *Journal of Kerala Studies* 5, part 1 (1978): 261–69.

Walding, Richard R., Helen Stone, and Achuthsankar S. Nair. 'The Russian Prince and the Maharajah of Travancore'. *Journal of Kerala Studies* 36 (2009): 10–87.

Washbrook, David. 'The Maratha Brahmin Model in South India: An Afterword'. *The Indian Economic and Social History Review* 47, no. 4 (2010): 597–615.

Watson, Robert Spence. 'Indian National Congresses'. *The Contemporary Review* 54 (London: Isbister and Company, 1888): 89–104.

Zaidi, S. Inayet A. 'European Mercenaries in the Indian Armies: AD 1750–1803'. *Studies in History* 27, no. 1 (2011): 55–83.

Zins, Max-Jean. 'Invented and Imported Traditions: Some Reflections on the Policy of Protocol during the British Raj'. *Proceedings of the Indian History Congress* 57 (1996): 659–79.

Acknowledgements

My interest in India's princely states began over a decade ago, when I first started researching Travancore. That culminated in *The Ivory Throne* (2015), but the project also taught me that princely territories have much to offer to the study of Indian history, if we rise above stereotypes. I hope *False Allies* will help generate interest in this direction among other students of history.

This project was made possible by the support and encouragement of several individuals and institutions. Early in 2019 in a remark to Gitanjali Maini in Bengaluru, I mentioned how Ravi Varma's portraits of princes might be a means to shortlist a few states from the intimidatingly large total and tell their stories. It was Gita who not only suggested that I turn this into a book, but also offered me a grant from the Sandeep and Gitanjali Maini Foundation. *False Allies* is the second book I have produced with the SGMF's support, the first being *Rebel Sultans* (2018). I remain most grateful to Gita and Sandeep Maini personally for their backing and their faith in my work.

On Ravi Varma, who has been of interest for about half my life now, over the years I was able to gather not only academic resources, but also anecdotal information and oral history from his relatives, both from the Kilimanoor and the Mavelikara–Travancore families. I must thank in particular Jay Varma, Prasanna Varma, Sethu Tampuratti, Dr R.P. Raja, Uma Varma, Dr Lakshmi Raghunandan, the late Divakara Varma, the late Kerala Varma (head of Kilimanoor until his demise last year) and others from the Varma family, who do not wish to be named. My friend Sharat Sunder Rajeev, with whom I have discussed Ravi Varma and much else over the last fourteen years, gave me valuable insights, for which I am grateful.

Thanks are also due to the following art collectors, scholars and friends: Archana Shenoy, Ravi Chakravarthy, Usha Balakrishnan, Rupika Chawla, Erwin Neumayer, Christine Schelberger, Nigel Chancellor, Sachin Kaluskar, Anil Relia, Chamundeshwari Bhogilal Chinai, Ashvin Rajagopalan, Brijeshwari Gohil, Dr V. Venu, Mir Muhammad Ali, S. Abu, Vivek Nair, Radhika Raje Gaekwad, Manda Hingurao, Jayanta Sengupta, Malavika Banerjee, David Gilmour, David Godwin, Niranjana Ramesh, Vignesh Karthik Rajahmani, Aparna Andhare, A. Ramachandran, B.B. Chand, S.K. Kakkad, Nanaji Shewale, Uma Thampuran, Radha Venuprasad, Colonel Anand, Premila Anand, Dr A.M. Tampi, the late Colonel Balasubramanian, Dr Biju G. Pillai, Paul Abraham, Timothy Prus, Mayank Gupta, Khyrunnisa A., Professor. P. Vijaya Kumar, Shrayana Bhattacharya, Palat Udayanan, Aditi Nayar, Ashok Mehta, Paliath Ravi Achan and Deepthi Sasidharan. I am also thankful to all the private collectors who have asked not to be named.

This book would not have been possible without the following institutions in India and overseas: the National Archives, New Delhi; the British Library, London; the Gokhale Institute of Politics and Economics, Pune; the Asiatic Society, Mumbai; the National Portrait Gallery, London; the Institute of Social and Economic Change, Bengaluru; the University of Michigan's Department of History of Art; the University of Berkeley; the Harvard Art Museums; the Central Library, Mumbai; the Maharana of Mewar Charitable Foundation, Udaipur; the Maharaja Fatesingh Museum, Vadodara; the Sree Chitra Art Gallery, Thiruvananthapuram; the Victoria Memorial Hall, Kolkata; the Piramal Foundation, Mumbai; the Rijksmuseum, Amsterdam; the Los Angeles County Museum, Los Angeles; the Metropolitan Museum of Art, New York; the Wellcome Collection, London; the British Museum, London; the Royal Collection Trust, London; The Times of India Group; the Archive of Modern Conflict, London; the Madhavan Nayar Foundation, Kochi; the Minneapolis Institute of Art; the EO Hoppé Estate Collection, Pasadena; and, finally, the Raja Ravi

Varma Heritage Foundation, Bengaluru. Online resources, particularly Getty Images, Archive.org and Wikimedia Commons have also been of tremendous value.

This book has benefited greatly from conversations with and inputs from friends and scholars working on related themes. Robin Jeffrey, whose seminal *Decline of Nayar Dominance* (1976) was among the earliest contributions to the study of the princely states, very generously read drafts and gave me detailed comments. Caleb Simmons's work on Krishnaraja Wadiyar III of Mysore has been both a delight and an inspiration, while Rahul Sagar, whose forthcoming biography of Sir Madhava Rao breaks new intellectual ground, gave me much to think about. I am grateful also to Manu Bhagavan, whose work on Baroda and Mysore has informed my own perspective. Smitha Nandakishoran, who was among the first class of students I taught, combed through the manuscript and pointed out everything from grammatical slips to ugly sentences, as did the young, remarkably well-read Ranvijay Singh Hada.

My editor and friend Parth Mehrotra has been a source of confidence and support for several years now. I also thank Chiki Sarkar, Nandini Mehta, Cincy Jose, Gavin Morris, R. Ajith Kumar, Shyama Warner, Manju Khanna and the team at Juggernaut Books for helping turn what was an unwieldy manuscript into a handsome volume. I hope it reaches many shelves in many places, besides my own.

This book is dedicated to my grandfathers, one of them an illiterate man who would have been somewhat amused with his grandson's decision to wield the pen; and the other, a gentle, intellectually inclined figure, whose patience and equanimity have helped me learn to negotiate life and work with optimism. My late father was present in picture form throughout the writing of this book, watching over my desk from his corner. And, of course, bearing with my chatter, mood swings and seasonal idiosyncrasies were my mother, sister and grandmother, without whom none of this would matter.

Manu S. Pillai
July 2021

Index

juggernaut

THE APP FOR INDIAN READERS

Fresh, original books tailored for mobile and for India. Starting at ₹10.

juggernaut.in

1

CRAFTED FOR MOBILE READING

Thought you would never read a book on mobile? Let us prove you wrong.

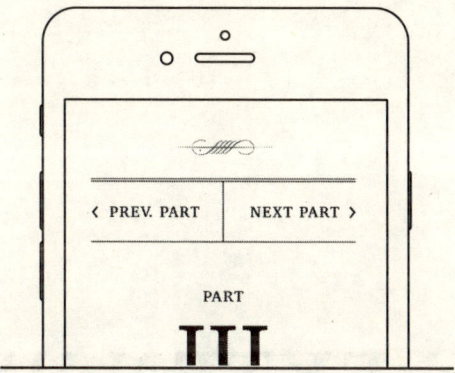

Beautiful Typography

The quality of print transferred
to your mobile. Forget ugly PDFs.

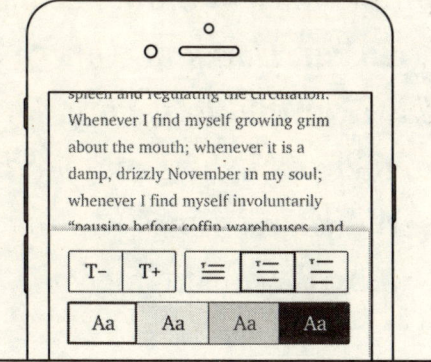

Customizable Reading

Read in the font size, spacing
and background of your liking.

AN EXTENSIVE LIBRARY

Including fresh, new, original Juggernaut books from the likes of Sunny Leone, Praveen Swami, Husain Haqqani, Umera Ahmed, Rujuta Diwekar and lots more. Plus, books from partner publishers and loads of free classics. Whichever genre you like, there's a book waiting for you.

DON'T JUST READ; INTERACT

We're changing the reading experience from passive to active.

juggernaut.in

Ask authors questions

Get all your answers from the horse's mouth.
Juggernaut authors actually reply to every
question they can.

Rate and review

Let everyone know of your favourite reads or
critique the finer points of a book – you will be
heard in a community of like-minded readers.

Gift books to friends

For a book-lover, there's no nicer gift than
a book personally picked. You can even
do it anonymously if you like.

Enjoy new book formats

Discover serials released in parts over
time, picture books including comics,
and story-bundles at discounted rates.
And coming soon, audiobooks.

juggernaut.in

4

LOWEST PRICES & ONE-TAP BUYING

Books start at ₹10 with regular discounts and free previews.

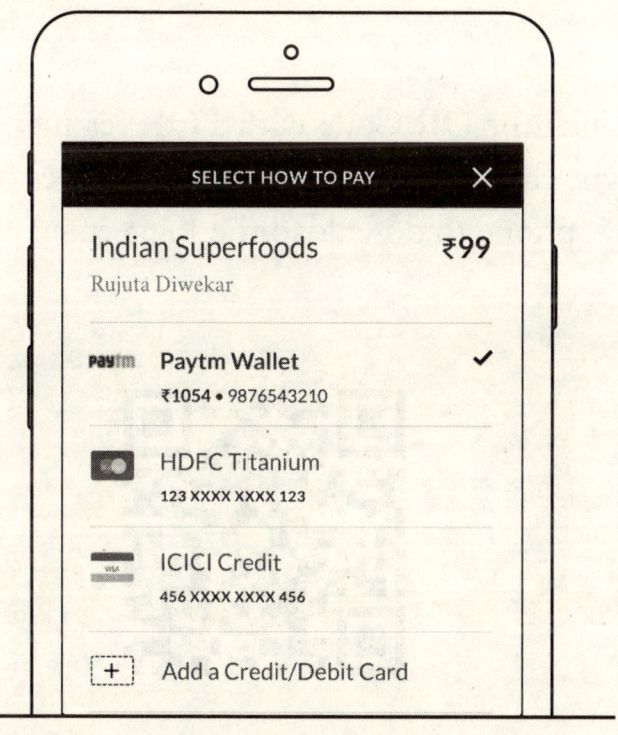

Paytm Wallet, Cards & Apple Payments

On Android, just add a Paytm Wallet once and buy any book with one tap. On iOS, pay with one tap with your iTunes-linked debit/credit card.

Click the QR Code with a QR scanner app or type the link into the Internet browser on your phone to download the Juggernaut app.

For our complete catalogue, visit www.juggernaut.in
To submit your book, send a synopsis and two
sample chapters to books@juggernaut.in
For all other queries, write to contact@juggernaut.in